FIFTH EDITION

# Theory and Practice of Counseling and Psychotherapy

GERALD COREY is Professor of Human Services and Professor of Counseling at California State University, Fullerton, and a licensed psychologist. He was the Coordinator of the Human Services Department at the university for nine years. Jerry received his doctorate in counseling from the University of Southern California. He is a Diplomate in Counseling Psychology, American Board of Professional Psychology; is a National Certified Counselor; is a Fellow of the American Psychological Association (Counseling Psychology); and is a Fellow of the Association for Specialists in Group Work.

In 1991 Jerry received the Outstanding Professor of the Year Award from California State University, Fullerton; in 1992 he was the recipient of an honorary doctorate in humane letters from National Louis University. He teaches courses in theories and techniques of counseling, professional ethics, and group counseling, and he trains and supervises students in group work. With his colleagues he has conducted workshops in the United States, Canada, Germany, Belgium, Scotland, Mexico, and China, with a special focus on training in group counseling. He regularly presents intensive courses, lectures, and workshops at various universities. He also gives presentations and workshops for professional organizations at state and national conferences. Along with his wife, Marianne Schneider Corey, and other colleagues, Jerry offers weeklong residential personal-growth groups and residential training and supervision workshops each summer. In addition, he enjoys traveling, hiking, and bicycling in the mountains and driving his family and friends in his 1931 Model A Ford.

Recent books that Jerry has authored or co-authored (all published by Brooks/Cole Publishing Company) are:

- *Case Approach to Counseling and Psychotherapy,* Fourth Edition (1996)
- *Theory and Practice of Group Counseling,* Fourth Edition (and *Manual* (1995)
- *I Never Knew I Had a Choice,* Fifth Edition (1993, with Marianne Schneider Corey)
- *Becoming a Helper,* Second Edition (1993, with Marianne Schneider Corey)
- *Issues and Ethics in the Helping Professions,* Fourth Edition (1993, with Marianne Schneider Corey and Patrick Callanan)
- *Group Techniques,* Second Edition (1992, with Marianne Schneider Corey, Patrick Callanan, and J. Michael Russell)
- *Groups: Process and Practice,* Fourth Edition (1992, with Marianne Schneider Corey)

FIFTH EDITION

# Theory and Practice of Counseling and Psychotherapy

GERALD COREY

*California State University, Fullerton*
*Diplomate in Counseling Psychology,*
*American Board of Professional Psychology*

Brooks/Cole Publishing Company
I(T)P™ An International Thomson Publishing Company

Pacific Grove • Albany • Bonn • Boston • Cincinnati • Detroit • London • Madrid • Melbourne
Mexico City • New York • Paris • San Francisco • Singapore • Tokyo • Toronto • Washington

 A CLAIREMONT BOOK

Sponsoring Editor: *Claire Verduin*
Marketing Team: *Margaret Parks and Nancy Kernal*
Editorial Associate: *Patsy Vienneau*
Production Coordinator: *Fiorella Ljunggren*
Production: *Cecile Joyner, The Cooper Company*
Manuscript Editor: *William Waller*

Permissions Editor: *Carline Haga*
Interior Design: *Vernon T. Boes*
Cover Design: *Sharon Kinghan*
Typesetting: *Bookends Typesetting*
Cover Printing: *Phoenix Color Corporation, Inc.*
Printing and Binding: *Quebecor Printing, Fairfield*

*Photo Credits*

P. ii: Ed Young; p. 91: National Library of Medicine; p. 133: courtesy of The Alfred Adler Institute of Chicago; p. 168: Harvard University Archives; p. 169: Mark Kaufman; p. 197: courtesy of The Carl Rogers Memorial Library; p. 223: © Esalen Institute/Photo by Paul Herbert; p. 258: courtesy of William Glasser; p. 281: courtesy of Arnold Lazarus; p. 317: courtesy of Albert Ellis.

COPYRIGHT © 1996, 1991, 1986, 1982, 1977 by Brooks/Cole Publishing Company
A division of International Thomson Publishing Inc.

ITP® The ITP logo is a registered trademark under license.

*2o334664*

*For more information, contact:*

BROOKS/COLE PUBLISHING COMPANY
511 Forest Lodge Road
Pacific Grove, CA 93950
USA

International Thomson Publishing Europe
Berkshire House 168–173
High Holborn
London WC1V 7AA
England

Thomas Nelson Australia
102 Dodds Street
South Melbourne, 3205
Victoria, Australia

Nelson Canada
1120 Birchmount Road
Scarborough, Ontario
Canada M1K 5G4

International Thomson Editores
Campos Eliseos 385, Piso 7
Col. Polanco
11560 México D. F. México

International Thomson Publishing GmbH
Königswinterer Strasse 418
53227 Bonn
Germany

International Thomson Publishing Asia
221 Henderson Road
#05–10 Henderson Building
Singapore 0315

International Thomson Publishing Japan
Hirakawacho Kyowa Building, 3F
2-2-1 Hirakawacho
Chiyoda-ku, Tokyo 102
Japan

Printed in the United States of America

10   9   8   7   6   5   4   3

**Library of Congress Cataloging-in-Publication Data**

Corey, Gerald
   Theory and practice of counseling and psychotherapy / Gerald
Corey. — 5th ed.
    p.   cm. p
   Includes bibliographical references and indexes.
   ISBN 0-534-33856-9
   1. Counseling.   2. Psychotherapy.   I. Title.
BF637.C6C574   1996                                    95-15145
158'3.—dc20                                                   CIP

MY APPRECIATION AND GRATITUDE TO THESE THREE PEOPLE WILL
BE WITH ME ALWAYS:

*Claire Verduin, publisher in counseling and psychology*
*Fiorella Ljunggren, production services manager*
*Bill Waller, manuscript editor*

# CONTENTS

# P R E F A C E

This book is intended for counseling courses for undergraduate and graduate students in psychology, counselor education, and the human-services and mental-health professions. It surveys the major concepts and practices of the contemporary therapeutic systems and addresses some ethical and professional issues in counseling practice. The book aims at teaching students to select wisely from various theories and techniques, which will help them develop a personal style of counseling.

I have found that students appreciate an overview of the divergent contemporary approaches to counseling and psychotherapy. They also consistently say that the first course in counseling means more to them when it deals with them as people. Therefore, I stress the practical application of the material and encourage reflection, so that using this book can be both a personal and an academic growth experience.

In this new fifth edition, every effort has been made to retain the major qualities that students and professors have found helpful in the previous editions: the succinct overview of the key concepts of each theory and their implications for practice, the straightforward and personal style, and the book's comprehensive scope. Care has been taken to present the theories in an accurate and fair way. I have also attempted to be simple, clear, and concise. Because many students want suggestions for supplementary reading as they study each therapy approach, I have included a reading list at the end of each chapter.

This edition updates the material and refines existing discussions. Part One deals with issues that are basic to the practice of counseling and psychotherapy. After the initial chapter, which puts the book into perspective, students are introduced to the counselor—as a person and a professional—in Chapter 2. It is fitting that this material be dealt with before introducing theoretical concepts and counseling techniques, because the role of the counselor as a person is highlighted throughout the text. Chapter 3, which has been updated and largely rewritten to focus on key controversies in counseling practice, offers an overview of a range of current ethical and professional issues facing counseling professionals. I have selected those contemporary ethical issues that tend to generate the most interesting discussions in my classes. This organization of chapters encourages students to think about basic issues in the counseling profession early in the course, and it also provides a mental set for their active and personal involvement with the book and their course.

Part Two is devoted to a consideration of the following theories and techniques in counseling: psychoanalytic, Adlerian, existential, person-centered, Gestalt, reality, behavior, cognitive-behavior, and family systems. Each chapter follows a common organizational pattern, so that students can easily compare and contrast the various models. This pattern includes core topics such as key concepts, the therapeutic process, therapeutic techniques and procedures, and summary and evaluation.

This edition contains an updated and expanded discussion of the contributions and limitations of each of the nine theories from a multicultural perspective. Both the client's and the counselor's cultural backgrounds are significant factors that have an influence on the therapeutic relationship. As readers review the theories, they are challenged to think of ways of adapting techniques from the various approaches to the unique needs of the person in the environment.

Family systems therapy has been added to this edition (Chapter 12), mainly because of the increased developments in the field. Although the book deals primarily with theories and techniques of individual counseling, the family systems perspective is another approach to working with individuals. Indeed, systems practitioners contend that to work effectively with clients, it is essential to consider the reciprocal influences between individuals and their family (and other systems of which they are a vital part).

In Part Three, readers are helped to put the concepts together in a meaningful way through a discussion of the integrative perspective and a consideration of a case study. Chapter 13 provides charts and other integrating material to help the student compare and contrast the nine approaches. There is more emphasis in this edition on providing a framework for a creative synthesis among the therapeutic models, and students are given guidelines for beginning to formulate their own integration and personal philosophy of counseling.

The "Case of Stan" has been retained in Chapter 14, because it helps readers see the application of a variety of techniques at various stages in the counseling process with the same client. The focus is on an integrative approach that draws from all the therapies and uses a thinking, feeling, and behaving model. This chapter offers a good review of the various theories as applied to a case example.

This text can be used in a flexible way. Some instructors will prefer to follow my sequencing of chapters. Others will prefer to begin with the theory chapters (Part Two) and then deal later with the student's personal characteristics and ethical issues. The topics can be covered in whatever order makes the most sense. Readers are offered some suggestions for using this book at the end of Chapter 1.

In this edition I have made every effort to incorporate those aspects that have worked best in the courses on counseling theory and practice that I regularly teach. To help readers apply theory to practice, I have also revised the student manual, which is designed for experiential work. The *Student Manual for Theory and Practice of Counseling and Psychotherapy* still contains open-ended questions and cases, structured exercises, self-inventories, and a variety of activities that can be done both in class and out of class. The fifth edition features a structured overview, as well as a glossary, for each of the theories and chapter quizzes for assessing the level of student mastery of basic concepts. The manual also contains the 1995 revision of the ACA's *Code of Ethics and*

*Standards of Practice* and the APA's *Ethical Principles of Psychologists and Code of Conduct.*

Also available is a revised and updated *Instructor's Resource Manual,* which includes suggestions for teaching the course, class activities to stimulate interest, and a variety of test questions and final examinations.

To complete this learning package, there is a newly revised and enlarged *Case Approach to Counseling and Psychotherapy* (Fourth Edition), which features several cases for each of the nine therapeutic approaches. Readers are provided with practical illustrations of the application of various techniques to these diverse cases. The casebook can either supplement this book or stand alone for use in certain courses. There is also a two-part videotape, in which I demonstrate an integrative approach in counseling Ruth (the central character in the casebook). Information about this videotape can be secured from the Brooks/Cole Publishing Company.

Some professors have found the textbook and the student manual to be ideal companions and realistic texts for a single course. Others like to use the textbook and the casebook as companions. And some use all three books as a package in their courses. The casebook can also be used in a case-management practicum or in fieldwork courses, because the cases include information extending from intake to termination. The integrated package affords instructors a great deal of flexibility to adapt the materials to their particular style of teaching and to the unique needs of their students.

## ACKNOWLEDGMENTS

The suggestions I received from the many readers of prior editions who took the time to complete the survey at the end of the book have been most helpful. Many other people have contributed ideas that have found their way into this fifth edition. I especially appreciate the time and efforts of the manuscript reviewers, who offered constructive criticism and supportive commentaries, as well as those professors who have used this book and provided me with feedback that has been most useful in these revisions. Those who reviewed the manuscript of the fifth edition are Bryan Farha, Oklahoma City University; Marcia Freer, Doane College; Barbara Herlihy, Loyola University, New Orleans; Thomas Hodgson, SUNY-Empire State College; and Beverly Palmer, California State University, Dominguez Hills.

Student reviewers, all in the undergraduate program in Human Services at California State University, Fullerton, who provided insightful comments include Sheila Bell, Pamela Cuervo, Renée Flory, and Michelle Muratori. Their input helped keep the book practical and readable. I would like to acknowledge Glennda Gilmour, who carefully prepared the indexes for this book.

The material on multicultural counseling was reviewed by Farah A. Ibrahim, University of Connecticut; Frederick T. L. Leong, Ohio State University, Columbus; Don C. Locke, North Carolina State University; Paul B. Pedersen, Syracuse University; Ronnie Priest, University of Memphis; Derald Wing Sue, California State University, Hayward, and California School of Professional Psychology, Alameda; and Julia R. J. Yang.

Special thanks are extended to the chapter reviewers, who provided consultation and detailed critiques. Their insightful and valuable comments have generally been incorporated into this edition:

- William Blau, private practice, El Monte, California, and California School of Professional Psychology; and J. Michael Russell of California State University, Fullerton (Chapter 4)
- James Bitter, East Tennessee State University (Chapter 5)
- Emmy van Deurzen-Smith, Regent's College, London; and J. Michael Russell, California State University, Fullerton (Chapter 6)
- David Cain, founder of the Person-Centered Association and a private practitioner in Carlsbad, California (Chapter 7)
- Lynne Jacobs, Los Angeles Institute of Gestalt Therapy; and Joseph Zinker, Cleveland Institute of Gestalt Therapy (Chapter 8)
- William Glasser, Institute for Control Theory, Reality Therapy, and Quality Management, Canoga Park, California; William H. Wheeler, Mississippi College; and Robert Wubbolding, Xavier University and Center for Reality Therapy, Cincinnati, Ohio (Chapter 9)
- Arnold A. Lazarus, Rutgers University (Chapter 10)
- Albert Ellis, Institute for Rational-Emotive Therapy, New York, and Frank M. Dattilio, Center for Cognitive Therapy, University of Pennsylvania School of Medicine (Chapter 11)
- Dorothy Stroh Becvar, Radford University; Ellen Rainbold Brt, Doane College; Donald Bubenzer, Kent State University; Marianne Schneider Corey; Irene Goldenberg, University of California, Los Angeles; Claudia Grauf-Grounds, University of San Diego; Michael P. Nichols, College of William and Mary; Mary Moline, Seattle Pacific University; Vanessa Vertin; John West, Kent State University; and Jon L. Winek, Appalachian State University (Chapter 12). James Bitter co-authored Chapter 12 with me.
- John C. Norcross, University of Scranton (Chapters 13 and 14)

This book is the result of a team effort, which includes the combined talents of the professional people in the Brooks/Cole family. I have appreciated the opportunity to work with Claire Verduin, publisher in counseling and psychology, who is always ready to listen and give her reactions to ideas regarding the evolution of this book; with Fiorella Ljunggren, production services manager, who oversees the production of our books; with Cecile Joyner, of The Cooper Company, who carried out the production of the book with efficiency; and with William Waller, the manuscript editor, whose careful attention has consistently ensured the concise and readable quality of our books. The efforts, dedication, and extra time of these special people certainly have contributed to the quality of this book. With the professional assistance of these people, the ongoing task of revising this book continues to bring more joy than pain.

*Gerald Corey*

# PART ONE
# BASIC ISSUES IN COUNSELING PRACTICE

# CHAPTER ONE

# Introduction and Overview

Introduction
Where I Stand
Suggestions for Using the Book
Overview of the Theory Chapters
Introduction to the Case of Stan

# Introduction

This heart of book surveys nine approaches to counseling and psychotherapy. Instead of emphasizing the theoretical foundations of these models, it presents the basic concepts of each and discusses features such as the therapeutic process (including goals), the client/therapist relationship, and specific procedures used in the practice of counseling. The book will help you develop a balanced view of the major ideas of various therapists and the practical techniques they employ.

I encourage you to keep an open mind and to seriously consider both the unique contributions and the particular limitations of each therapeutic system presented in Part Two of this book. From my perspective no single model is comprehensive enough to explain all facets of human experience. Although attempts have been made to integrate various approaches, those practitioners who align themselves with one theoretical viewpoint still tend to view their system as complete in itself. Some proponents operate on the assumption that their approach is the best available theory to guide practice. A psychoanalytic practitioner, for instance, may view behavior therapy as a superficial, technique-oriented approach that cannot produce long-term changes in clients. Some behavior therapists, in turn, are convinced that psychoanalysis is based on unfounded premises and simply does not work. And some existential psychologists criticize both psychoanalytic therapy and behavior therapy on the grounds that they are mechanistic and reductionistic and are therefore limited in dealing with human struggles.

This book assumes that beginning students of counseling can start to acquire a counseling style tailored to their own personality if they familiarize themselves with the major approaches to therapeutic practice. I emphasize to my students that they will not gain the knowledge and experience needed to synthesize various approaches merely by completing an introductory course in counseling theory. This process will take many years of study, training, and practical counseling experience. I nevertheless recommend a personal synthesis as a framework for the professional education of counselors. The danger in presenting one model to which all students are expected to subscribe is that it could limit their effectiveness in working with future clients. Valuable dimensions of human behavior can be overlooked if the counselor is restricted to a single theory.

On the other hand, an undisciplined eclectic approach can be an excuse for failing to develop a sound rationale for systematically adhering to certain concepts and to the techniques that are extensions of them. It is easy to pick and choose fragments from the various therapies that merely support one's biases and preconceptions. Nevertheless, a study of the various models presented in this book will show that some kind of integration of concepts and techniques from the various approaches is possible.

As I continue to develop the material for this book, I become increasingly aware that each therapeutic approach has useful dimensions and that accepting the validity of one model does not necessarily imply a rejection of seemingly divergent models. It is not a matter of a theory being "right" or "wrong," for every theory offers a unique contribution to understanding human behavior and has unique implications for counseling practice. There is a clear place for theoretical pluralism, especially in a society that is becoming increasingly pluralistic.

# Where I Stand

My own philosophical orientation is strongly influenced by the existential approach. Because this approach does not specify techniques and procedures, I feel the freedom to draw techniques from the other models of therapy. I particularly like to use role-playing techniques. I find that when people can reenact scenes from their lives, they become far more involved than when they merely report anecdotes about themselves. In addition, many techniques in my approach are derived from cognitive-behavior therapy: assertiveness training and social-skills training, behavior rehearsal, modeling, and a variety of coaching techniques.

I respect the psychoanalytic emphasis on early psychosexual and psychosocial development. I believe that one's past plays a crucial role in shaping one's current personality and behavior. Although I reject the deterministic notion that humans are the product of their early conditioning and, thus, are victims of their past, I think that an exploration of the past is essential, particularly to the degree that the past is related to their present emotional or behavioral difficulties.

From the cognitive-behavioral approaches I value the focus on how our thinking affects the way we feel and behave. These therapies also give weight to current behavior. Although thinking and feeling are important dimensions, it can be a mistake to overemphasize them and not explore how clients are behaving. What people are doing often gives us a good clue to what they really want. I also value the emphasis on specific goals and on encouraging clients to formulate concrete aims for their own therapy sessions and in life. I find that "contracts" developed by clients are extremely useful, and I frequently either suggest specific "homework assignments" or ask my clients to devise their own. More approaches have been developing methods that involve a collaboration between the therapist and client, making the therapeutic venture a sharing of responsibility. This collaborative relationship, coupled with teaching clients ways to use what they learn in therapy in their everyday lives, empowers clients to go into the world and take an active stance. Although I accept the value of increasing clients' insight and awareness, I consider it essential that they put into practice what they are learning in therapy.

A related assumption of mine is that clients can exercise increasing freedom to choose their future. Although we are surely influenced by our social environment and although much of our behavior is a product of learning and conditioning, an increased awareness of these forces allows us to transcend them. Most of the contemporary models of counseling and therapy assume that clients are able to accept personal responsibility and that their failure to do so has largely resulted in their present emotional and behavioral difficulties.

This focus on acceptance of personal responsibility does not imply that we can be anything that we want. We need to recognize that there are social, environmental, cultural, and biological realities that limit our freedom of choice. What seems crucial is learning how to cope with the external and internal forces that limit our decisions and behavior. Thus, a comprehensive approach to counseling goes beyond focusing on our internal dynamics by addressing those environmental realities that influence us. Those therapies that focus exclusively on intrapsychic dimensions have limited utility in working with culturally diverse populations.

My philosophy of counseling does not include the assumption that therapy is exclusively for the "sick" and is aimed at "curing" psychological "ailments." Such a focus on psychopathology severely restricts therapeutic practice, mainly because it stresses one's deficits rather than one's strengths. In Chapters 5 and 6, the limitations of this notion of therapy based on a medical model are explored. For example, counselors with an Adlerian orientation contend that people are not emotionally sick and in dire need of curing; rather, people become discouraged and need encouragement. This is a positive and growth-oriented model that is focused on the future, on the goals that provide direction in life, and on the ability of clients to create their destiny. Counseling, then, is viewed as a vehicle for helping "normal" people get more from life. The clients with whom I work in group situations are, for the most part, relatively healthy people who see counseling as a self-exploratory experience. With this population (whom I refer to as "normal neurotics") the Adlerian, existential, person-centered, Gestalt, and cognitive-behavioral perspectives offer valuable tools for helping people make their own changes, both during the therapeutic hour and in their outside existence.

The existential approach and person-centered therapy both emphasize the client/therapist relationship as the major factor that leads to constructive personal change. These approaches stress that therapists' techniques are far less important than the quality of the therapeutic relationship that they develop. Indeed, therapists are not in business to change clients, to give them quick advice, or to solve their problems for them. Instead, therapists heal through a process of genuine dialogue with their clients. The kind of person a therapist is, or the ways of being that he or she models, is the most critical factor affecting the client and promoting change. If practitioners possess wide knowledge, both theoretical and practical, yet lack human qualities of compassion, caring, good faith, honesty, realness, and sensitivity, they are merely technicians. In my judgment those who function exclusively as technicians do not make a significant difference in the life of their clients. It seems essential to me that counselors explore their own values, attitudes, and beliefs in depth and that they work to increase their own awareness. Throughout the book I encourage you to find ways of personally relating to each of the therapies, for unless you apply this material to yourself personally, an academic understanding is the best that you can hope for.

I see the process of psychotherapy as an engagement between two persons, both of whom are bound to change through the therapeutic venture. Perhaps one of the most significant characteristics of an effective therapist is the quality of *presence,* which is discussed in some detail in Chapters 6, 7, and 8. Therapists must be willing to remain open to their own growth and to struggle in their lives if their clients are to believe in them and the therapeutic process. Why should clients seek therapists who are "finished products" and who do not do in their own life what they expect clients to do in theirs? In short, counselors teach clients by the behavior they model.

With respect to mastering the techniques of counseling and being able to apply them appropriately and effectively, it is my belief that, as a counselor, you are your very best technique. Your reactions to your clients, including sharing how you are affected in the relationship with them, can be the most useful catalyst in the therapeutic process. I think it is misleading to imbue students with the idea that counseling is a science that is distinct from the behavior and personality of the counselor. There is no substitute for developing techniques that are an expression of your personality and that work for you. It is really impossible to separate the techniques you use from your personality and the relationship you have with your clients. There is the ever-present danger of becoming a mechanical technician and simply administering techniques to clients without regard for the relationship variables. Techniques should not be used as a substitute for the hard work that it takes to develop a constructive client/ therapist relationship. Although counselors can learn attitudes and skills and acquire certain knowledge about personality dynamics and the therapeutic process, much of effective therapy is the product of artistry. Thus, counseling entails far more than becoming a skilled technician. It implies that you are able to establish and maintain a good working relationship with your clients, that you can draw upon your own experiences and reactions, and that you can use techniques that are suited to the needs of your clients.

I encourage students and those with whom I consult to experience a wide variety of techniques themselves *as clients*. Reading about a technique in a book is one thing; actually experiencing it from the vantage point of a client is quite another. If you have practiced relaxation exercises, for example, you will have a much better feel for how to administer them and will know more about what to look for as you work with clients. If you have carried out real-life homework assignments as a part of your own self-change program, you will have a lot more empathy for your clients and their potential problems. If you have experienced guided imagery, you are likely to suggest fantasy exercises to your clients in a more sensitive and effective manner. Your own anxiety over self-disclosing and confronting personal concerns can be a most useful anchoring point as you work with the anxieties of your clients. The courage you display in your therapy will help you appreciate how essential courage is for your clients.

Although I emphasize that the human qualities of a therapist are of primary importance, I do not think it is sufficient to be merely a good person with good intentions. To be effective, the therapist also requires supervised experiences in counseling and a knowledge of counseling theory and techniques. Further, it is essential to be well grounded in the various *theories of personality* and to learn how they are related to theories of counseling. Your conception of the person affects the interventions that you make. Another factor, of course, is the individual characteristics of the client. Some practitioners make the mistake of relying on one type of intervention (supportive, confrontational, information-giving) for most of the clients with whom they work. In reality, different clients may respond to various types of intervention. Even in the course of an individual's therapy, he or she may need various interventions. Practitioners need to acquire a broad base of counseling techniques that are suitable for an individual client, rather than forcing the client to fit their specialized form of intervention.

# Suggestions for Using the Book

Here are some specific recommendations on how to get the fullest value from this book. The personal tone of the book invites you to relate what you are reading to your own experiences. As you read Chapter 2, "The Counselor: Person and Professional," begin the process of reflecting on your needs, motivations, values, and life experiences, considering how you are likely to bring the person you are becoming into your professional work. You will assimilate much more knowledge about the various therapies if you make a conscious attempt to apply their key concepts and techniques to your personal growth. Chapter 2 can also help you think about how to use yourself as a person as your single most important therapeutic instrument. Merely memorizing the ideas and procedures of the models is of little value. What *will* make a difference is your ability to incorporate selected concepts and procedures into a personalized style of counseling that expresses your own uniqueness. Chapter 3 deals with significant ethical issues in counseling practice, and it is useful to begin considering them early in the course. These topics include the rights and responsibilities of clients, the ethics of the client/therapist relationship, ethical issues in multicultural perspective, and dealing with counseling goals.

Students learn a lot by seeing a theory in action, preferably in a live demonstration or as part of experiential activities in which they function in the alternating roles of client and counselor. Many students find the case history of a hypothetical client, "Stan," helpful in understanding how various techniques are applied to the same person. The introduction to Stan's case, which describes his life and struggles, is found at the end of this chapter. In each of the nine theory chapters, there is a discussion of how a therapist with the orientation in question is likely to proceed with Stan. In Chapter 14, which I recommend reading early, I present how I would work with Stan, suggesting concepts and techniques that I would draw on from many of the models (forming an integrative approach).

Next, and also before you study each therapy in depth in Part Two, Chapters 4–12, I suggest that you at least skim Chapter 13, which is a comprehensive review of the key concepts from all nine of the theories you will study. I attempt to show how an integration of these perspectives can form the basis for creating your own personal synthesis to counseling. In developing an integrative perspective, it is essential to think holistically. To understand human functioning, it is imperative to account for the physical, emotional, mental, social, cultural, political, and spiritual dimensions. If any of these facets of human experience is neglected, a theory is limited in explaining how we think, feel, and act.

To provide you with a consistent framework for comparing and contrasting the various therapies, the nine theory chapters share a common format. This format includes a few notes on the personal history of the founder or another key figure; a brief historical sketch showing how and why each theory developed at the time it did; a discussion of the approach's key concepts; an overview of the therapeutic process (including the therapist's role and client's work); therapeutic techniques and procedures; a summary and evaluation; suggestions of how to continue your learning about each approach; and suggestions for further reading.

# Overview of the Theory Chapters

This section explains why I have selected the nine therapeutic approaches discussed in this book. Table 1-1 presents an overview of these approaches, which are explored in Chapters 4–12. I have classified them in four general categories.

First are the *analytic approaches. Psychoanalytic therapy* is based largely on insight, unconscious motivation, and reconstruction of the personality. The reason for including the psychoanalytic model (and placing it first) is its major influence on all of the other formal systems of psychotherapy. Some of the therapeutic models are basically extensions of psychoanalysis, others are modifications of analytic concepts and procedures, and still others are positions that emerged as a reaction against psychoanalysis. Many of the other theories of counseling and psychotherapy have borrowed and integrated principles and techniques from psychoanalytic approaches.

*Adlerian therapy* differs from psychoanalytic theory in many respects, but it can broadly be considered an analytic perspective. Adlerians focus on meaning, goals, purposeful behavior, conscious action, belonging, and social interest. Although Adlerian theory accounts for present behavior by studying childhood experiences, it does not focus on unconscious dynamics. There has been a reawakening of interest in Alfred Adler's ideas, and greater credit is now being given to his contributions to all of the contemporary therapies. In the 1920s and 1930s Adler was truly a pioneering genius, and his approach was a precursor of many of the cognitive therapies that have been thriving since the 1980s.

The second category comprises the *experiential and relationship-oriented therapies,* the existential approach, the person-centered approach, and Gestalt therapy. The *existential approach* stresses a concern for what it means to be fully human. It suggests certain themes that are a part of the human condition, such as freedom and responsibility, anxiety, guilt, awareness of being finite, creating meaning in the world, and shaping one's future by making active choices. This approach is not a unified school of therapy with a clear theory and a systematic set of techniques. Rather, it is a philosophy of counseling that stresses the divergent methods of understanding the subjective world of the person. The *person-centered approach,* which is rooted in a humanistic philosophy, places emphasis on the basic attitudes of the therapist. It maintains that the quality of the client/therapist relationship is the prime determinant of the outcomes of the therapeutic process. Philosophically, this model assumes that clients have the capacity for self-direction without active intervention and direction

TABLE 1-1
Overview of Contemporary Counseling Models

| | |
|---|---|
| *Psychoanalytic psychotherapy* | Key figure: Sigmund Freud. A theory of personality development, a philosophy of human nature, and a method of psychotherapy, it focuses on unconscious factors that motivate behavior. Attention is given to the events of the first six years of life as determinants of the later development of personality. |
| *Adlerian therapy* | Key figure: Alfred Adler. Following Adler, Rudolf Dreikurs is credited with popularizing the approach in the United States. A growth model, it stresses taking responsibility, creating one's own destiny, and finding meaning and goals to give life direction. Key concepts are used in most other current therapies. |
| *Existential therapy* | Key figures: Viktor Frankl, Rollo May, and Irvin Yalom. It reacts against the tendency to view therapy as a system of well-defined techniques. Instead, it stresses building therapy on the basic conditions of human existence, such as choice, the freedom and responsibility to shape one's life, and self-determination. It focuses on the quality of the person-to-person therapeutic relationship. |
| *Person-centered therapy* | Founder: Carl Rogers. This approach was developed during the 1940s as a nondirective reaction against psychoanalysis. Based on a subjective view of human experiencing, it places faith in and gives responsibility to the client in dealing with problems. |
| *Gestalt therapy* | Founder: Fritz Perls. An experiential therapy stressing awareness and integration, it grew as a reaction against analytic therapy. It integrates the functioning of body and mind. |
| *Reality therapy* | Founder: William Glasser. A short-term approach focusing on the present, it stresses a person's strengths. Clients learn more realistic behavior and thus achieve success. |
| *Behavior therapy* | Key figures: Arnold Lazarus and Albert Bandura. It applies the principles of learning to the resolution of specific behavioral disorders. Results are subject to continual experimentation. This technique is always in the process of refinement. |
| *Cognitive-behavior therapy* | Key figures: Albert Ellis founded rational emotive behavior therapy, a highly didactic, cognitive, action-oriented model of therapy that stresses the role of thinking and belief systems as the root of personal problems. A. T. Beck founded cognitive therapy. |
| *Family systems therapy* | The systemic approach is based on the assumption that the key to changing the individual is understanding and working with the family. |

on the therapist's part. It is in the context of a living and authentic relationship with the therapist that this growth force within the client is released. The final experiential approach is *Gestalt therapy.* It offers a range of techniques for helping clients focus on what they are experiencing now.

Third are the *action therapies,* which include reality therapy, behavior therapy, rational emotive behavior therapy, and cognitive therapy. *Reality therapy* focuses on clients' current behavior. It stresses their personal responsibility for changing themselves by developing clear plans for new behaviors. Like reality therapy, *behavior therapy* puts a premium on *doing* and on taking steps to make concrete changes. A current trend in behavior therapy is toward paying increased attention to cognitive factors as an important determinant of behavior. *Rational emotive behavior therapy* and *cognitive therapy* highlight the necessity of learning how to challenge dysfunctional beliefs and automatic thoughts that lead to human misery. These approaches are used to help people undermine their faulty and self-defeating assumptions and form a rational philosophy of life.

The fourth general approach is the *systems perspective,* of which family therapy is a part. This orientation stresses the importance of understanding individuals in the context of the surroundings that influence their development. In order to bring about individual change, it is essential to pay attention to the way in which the individual's personality has been affected by his or her family and other systems.

In my view, practitioners need to pay attention to what their clients are *thinking, feeling,* and *doing.* Thus, a complete therapy system must address all three of these facets. Some of the therapies included in this book highlight the role that cognitive factors and thinking play in counseling; others place emphasis on the experiential aspects of counseling and the role of feelings, and others emphasize putting plans into action and learning by doing. Combining all of these dimensions provides the basis for a powerful and comprehensive therapy. If any of these dimensions is excluded, the therapy approach is incomplete.

# Introduction to the Case of Stan

In each of the nine theory chapters in Part Two, as mentioned, I illustrate how the various therapies can be used to deal with the same client, Stan. We will examine their answers to questions such as these: What themes in Stan's life merit special attention in therapy? What concepts explain the nature of his problems? What are the general goals of his therapy? What possible techniques and methods would best meet these goals? What are some characteristics of the relationship between Stan and his therapist? How might the therapist proceed?

A single case can illustrate both contrasts and parallels among the approaches. It will also help you understand the practical applications of the nine models and will provide some basis for integrating them. Try to sharpen your focus on certain attributes of each approach that can be incorporated into a personalized style of counseling.

The setting is a community mental-health agency, where both individual and group counseling by a qualified staff are available. Stan is coming to counseling because of a court order as a stipulation of his probation. He was convicted of driving under the influence of alcohol. Although he does not think he has a serious drinking problem, the judge determined that he needed professional help. Stan arrives for an intake interview and provides the counselor with this information:

> At 25 years old I'm working in construction. I like building houses, but I'm pretty sure I don't want to stay in construction for the rest of my life. When it comes to my personal life, I've always had a rough time getting along with people. I suppose you could call me a "loner." I like having people in my life, but I just don't seem to know how to go about making friends or getting close to people. Probably the reason I sometimes drink a bit too much is because I'm so scared when it comes to mixing with people. Even though I hate to admit it, when I've been drinking, things don't seem quite so overwhelming. When I look at others, they seem to know the right things to say. Next to them I feel so dumb. I'm afraid that people will be bored with me and that if they really knew me, they wouldn't want anything to do with me. Sure, I'd like to turn my life around, and I'm trying, but sometimes I just don't know where to begin. That's why I went back to school. Besides my work in construction I'm also a part-time college student majoring in psychology. I want to better myself. In one of my classes, Psychology of Personal Adjustment, we talked about ourselves and how we wanted to change, and we also had to write an autobiographical paper. Should I bring it in?

That is the essence of Stan's introduction. The counselor says that she very much wants to read his autobiography. He hopes it will give her a better understanding of where he has been, where he is now, where he would like to go, and what he wants for himself. It reads as follows:

> Where I am currently in my life? At 25, I feel that I've wasted most of my life. By now I should be finished with college and into a good job, but instead I'm only a junior. I can't afford to really commit myself to pursuing college full time, because I need to work to support myself. Even though construction work is hard, I like the satisfaction I get when I look at what I helped build.
>
> Although I'd like to build things as a hobby, I want to get into some profession where I could work with people, if I can ever get over my fears of what people think of me. Someday, I'm hoping to get a master's degree in counseling or in social work and eventually work as a counselor with kids who are in trouble. I feel I was helped by someone who cared about me, and I would like to have a similar influence on young people.
>
> At this time I live alone, have very few friends, and feel scared with people my own age or older. I feel good when I'm with kids, because they're so honest. But I worry a lot whether I'm smart enough to get through all the studies I'll need to do before I can become a counselor.
>
> One of my problems is that I drink heavily and frequently get drunk. This happens mostly when I feel alone and scared that I'll always feel as lonely and isolated as I do now. At first drinking makes me feel better, but later on I really feel rotten. I used to do drugs heavily, and once in a while I still get loaded.

People really scare me, and I feel overwhelmed when I'm around strong and attractive women. I feel all cold, sweaty, and terribly uptight when I'm with a woman. Maybe I think they're judging me, and I know they'll find out that I'm not much of a man. I'm afraid I won't measure up to being a man—*always* having to be strong, tough, and perfect. I'm not any of those, so I often wonder if I'm adequate as a man. I really have trouble seeing myself as sexually adequate. When I do have sex, I get uptight and worry that I won't be able to perform, and then I really feel terrible.

I feel anxiety much of the time, particularly at night. Sometimes I get so scared that I feel like running, but I just can't move. It's awful, because I often feel as if I'm dying at times like this. And then I fantasize about committing suicide and wonder who would care. Sometimes I see my family coming to my funeral feeling very sorry that they didn't treat me better. I even made a weak attempt to do myself in a couple of years ago. Much of the time I feel guilty that I haven't worked up to my potential, that I've been a failure, that I've wasted much of my time, and that I let people down a lot. I can really get down on myself and wallow in my guilt, and I feel very *depressed*. At times like this I think about how rotten I am, how I'll never to able to change, and how I'd be better off dead. Then I wouldn't have to hurt anymore, and I wouldn't want anything either. It's very difficult for me to get close to anyone. I can't say that I've ever loved a person, and I know that I've never felt fully loved or wanted.

Everything is not bleak, because I did have enough guts to leave a lot of my shady past behind me, and I did get into college. I like my determination—I *want* to change. I'm tired of feeling like a loser, and I know that nobody is going to change my life for me. It's up to me to get what I want. Even though I feel scared a lot, I like it that I can *feel* my feelings and that I'm willing to take risks. I hate being a quitter.

What was my past like? What are some significant events and turning points in my life? A major turning point was the confidence my supervisor had in me at the youth camp where I worked the past few summers. He helped me get my job, and he also encouraged me to go to college. He said he saw a lot of potential in me for being able to work well with young people. That was hard for me to really believe, but his faith inspired me to begin to believe in myself. Another turning point was my marriage and divorce. This "relationship" didn't last long before my wife left me. Wow, that really made me wonder about what kind of man I was! She was a strong and dominant woman who was always telling me how worthless I was and how she couldn't stand to get near me. We met in a gambling casino in Las Vegas, and we tied the knot shortly after that. We had sex only a few times, and most of the time I was impotent. That was hard to take—a real downer! I'm so afraid to get close to a woman. I'm afraid she'll swallow me up. My parents never got a divorce, but I wish they had. They fought most of the time. I should say, my mother did most of the fighting. She was dominant and continually bitching at my father, whom I always saw as weak, passive, and mousy next to her. He would *never* stand up to her. There were four of us kids at home. My folks always compared me unfavorably with my older sister (Judy) and older brother (Frank). They were "perfect" children, successful honor students. My younger brother (Karl) and I fought a lot, and he was the one who was spoiled rotten by them. I really don't know what happened to me and how I turned out to be the failure of the bunch.

In high school I got involved with the wrong crowd and took a lot of drugs. I was thrown into a youth rehabilitation facility for stealing. Later I was expelled from regular school for fighting, and I landed in a continuation high school, where I would go to school in the mornings and have afternoons for on-the-job training. I got into auto mechanics and was fairly successful and even managed to keep myself employed for three years as a mechanic.

Back to my parents. I remember my father telling me: "You're really dumb. Why can't you be like your sister and brother? You'll never amount to a hill of beans! Why can't you ever do anything right?" And my mother treated me much the way she treated my father. She would say: "Why do you do so many things to hurt me? Why can't you grow up and be a man? You were a mistake— I wish I hadn't had you! Things are so much better around here when you're gone." I recall crying myself to sleep many nights, feeling so terribly alone and filled with anger and hate. And feeling so disgusted with myself. There was no talk of religion in my house, nor was there any talk about sex. In fact, I always find it hard to imagine my folks ever having sex.

Where would I like to be five years from now? What kind of person do I want to become, and what changes do I most want in my life? Most of all, I would just like to start feeling better about myself. I would really like to be able to stop drinking altogether and still feel good. I have an inferiority complex, and I know how to put myself down. I want to like myself much more than I do now. I hope I can learn to love at least a few other people, most of all, women. I want to lose my fear that women can destroy me. I would like to feel equal with others and not always have to feel apologetic for my existence. I don't want to suffer from this anxiety and guilt. And I hope that I can begin to think of myself as an OK person. I really want to become a good counselor with kids, and to do this I know I'm going to have to change. I'm not certain how I'll change or even what all the changes are I hope for. I do know that I want to get free of my self-destructive tendencies and learn to trust people more. Maybe when I begin to like myself more, I'll be able to trust that others might find something about me that is worth liking.

Effective therapists, regardless of their theoretical orientation, would pay attention to suicidal ideation. In his autobiography Stan says that "I fantasize about committing suicide and wonder who would care." At times, he also doubts that he will ever change and wonders if he'd be better off dead. The therapist, before embarking on the therapeutic journey, would certainly make an assessment of Stan's current ego strength, which would include a discussion of his suicidal thoughts and feelings. (There is a discussion of specific guidelines for the assessment of suicidal risk in Chapter 3.)

In Chapters 4–12, you can assume that a practitioner representing each of the theories has read Stan's case and is familiar with key themes in his life. Each therapist will illustrate the concepts and techniques of the particular approach as it applies to working with him. In addition, in these chapters you are asked to think about how you would continue counseling him from the different perspectives. In doing so, you will find it useful to refer back to Stan's autobiography and also to some of the material in Chapter 14.

CHAPTER TWO

# The Counselor:
# Person and Professional

# Introduction

In this chapter I ask you to examine my assumption that one of the most important instruments you have to work with as a counselor is *yourself as a person*. In preparing for counseling, you can acquire a knowledge of the theories of personality and psychotherapy, you can learn diagnostic and intervention techniques, and you can learn about the dynamics of human behavior. Although such knowledge and skills are essential, I do not believe that they are, by themselves, sufficient for establishing and maintaining effective therapeutic relationships. To every therapy session we bring our human qualities and the experiences that have influenced us. In my judgment this human dimension is one of the most powerful determinants of the therapeutic encounter that we have with clients. If we hope as counselors to promote growth and change in our clients, we must be willing to promote growth in our own life. Our most powerful source of influencing clients in a positive direction is our living example of who we are and how we continually struggle to live up to our potential.

A good way to begin your study of contemporary counseling theories is by reflecting on the personal issues that are raised in this chapter. Then, after you have studied the nine theories of counseling, this chapter deserves another reading. I suggest that you reevaluate ways in which you can work on your development as a person, considering especially your needs, motivations, values, and personality traits that could either enhance or interfere with your effectiveness as a counselor. By remaining open to self-evaluation, you not only expand your awareness of self but also build the foundation for developing your abilities as a professional. The theme of this chapter is that the *person* and the *professional* are intertwined entities that cannot be separated in reality.

# Personal Characteristics of Effective Counselors

The trend in counseling today is toward stressing the values and behavior of the counselor. What is crucial is therapists' ability to look at, understand, and accept themselves as well as their clients. Because the quality of the client/counselor relationship seems to be the most important factor fostering growth, we will examine in this section the personal characteristics of counselors that contribute most to this relationship.

## THE AUTHENTICITY OF THE COUNSELOR

Therapy, because it is an intimate form of learning, demands a practitioner who is willing to shed stereotyped roles and be a real person in a relationship. It is precisely within the context of such a person-to-person relationship that the client experiences growth. If as counselors we hide behind the safety of our professional role, our clients will keep themselves hidden from us. If we become merely technical experts and leave our own reactions, values, and self out of our work, the result will be sterile counseling. It is through our own genuineness and our aliveness that we can significantly touch our clients. If we make life-oriented choices, radiate a zest for life, are real in our relationships with our clients, and let ourselves be known to them, we can inspire and teach them in the best sense of the words. This does not mean that we are self-actualized persons who have "made it" or that we are without our problems. Rather, it implies that we are willing to look at our lives and make the changes we want. Because we affirm that changing is worth the risk and the effort, we hold out hope to our clients that they can become their own person and can like the person they are becoming.

In short, as therapists we serve as models for our clients. If we model incongruent behavior, low-risk activity, and deceit by remaining hidden and vague, we can expect our clients to imitate this behavior. If we model realness by engaging in appropriate self-disclosure, our clients will tend to be honest with us in the therapeutic relationship. To be sure, counseling can be for better or for worse. Clients can become more of what they are capable of becoming, or they can become less than they might be. In my judgment the degree of aliveness and psychological health of the counselor is the crucial variable that determines the outcome.

## THE COUNSELOR AS A THERAPEUTIC PERSON

How can counselors be therapeutic persons and model awareness and growth for their clients? In thinking about counselors who are therapeutic, I have isolated a cluster of personal qualities and characteristics. I do not expect any therapist to fully exemplify all these traits, and I am not proposing a fixed model of perfection. Rather, for me the willingness to struggle to become a more therapeutic person is the crucial quality. The following list is not a dogmatic itemizing of the "right" ways to be a therapist. It is intended to stimulate you to examine your ideas of what kind of person can make a significant difference in the lives of others.

- *Effective counselors have an identity.* They know who they are, what they are capable of becoming, what they want out of life, and what is essential. Although they have a clear sense of their priorities, they are willing to reexamine their values and goals. They are not mere reflections of what others expect or want them to be but strive to live by internal standards.
- *They respect and appreciate themselves.* They can give help and love out of their own sense of self-worth and strength. They are also able to ask and to receive from others, and they do not isolate themselves from others as a false demonstration of strength.
- *They are able to recognize and accept their own power.* They feel adequate with others and allow others to feel powerful with them. They do not diminish others so that they can feel a relative sense of power. They use their power and model its healthy uses for clients, but they avoid abusing it.

- *They are open to change.* Rather than settling for less, they extend themselves to become more. They exhibit a willingness and courage to leave the security of the known if they are not satisfied with what they have.
- *They are expanding their awareness of self and others.* They realize that if they have limited awareness, they also have limited freedom. Instead of investing energy in defensive behavior designed to block out experiences, they focus on reality-oriented tasks.
- *They are willing and able to tolerate ambiguity.* Most of us have a low threshold for coping with a lack of clarity. Because growth depends on leaving the familiar and entering unknown territory, people who are committed to personal development are willing to accept some degree of ambiguity in their lives. As they build their ego strength, they develop more self-trust—that is, trust in their intuitive processes and judgments and willingness to experiment with novel behavior. They eventually come to realize that they are trustworthy.
- *They are developing their own counseling style.* It is an expression of their philosophy of life and an outgrowth of their life experiences. Although they may freely borrow ideas and techniques from many other therapists, they do not mechanically imitate another's style.
- *They can experience and know the world of the client, yet their empathy is nonpossessive.* They are aware of their own struggles and pain, and they have a frame of reference for identifying with others while at the same time not losing their own identity by overidentifying with others.
- *They feel alive, and their choices are life-oriented.* They are committed to living fully rather than settling for mere existence. They do not allow events to shape them, for they take an active stance toward life.
- *They are authentic, sincere, and honest.* They do not live by pretenses but attempt to *be* what they think and feel. They are willing to appropriately disclose themselves to selected others. They do not hide behind masks, defenses, sterile roles, and facades.
- *They have a sense of humor.* They are able to put the events of life in perspective. They have not forgotten how to laugh, especially at their own foibles and contradictions. Their sense of humor enables them to put their problems and imperfections in perspective.
- *They make mistakes and are willing to admit them.* Although they are not overburdened with guilt over how they could or should have acted, they learn from mistakes. They do not dismiss their errors lightly, yet they do not choose to dwell on misery.
- *They generally live in the present.* They are not riveted to the past, nor are they fixated on the future. They are able to experience the "now" and be present with others in the now. They can be with others in their pain or their joy, for they are open to their own emotional experience.
- *They appreciate the influence of culture.* They are aware of the ways in which their own culture affects them, and they have a respect for the diversity of values espoused by other cultures. They are also sensitive to the unique differences arising out of social class, race, and gender.
- *They are able to reinvent themselves.* They can revitalize and recreate significant relationships. They make decisions about how they would like

to change, and they work toward becoming the person they would like to become.

- *They are making choices that shape their lives.* They are aware of early decisions they made about themselves, others, and the world. They are not the victims of these early decisions, for they are willing to revise them if necessary. Because they are continually evaluating themselves, they are not restrained by limited self-definitions.

- *They have a sincere interest in the welfare of others.* This concern is based on respect, care, trust, and a real valuing of others. It implies that they are willing to challenge people who are significant in their lives to also remain open to growth.

- *They become deeply involved in their work and derive meaning from it.* They can accept the rewards flowing from their work, and they can honestly admit the ego needs that are gratified by it. Yet they are not slaves to their work, and they do not depend on it exclusively to live a full life. They have other interests that provide them with a sense of purpose and fulfillment.

- *They are able to maintain healthy boundaries.* Although they strive to be fully present for their clients, they don't carry the problems of their clients around with them during leisure hours. They know how to say no, which allows them to keep a balance in their lives. They are alert to signs of burnout and take good care of themselves. Being an effective counselor does not involve unbounded giving and altruism.

This picture of the characteristics of the therapeutic person might appear monumental and unrealistic. Who could ever be all those things? Certainly I do not fit this bill! Do not think of these personal characteristics from an all-or-nothing perspective; rather, consider them on a continuum. A given trait may be very characteristic of you, at one extreme, or it may be very uncharacteristic of you, at the other extreme. For example, it is not a question of either being emotionally present for others or being completely detached and distant. To some extent you can learn to become more present when you are with others. I have presented this picture of the therapeutic person with the hope that you will examine it and develop your own concept of what personality traits you think are essential to strive for in order to promote personal growth.

# Personal Counseling for the Counselor

Discussion of the counselor as a therapeutic person raises another issue debated in counselor education: whether people should participate in counseling or therapy before they become practitioners. My view is that counselors should have the experience of being a client at some time, because such self-exploration can increase their level of self-awareness. This experience can be obtained before their training, during it, or both, but I strongly support some form of personal exploration as a prerequisite to counseling others.

Such counseling should be viewed not as an end in itself but as a means to help a potential counselor become a more therapeutic person who will have a greater chance of positively influencing clients. Opportunities for self-exploration can be instrumental in helping counselors-in-training assess their motivations for pursuing this profession. Examining our values, needs, attitudes, and experiences can illuminate what we are getting from helping others. It is important that we know why we want to intervene in the lives of others, so that we can avoid the pitfalls of continually giving to others yet finding little personal satisfaction from our efforts. There is value in continuing individual or group counseling as we begin to practice as professionals. At this time we often feel a sense of professional impotence, and we frequently feel like quitting. Student counselors would do well to recognize their helplessness and despair but to avoid deciding too soon that they are unsuited to be a counselor. Personal counseling is an ideal place for beginning counselors to express and explore their concerns over whether they are able to help anyone. Issues such as the hazards of the counseling profession, as well as those related to the therapist's personal life, can be profitably explored in a counselor's personal therapy as the need arises (Guy, 1987; Kottler, 1993).

Being therapists forces us to confront our unexplored blocks related to loneliness, power, death, sexuality, our parents, and so on. This does not mean that we need to be free of conflicts before we can counsel others, but it does mean that we should be aware of what these conflicts are and how they are likely to affect us as counselors. For example, if we have great difficulty in dealing with anger and guilt in ourselves, the chances are that we will do something to dilute these emotions when they occur in our clients. How can we be present for our clients and encourage them to express feelings that we are so intent on denying in ourselves?

When I began counseling others, old wounds were opened, and feelings that I had not explored in depth came to the surface. It was difficult for me to encounter a client's depression, because I had failed to come to terms with the way I had escaped from my own depression. Thus, I did my best to cheer up depressed clients by talking them out of what they were feeling, mainly because of my own inability to deal with such feelings. In the years when I began working as a counselor in a university counseling center, I frequently wondered what I could do for my clients. I often had no idea of what, if anything, my clients were getting from our sessions. I couldn't tell if they were getting better, staying the same, or getting worse. It was very important to me to note progress and see change in my clients. Because I did not see immediate results, I had many doubts whether I could become an effective counselor. What I did not understand at the time was that my clients needed to struggle to find their own answers. It was *my* need to see them feel better quickly, for then I would know that I was helping them. It never occurred to me that clients often feel worse as they give up their defenses and open themselves to their pain. It took me some time to appreciate the courage involved in becoming fully engaged in the therapeutic venture.

Personal therapy can be instrumental, then, in healing the healer. If student counselors are not actively involved in the pursuit of healing their own psychological wounds, they will probably have considerable difficulty entering the world of a client. As counselors we can take our clients no further than we have been willing to go in our own life. If we are not committed personally to the value of struggling, we will not convince clients that they should pay the price of their struggle. Through being clients ourselves, we have an experiential frame of reference to view ourselves as we are. It gives us a basis for compassion for our clients, for we can draw on our own memories of reaching impasses in our therapy, of both wanting to go further and at the same time wanting to stay where we were. Our own therapy can help us develop patience with our patients! We learn what it feels like to deal with anxieties that are aroused by self-disclosure and self-exploration. We may experience transference and thus know firsthand how it is to view our therapist as a parent figure. Being willing to participate in a process of self-exploration can reduce the chances of assuming an attitude of arrogance or of being convinced that we have "arrived" as a person. Indeed, experiencing counseling as a client is very different from merely reading about the counseling process.

The main reason for having students receive some form of psychotherapy is to help them learn to deal with countertransference (the process of seeing themselves in their clients, of overidentifying with their clients, or of meeting their needs through their clients). Recognizing the manifestations of their countertransference reactions is one of the most essential abilities of effective counselors. Unless counselors are aware of their own conflicts, needs, assets, and liabilities, they can use the therapy hour more for their own purposes than for being available for their clients, which becomes an ethical issue. Unaware counselors are in danger of being carried away on the client's emotional tidal wave, which is of no help to themselves or their clients. It is unrealistic to think that counselors can completely rid themselves of any traces of counter-transference or that they can ever fully resolve certain issues from the past. But they can become aware of the signs of these reactions and can deal with these feelings in their own therapy and supervision sessions.

Ideally, individual counseling is combined with group-oriented growth experiences. My preference is for personal-growth groups, for here counselor candidates can benefit from the reactions of other members. The group can focus on helping the participants clarify their motivations for wanting to become a counselor. Some questions for exploration are these: "Why do I want to pursue a career in the helping professions? What are my own needs and motivations? What rewards do I receive from being a counselor? How can I differentiate between satisfaction of clients' needs and satisfaction of my own needs?" Other questions that might profitably be asked in a personal-growth experience are as follows: "What are some of my problems, and what am I doing to resolve them? How might my own problems get in the way of working as a counselor? What are my values, where did they originate, and how will they affect my counseling style? How willing am I to take risks? Am I willing to do what I encourage my clients to do? What are some ways in which I avoid using my own strengths, and how can I more fully utilize my potential power? What keeps me from being as open, honest, and real as I might be? How do others experience me? What impact do I have on others?"

These questions reflect but a few of the possible areas of exploration in a personal-growth experience. The aim is to provide a situation in which counselors can come to greater self-understanding. I never cease to be surprised by the amount of resistance I encounter from the ranks of professionals on this issue. I hear this argument: "Requiring the therapist to be a client in personal counseling is based on a medical model of sickness. It's like saying that a surgeon can't perform an operation that he or she has not also undergone." I simply cannot accept that analogy. I am left with the strong conviction that therapists cannot hope to open doors for clients that they have not opened for themselves. If we are fearful of facing ourselves, how can we help others look at their lives? If we have limited vision, how can we help our clients expand their vision of what they might become?

Some practitioners view themselves as beyond making personal use of the kind of therapy they offer to others, which makes me wonder whether they truly believe in therapy as an agent for change. It is as though they think that they should be able to work out all of their problems by themselves and that seeking professional help is a sign of personal and professional weakness. It is obvious that experienced practitioners occasionally go through a crisis or an impairment. People do not have total control over their lives. They must face unexpected events such as illness and death. Thus, anyone may need help at a given time to work through a crisis. Being open to periodic self-review with the help of another professional can be a resource for acquiring a new perspective on a problem. Although supervision with a personal focus on the counselor as a person may not be available in some educational and professional settings, it is essential that practitioners learn how to ask for supervision that involves self-review and the care of the counselor as well as supervision that focuses largely on case management or the dynamics of dealing with clients.

# The Counselor's Values and the Therapeutic Process

As alluded to in the last section, the importance of self-exploration for counselors carries over to the values and beliefs they hold. My experience in teaching and supervising students of counseling shows me how crucial it is that they be aware of their values, of where and how they acquired them, and of how their values influence their interventions with clients. An excellent focus for the process of self-searching is examining how your values are likely to affect your work as a counselor. Counseling and therapy are not forms of indoctrination whereby practitioners persuade clients to act or feel in the "right way." Unfortunately, many well-intentioned counselors are overzealous in their mission of helping to "straighten people out." The implication is that by virtue of their greater wisdom they will provide answers for the troubled client. But counseling is not synonymous with preaching or teaching.

## THE ROLE OF VALUES IN COUNSELING

A core issue is the degree to which the counselor's values should enter into a therapeutic relationship. As counselors we are often taught not to let our values show, lest they bias the direction clients are likely to take. Yet we are simply not value-neutral, nor are we value-free; our therapeutic interventions rest on core values. Although our values do influence the way we practice, it is possible to maintain a sense of objectivity. Let me pose a series of questions designed to help you search yourself for your own tentative answers about the role of values in counseling:

- Is it desirable for counselors to hold back their value judgments about their clients' choices? Is it possible for therapists to make value judgments only about events that affect their own personal life and pass no judgments on to clients?
- Is it possible for counselors to disagree with a client's values and still accept him or her as a person?
- Can counselors remain "neutral" and still challenge their clients to make an honest assessment of whether their behavior is getting them what they want? Is there a difference between neutrality and objectivity?
- How can practitioners retain their own sense of values and remain true to themselves yet at the same time allow their clients the freedom to select values and behavior that differ sharply from theirs?
- What is the essential difference between counselors who honestly expose their core values, when appropriate, and those who in subtle ways "guide" their clients to accept the values that they deem to be good for them?
- Is it possible to separate a discussion of values from the therapeutic process?
- What is the best course of action to take when you become aware of sharp value conflicts with certain clients?
- Is it ever justifiable for counselors to impose their values on clients? What about those situations in which the counselor is convinced that the client's values result in self-destructive behavior?

From my perspective, your role as a counselor is to create a climate in which clients can examine their thoughts, feelings, and actions and eventually arrive at solutions that are best for them. Your job is to *assist* individuals in finding answers that are most congruent with their own values. What seems critical is that you be aware of the nature of your values and how your beliefs and standards operate on the interventions you make with clients. Your function as a counselor is not to persuade or convince clients of the proper course to take but to help them assess their behavior so that they can determine the degree to which it is working for them. If clients acknowledge that what they are doing is not working, it is appropriate to challenge them to develop new ways of behaving to help them move closer to their goals. Of course, this process of challenging clients is done with full respect given to their right to decide which values they will use as a framework for living. Individuals seeking counseling are the ones who need to wrestle with clarifying their own values and goals, making informed decisions, choosing a course of action, and assuming the responsibility and accountability for the decisions they make. Because counseling is a process that involves teaching clients how to deal with their problems and find their own solutions based on their value system, it is essential that the counselor not short-circuit a client's exploration.

One national survey revealed a consensus among a representative group of mental-health professionals that certain basic values are important for healthy lifestyles and for guiding and evaluating psychotherapy (Jensen & Bergin, 1988). The following ten values were thought by these professionals to contribute to a positive, mentally healthy lifestyle: (1) competent perception and expression of feelings; (2) a sense of being a free and responsible agent; (3) developing strategies for managing stress; (4) self-awareness and growth; (5) being committed in marriage, family, and other relationships; (6) self-maintenance and physical fitness; (7) having orienting goals and a meaningful purpose; (8) forgiveness; (9) regulated sexual fulfillment; and (10) spirituality/religiosity. This study implies that the value systems of practitioners are an integral part of therapeutic theory and practice, challenging the view that therapists should be neutral with respect to values.

The question of the influence of the counselor's values on the client has ethical implications when we consider that goals and therapeutic methods are expressions of the counselor's philosophy of life. Even though therapists should not directly teach the client or impose specific values, they do implement a philosophy of counseling, which is, in effect, a philosophy of life. Counselors communicate their values by the therapeutic goals to which they subscribe and by the procedures they employ to reach these goals. Counselors' views of what they want their clients to be like, or their views of a healthy and optimally functioning person, *do* reveal their values. Because ethically sensitive therapists respect their clients' self-determination, they help them decide whether they are truly living by their values or merely incorporating parental and societal values without evaluating them. Professionals need to be alert to the possibility of manipulating a client to accept values wholesale, for to do so would mean that they were simply becoming another parent substitute.

## DEALING WITH VALUE CONFLICTS

As an example of the influence that the counselor's philosophy of life can have on a client and of possible clashes over values between the client and the counselor, consider this case: The client, Joyce, is a married woman in her late 30s with three children. She has been in weekly individual therapy for six months. She is struggling to decide whether she wants to remain married to her husband, whom she perceives as boring, uninvolved with their children, complacent, and overly involved in his work. Although Joyce has urged him to join her in marriage counseling or undertake some form of therapy for himself, he has consistently refused. He maintains that he is fine and that she is the one with the problems. She tells the therapist that she would divorce him immediately "if it weren't for the kids" and that when the children finish high school, she will surely leave him. For now, however, she is ambivalent; she cannot decide whether she wants to accept the security that she now has (along with the deadness of her relationship with her husband) or whether she is willing to leave this security and risk making a better life for herself (as well as risk being stuck with even less than she has now). She has been contemplating having an affair so that someone other than her husband can meet her physical and emotional needs. She is also exploring the possibility of finding a job so that she will be less dependent on her husband. By getting a job, she could have outside opportunities for personal satisfaction and still remain in the marriage by deciding to accept what she has with him.

Consider the following questions, and decide what value judgments can be made:

- One of Joyce's reasons for staying married is "for the sake of the children." What if you, as her therapist, accept this value and believe that she should not challenge her marriage because children need both parents and a divorce is damaging? Might she be using the children as an excuse? What if your judgment is that she would be better off by divorcing now? What do your beliefs about divorce, marriage, and children have to do with her possible decisions?
- Joyce is talking about an affair as a possibility. What are your values concerning monogamy and extramarital sex? Do you believe that having an affair would be helpful or destructive for your client? Would you be able to allow her to make this decision? What influence might your views have on her? Could you objectively counsel her if your values differed from hers in this area?
- Joyce must weigh the value of security against the value of possible growth. If you are conservative and place primary value on security, what effects might your view have on your client? What life experiences of yours might have a bearing on her decisions?

At times you are likely to be faced with ethical issues involving sharp differences between your own values and certain values of your clients. There are some situations in which these value conflicts do not become apparent until the therapeutic alliance is well established. Thus, it is not simply a matter of referring clients in cases of value clashes. Let's return to the case of Joyce and give her a new problem. Assume that she initially seeks counseling because of problems in her marriage. As you work with her, it becomes clear that she has a good deal of respect for you, that she wants to be liked by you, and that she seeks your acceptance and approval. One day she informs you that she has been having an affair, that she has not had sex with her husband for over a year, and that she has just found out that she is pregnant. Joyce is in a turmoil because none of her options appear satisfactory to her. She tells you that she is not in a financial or psychological position to support a child, especially if she decides to divorce her husband. She is becoming clearer that she does not want to remain in a relationship with him. Although she says that she is morally opposed to abortion, this is the path that she is inclined to take.

Assume that as Joyce's counselor you are personally opposed to abortion on moral or religious grounds. If so, the following are some questions for reflection: Would you be in a position to encourage her to explore all of her alternatives? Would you see it as your task to persuade her to accept another option besides abortion? Given the fact that you have been counseling her for several months, if you were to refer her to another counselor because of your beliefs and values on abortion, would this constitute abandonment? Would a referral be in her best interest? Can you respect your client's right to have a different value system from yours and help her decide what course to follow?

If you are morally opposed to abortion on the ground that it is taking the life of an innocent human being, it may be difficult to maintain objectivity if you see it as essential that your client accept your belief in this area. In my discussions with students in my classes, I find that many of them say they have difficulty in accepting the right of their clients to think differently from them with respect to moral beliefs and values in areas such as abortion, extramarital affairs, premarital sex, divorce, and gay male and lesbian lifestyles. Some students say that if they see a behavior as being morally wrong, they would not be able to condone it in clients. Thus, these students are likely to steer the client in the direction of adopting the values they deem to be morally correct.

As a counselor, if you view it as your role to use your value system as the standard for decision making for your clients, ask yourself why you see it as your place to persuade your clients to live according to what you believe to be right and wrong. Consider Joyce's case from several different perspectives. Assume that abortion is not the issue but that you are working with her in each of the following situations:

- Joyce is single and is engaging in unprotected premarital sex. If you were morally opposed to premarital sex, would you attempt to change her behavior? If she were using birth control measures and restricting her sexual behavior to one man, would this make a difference in the way you might counsel her?
- Assume that Joyce is a lesbian. She is not coming to you to change her sexual orientation but to work out difficulties she is experiencing in being true to herself with members of her family. If you believe that homosexuality is morally wrong, would you be able to respect her beliefs and her right to live differently? Would you accept her as a client?
- Assume that Joyce wants to divorce her husband and marry another man whom she recently met. If you believe that in her case divorce is wrong, because of the impact on her children, could you work with her? What course might your counseling take with her?

We engage in self-deception when we attempt to convince ourselves that our own experiences and systems of values do not enter our therapeutic relationships and that they do not have an influence on a client's decision making and behavior. It is essential that we clarify our positions on such other controversial issues as the following:

- *Religion.* If therapists call themselves "Christian counselors" and see their beliefs about sin, salvation, and the client's relationship with Christ as a central part of the therapeutic process, how does their view influence clients who are nonreligious? who are non-Christian? who are Christian but do not accept the therapist's religious beliefs? What potential impact does a nonreligious therapist have on a client with a definite religious persuasion? Can the nonreligious therapist allow clients to maintain their religious values, or will the therapist confront these values as forms of "immature defenses"? What are your views on religion, and how do you see them as influencing your work as a counselor?
- *Alternative lifestyles.* In working with gay male or lesbian clients, how might your values influence what you say or do? If you saw a gay lifestyle as

immoral or as a form of psychopathology, would you be genuinely able to encourage clients to retain their behavior and values? Would you encourage such clients to define their own goals, or would you be inclined to direct them toward the goals you think they should have? If a gay male client fully accepted being gay, would you still be able to work with him on meeting his personal goals for therapy? When would you be inclined to refer him? What would be your reasons for making a referral?

• *Right to die.* Assume that you are involved with a client who is in the advanced stages of AIDS and who has been given no hope. He wants to talk about ways of ending his misery, rather than going through what seems to be an expensive and futile treatment. What are your values pertaining to a person's right to die, and how do you think they would come into play in this situation? How would legal mandates influence you in following what you believed to be an ethical course? Are you prepared to address an internal struggle between answering his request for options on euthanasia and violating a professional ethical standard?

## THE ROLE OF VALUES
## IN DEVELOPING THERAPEUTIC GOALS

The counselor's values have implications for establishing goals to guide the counseling process. A fundamental question is who should establish the goals of counseling. Almost all theories are in accord that it is largely the client's responsibility to decide these objectives, collaborating with the therapist as therapy proceeds. Counselors have general goals, which are reflected in their behavior during the therapy session, in their observations of the client's behavior, and in the interventions they make. It is critical that the general goals of counselors be congruent with the personal goals of the client.

In my view therapy ought to begin with an exploration of the client's expectations and goals. Clients initially tend to have vague ideas of what they expect from therapy. They may be seeking solutions to problems, they may want to stop hurting, they may want to change others so they can live with less anxiety, or they may seek to be different so that some significant persons in their lives will be more accepting of them. In some cases clients may have no goals; they are in the therapist's office simply because they were sent there by their parents, probation officer, or teacher, and all they want is to be left alone. So where can a counselor begin? The intake session can be used most productively to focus on the client's goals or lack of them. The therapist may begin by asking such questions as these: "What do you expect from counseling? Why are you here? What do you want? What do you hope to leave with? How is what you are presently doing working for you? What aspects of yourself or your life situations would you most like to change?"

It is frustrating for therapists to hear clients make statements such as "I'd just like to understand myself more, and I'd like to be happy." Counselors can bring such global and diffuse wishes into sharper focus by asking: "What is keeping you from feeling happy? What *do* you understand about yourself now?

What would you like to understand about yourself that you don't now understand?" The main point is that setting goals seems unavoidable, and if there is to be any productive direction, the client and counselor need to explore what they hope to obtain from the counseling relationship. The two need to decide from the outset whether they can work with each other and whether their goals are compatible. Even more important, it is essential that counselors be able to understand, respect, and work within the framework of the client's world, rather than forcing the client to fit neatly into their scheme of values.

## SOME RECOMMENDATIONS

My colleagues and I take the position that it is neither possible nor desirable for counselors to be scrupulously neutral with respect to values in the counseling relationship (G. Corey, Corey, & Callanan, 1993). We contend that counselors should be willing to express their values openly when they are relevant to the questions that come up in their sessions with clients. We caution counselors against the tendency to assume either of two extreme positions. At one extreme are counselors who hold definite and absolute beliefs and see it as their job to exert influence on clients to adopt their values. These counselors tend to direct their clients toward the attitudes and values they judge to be "right." At the other extreme are counselors who maintain that they should keep their values out of their work and that the ideal is to strive for value-free counseling. Because these counselors are so intent on remaining "objective" and because they are so anxious not to influence their clients, they run the risk of immobilizing themselves.

Furthermore, we take the position that clients often want and need to know where their therapist stands in order to critically examine their own thinking. Thus, clients deserve an honest involvement on the part of their counselor. We also believe that it seems arrogant, and probably inaccurate, to assume that counselors know what is best for others. Therefore, counselors would do well to avoid equating therapy with pushing people to conform to certain "acceptable" standards. Counseling is a process whereby clients are challenged to honestly evaluate their values and then decide for themselves in what ways they will modify these values and their behavior.

If you have definite values in certain areas such as those listed earlier and if you are intent on directing your clients toward your goals, ethical practice dictates that you inform your potential clients of those values that will certainly influence your interventions with them. Through your professional disclosure statement, in which you describe your philosophy of the counseling relationship, it is a good idea to let potential clients know from the outset whether you are opposed to abortion, object to a gay male or lesbian lifestyle, or have any other values that are likely to influence their decisions and behavior. They have a right to know your perspectives before they get involved with you professionally. I am not suggesting that you have to give up your values, for you do need to be true to yourself. Neither am I suggesting that you should be able to work with all clients or with all problems. If you are unable or unwilling to be objective in areas where there are value conflicts between you and a client, a referral is often the ethical alternative.

Many experienced counselors have resolved these and many other issues related to values and the therapeutic process. As a student counselor or beginning practitioner, however, you will probably have to address many previously unexamined issues to increase your effectiveness.

# Becoming an Effective Multicultural Counselor

Part of the process of becoming an effective counselor involves learning how to recognize diversity and shaping your counseling practice to fit the client's world. It is essential for counselors to develop sensitivity to cultural differences if they hope to make interventions that are congruent with the values of their clients. Counselors bring their own heritage with them to their work, so they must know how cultural conditioning has influenced the directions they take with their clients. Moreover, unless the social and cultural context of clients is taken into consideration, it is most difficult to appreciate the nature of their struggles. Many counseling students have come to value characteristics such as making their own choices, expressing what they are feeling, being open and self-revealing, and striving for independence. Yet some of their clients may not share these goals. Certain cultures emphasize being emotionally reserved or being selective about sharing personal concerns. Counselors need to determine whether the assumptions they have made about the nature and functioning of therapy are appropriate for culturally diverse populations. We will look at the various theories presented in this book in light of their applications in a multicultural society.

Clearly, effective counseling must take into account the impact of culture. Culture is, quite simply, the values and behaviors shared by a group of individuals. It is important to realize that culture does not refer just to an ethnic or racial heritage but includes age, gender, religion, lifestyle, physical and mental ability, and socioeconomic status. Pedersen (1994) maintains that counselors have two choices: to ignore the influence of culture or to attend to it. Whatever choice is made, culture will continue to influence both the client's and the counselor's behavior, with or without the counselor's awareness.

## ACQUIRING COMPETENCIES IN MULTICULTURAL COUNSELING

Effective counselors understand their own cultural conditioning, the conditioning of their clients, and the sociopolitical system of which they are a part. Acquiring this understanding begins with counselors' awareness of any cultural values, biases, and attitudes that may hinder their development of a positive view of pluralism.

Sue, Arredondo, and McDavis (1992) have developed a conceptual framework for competencies and standards in multicultural counseling. Their dimensions of competency involve three areas: beliefs and attitudes, knowledge, and skill.

BELIEFS AND ATTITUDES OF CULTURALLY SKILLED COUNSELORS.   First, effective counselors have moved from being culturally unaware to ensuring that their personal biases, values, or problems will not interfere with their ability to work with clients who are culturally different from them. They do not allow their fear of discovering and owning up to their prejudices to block them from a multicultural perspective. They seek to examine and understand the world from the vantage point of their clients. They respect clients' religious and spiritual beliefs and values. They are comfortable with differences between themselves and others in terms of race, ethnicity, culture, and beliefs. Because these therapists welcome diverse value orientations and diverse assumptions about human behavior, they have a basis for sharing the worldview of their clients, as opposed to being culturally encapsulated. They value bilingualism and do not view another language as an impediment to counseling.

KNOWLEDGE OF CULTURALLY SKILLED COUNSELORS.   Second, culturally effective practitioners possess certain knowledge. They know specifically about their own racial and cultural heritage and how it affects them personally and professionally. Because they understand the dynamics of oppression, racism, discrimination, and stereotyping, they are in a position to detect their own racist attitudes, beliefs, and feelings. They understand the worldview of their clients, and they learn about their clients' cultural backgrounds. Because they understand the basic values underlying the therapeutic process, they know how these values may clash with the cultural values of some minority groups. They understand that external sociopolitical forces influence all groups, and they know how these forces operate with respect to the treatment of minorities. These practitioners are aware of the institutional barriers that prevent minorities from utilizing the mental-health services available in their community. They possess knowledge about the historical background, traditions, and values of the client populations with whom they are working. They know about minority family structures, hierarchies, values, and beliefs. Furthermore, they are knowledgeable about community characteristics and resources. Culturally skilled counselors know how to help clients make use of indigenous support systems. In areas where they are lacking in knowledge, they seek resources to assist them. The greater their depth and breadth of knowledge of culturally diverse groups, the more likely they are to be effective practitioners.

SKILLS AND INTERVENTION STRATEGIES OF CULTURALLY SKILLED COUNSELORS.   Third, effective counselors have acquired certain skills in working with culturally diverse populations. Multicultural counseling is enhanced when practitioners use methods and strategies and define goals consistent with the life experiences and cultural values of their clients. Such practitioners modify and adapt their interventions so as to accommodate cultural differences. They do not force their clients to fit within one counseling approach. They are able to send and receive both verbal and nonverbal messages accurately and appro-priately. They are willing to seek out educational, consultative, and training expe-riences to enhance their ability to work with culturally diverse client populations.

## INCORPORATING CULTURE INTO COUNSELING PRACTICE

Although practitioners can acquire general knowledge and skills that will enable them to function effectively with diverse client populations, it is not realistic to expect that they will know everything about the cultural background of a client. There is much to be said for letting clients teach counselors about rele-vant aspects of their culture. It is a good idea for counselors to ask clients to provide them with the information they will need to work effectively. It helps to assess the degree of acculturation and identity development that has taken place. This is especially true for individuals who have the experience of living in more than one culture. They often have allegiance to their own culture, and yet they may find certain characteristics of their new culture attractive. They may experience conflicts in integrating the two cultures in which they live. These core struggles can be productively explored in the therapeutic context if the counselor understands and respects this cultural conflict.

WELCOMING DIVERSITY.   Counseling is by its very nature diverse in the con-text of a multicultural society, so it is easy to see that there are no ideal therapeutic approaches. Instead, different theories have distinct features that have appeal for different cultural groups. There are also distinct limitations of some theoretical approaches when they are applied to certain populations. Effective multicultural practice demands an open stance on the part of the practitioner, a flexibility, and a willingness to modify strategies to fit the needs and the situation of the individual client. Practitioners who truly respect their clients will be aware of a client's hesitation and will not be too quick to misinterpret this behavior. In-stead, they will patiently attempt to enter the world of their client as much as they can. It is not necessary for practitioners to have the same experiences as their clients; what is more important is that they attempt to be open to a similar set of feelings and struggles. It is not always by similarity, but rather by differences, that we are challenged to look at what we are doing.

SOME PRACTICAL GUIDELINES.   Reflecting on the following guidelines may increase your effectiveness in serving diverse client populations:

- Learn more about ways in which your own cultural background has an influence on your thinking and behaving. What specific steps can you take to broaden your base of understanding, both of your own culture and of other cultures?
- Identify your basic assumptions—especially as they apply to diversity in culture, ethnicity, race, gender, class, religion, and lifestyle—and think about how your assumptions are likely to affect your practice as a counselor.

- Where did you obtain your knowledge about culture? Are your attitudes about diverse cultures your own, and have you carefully examined them?
- Learn to pay attention to the common ground that exists among people of diverse backgrounds. What are some of the ways in which we all share universal concerns?
- Realize that it is not necessary to learn everything about the cultural backgrounds of your clients before you begin working with them. Allow them to teach you how you can best serve them.
- Spend time preparing clients for counseling. Teach them how to use their therapeutic experience to meet the challenges they face in their every-day lives.
- Recognize the importance of being flexible in applying the methods you use with clients. Don't be wedded to a specific technique if it is not appropriate for a given client.
- Remember that practicing from a multicultural perspective can make your job easier and can be rewarding for both you and your clients.

It is important to realize that it takes time, study, and experience to become an effective multicultural counselor. Multicultural competence cannot be reduced simply to cultural awareness and sensitivity, to a body of knowledge, or to a specific set of skills. This multicultural expertise requires that counselors have sufficient breadth and depth in all three areas (Leong & Kim, 1991).

# Issues Faced by Beginning Therapists

This section is based on my observation and work with counselors-in-training and on my own struggles when I began practicing. It identifies some of the major issues that most of us typically face, particularly during the beginning stages of learning how to be therapists. I have become aware of a recurring pattern of questions, conflicts, and issues that provide the substance of seminars and practicum experiences in counseling. When counselor interns complete their formal course work and begin facing clients, they are put to the test of integrating and applying what they have learned. They soon realize that all they really have to work with is themselves—their own life experiences, values, and humanity. At that point some real concerns arise about their adequacies as a counselor and as a person and about what they can bring of themselves to the counseling relationship. In what follows I attempt to formulate some useful guidelines for beginning counselors.

## DEALING WITH OUR ANXIETIES

Most beginning counselors, regardless of their academic and experiential backgrounds, anticipate meeting their initial clients with ambivalent feelings. As beginners, if we have enough sense, we are probably anxiety ridden and ask ourselves such questions as "What will I say? How will I say it? Will I be able to help? What if I make mistakes? Will my clients return, and if they do, what will I do next?'' In my view a certain level of anxiety demonstrates that we are aware of the uncertainties of the future with our clients and of our abilities to really be there and stay with them. Because therapy is serious business and can have a strong impact on clients, we can accept our anxieties as normal. Whereas too much anxiety can torpedo any confidence we might have and cause us to be frozen, we have every right to experience some trepidation. We may also fear that our peers know far more than we do, that they are much more skilled and perceptive, and that they will see us as incompetent.

The willingness to recognize and deal with these anxieties, as opposed to denying them by pretenses, is a mark of courage. That we have self-doubts seems perfectly normal; it is how we deal with them that counts. One way is to openly discuss them with a supervisor and peers. The possibilities are rich for meaningful exchanges and for gaining support from fellow interns, who probably have many of the same concerns, fears, and anxieties.

## BEING AND DISCLOSING OURSELVES

Because we are typically self-conscious and anxious when we begin counseling, we tend to be overconcerned with what the books say and with the mechanics of how we should proceed. Inexperienced therapists too often fail to appreciate the values inherent in simply being themselves.

A common tendency is for counselors to become passive. They listen. They reflect. They have insights and hunches but mull over them so long that even if they decide to act on a hunch, the appropriate time for action has already passed. So they sit back, passively wondering whether their internal reactions are correct. Thus, I tend to encourage an active stance for the student counselor, because I believe that it is generally better to risk being inappropriate than to almost ensure bland results by adopting passive, nondirective stances.

Let me push further with the issue of being oneself. I do not believe that we should be either of two extremes: at one end are counselors who lose themselves in their fixed role and who hide behind a professional facade; at the other end are therapists who strive too hard to prove that they, too, are human. If we are at either of these poles, we are not being ourselves.

Take the first extreme. Here counselors are so bound up in maintaining stereotyped role expectations that little of them as a person shows through. Although we do have role functions, it is possible for us to responsibly perform them without blurring our identity and becoming lost in our role. I believe that the more insecure, frightened, and uncertain we are in our professional work, the more we will cling to the defense afforded by a role. The unrealistic expectation that we must be superhuman leads to becoming ossified in fixed roles.

At this extreme of too little self-disclosure, counselors are unwilling to discuss the reactions they are having toward clients or what has been going on with them during the session. They focus too much on the clients, often by questioning or probing, which is a subtle demand for them to be open and revealing. At the same time they are modeling closed behavior. They expect their clients to do what they are not doing themselves in the therapy relationship. Their clients are left guessing about what the counselor is experiencing during the session; thus, a valuable basis for an honest dialogue is lost.

At the other extreme, counselors actively work at demonstrating their humanness. Instead of getting lost in a professionally aloof and nondisclosing role, such counselors overreact and blur any distinction between the helper and the one who is helped. They would rather be seen as a buddy with similar hang-ups than as a therapist.

At this extreme we tell clients too much about ourselves, and thus we take the focus off of them and put it on ourselves as therapists. We might make the mistake of inappropriately burdening them with fleeting reactions or impressions we are having toward them; our disclosures in these cases have the effect of closing them up. The key point is that disclosure should have the effect of encouraging clients to deepen their level of self-exploration or to enhance the therapeutic relationship. Excessive counselor disclosure often originates from the counselor's own needs, and in these cases the client's needs are secondary.

I have found the following guidelines useful in determining when self-disclosure is facilitative: First, disclosing my persistent feelings that are directly related to the present transaction can be useful. If I am consistently bored or irritated in a session, it becomes essential to reveal my feeling. On the other hand, I think it is unwise to share every fleeting fantasy or feeling that I experience. Timing is important. Second, I find it helpful to distinguish between disclosure that is relating history and disclosure that is an unrehearsed expression of my present experiencing. For me to mechanically report events of my past might be pseudodisclosure. If it is easy to relate or if it sounds rehearsed and mechanical to me, I have a clue that I am trying too hard to be authentic. However, if my disclosure is an outgrowth of something I am feeling in the moment and if, as I share this feeling, it has some freshness of expression, I can be more sure that it is facilitative. Last, I often ask myself why I am revealing myself and to what degree it is appropriate to the task of helping the client.

## AVOIDING PERFECTIONISM

Both undergraduate students in human services and graduate students in counseling are prone to putting themselves under tremendous pressure. They tell themselves things such as "I have to be the perfect counselor, and if I'm not, I could do severe damage"; "I should know everything there is to know about my profession, and if I show that there is something I don't know, others will see me as incompetent"; "I ought to be able to help everybody who seeks my help. If there is someone I can't help, that just proves my incompetence"; "If a client doesn't get better, it must be my fault"; "Making a mistake is horrible, and failure is always fatal. If I were really professional, I wouldn't make mistakes"; "I should always radiate confidence; there is no room for self-doubt."

Perhaps one of the most common self-defeating beliefs with which we burden ourselves is that we must be perfect. Although we may well know intellectually that humans are not perfect, emotionally we often feel that there is little room for error. I attempt to teach counseling interns and students that they need not burden themselves with the idea that they must be perfect. They do not have to know everything, and there is no disgrace in revealing their lack of knowledge. Rather than trying to impress others and bluffing their way through difficult situations, they can always admit the truth and then set out to find information or answers (if indeed there is an answer). It takes courage for them to admit their imperfections, but there is a value in being open about them.

To be sure, we *will* make mistakes, whether we are beginning or seasoned therapists. If our energies are tied up with presenting an image of perfection, we will have little energy left to be present for our clients. What is more important than our mistakes is the lesson that we learn from each mistake. In working with students, I tell them to challenge their notion that they should know everything and should be perfectly skilled. I encourage them to share their mistakes or what they perceive as errors. If they are willing to risk making mistakes in supervised learning situations and are willing to reveal their self-doubts, they will find a direction that leads to growth.

## BEING HONEST ABOUT OUR LIMITATIONS

A related fear that most of us have is of facing our limitations as counselors. We fear losing the client's respect if we say, "I really feel that I can't help you on this point" or "I just don't have the kind of information or skill to help you with this problem." Clients' responses overwhelmingly confirm the value of honesty as opposed to an attempt to fake competence. Not only will we perhaps not lose our clients' respect, but we may gain their respect by frankly admitting our limitations. An illustration comes to mind. A counselor-in-training had intake duty in a college counseling center. Her first client came in wanting to discuss the possibilities of an abortion for his girlfriend. Many questions raced through her mind: "Should I admit to him my lack of awareness and skill in dealing with this problem, or should I somehow bluff my way through to avoid looking like a neophyte? Should I know how to help him? Will he get a negative impression of the counseling center if I tell him I don't have the skill for this case? What about the girl in this situation? Is it really enough to work only with him? Is all that he really needs at this point simply information? Will information resolve the issue?" Fortunately, the counselor-in-training let the client know that the matter was too complicated for her to tackle, and she got another counselor on duty to help him. A point of this illustration is that we sometimes burden ourselves with the expectation that we should be all-knowing and skillful, even without experience. This counselor-in-training's willingness to be realistic helped her avoid the pitfalls of trying to look good for the client and of presenting a false image.

We cannot realistically expect to succeed with every client. Even experienced counselors at times become glum and begin to doubt their value when they are forced to admit that there are clients whom they are not able to touch, much less reach in a significant way. Be honest enough with yourself and with your client to admit that you cannot work successfully with everyone.

There is a delicate balance between learning our realistic limits and challenging what we sometimes think of as being "limits." For example, we may tell ourselves that we could never work with the elderly because we cannot identify with them, because they would not trust us, because we might find it depressing, and so forth. In this case, however, it might be good to test what we see as limits and open ourselves to this population. If we do, we may find that there are more grounds for identification than we thought. Before deciding that we do not have the life experiences or the personal qualities to work with a given population, we might do well to try working in a setting with a population we do not intend to specialize in. This can be done through diversified field placements or visits to agencies.

## UNDERSTANDING SILENCE

Those silent moments during a therapeutic session may seem like silent hours to a beginning therapist. It is not uncommon to be threatened by silences to the point that we frequently do something counterproductive to break the silence and thus relieve our anxiety. I recall a time when I was a counselor intern and was tape-recording an individual session with a highly verbal high school girl. Toward the end of the session she became silent for a moment, and my anxiety level rose to the degree that I felt compelled to rush in and give several interpretations to what she had been saying earlier. When my supervisor heard the tape he exclaimed: "Hell, your talk really got in her way. You didn't hear what she was saying! I'll bet she doesn't come back for her session next week." Well, she came back, and by that time I was determined not to intervene and talk my anxiety away. So, rather than taking the initiative of beginning the session, I waited for her to begin. We waited for about half an hour. We played a game of "you first." Each of us sat and stared at the other. Finally, we began exploring what this silence felt like for each of us.

    Silence can have many meanings: the client may be quietly thinking about some things that were discussed earlier or evaluating some insight just acquired; the client may be waiting for the therapist to take the lead and decide what to say next, or the therapist may be waiting for the client to do this; either the client or the therapist may be bored, distracted, or preoccupied or may just not have anything to say for the moment; the client may be feeling hostile toward the therapist and thus be playing the game of "I'll just sit here like a stone and see if he [she] can get to me"; the client and the therapist may be communicating without words, the silence may be refreshing, or the silence may say much more than words; and perhaps the interaction has been on a surface level, and both persons have some fear or hesitancy about getting to a deeper level.

    I suggest that when silences occur, you explore with your client what they mean. You could first acknowledge the silence and your feelings about it and then, rather than talking noisily simply to make each other comfortable, pursue its meanings.

## DEALING WITH DEMANDING CLIENTS

A major issue that puzzles many beginning counselors is how to deal with the overdemanding client. Typically, because therapists feel that they should extend themselves in being helpful, they often burden themselves with the unrealistic standard that they should give unselfishly regardless of how great the demands on them are. The demands may manifest themselves in a variety of ways. Clients may call you frequently at home and expect you to talk at length; demand to see you more often or for a longer period than you can provide; want to see you socially; want you to adopt or in some other way take care of them and assume their responsibilities; expect you to manipulate another person (spouse, child, parent) to see and accept their point of view; demand that you not leave them and that you continually demonstrate how much you care; or demand that you tell them what to do and how to solve a problem. One way of heading off these demands is to make your expectations clear during the initial counseling session or in the disclosure statement.

It could be useful for you to review some of your encounters with clients to assess the ways you feel that you have been the victim of excessive demands. What are some demands that were placed on you? How did you handle those situations? Can you say no to clients when you want to? Are you able to value yourself enough that you can made demands for yourself? Do you confront demanding clients, or do you allow them to manipulate you in the same way that they have manipulated others? If you let them manipulate you, are you doing them a favor? For a more detailed discussion on this subject, see Kottler's (1992) *Compassionate Therapy: Working with Difficult Clients.*

## DEALING WITH UNCOMMITTED CLIENTS

At the other extreme are clients who have very little investment in counseling. Many clients are involuntary in that they are required by a court order to obtain therapy. In these cases you may well be challenged in your attempt to establish a working relationship. But it is possible to do effective work with clients who are sent to you.

Practitioners who work with involuntary clients must begin by openly discussing the nature of the relationship. They should not promise what they cannot or will not deliver. It is good practice to make clear the limits of confidentiality as well as any other factors that may affect the course of therapy. In working with involuntary clients, it is especially important to prepare them for the process. Questions to take up include these: What is the therapy about? What are the joint responsibilities of the two parties? How might therapy help clients get what they want? What can clients do to increase the chances that the therapy experience will be positive? What are the potential risks and dangers? What can clients expect in the general course of treatment? This kind of preparation can go a long way toward dealing with resistance. Often, in fact, resistance is brought about by a counselor who omits preparation and merely assumes that all clients are open and ready to benefit from therapy.

As a beginning counselor you can easily be drawn into unproductive games with uncommitted clients, to the extent that you show far more investment in these clients than they manifest. It is possible for you to try too hard to be understanding and accepting, and therefore you may make few demands on such clients. There are also situations in which a therapist completely blames "un-committed clients" for a lack of progress in counseling. What appears to be a lack of commitment may be a failure to understand the nature of counseling. Cultural and developmental variables play an important role in a client's readiness to participate in the therapeutic process.

Yet some clients have little motivation for seeking counseling. It is especially difficult for beginning counselors to confront such a client, for they fear that if they do, the client will surely not return. Perhaps a direct and caring confrontation is the very factor that can lead to an increased level of commitment from clients. If they persistently seem to "forget" appointments or fail to do much work during or outside of the therapy session, they can be asked if they want to continue coming for counseling. If they make a decision not to continue, this is at least some step toward assuming responsibility for their actions. In the case of clients who are sent to counseling by the court, the therapist can still tell them that although they are required to attend sessions, it is up to them to decide how they will use this time. They can eventually be shown that even though they are involuntary clients, they can use this time well.

## ACCEPTING SLOW RESULTS

Do not expect instant results. You will not "cure" clients in a few sessions. So many beginning therapists experience the anxiety of not seeing the fruits of their labor. They ask themselves: "Am I really doing my client any good? Is the client perhaps getting worse? Is anything really occurring as a result of our sessions, or am I just deceiving myself into believing we're making progress?" I hope that you will learn to tolerate the ambiguity of not knowing for sure whether your client is improving, at least during the initial sessions. Understand that clients may apparently "get worse" before they show therapeutic gains. After clients have decided to work toward self-honesty and drop their defenses and facades, they can be expected to experience an increase of personal pain and disorganization, which may result in a depression or a panic reaction. Many a client has uttered: "My God, I was better off before I started therapy. Now I feel more vulnerable than before. Maybe I was happier when I was ignorant." Also, realize that the fruitful effects of the joint efforts of the therapist and the client may not be manifest for months (or even years) after the conclusion of therapy.

The year I began doing full-time individual and group counseling in a college counseling center was, professionally, the most trying year for me. Up until that time I was teaching a variety of psychology courses, and I could sense relatively quick results or the lack of them. I found teaching gratifying, reinforcing, and many times exciting; by contrast, counseling seemed like a laborious and thankless task. The students who came to the counseling center did not evidence any miraculous cures, and some would come each week with the same complaints. They saw little progress, sought answers, wanted some formula for feeling better, or wanted a shot of motivation. I was plagued with self-doubts and skepticism. My needs for reinforcement were so great that I was anti-therapeutic for some. I needed them to need me, to tell me that I was effective, to assure me that they were noticing positive changes, and so on. I became aware that I had attempted to refer the depressed male students to other counselors, whereas I had put effort into encouraging a bright, attractive young woman to continue in counseling. Learning the dynamics of my motivation did not come easily, and I appreciated the confrontation that several of my colleagues provided in helping me become more honest about whose needs were really being met. Eventually I discovered that growth and change did occur in a number of my clients as a result of our joint efforts. They were willing to assume their responsibilities for taking risks, and I became more willing to stay with them, even though I was not at all sure of the results.

My beginning experiences taught me that I needed to be able to tolerate not knowing whether a client was progressing or whether I was being instrumental in that person's growth or change. I learned that the only way to acquire self-trust as a therapist was to allow myself to feel my self-doubts, uncertainty about my effectiveness, and ambivalence over whether I wanted to continue as a counseling psychologist. As I became less anxious over my performance, I was able to pay increasing attention both to the client and to myself in the therapeutic relationship.

## AVOIDING SELF-DECEPTION

No discussion of guidelines for beginning counselors could be complete without mentioning the phenomenon of self-deception—both by the counselor and by the client. Self-deception is not necessarily conscious lying, for it can be subtle and unconscious. For both parties the motivation for deception may be the need to make the relationship worthwhile and productive; both have invested in seeing positive results. Our need to witness personal changes may blur reality and cause us to be less skeptical than we should be.

Our need to feel that we are instrumental in assisting another to enjoy life more fully and our need to feel a sense that we do make significant differences can at times lead to self-deception. We look for evidence of progress, and we rationalize away elements of failure. Or we give ourselves credit for our clients' growth when it may be due largely to another variable, perhaps to something unrelated to the therapeutic relationship. My point is that being aware of a tendency toward self-deception in a counseling relationship can lead to an exploration of the phenomenon and thus lessen the chances of its occurring.

## AVOIDING LOSING OURSELVES IN OUR CLIENTS

A common mistake for beginners is to worry too much about clients. There is a danger of incorporating clients' neuroses into our own personality. We lose sleep wondering what decisions they are making. We sometimes identify so closely with clients that we lose our own sense of identity and assume their identity. Empathy becomes distorted and militates against a therapeutic intervention. We need to learn how to "let clients go" and not carry around their problems until we see them again. The most therapeutic thing is to be as fully present as we are able to be (feeling with our clients and experiencing their struggles with them) but to let them assume the responsibility of their living and choosing outside of the session. If we become lost in clients' struggles and confusion, we cease being an effective agent in helping them find their way out of the darkness. If we take on ourselves the responsibility our clients need to learn to direct their lives, we are blocking rather than fostering their growth.

This discussion relates to an issue that we all need to recognize and face in our work as counselors—namely, *countertransference,* which occurs when a counselor's own needs or unresolved personal conflicts become entangled in the therapeutic relationship. Because countertransference that is not recognized and not successfully dealt with has the effect of blurring therapist objectivity (and actually intruding in the counseling process), it is essential that counselor trainees focus on *themselves* in supervision sessions. By dealing with the reactions that are stirred up in them in their relationship with a particular client, they can learn a lot about how their needs and unfinished business in their own life can bog down the progress of a client. Here are a few illustrations of common forms of countertransference.

- the need to be liked, appreciated, and approved of by clients
- the therapist's fear of challenging clients lest they leave and think poorly of the therapist
- sexual feelings and sexually seductive behavior on the therapist's part toward clients (to the extent that the therapist becomes preoccupied with sexual fantasies or deliberately focuses clients' attention on sexual feelings toward the therapist)
- extreme reactions to certain clients who evoke old feelings in the therapist—for example, clients who are perceived by the therapist as judgmental, domineering, paternalistic, maternalistic, controlling, and the like
- the therapist's need to take away clients' pain or struggles because their experience is opening up old wounds or unrecognized conflicts in the therapist
- compulsive giving of advice, with the counselor assuming a superior position of wanting to dictate how clients should live and the choices they should make

This brief discussion is not a complete treatment of the issue of learning how to work through our feelings toward clients. Because it may not be appropriate for us to use clients' time to work through our reactions to them, it makes it all the more important that we be willing to work on ourselves in our own sessions with another therapist, supervisor, or colleague. Although recognizing how our needs can intrude in our work as counselors is one beginning step, we need to be willing to continually explore what we are seeing in ourselves. If we do not, we increase the danger of losing ourselves in our clients and using them to meet our unfulfilled needs.

## DEVELOPING A SENSE OF HUMOR

Although therapy is a responsible matter, it need not be deadly serious. Both clients and counselors can enrich a relationship by laughing. I have found that humor and tragedy are closely linked and that after allowing ourselves to feel some experiences that are painfully tragic, we can also genuinely laugh at how seriously we have taken our situation. We secretly delude ourselves into believing that we are unique in that we are alone in our pain and we alone have experienced the tragic. What a welcome relief when we can admit that pain is not our exclusive domain. The important point is that therapists recognize that laughter or humor does not mean that work is not being accomplished. There are times, of course, when laughter is used to cover up anxiety or to escape from the experience of facing threatening material. The therapist needs to distinguish between humor that distracts and humor that enhances the situation.

## ESTABLISHING REALISTIC GOALS

Realistic goals are essential for a relationship with a client. Assume that your client is truly in need of a major overhaul. He presents himself as a man who is intensely dissatisfied with life, rarely accomplishes what he begins, and feels inadequate and helpless. Now for the reality of the situation. He comes into a community crisis-counseling clinic where you work. Your agency has a policy of limiting a person to a series of six counseling sessions. There are long lines, waiting lists, and many people in need of crisis counseling. The man comes to you because of his personal inability to function; his wife has just abandoned him. Even though both of you may agree that he needs more than a minor tune-up, the limitations of the services at hand prevent exploring his problems in depth. Both counselor and client need to decide on realistic goals. This does not mean that the two need to settle on patch-up work. One possibility is to explore the underlying dynamics of the presenting problem, with attention to what alternatives are open beyond the six sessions. If our aims are realistic, we may be sad that we could not accomplish more, but at least we will not be steeped in frustration for not accomplishing miracles.

## SHARING OF RESPONSIBILITY WITH THE CLIENT

The way in which counselors structure their sessions has implications for the balance of responsibility that will characterize the client/therapist relationship. In your work as a counselor, it is essential that you become aware of the subtle ways in which your behavior can influence your clients. It is critical that you monitor what you say and do in terms of its impact, frequently asking yourself: "What am I doing? Whose needs are being met—my client's or my own? What is the effect of my behavior on my client?"

You will probably struggle with finding the optimum balance in sharing responsibility with your clients. One mistake is to assume full responsibility for the direction and outcomes of therapy. This will lead to taking from your clients the rightful responsibility they need if they are to become empowered by making their own decisions. It could also increase the likelihood of your early burnout. Another mistake is for you to refuse to accept the responsibility for making accurate assessments and designing appropriate treatment plans for your clients. The topic of this sharing of responsibility needs to be addressed at the beginning of the therapeutic relationship. Early during the course of counseling, it is your responsibility to discuss specific matters such as length and overall duration of the sessions, confidentiality, general goals, and methods used to achieve goals. (I will deal in more detail with this matter of discussing informed consent in Chapter 3.)

It is important to be alert to your clients' efforts to get you to assume responsibility for directing their lives. Many clients seek a "magic answer" as a way of escaping the anxiety of making their own decisions. Yet it is not your role to assume responsibility for directing your clients' lives. Client-initiated contracts and specific assignments are helpful in keeping the focus of responsibility on the client. Contracts can be changed, and new ones can be developed. Formulating contracts can continue during the entire counseling relationship. You might ask yourself: "Are my clients doing now what will move them toward greater independence and toward increasingly finding their answers within?" Perhaps the best measure of our general effectiveness as counselors is the degree to which clients are able to say to us, "I appreciate what you've been to me, and because of your faith in me, I feel I can now go it alone." Eventually, if we are good enough, we will be out of business!

## DECLINING TO GIVE ADVICE

A common mistaken notion is that giving advice is the same as counseling. It is not unusual to hear prospective students who are interviewing for admission to a graduate counseling program say: "I want a master's degree in counseling because my friends often come to me for advice. I've always have been one who likes to help others." Quite often clients who are suffering come to a therapy session seeking and even demanding advice. They want more than direction; they want a wise counselor to make a decision or resolve a problem for them. Counseling should not be confused with the dispensing of information. As I view it, a therapist's tasks are to help clients discover their own solutions and recognize their own freedom to act, not to deprive them of the opportunity to act freely. A common escape by many clients is not trusting themselves to find solutions, use their freedom, or discover their own direction. Even if we, as therapists, were able to resolve their struggles for them, we would be fostering their dependence on us. They would continually need to seek our counsel for every new twist in their difficulties. Our job is to help them independently make choices and have the courage to accept the consequences of their choices. Giving advice (as a style) does not work toward this end.

I am not ruling out occasional use of the technique of giving advice. There are appropriate times for direct advice, particularly when clients are clearly in danger of harming themselves or others or when for the time being they are unable to make clear choices. Also, information can be used legitimately in therapy as a basis for helping clients make their own choices. Essential to decision making is having pertinent information.

My caution is against overusing the technique of giving information and advice as the main diet of counseling. Far too many inexperienced counselors fall into the trap of believing that they are not doing their job unless they are being prescriptive and meeting clients' apparent demands for advice. I recommend that instead of merely being advice givers, we ask our clients questions such as "What alternatives are open to you? What possibilities do you see? If I were able to solve this particular problem, how would that help you with future problems? Are you asking me to assume your responsibility for you? How have you avoided accepting the responsibility for directing your own life in the past? Can part of your present problem stem from depending too much on others to direct your life?"

## DEFINING YOUR ROLE AS A COUNSELOR

One of your challenges as a counselor will be to define and clarify your professional role. As you read about the various theoretical orientations in Part Two, reflect on the counselor's role from each of these perspectives. Think about what role or roles you would most want to assume. At this point, how might you define the basic role of a therapist? Is the therapist a friend? an expert? a teacher? an advice giver? an information giver? a provider of alternatives? a confronter? As a counselor, might you have each of these functions at various times, and if so, what is your *basic* role in the counseling process? What influence might the setting in which you practice have on your role? What might you do when you are in conflict with the agency's view of what you should be doing?

The fact that a range of appropriate roles exists often confuses beginning counselors. There is no simple and universal answer to the question of the therapist's proper role. Factors such as the type of counseling, the counselor's level of training, the clientele to be served, and the therapeutic setting all need to be considered.

Mental-health workers often find themselves in jobs that demand that they function in multiple roles and perform tasks that do not mix well. In a state hospital where my colleagues and I provided training workshops for the treatment staff, we learned that employees had to switch among several diverse roles. Psychiatric technicians, psychologists, and social workers were expected to function as therapists to a group of involuntarily committed clients, many of whom had been diagnosed as mentally disordered sex offenders or sociopaths. In addition to providing one-to-one contacts, they were expected to regularly hold group-therapy sessions. Yet at the same time they were responsible for making a determination of when the patients were ready to be released and returned to the community. These mental-health workers were expected to carry out multiple functions: therapist, sponsor, nurse, friend, teacher, parent, administrator, guard, and judge.

This mixture of responsibilities proved to be a major burden for many of these workers, because they knew that some of their clients might commit future offenses (including rape, child molestation, or murder). Clients were aware that these workers would make judgments concerning their detention or release. In many cases these clients learned the "right" language aimed at impressing the treatment team, even though many of them had not made any substantial changes in their attitudes or behavior.

Although having to perform the dual roles of therapist and evaluator may be far less than ideal, it is often impractical and unrealistic to think that such workers can involve themselves strictly in therapeutic functions. Like it or not, the reality of most institutions demands that workers participate in treatment-team staffings and meetings in which they make evaluative judgments about their clients and decisions that may affect their ability to create a climate of trust in which they can function ideally. Therefore, it is probably best that these workers frankly tell their clients at the outset about this situation and then not apologize for it. This type of directness with clients can go a long way in establishing trust.

From my perspective, the central function of counseling is to help clients recognize their own strengths, discover what is preventing them from using their strengths, and clarify what kind of person they want to be. Counseling is a process by which clients are invited to look honestly at their behavior and lifestyle and make certain decisions about the ways in which they want to modify the quality of their life. In this framework counselors need to provide support and warmth, yet care enough to challenge and confront so that clients will be enabled to take the actions necessary to bring about significant change.

In your work as a counselor, you would do well to make a critical evaluation of appropriate counseling functions. You can benefit from deciding in advance those functions that you feel are inconsistent with genuine counseling. It will help you to realize that the professional roles that you assume are likely to be dependent on factors such as the client populations with whom you are working, the specific therapeutic services that you are providing, the particular stage of counseling, and the setting in which you work. Your role will not be defined once and for all, but you will have to reassess the nature of your professional commitments and redefine your role at various times.

## LEARNING TO USE TECHNIQUES APPROPRIATELY

A question that counselors need to ask themselves is *why* they use a certain technique. When counselors are at an impasse with a client, they sometimes have a tendency to look for the "right" techniques to get the sessions moving. As we saw in Chapter 1, relying on techniques too much can lead to mechanical counseling. Ideally, the techniques that therapists use should evolve from the therapeutic relationship and should enhance the client's awareness or suggest possibilities for experimenting with new behavior. It is essential that there be a rationale for the techniques used and that they be tied into the goals of therapy. This does not mean that counselors need to restrict themselves to drawing on accepted techniques and procedures within a single model; quite the contrary.

However, effective counselors avoid using techniques in a hit-or-miss fashion, to fill time, to meet their own needs, or to get things moving.

As you study the theories in the coming chapters, pay attention to the techniques you favor, and examine your motivations for using or avoiding certain techniques. This process is a continuing one. Reflect on the following questions to determine your view of the place of techniques in counseling:

- Do you use a lot of questions in your counseling? If so, are they *open* questions, which encourage further client talk and exploration, or *closed* questions, which have a simpler answer or do not lead to deeper self-exploration?
- Do your techniques intensify what a client is feeling, or do they have the effect of closing up certain feelings? How comfortable are you with pain? anger? jealousy? conflict?
- How do you decide which techniques to use with a particular client? How do you evaluate the usefulness of the interventions that you make?
- What techniques have you personally experienced from the vantage point of a client? What were some of your positive experiences? Did you have any negative experiences?
- How do you imagine it would be if you avoided using any techniques or counseling procedures other than simply being with your clients and relating to them through dialogues?

## DEVELOPING YOUR OWN COUNSELING STYLE

Counselors-in-training need to be cautioned about the tendency to mimic the style of their supervisor, therapist, or some other model. It is important that we accept that there is no "right" way to conduct therapy and that wide variations in approach can be effective. We inhibit our potential effectiveness in reaching others when we attempt to imitate another therapist's style or when we fit most of our behavior during the session into the Procrustean bed of some expert's theory. Although I am fully aware that one's style as a counselor will be influenced by teachers, therapists, and supervisors, I caution against blurring one's own potential uniqueness by trying to imitate them. At best one becomes a carbon copy, a poor imitation of the other. I do not have any formula for the way to develop a unique therapeutic style, but I do think that the awareness of our tendency to copy our teachers is critical in freeing ourselves and finding a direction that is compatible with our personality. I advocate borrowing from others but, at the same time, finding a way that is distinctive to yourself.

# Staying Alive as a Person and as a Professional

If the thesis that I have presented in this chapter is valid—that ultimately our single most important instrument is the person who we are and that our most powerful technique is our ability to model aliveness and realness—then taking care of ourselves so that we remain fully alive is essential. We need to work at dealing with those factors that threaten to drain life from us and render us helpless. I am presenting a discussion of this issue early in the book because I encourage you to consider how you can apply the theories that you will be studying to enhancing your life from both a personal and a professional standpoint. My assumption is that if you are aware of those factors that contribute to sapping your vitality as a person, you are in a better position to prevent the condition that is known as *professional burnout.*

What is burnout? I have heard counselors complain that they are just going through the motions on their job. They feel that whatever they are doing makes no difference at all and that they have nothing left to give. Some of these practitioners have convinced themselves that this feeling of burnout is one of the inevitable hazards of the profession and that there is not much they can do to revitalize themselves. This assumption is lethal, for it cements the feeling of impotence and leads to a giving up of hope. Equally bad are those practitioners who do not realize that they are burned out!

Burnout manifests itself in many ways. Those who experience this syndrome typically find that they are tired, drained, and without enthusiasm. They talk of feeling pulled by their many projects, most of which seem to have lost meaning. They feel that what they do have to offer is either not wanted or not received; they feel unappreciated, unrecognized, and unimportant, and they go about their jobs in a mechanical and routine way. They tend not to see any concrete results or fruits from their efforts. Often they feel oppressed by the "system" and by institutional demands, which, they contend, stifle any sense of personal initiative. A real danger is that the burnout syndrome can feed off of itself, so that practitioners feel more and more isolated. They may fail to reach out to one another and to develop a support system. Because burnout can rob us of the vitality we need personally and professionally, it is important to look at some of its causes, possible remedies, and ways of preventing it.

## CAUSES OF BURNOUT

Rather than having a single cause, burnout results from a combination of factors. It is best understood by considering the individual, interpersonal, and organizational factors that contribute to the condition. Recognizing the causes of burnout can itself be a step in dealing with it. A few of them are:

- doing the same type of work with little variation, especially if this work seems meaningless
- giving a great deal personally and not getting back much in the way of appreciation or other positive responses
- lacking a sense of accomplishment and meaning in work
- being under constant and strong pressure to produce, perform, and meet deadlines, many of which may be unrealistic
- working with a difficult population, such as those who are highly resistant, who are involuntary clients, or who show very little progress

- conflict and tension among a staff; an absence of support from colleagues and an abundance of criticism
- lack of trust between supervisors and mental-health workers, leading to a condition in which they are working against each other instead of toward commonly valued goals
- not having opportunities for personal expression or for taking the initiative in trying new approaches, a situation in which experimentation, change, and innovation are not only unrewarded but also actively discouraged
- facing unrealistic demands on your time and energy
- having a job that is both personally and professionally taxing without much opportunity for supervision, continuing education, or other forms of in-service training
- unresolved personal conflicts beyond the job situation, such as marital tensions, chronic health problems, financial problems, and so on

Rather than looking at burnout as something that could afflict you, you may find it useful to consider your own role in increasing the risk of burnout. Certain personality traits and characteristics can increase the risk factor. For instance, a strong need for approval for all that you do or an inordinate desire to be needed can lead to burnout. As long as the source of your value lies outside of yourself, you are in a tentative position, because once this external validation ceases, you begin to starve emotionally.

## REMEDIES FOR BURNOUT

Learning ways to take care of ourselves is a necessary step beyond this initial recognition of the problem of burnout. I see acceptance of *personal responsibility* as one of the most critical factors. In my experience in conducting training workshops, it has become almost standard to hear mental-health workers blame the system and other external factors for their condition; the more they look outside of themselves for the reasons that they feel dead, the greater becomes their sense of impotence and hopelessness. At these workshops I often hear statements such as these:

- "I'm failing as a counselor because my clients are highly resistive and don't really want to change. Besides, they're not capable of much change!"
- "The system here keeps us down. We're merely small cogs that need to keep functioning if this big machine is to continue working."
- "I have far too many clients, and I also have too many demands on my time. All these demands make me feel useless, because I know I'll never be able to meet them."

Notice that these professionals are placing responsibility *outside* of themselves and that someone else or some impersonal factor is *making* them ineffective. This is the passive stance that so often contributes to general feelings of hopelessness and powerlessness. To the degree that professionals continue to blame external factors, they also surrender their own personal power and assume the position of a victim. This very passive state lends itself to the development of cynicism that makes it difficult to harness energy and apply it to performing tasks. It is essential that counselors recognize that even though external realities do exert a toll on personal energy, they themselves are playing a role in remaining passive. Although bureaucratic obstacles can make it difficult to function effectively, it is possible to learn ways to survive with dignity within an institution and to engage in meaningful work. This means that counselors will have to become active and stop blaming the system for all that they cannot do. Instead, as a place to begin, they can focus on what they *can* do to bring about *some* changes and to create a climate in which they can do work that has meaning for them.

## PREVENTING BURNOUT

Learning to look within yourself to determine what choices you are making (and not making) to keep yourself alive can go a long way in preventing what some people consider to be an inevitable condition associated with the helping professions. It is crucial to recognize that you have considerable control over whether you become burned out. Although you cannot always control stressful events, you do have a great deal of control over how you interpret and react to these events. What is so important to realize is that you cannot continue to give and give while getting little in return. There is a price to pay for always being available and for assuming that you are able to control the lives and destinies of others. Become attuned to the subtle signs of burnout, rather than waiting for a full-blown condition of emotional and physical exhaustion to set in. Develop your own strategy for keeping yourself alive personally and professionally. A few suggestions for preventing burnout follow:

- Evaluate your goals, priorities, and expectations to see if they are realistic and if they are getting you what you want.
- Recognize that you can be an active agent in your life.
- Find other interests besides work, especially if your work is not meeting your most important needs.
- Think of ways to bring variety into work.
- Take the initiative to start new projects that have personal meaning, and do not wait for the system to sanction this initiative.
- Learn to monitor the impact of stress, on the job and at home.
- Attend to your health through adequate sleep, an exercise program, proper diet, and meditation or relaxation.
- Develop a few friendships that are characterized by a mutuality of giving *and* receiving.
- Learn how to ask for what you want, though don't expect always to get it.
- Learn how to work for self-confirmation and for self-rewards, as opposed to looking externally for validation.
- Find meaning through play, travel, or new experiences.

- Take the time to evaluate the meaningfulness of your projects to determine where you should continue to invest time and energy.
- Avoid assuming burdens that are properly the responsibility of others. If you worry more about your clients than they do about themselves, for example, it would be well for you to reconsider this investment.
- Take classes and workshops, attend conferences, and read to gain new perspectives on old issues.
- Rearrange your schedule to reduce stress.
- Learn your limits, and learn to set limits with others.
- Learn to accept yourself with your imperfections, including being able to forgive yourself when you make a mistake or do not live up to your ideals.
- Exchange jobs with a colleague for a short period, or ask a colleague to join forces in a common work project.
- Form a support group with colleagues to share feelings of frustration and to find better ways of approaching the reality of difficult job situations.
- Cultivate some hobbies that bring pleasure.
- Make time for your spiritual growth.
- Become more active in your professional organization.
- Seek counseling as an avenue of personal development.

Although this is not an exhaustive list, it does provide some direction for thinking about ways in which to keep ourselves alive. Our attempts to keep ourselves professionally updated will not mean much if we feel dead personally. This is why we must make periodic assessments of the direction of our own life to determine if we are living the way we want. If we are not, we must decide what we are willing to actually do to *make* changes occur, rather than simply wait for new life to enter us. By being in tune with ourselves, by having the experience of centeredness and solidness, and by feeling a sense of personal power, we have the basis for integrating our life experiences with our professional experiences. Such a synthesis can provide the basis for being an effective professional.

# Summary

One of the basic issues in the counseling profession concerns the significance of the counselor as a person in the therapeutic relationship. Since counselors are asking people to take an honest look at themselves and to make choices concerning how they want to change, it is critical that counselors themselves be searchers who hold their own lives open to the same kind of scrutiny. Counselors should repeatedly ask themselves such questions as "What do I personally have to offer others who are struggling to find their way? Am I doing in my own life what I urge others to do?"

Counselors can acquire an extensive theoretical and practical knowledge and can make that knowledge available to their clients. But to every therapeutic session they also bring themselves as persons. They bring their human qualities and the life experiences that have molded them. It is my belief that professionals can be well versed in psychological theory and can learn diagnostic and inter-viewing skills and still be ineffective as helpers. If counselors are to promote growth and change in their clients, they must be willing to promote growth in their own life by exploring their own choices and decisions and by striving to become aware of the ways in which they have ignored their own potential for growth. This willingness to attempt to live in accordance with what they teach and thus to be positive models for their clients is what makes counselors "therapeutic persons."

# CHAPTER THREE

# Ethical Issues in Counseling Practice

# Introduction

This chapter introduces you to some of the ethical principles and issues that will be a basic part of your professional practice. Its purpose is to stimulate you to think further about these issues so that you can form a sound basis for making ethical decisions. Topics that are addressed include balancing the client's needs against your own needs, ways of making sound ethical decisions, educating clients about their rights, parameters of confidentiality, guidelines for assessing suicidal tendencies, ethical concerns in counseling diverse client populations, ethical issues involving diagnosis and testing, dealing with dual relationships, and developing and maintaining competence as a practitioner.

As you become involved in counseling, you will find that interpreting the ethical guidelines of your professional organization and applying them to particular situations demand the utmost ethical sensitivity. Even responsible practitioners differ over how to apply established ethical principles to specific situations. It is clear that therapists are challenged to deal with questions that do not always have obvious answers. You will have to struggle with yourself to decide how to act in ways that will further the best interests of your clients. To help you make such decisions, consult with colleagues, keep yourself informed about laws affecting your practice, keep up to date in your specialty field, stay abreast of developments in ethical practice, reflect on the impact that your values have on your practice, and be willing to engage in honest self-examination.

One practical way to keep yourself informed on matters pertaining to ethical and professional issues is to read about these issues and discuss them with fellow students and colleagues. Another good way is to join one or more of the professional organizations, which provide members with current information. Within the past decade there has been a definite increase in professional articles dealing with ethics, and the number of books on ethical issues has significantly increased. (See the References and Suggested Readings at the end of Part One).

The ethical issues raised in this chapter need to be reexamined periodically throughout your professional life. You can benefit from both formal and informal opportunities to discuss ethical dilemmas during your training program. Even if you resolve some ethical issues while completing a graduate program, there is no guarantee that they have been settled once and for all. These issues are bound to take on new dimensions as you gain more experience. I have found that students often burden themselves unnecessarily with the expectation that they should resolve all problem issues before they are ready to practice. Ethical decision making is an evolutionary process that requires you to be continually open and self-critical.

In recent years there has been an increased awareness of the ethical responsibility of counselors to alleviate human suffering on a broader scale. No longer can practitioners afford to confine themselves to their offices if they hope to reach a wide group of people who are in need of services. Many mental-health professionals now emphasize social action by exerting their influence against such wrongs as discrimination against women and minority groups, the continuation of racism in society, the neglect of the aged, and inhumane practices against children. Seminars and workshops are conducted to awaken professionals to pressing needs in the community. In sum, counselors are discovering that to bring about significant individual change, they cannot ignore the major social ills that often create and exacerbate problems for individuals; they must become active agents of constructive social change.

# Putting the Client's Needs before Your Own

Issues pertaining to counselors meeting their needs through their professional work were examined in Chapter 2. The ethical dimensions of this topic are addressed here. I do not think that as counselors we can keep our personal needs completely separate from our relationships with clients. Ethically, it is essential that we become aware of our own needs, areas of unfinished business, potential personal conflicts, and defenses. We need to realize how such factors could interfere with helping our clients.

Our professional relationships with our clients exist for their benefit. A useful question that we can frequently ask ourselves is "Whose needs are being met in this relationship, my client's or my own?" It takes considerable professional maturity to make an honest appraisal of your behavior and its impact on clients. I do not think it is unethical for us to meet our personal needs through our professional work, yet it is essential that these needs be kept in perspective. For me, the ethical issue exists when we meet our needs, in either obvious or subtle ways, at the expense of our clients. The crux of the matter is to avoid exploiting clients.

What kind of awareness is crucial? We all have certain blind spots and distortions of reality. As helping professionals we have responsibilities to work actively toward expanding our own self-awareness and to learn to recognize areas of prejudice and vulnerability. If we are aware of our personal problems and are willing to work them through, there is less chance that we will project them onto clients. If certain areas of struggle surface and old conflicts become reactivated, we have an ethical obligation to seek our own therapy, so that we will be able to assist clients in confronting these same struggles.

As counselors we must also examine other, less obviously harmful, personal needs that can get in the way of creating growth-producing relationships. These other aspects of our personality include the need for control and power; the need to be nurturing and helpful; the need to change others in the direction of our own values; the need to teach and preach and to persuade as well; the need for feeling adequate, particularly when it becomes overly important that the client confirm our competence; and the need to be respected and appreciated. I am not asserting that these needs are neurotic; on the contrary, it is essential that our needs be met if we are to be involved with helping others find satisfaction in their life. Nor do I think that there is anything amiss in our deriving deep personal satisfaction from our work. And surely many of our needs for feeling worthwhile, important, respected, and adequate may enhance the quality of our work with others.

Personal power is a quality that every effective helping person possesses. It is a vital component of good therapy, and many clients improve as a result of sharing in the power of their therapist. One aspect of modeling is for therapists to be powerful persons. People who genuinely feel powerful do not dominate the lives of others and do not encourage others to remain in a dwarfed state so that they can feel superior. They are able to appreciate other people's potency and their own at the same time. The impotent therapist uses clients in an attempt to achieve a sense of power. To a powerful therapist, the client's accomplishments and strengths are a source of joy.

Clearly, the fact that power can be used against the client is an ethical concern. For example, consider the therapist's use of control (both consciously and unconsciously) as a way of reducing personal threat and anxiety. If a counselor is unsure of his own sexuality, he may use power to keep his female clients from threatening him. For instance, he may distance a woman with abstract, intellectual interpretations or by assuming an aloof, "professional" stance. If she desires to become a mature and assertive woman and he feels uncomfortable in the presence of powerful women, he may subvert her attempts and encourage her to remain dependent.

Consider also the counselor's need to nurture, which certainly attracts some students to the helping professions. These are the people who may be inclined to "teach people how to live the good life," to "straighten people out," and to "solve others' problems," all with the intention of being nurturing. Others at one point recognized that they were miserable, or at least that they wanted to make basic changes in their life, and then embarked on a successful journey of self-exploration. Such people may now deeply desire to help others find their own way and, in so doing, provide for themselves a sense of meaningfulness and personal significance. One aspect of therapists' need to nurture is their need for others to nurture *them* through respect, admiration, approval, appreciation, affection, and caring. The helping person quickly learns that the rewards for nurturing others are abundant.

Again, I see nothing amiss in counselors' need to be nurtured. The ethical questions are these: What are the dangers to the client's well-being when the therapist has an exaggerated need for nurture from the client? Can counselors distinguish between counseling for the client's benefit and that for their own gains? Are therapists sufficiently aware of their needs for approval and appreciation? Do they base their perceptions of adequacy strictly on reactions from clients?

In summary, I believe that many are motivated to enter the counseling profession because of their needs for power, for feeling useful and significant, and for reinforcing their feelings of adequacy. If helpers depend inordinately on others for their psychological gratification, they are likely to keep others in a dependent position. Because of their own emotional hunger and their own need to be psychologically fed, they are unable to focus genuine attention on the client's deprivations. At the extreme, the helper is in greater need of the "helpee" than the other way around. For these reasons ethical practice demands that counselors recognize the central importance of continuously evaluating in which direction their personality might influence clients—for progress or for stagnation.

# Ethical Decision Making

As a practitioner you will ultimately have to apply the ethical codes of your profession to the many practical problems you face. You will not be able to rely on ready-made answers or prescriptions given by professional organizations, which typically provide only broad guidelines for responsible practice. The following organizations all have codes of ethics that offer guidance to practitioners: the American Counseling Association ([ACA], 1995), the American Association for Marriage and Family Therapy ([AAMFT], 1991), the American Psychiatric Association (1989), the American Psychoanalytic Association (1983), the American Psychological Association ([APA], 1992), the National Association of Social Workers ([NASW], 1990), the National Board for Certified Counselors ([NBCC], 1989), and the National Organization for Human Service Education ([NOHSE], 1994). (The addresses of most of these organizations are found in Appendix 2 of the student manual of this textbook.)

Most of the 42 state counselor-licensing statutes contain codes of ethics. Part of the process of making ethical decisions involves learning about the resources from which you can draw when you are struggling with an ethical question. Although you are ultimately responsible for making ethical decisions, you do not have to do so in a vacuum. You should also be aware of the consequences of practicing in ways that are not sanctioned by organizations of which you are a member or the state in which you are licensed to practice.

## BASIC PRINCIPLES OF CODES OF ETHICS

Although ethics codes are living documents that change over time, certain constant moral principles form the foundation of all professional codes. One way of viewing codes is to look at their underlying principles. Welfel and Kitchener (1992) and Kitchener (1984) have described five basic moral principles that are reflected in all professional codes: benefit others, do no harm, respect others' autonomy, be just or fair, and be faithful. Each of these principles is defined below.

1. *Beneficence* implies accepting responsibility for promoting what is good for others. In counseling relationships, it refers to doing what enhances the client's well-being. When clients enter into a therapeutic venture, they do so with the expectation that they will benefit from the services.

2. *Nonmaleficence,* which means doing no harm, involves the commitment of practitioners to exercise care in avoiding activities (such as situations involving conflicts of interest) that have a high risk of hurting clients, even inadvertently.

3. *Autonomy* refers to the client's self-determination. It pertains to the belief that clients have freedom of thought and freedom to choose their direction. Counselors have an ethical obligation to decrease client dependency and to foster independent decision making. This principle implies that therapists do not have the right to interfere in the lives of their clients by making decisions for them.

Instead, counselors are charged with helping their clients think clearly and weigh the consequences of their actions.

4. *Justice* refers to the commitment of counselors to provide equal and fair treatment to all clients. This includes doing what is possible to ensure that all people are given equal access to counseling services, regardless of factors such as age, sex, race, ethnicity, cultural background, disability, socioeconomic status, lifestyle orientation, and religion. This principle also refers to the fair treatment of an individual when his or her interests need to be considered in the context of the rights and interests of others.

5. *Fidelity* refers to making honest promises and faithfully honoring these commitments to clients. This involves a counselor's willingness to do what is necessary to create a trusting and therapeutic climate in which people can search for their own solutions. This principle involves being careful not to deceive or exploit clients.

## THE ROLE OF ETHICAL CODES
## AS A CATALYST FOR IMPROVING PRACTICE

Professional codes of ethics serve a number of purposes. They educate counseling practitioners and the general public about the responsibilities of the profession. They provide a basis for accountability, and through their enforcement, clients are protected from unethical practices. Perhaps most importantly, codes can provide a basis for reflecting on and improving one's professional practice. Self-monitoring is a better route for professionals to take than being policed by an outside agency (Herlihy & Corey, 1994).

It should be emphasized that codes of ethics typically address a broad range of issues and behaviors. Thus, they describe minimal standards of behavior and identify and prohibit those behaviors that are unethical. There is a real difference between merely following the ethical codes and making a commitment to practicing with the highest ideals. *Mandatory ethics* entails a level of ethical functioning at which counselors simply act in compliance with minimal standards. *Aspirational ethics* pertains to striving for the optimum standards of conduct. Rather than merely focusing on ways to avoid a malpractice suit, therapists who are committed to aspirational ethics are primarily concerned with doing what is in the best interests of their clients. When we carefully study the ethical codes of our profession, apply relevant standards to situations that we encounter, and periodically review them, codes of ethics can become a vehicle to improve and enhance our professional practice (Herlihy & Corey, 1994).

From my perspective, one of the unfortunate trends is for ethics codes to increasingly take on legalistic dimensions. Many practitioners are so anxious about becoming embroiled in a lawsuit that they gear their practices mainly toward fulfilling legal minimums, rather than thinking of what is right for their clients. In this era of litigation it makes sense to be aware of the legal aspects of practice and do what is possible to reduce the chances of malpractice action, but it is a mistake to confuse legal behavior with being ethical. Although following the law is part of ethical behavior, being an ethical practitioner involves far more. One of the best ways to prevent being sued for malpractice rests in demonstrating respect for clients, having their welfare as a central concern, and practicing within the framework of professional codes.

Ethics codes are necessary, yet they are not sufficient for exercising ethical responsibility. Although it is essential that you know the contents of the codes of your profession, it is also important that you be aware of their limitations. By their very nature, codes provide general guidance on what constitutes behavior that is in the client's best interests. In writing about their limits, Welfel and Kitchener (1992) indicate that codes are conservative by nature, balancing the protection of the consumer against the protection of the professional from outside regulation. Codes become outdated and thus need to be revised periodically. They tend to be reactive in nature, meaning that some specific clauses are drafted after certain problem areas become evident. For instance, at one time there were no explicit sanctions prohibiting sex with clients. When it became evident that sexual misconduct was a major problem within the profession, the codes specified this form of unethical behavior.

Over time, most of the ethical codes of various mental-health professions have evolved into lengthy documents, setting forth what is desired behavior and proscribing behavior that may not serve the client's welfare. Even though codes are becoming more specific, they do not convey ultimate truth, nor do they provide ready-made answers for the ethical dilemmas that practitioners will encounter. Ultimately, professionals are expected to exercise prudent judgment when it comes to interpreting and applying ethical principles to specific situations. In my view, ethical codes are best used as guidelines to formulate sound reasoning and serve practitioners in making the best judgments possible. Because ethics codes are creations of human beings, and because they are evolving documents that are modified over time, some degree of flexibility is essential in applying them. No code of ethics can delineate what would be the appropriate or best course of action in each problematic situation a professional will face.

Many standards within ethics codes are extremely difficult to enforce. This places the focus on the goodwill and commitment of individual practitioners in monitoring the quality of their actions in professional practice. A few ways in which counselors might engage in ethically questionable behavior that would be difficult to detect by others, and thus difficult to enforce, include:

- prolonging client dependency on the therapist to the extent that autonomy of the client becomes difficult
- being unaware of countertransference reactions to a client and thus increasing resistance and thwarting therapeutic progress
- imposing values, goals, and strategies on clients that are not congruent with their cultural background
- using techniques that are aimed at therapist comfort rather than at helping clients achieve their therapeutic goals
- prolonging the number of counseling sessions because of the therapist's emotional or financial needs

- practicing with little enthusiasm or tolerating boredom, apathy, and even burnout

At this point, reflect on any ways in which you might engage in less than the highest ethical behavior. What are some subtle ways in which your behavior might be self-serving? How might you fail to render the best professional service in spite of your intentions to do what is right? What paths can you take to best monitor your behavior?

## SOME STEPS IN MAKING ETHICAL DECISIONS

There are a number of different models for ethical decision making, most of which tend to focus on the application of principles to ethical dilemmas. After reviewing a few of these models, my colleagues and I have identified the following steps as a procedural way to help you think through ethical problems (see G. Corey, Corey, & Callanan, 1993):

- Identify the problem or dilemma. Gather information that will shed light on the nature of the problem. This will help you decide whether the problem is mainly ethical, legal, or moral.
- Identify the potential issues. Evaluate the rights, responsibilities, and welfare of all those who are involved in the situation. Apply the underlying principles of autonomy, beneficence, nonmaleficence, justice, and fidelity to the specific situation.
- Look at the relevant ethical codes for general guidance on the matter. Consider whether your own values and ethics are consistent with or in conflict with the relevant guidelines.
- Seek consultation from more than one source to obtain various perspectives on the dilemma.
- Brainstorm various possible courses of action. Continue discussing options with other professionals.
- Enumerate the consequences of various decisions, and reflect on the implications of each course of action for your client. Again, consider the five ethical principles of autonomy, beneficence, nonmaleficence, justice, and fidelity as a framework for evaluating the consequences of a given course of action.
- Decide on what appears to be the best possible course of action. Recognize that the more subtle the ethical dilemma, the more difficult the decision-making process will be. Be aware that in reasoning through any ethical issue, different practitioners will make a variety of decisions.

Professional maturity implies that you are open to questioning and that you are willing to discuss your quandaries with colleagues. Recognize that there is rarely one ideal course of action to follow. Because ethical codes do not make decisions for you, demonstrate a willingness to struggle, to raise questions, to discuss ethical concerns with others, and to continually clarify your values and examine your motivations.

# Some Basic Rights of Clients

As mentioned earlier, it is ethical practice to focus more on promoting the welfare of your clients than on making minimal interventions that will protect you from a malpractice suit. By educating your clients about their rights and responsibilities, you are both empowering them and at the same time reducing your chances of being sued. When clients give their informed consent, for example, they do not have to remain in the dark about the therapy process, and they increase their chances of working collaboratively with you. Attending to the rights of your clients is an excellent foundation for building a trusting relationship with them. This section examines the right of informed consent, the rights of minors, and the right to a referral.

## THE RIGHT OF INFORMED CONSENT

One of the best ways of protecting the rights of clients is to develop procedures to help them make informed choices. This process of providing clients with the information they need to become active participants in the therapeutic relationship begins with the initial session and continues throughout counseling. The challenge of fulfilling the spirit of informed consent is to strike a balance between giving clients too much information and giving them too little. For example, it is too late to tell minors that you intend to consult with their parents after they have disclosed that they are considering an abortion. In such a case both the girlfriend and the boyfriend have a right to know about the limitations of confidentiality before they make such highly personal disclosures. On the other hand, clients can be overwhelmed if counselors go into too much detail initially about the interventions they are likely to make. It takes both intuition and skill for practitioners to strike a balance.

Providing for informed consent tends to promote the active cooperation of clients in their counseling plan. Clients often do not realize that they have any rights and do not think about their own responsibilities in solving their problems. Those who feel desperate for help may unquestioningly accept whatever their counselor says or does. They seek the expertise of a professional without realizing that the success of this relationship depends largely on their own investment in the process.

Most professional codes of ethics provide that clients have the right to be presented with enough data to make informed choices about entering and continuing the client/therapist relationship. Depending on the setting and the situation, this discussion can involve those issues that may affect the client's decision to enter the therapeutic relationship. Some of these factors are the general goals of counseling, the responsibilities of the counselor toward the client, the responsibilities of clients, limitations of and exceptions to confidentiality, legal and ethical parameters that could define the relationship, the qualifications and background of the practitioner, the fees involved and the services one can expect, and the approximate length of the therapeutic process. Further areas might include the benefits of counseling, the risks involved, and the possibility that one's case will be discussed with the therapist's colleagues or supervisors. Providing this kind of information in writing is a good method of helping clients understand what is involved in the counseling process. Clients can take this written information home and can then bring up questions at the following session. (A sample "informed-consent document" is reproduced in the student manual that accompanies this textbook.)

The ACA (1995) guideline on the issue of the client/counselor relationship is "When counseling is initiated, and throughout the counseling process as necessary, counselors inform clients of the purposes, goals, techniques, procedures, limitations, potential risks and benefits of services to be performed and other pertinent information." Several factors in addition to those already mentioned are likely to affect the client's decision to enter the relationship. For example, the recording of an interview by audio- or videotape would be an issue, because others besides the client and the therapist might listen to or view the tapes. Some school districts have a policy that if clients reveal that they use drugs, the counselor is obliged to report their names to the principal. In other cases, clients do not voluntarily initiate a therapeutic relationship but are recipients of "mandatory counseling." It is clear that in each of these instances certain policies or conditions can affect the client's decision to enter a therapeutic relationship. Thus, it is ethical practice for the therapist to make known to the potential client the limitations of the relationship.

## THE RIGHTS OF MINORS

What are some of the ethical and legal issues in counseling children and adolescents? Can minors consent to treatment without parental knowledge and consent? To what degree should they be allowed to participate in setting the goals for counseling? What are the limits of confidentiality? In most states, parental knowledge and consent are legally required for a minor to enter into a relationship with a health-care professional. There are some exceptions, however: Some states have laws that grant adolescents the right to seek counseling about birth control, abortion, substance abuse, child abuse, and other crises. The justification for allowing children and adolescents to seek a therapeutic relationship without parental consent is that they otherwise might not obtain this crucial treatment. This is particularly true in cases involving drug or alcohol abuse, family conflict, physical or psychological abuse, and pregnancy or abortion counseling. In such cases therapists who work with minors frequently find themselves in the role of an advocate.

## THE RIGHT TO A REFERRAL

What should therapists do when they judge that a client should be referred, either because they feel unqualified to continue working with the client or because they believe that the type or duration of treatment at hand is too limited for what the client should receive? For example, Sherri has been seeing her high school counselor, Monica, weekly for two months, and she feels that the sessions are extremely helpful. The counselor agrees that Sherri is making progress but is also aware of some other realities: Her time is limited, because she has 450 counselees; the school has a policy that long-term counseling should not be provided and that a referral should be made when indicated; and Sherri's emotional problems are deep enough to indicate intensive psychotherapy. Because of these realities, Monica suggests a referral and gives Sherri the reasons. Assume that Sherri responds in one of these two ways: One, she may agree to accept the referral and see a private therapist. In this case when does Monica's responsibility to Sherri end? The guideline is that the responsibility for the client's welfare continues until she begins seeing the other therapist. Even after that some form of consultation with the other therapist may be in order. Two, Sherri may refuse to be referred and say that she does not want to see anyone else. Should Monica terminate the relationship? Should she continue but still encourage Sherri to accept an eventual referral? What if the counselor feels that she is "getting in over her head" with Sherri?

This case raises two questions for consideration: (1) What criteria can be used to determine whether the client is benefiting from a counseling relationship? (2) If clients believe that they are profiting but no signs of progress are seen, how can this ethical dilemma be resolved?

# Dimensions of Confidentiality

Confidentiality, which is central to developing a trusting and productive client/therapist relationship, is both a legal and an ethical issue. State laws now address confidentiality in therapy, as do the ethical codes of all the mental-health professions. Because no genuine therapy can occur unless clients trust in the privacy of their revelations to their therapists, professionals have the responsibility to define the degree of confidentiality that can be promised. Counselors have an ethical responsibility to discuss the nature and purpose of confidentiality with their clients early in the counseling process. In addition, clients have a right to know that their therapist may be discussing certain details of the relationship with a supervisor or a colleague. Both the APA and the ACA have codes relevant to this subject. The APA's (1992) principle is: "Unless it is not feasible or is contraindicated, the discussion of confidentiality occurs at the outset of the relationship and thereafter as new circumstances may warrant." The ACA's (1995) ethics code states: "When counseling is initiated and throughout the counseling process as necessary, counselors inform clients of the limitations of confidentiality and identify forseeable situations in which confidentiality must be breached."

Although most counselors agree on the essential value of confidentiality, they realize that it cannot be considered an absolute. There are times when confidential information must be divulged, and there are many instances in which whether to keep or to break confidentiality becomes a cloudy issue. In making their determinations of when to breach confidentiality, therapists must consider the requirements of the institution in which they work and the clientele they serve.

Because these circumstances are frequently not clearly defined by accepted ethical codes, counselors must exercise professional judgment. In general, confidentiality must be broken when it becomes clear that clients might do serious harm to either themselves or others. There is a legal requirement to break confidentiality in cases involving child abuse, abuse of the elderly, and danger to others. All mental-health practitioners and interns need to be aware of their duty to report such abuse. The ACA's code of ethics offers this general guidance: "Counselors must keep information related to counseling services confidential unless disclosure is in the best interests of clients, is required for the welfare of others, is in response to obligations to society, or is required by law. When disclosure is required, only information that is essential is revealed."

The crux of the matter often comes down to *when* disclosure is in the client's best interest or when it is required to protect others. For example, are all threats by a client to be followed up with a report to the authorities? What if the client does not make a verbal threat but the counselor has a strong hunch that the person could be homicidal or suicidal?

## GENERAL GUIDELINES ON CONFIDENTIALITY

Following are some of the circumstances that dictate when information *must* legally be reported by counselors:

- when clients pose a danger to others or themselves
- when the therapist believes that a client under the age of 16 is the victim of incest, rape, child abuse, or some other crime
- when the therapist determines that the client needs hospitalization
- when information is made an issue in a court action
- when clients request that their records be released to themselves or a third party

In general, however, it is a counselor's primary obligation to protect the client's disclosures as a vital part of the therapeutic relationship. When assuring clients that what they reveal in sessions will generally be kept confidential, counselors should also tell them of any limitations on confidentiality. This practice does not necessarily inhibit successful counseling.

Therapists should discuss with their clients how certain information about them might be shared with others at times. It is generally accepted that therapists will have no professional contact with the family or friends of a client without first securing the client's permission. It is accepted, in addition, that information obtained in therapeutic relationships should be discussed with others for professional purposes only and with persons who are clearly related to the case.

The issue of confidentiality takes on added dimensions for students who are involved in a fieldwork placement or internship as part of their program. In most cases these counselor interns are required to keep notes on the proceedings with their individual clients or the members of their group. Also, group-supervision sessions at a clinic or university typically entail open discussions about the clients with whom these counselor interns are working. These discussions should always be conducted in a professional manner. If a particular individual client is being discussed, it is important that this person's identity be protected, if at all possible. In many situations interns can actually show their clients what they are writing and discuss these notes with them. If clients receive this type of openness from their counselors, I have found, they respond with greater frankness, for they feel that information will be used *for* them, not *against* them.

## SPECIAL CONSIDERATIONS IN CONFIDENTIALITY

Legislators and judges seem inclined to bind all mental-health practitioners to confidentiality while at the same time limiting its scope. They appear to believe that confidentiality is necessary for a counseling relationship to be effective but that it need not be absolute.

As we have seen, counselors must become familiar with local and state laws that govern their specialization. Yet this knowledge alone will not settle difficult situations. There are various and sometimes conflicting ways to interpret a law, and professional judgment does play a critical role in resolving most cases.

DUTY TO WARN AND PROTECT.    As a result of a number of court decisions, mental-health practitioners have become increasingly aware of and concerned about their double duty: to protect other people from potentially dangerous clients and to protect clients from themselves. These court decisions have mandated that practitioners have a responsibility to protect the public from potentially dangerous clients. This responsibility entails liability for civil damages when practitioners neglect this duty by failing to diagnose or predict dangerousness, failing to warn potential victims of violent behavior, failing to commit dangerous individuals, and prematurely discharging dangerous clients from the hospital (APA, 1985).

What is expected is that counselors use sound professional judgment and that they seek consultation when they are in doubt about a given individual or situation. Further, those practitioners who work in mental-health clinics or agencies should inform their supervisor or director and document in writing the nature of these consultations. If they determine that a client poses a serious danger of violence to others, they are obliged to use reasonable care to protect the potential victims. In addition to notifying the proper authorities, they should warn the intended victims if the law in their state allows them to do so. In the case of a minor, the parents should be notified. In this regard counselors need to inform their clients of the possible actions they must take to protect a third party. Once again, because there are frequently no clear-cut answers, as these situations are often unique, it is a good policy for counselors to consult with colleagues for other opinions and suggestions concerning the gravity of a case, as well as for suggestions on how to proceed. It is also sound practice to document in the client's case notes the results of these consultations.

CONFIDENTIALITY WITH HIV-POSITIVE CLIENTS.    Mental-health professionals will be increasingly confronted with ethical issues involving clients who have AIDS or who are infected with its virus. The issues surrounding the limits of confidentiality with HIV clients pose new challenges for counselors. Questions arise: Who is the client—the individual, the uninformed sexual partner(s), the family, or society? What are the responsibilities of helpers when education and appeals to reason fail with clients who are HIV-positive and do not practice safe sex? Will the practice of reporting such individuals, especially those who have anonymous partners, result in the termination of counseling? Should informing public-health and mental-health personnel be a mandatory practice, or should it be used as a last resort?

The professional literature and the ethical codes of various professional organizations are beginning to define the limits of confidentiality raised by the life-threatening activities of HIV clients who continue to be sexually active without informing their partners. To what degree do therapists have the duty to protect others from HIV infection by a client? For example, must counselors break confidentiality and even take coercive action in cases where an HIV-infected person is believed to be sexually active or sharing needles with partners who are not aware of the client's infection? It is difficult to determine the balance between maintaining the confidentiality and privacy of the client and protecting others from potential infection.

# Guidelines for Dealing with Suicidal Clients

Practitioners have an obligation not only to warn and to protect others from the acts of dangerous people but also to protect suicidal clients. There are definite limitations to confidentiality when the counselor determines that a client is a suicide risk. The assessment and management of suicidal clients are typically stressful for counselors. The possibility of a client's suicide raises a number of difficult issues that practitioners must face, such as their degree of influence, competence, level of involvement with a client, responsibility, and legal obligations. Counselors need to demonstrate the ability to make appropriate interventions in critical situations.

When practitioners are faced with suicide threats by clients, what steps can they take to increase their chances of behaving ethically and legally? First, it is essential to make a decision about the seriousness of the situation. Second, if therapists judge that a foreseeable risk does exist, they are *required* to take action. They are expected to use direct intervention that is consistent with the standard of practice common to their profession. The client's right to confidentiality assumes secondary importance when his or her life is at risk.

Certain characteristics are associated with suicide-prone behavior, including chronic depression, hopelessness, a clear plan for taking one's life, and prior suicidal attempts. Wubbolding (1988a) suggests that therapist use direct questioning about the suicide threat to assess what kind of intervention is necessary. He suggests questions such as the following: "Are you thinking about killing yourself?" "Have you tried previously to kill yourself?" "Do you have a plan?"

"Do you have the means to kill yourself?" "Will you make a unilateral contract not to kill yourself accidentally or on purpose? For how long?"

Although there is no typical suicidal person, there are common warning signs. According to Morrissey (1994), a suicidal person may:

- talk about committing suicide
- give away prized possessions
- take unnecessary risks
- be preoccupied with death and dying
- have made previous suicide attempts or gestures
- lose interest in hobbies, school, or work
- have had a recent severe loss
- increase the use of alcohol or drugs

Once the therapist makes the assessment of forseeable risk, what are some possible courses of action? What are some ethical and legal options to consider? How can counselors take appropriate steps to demonstrate that a reasonable attempt was made to control the suicidal client? Consultation is most important, both in the assessment and intervention phases. The practice of consultation offers protection to both the client and the counselor. The counselor's course of action should follow a predetermined, agreed-upon, and flexible policy (Wubbolding, 1988a).

Fujimura, Weis, and Cochran (1985) maintain that counselors must take their clients' "cry for help" seriously and must also have the necessary knowledge and skills to intervene once they make the determination that a client is suicidal. Many of these clients are facing a short-term crisis, and if they can be given help in coping with this crisis, they can be saved. These authors also stress the importance of knowing how, when, and where to appropriately refer clients whose concerns are beyond the counselor's boundary of competence.

At this point, you might reflect on your own views about suicide and how you would react to suicide threats in a counseling session. Therapists are bound by the law to make assessments and intervene in professionally appropriate ways. If you were not under this legal imperative, however, how might you handle suicide threats? Do you think that ethical practice always involves taking those steps that are legally required? As you think about this issue, do you see any potential conflict between ethics and the law?

# Ethical Issues in a Multicultural Perspective

In Chapter 2, as you will recall, I stressed that ethical practice requires counselors to have the education and training that will allow them to practice as effective multicultural counselors. We also considered the importance of taking the client's cultural context into account in counseling. Certainly, the ethical codes in our field need to incorporate an all-embracing perspective, rather than being geared to a specific population or a single set of value standards. In this section we look at how it is possible that conscientious and well-intentioned practitioners who follow their professional codes of ethics can still be practicing unethically if they do not address cultural differences.

## ETHICAL CODES AND MULTICULTURAL COUNSELING

The ACA's (1995) Code of Ethics and Standards of Practice encourages practitioners who counsel clients from bacgrounds different from their own to respect these differences; gain knowledge, personal awareness, and sensitivity pertinent to these clients; and incorporate culturally relevant practices into their work. In addition, in the preamble is the declaration that "association members recognize diversity in our society and embrace a cross-cultural approach in support of the worth, dignity, potential, and uniqueness of each individual."

If counselors do not have a frame of reference for being sensitive to various forms of diversity, they lessen the possibilities of establishing an effective client/ counselor relationship. It is neither ethical nor clinically sound for counselors to use techniques that are based on a monocultural model without attempting to develop strategies that will reflect awareness of and sensitivity to culture and gender concerns.

Because some contemporary ethical guidelines are still based on a culturally narrow perspective of counseling, it may be necessary for the multicultural counselor to reframe particular standards in order to counsel in an ethically appropriate manner. For example, Pedersen (1994) contends that the *Ethical Principles of Psychologists and Code of Conduct* (APA, 1992) are culturally encapsulated. He argues that to the extent that these principles are based on stereotyped values from the dominant culture's perspective, they need to be revised so that the interests of minority groups are taken into account. Furthermore, to the extent that they are grounded on a single standard of normal and ethical behavior, they require revision to incorporate a variety of culturally defined alternatives.

It should be pointed out that the APA has developed a separate set of useful guidelines for providers of psychological services to ethnic, linguistic, and culturally diverse populations (see APA, 1993). Examples of two of these guidelines are as follows:

- "Psychologists, regardless of ethnic/racial background, are aware of how their own cultural background/experiences, attitudes, values, and biases influence psychological processes. They make efforts to correct any prejudices and biases."
- "Psychologists' practice incorporates an understanding of the client's ethnic and cultural background. This includes the client's familiarity and comfort with the majority culture as well as ways in which the client's culture may add to or improve various aspects of a majority culture and/or of society at large."

# HAVE CURRENT THEORIES OUTLIVED THEIR USEFULNESS?

Some writers allege that current theories of counseling and psychotherapy—
including the nine theories that constitute Part Two of this textbook—are
inadequate to describe, explain, predict, and deal with the richness and complexity of a culturally diverse population (Sue, Ivey, & Pedersen, 1996). It
has also been asserted that contemporary theories cannot be easily adapted to
a wide range of cultures and that the helping professions need to develop a
theory of multicultural counseling and therapy.

I agree only to a point with this assertion, for my position is that current
theories can be expanded to include a multicultural perspective.

With respect to many of the traditional theories, assumptions made about
mental health, optimum human development, the nature of psychopathology,
and the nature of effective treatment often do not have relevance for some clients.
In order for traditional theories to be relevant in a multicultural society, they
need to incorporate an interactive person-in-the-environment focus and to account for salient cultural variables. It is essential for therapists to create therapeutic strategies that are congruent with the range of values and behaviors that
are characteristic of a pluralistic society.

# ARE COUNSELING AND THERAPY CULTURE-BOUND?

Multicultural specialists have asserted that theories of counseling and psychotherapy represent different worldviews, each with its own values, biases, and
assumptions about human behavior. Some counselors have criticized traditional
therapeutic practices as irrelevant for people of color and other special populations such as the elderly. Most techniques are derived from counseling approaches developed by and for white, male, middle-class, Western clients and
therefore may not be applicable to clients from different racial, ethnic, and
cultural backgrounds. The Western models of counseling have major limitations
when they are applied to certain special populations and minority groups such
as Asian and Pacific Islanders, Latinos, Native Americans, and African Americans.
Moreover, value assumptions made by culturally different counselors and clients
have resulted in culturally biased counseling and have led to underuse of
mental-health services (Pedersen, 1994).

Some of the values implicit in contemporary counseling theories include
an emphasis on individualism, the separate existence of the self, individuation
as the foundation for maturity, and decision making and responsibility as resting
with the individual rather than the group. By contrast, an Asian perspective
would play down individuality and focus on interdependence and the losing
of oneself in the totality of the cosmos.

It cannot be denied that the psychoanalytic, behavioral, cognitive-behavioral,
and existential approaches originated in the Euro-American culture and are
grounded on a core set of values. I think it is a myth that these approaches are

value-neutral and are applicable to all human beings. There is a danger of imposing these values as being the only right ones and as having universal applicability.
The relationship-oriented therapies—such as person-centered theory, existential therapy, and Gestalt therapy—emphasize freedom of choice and self-
actualization. Practitioners with such an orientation tend to focus on individual
responsibility for making internal changes as a way to cope with problems, and
they view individuation as the foundation for healthy functioning. In some
cultures, however, the key values are collectivist. Rather than emphasizing the
development of the individual, they focus on what is good for the group. Certainly, therapists who operate on the assumption that all clients should embrace
individualism are in error. Regardless of the therapist's orientation, it is crucial
to listen to clients and determine why they are seeking help and how best to
deliver the help that is appropriate for them.

## FOCUSING ON BOTH
## INDIVIDUAL AND ENVIRONMENTAL FACTORS

A theoretical orientation provides practitioners with a map to guide them in
a productive direction with their clients. Hopefully, their theory orients them
and does not control what they attend to in the therapeutic venture. Counselors
who operate from a multicultural framework also have certain assumptions and
a focus that guides their practice. They view individuals in the context of the
family and the culture, and their aim is to facilitate social action that will lead
to change within the client's community, rather than merely increasing the
individual's insight. Some multicultural practitioners maintain that therapeutic
practice will be effective only to the extent that interventions are tailored toward
social action aimed at changing those factors that are creating the client's problem, rather than blaming the client for his or her condition.

An adequate theory of counseling does deal with the social and cultural
factors of an individual's problems. However, there is something to be said for
helping clients deal with their response to environmental realities. Counselors
may well be at a loss in trying to bring about social change when they are sitting with a client who is in pain because of social injustice. By using techniques
from many of the traditional therapies, counselors can help clients increase their
awareness of their options in dealing with barriers and struggles. It is not a matter of focusing strictly on an individual's intrapsychic dynamics and forgetting
about bringing about change in the environment; rather, it is a matter of aiding
clients in clarifying how they are personally affected by external conditions and
challenging them to make decisions about what they can do to change themselves
if they cannot directly change the outside world. It is essential to focus on *both*
individual and social factors if change is to occur. Indeed, the person-in-the-
environment perspective acknowledges the interactive reality. (For a more
detailed treatment of ethical issues in multicultural counseling see LaFromboise
and Foster, 1989, Pedersen, 1994, and G. Corey et al., 1993.)

# Ethical Issues in the Assessment Process

As you will see when you study the various theories of counseling, some approaches place heavy emphasis on the role of assessment as a prelude to the treatment process. Other theories—mainly the relationship-oriented and experiential therapies such as existential therapy, person-centered therapy, and Gestalt therapy—tend to view diagnosis and testing as an external frame of reference that can remove the therapist from understanding the deeply personal and subjective world of the client. Both clinical and ethical issues are associated with the use of diagnostic and testing procedures.

## THE ROLE OF DIAGNOSIS IN COUNSELING

*Psychodiagnosis* is the analysis and explanation of a client's problems. It may include an explanation of the causes of the client's difficulties, an account of how these problems developed over time, a classification of any disorders, a specification of preferred treatment procedure, and an estimate of the chances for a successful resolution. The purpose of diagnosis in counseling and psychotherapy is to identify disruptions in a client's present behavior and lifestyle. Once problem areas are clearly identified, the counselor and client are able to establish the goals of the therapy process, and then a treatment plan can be tailored to the unique needs of the client. A diagnosis is not a final category; rather, it provides a working hypothesis that guides the practitioner in understanding the client. The therapy sessions provide useful clues about the nature of the client's problems. Thus, diagnosis begins with the intake interview and continues throughout the duration of therapy.

The "bible" for guiding practitioners in making diagnostic assessments is the fourth edition of the American Psychiatric Association's (1994) *Diagnostic and Statistical Manual of Mental Disorders,* (DSM-IV). Clinicians who work in community mental-health agencies, private practice, and other human-service settings are generally expected to assess client problems within the framework of the DSM-IV. This manual advises practitioners that it represents only an initial step in a comprehensive evaluation. There is also a caution about the necessity of gaining additional information about the person being evaluated beyond that which is required to make a DSM-IV diagnosis.

Although some clinicians view diagnosis as central to the counseling process, others view it as unnecessary and even a detriment. They contend that diagnosis is an inappropriate application of the medical model of mental health to therapeutic practice. Some assert that practitioners can become too focused on the client's history and thus fail to pay sufficient attention to present attitudes and behavior. They maintain that the diagnostic process needs to be rooted in the individual's current lifestyle if it is to be effective (Brammer, Shostrom, & Abrego, 1989). Brammer and his colleagues contend that practitioners must make some decisions, do some therapeutic planning, be alert for signs of pathology in order to avoid serious mistakes in therapy, and be in a position to make some prognoses. They propose that a therapist "simultaneously understand diagnostically and understand therapeutically" (p. 148).

CONSIDERING ETHNIC AND CULTURAL FACTORS IN ASSESSMENT AND DIAGNOSIS.  A danger of the diagnostic approach is the possible failure of counselors to consider ethnic and cultural factors in certain patterns of behavior. Unless cultural variables are considered, some clients may be subjected to an erroneous diagnosis. Certain behaviors and personality styles may be labeled neurotic or deviant simply because they are not characteristics of the dominant culture. Sue and Sue (1990) give the example of some mental-health professionals' assertions that Asian Americans are the most repressed of all clients. Such statements indicate that these therapists expect all clients to be self-disclosing, emotionally expressive, and assertive. These counselors do not recognize that the cultural upbringing of many Asian Americans places a value on restraint of strong feelings and on a reluctance to discuss personal matters with anyone outside the family. Thus, counselors who work with African Americans, Asian Americans, Latinos, and Native Americans may erroneously conclude that a client is repressed, inhibited, passive, and unmotivated, all of which are seen as undesirable by Western standards.

In its revision of its Code of Ethics and Standards of Practice, the ACA (1995) recognizes that there are cultural implications of making proper diagnoses and of using tests:

> Counselors are cautious in using assessment techniques, making evaluations, and interpreting the performance of populations not represented in the norm group on which an instrument was standardized. They recognize the effects of age, color, culture, disability, ethnic group, gender, race, religion, sexual orientation, and socioeconomic status on test administration and interpretation and place test results in proper perspective with other relevant factors.

In assessments of clients with different backgrounds, the DSM-IV emphasizes the importance of being aware of unintentional bias and keeping an open mind to the presence of distinctive ethnic and cultural patterns that could influence the diagnostic process. Evidence suggests that the symptoms and course of a number of DSM-IV disorders are influenced by such factors. As a way to understand the nature of diversity among individuals, the DSM-IV includes a new section that addresses culture-related features and incorporates cautions so that misdiagnoses are less likely:

> Diagnostic assessment can be especially challenging when a clinician from one ethnic or cultural group uses the DSM-IV classification to evaluate an individual from a different ethnic or cultural group. A clinician who is unfamiliar with the nuances of an individual's cultural frame of reference may incorrectly judge as psychopathology those normal variations in behavior, belief, or experience that are particular to the individual's culture.

A PERSONAL COMMENTARY ON DIAGNOSIS.    Is there a way to bridge the gap between the extreme view that diagnosis is the essential core of therapy and the extreme view that it is a detrimental factor? I conceive of diagnosis as a continuing process that focuses on understanding the client. Both the therapist and the client are engaged in this search-and-discovery process from the first session to the last. Even though practitioners may avoid formal diagnostic procedures and terminology, it seems that they do raise certain questions, such as: What is going on in the client's life now, and what does the client want from therapy? What are the client's strengths and limitations? What is the client like in the counseling setting, and what does this behavior reveal about the client's actions outside of therapy? How far should therapy go? What is the client learning from therapy, and to what degree is he or she applying this learning to daily living? In dealing with these questions, the therapist is formulating some conception about what clients want and how they might best attain their goals. Thus, diagnosis becomes a form of making tentative hypotheses, and these hunches can be formed with clients and shared with them throughout the process.

From my perspective, diagnosis should be associated with treatment, and it should help the practitioner conceptualize a case. Ethical dilemmas are created when diagnosis is done strictly for insurance purposes, which often entails arbitrarily assigning a client a diagnostic classification. However, it is a clinical, legal, and ethical obligation of therapists to screen clients for life-threatening problems such as organic disorders, schizophrenia, bipolar disorder, and suicidal types of depression. Students need to learn the clinical skills necessary to do this type of screening, which is a form of diagnostic thinking. In order to function in most mental-health agencies, practitioners need to become skilled in understanding and utilizing diagnostic procedures.

## GUIDELINES FOR THE USE OF TESTS IN COUNSELING

The place of testing in counseling and therapy is another controversial issue. Models that emphasize the objective view of counseling are inclined to use testing procedures to get information about clients or to provide them with information so that they can make more realistic decisions. The person-centered and existential orientations view testing much as they do diagnosis, as an external form of understanding that has little to do with effective counseling.

A wide variety of tests can be used for counseling purposes, including measures of interest, aptitude, achievement, attitudes and values, and personal characteristics. In my view tests can be used as an adjunct to counseling; valuable information, which can add to a client's capacity to make decisions, can be gleaned from them. Some cautions and guidelines regarding the use of tests are listed below:

- Clients should be involved in the test-selection process. They should decide which categories of tests, if any, they wish to take.

- Clients' reasons for wanting tests, as well as their past experience with tests, should be explored.
- A client needs to be aware that tests are only tools, and imperfect ones at that. As means to an end, tests do not provide "the answer," but at best they provide additional information that can be explored in counseling and used in coming to certain decisions.
- The counselor needs to clarify the purposes of the tests and point out their limitations. This role implies that the counselor has a good grasp of what the test is about and that he or she has taken it.
- The test results, not simply scores, should be given to the client, and their meanings should be explored. In interpreting the results, the counselor should be tentative and neutral, refraining from judgments as much as possible and allowing clients to formulate their own meanings and conclusions.
- It is especially important to consider the ways in which socioeconomic, ethnic, and cultural factors can affect test scores (ACA, 1995).

# Dual Relationships in Counseling Practice

Dual (or multiple) relationships, either sexual or nonsexual, occur when counselors assume two (or more) roles simultaneously or sequentially with a client. Some examples of dual relationships are combining the roles of teacher and therapist or of supervisor and therapist; bartering for goods or therapeutic services; borrowing money from a client; providing therapy to a friend, an employee, or a relative; engaging in a close personal relationship with a client; becoming emotionally or sexually involved with a former client; and going into a business venture with a client.

Although sexual relationships initially received the most attention from both the media and professional groups, nonsexual dual relationships are becoming a lively topic of discussion at professional conventions. Because dual relationships are necessarily complex and multidimensional, there are few simple and absolute answers to neatly resolve them. It is not always possible to play a single role in your work as a counselor, nor is it always desirable. You will probably have to wrestle with balancing more than one role, regardless of the setting in which you work or the client population you serve. Thus, it is critical that you give careful thought to the complexities of multiple relationships before embroiling yourself in ethically questionable situations.

Dual relationships are rarely a clear-cut matter, for ethical reasoning and judgment come into play when ethical codes are applied to specific situations (G. Corey & Herlihy, 1993; Herlihy & Corey, 1992). Although dual relationships do carry inherent risks, they are not always harmful, unethical, and unprofessional. Some dual relationships are clearly exploitative and do serious harm both to clients and to the professional, but others may have more potential benefits to clients than potential risks.

## ETHICAL CODES AND DUAL RELATIONSHIPS

What guidance do codes of ethics offer on handling dual relationships? Almost all of the codes of the professional organizations now warn against such relationships. These codes typically caution professionals against entering into those relationships "that could impair objectivity." The problem is that the codes are usually written in general terms, which demands that practitioners use their best judgment in each situation to determine if there is a potential for harm.

The APA (1992) has replaced "dual relationships" with "multiple relationships" in its code. The current ethical focus is on keeping alert to the possibilities of damaging exploitation, rather than a universal prohibition of all dual relationships. The section reads as follows:

> In many communities and situations, it may not be feasible or reasonable for psychologists to avoid social or other nonprofessional contacts with persons such as patients, clients, students, supervisees, or research participants. Psychologists must always be sensitive to the potential harmful effects of other contacts on their work and on those persons with whom they deal. A psychologist refrains from entering into or promising another personal, scientific, professional, financial, or other relationship with such persons if it appears likely that such a relationship reasonably might impair the psychologist's objectivity or otherwise interfere with the psychologist's effectively performing his or her functions as a psychologist, or might harm or exploit the other party.

In the sections that follow, the focus is on various aspects of dual relationships and special issues pertaining to the client/therapist relationship. Some of these topics are: Can social and personal relationships ever mix with the therapeutic relationships? What are some clinical and ethical considerations in the use of touching in therapy? Why are sexual intimacies with clients unethical and harmful? Are sexual intimacies with former clients always unethical? How can practitioners learn to deal with sexual attractions?

## PERSONAL RELATIONSHIPS WITH CLIENTS

A special issue is how social relationships mix with therapeutic ones. In general, although friendships can be therapeutic, it is difficult to be primarily concerned with counseling someone while maintaining a personal relationship with the client outside of the sessions. By the very nature of the therapeutic relationship, counselors are in a more powerful position than clients; thus, there is the danger of subtle exploitation of clients (Kitchener, 1988; Kitchener & Harding, 1990). Three questions can be raised: (1) "Will I confront and challenge a client with whom I am involved socially as much as or more than I do clients with whom I have a strictly professional relationship?" (2) "Will my own needs for maintaining the social relationship interfere with my therapeutic activities and thus defeat the purposes of therapy?" and (3) "How will my client react to combining a personal and a professional relationship?"

These questions do not have simple answers. There are many forms of socializing, ranging from dating a client to simply attending a social function where the client is present. There are also differences between a social involvement initiated by a client and one instigated by a therapist. The specific context must always be taken into consideration. For example, some counselors who work with adolescents organize outdoor activities, such as hiking and camping, that are considered a basic part of the therapy program. The rationale is that interacting with clients in informal ways has advantages over a 50-minute therapy session. Some peer counselors contend that the friendships they have with people before counseling are a positive factor in building trust that leads to productive therapeutic results.

What is essential is that counselors develop an awareness of their own motivations as well as the motivations of their clients. They must honestly and accurately assess the impact that a social relationship might have on the client/therapist relationship. Further, counselors who as a matter of course tend to develop most of their friendships from their relationships with clients would do well to examine the degree to which they are using the power of their position to make social contacts.

## TOUCHING AS A PART OF THE CLIENT/THERAPIST RELATIONSHIP

A topic that students inevitably raise is whether to engage in touching their clients. Touching is not necessarily a part of a dual relationship, but certain touching practices can lead to sexual relationships. Students ask: "How can I tell when touching will be helpful or not? Is touching for the client's benefit or my own? Do I have to hold myself back from expressing affection or compassion in a physical way? What if my touch is misinterpreted? If I feel sexually drawn to certain clients, is it dangerous to express physical closeness?" Unfortunately, we live in an era when touching in a professional relationship is fraught with potential risks. Some counselors have taboolike attitudes against touching clients. Therapists may inhibit themselves when they feel a compassionate or empathetic urge to touch, lest their actions be misinterpreted as sexual or exploitive. A reality is that insurance carriers often discourage practitioners from touching clients beyond a routine handshake. They react in this way because therapists' sexual misconduct often begins with inappropriate touching of clients. Other practitioners oppose any form of physical contact in the therapeutic relationship on the grounds that it can promote dependency, can interfere with the transference relationship, and can be misunderstood by clients.

Although I agree with the position that erotic contact with clients is unethical, I think that nonerotic touching can be therapeutically valuable. What is important is that touching not be done as a technique or as something that is not genuinely felt. Touching should be a spontaneous and honest expression that is appropriate in the particular therapeutic context. Touches that are not authentic and not spontaneous are detected as such; if clients cannot believe your touch, why should they believe your words? Counselors need to be sensitive to situations where touching is likely to be counterproductive. A central factor is the client's readiness and need to be touched. In some cases, victims of incest may be resistant to physical contact and may be offended and frightened by a counselor's well-intended touch. Other clients, because of their cultural background, may be uncomfortable with any physical expressions of concern.

Counselors sometimes reach out too soon to comfort clients who are crying and expressing pain. Clients do need at times to fully experience and express their pain, and touching them may serve to cut off what they are feeling. Some counselors reach out physically not to meet the needs of their clients but to comfort themselves, because they are distressed by the pain their clients are expressing. Once clients have an opportunity to express their struggle, however, they may welcome touching. Although this is a complex issue, therapists need to be honest with themselves and their clients. The question "Whose needs are being met—my client's or my own?" is a good one to raise time and again.

## EROTIC AND SEXUAL CONTACT WITH CLIENTS

The topic of sexual intimacy between the counselor and client is receiving a great deal of attention in the professional literature. Sexual relationships are among the most serious of all ethical violations, for they can have devastating effects on clients. Most professional codes clearly state, for instance, that sexual intimacies with clients are unethical.

Research indicates that sexual misconduct is one of the major causes for malpractice actions against mental-health providers. The rate of these unethical practices is alarming, and reports of sexual intimacies and sexual harrassment have been increasing (Brodsky, 1986; Gottlieb, Sell, & Schoenfeld, 1988; Holroyd & Bouhoutsos, 1985; Pope, 1988; Pope & Bouhoutsos, 1986; Pope, Sonne, & Holroyd, 1993; Vasquez & Kitchener, 1988). This increase may be due in part to a greater sense of awareness of the problem by the public, as well as better reporting procedures.

Sexual intimacy between counselors and clients is both unethical and professionally inappropriate for several reasons. Clients are usually more vulnerable than the therapist. They are the ones who are revealing themselves in deeply personal ways. They are sharing their fears, past secrets, fantasies, hopes, sexual desires, and conflicts, and it can be easy to take advantage of them. Counseling rests on the foundation of trust. When clients initiate counseling, they trust that their well-being will be given primary consideration. Counselors who enter into sexual alliances with clients violate this basic trust, and clients may well say, "Look at what happened when I *did* trust."

If counselors become sexually active with clients, they lose their capacity for objectivity. These therapists will probably be far more concerned about the feelings their clients have for them than about challenging them to take an honest look at their life. Clients who feel used may discount the value of anything they have learned in their therapy and may also be closed to any further psychological assistance out of their bitterness and resentment. This is true even if some clients actually provoke and in some ways invite a sexual relationship. Therefore, it becomes vital that therapists recognize their own areas of countertransference (for example, the extreme need to be needed or to be seen as sexually attractive).

Although the existing codes are explicit with respect to sex in therapy relationships, they cannot define some of the more subtle ways in which sexuality may be a part of a client/therapist relationship. Sexual attractions may be dealt with poorly. Therapists may behave inappropriately and unethically by acting seductively with certain clients, they may influence clients to focus on romantic or sexual feelings toward them, or they may initiate physical contact that is mainly aimed at satisfying their own desires. In many subtle ways, sexual overtones can distort the therapy relationship, and a therapist's behavior can have much the same effect as direct sexual involvement.

## SEX WITH FORMER CLIENTS

What of the ethics of therapists who become intimately involved with their clients once the therapy relationship has been terminated? In addition to prohibiting sex with current clients, most ethics codes also state that therapists do not provide counseling services to persons with whom they have had a sexual relationship. The codes of some professional organizations, such as the APA (1992), the ACA (1995), and the AAMFT (1991), prohibit therapists from engaging in sexual relationships with former clients for at least two years after ending the professional relationship. Many licensing boards now also specify a minimum two-year "waiting period." Some state licensing boards have a clear prohibition against sexual intimacies with former clients, regardless of the time elapsed. In certain states, it is a felony for a therapist to have sex with a client or a former client.

For those practitioners who are considering entering into a sexual relationship with a former client, Bennett and his colleagues (1990) point out that therapists have been sued for malpractice for engaging in this practice. They suggest that counselors reflect on the reasons for terminating therapy and that they weigh the potential benefits and risks of developing a personal relationship with a client. They recommend that before initiating such a relationship, counselors seek consultation and supervision.

## LEARNING TO DEAL WITH SEXUAL ATTRACTIONS

In their pioneering book, *Sexual Feelings in Psychotherapy,* Pope and his colleagues (1993) emphasize that the matter of sexual attraction in the client/therapist relationship is difficult to acknowledge and even more difficult to explore. Indeed, the majority of therapists apparently do experience sexual attraction to clients, and most are troubled by this phenomenon. Research indicates that attractions to clients make most therapists feel guilty, anxious, or confused (Pope, Keith-Spiegel, & Tabachnick, 1986).

Although most of my students seem intellectually clear on their position of engaging in sex with clients, they do struggle with their sexual attractions toward clients, the attractions of their clients to them, and sexual fantasies. Unfortunately, the role of sexual attractions in therapy is shrouded with taboos, which means that counselor trainees are generally poorly equipped to deal with these feelings when they occur.

I agree with Pope and his colleagues (1986, 1993) when they write that the taboo must be lifted so that therapy trainees can recognize and accept their sexual attractions as human responses. Vasquez (1988) makes an excellent case for the need for training strategies to prevent counselor/client sexual contact. These strategies include activities that promote self-awareness and creating a climate that enhances the development of moral values and behavior. She also emphasizes that instructors and supervisors can best teach ethical behavior not by lecturing but by modeling sensitive and nonexploitive behavior with their students and supervisees. In such a training context, students are encouraged to plan steps that would prevent becoming involved in sexual misconduct.

Educational programs must provide a safe environment in which trainees can acknowledge and discuss feelings of sexual attraction. Pope and his colleagues (1993) describe the importance of creating conditions in which counselors in training can learn about sexual feelings toward clients with the help, support, encouragement, and acceptance of other people.

If counselors do not learn how to deal with the full range of their feelings toward their clients, there is greater likelihood of getting involved in seductive interchanges. Ideally, practitioners will be able to accept their sexual feelings and desires toward certain clients and at the same time see the distinction between *having* these feelings and *acting* on them. This is an area in which beginning counselors can greatly benefit from consultation sessions with a supervisor.


## PERSPECTIVES ON DUAL RELATIONSHIPS

Some of the problematic aspects of engaging in dual relationships are that they are pervasive, they can be difficult to recognize, they are unavoidable at times, they are potentially harmful, and they are the subject of conflicting advice from various experts. A review of the literature reveals that dual relationships are hotly debated. Except for sexual intimacy with current clients, there is not much consensus regarding the appropriate way to manage dual relationships.

A consensus of many writers is that since dual relationships are inevitable in some situations, a global prohibition does not seem to be a realistic answer. Because interpersonal boundaries are not static but undergo redefinition over time, the challenge for practitioners is to learn how to manage boundary fluctuations and to deal effectively with overlapping roles. One key to learning how to manage dual relationships is to think of ways to minimize the risks involved.

WAYS OF MINIMIZING RISK.    In determining whether to proceed with a dual relationship, it is critical to consider whether the potential benefit of such a relationship outweighs the potential harm. It is your responsibility to develop safeguards aimed at reducing the potential for negative consequences. Herlihy and Corey (1992) identify the following guidelines:

- Fully inform clients about any potential risks.
- Discuss and clarify issues of concern.
- Consult with colleagues on a regular basis.
- Work under supervision in cases where the potential for harm is high.
- Document discussions regarding any dual relationships and the steps taken to reduce risks to the client.

It may be necessary to refer a client to another professional if problems develop or if harm seems likely.

A DECISION-MAKING MODEL.   In working through a dual relationship concern, it is best to begin by ascertaining whether such a relationship can be avoided. Sometimes dual relationships are avoidable, and to get involved in them may be putting the client needlessly at risk. In other cases, dual relationships are unavoidable. For instance, a counselor in a rural community may have as clients the local banker, merchant, and minister. In this setting, mental-health practitioners may have to blend several professional roles and functions. They may also attend the same church or belong to the same community organization as their clients. These professionals are likely to find it more difficult to maintain clear boundaries than practitioners who work in a large city.

The decision-making model proposed by Herlihy and Corey (1992) differentiates between unavoidable and avoidable relationships. In cases where a dual relationship is *unavoidable,* the guidelines for minimizing risks discussed in the previous section apply. If the dual relationship is *avoidable,* the counselor has a choice of what course of action to take. If the potential benefits outweigh the risks, it is still sound practice to follow all of the procedures listed earlier. If the risks outweigh the benefits, ethical practice demands that we decline to enter into a conflicting relationship.

You are likely to encounter many forms of nonsexual dual relationships. One way of dealing with any potential problems is to do whatever is possible to completely avoid such relationships. Another alternative is to deal with each dilemma as it surfaces, making full use of informed consent and at the same time seeking consultation and supervision in dealing with the situation. This second alternative provides a professional challenge for self-monitoring. It is one of the hallmarks of professionalism to be willing to grapple with these ethical complexities of day-to-day practice.

# Therapist Competence, Education, and Training

As a basic ethical principle, therapists are expected to recognize their own personal and professional limitations. Ethical counselors do not employ diagnostic or treatment procedures that are beyond the scope of their training, nor do they accept clients whose personal functioning is seriously impaired unless they are qualified to work with those clients. Counselors who become aware of their lack of competence in a particular case have the responsibility to consult with colleagues or a supervisor, or to make a referral.

## CRITERIA FOR DETERMINING COMPETENCE

As a practitioner, on what basis can you decide whether you are qualified to offer specific professional services? You will probably grapple with the question "How can I recognize the boundaries of my competence, and how can I know when I have exceeded them?" This issue is not solved by possessing advanced degrees, licenses, and credentials. In reality, many people who complete master's and doctoral programs in a mental-health specialty still lack the skills, training, practical experience, or personal characteristics needed to counsel certain populations.

Practitioners must continually assess their competence to help particular clients. There will be times when experienced counselors or therapists need to consult colleagues or a specialist in a related field. It is possible for therapists who have worked with clients over a long period to lose their perspective with these clients. At times it is wise for therapists to confer with colleagues to share their perceptions of what is occurring with their clients, within themselves, and between them and their clients. If a client complains often of physical symptoms (such as headaches), it seems essential that any organic problem be ruled out by a physician before the assumption is made that the client's problem is psychologically caused. What if the client had a brain tumor and the psychological counselor failed to refer him or her to a physician for a physical examination? It is also a good practice for counselors to find a psychiatrist with whom they can consult, especially regarding those clients who could benefit from medication.

## TRAINING AND SUPERVISION

Related to the issue of competence are the questions "What education, training, and supervision are necessary for ensuring competent practice?" and "What experiences are necessary for prospective counselors?"

If experienced practitioners need occasional consultation, it goes without saying that beginning therapists need supervision and continuing consultation. In working with undergraduate human-services students and with graduate students in counseling programs, I have found most of them eager for direction and supervision. They often ask for extra time and are quite willing to discuss their reactions, blockages, frustrations, and confusions in supervision meetings. Realizing that they need skills in working effectively with the problems that clients bring, they tend to want a chance to discuss their fieldwork experiences. It thus becomes an ethical and practical concern that appropriate supervision be given to the intern, for the sake of both the client's welfare and the intern's professional growth. A problem can arise when the counselor intern is placed in a community agency and the on-the-job supervisor is so busy that he or she has little time for such supervising. I encourage interns to be active and assertive in seeking the supervision they need to carry out the duties of their field placement. If the supervisor does not initiate close supervision, trainees need to continue to ask for what they need.

## CONTINUING EDUCATION

Professional competence is not something that we attain once and for all, even by earning advanced degrees and licenses. Continuing professional education is essential in keeping up to date with knowledge in your professional specialty, as well as in sharpening your skills. Although most professions support efforts to make continuing education a mandatory condition of relicensing, it is still possible for some to stop their learning process once an advanced degree has been earned. Some professional organizations have a voluntary program, even if state licensure laws do not mandate continuing education. For example, all clinical members of the AAMFT are encouraged to complete 150 hours of education every three years.

Those counselors who fail to keep abreast of developments are certainly vulnerable on both ethical and legal grounds. Personally, I would like to see practitioners decide for themselves the kind of in-service and continuing education that would be most meaningful. They might choose a combination of formal course work, attendance at professional workshops, participation in professional conferences where one can be challenged and stimulated, and opportunities for having their work observed and critiqued by colleagues.

Continuing education is particularly essential in the area of developing awareness, knowledge, and skills for counseling in a multicultural society. Although graduate counseling programs are giving increased emphasis to cultural factors, there are still too many counselors who ignore the reality of cultural diversity (Pedersen, 1994).

# Guidelines for Ethical Practice: A Review

Without setting out the following guidelines as absolute decrees, I would like to summarize this chapter by putting into focus some principles that I believe are important for counselors to review throughout their professional practice. My hope is that you will think about these as guidelines, apply them to yourself, and attempt to formulate your own views and positions on some of the topics raised in this chapter. The task of developing a sense of professional and ethical responsibility is never really finished, and new issues will constantly be surfacing. As I implied earlier, these ethical issues demand periodic reflection and an openness to change.

1. Counselors need to be aware of what their own needs are, what they are getting from their work, and how their needs and behaviors influence their clients. It is essential that the therapist's own needs not be met at the client's expense.

2. Counselors should have the training and experience necessary for the assessments they make and the interventions they attempt.

3. Counselors need to become aware of the boundaries of their competence, and they should seek qualified supervision or refer clients to other professionals when they recognize that they have reached their limit with a given client. They should make themselves familiar with the resources in the community so that they can make appropriate referrals.

4. Although practitioners know the ethical standards of their professional organizations, they are also aware that they must exercise their own judgment in applying these principles to particular cases. They realize that many problems have no clear-cut answers, and they accept the responsibility of searching for appropriate solutions.

5. It is important for counselors to have some theoretical framework of behavior change to guide them in their practice.

6. Counselors need to recognize the importance of finding ways to update their knowledge and skills through various forms of continuing education.

7. Counselors should avoid any relationships with clients that are clearly a threat to therapy.

8. It is the counselor's responsibility to inform clients of any circumstances that are likely to affect the confidentiality of their relationship and of any other matters that are likely to negatively influence the relationship.

9. It is imperative that counselors be aware of their own values and attitudes, recognize the role that their belief system plays in their relationships with their clients, and avoid imposing these beliefs, either subtly or directly.

10. It is important for counselors to inform their clients about matters such as the goals of counseling, techniques and procedures that will be employed, possible risks associated with entering the relationship, and any other factors that are likely to affect the client's decision to begin therapy.

11. Counselors must realize that they teach their clients through a modeling process. Thus, they should attempt to practice in their own lives what they encourage in their clients.

12. Counseling takes place in the context of the interaction of cultural backgrounds. You bring your culture to the counseling relationship, and your client's cultural values also operate in the process.

13. Counselors need to learn a process for thinking about and dealing with ethical dilemmas, realizing that most ethical issues are complex and defy simple solutions. The willingness to seek consultation is a sign of professional maturity.

Resolving the ethical dilemmas you will face requires a commitment to question your own behavior and motives. A sign of good faith on the part of counselors is their willingness to share struggles with colleagues. Such consultation can be of great help in clarifying issues by giving you another perspective on a situation. I want to emphasize that being a professional counselor does not imply that you are perfect or superhuman. If you are willing to risk doing anything worthwhile in your work, you are bound to make some mistakes. What seems crucial is your willingness to reflect on what you are doing and on whose needs are being given priority.

If there is one fundamental question that can serve to tie together all the issues discussed in this chapter, it is this: Who has the right to counsel another person? This question can be the focal point of your reflection on ethical and professional issues. It can also be the basis of your self-examination each day that you meet with clients. You can continue to ask yourself: "What makes me think I have a right to counsel others? What do I have to offer the people I'm counseling? Am I doing in my own life what I'm encouraging my clients to do?" If you answer these questions honestly, you may be troubled. At times you may feel that you have no ethical right to counsel others, perhaps because your own life isn't always the model you would like it to be for your clients. More important than resolving all of life's issues is knowing what kinds of questions to ask and then remaining open to reflection.

# Where to Go from Here

This chapter has introduced you to a wide range of ethical and legal issues that you are bound to face at some point in your counseling practice. One chapter cannot begin to give in-depth coverage of these topics. Now that your interest has been piqued, you can continue by getting a copy of the ACA's *Ethical Standards Casebook* (Herlihy & Corey, 1996) which is listed in the Recommended Supplementary Readings, along with several textbooks on ethics in counseling that will give you a broader perspective on these issues. Reading selected journal articles on professional ethics is another way to increase your awareness of the ethical dimensions of practice. There is a comprehensive and updated list of these journal articles in the References and Suggested Readings at the end of Part One. In addition to reading, taking a separate course in ethical and professional issues in the counseling profession would be most helpful in stimulating your thinking and giving you a framework for ethical decision making. As you read the rest of the chapters in this textbook, be alert for ethical issues as they relate to the various therapeutic approaches.

# Recommended Supplementary Readings for Part One

*The Imperfect Therapist: Learning from Failure in Therapeutic Practice* (Kottler & Blau, 1989) describes how unrealistic expectations and perfectionism can influence the way therapists experience failure. The work details the common mistakes of beginning therapists and shows how to learn from these experiences.

*On Being a Therapist* (Kottler, 1993) shows how the professional work in which therapists engage directly affects their personal lives. By becoming involved in the exploration of their clients' pain, therapists open up their own psychological wounds. Examples are given of the prices that therapists pay for working with high levels of stress.

*I Never Knew I Had a Choice* (G. Corey & Corey, 1993) is a good resource with which to continue a reading program on the counselor as a person. Topics include our struggle to achieve autonomy; the roles that work, love, sexuality, intimacy, and solitude play in our lives; the meaning of loneliness, death, and loss; and the ways in which we choose our values and philosophy of life.

*Becoming a Helper* (M. Corey & Corey, 1993) has chapters that expand on issues dealing with the personal and professional lives of helpers. Some of the topics emphasized include the motivations for becoming helper, the helper in the helping process, value issues, common concerns facing counselors, dealing with life transitions, self-exploration and personal growth, understanding your family history, managing stress, the challenge of retaining your vitality, and dealing with professional burnout.

*The Personal Life of the Psychotherapist* (Guy, 1987) deals with the impact of clinical practice on the therapist's intimate relationships and psychological well-being. The author covers topics such as training to become a therapist, significant events in the life of the therapist, impairment among psychotherapists, and future trends in the practice of psychotherapy.

*Counseling American Minorities: A Cross-Cultural Perspective* (Atkinson, Morten, & Sue, 1993) describes a minority-identity development model. This edited book has excellent sections dealing with counseling for Native Americans, Asian Americans, African Americans, and Latinos.

*A Handbook for Developing Multicultural Awareness* (Pedersen, 1994) is based on the assumption that all counseling is to some extent multicultural. In this useful handbook, the author deals with topics such as developing multicultural awareness; becoming aware of our culturally biased assumptions; acquiring knowledge for effective multicultural counseling; and learning skills to deal with cultural diversity.

*A Theory of Multicultural Counseling and Psychotherapy* (Sue, Ivey, & Pedersen, 1996) presents a rationale for a theory of multicultural counseling and sets forth a series of propositions and corollaries related to multicultural counseling that have implications for theory development, research, practice, and training. It also contains separate chapters dealing with specific populations.

*Ethical Standards Casebook* (Herlihy & Corey, 1996) contains a variety of useful cases that are geared to the ACA *Code of Ethics and Standards of Practice.* The examples illustrate and clarify the meaning and intent of the standards.

*Dual Relationships in Counseling* (Herlihy & Corey, 1992) puts the dual-relationship controversy into perspective. It deals with issues in counselor preparation and focuses on dual relationships in a variety of work settings, such as private practice, school counseling, rehabilitation counseling, consultation, and group counseling. (Both this book and the one above can be purchased from the ACA, 5999 Stevenson Avenue, Alexandria, VA 22304; telephone: 703-823-9800.)

*Issues and Ethics in the Helping Professions* (G. Corey, Corey, & Callanan, 1993) is devoted entirely to the issues that were introduced briefly in Chapter 3. Some relevant deal with the role of values in the client/counselor relationship, therapist responsibilities, therapist competence, factors influencing the client/therapist relationship, dual relationships, and dealing with transference and countertransference. The book is designed to involve readers in a personal and active way, and many open-ended cases are presented to help them formulate their thoughts on various issues.

*Manual for Theory and Practice of Counseling and Psychotherapy* (G. Corey, 1996b) is designed to help you integrate theory with practice and to make the concepts covered in the book come alive. It consists of self-inventories, overview summaries of the theories, a glossary of key concepts, study questions, issues and questions for personal application, activities and exercises, comprehension checks and quizzes, case examples, a code of professional ethics, and a list of professional organizations to contact for resources. The manual is fully coordinated with the textbook to make it a personal study guide.

*Case Approach to Counseling and Psychotherapy* (G. Corey, 1996a) is structured along the same chapter lines as this textbook. Thus, if you want to focus more on case applications and see how each of the theories works in action, this casebook will be a handy supplement to the course. A hypothetical client, Ruth, experiences counseling from all of the therapeutic vantage points. There are other cases for each theory, and you are invited to test your thinking in applying techniques from the theories to a variety of cases.

# References and Suggested Readings for Part One*

AKAMATSU, T. J. (1988). Intimate relationships with former clients: National survey of attitudes and behavior among practitioners. *Professional Psychology: Research and Practice, 19*(4), 454–458.

AMERICAN ASSOCIATION FOR MARRIAGE AND FAMILY THERAPY. (1991). *AAMFT code of ethics.* Washington, DC: Author.

AMERICAN COUNSELING ASSOCIATION. (1995). *Proposed revision: American Counseling Association code of ethics and standards of practice.* Alexandria, VA: Author.

AMERICAN MENTAL HEALTH COUNSELORS ASSOCIATION. (1987). *Code of ethics for certified clinical mental health counselors.* Alexandria, VA: Author.

AMERICAN PSYCHIATRIC ASSOCIATION. (1989). *Principles of medical ethics with annotations especially applicable to psychiatry.* Washington, DC: Author.

AMERICAN PSYCHIATRIC ASSOCIATION. (1994). *Diagnostic and statistical manual of mental disorders* (4th Ed.). Washington, DC: Author.

AMERICAN PSYCHOANALYTIC ASSOCIATION. (1983). *Principles of ethics for psychoanalysts and provisions for implementation of the principles of ethics for psychoanalysts.* New York: Author.

AMERICAN PSYCHOLOGICAL ASSOCIATION. (1985). *White paper on duty to protect.* Washington, DC: Author.

AMERICAN PSYCHOLOGICAL ASSOCIATION. (1992). Ethical principles of psychologists and code of conduct. *American Psychologist, 47,* 1597–1611.

AMERICAN PSYCHOLOGICAL ASSOCIATION. (1993). Guidelines for providers of psychological services to ethnic, linguistic, and culturally diverse populations. *American Psychologist, 48*(1), 45–48.

*ATKINSON, D. R., MORTEN, G., & SUE, D. W. (Eds.). (1993). *Counseling American minorities: A cross cultural perspective* (4th ed.). Madison, WI: Brown & Benchmark.

BALDWIN, M., & SATIR, V. (Eds.). (1987). *The use of self in therapy.* New York: Haworth Press.

*BATES, C. M., & BRODSKY, A. M. (1989). *Sex in the therapy hour: A case of professional incest.* New York: Guilford Press.

BENNETT, B. E., BRYANT, B. K., VANDENBOS, G. R., & GREENWOOD, A. (1990). *Professional liability and risk management.* Washington, DC: American Psychological Association.

BOGRAD, M. (1993, January/February). The duel over dual relationships. *The California Therapist, 5*(1) 7–16.

BOUHOUTSOS, J., HOLROYD, J., LERMAN, H., FORER, B. R., & GREENBERG, M. (1983). Sexual intimacy between psychotherapists and patients. *Professional Psychology: Research and Practice, 14*(2), 185–196.

BRAMMER, L. M., SHOSTROM, E. L., & ABREGO, P. J. (1989). *Therapeutic psychology: Fundamentals of counseling and psychotherapy* (5th ed.). Englewood Cliffs, NJ: Prentice-Hall.

*BRODSKY, A. M. (1986). The distressed psychologist: Sexual intimacies and exploitation. In R. R. Kilburg, P. E. Nathan, & R. W. Thoreson (Eds.), *Professionals in distress: Issues, syndromes, and solutions in psychology* (pp. 153–172). Washington, DC: American Psychological Association.

*BUGENTAL, J. F. T. (1987). *The art of the psychotherapist.* New York: Norton.

*Books and articles marked with an asterisk are suggested for further study.

COMAS-DIAZ, L. (1990). The future of psychotherapy with ethnic minorities. *Psychotherapy, 29*(1), 88–94.

COREY, G. (1996a). *Case approach to counseling and psychotherapy* (4th ed.). Pacific Grove, CA: Brooks/Cole.

COREY, G. (1996b). *Manual for theory and practice of counseling and psychotherapy* (4th ed.). Pacific Grove, CA: Brooks/Cole.

COREY, G., & COREY, M. (1993). *I never knew I had a choice* (5th ed.). Pacific Grove, CA: Brooks/Cole.

*COREY, G., COREY, M., & CALLANAN, P. (1993). *Issues and ethics in the helping professions* (4th ed.). Pacific Grove, CA: Brooks/Cole.

COREY, G., & HERLIHY, B. (1993). Dual relationships: Associated risks and potential benefits. *Ethical Issues in Professional Counseling, 1*(1), 4–11.

*COREY, M., & COREY, G. (1993). *Becoming a helper* (2nd ed.). Pacific Grove, CA: Brooks/Cole.

FUJIMURA, L. E., WEIS, D. M., & COCHRAN, J. R. (1985). Suicide: Dynamics and implications for counseling. *Journal of Counseling and Development, 63*(10), 612–615.

GABBARD, G., & POPE, K. (1988). Sexual intimacies after termination: Clinical, ethical, and legal aspects. *The Independent Practitioner, 8*(2), 21–26.

GOTTLIEB, M. C., SELL, J. M., & SCHOENFELD, L. S. (1988). Social/romantic relationships with present and former clients: State licensing board actions. *Professional Psychology: Research and Practice, 19*(4), 459–462.

*GUY, J. D. (1987). *The personal life of the psychotherapist.* New York: Wiley.

*HERLIHY, B., & COREY, G. (1992). *Dual relationships in counseling.* Alexandria, VA: American Counseling Association.

*HERLIHY, B., & COREY, G. (1994). Code of ethics as catalysts for improving practice. *Ethical Issues in Professional Counseling, 2*(1), 1–12.

*HERLIHY, B., & COREY, G. (1996). *Ethical standards casebook* (5th ed.). Alexandria, VA: American Counseling Association.

HOLROYD, J. C., & BOUHOUTSOS, J. C. (1985). Sources of bias in reporting effects of sexual contact with patients. *Professional Psychology: Research and Practice, 16*(5), 701–709.

*IVEY, A. E., IVEY, M. B., & SIMEK-MORGAN, L. (1993). *Counseling and psychotherapy: A multicultural perspective.* Boston: Allyn & Bacon.

JENSEN, J. P., & BERGIN, A. E. (1988). Mental health values of professional therapists: A national interdisciplinary survey. *Professional Psychology: Research and Practice, 19*(3), 290–297.

KEITH-SPIEGEL, P., & KOOCHER, G. (1985). *Ethics in psychology: Professional standards and cases.* New York: Random House.

KILBURG, R. R., NATHAN, P. E., & THORESON, R. W. (Eds.). (1986). *Professionals in distress: Issues, syndromes, and solutions in psychology.* Washington, DC: American Psychological Association.

KITCHENER, K. S. (1984). Intuition, critical evaluation, and ethical principles: The foundation for ethical decisions in counseling psychology. *The Counseling Psychologist, 12*(3), 43–55.

KITCHENER, K. S. (1988). Dual role relationships: What makes them so problematic? *Journal of Counseling and Development, 67*(4), 217–221.

KITCHENER, K. S., & Harding, S. S. (1990). Dual role relationships. In B. Herlihy & L. Golden, *Ethical standards casebook* (4th ed.). Alexandria, VA: American Counseling Association.

* KOTTLER, J. A. (1992). *Compassionate therapy: Working with difficult clients.* San Francisco: Jossey-Bass.

* KOTTLER, J. A. (1993). *On being a therapist* (Rev. ed.). San Francisco: Jossey-Bass.

KOTTLER, J. A. (1994). *Beyond blame: A new way of resolving conflicts in relationships.* San Francisco: Jossey-Bass.

* KOTTLER, J. A., & Blau, D. (1989). *The imperfect therapist: Learning from failure in therapeutic practice.* San Francisco: Jossey-Bass.

LaFROMBOISE, T. D., & FOSTER, S. L. (1989). Ethics in multicultural counseling. In P. Pedersen, J. Draguns, W. Lonner, & J. Trimble (Eds.), *Counseling across cultures* (3rd ed.) (pp. 115–136). Honolulu: University of Hawaii Press.

LEE, C. C., & KURILLA, V. (1993). Ethics and multiculturalism: The challenge of diversity. *Ethical Issues in Professional Counseling, 1*(3), 1–11.

LEONG, F. T. L., & KIM, H. H. W. (1991). Going beyond cultural sensitivity on the road to multiculturalism: Using the intercultural sensitizer as a counselor training tool. *Journal of Counseling and Development, 70,* 112–118.

MASLACH, C. (1982). *Burnout: The cost of caring.* Englewood Cliffs, NJ: Prentice-Hall (Spectrum).

MORRISSEY, M. (1994). Help me. *Guidepost, 37*(1), 1, 10.

NATIONAL ASSOCIATION OF SOCIAL WORKERS. (1990). *Code of Ethics* (Rev. ed.). Silver Spring, MD: Author.

NATIONAL BOARD FOR CERTIFIED COUNSELORS. (1989). *Code of ethics.* Alexandria, VA: Author.

NATIONAL FEDERATION OF SOCIETIES FOR CLINICAL SOCIAL WORK. (1985). *Code of ethics.* Silver Spring, MD: Author.

NATIONAL ORGANIZATION FOR HUMAN SERVICE EDUCATION. (1994). *Ethical standards of human service professionals (proposed).* Author.

PATE, R. H., & BONDI, A. M. (1992). Religious beliefs and practice: An integral aspect of multicultural awareness. *Counselor Education and Supervision, 32*(2), 108–115.

* PEDERSEN, P. (1994). *A handbook for developing multicultural awareness* (2nd ed.). Alexandria, VA: American Counseling Association.

POPE, K. S. (1985). Dual relationships: A violation of ethical, legal, and clinical standards. *California State Psychologist, 20*(3), 3–5.

POPE, K. S. (1988). How clients are harmed by sexual contact with mental health professionals: The syndrome and its prevalence. *Journal of Counseling and Development, 67*(4), 222–226.

POPE, K. S., & BOUHOUTSOS, J. C. (1986). *Sexual intimacy between therapists and patients.* New York: Praeger.

POPE, K. S., KEITH-SPIEGEL, P., & TABACHNICK, B. G. (1986). Sexual attraction to clients: The human therapist and the (sometimes) inhuman training system. *American Psychologist, 41*(2), 147–158.

* POPE, K. S., SONNE, J. L., & HOLROYD, J. (1993). *Sexual feelings in psychotherapy: Explorations for therapists and therapists-in-training.* Washington, DC: American Psychological Association.

POPE, K. S., TABACHNICK, B. G., & KEITH-SPIEGEL, P. (1987). Ethics of practice: The beliefs and behaviors of psychologists as therapists. *American Psychologist, 42*(11), 993–1006.

POPE, K. S., TABACHNICK, B. G., & KEITH-SPIEGEL, P. (1988). Good and poor practices in psychotherapy: National survey of beliefs of psychologists. *Professional Psychology: Research and Practice, 19*(5), 547–552.

* POPE, K. S., & VASQUEZ, M. J. T. (1991). *Ethics in psychotherapy and counseling: A practical guide for psychologists.* San Francisco: Jossey-Bass.

ST. GERMAINE, J. (1993). Dual relationships: What's wrong with them? *American Counselor, 2*(3), 25–30.

SELL, J. M., GOTTLIEB, M. C., & SCHOENFELD, L. (1986). Ethical considerations of social/romantic relationships with present and former clients. *Professional Psychology: Research and Practice, 17*(6), 504–508.

SUE, D. W., ARREDONDO, P., & McDAVIS, R. J. (1992). Multicultural counseling competencies and standards. A call to the profession. *Journal of Counseling and Development, 70*(4), 477–486.

SUE, D. W., BERNIER, J. E., DURRAN, A., FEINBERG, L., PEDERSEN, P., SMITH, E. J., & NUTTALL, E. V. (1982). Position paper: Cross-cultural counseling competencies. *The Counseling Psychologist, 10*(2), 45–52.

*SUE, D. W., IVEY, A. E., & PEDERSEN, P. (1996). *A theory of multicultural counseling and therapy.* Pacific Grove, CA: Brooks/Cole.

*SUE, D. W., & SUE, D. (1990). *Counseling the culturally different: Theory and practice* (2nd ed.). New York: Wiley.

SZASZ, T. (1986). The case against suicide prevention. *American Psychologist, 41*(7), 806–812.

TAGGART, S. (1994). *Living as if: Belief systems in mental health practice.* San Francisco: Jossey-Bass.

TOMM, K. (1993, January/February). The ethics of dual relationships. *The California Therapist, 5*(1) 7–19.

VAN HOOSE, W. H., & KOTTLER, J. A. (1985). *Ethical and legal issues in counseling and psychotherapy* (2nd ed.). San Francisco: Jossey-Bass.

VASQUEZ, M. J. T. (1988). Counselor-client sexual contact: Implications for ethics training. *Journal of Counseling and Development, 67*(4), 238–241.

VASQUEZ, M. J. T., & KITCHENER, K. S. (1988). Introduction to special feature. *Journal of Counseling and Development, 67*(4), 214–216.

WELFEL, E. R., & KITCHENER, K. S. (1992). Introduction to the special section: Ethics education—An agenda for the 90s. *Professional Psychology: Research and Practice, 23*(3), 179–181.

WILSON, L. S., & RANFT, V. A. (1993). The state of ethics for counseling psychology doctoral students. *The Counseling Psychologist, 21*(3), 445–456.

WRENN, C. G. (1962). The culturally encapsulated counselor. *Harvard Educational Review, 32,* 444–449.

WRIGHT, J., COLEY, S., & COREY, G. (1989). Challenges facing human services education today. *Journal of Counseling and Human Service Professions, 3*(2), 3–11.

WUBBOLDING, R. E. (1988a). Intervention in suiciding behaviors. *Journal of Reality Therapy, 7*(2), 13–17.

WUBBOLDING, R. E. (1988b). Signs and myths surrounding suiciding behaviors. *Journal of Reality Therapy, 8*(1), 18–21.

ZEIG, J. K., & MUNION, W. M. (Eds.). (1990). *What is psychotherapy? Contemporary perspectives.* San Francisco: Jossey-Bass.

PART TWO

# THEORIES AND TECHNIQUES OF COUNSELING

CHAPTER FOUR
## Psychoanalytic Therapy

CHAPTER FIVE
## Adlerian Therapy

CHAPTER SIX
## Existential Therapy

CHAPTER SEVEN
## Person-Centered Therapy

CHAPTER EIGHT
## Gestalt Therapy

CHAPTER NINE
## Reality Therapy

CHAPTER TEN
## Behavior Therapy

CHAPTER ELEVEN
## Cognitive-Behavior Therapy

CHAPTER TWELVE
## Family Systems Therapy

CHAPTER FOUR

# Psychoanalytic Therapy

# S I G M U N D   F R E U D

SIGMUND FREUD (1856–1939) was the firstborn in a Viennese family of three boys and five girls. His father, like many others of his time and place, was very authoritarian. Freud's family background is a factor to consider in understanding the development of his theory.

Even though Freud's family had limited finances and was forced to live in a crowded apartment, his parents made every effort to foster his obvious intellectual capacities. He had many interests, but his career choices were restricted because of his Jewish heritage. He finally settled on medicine. Only four years after earning his medical degree from the University of Vienna at the age of 26, he attained a prestigious position there as a lecturer.

Freud devoted most of the rest of his life to formulating and extending his theory of psychoanalysis. Interestingly, the most creative phase of his life corresponded to a period when he was experiencing severe emotional problems of his own. When he was in his early 40s, he had numerous psychosomatic disorders, as well as exaggerated fears of dying and other phobias. During this time he was involved in the difficult task of self-analysis. By exploring the meaning of his own dreams, he gained insights into the dynamics of personality development. He first examined his childhood memories and came to realize the intense hostility that he had felt for his father. He also recalled his childhood sexual feelings for his mother, who was attractive, loving, and protective. He then clinically formulated his theory as he observed his patients work through their own problems in analysis.

Freud had very little tolerance for colleagues who diverged from his psychoanalytic doctrines. He attempted to keep control over the movement by expelling those who dared to disagree. Carl Jung and Alfred Adler, for example, worked closely with Freud, but each founded his own therapeutic school after repeated disagreements with him on theoretical and clinical issues.

Freud was highly creative and productive, frequently putting in an 18-hour day. His collected works fill 24 volumes. Freud's productivity remained at this prolific level until late in his life, when he contracted cancer of the jaw. During his last two decades he underwent 33 operations and was in almost constant pain. He died in London in 1939.

As the originator of psychoanalysis, Freud distinguished himself as an intellectual giant. He pioneered new techniques for understanding human behavior, and his efforts resulted in the most comprehensive theory of personality and psychotherapy ever developed.

# Introduction

Freud's views continue to influence contemporary practice. Many of his basic concepts are still part of the foundation on which other theorists build and develop. Indeed, most of the other theories of counseling and psychotherapy discussed later in this book have been influenced by psychoanalytic ideas. Some of these therapeutic approaches extended the psychoanalytic model, others modified its concepts and procedures, and others emerged as a reaction against it. Many borrowed and integrated its principles and techniques.

Freud's psychoanalytic system is a model of personality development, a philosophy of human nature, and a method of psychotherapy. He gave psychotherapy a new look and new horizons. He called attention to psychodynamic factors that motivate behavior, focused on the role of the unconscious, and developed the first therapeutic procedures for understanding and modifying the structure of one's basic character. His theory is a benchmark against which many other theories are measured.

In this relatively short chapter it is impossible to capture the diversity of the psychodynamic approaches that have arisen since Freud. The main focus of this chapter, rather, is on the basic psychoanalytic concepts and practices, many of which originated with him. The chapter sketches therapies that apply classical psychoanalytic concepts to practice less rigorously than he did. The chapter also summarizes Erik Erikson's theory of psychosocial development, which extends Freudian theory in several ways. I also devote brief attention to Jung's approach and to contemporary psychoanalytic theory and practice, including some of the concepts of object-relations theory.*

# Key Concepts

## VIEW OF HUMAN NATURE

The Freudian view of human nature is basically deterministic. According to him, our behavior is determined by irrational forces, unconscious motivations, biological and instinctual drives, as these evolve through key psychosexual stages in the first six years of life. As Kovel notes, however: "Given the dialectic between conscious and unconscious, the strict determinism that has been ascribed to Freudianism . . . melts away. True, thoughts are determined, but not in a linear way. Psychoanalysis teaches a person that his behavior is far more complex than had been imagined" (1976, p. 77). Indeed, psychoanalysis teaches that one may, through insight, free oneself from the tyranny of past experience. As the unconscious becomes conscious, blind habit is replaced by choice. This is an unusually liberated form of determinism.

Instincts are central to the Freudian approach. Although he originally used the term *libido* to refer to sexual energy, he later broadened it to include the

---

*I want to acknowledge the contributions of William Blau and J. Michael Russell to the updating and refining of the ideas in this chapter, especially those dealing with contemporary trends in psychoanalytic practice.

energy of all the *life instincts*. These instincts serve the purpose of the survival of the individual and the human race; they are oriented toward growth, development, and creativity. Libido, then, should be understood as a source of motivation that encompasses sexual energy but goes beyond it. Freud includes all pleasurable acts in his concept of the life instincts; he sees the goal of much of life as gaining pleasure and avoiding pain.

Freud also postulates *death instincts,* which account for the *aggressive drive.* At times, he asserts, people manifest through their behavior an unconscious wish to die or to hurt themselves or others. In his view both the sexual and aggressive drives are powerful determinants of why people act as they do.

Although there may be conflicts between the life instincts (known as Eros) and the death instincts (known as Thanatos), human beings are not condemned to be the victims of aggression and self-destruction. In his book *Civilization and Its Discontents* (1930/1962) Freud gives an indication that the major challenge facing the human race is how to manage the aggressive drive. For him, the unrest and anxiety of people are related to their knowledge that the human race can be exterminated. How much more true is this today than it was in Freud's time?

## STRUCTURE OF PERSONALITY

According to the psychoanalytic view, the personality consists of three systems: the id, the ego, and the superego. These are names for psychological structures and should not be thought of as manikins that separately operate the personality; one's personality functions as a whole rather than as three discrete segments. The id is the biological component, the ego is the psychological component, and the superego is the social component.

From the orthodox Freudian perspective, humans are viewed as energy systems. The dynamics of personality consist of the ways in which psychic energy is distributed to the id, ego, and superego. Because the amount of energy is limited, one system gains control over the available energy at the expense of the other two systems. Behavior is determined by this psychic energy.

THE ID.   The id is the original system of personality; at birth a person is all id. The id is the primary source of psychic energy and the seat of the instincts. It lacks organization, and it is blind, demanding, and insistent. A cauldron of seething excitement, the id cannot tolerate tension, and it functions to discharge tension immediately and return to a homeostatic condition. Ruled by the *pleasure principle,* which is aimed at reducing tension, avoiding pain, and gaining pleasure, the id is illogical, amoral, and driven by one consideration: to satisfy instinctual needs. The id never matures, remaining the spoiled brat of personality. It does not think but only wishes or acts. The id is largely unconscious, or out of awareness.

THE EGO.   The ego has contact with the external world of reality. It is the "executive" that governs, controls, and regulates the personality. As a "traffic cop," it mediates between the instincts and the surrounding environment. The ego controls consciousness and exercises censorship. Ruled by the *reality principle,* the ego does realistic and logical thinking and formulates plans of action for satisfying needs. What is the relation of the ego to the id? The ego, as the seat of intelligence and rationality, checks and controls the blind impulses of the id. Whereas the id knows only subjective reality, the ego distinguishes between mental images and things in the external world.

THE SUPEREGO.    The superego is the judicial branch of personality. It includes a person's moral code, the main concern being whether action is good or bad, right or wrong. It represents the ideal, rather than the real, and strives not for pleasure but for perfection. It represents the traditional values and ideals of society as they are handed down from parents to children. It functions to inhibit the id impulses, to persuade the ego to substitute moralistic goals for realistic ones, and to strive for perfection. The superego, then, as the internalization of the standards of parents and society, is related to psychological rewards and punishments. The rewards are feelings of pride and self-love; the punishments are feelings of guilt and inferiority.

## CONSCIOUSNESS AND THE UNCONSCIOUS

Perhaps Freud's greatest contributions are his concepts of the unconscious and of the levels of consciousness, which are the keys to understanding behavior and the problems of personality. The unconscious cannot be studied directly; it is inferred from behavior. Clinical evidence for postulating the unconscious includes the following: (1) dreams, which are symbolic representations of unconscious needs, wishes, and conflicts; (2) slips of the tongue and forgetting, for example, a familiar name; (3) posthypnotic suggestions; (4) material derived from free-association techniques; (5) material derived from projective techniques; and (6) the symbolic content of psychotic symptoms.

For Freud, consciousness is a thin slice of the total mind. Like the greater part of the iceberg that lies below the surface of the water, the larger part of the mind exists below the surface of awareness. The unconscious stores up all experiences, memories, and repressed material. Needs and motivations that are inaccessible—that is, out of awareness—are also outside the sphere of conscious control. Most psychological functioning exists in the out-of-awareness realm. The aim of psychoanalytic therapy, therefore, is to make the unconscious motives conscious, for only then can one exercise choice. Understanding the role of the unconscious is central to grasping the essence of the psychoanalytic model of behavior. The unconscious, even though out of awareness, does influence behavior. Unconscious processes are the roots of all forms of neurotic symptoms and behaviors. From this perspective, a "cure" is based on uncovering the meaning of symptoms, the causes of behavior, and the repressed materials that interfere with healthy functioning. It is to be noted, however, that intellectual insight alone does not resolve the symptom. The client's need to cling to old patterns (repetition) must be confronted by working through transference distortions, a process that will be discussed later in this chapter.

# ANXIETY

Also essential to the psychoanalytic approach is its concept of anxiety. Anxiety is a state of tension that motivates us to do something. It develops out of a conflict among the id, ego, and superego over control of the available psychic energy. Its function is to warn of impending danger.

There are three kinds of anxiety: reality, neurotic, and moral. Reality anxiety is the fear of danger from the external world, and the level of such anxiety is proportionate to the degree of real threat. Neurotic and moral anxiety are evoked by threats to the "balance of power" within the person. They signal to the ego that unless appropriate measures are taken, the danger may increase until the ego is overthrown. Neurotic anxiety is the fear that the instincts will get out of hand and cause one to do something for which one will be punished. Moral anxiety is the fear of one's own conscience. People with a well-developed conscience tend to feel guilty when they do something contrary to their moral code. When the ego cannot control anxiety by rational and direct methods, it relies on unrealistic ones—namely, ego-defense behavior.

# EGO-DEFENSE MECHANISMS

Ego-defense mechanisms help the individual cope with anxiety and prevent the ego from being overwhelmed. These ego defenses, rather than being pathological, are normal behaviors. They can have adaptive value if they do not become a style of life to avoid facing reality. The defenses one uses depend on one's level of development and degree of anxiety. Defense mechanisms have two characteristics in common: They either deny or distort reality, and they operate on an unconscious level. Following are brief descriptions of some common ego defenses:

- *Repression.* The mechanism of repression is one of the most important Freudian processes, and it is the basis of many other ego defenses and of neurotic disorders. It is a means of defense through which threatening or painful thoughts and feelings are excluded from awareness. Freud explained repression as an involuntary removal of something from consciousness. It is assumed that most of the painful events of the first five years of life are so excluded, yet these events do influence later behavior.
- *Denial.* Denial plays a defensive role similar to that of repression, yet it generally operates at preconscious and conscious levels. Denial of reality is perhaps the simplest of all self-defense mechanisms; it is a way of distorting what the individual thinks, feels, or perceives in a traumatic situation. It consists of defending against anxiety by "closing one's eyes" to the existence of threatening reality. In tragic events such as wars and other disasters, people often tend to blind themselves to realities that would be too painful to accept.
- *Reaction formation.* One defense against a threatening impulse is to actively express the opposite impulse. By developing conscious attitudes and behaviors that are diametrically opposed to disturbing desires, people do not have

to face the anxiety that would result if they were to recognize these dimensions of themselves. Individuals may conceal hate with a facade of love, be extremely nice when they harbor negative reactions, or mask cruelty with excessive kindness.

• *Projection.* Another mechanism of self-deception consists of attributing to others one's own unacceptable desires and impulses. Lustful, aggressive, or other impulses are seen as being possessed by "those people out there, but not by me." Thus, a man who is sexually attracted to his daughter may maintain that it is *she* who is behaving seductively with him. Thus, he does not have to recognize or deal with his own desires.

• *Displacement.* One way to cope with anxiety is to discharge impulses by shifting from a threatening object to a "safer target." Displacement consists of directing energy toward another object or person when the original object or person is inaccessible. For example, the meek man who feels intimidated by his boss comes home and unloads inappropriate hostility onto his children.

• *Rationalization.* Some people manufacture "good" reasons to explain away a bruised ego. Rationalization involves explaining away failures or losses. Thus, it helps justify specific behaviors, and it aids in softening the blow connected with disappointments. When people do not get positions they have applied for in their work, they think of logical reasons why they did not succeed, and they sometimes attempt to convince themselves that they really did not want the position anyway.

• *Sublimation.* From the Freudian perspective, many of the great artistic contributions resulted from a redirection of sexual or aggressive energy into creative behaviors. Sublimation involves diverting sexual or aggressive energy into other channels, ones that are usually socially acceptable and sometimes even admirable. For example, aggressive impulses can be channeled into athletic activities, so that the person finds a way of expressing aggressive feelings and, as an added bonus, is often praised.

• *Regression.* Some people revert to a form of behavior that they have outgrown. In this regression to an earlier phase of development, the demands are not so great. In the face of severe stress or extreme challenge, individuals may attempt to cope with their anxiety by clinging to immature and inappropriate behaviors. For example, children who are frightened in school may indulge in infantile behavior such as weeping, excessive dependence, thumbsucking, hiding, or clinging to the teacher. They are seeking to return to a time in their life when there was security.

• *Introjection.* The mechanism of introjection consists of taking in and "swallowing" the values and standards of others. For example, in concentration camps some of the prisoners dealt with overwhelming anxiety by accepting the values of the enemy through an identification with the aggressor. Another example is the abused child, who assumes the abusing parent's way of handling stresses and thus continues the cycle of child beating. It should be noted that there are also positive forms of introjection, such as the incorporation of parental values or the attributes and values of the therapist (assuming that these are not merely uncritically accepted).

• *Identification.* Although identification is part of the developmental process by which children learn sex-role behaviors, it can also be a defensive reaction. It can enhance self-worth and protect one from a sense of being a failure. Thus, people who feel basically inferior may identify themselves with successful causes, organizations, or people in the hope that they will be perceived as worthwhile.

• *Compensation.* Compensation consists of masking perceived weaknesses or developing certain positive traits to make up for limitations. Thus, children who do not receive positive attention and recognition may develop behaviors designed to at least get negative attention. People who feel intellectually inferior may direct an inordinate degree of energy to building up their bodies; those who feel socially incompetent may become "loners" and develop their intellectual capacities. This mechanism can have direct adjustive value, and it can also be an attempt by the person to say "Don't see the ways in which I am inferior, but see me in my accomplishments."

## DEVELOPMENT OF PERSONALITY

IMPORTANCE OF EARLY DEVELOPMENT.   A significant contribution of the psychoanalytic model is the delineation of the stages of psychosocial and psychosexual development from birth through adulthood. It provides the counselor with the conceptual tools for understanding trends in development, key developmental tasks characteristic of the various stages, normal and abnormal personal and social functioning, critical needs and their satisfaction or frustration, origins of faulty personality development that lead to later adjustment problems, and healthy and unhealthy uses of ego-defense mechanisms.

In my opinion, an understanding of the psychoanalytic view of development is essential if a counselor is to work in depth with clients. I have found that the most typical problems that people bring to counseling are (1) the inability to trust oneself and others, the fear of loving and forming close relationships, and low self-esteem; (2) the inability to recognize and express feelings of hostility, anger, rage, and hate, the denial of one's own power as a person, and the lack of feelings of autonomy; and (3) the inability to fully accept one's own sexuality and sexual feelings, difficulty in accepting oneself as a man or woman, and fear of sexuality. According to the Freudian psychoanalytic view, these three areas of personal and social development (love and trust, dealing with negative feelings, and developing a positive acceptance of sexuality) are all grounded in the first six years of life. This period is the foundation on which later personality development is built.

ERIKSON'S PSYCHOSOCIAL PERSPECTIVE.   Erikson (1963) built on Freud's ideas and extended his theory by stressing the *psychosocial* aspects of development beyond early childhood. His theory of development holds that psychosexual growth and psychosocial growth take place together, and that at each stage of life we face the task of establishing an equilibrium between ourselves and our social world. He describes development in terms of the entire life span, divided by specific crises to be resolved. According to Erikson, a *crisis* is equivalent to a turning point in life, when we have the potential to move forward or to regress.

At these turning points we can either resolve our conflicts or fail to master the developmental task. To a large extent our life is the result of the choices we make at these stages.

Erikson is often credited with bringing an emphasis on social factors to contemporary psychoanalysis. Classical psychoanalysis is grounded on *id psychology,* and it holds that instincts and intrapsychic conflicts are the basic factors shaping personality development (both normal and abnormal). Contemporary psychoanalytic thinking tends to be based on *ego psychology,* which does not deny the role of intrapsychic conflicts but does emphasize the striving of the ego for mastery and competence throughout the human life span. Erickson's focus is on the ego, which is seen as possessing strength and offering ways of dealing with life's tasks in competent and creative ways. Ego psychology deals with both the early and the later developmental stages, for the assumption is that current problems cannot simply be reduced to repetitions of unconscious conflicts from early childhood. The stages of adolescence, mid-adulthood, and later adulthood all involve particular crises that must be addressed. As one's past has meaning in terms of the future, there is a continuity in development, reflected by stages of growth; each stage is related to the other stages.

Because I believe in the value of viewing an individual's development from a combined perspective that includes both psychosexual and psychosocial factors, I have included both Freud's and Erikson's views of the development of personality. This integration is possible because Erikson's ideas are consistent with Freud's. Erikson would contend, however, that Freud did not go far enough in explaining the ego's place in development and did not give enough attention to social influences throughout the life span (see Table 4-1 on pp. 100–101).

THE FIRST YEAR OF LIFE: THE ORAL STAGE.   Freud postulates infantile sexuality. Society's failure to recognize this phenomenon can be explained by cultural taboos and the individual's repression of early experiences in this area.

The oral stage goes from birth to the end of the first year. Sucking the mother's breasts satisfies the infant's need for food and pleasure. As the mouth and lips are sensitive erogenous zones, sucking produces erotic pleasure. Two activities during this developmental period are oral-incorporative behavior and oral-aggressive behavior. These early behaviors are considered to be the prototypes of some of the character traits of adulthood.

First to appear is *oral-incorporative* behavior, which involves pleasurable stimulation of the mouth. Libidinal energy is at first focused on the mouth, and then with maturity other areas of the body develop and become the focal points of gratification. However, adults who exhibit excessive oral needs (such as excessive eating, chewing, talking, smoking, and drinking) may have an *oral fixation.* Deprivation of oral gratification during infancy is assumed to lead to problems in adulthood.

As the infant teethes, the *oral-aggressive* period begins. Biting is one activity at this time. Adult characteristics such as sarcasm, hostility, aggression, gossip, and making "biting" comments to others are related to events of this developmental period.

Greediness and acquisitiveness may develop as a result of not getting enough food or love during the early years of life. Material things that children seek become substitutes for what they really want—namely, food and love from the mother. Later personality problems that stem from the oral stage are the development of a view of the world based on mistrust, fear of reaching out to others, rejection of affection, fear of loving and trusting, low self-esteem, isolation and withdrawal, and inability to form or maintain intense relationships.

In Erikson's psychosocial view this stage of infancy is characterized by a struggle between *trust* and *mistrust*. An infant's basic task is to develop a sense of trust in self, others, and the world. The infant needs to count on others and to develop a sense of being wanted and secure. This sense of trust is learned by being caressed and cared for.

From Erikson's viewpoint if the significant others in an infant's life provide the necessary love, the infant develops a sense of trust. When love is absent, the result is a general sense of mistrust of others. Clearly, infants who feel accepted are in a more favorable position to successfully meet future developmental crises than are those who do not receive adequate nurturing.

AGES 1–3: THE ANAL STAGE.   The anal stage marks another step in development. The tasks to be mastered during this stage are learning independence, personal power, and autonomy and learning how to recognize and deal with negative feelings.

Beginning in the second year and extending into the third year, the anal zone comes to be of major significance in the formation of personality. Now children continually face parental demands, experience frustrations when they handle objects and explore their environment, and are expected to master control of their bowels. When toilet training begins during the second year, children have their first major experience with discipline. The method of toilet training and the parents' feelings, attitudes, and reactions toward the child can have far-reaching effects on the formation of personality traits. Many of the attitudes children learn about their own bodily functions are the direct result of the attitudes of their parents. Later personality problems such as compulsivity have roots in the ways parents rear their children during this stage.

Children may attempt to control their parents by either withholding their feces or defecating at inappropriate times. If strict toilet-training methods are used, children may express their anger by expelling their feces at inappropriate places and times. This behavior can lay the foundation for later adult characteristics such as cruelty, inappropriate displays of anger, and extreme disorderliness. Freud describes this as the *anal-aggressive* personality. In contrast, other parents might focus too much attention on their children's bowel movements by giving praise whenever they defecate, which can contribute to a child's exaggerated view of the importance of this activity. This focus might be associated with a person's need for being productive. Again, certain adults develop fixations revolving around extreme orderliness, hoarding, stubbornness, and stinginess. This is known as the *anal-retentive* personality. The important point is that later adult characteristics have their roots in the experiences of this period.

T A B L E    4-1
Comparison of Freud's Psychosexual Stages and Erikson's Psychosocial Stages

| PERIOD OF LIFE | FREUD | ERIKSON |
|---|---|---|
| *First year of life* | *Oral stage* Sucking at mother's breasts satisfies need for food and pleasure. Infant needs to get basic nurturing, or later feelings of greediness and acquisitiveness may develop. Oral fixations result from deprivation of oral gratification in infancy. Later personality problems can include mistrust of others, rejecting others' love, and fear of and inability to form intimate relationships. | *Infancy: Trust versus mistrust* If significant others provide for basic physical and emotional needs, infant develops a sense of trust. If basic needs are not met, an attitude of mistrust toward the world, especially toward interpersonal relationships, is the result. |
| *Ages 1–3* | *Anal stage* Anal zone becomes of major significance in formation of personality. Main developmental tasks include learning independence, accepting personal power, and learning to express negative feelings such as rage and aggression. Parental discipline patterns and attitudes have significant consequences for child's later personality development. | *Early childhood: Autonomy versus shame and doubt* A time for developing autonomy. Basic struggle is between a sense of self-reliance and a sense of self-doubt. Child needs to explore and experiment, to make their mistakes, and to test limits. If parents promote dependency, child's autonomy is inhibited, and capacity to deal with world successfully is hampered. |
| *Ages 3–6* | *Phallic stage* Basic conflict centers on unconscious incestuous desires that child develops for parent of opposite sex and that, because of their threatening nature, are repressed. *Male phallic stage,* known as *Oedipus complex,* involves mother as love object for boy. *Female phallic stage,* known as *Electra complex,* involves girl's strivings for father's love and approval. How parents respond, verbally and nonverbally, to child's emerging sexuality has an impact on sexual attitudes and feelings that child develops. | *Preschool age: Initiative versus guilt* Basic task is to achieve a sense of competence and initiative. If children are given freedom to select personally meaningful activities, they tend to develop a positive view of self and follow through with their projects. If they are not allowed to make their own decisions, they tend to develop guilt over taking initiative. They then refrain from taking an active stance and allow others to choose for them. |

| PERIOD OF LIFE | FREUD | ERIKSON |
| --- | --- | --- |
| *Ages 6–12* | *Latency stage*<br>After the torment of sexual impulses of preceding years, this period is relatively quiescent. Sexual interests are replaced by interests in school, playmates, sports, and a range of new activities. This is a time of socialization as child turns outward and forms relationships with others. | *School age: Industry versus inferiority*<br>Child needs to expand understanding of world, continue to develop appropriate sex-role identity, and learn the basic skills required for school success. Basic task is to achieve a sense of industry—to set and attain personal goals. Failure to do so results in a sense of inadequacy. |
| *Ages 12–18* | *Genital stage*<br>Old themes of phallic stage are revived. This stage begins with puberty and lasts until senility sets in. Despite societal restrictions and taboos, adolescents can deal with sexual energy by investing it in various socially acceptable activities such as forming friendships, engaging in art or in sports, and preparing for a career. | *Adolescence: Identity versus role confusion*<br>A time of transition between childhood and adulthood. A time for testing limits, breaking dependent ties, and establishing a new identity. Major conflicts over clarification of self-identity, life goals, and life's meaning. Failure to achieve a sense of identity results in role confusion. |
| *Ages 18–35* | *Genital stage continues*<br>Core characteristic of mature adult is the freedom "to love and to work." This move toward adulthood involves freedom from parental influence and capacity to care for others. | *Young adulthood: Intimacy versus isolation*<br>Developmental task at this time is to form intimate relationships. Failure to achieve intimacy can lead to alienation and isolation. |
| *Ages 35–60* | *Genital stage continues* | *Middle age: Generativity versus stagnation*<br>There is a need to go beyond self and family and to help the next generation. This is a time of adjusting to the discrepancy between one's dreams and one's actual accomplishments. Failure to achieve a sense of productivity can lead to psychological stagnation. |
| *Ages 60+* | *Genital stage continues* | *Later life: Integrity versus despair*<br>If one has few regrets and feels personally worthwhile, ego integrity results. Failure to achieve ego integrity can lead to feelings of despair, hopelessness, guilt, resentment, and self-rejection. |

During the anal period of development, the child will surely experience so-called "negative" feelings such as hostility, destructiveness, anger, rage, hatred, and so on. It is important that children learn that these are acceptable feelings. Many clients in therapy have not yet learned to accept their anger and hatred toward those they love. Because they were either directly or indirectly taught that these feelings were bad and that parental acceptance would be withheld if they expressed them, they repressed them.

According to Erikson, early childhood is a time for developing *autonomy;* children who do not master the task of gaining some measure of self-control and ability to cope with the world develop a sense of *shame* and *doubt* about their abilities. Parents who do too much for their children hamper their independence. Children who are encouraged to stay dependent will doubt their capacities for successfully dealing with the world.

It is important at this stage that children begin to acquire a sense of their own power. If parents do too much for their children, the message transmitted is "Here, let me do thus-and-so for you, because you are too weak or helpless to do these things for yourself." During this time children need to experiment, to make mistakes and feel that they are still acceptable persons, and to recognize some of their own power as separate and distinct individuals. So many clients are in counseling precisely because they have lost touch with their potential for power; they are struggling to define who they are and what they are capable of doing.

AGES 3–6: THE PHALLIC STAGE.    We have seen that between the ages of 1 and 3 the child discards infantile ways and actively carves a distinctive niche in the world. This is the period when capacities for walking, talking, thinking, and controlling the sphincters develop rapidly. As increased motor and perceptual abilities develop, so also do interpersonal skills. The child's progression from a period of passive/receptive mastery to a period of active mastery sets the stage for the next psychosexual developmental period—the phallic stage. During this period sexual activity becomes more intense, and the now the focus of attention is on the genitals—the boy's penis and the girl's clitoris.

According to the orthodox Freudian view, the basic conflict of the phallic stage centers on the unconscious incestuous desires that children develop for the parent of the opposite sex. Because these feelings are of such a threatening nature, they are typically repressed; yet they are powerful determinants of later sexual development and adjustment. Along with the wish to possess the parent of the opposite sex comes the unconscious wish of the child to "do away with" the competition—the parent of the same sex.

According to Freudian theory, boys and girls both experience sexual longings and conflicts, which they repress. In the *male phallic stage* the boy craves the attention of his mother, feels antagonistic toward his father, and develops fears that his father will punish him for his incestuous feelings toward his mother. This is known as the *Oedipus complex.* Thus, the mother becomes the love object for the boy. Both in his fantasy and his behavior, he exhibits sexual longings for her. He soon realizes that his more powerful father is a rival for the exclusive attention he desires from her. About the time when the mother becomes the object of love for the boy, however, repression is already operating, which prevents a conscious awareness of a part of his sexual aims.

At this time the boy typically develops specific fears related to his penis. Freud describes the condition of *castration anxiety,* which is said to play a central role in the boy's life at this time. His ultimate fear is that his father will retaliate by cutting off his offending organ. The reality of castration is emphasized when the boy notices the absence of the penis in girls. As a result of this anxiety of losing his prized possession, the boy is said to repress his sexual desire for his mother. If the oedipal conflict is properly resolved, the boy replaces his sexual longings for his mother with more acceptable forms of affection; he also develops strong identification with his father. In a sense, it is a matter of realizing that if he cannot beat his father, he might as well join him. Through this identification with his father, the boy experiences vicarious satisfaction. He becomes more like his father, and he may adopt many of his father's mannerisms.

The *female phallic stage* is not so clearly described by Freud as is the male stage. Also, the orthodox Freudian view of female development has stirred up considerable controversy and has met with negative reactions from many women. The *Electra complex* is the girl's counterpart to the Oedipus complex. The girl's first love object is her mother, but love is transferred to her father during this stage. She is said to develop negative feelings toward her mother when she discovers the absence of a penis, the condition known as *penis envy.* This is the girl's counterpart to the boy's castration anxiety. She is said to have a desire to compete with her mother for the father's attention, and when she realizes that she cannot replace her mother, she begins an identification process by taking on some of the characteristics of her mother's behavior.

The development of sexual attitudes assumes critical importance during this period of life. Perhaps one of the most frequently misunderstood terms in Freud's theory is *sexuality.* He uses it much more broadly than it is typically used. Sexuality refers to organ pleasure of any kind. The type of sexuality that becomes evident during the phallic stage does not necessarily refer to the child's desire for sexual intercourse with the opposite-sex parent. Although the boy's feelings toward his mother are erotically tinged, this kind of sexuality is more diffuse than sexual intercourse, and the child's concept of actual sexual intercourse is often undefined. It is during this period of psychosexual development that behaviors such as the following become increasingly evident: curiosity about sexual matters, sexual fantasies, masturbation, sex-role identification patterns, and sex play.

The phallic period has significant implications for the therapist who works with adults. Many clients have never fully resolved their feelings about their own sexuality. They may have confused feelings about sex-role identification, and they may be struggling to accept their sexual feelings and behavior. In my judgment it is important that therapists give just recognition to early experiences when they are working with adult clients. I am not suggesting that therapists view people as condemned to a lack of sexual responsiveness or impotence if they have not successfully mastered the developmental tasks of the phallic period. What I do see as important, however, is that clients become aware of their childhood experiences in this area, perhaps even relive and reexperience them in fantasy. As they relive events and feel again many of their buried feelings, they become increasingly aware that they are capable of inventing new endings to dramas they experienced as children. Thus, they come to realize that although their present attitudes and behavior are surely shaped by the past, they are not doomed to remain victims of the past.

From the psychosocial perspective, the core struggle of the preschool phase is between *initiative* and *guilt.* Erikson contends that the basic task of the preschool years is to establish a sense of competence and initiative. He places more stress on social development than on concerns relating to sexuality. During this time children are psychologically ready to pursue activities of their own choosing. If they are allowed the freedom to select meaningful activities, they tend to develop a positive outlook characterized by the ability to initiate and follow through. If they are not allowed to make some of their own decisions, however, or if their choices are ridiculed, they develop a sense of guilt over taking the initiative. Typically, they withdraw from taking an active stance and permit others to make decisions for them.

AGES 6–12: THE LATENCY STAGE.   With the passing of the turbulence of the first expression of the Oedipus complex and the combined stresses of the oral, anal, and phallic stages of psychosexual development, the individual can enjoy a period of relative rest. The major structures of personality (id, ego, superego) are largely formed, as are the relationships between these subsystems.

During this latency period new interests replace infantile sexual impulses. Socialization takes place, and children direct their interests to the larger world. The sexual drive is sublimated, to some extent, to activities in school, hobbies, sports, and friendships with members of the same sex.

The oral, anal, and phallic stages taken together are known as the pregenital period. A major characteristic of this period is a *narcissistic* orientation, or an inward and self-centered preoccupation. During the middle-childhood years there is a turning outward toward relationships with others. Children of this age have an interest in the things of the external world as well as of their internal world. This period prevails until the onset of puberty; it is during adolescence that the individual begins to establish an adult identity, along with a genital orientation.

Corresponding to the latency stage is Erikson's school-age stage, marked by a need to resolve the conflict between *industry* and *inferiority.* Some of the unique psychosocial tasks that must be met if healthy development is to proceed are expanding one's understanding of the physical and social worlds; continuing to develop an appropriate sex-role identity; continuing to develop a sense of values; engaging in social tasks; learning how to accept people who are different; and learning basic skills needed for schooling.

According to Erikson, the central task of middle childhood is to achieve a sense of industry; failure to do so results in feelings of inadequacy and inferiority. A sense of industry is associated with creating goals that are personally meaningful and achieving them. If this is not done, it will be difficult to experience a sense of adequacy in later years, and future developmental stages will be negatively influenced.

Some of the following problems originate during middle childhood; they are often manifested in later problems that counselors deal with:

- a negative self-concept
- feelings of inadequacy relating to learning
- feelings of inferiority in establishing social relationships
- conflicts over values
- a confused sex-role identity
- unwillingness to face new challenges
- a lack of initiative
- dependency

AGES 12–18: THE GENITAL STAGE.   Young adults move into the genital stage unless they become fixated at an earlier period of psychosexual development. During adolescence oedipal and Electra conflicts are among the old themes of the phallic stage that are revived and recapitulated. Adolescents typically develop interest in the opposite sex, engage in some sexual experimentation, and begin to assume adult responsibilities. As they move out of adolescence and into mature adulthood, they form intimate relationships, become free of parental influence, and develop the capacity to be interested in others. There is a trend away from narcissism and toward altruistic behavior and concern for others. According to Freud, the goals of *lieben und arbeiten* are core characteristics of the mature adult; that is, the freedom "to love and to work" and to derive satisfaction from loving and working is of paramount importance.

Freud was primarily concerned with the impact of resolving sexual issues during the first six years of life. He did not go into great detail in discussing the crises associated with adolescence or the stages of adulthood. Erikson's view of development, however, continues where Freud left off. It accounts for forces influencing adolescent development and various phases of adulthood. According to Erikson, the major developmental conflicts of the adolescent years are related to the formation of a *personal identity.* Adolescents struggle to define who they are, where they are going, and how to get there. If they fail to achieve a sense of identity, *role confusion* is the result. Because they experience diverse pressures—from parents, peers, and society—they often find it difficult to gain a clear sense of identity.

Adolescents have the task of integrating a system of values that will give their life direction. In the formation of a personal philosophy of life, they must make key decisions relating to religious beliefs, sexual ethics, values, and so forth. In this search for identity, models are especially important.

ADULTHOOD.   For Freud, the genital stage continues through adulthood. Erikson has delineated three stages that cover the adult period: young adulthood, middle age, and later life. He sets forth the psychosocial experiences, expectations, and developmental tasks typical of these stages:

1. *Young adulthood: intimacy versus isolation.* In Erikson's view we approach adulthood after we master the adolescent conflicts over identity and role confusion. During young adulthood our sense of identity is tested again by the

challenge of *intimacy* versus *isolation.* One of the key characteristics of the psychologically mature person is the ability to form intimate relationships. A prerequisite to establishing this intimacy with others is a confidence in our own identity. Intimacy involves an ability to share with others and to give to others from our own centeredness.

2. *Middle age: generativity versus stagnation.* This is a time for learning how to live creatively with both ourselves and others. On the one hand, it can be one of the most productive periods of life. On the other hand, we may painfully experience the discrepancy between our dreams of young adulthood and the reality of what we have accomplished. Erikson sees the stimulus for continued growth in middle age as the crisis between *generativity* and *stagnation.* He considers generativity in the broad sense to include creating through a career, family, leisure-time activities, and so on. The main quality of productive adults is their ability to love well, to work well, and to play well. If adults fail to achieve a sense of productivity, they begin to stagnate and to die psychologically.

3. *Later life: integrity versus despair.* According to Erikson, the core crisis of the elderly is *integrity* versus *despair.* Ego integrity is achieved by those who feel few regrets; they have lived a productive and worthwhile life and have coped with their failures as well as their successes. They are not obsessed with what might have been, and they are able to derive satisfaction from what they have done. They are able to view death as a part of the life process, and they can still find meaning in how they are now living. The failure to achieve ego integrity tends to lead to feelings of despair, hopelessness, guilt, resentment, and self-disgust. Such people think about all of the things they could have done, and they may yearn for "another chance." This realization that they have wasted their life leads to a sense of despair.

COUNSELING IMPLICATIONS.   By taking a combined psychosexual and psychosocial perspective, counselors have a useful conceptual framework for understanding developmental issues as they appear in therapy. Regardless of a counselor's theoretical preference, relevant questions such as the following can give direction to the therapeutic process:

- What are some major developmental tasks at each stage in life, and how are these tasks related to counseling?
- What are some themes that give continuity to this individual's life?
- What are some universal concerns of people at various points in life? How can people be challenged to make life-affirming choices at these points?
- What is the relationship between an individual's current problems and significant events from earlier years?
- What influential factors have shaped one's life?
- What choices were made at these critical periods, and how did the person deal with these various crises?

Counselors who work with a developmental perspective are able to see a continuity in life and to see certain directions their clients have taken. This perspective gives a broader picture of the individual's struggle, and clients are able to discover some significant connections among the various stages of their life.

# JUNG'S PERSPECTIVE ON
# THE DEVELOPMENT OF PERSONALITY

Carl Jung made monumental contributions to our deep understanding of the human personality. His pioneering work sheds light on human development, particularly during middle age. Jung places central importance on the psychological changes that are associated with midlife. He maintains that we need to let go of many of the values and behaviors that guided the first half of our life and confront our unconscious. We can best do this by paying attention to the messages of our dreams and by engaging in creative activities such as writing or painting. The task facing us during the midlife period is to be less influenced by rational thought and to instead give expression to these unconscious forces and integrate them into our conscious life (Schultz & Schultz, 1994).

Jung himself learned a great deal from his own midlife crisis. At age 81 he wrote about his recollections in his autobiography, *Memories, Dreams, Reflections* (1961), in which he also identified some of his major contributions. Jung made a choice to focus on the unconscious realm in his personal life, which also influenced the development of his theory of personality. However, he had a very different conception of the unconscious than did Freud. Although he was a colleague of Freud's and valued many of his contributions, he eventually came to the point of not being able to support some of his basic concepts, especially his theory of sexuality. Jung recalls Freud's words to him: "My dear Jung, promise me never to abandon the sexual theory. This is the most essential thing of all. You see, we must make a dogma of it, an unshakable bulwark" (Jung, 1961, p. 150). Jung became convinced that he could no longer collaborate with Freud because he believed that Freud placed his own authority over truth. Freud had little tolerance for other theoreticians, such as Jung and Adler, who dared to challenge his theories. Although Jung had a lot to lose professionally by withdrawing from Freud, he saw no other choice. He subsequently developed a spiritual approach that places great emphasis on being impelled to find meaning in life, rather than being driven by the psychological and biological forces described by Freud.

In contrast to Freudian determinism, Jung maintains that humans are not merely shaped by past events but also progress beyond their past. Part of the nature of humans is to be constantly developing, growing, and moving toward a balanced and complete level of development. For Jung, our present personality is determined both by who and what we have been and also by the person we hope to become. The process of self-actualization is oriented toward the future. His theory is based on the assumption that humans tend to move toward the fulfillment or realization of all of their capabilities. Achieving individuation, or the harmonious integration of the conscious and unconscious aspects of personality, is viewed as being an innate and primary goal. For Jung, we have both constructive and destructive forces, and to become integrated, it is essential to accept the dark side of our nature with its primitive impulses such as selfishness and greed. Acceptance of this dark side (or shadow) does not imply being dominated by this dimension of our being but simply recognizing that this is a part of our nature.

Jung teaches that many dreams contain messages from the deepest layer of the unconscious, which he describes as the source of creativity. He calls this deep layer the *collective unconscious,* the "all-controlling deposit of ancestral experiences" (Schultz & Schultz, 1994, p. 85). Jung sees a connection between each person's personality and the past, not only childhood events but also the history of the species. Dreams thus reflect both an individual's personal unconscious and the collective unconscious. This means that some dreams deal with an individual's relationship to a larger whole such as the family, universal humanity, or generations over time. The contents of the collective unconscious are called *archetypes.* Among the most important archetypes are the persona, the anima and animus, and the shadow. The *persona* is a mask, or public face, that we wear to protect ourselves. The *animus* and the *anima* represent both the biological and psychological aspects of masculinity and femininity, which are thought to coexist in both sexes. The *shadow* has the deepest roots and is the most dangerous and powerful of the archetypes. As mentioned, it represents our dark side, the thoughts, feelings, and actions that are socially reprehensible and that we tend to disown by projecting them outward. In a dream all of these parts can be considered manifestations of who and what we are.

Jung agrees with Freud that dreams provide a pathway into the unconscious, but he differs from Freud on their functions. He writes that dreams have two purposes: They are prospective, in that they help people prepare themselves for the experiences and events they anticipate in the near future. They also serve a compensatory function; that is, they work to bring about a balance between opposites within the person. They compensate for the overdevelopment of one facet of the individual's personality (Schultz & Schultz, 1994).

Jung views dreams more as an attempt to express than an attempt to repress and disguise. They are a creative effort of the dreamer in struggling with contradiction, complexity, and confusion. The aim of the dream is resolution and integration. According to Jung, each part of the dream can be understood as some projected quality of the dreamer. His method of interpretation draws on a series of dreams obtained from a person, during the course of which the meaning gradually unfolds. If you are interested in further reading, I suggest Jung (1961) and Singer Harris (1996).

## CONTEMPORARY TRENDS:
## SELF PSYCHOLOGY AND OBJECT-RELATIONS THEORY

Psychoanalytic theory, rather than being closed or static, is continually evolving. As we have seen, Freud emphasized intrapsychic conflicts pertaining to the gratification of basic needs. Later, writers in the neo-Freudian school moved away from his orthodox position and contributed to the growth and expansion of the psychoanalytic movement by incorporating the cultural and social influences on personality. Then ego psychology, with its stress on psychosocial development throughout the life span, was developed, largely by Erikson.

The evolution of psychoanalytic theory and practice did not cease with these developments. A new trend in psychoanalytic thinking characterized the 1970s and the 1980s. Hedges (1983) writes that this newer thinking emphasizes:

- the origins, transformations, and organizational functions of the self
- one's experiences of others
- the differentiation between and integration of the self and others
- the influence of critical factors in early development on later development

These newer approaches are often classified under the labels *self psychology* or *object-relations theory*. Object relations are interpersonal relationships as they are represented intrapsychically. The term *object* was used by Freud to refer to that which satisfies a need, or to the significant person or thing that is the object, or target, of one's feelings or drives. It is used interchangeably with the term *other* to refer to an important person to whom the child, and later the adult, becomes attached. Rather than being individuals with a separate identity, others are perceived by an infant as objects for gratifying needs. Thus, object relations are interpersonal relationships that shape the individual's current interactions with people, both in reality and in fantasy. Object-relations theories have diverged from orthodox psychoanalysis, although some theorists attempt to integrate the increasingly varied ideas that characterize this school of thought (St. Clair, 1996).

SUMMARY OF STAGES OF DEVELOPMENT.   These recent psychoanalytic theories center on predictable developmental sequences in which the early experiences of the self shift in relation to an expanding awareness of others. Once self/other patterns are established, it is assumed, they influence later interpersonal relationships. Specifically, people search for relationships that match the patterns established by their earlier experiences. People who are either overly dependent or overly detached, for example, can be repeating patterns of relating that they established with their mother when they were toddlers (Hedges, 1983). These newer theories provide insight into how an individual's inner world can cause difficulties in living in the actual world of people and relationships (St. Clair, 1996).

A central influence on contemporary object-relations theory is Margaret Mahler (1968), a pediatrician who emphasized the observation of children. In her view, the resolution of the Oedipus complex is less critical than the child's progression from a symbiotic relationship with a maternal figure toward separation and individuation. Her studies focus on the interactions between the child and the mother in the first three years of life. According to Mahler, the self develops through four broad stages, which she conceptualizes somewhat differently from the traditional Freudian psychosexual stages. Her belief is that the individual begins in a state of psychological fusion with the mother and progresses gradually to separation. The unfinished crises and residues of the earlier state of fusion, as well as the process of separating and individuating, have a profound influence on later relationships. Object relations of later life build on the child's search for a reconnection with the mother (St. Clair, 1996). Psychological development can be thought of as the evolution of the way in which individuals separate from and differentiate themselves from others.

The first phase of development of the self, in the first three or four weeks of life, Mahler calls *normal infantile autism.* Here the infant is presumed to be responding more to states of physiological tension than to psychological processes. The infant is, in many respects, unable to differentiate itself from its mother, and, according to Melanie Klein (1975), perceives parts—breasts, face, hands, and mouth—rather than a unified self. In this undifferentiated state there is no whole self, and there are no whole objects. When adults show the most extreme forms of lack of psychological organization and sense of self, they may be thought of as revealing fixations at this most primitive infantile stage.

Mahler's second phase, called *symbiosis,* is recognizable by the third month and extends roughly through the eighth month. Here, as with the first stage, the infant has a pronounced dependency on the mother. She (or the primary caregiver) is clearly a partner and not just an interchangeable part. The infant seems to expect a very high degree of emotional attunement with its mother. Psychoanalysts think that psychotic disorders are linked to the failure to pass beyond the symbiotic phase.

Mahler's third phase starts by the fourth or fifth month, thus overlapping the second stage. This third phase she calls the *separation/individuation* process. It involves the child's moving through several subphases, away from symbiotic forms of relating. During this time of differentiation the child experiences separation from significant others yet still turns to them for a sense of confirmation and comfort. The child may demonstrate ambivalence, torn between enjoying separate states of independence and dependence. The toddler who proudly steps away from the parents and then runs back to be swept up in approving arms can be said to illustrate some of the main issues of this period (Hedges, 1983, p. 109). Others are looked to as approving mirrors for the child's developing sense of self; optimally, these relationships can provide a healthy self-esteem.

Children who do not experience the opportunity to differentiate, and also those who lack the opportunity to idealize others while also taking pride in themselves, may later suffer from *narcissistic* character disorders and problems of self-esteem. The narcissistic personality is characterized by a grandiose and exaggerated sense of self-importance and an exploitive attitude toward others, which serve the function of masking a frail self-concept. Such individuals seek attention and admiration from others. They unrealistically exaggerate their accomplishments, and they have a tendency toward extreme self-absorption. Kernberg (1975) characterizes narcissistic people as focusing on themselves in their interactions with others, having a great need to be admired, possessing shallow affect, and being exploitive and, at times, parasitic in their relationships with others. Kohut (1971) characterizes such people as perceiving threats to their self-esteem and as having feelings of emptiness and deadness.

"Borderline" conditions are also rooted in the period of separation/individuation. People with a *borderline personality disorder* have moved into the separation process but have been thwarted by maternal rejection of their individuation.

In other words, a crisis ensues when the child does develop beyond the stage of symbiosis but the mother (or the mothering figure) is unable to tolerate this beginning individuation and withdraws emotional support. Borderline people are characterized by instability, irritability, self-destructive acts, impulsive anger, and extreme mood shifts. They typically experience extended periods of disillusionment, punctuated by occasional euphoria. Kernberg describes the syndrome as including a lack of clear identity, a lack of deep understanding of other people, poor impulse control, and the inability to tolerate anxiety (1975, pp. 161–162).

Mahler's fourth and final phase involves a move toward constancy of self and object. This development is typically pronounced by the 36th month (Hedges, 1983). By now others are more fully seen as separate from the self. Ideally, children can begin to relate without being overwhelmed with fears of losing their sense of individuality, and they may enter into the later psychosexual and psychosocial stages with a firm foundation of selfhood.

TREATING BORDERLINE AND NARCISSISTIC DISORDERS.    Borderline and narcissistic disorders seem to be rooted in traumas and developmental disturbances during the separation/individuation phase. However, the full manifestations of the personality and behavioral symptoms tend to develop in early adulthood. Borderline and narcissistic symptoms such as splitting (a defensive process of keeping incompatible perceptions separate) and notions of grandiosity are behavioral manifestations of developmental tasks that were disturbed or not completed earlier (St. Clair, 1996).

A great deal of recent psychoanalytic writing deals with the nature and treatment of borderline and narcissistic personality disorders. Object-relations theory sheds new light on the understanding of these disorders. Among the most significant theorists in this area are Kernberg (1975, 1976), Kohut (1971, 1977, 1984), and Masterson (1976). Kohut has maintained that people are their healthiest and best when they can feel both independence and attachment, taking joy in themselves and also being able to idealize others. Since mature adults feel a basic security grounded in a sense of freedom, self-sufficiency, and self-esteem, they are not compulsively dependent on others but also do not have to fear closeness.

This chapter permits only a brief treatment of the newer formulations in psychoanalytic theory. If you would like to pursue this emerging approach, an overview of this vast and growing literature can be found in Hedges (1983), Kaplan (1978), and St. Clair (1996).

# The Therapeutic Process

## THERAPEUTIC GOALS

Two goals of Freudian psychoanalytic therapy are to make the unconscious conscious and to strengthen the ego so that behavior is based more on reality and less on instinctual cravings. Successful analysis is believed to result in significant modification of the individual's personality and character structure. The focus is on using therapeutic methods to bring out unconscious material that can be worked through. Childhood experiences are reconstructed, discussed, interpreted, and analyzed. It is clear that the process is not limited to solving problems and learning new behaviors. Rather, there is a deeper probing into the past in order to develop the level of self-understanding that is assumed to be necessary for a change in character. Analytic therapy is oriented toward achieving insight, but not just an intellectual understanding; it is essential that the feelings and memories associated with this self-understanding be experienced.

## THERAPIST'S FUNCTION AND ROLE

Classical analysts typically assume an anonymous stance, which is sometimes called the "blank-screen" approach. They engage in very little self-disclosure and maintain a sense of neutrality, because they are attempting to foster a *transference relationship,* in which their clients will make *projections* onto them. Therapists believe that if they say little about themselves and rarely share their personal reactions, whatever the client feels toward them is largely the product of feelings associated with other significant figures from the past. These projections, which have their origins in unfinished and repressed situations, are considered "grist for the mill," and their analysis is the very essence of therapeutic work.

One of the central functions of analysis is to help the analysand acquire the freedom to love, work, and play. There are other functions. Analysts are concerned with assisting their analysands in achieving self-awareness, honesty, and more effective personal relationships; in dealing with anxiety in a realistic way; and in gaining control over impulsive and irrational behavior. Of course, these issues are problems to the degree that they impair one's capacity to fully love and work in the broad sense of the terms as used by Freud. The analyst must first establish a working relationship with the analysand and then do a lot of listening and interpreting. Particular attention is given to the client's resistances. While the analysand does most of the talking, the analyst listens, learns, and decides when to make appropriate interpretations. A major function of interpretation is to accelerate the process of uncovering unconscious material. The analyst listens for gaps and inconsistencies in the analysand's story, infers the meaning of reported dreams and free associations, carefully observes during the therapy session, and remains sensitive to clues concerning the analysand's feelings toward the analyst.

Organizing these therapeutic processes within the context of understanding personality structure and psychodynamics enables the analyst to formulate the nature of analysands' problems. One of the central functions of the analyst is to teach clients the meaning of these processes so that they are able to achieve insight into their problems, increase their awareness of ways to change, and thus gain more rational control over their lives.

As Saretsky (1978) notes, the process of psychoanalytic therapy does not neatly follow a direct path from an insight to a cure. It is more like putting the pieces of a puzzle together. Whether clients change depends considerably more on their readiness to change than on the accuracy of the therapist's interpretations. If the therapist pushes clients too rapidly or offers ill-timed interpretations, therapy is likely to become counterproductive.

## CLIENT'S EXPERIENCE IN THERAPY

Clients interested in psychoanalysis must be willing to commit themselves to an intensive and long-term therapy process. Typically, they come to therapy several times weekly for three to five years. After some face-to-face sessions with the analyst, analysands lie on a couch and free-associate; that is, they say whatever comes to mind without self-censorship. This process of free association is known as the "fundamental rule." Clients report their feelings, experiences, associations, memories, and fantasies to the analyst. Lying on the couch encourages deep, uncensored reflections and reduces the stimuli that might interfere with their getting in touch with their internal conflicts and productions. It also reduces their ability to "read" their analyst's face for reactions and, hence, fosters the projections characteristic of a regressive transference. At the same time, the analyst is freed from having to carefully monitor facial clues.

What has just been described is classical psychoanalysis. It should be noted that many psychoanalytically oriented practitioners (as distinct from analysts) do not use all these techniques. Yet they do remain alert to transference manifestations and work with dreams and with unconscious material.

Clients in psychoanalytic therapy make a commitment with the therapist to stick with the procedures of an intensive therapeutic process. They agree to talk, because their verbal productions are the heart of psychoanalytic therapy. They are typically asked not to make any radical changes in their lifestyle during the period of analysis, such as getting a divorce or quitting their job.

Psychoanalytic clients are ready to terminate their sessions when they and their analyst agree that they have clarified and accepted their emotional problems, have understood the historical roots of their difficulties, and can integrate their awareness of past problems with their present relationships. Successful analysis answers a client's "why" questions regarding his or her life. For example, a lawyer in psychoanalytic therapy should develop an understanding of why he or she chose law as a profession, as well as resolving conflicts associated with the choice. Clients who emerge successfully from analytic therapy report that they have achieved such things as an understanding of their symptoms and the func tions they serve, an insight into how their environment affects them and how they affect the environment, and a reduced defensiveness (Saretsky, 1978).

## RELATIONSHIP BETWEEN THERAPIST AND CLIENT

The client's relationship with the analyst is conceptualized in the transference process, which is the core of the psychoanalytic approach. Transference is the client's unconscious shifting to the analyst of feelings and fantasies that are reactions to significant others in the client's past. Transference allows clients to understand and resolve "unfinished business" from these past relationships. The treatment process involves their reconstruction and reliving of the past. As therapy progresses, childhood feelings and conflicts begin to surface from the depths of the unconscious. Clients regress emotionally. Some of their feelings arise from conflicts such as trust versus mistrust, love versus hate, dependence versus independence, and autonomy versus shame and guilt. Transference takes place when clients resurrect from their early years intense conflicts relating to love, sexuality, hostility, anxiety, and resentment; bring them into the present; reexperience them; and attach them to the analyst. For example, clients may transfer unresolved feelings toward a stern and unloving father to the analyst, who, in their eyes, becomes stern and unloving. Hostile feelings are the product of negative transference, but clients may also develop a positive transference and, for example, fall in love with the analyst, wish to be adopted, or in many other ways seek the love, acceptance, and approval of an all-powerful therapist. In short, the analyst becomes a current substitute for significant others.

If therapy is to produce change, the transference relationship must be worked through. The *working-through* process consists of an exploration of unconscious material and defenses, most of which originated in early childhood. Working through is achieved by repeating interpretations and by exploring forms of resistance. It results in a resolution of old patterns and allows clients to make new choices. In the process of working through there is a constant going back to the raw data of the session in an attempt to gain new understandings of present experience. Clients have many opportunities to see the variety of ways in which their core conflicts and core defenses are manifested in their daily life. It is assumed that for clients to become psychologically independent, they must not only become aware of this unconscious material but also achieve some level of freedom from behavior motivated by infantile strivings, such as the need for total love and acceptance from parental figures. If this demanding phase of the therapeutic relationship is not properly worked through, clients simply transfer their infantile wishes for universal love and acceptance to other figures they deem powerful. It is precisely in the client/therapist relationship that the manifestation of these childhood motivations becomes apparent. Because the transference relationship takes time to build in intensity and additional time to understand and resolve, working through requires a lengthy period in the total therapeutic process.

Among modern psychoanalytic writers there is agreement that reconstructive therapy is a lengthy process, ranging from three to five years or more. There is also widespread awareness that short-term individual and group techniques (such as crisis and supportive interventions) can be of therapeutic value. These strategies have been found to be effective with clients with borderline personality disorders (Hedges, 1983). Such briefer therapy strategies aim at increasing self-awareness and strengthening an individual's adaptive or coping skills.

With respect to therapy with the narcissistic client, the focus is on the development of mirror and idealizing transferences to the therapist. Narcissistic disorders improve as the therapist repeatedly acknowledges ways in which the client has been emotionally wounded in the past as well as the client's present disappointments in relationship to the therapist. Therapy is seen as a process in which clients learn to provide themselves with reassurance, rather than seeking confirmation from others in the environment. The focus is on improving self-esteem and repairing original psychological wounds received at an early age (Kohut, 1971, 1977, 1984). Thus, with narcissistic personalities the course of therapy consists of establishing an emotional bond with the therapist. Earlier symbiotic relationships now become emotionally *replicated* with the therapist. As this replication of past emotional experiences occurs, a separation/individuation process begins in relation to the therapist. Through this therapeutic relationship, the client experiences changes.

It must be emphasized, however, that all traces of our childhood needs and traumas will never be completely erased. Thus, our infantile conflicts may not be fully resolved, even though many aspects of transference are worked through with a therapist. We may need to struggle at times throughout our life with feelings that we project onto others as well as with unrealistic demands that we expect others to fulfill. In this sense we experience transference with many people, and our past is always a vital part of the person whom we are presently becoming.

This notion of never becoming completely free of past experiences has significant implications for therapists who become intimately involved in the unresolved conflicts of their clients. This intense relationship is bound to ignite some of the unconscious conflicts within therapists. Even if these conflicts have surfaced to awareness, and even if the therapists have dealt with these personal issues in their own intensive therapy, they may still project distortions onto clients. *Countertransference* refers to the reactions therapists have toward their clients that may interfere with their objectivity. For example, a client may become excessively dependent on his therapist. He may look to her to direct him and tell him how to live, and he may look to her for the love and acceptance that he felt he was unable to secure from his mother. The therapist herself may have unresolved needs to nurture, to foster a dependent relationship, and to be told that she is significant, and she may be meeting her own needs by in some way making her client infantile. Unless she is aware of her own needs as well as her own dynamics, it is very likely that her dynamics will interfere with the progress of therapy.

Therapists are expected to develop some level of objectivity and not to react irrationally and subjectively in the face of anger, love, adulation, criticism, and other intense feelings of their clients. Most psychoanalytic training programs require that trainees undergo their own extensive analysis as a client. If analysts become aware of symptoms (such as strong aversion to certain types of clients, strong attraction to other types of clients, developing psychosomatic reactions at definite times in therapeutic relationships, and the like) it behooves them to seek professional consultation or enter their own therapy for a time to work out unresolved personal issues that stand in the way of their being effective therapists.

It is a mistake to assume that all feelings that clients have toward their therapists are manifestations of transference. Many of these reactions may have a reality base, and clients' feelings may well be directed to the here-and-now style that the therapist exhibits. On the one hand, every positive response (such as liking of the therapist) should not be labeled "positive transference." On the other hand, a client's anger toward the therapist may be a function of the therapist's behavior; it is a mistake to label all negative reactions as signs of "negative transference." Likewise, therapists have feelings toward their clients, and they do not react uniformly to all clients. So it is not precise to contend that all positive and negative feelings of therapists toward their clients are merely countertransference. Countertransference is the phenomenon that occurs when there is an inappropriate affect, when therapists respond in irrational ways, or when they lose their objectivity in a relationship because their own conflicts are triggered—specifically, when they relate to the client as if this person were mother, father, or lover.

Searles (1979) suggests that there can be some positive outcomes to countertransference. A growing number of psychoanalysts are maintaining that countertransference reactions can provide an important means for understanding the world of the client. The analyst who notes a countertransference mood of irritability, for instance, may learn something about a client's pattern of being demanding. In this light countertransference can be seen as potentially useful, if it is explored in analysis. As the focus on the analytic process moves into material that is rooted in what Mahler calls symbiosis, issues emerge that deal with the early mother/infant partnership. Like this early relationship, the therapist/client relationship requires an especially high degree of emotional attunement. Viewed in this more positive way, countertransference becomes a key means of potentially helping the client. For a more detailed discussion of countertransference, see Searles (1979), who has done pioneering work in this area.

It should be clear that the client/therapist relationship is of vital importance in psychoanalytic therapy. As a result of this relationship, particularly in working through the transference situation, clients acquire insights into their own unconscious psychodynamics. Awareness of and insights into repressed material are the bases of the analytic growth process. Clients are able to understand the association between their past experiences and their current behavior and character structure. The psychoanalytic approach assumes that without this dynamic self-understanding there can be no substantial personality change or resolution of present conflicts.

# Application: Therapeutic Techniques and Procedures

This section deals with the techniques most commonly used by psychoanalytically oriented therapists. Some features of psychoanalytic therapy (as opposed to traditional psychoanalysis) are:

- The therapy is geared more to limited objectives than to restructuring of one's personality.
- The therapist is less likely to use the couch.
- There are probably fewer sessions.
- There is more frequent use of supportive interventions—such as reassurance, expressions of empathy and support, and suggestions—and of self-disclosure by the therapist.

- There is more focus on pressing practical issues than on working with fantasy material.

The techniques of psychoanalytic therapy are aimed at increasing awareness, fostering insights into the client's behavior, and understanding the meanings of symptoms. The therapy proceeds from the client's talk to catharsis to insight to working through unconscious material. This work is done to attain the goals of intellectual and emotional understanding and reeducation, which, it is hoped, lead to personality change. The six basic techniques of psychoanalytic therapy are (1) maintaining the analytic framework, (2) free association, (3) interpretation, (4) dream analysis, (5) analysis of resistance, and (6) analysis of transference.

## MAINTAINING THE ANALYTIC FRAMEWORK

The psychoanalytic process stresses maintaining a particular framework aimed at accomplishing the goals of this type of therapy. "Maintaining the analytic framework" refers to a whole range of procedural and stylistic factors, such as the analyst's relative anonymity, the regularity and consistency of meetings, and starting and ending the sessions on time. One of the most powerful features of psychoanalytically oriented therapy is that the consistent framework is itself a therapeutic factor, comparable on an emotional level to the regular feeding of an infant. Analysts attempt to minimize departures from this consistent pattern (such as vacations, changes in fees, or changes in the meeting environment).

## FREE ASSOCIATION

Free association plays a central role in the process of maintaining the analytic framework. At the initial phase the analyst will explain the fundamental rule of psychoanalysis, which involves clients' saying whatever comes to mind, regardless of how painful, silly, trivial, illogical, or irrelevant it may be. Such *free association* is the central technique in psychoanalytic therapy. In essence, clients flow with any feelings or thoughts by reporting them immediately without censorship. As the analytic work progresses, most clients will occasionally depart from adhering to this basic rule, and these resistances will be interpreted by the therapist when it is timely to do so. In classical psychoanalysis clients typically lie on the couch while the analyst sits behind them so as not to distract them during the free flow of associations; in psychoanalytic therapy the couch is less regularly part of the usual procedure.

Free association is one of the basic tools used to open the doors to unconscious wishes, fantasies, conflicts, and motivations. This technique often leads to some recollection of past experiences and, at times, a releasing of intense feelings that have been blocked off. This release is not seen as crucial in itself, however. During the free-association process the therapist's task is to identify the repressed material that is locked in the unconscious. The sequence of associations guides the therapist in understanding the connections that clients make among events. Blockings or disruptions in associations serve as cues to anxiety-arousing material. The therapist interprets the material to clients, guiding them toward increased insight into the underlying dynamics.

As analytic therapists listen to their clients' free associations, they hear not only the surface content but also the hidden meaning. This awareness of the language of the unconscious has been termed "listening with the third ear" (Reik, 1948). Nothing the client says is taken at face value. For example, a slip of the tongue can suggest that an expressed affect is accompanied by a conflicting affect. Areas that clients do not talk about are as significant as the areas they do discuss. Although psychoanalytic theory offers guidelines, the individual client must determine the actual meanings of specific content through associations.

## INTERPRETATION

Interpretation consists of the analyst's pointing out, explaining, and even teaching the client the meanings of behavior that is manifested in dreams, free association, resistances, and the therapeutic relationship itself. The functions of interpretations are to allow the ego to assimilate new material and to speed up the process of uncovering further unconscious material.

Interpretation is grounded in the therapist's assessment of the client's personality and of what factors in the client's past contributed to his or her difficulties. Under contemporary definitions interpretation includes identifying, clarifying, and translating the client's material.

In making an appropriate interpretation, the therapist must be guided by a sense of the client's readiness to consider it (Saretsky, 1978). The therapist uses the client's reactions as a gauge. It is important that interpretations be well timed, because clients will reject ones that are inappropriately timed. A general rule is that interpretation should be presented when the phenomenon to be interpreted is close to conscious awareness. In other words the analyst should interpret material that clients have not yet seen for themselves but are capable of tolerating and incorporating as their own. Another general rule is that interpretation should always start from the surface and go only as deep as clients are able to go. A third general rule is that it is best to point out a resistance or defense before interpreting the emotion or conflict that lies beneath it.

## DREAM ANALYSIS

Dream analysis is an important procedure for uncovering unconscious material and giving the client insight into some areas of unresolved problems. During sleep, defenses are lowered, and repressed feelings surface. Freud sees dreams as the "royal road to the unconscious," for in them one's unconscious wishes, needs, and fears are expressed. Some motivations are so unacceptable to the person that they are expressed in disguised or symbolic form rather than being revealed directly.

Dreams have two levels of content: the latent content and the manifest content. The *latent content* consists of hidden, symbolic, and unconscious motives, wishes, and fears. Because they are so painful and threatening, the unconscious sexual and aggressive impulses that make up the latent content are transformed into the more acceptable *manifest content,* which is the dream as it appears to the dreamer. The process by which the latent content of a dream is transformed into the less threatening manifest content is called *dream work.* The therapist's task is to uncover disguised meanings by studying the symbols in the manifest content of the dream. During the session the therapist may ask clients to free-associate to some aspect of the manifest content of a dream for the purpose of uncovering the latent meanings. Therapists participate in the process by exploring the clients' associations with them. Interpreting the meanings of the dream elements helps clients unlock the repression that has kept the material from consciousness and relate the new insight to their present struggles. Rather than simply serving as a pathway to repressed material, dreams can also provide an understanding of the client's current functioning.

## ANALYSIS AND INTERPRETATION OF RESISTANCE

Resistance, a concept fundamental to the practice of psychoanalysis, is anything that works against the progress of therapy and prevents the client from producing previously unconscious material. Specifically, in analytic therapy resistance is the client's reluctance to bring to the surface of awareness unconscious material that has been repressed. Resistance refers to any idea, attitude, feeling, or action (conscious or unconscious) that fosters the status quo and gets in the way of change. During free association or association to dreams, the client may evidence an unwillingness to relate certain thoughts, feelings, and experiences. Freud views resistance as an unconscious dynamic that people use to defend against the intolerable anxiety and pain that would arise if they were to become aware of their repressed impulses and feelings.

As a defense against anxiety, resistance operates specifically in psychoanalytic therapy to prevent the client and therapist from succeeding in their joint effort to gain insights into the dynamics of the unconscious. Because resistance blocks threatening material from entering awareness, the analytic therapist points it out, and clients must confront it if they hope to deal with conflicts realistically. The therapist's interpretation is aimed at helping clients become aware of the reasons for the resistance so that they can deal with them. As a general rule, the therapist points out and interprets the most obvious resistances in order to lessen the possibility of clients' rejecting the interpretation and to increase the chance that they will begin to look at their resistive behavior.

Resistances are not just something to be overcome. Because they are representative of usual defensive approaches in daily life, they need to be recognized as devices that defend against anxiety but that interfere with the ability to accept change that could lead to experiencing a more gratifying life. It is extremely important that therapists respect the resistances of clients and assist them in working therapeutically with their defenses. If handled properly, resistance can be one of the most valuable tools in understanding the client.

# ANALYSIS AND INTERPRETATION OF TRANSFERENCE

As was mentioned earlier, transference manifests itself in the therapeutic process at the point where clients' earlier relationships contribute to their distorting the present with the therapist. It makes sense that clients often react to their therapist as they did to a significant person. The transference situation is considered valuable because its manifestations provide clients with the opportunity to reexperience a variety of feelings that would otherwise be inaccessible. Through the relationship with the therapist, clients express feelings, beliefs, and desires that they have buried in their unconscious. Through appropriate interpretations and working through of these current expressions of early feelings, clients are able to change some of their long-standing patterns of behavior.

The analysis of transference is a central technique in psychoanalysis and psychoanalytically oriented therapy, for it allows clients to achieve here-and-now insight into the influence of the past on their present functioning. Interpretation of the transference relationship enables clients to work through old conflicts that are keeping them fixated and retarding their emotional growth. In essence, the effects of early relationships are counteracted by working through a similar emotional conflict in the therapeutic relationship.

These remarks about basic techniques can be brought together by a brief illustration. A client enters the office, saying to the therapist: "Sorry, I forgot my checkbook again. I'll get you next week." He lies down and starts in with, "Well, I had a dream, but I don't think there's much to learn from it. All I remember was that there was some elderly woman who got run over by a bus, and I couldn't decide whether I wanted to help her." He says that he does not have any ideas about the dream. As the session progresses, this client talks about how he is going to need to miss the next few sessions, because he wants to go out of town for a few days on a spur-of-the-moment vacation. Later, he mentions how much he enjoyed watching the football game the night before. The home team soundly defeated the opposition, whom he describes as "a bunch of old ladies."

The therapist notes at the outset of the session that she feels a bit of irritation at this client's habit of "forgetting" to pay regularly. She then notes her surprise at the rather sudden announcement that the next sessions are going to be missed. Prompted by her own associations rooted in her knowledge of this client's previous work on his feelings about his passive mother, she says, "I wonder whether there is anything going on between you and me that comes out in your forgetting your checkbook and then announcing that you won't be coming for a few days?" The client's subsequent remarks suggest that other matters have higher priority than bringing along his checkbook. "I just assumed it would be OK if I didn't pay you for a week or so." The analyst asks, "Were you hoping this old lady would be flattened by the bus?"

In this vignette the therapist made use of her own reactions as well as her knowledge of the client's past. Her interpretations highlighted the departures from the analytic framework, represented by irregularity in payment and attendance. She treated the dream as a reference to the transference, with the associations expressing ambivalence about the weakness and passivity that the client attributes to his mother and his therapist.

## PSYCHOANALYTIC THERAPY APPLIED TO THE CASE OF STAN

In each of the chapters in Part Two, the case of Stan is used to demonstrate the practical applications of the theory in question. In order to give you a focus on Stan's central concerns, refer to the end of Chapter 1, where his biography is given. I also recommend that you at least skim Chapter 14, which deals with an integrative approach as applied to Stan.

In Chapters 4–11, you will notice that Stan is working with a female therapist. Given his feelings toward women, it may seem odd that he selected a woman for his therapist. However, knowing that he had difficulty with women, he deliberately made this choice as a way to challenge himself, both in his therapy and in his everyday life. As you will see, one of his goals is to learn how to become less intimidated in the presence of women and to be more himself around them.

The psychoanalytic approach focuses on the unconscious psychodynamics of Stan's behavior. Considerable attention is given to material that he has repressed, such as his anxiety related to the threatened breakthrough of his sexual and aggressive impulses. In the past he had to rigidly control both these impulses, and when he did not, he got into trouble. He also developed a strong superego by introjecting parental values and standards and making them his own. These aspirations were unrealistic, for they were perfectionistic goals. He could be loved only if he became perfect; yet no matter what he attempted, it never seemed adequate. He internalized his anger and guilt, which became depression. At the extreme he demonstrated a self-destructive tendency, which is a way of inflicting punishment on himself. Instead of directing his hostility toward his parents and siblings, he turned it inward toward himself. Stan's preoccupation with drinking could be hypothesized as evidence of an oral fixation. Because he never received love and acceptance during his early childhood, he is still suffering from this deprivation and still desperately searching for approval and acceptance from others. Stan's sex-role identification was fraught with difficulties. He learned the basis of female/male relationships through his early experiences with his parents. What he saw was fighting, bickering, and discounting. His father was the weak one who always lost, and his mother was the strong, domineering force who could and did hurt men. He identified with his weak and impotent father; he generalized his fear of his mother to all women. It could be further hypothesized that he married a woman who was similar to his mother and who reinforced his feelings of impotence in her presence.

The opportunity to develop a transference relationship and work through it is the core of the therapy process. An assumption is that Stan will eventually relate to his therapist as he did to his mother and that the process will be a valuable means of gaining insight into the origin of his difficulties with women. The analytic process stresses an intensive exploration of his past. The goal is to make the unconscious conscious, so that he will no longer be determined by unconscious forces. He devotes much therapy time to reliving and exploring his early past. As he talks, he gains increased understanding of the dynamics of his behavior. He begins to see connections between his present problems and early experiences in his childhood. Thus, he explores memories of relationships with his siblings and with his mother and father and also explores how he has generalized his view of women and men from his view of these family members. It is expected that he will reexperience old feelings and uncover buried feelings related to traumatic events. Some questions for Stan could include "What did you do when you felt unloved? What did you have to do as a child with your negative feelings? Could you express your rage, hostility, hurt, and fears? What effects did your relationship with your mother have on you? What did this teach you about all women?"

The analytic process focuses on key influences in Stan's developmental years. As he comes to understood how he has been shaped by these past experiences, he is increasingly able to exert control over his present functioning. Many of his fears become conscious, and then his energy does not have to remain fixed on defending himself from unconscious feelings. Instead, he can make new decisions about his current life. He can do this only if he works through the transference relationship, however, for the depth of his endeavors in therapy largely determines the depth and extent of his personality changes.

If the therapist is operating from a contemporary psychoanalytic orientation, her focus will be on Stan's developmental sequences. Particular attention is paid to understanding his current behavior in the world as largely a repetition of one of his earlier developmental phases. Because of his dependency it is useful in understanding his behavior to see that he is now repeating patterns that he formed with his mother during his infancy. Viewed from this perspective, he has not accomplished the task of separation and individuation. He is still "stuck" in the symbiotic phase on some levels, he is unable to obtain his confirmation of worth from himself, and he has not resolved the dependence/independence struggle. Looking at his behavior from the viewpoint of self psychology can help the therapist deal with his difficulties in forming intimate relationships.

FOLLOW-UP: YOU CONTINUE AS STAN'S PSYCHOANALYTIC THERAPIST.    With each of the nine theoretical orientations, you will be encouraged to try your hand at applying the principles and techniques that you have just studied in the chapter to working with Stan from that particular perspective. The information presented about Stan from each of these theory chapters will provide you with some ideas of how you might continue working with him if he were referred to you. Do your best to stay within the general spirit of each theory by identifying specific concepts you would draw from and techniques that you might use in helping him explore the struggles that he identifies. To guide you in this follow-up process, a series of questions provides some structure in thinking about his case:

- How much interest would you have in Stan's early childhood? What are some ways you'd help him see patterns between his childhood issues and his current problems?

- Consider the transference relationship that is likely to be established between you and Stan. How might you react to his making you into a significant person in his life?
- In working with Stan, what countertransference issues might arise for you?
- What resistances might you predict in your work with Stan? From a psychoanalytic perspective, how would you interpret this resistance? What might it be like for you to encounter his resistance?

# Summary and Evaluation

## SUMMARY

The major concepts of Freudian psychoanalytic theory include the struggle between the life and death instincts at the heart of human nature; the tripartite structure of personality, with its systems of the id, the ego, and the superego; the dynamics of the unconscious and its influence on behavior; the role of anxiety; and the development of personality at various life periods, including the oral, anal, phallic, latency, and genital stages.

Building on many of Freud's basic ideas, Erikson broadened the developmental perspective by including psychosocial trends. In his model, each of the eight stages of human development is characterized by a crisis, or turning point. We can either master the developmental task or fail to resolve the core struggle. These eight stages of the life span are infancy, early childhood, preschool age, school age, adolescence, young adulthood, middle age, and later life. (As a succinct review of these developmental turning points, Table 4-1 compares Freud's and Erikson's views of growth and development.)

Unlike Freudian theory, Jungian theory is not reductionistic. Jung views humans positively and focuses on individuation, the capacity of humans to move toward wholeness and self-realization. To become what they are capable of becoming, individuals must explore the unconscious aspects of their personality, both the personal unconscious and the collective unconscious. In Jungian analytical therapy, the therapist assists the client in tapping his or her inner wisdom. The goal of therapy is not merely the resolution of immediate problems but the transformation of personality.

The contemporary trend in psychoanalytic theory is reflected in self psychology and object-relations theory. These approaches are based on the notion that at birth there is no differentiation between others and self and that others represent objects of need gratification for the infant. Through the process of attachment, the child enters the second stage of normal symbiosis, during which there is still a lack of clarity between what is self and what is object. In the third stage children begin to draw away from this symbiosis and individuate, differentiating themselves as separate from the parents to whom they are attached. The fourth stage is one of integration. Others are perceived as both separate and related. In normal development children are able to relate to their parents without fearing a loss of their sense of autonomy.

Psychoanalytic therapy consists largely of using methods to bring out unconscious material that can be worked through. It focuses primarily on childhood experiences, which are discussed, reconstructed, interpreted, and analyzed. The assumption is that this exploration of the past, which is typically accomplished by working through the transference relationship with the therapist, is necessary for character change. The most important techniques typically employed in psychoanalytic practice are maintaining the analytic framework, free association, interpretation, dream analysis, analysis of resistance, and analysis of transference.

## CONTRIBUTIONS OF THE PSYCHOANALYTIC APPROACH

I believe that counselors can broaden their understanding of clients' struggles by appreciating Freud's many significant contributions. It must be emphasized that competent use of psychoanalytic techniques requires training beyond the scope of most counselors. Regardless of their theoretical orientation, however, it is well for counselors to be trained so that they will understand such psychoanalytic phenomena as transference, countertransference, resistance, and the use of ego-defense mechanisms as reactions to anxiety. The psychoanalytic approach provides counselors with a conceptual framework for looking at behavior and for understanding the origins and functions of symptoms. If counselors ignore the early history of the client, they are limiting their vision of the causes of the client's present suffering and the nature of the client's present functioning. Although there is little to be gained from blaming the past for the way a person is now or from dwelling on the past, it is very useful to understand and work with the past as it pertains to the client's current situation.

For therapeutic practice the psychoanalytic point of view is particularly useful in (1) understanding resistances that take the form of canceling appointments, fleeing from therapy prematurely, and refusing to look at oneself; (2) understanding that unfinished business can be worked through, so that clients can provide a new ending to some of the events that have crippled them emotionally; (3) understanding the value and role of transference; and (4) understanding how the overuse of ego defenses, both in the counseling relationship and in daily life, can keep clients from functioning effectively.

My teaching experience has demonstrated that students sometimes have a difficult time understanding and accepting some of the Freudian notions about the stages of development. The Oedipus complex, penis envy, castration anxiety, incestuous feelings, and connections between past situations and current character may seem rather obscure on initial presentation. I recall that I had many doubts about the validity of these concepts when I first studied them in my undergraduate days. However, my professional work has given me a wider perspective on the Freudian view of psychosexual development. It is essential to keep in mind that this view must be understood from the vantage point of the time in which Freud wrote, during the Victorian era of the authoritarian father. Much of what he described makes sense when it is seen in historical and cultural perspective.

The psychoanalytic approach provides a framework for a dynamic understanding of the role of early childhood events and the impact of these experiences on the contemporary struggles faced by clients. Without completely accepting the orthodox Freudian position, we can still draw on many of these analytic concepts as a framework for understanding clients and for helping them achieve a deeper understanding of the roots of their conflicts.

If the psychoanalytic approach is considered in a broader context than its initial Freudian perspective, it becomes a more powerful model for understanding human behavior. Although I find Freud's *psychosexual* concepts of great value, I think that adding Erikson's stress on *psychosocial* factors gives a more complete picture of the critical turning points at each stage of development. Integrating these two perspectives is, in my view, most useful for understanding key themes in the development of personality. Erikson's developmental schema does not avoid the psychosexual issues and stages postulated by Freud; rather, Erikson extended the stages of psychosexual development throughout life. His perspective integrates psychosexual and psychosocial concepts without diminishing the import of either.

Sociocultural factors provide practitioners with a framework for understanding the major tasks and crises of each stage of development. According to Hamachek (1988), the principal strength of psychosocial theory is that it acknowledges that humans are biological, psychological, and social beings and that an interactive mix of these inner and outer forces shapes humans. The key needs and developmental tasks, along with the challenges inherent at each stage of life, provide a model for understanding some of the core conflicts that clients explore in their therapy sessions. This approach gives special weight to childhood and adolescent factors that are significant in later stages of development while recognizing that the later stages also have their significant crises. Themes and threads can be found running through a client's life.

CONTRIBUTIONS OF RECENT THEORISTS.    The contemporary trends in psychoanalytic thinking have contributed to the understanding of how our current behavior in the world is largely a repetition of patterns set during one of the early phases of development. Object-relations theory helps us see the ways in which clients interacted with significant others in the past and how they are superimposing these early experiences on present relationships. For the many clients in therapy who are struggling with issues such as separation and individuation, intimacy, dependence versus independence, and identity, these newer formulations can provide a framework for understanding how and where aspects of development have been fixated. They have significant implications for many areas of human interaction such as intimate relationships, the family and child rearing, and the therapeutic relationship.

In my opinion it is possible to have an analytic framework that gives structure and direction to a counseling practice and at the same time to draw on other therapeutic techniques. I find value in the contributions of those writers who have built on the basic ideas of Freud and have added an emphasis on the social forces affecting personality development. In contemporary psychoanalytic practice more latitude is given to the therapist in using techniques and in developing the therapeutic relationship. The newer psychoanalytic theorists have enhanced, extended, and refocused classical analytic techniques. They are concentrating on the development of the ego and are paying attention to the social factors that influence the differentiation of an individual from others.

In a critique of long-term psychodynamic therapy, Strupp (1992) assumes that this approach will remain a luxury for most people in our society. But he contends that the various modifications of psychoanalysis "have infused psychodynamic psychotherapy with renewed vitality and vigor." Recognizing that most practitioners have been influenced by an eclectic spirit, he predicts the following outlook for psychodynamic practice: "This movement reflects a decisive departure from orthodoxy, together with much greater openness by most therapists to adapt to changing circumstances and to tailor techniques to the changing needs of patients as well as to the demands of our multifaceted society" (p. 25). He suggests that this approach will undergo further revisions and that it will maintain its prominence in individual, group, marital, and family therapy. Although contemporary psychodynamic forms diverge considerably in many respects from the original Freudian emphasis on drives, his basic concepts of unconscious motivation, the influence of early development, transference, countertransference, and resistance are still central to the newer modifications. Strupp notes a decline in practices based on the classical analytic model due to reasons such as time commitment, expense, limited applications to diverse client populations, and questionable benefits. He acknowledges that the realities stemming from *managed care* will mean increasing emphasis on short-term treatments for specific disorders, limited goals, and containment of costs. Some of the current trends and directions in psychodynamic theory and practice that Strupp identifies are summarized below:

- The emphasis on treatment has shifted from the "classical" interest in curing neurotic disorders to the problems of dealing therapeutically with chronic personality disorders, borderline conditions, and narcissistic personality disorders. There is also a movement toward devising specific treatments for specific disorders.
- Increased attention is being paid to establishing a good therapeutic alliance early in therapy. A collaborative working relationship is now viewed as a key factor in a positive therapeutic outcome.
- There is a renewed interest in the development of briefer forms of psychodynamic therapy, largely due to societal pressures for accountability and cost-effectiveness. The indications are that time-limited therapy will be used more in the future.
- Psychodynamic group therapy is becoming more popular. It has received widespread acceptance for a number of reasons: It is more economical, it provides clients with opportunities to learn how they function in groups, and it offers a unique perspective on understanding problems and working them through therapeutically.

In basic agreement with Strupp is Marmor (1989), who believes that the psychoanalytic orientation will move toward the development of short-term techniques: "Only the short-term approaches provide a reasonable hope for

dealing economically and effectively with the deluge of emotional and
problems that our complicated society seems to be spawning in ever
numbers" (p. 257).

CONTRIBUTIONS TO MULTICULTURAL COUNSELING. Psychoanalytically oriented therapy, if modified to include short-term strategies, can be appropriate
for culturally diverse populations. Comas-Diaz and Minrath (1985) recommend
that the diffused sense of identity prevalent among borderline clients from ethnic
minorities be examined from both a sociocultural and a developmental perspective. One aid to helping clients rebuild their identity is to emphasize strengths
rather than deficiencies among ethnically different groups. Racial and ethnic
minorities have to simultaneously develop two sets of identity: a general overall
ego identity as well as a cultural identity. In this sense, minority youths have
a more complex adolescent experience because of this dual identity. Erikson's
psychosocial approach, with his emphasis on critical issues in stages of development, has particular application to people of color. Counselors can help these
clients review environmental situations at the various critical turning points in
their lives to determine how certain events have affected them either positively
or negatively.

Psychotherapists need to recognize and confront their own potential sources
of bias. Countertransference may involve prejudices that are conveyed uninten-
tionally through the therapist's interventions (Julia Yang, personal communication, June 14, 1993). To the credit of the psychoanalytic approach, it stresses
the value of intensive psychotherapy as part of the training of therapists, which
helps them become aware of their own sources of countertransference.

## LIMITATIONS AND CRITICISMS
## OF THE PSYCHOANALYTIC APPROACH

What are the limitations of the psychoanalytic approach as a view of human
nature, as a model for understanding behavior, and as a method of therapy? How
applicable is this approach to counseling in a mental-health clinic? in a school?
in other public and private human-services agencies? In general, considering
factors such as time, expense, and availability of trained psychoanalytic therapists,
I think the practical applications of many analytic techniques are limited. This
is especially true of methods such as free association on the couch, dream
analysis, and analysis of the transference relationship. A major limitation of
psychoanalysis as a practical technique is that many severely disturbed clients
lack the level of ego strength needed for this treatment.

In fairness, some psychoanalytic therapists have developed modifications
of techniques that allow for treating of clients with limited ego strength. Severely
disturbed people, including those with psychoses, may be amenable to variations of psychoanalytic approaches.

A notion that I find limiting is the anonymous role of the therapist. Although
the analyst's anonymity can be justified on theoretical grounds, I think that in

therapy situations other than classical psychoanalysis this stance is unduly restrictive. The classical technique of nondisclosure can be misused in short-term individual therapy and assessment. Therapists in these situaitons who adopt the blank-screen aloofness that is called for theoretically only in the "pure" context of classical psychoanalysis may actually be keeping themselves hidden as persons in the guise of "being professional." Whereas the analyst who practices classical analysis is intentionally frustrating the client's relationship needs in the service of inducing regression and a transference neurosis, the nonclassical psychoanalytical practitioner has more freedom to interact with clients. The variation in technique results from different intents rather than from different styles.

From a feminist perspective, there are distinct limitations to a number of Freudian concepts, especially the Oedipus and Electra complexes. In her review of feminist counseling and therapy, Enns (1993) also notes that the object-relations approach has been criticized for its emphasis on the role of the mother/child relationship in determining later interpersonal functioning. The approach gives great responsibility to mothers for deficiencies and distortions in development. Whereas fathers are conspicuously absent from the hypothesis about patterns of early development, mothers are blamed for inadequate parenting. Enns indicates that some feminist therapists have addressed the limitations of psychoanalysis by incorporating family systems work within their psychoanalytic model.

LIMITATIONS FOR MULTICULTURAL COUNSELING.    One practical limitation of conducting traditional psychoanalysis in multicultural situations is that most clients do not want or cannot afford to devote five years to intensive treatment. Few people have the motivation, time, and money for a therapy that involves this degree of commitment. Psychoanalytic therapy is generally perceived as being based on upper- and middle-class values. Another limitation pertains to the ambiguity inherent in most psychoanalytic approaches. This can be problematic for ethnic minority clients, particularly many Asian Americans, who may prefer a more structured and problem-oriented approach to counseling.

Another difficulty is that intrapsychic analysis may be in direct conflict with some clients' social framework and environmental perspective. Atkinson, Thompson, and Grant (1993) underscore the need for therapists to consider possible external sources of a client's problems, especially if they have experienced an oppressive environment. If there is no balance between the external and internal perspectives, clients will be blamed for their condition. The concerns that many clients bring to therapy often center on environmental issues related to survival and security. Many individuals are not inclined to see value in a long-term process of personality restructuring. Many clients are concerned about dealing with a crisis situation and with finding answers, or at least some direction, in addressing survival needs pertaining to housing, employment, and child care. They tend to want help in getting information and finding resources to solve immediate and pressing problems, rather than major restructuring of their personality. This does not imply that ethnic-minority clients are unable to profit from analytic therapy but, rather, that this particular orientation could be more beneficial *after* more pressing issues and concerns have been resolved. A systems perspective, including the role of the family, one's network of friends and extended family, and social and environmental factors, may be more often suitable for the concerns that many clients bring to therapy.

# Where to Go from Here

If this chapter has provided the impetus for you to learn more about the psychoanalytic approach or the contemporary offshoots of psychoanalysis, select a few books from the Recommended Supplementary Readings and References and Suggested Readings. Various colleges and universities offer special workshops or short courses through continuing education on topics such as therapeutic considerations in working with borderline and narcissistic personalities. Such workshops could give you a new perspective on the range of applications of contemporary psychoanalytic therapy. An organization to contact for further information about training programs, workshops, and graduate programs in various states is:

> American Psychoanalytic Association
> 309 East 49th Street
> New York, NY 10017

This organization has a code of ethics, revised in 1983, that deals with many aspects of the practice of psychoanalytic therapy.

## *Recommended Supplementary Readings*

If you are interested in expanding your knowledge of the Freudian approach, a good place to begin is *A Primer of Freudian Psychology* (Hall, 1954), a concise overview. The next step would be to consult *An Elementary Textbook of Psychoanalysis* (Brenner, 1974), an excellent orientation text for those who want to acquaint themselves with psychoanalytic theory. Chapter topics include basic hypotheses, drives, the psychic apparatus, dreams, psychopathology, and conflict.

   I highly recommend two textbooks, with identical titles. *Theories of Personality* (Schultz & Schultz, 1994) is a concise overview of the major personality theories; it would be a good place to begin. Theories are clearly presented, as well as techniques of inquiry and therapeutic implications. *Theories of Personality* (Hall & Lindzey, 1978) is an advanced treatment of the major contemporary theories. The chapter on Jung's analytic theory is excellent. This book is a superb resource.

## *References and Suggested Readings**

ATKINSON, D. R., THOMPSON, C. E., & GRANT, S. K. (1993). A three-dimensional model for counseling racial/ethnic minorities. *The Counseling Psychologist, 21*(2), 257–277.
BRENNER, C. (1974). *An elementary textbook of psychoanalysis* (Rev. ed.). Garden City, NY: Doubleday (Anchor).
CASEMENT, P. J. (1991). *Learning from the patient*. New York: Guilford Press.

*Books marked with an asterisk are recommended for further reading.

COMAS-DIAZ, L., & MINRATH, M. (1985). Psychotherapy with ethnic minority borderline clients. *Psychotherapy, 22*(25), 418–426.

COREY, G. (1995). *Theory and practice of group counseling* (4th ed.). Pacific Grove, CA: Brooks/Cole.

* COREY, G. (1996). *Case approach to counseling and psychotherapy* (4th ed.). Pacific Grove, CA: Brooks/Cole.

EAGLE, M. N., & WOLITZKY, D. L. (1992). Psychoanalytic theories of psychotherapy. In D. K. Freedheim (Ed.), *History of psychotherapy: A century of change* (pp. 109–158). Washington, DC: American Psychological Association.

ENNS, C. Z. (1993). Twenty years of feminist counseling and therapy: From naming biases to implementing multifaceted practice. *The Counseling Psychologist, 21*(1), 3–87.

* ERIKSON, E. H. (1963). *Childhood and society* (2nd ed.). New York: Norton.

FREUD, S. (1949). *An outline of psychoanalysis.* New York: Norton.

* FREUD, S. (1955). *The interpretation of dreams.* London: Hogarth Press.

FREUD, S. (1962). *Civilization and its discontents.* New York: Norton. (Original work published 1930.)

FROMM, E. (1980). *Greatness and limitations of Freud's thought.* New York: New American Library (Mentor).

GOLDMAN, G. D., & MILMAN, D. S. (1978). *Psychoanalytic psychotherapy.* Reading, MA: Addison-Wesley.

* GREENBERG, J. R., & MITCHELL, S. A. (1983). *Object relations in psychoanalytic theory.* Cambridge, MA: Harvard University Press.

HALL, C. (1954). *A primer of Freudian psychology.* New York: New American Library (Mentor).

* HALL, C., & LINDZEY, G. (1978). *Theories of personality* (3rd ed.). New York: Wiley.

HAMACHEK, D. F. (1988). Evaluating self-concept and ego development within Erikson's psychosocial framework: A formulation. *Journal of Counseling and Development, 66*(8), 354–360.

HEDGES, L. E. (1983). *Listening perspectives in psychotherapy.* New York: Aronson.

JUNG, C. G. (1961). *Memories, dreams, reflections.* New York: Vintage.

KAPLAN, L. (1978). *Oneness and separateness.* New York: Simon & Schuster.

* KERNBERG, O. F. (1975). *Borderline conditions and pathological narcissism.* New York: Aronson.

KERNBERG, O. F. (1976). *Object-relations theory and clinical psychoanalysis.* New York: Aronson.

KLEIN, M. (1975). *The psycho-analysis of children.* New York: Dell.

KOHUT, H. (1971). *The analysis of the self.* New York: International Universities Press.

KOHUT, H. (1977). *Restoration of the self.* New York: International Universities Press.

KOHUT, H. (1984). *How does psychoanalysis cure?* Chicago: University of Chicago Press.

KOVEL, J. (1976). *A complete guide to therapy.* New York: Pantheon.

KUTASH, I. L., & Greenberg, J. C. (1986). Psychoanalytic psychotherapy. In I. L. Kutash & A. Wolf (Eds.), *Psychotherapist's casebook.* San Francisco: Jossey-Bass.

LIFF, Z. A. (1992). Psychoanalysis and dynamic techniques. In D. K. Freedheim (Ed.), *History of psychotherapy: A century of change* (pp. 571–586). Washington, DC: American Psychological Association.

LINDER, R. (1955). *The fifty-minute hour.* New York: Bantam Books.

MAGNAVITA, J. J. (1993). The evolution of short-term dynamic psychotherapy: Treatment of the future? *Professional Psychology: Research and Practice, 24*(3), 360–365.

MAHLER, M. S. (1968). *On human symbiosis or the vicissitudes of individuation.* New York: International Universities Press.

MAHLER, M. S. (1971). A study of the separation and individuation process. In *The psychoanalytic study of the child: Vol. 26* (pp. 403–422). New York: Quadrangle.

* MALCOLM, J. (1981). *Psychoanalysis: The impossible profession*. New York: Random House (Vintage).

MARMOR, J. (1989). The future of dynamic psychotherapy. *International Journal of Short-Term Psychotherapy, 4*(4), 259–284.

* MASTERSON, J. F. (1976). *Psychotherapy of the borderline adult: A developmental approach*. New York: Brunner/Mazel.

* MASTERSON, J. F. (1982). *The narcissistic and borderline disorders: An integrated developmental approach*. New York: Brunner/Mazel.

MASTERSON, J. F. (1983). *Countertransference and psychotherapeutic technique*. New York: Brunner/Mazel.

MASTERSON, J. F. (1985). *The real self: A developmental, self, and object relations approach*. New York: Brunner/Mazel.

* MASTERSON, J. F. (1987). The evolution of the developmental object relations approach to psychotherapy. In J. K. Zeig (Ed.), *The evolution of psychotherapy* (pp. 236–242). New York: Brunner/Mazel.

* NYE, R. (1996). *Three psychologies: Perspectives from Freud, Skinner, and Rogers* (5th ed.). Pacific Grove, CA: Brooks/Cole.

REIK, T. (1948). *Listening with the third ear*. New York: Pyramid.

* ST. CLAIR, M. (1996). *Objects relations and self psychology: An introduction.*(2nd ed.) Pacific Grove, CA: Brooks/Cole.

SARETSKY, T. (1978). The middle phase of treatment. In G. D. Goldman & D. S. Milman (Eds.), *Psychoanalytic psychotherapy*. Reading, MA: Addison-Wesley.

* SCHULTZ, D., & SCHULTZ, S. E. (1994). *Theories of personality* (5th ed.). Pacific Grove, CA: Brooks/Cole.

* SEARLES, H. F. (1979). *Countertransference and related subjects. Selected papers*. New York: International Universities Press.

SINGER HARRIS, A. (1996). *Living with paradox: An introduction to Jungian psychology*. Pacific Grove, CA: Brooks/Cole.

STRUPP, H. H. (1992). The future of psychodynamic psychotherapy. *Psychotherapy, 29*(1), 21–27.

SULLIVAN, H. S. (1956). *The psychiatric interview*. New York: Norton.

* WOLBERG, L. R. (1987). The evolution of psychotherapy: Future trends. In J. K. Zeig (Ed.), *The evolution of psychotherapy* (pp. 250–259). New York: Brunner/Mazel.

CHAPTER FIVE

# Adlerian Therapy

# ALFRED ADLER

ALFRED ADLER (1870–1937) was the third child in a Vienna family of five boys and two girls. One of his brothers died as a young boy. Adler's early childhood was not a happy time, for he was sickly and very much aware of death. At 4 he almost died of pneumonia, and at that time he made a significant decision to become a doctor himself.

Because he was ill so much during the first few years of his life, Adler was pampered by his mother. Later he was "dethroned" by a younger brother. It appears that he developed a trusting relationship with his father and that he did not feel very close to his mother. He was jealous of his oldest brother, which led to strained relationships between the two during childhood and adolescence. His early years were characterized by struggling to overcome childhood weaknesses and feelings of inferiority. It is clear that these family experiences had an impact on the formation of his theory. Nevertheless, he is an example of a person who shaped his own life as opposed to being determined by his fate.

Adler was a poor student, and his teacher advised his father that he would be fit to be a shoemaker but not much else. With determined effort Adler eventually rose to the top of his class. He went on to study medicine at the University of Vienna, entered private practice as an ophthalmologist, and then shifted to general medicine. He eventually specialized in neurology and psychiatry, and he had a keen interest in incurable childhood diseases.

Adler had a passionate concern for the common person. He expressed his social interest by being outspoken on matters of child-rearing pratices, school reforms, and prejudices that resulted in conflict. He spoke and wrote in simple and nontechnical language so that the public could understand and apply the principles of his Individual Psychology. After serving in World War I as a medical officer, he created numerous child-guidance clinics in the Vienna public schools and began training teachers, social workers, physicians, and other professionals. He pioneered the practice of teaching professionals through live demonstrations with parents and children before large audiences. The clinics he founded grew in number and in popularity, and he was indefatigable in lecturing and demonstrating his work.

Adler lived by this overcrowded work schedule, yet he still took some time to sing, enjoy music, and be with friends. He ignored the warning of his friends to slow down. In the mid-1920s he began lecturing in the United States, and he later made frequent visits and tours. His packed schedule continued, and on May 28, 1937, while taking a walk before a scheduled lecture in Aberdeen, Scotland, he collapsed and died of heart failure.

# Introduction

Along with Freud and Jung, Adler was a major contributor to the development of the psychodynamic approach to therapy. After eight to ten years of collaboration, Freud and Adler parted company, with Freud taking the position that Adler was a heretic and had deserted him. Adler resigned as president of the Vienna Psychoanalytic Society in 1911 and founded the Society for Individual Psychology in 1912. Freud then asserted that it was not possible to support Adlerian concepts and still remain in good standing as a psychoanalyst.

Later, as we saw in Chapter 4, a number of other psychoanalysts deviated from Freud's orthodox position. These Freudian revisionists, who included Karen Horney, Erich Fromm, and Harry Stack Sullivan, agreed that social and cultural factors were of great significance in the shaping of personality. Even though these three therapists are typically called neo-Freudians, it would be more appropriate, as Heinz Ansbacher (1979) has suggested, to refer to them as neo-Adlerians, because they moved away from Freud's biological and deterministic point of view and toward Adler's social-psychological and teleological view of human nature.

Adler stresses the unity of personality, contending that people can be understood as integrated and complete beings. This view emphasizes the purposeful nature of behavior, maintaining that where we are striving to go is more important than where we have come from. Adler saw humans as both the creators and the creations of their own lives; that is, they develop a unique style of living that is both a movement toward and an expression of their selected goals. In this sense, we create ourselves rather than merely being shaped by our childhood experiences.

After Adler's death in 1937, Rudolf Dreikurs was the most significant figure in bringing Adlerian psychology to the United States, especially as its principles applied to education, individual and group therapy, and family counseling. Dreikurs is credited with giving impetus to the idea of child-guidance centers and to the training of professionals to work with a wide range of clients. More recently, Kurt Adler, Oscar Christensen, Raymond Corsini, Don Dinkmeyer, Bronia Grunwald, Ray Lowe, Harold Mosak, Bill and Mim Pew, Bob Powers, Bernard Shulman, Manford Sonstegard, and Frank Walton have contributed to translating Adler's and Dreikurs's principles into practical approaches in working with children, parents, teachers, and other human-services workers in the United States.*

# Key Concepts

## VIEW OF HUMAN NATURE

Adler abandoned Freud's basic theories because he believed that Freud was excessively narrow in his stress on biological and instinctual determination. Like Freud, Adler holds that what the individual becomes in adult life is largely

---

*I want to acknowledge the diligent efforts and contributions of James Bitter in bringing this chapter up to date.

influenced by the first six years of life, but Adler's focus is not simply on exploring past events. Rather, he is interested in the person's perception of the past
and how this interpretation of early events has a continuing influence. On many
theoretical grounds he was in opposition to Freud. According to Adler, for example, humans are motivated primarily by social urges rather than by sexual
urges. For him, behavior is purposeful and goal-directed. Consciousness, not
the unconscious, is the center of personality. Unlike Freud, Adler stresses choice
and responsibility, meaning in life, and the striving for success or perfection.

Adler's theory focuses on inferiority feelings, which he sees as a normal condition of all people and as a source of all human striving. Rather than being
considered as a sign of weakness or abnormality, feelings of inferiority can be
the wellspring of creativity. They motivate us to strive for mastery, success
(superiority), and even perfection. We are driven to overcome our sense of inferiority and strive for increasingly higher levels of development (Schultz &
Schultz, 1994). Indeed, at around 6 years of age, our fictional vision of ourselves
as perfect is formed into a life goal. The life goal unifies the personality and
becomes the source of human motivation; every striving and every effort to
overcome inferiority is now in line with this goal.

From the Adlerian perspective, humans are not merely determined by
heredity and environment. Instead, they have the capacity to interpret, influence,
and create events. Adler asserts that *what* we were born with is not the central
issue. What is crucial is what we *do* with the abilities we possess. Adlerians
recognize that biological and environmental conditions limit our capacity to
choose and to create. Although they reject the deterministic stance of Freud,
they do not go to the other extreme by maintaining that individuals can become
whatever they want.

Because their approach is grounded on a growth model, Adlerians put the
focus on reeducating individuals and reshaping society. Adler was the forerunner
of a subjective approach to psychology, which focuses on internal determinants
of behavior such as values, beliefs, attitudes, goals, interests, and the individual
perception of reality. He was a pioneer of an approach that is holistic, social,
goal-oriented, and humanistic.

## SUBJECTIVE PERCEPTION OF REALITY

Adlerians attempt to view the world from the client's subjective frame of reference, an orientation described as phenomenological. It is phenomenological
in that it pays attention to the individual way in which people perceive their
world. This "subjective reality" includes the individual's perceptions, thoughts,
feelings, values, beliefs, convictions, and conclusions. Behavior is understood
from the vantage point of this subjective perspective. How life is in reality is
less important than how the individual believes life to be.

As you will see in chapters that follow, many contemporary theories have
incorporated this notion of the client's subjective worldview as a basic factor
explaining behavior. Some of the other approaches that have a phenomenological
perspective are existential therapy, person-centered therapy, Gestalt therapy, the
cognitive-behavioral therapies, and reality therapy.

## UNITY AND PATTERNS OF HUMAN PERSONALITY

A basic premise of the Adlerian approach, also known as *Individual Psychology*, is that personality can only be understood holistically and systematically; that is, the individual is seen as an indivisible whole, born, reared, and living in specific familial, social, and cultural contexts. People are social, creative, decision-making beings who have a unified purpose and cannot be fully known outside of the contexts that have meaning in their lives (Sherman & Dinkmeyer, 1987).

The human personality becomes unified through the life goal. An individual's thoughts, feelings, beliefs, convictions, attitudes, character, and actions are expressions of his or her uniqueness, and all reflect a plan of life that allows for the movement toward a self-selected life goal. An implication of this holistic view of personality is that the client is an integral part of a social system. There is more focus on interpersonal relationships than on the individual's internal psychodynamics.

BEHAVIOR AS PURPOSEFUL AND GOAL-ORIENTED.    Individual Psychology assumes that all human behavior has a purpose. Humans set goals for themselves, and behavior becomes unified in the context of these goals. Adler replaced deterministic explanations with teleological (purposive, goal-oriented) ones. A basic assumption of Individual Psychology is that what we are striving for is crucial. Thus, Adlerians are interested in the future, without minimizing the importance of past influences. They assume that decisions are based on the person's experiences, on the present situation, and on the direction in which the person is moving. They look for continuity by paying attention to themes running through a person's life.

Adlerians use the term *fictional finalism* to refer to an imagined central goal that guides a person's behavior. Adler was influenced by the philosopher Hans Vaihinger's view that people live by fictions (or views of how the world should be). The guiding fiction might be expressed as: "Only when I am perfect can I be secure," or "Only when I am important can I be accepted." The fictional goal represents an individual's image of a perfected position, for which he or she strives in any given situation. The term *finalism* refers to the ultimate nature of the person's goal and the ever-present tendency to move in a certain direction. Because of this ultimate goal, we have the creative power to choose what we will accept as truth, how we will behave, and how we will interpret events. Sometimes, of course, we make mistakes.

THE STRIVING FOR SIGNIFICANCE AND SUPERIORITY.    Adler stresses that striving for perfection and coping with inferiority by seeking mastery are innate (Adler, 1979, p. 29). To understand human behavior it is essential to grasp the ideas of basic inferiority and compensation. According to Adler, the second we experience inferiority, we are pulled by the striving for superiority. He maintains that the goal of success pulls people forward toward mastery and enables them to overcome obstacles. The goal of superiority contributes to the development of human community. However, it is important to note that *superiority*, as used by Adler, does not mean being superior to others but, rather, attaining a perceived better position in life. Superiority is a striving from a perceived lower position to a perceived higher position, from a felt minus to a felt plus. We cope with feelings of helplessness by striving for competence, mastery, and perfection. We can seek to change a weakness into a strength, for example, or we can excel in one area of concentration to compensate for defects in other areas. The unique way in which we develop a style of striving for competence is what constitutes individuality.

LIFESTYLE.   The term *lifestyle* refers to an individual's basic orientation to life, or one's personality, and includes the themes that characterize the person's existence. Synonyms are plan of life, life movement, strategy for living, and road map of life. It is through our lifestyle that we move toward our life goal. Adler saw us as actor, creator, and artist of our life. In striving for goals that have meaning to us, we develop a unique style of life (Ansbacher, 1974). This concept accounts for why all of our behaviors fit together so that there is some consistency to our actions. Understanding one's lifestyle is somewhat like understanding the style of a composer: "We can begin wherever we choose: every expression will lead us in the same direction—toward the one motive, the one melody, around which the personality is built" (Adler, 1964a, p. 332).

No two people develop exactly the same lifestyle. In striving for the goal of superiority, some develop their intellect; others, their artistic talent; others, athletic skills; and so on. These styles of life consist of people's views about themselves and the world and their distinctive behaviors and habits as they pursue their personal goals. Everything we do is influenced by this unique lifestyle, which is assumed to be influenced by forces during the first six years of life. Experiences within the family and relationships between siblings contribute to the development of the lifestyle (Sherman & Dinkmeyer, 1987). But it is not the childhood experiences in themselves that are crucial; rather, it is our present interpretation of these events.

## SOCIAL INTEREST

*Social interest,* or *Gemeinschaftsgefühl,* is probably Adler's most significant and distinctive concept. The term refers to an individual's awareness of being a part of the human community and to the individual's attitudes in dealing with the social world; it includes striving for a better future for humanity. The socialization process, which begins in childhood, involves finding a place in one's society and acquiring a sense of belonging and of contributing (Kefir, 1981). Adler equated social interest with a sense of identification and empathy with others: "to see with the eyes of another, to hear with the ears of another, to feel with the heart of another" (1979, p. 42). The degree to which we successfully share with others and are concerned with the welfare of others is a measure of mental health (Sherman & Dinkmeyer, 1987). From the Adlerian perspective, as social interest develops, the individual's feelings of inferiority and alienation diminish. Social interest will develop if it is taught, learned, and used. People express social interest through shared activity and mutual respect. Those without social interest become discouraged and end up on the useless side of life.

Individual Psychology rests on a central belief that our happiness and success are largely related to this social connectedness. Because we are part of a society, we cannot be understood in isolation from the social context. Humans seek a place in the family and in society. There is a basic need to feel secure, accepted, and worthwhile. People need to discover their unique way of contributing and sharing in activities and responsibilities. Many of the problems we experience are related to the fear of not being accepted by the groups we value. If our sense of belonging is not fulfilled, anxiety is the result. Only when we have a sense of belonging are we able to act with courage in facing and dealing with our problems.

Mosak (1977) contends that we must face and master five life tasks: relating to others (friendship), making a contribution (work), achieving intimacy (love and family relationships), getting along with ourselves (self-acceptance), and developing our spiritual dimension (including values, meaning, life goals, and our relationship with the universe, or cosmos). Furthermore, it is essential that we define our sex roles and learn to relate to others. Because we are not self-sufficient, we need to learn to become interdependent. Work is basic to survival, and therefore it is important that we create meaning in work and that we accept our part in this social enterprise. Our feelings about ourselves and our level of self-acceptance are determinants of how effectively we are able to form interpersonal relationships.

## BIRTH ORDER AND SIBLING RELATIONSHIPS

The Adlerian approach is unique in giving special attention to the relationships between siblings and the position in one's family. Adler identified five psychological positions: oldest, second of only two, middle, youngest, and only. It should be noted that actual birth order itself is less important than the individual's interpretation of his or her place in the family. Since Adlerians view most human problems as social in nature, they emphasize intrafamily relationships.

Adler (1958) observes that many people wonder why children in the same family often differ so widely. It is a fallacy to assume that children of the same family are formed in the same environment. Although they share aspects in common in the family constellation, the psychological situation of each child is different from that of the others because of the order of their birth. The following description of the influence of birth order is based on Ansbacher and Ansbacher (1964), Dreikurs, (1953), and Adler (1958):

1. The *oldest child* generally receives a good deal of attention, and during the time she is the only child, she is typically somewhat spoiled as the center of attention. She tends to be dependable and hard working and strives to keep ahead. When a new brother or sister arrives on the scene, however, she finds herself ousted from her favored position. She is no longer unique or special. She may readily believe that the newcomer (or intruder) will rob her of the love to which she is accustomed.

2. The *second child* is in a different position. From the time he is born, he shares the attention with another child. The typical second child behaves

as if he were in a race and is generally under full steam at all times. It is as though this second child were in training to surpass the older brother or sister. This competitive struggle between the two first children influences the later course of their lives. The younger child develops a knack for finding out the elder child's weak spots and proceeds to win praise from both parents and teachers by achieving successes where the older sibling has failed. If one is talented in a given area, the other strives for recognition by developing other abilities. The second-born is often opposite to the firstborn.

3. The *middle child* often feels squeezed out. She may become convinced of the unfairness of life and feel cheated. This person can assume a "poor me" attitude and can become a problem child. On the other hand, especially in families characterized by conflict, the middle child will become the switchboard and the peacemaker, the person who holds things together.

4. The *youngest child* is always is the baby of the family and tends to be the most pampered one. He has a special role to play, for all the other children are ahead of him. Youngest children tend to go their own way. They often develop in ways no others in the family have thought about.

5. The *only child* has a problem of her own. Although she shares some of the characteristics of the oldest child (namely, high achievement drive), she may not learn to share or cooperate with other children. She will learn to deal with adults well, as they make up her original familial world. Often, the only child is pampered by her parents and may become dependently tied to one or both of them. She may want to have center stage all of the time, and if her position is challenged, she will feel it is unfair.

The birth order and the interpretation of one's position in the family have a great deal to do with how adults interact in the world. They acquired a certain style of relating to others in childhood, and they formed a definite picture of themselves that they carry into their adult interactions. In Adlerian therapy, working with family dynamics, especially relationships among siblings, assumes a key role. Although it is important to avoid stereotyping individuals into a category, it does help to see how certain personality trends that began in childhood as a result of sibling rivalry do have a way of following one throughout the rest of one's life.

# The Therapeutic Process

## THERAPEUTIC GOALS

Adlerian counseling rests on a collaborative arrangement between the client and the counselor. In general, the therapeutic process includes identifying and exploring *mistaken goals* and *faulty assumptions,* followed by a reeducation of the client toward more constructive goals. The main aim of therapy is to develop clients' social interest, which is accomplished by increasing their self-awareness and challenging and modifying their fundamental premises, life goals, and basic concepts (Dreikurs, 1967).

Adlerians do not see clients as being "sick" and in need of being "cured." Rather, the goal is to reeducate clients so that they can live in society as an equal, both giving to society and receiving from others (Mosak, 1995). Therefore, the counseling process focuses on providing information, teaching, guiding, and offering encouragement to discouraged clients. Encouragement is the most powerful method available for changing a person's beliefs. It helps clients build self-confidence and stimulates courage. Courage is the willingness to act *even when fearful* in ways that are consistent with social interest. Fear and courage always go hand in hand, because without fear, there would be no need for courage. The loss of courage, or discouragement, results in mistaken and dysfunctional behavior. Discouraged people do not act in line with social interest on the useful side of life.

Adlerian counselors are educating clients in new ways of looking at themselves, others, and life. Through the process of providing clients with a new cognitive map, or a fundamental understanding of the purpose of their behavior, counselors assist them in changing their perceptions. Mosak (1995, p. 67) lists the following as the goals of the educational process of therapy:

- fostering social interest
- helping clients overcome feelings of discouragement and inferiority
- modifying clients' views and goals—that is, changing their lifestyle
- changing faulty motivation
- assisting clients to feel a sense of equality with others
- helping people become contributing members of society

## THERAPIST'S FUNCTION AND ROLE

Adlerian counselors focus on the cognitive aspects of therapy. They realize that clients are discouraged emotionally and are functioning ineffectively on a behavioral level because of their faulty cognitions (beliefs and goals). They operate on the assumption that clients will feel and behave better if they discover and correct their basic mistakes. Therapists tend to look for major mistakes in thinking and valuing such as mistrust, selfishness, unrealistic ambitions, and lack of confidence.

A major function of the therapist is to make a comprehensive assessment of the client's functioning. Therapists gather information on the client's *family constellation,* which includes parents, siblings, and others living in the home. They do this by means of a questionnaire, which when summarized and interpreted gives a picture of the individual's early social world. From this information therapists are able to get a perspective on the client's major areas of success and failure and on the critical influences that have had a bearing on the role the client has decided to assume in the world. The counselor also uses *early recollections* as a diagnostic tool. These recollections are of single incidents from childhood that we are able to reexperience. They reflect our current convictions, evaluations, attitudes, and biases (Griffith & Powers, 1984). These memories provide a brief picture of how we see ourselves and others and what we anticipate for our future. After these early recollections are summarized and interpreted, the therapist identifies some of the major successes and mistakes in the client's life. The aim is to provide a point of departure for the therapeutic venture. This process is called a lifestyle assessment.

By way of summary, in making this diagnostic assessment, therapists do the following: They extract major patterns that appear in the family-constellation questionnaire and thereby get a picture of the client's basic personality. Then, by means of interpreting early recollections, they get a sense of the person's present outlook on life. Mistaken aspects of the client's view of life are identified by comparing his or her current convictions with the framework of social-interest concepts. When this process is completed, the counselor and the client have targets for therapy (Gushurst, 1971).

## CLIENT'S EXPERIENCE IN THERAPY

Clients in Adlerian counseling focus their work on their lifestyle, which provides the blueprint for their actions. How do clients maintain their lifestyle, and why do they resist changing it? Generally, people fail to change because they do not recognize the errors in their thinking and behavior, do not know what to do differently, and are fearful of leaving old patterns for new and unpredictable outcomes. Thus, even though their ways of thinking and behaving are not successful, they tend to cling to the familiar patterns (Manaster & Corsini, 1982).

In therapy clients explore what Adlerians call *private logic,* the concepts about self, others, and life that constitute the philosophy on which an individual's lifestyle is based. Clients' problems arise because the conclusions based on their private logic often do not conform to the requirements of social living. The core of the therapy experience consists of clients' discovering their basic mistakes and then learning how to correct these faulty assumptions and conclusions.

To provide a concrete example, think of a chronically depressed middle-aged man who begins therapy. After a lifestyle investigation is completed, the following patterns of basic mistakes are identified:

- He has convinced himself that nobody could really care about him.
- He rejects people before they have a chance to reject him.
- He is harshly critical of himself, expecting perfection.
- He has expectations that things will rarely work out well.
- He burdens himself with guilt, since he is convinced that he is letting everyone down.

Even though this man developed these mistaken ideas about life as a small child, he is still clinging to them as rules for living. His expectations, most of which are pessimistic, tend to be fulfilled, because on some level he is seeking to validate his beliefs. In therapy this man will learn how to challenge the structure of his private logic. In his case the syllogism goes as follows:

- "I am basically unlovable."
- "The world is filled with people who are likely to be rejecting."
- "Therefore, I must keep to myself so I won't be hurt."

This person has held onto several basic mistakes. His private logic provides central psychological unity for him. Mosak (1977) would say that there are central themes or convictions in this client's life, some of which may be: "I must get what I want in life." "I must control everything in my life." "I must know everything there is to know, and a mistake would be catastrophic." "I must be perfect in everything I do." It is important for the therapist to listen for the underlying purposes of this client's behavior. Adlerian therapists do not focus directly on *feelings* of depression. Instead, they devote attention to beliefs and convictions, which result in emotional and behavioral disturbances. It is not true that Adlerians discount the role of feelings; rather, they see feelings as being the result of (rather than the cause of) thinking and behaving. So first we think, then feel, and then act. Because emotions are at the service of our cognitive processes, it follows that clients will spend much of their time discussing thoughts, beliefs, and what they are currently doing based on their conceptual framework for living. In short, if clients hope to begin to *feel* better and to *act* better, they must learn better ways of *thinking*. Further, because clients are not perceived by the therapist as "sick," but mainly discouraged, they will receive much encouragement that change is possible. Through the therapeutic process, they will discover that they have resources and options to draw on in dealing with significant life issues and life tasks.

## RELATIONSHIP BETWEEN THERAPIST AND CLIENT

Adlerians consider a good client/therapist relationship to be one between equals that is based on cooperation, mutual trust, respect, confidence, and alignment of goals. They place special value on the counselor's modeling of communication and acting in good faith. From the beginning of therapy the relationship is a collaborative one, characterized by two persons working equally toward specific, agreed-on-goals. Dinkmeyer, Dinkmeyer, and Sperry (1987) maintain that at the outset of counseling, clients should begin to formulate a plan, or contract, detailing what they want, how they plan to get where they are heading, what is preventing them from successfully attaining their goals, how they can change nonproductive behavior into constructive behavior, and how they can make full use of their assets in achieving their purposes. The therapeutic contract sets forth the goals of the counseling process and specifies the responsibilities of both the therapist and the client. However, developing a contract is not a requirement of Adlerian therapy.

The client is not viewed as a passive recipient; rather, the client is an active party in a relationship between equals in which there is no superior and no inferior. Through this *collaborative* partnership clients recognize that they are responsible for their behavior. Although Adlerians view the quality of the therapeutic relationship as relevant to the outcomes of therapy, they do not assume that this relationship, alone, will bring about change. It is the starting point in the process of change. Without initial trust and rapport, the difficult work of changing one's lifestyle is not likely to occur.

# Application: Therapeutic Techniques and Procedures

Adlerian counseling is structured around four central objectives, which correspond to the four phases of the therapeutic process (Dreikurs, 1967). These phases are not linear and do not progress in rigid steps; rather, they can best be understood as a weaving that leads to a tapestry. These stages are:

1. establishing the proper therapeutic relationship
2. exploring the psychological dynamics operating in the client (analysis and assessment)
3. encouraging the development of self-understanding (insight)
4. helping the client make new choices (reorientation and reeducation)

## PHASE 1: ESTABLISHING THE RELATIONSHIP

As noted previously, the Adlerian counselor works in a collaborative way with clients, thus increasing their sense of responsibility for their life. This relationship is based on a sense of deep caring, involvement, and friendship. Mozdzierz, Lisiecki, Bitter, and Williams (1984) see the therapist as a friend on whom the client can count in time of need. Therapeutic progress is possible only when there is an alignment of clearly defined goals between the therapist and the client. The counseling process, to be effective, must deal with the personal issues that the client recognizes as significant and is willing to discuss and change.

One way to create a working therapeutic relationship is for counselors to help clients become aware of their assets and strengths, rather than dealing continually with their deficits and liabilities. During this initial phase the relationship is created by listening, responding, demonstrating respect in the client's capacity to change, and exhibiting genuine enthusiasm. When clients enter therapy, they typically have a diminished sense of self-worth and self-respect, and they lack faith in their ability to cope with the tasks of life. Therapists provide support, which is an antidote to despair and discouragement. For some people this may be one of the few times that they have truly experienced a caring human relationship. Encouragement consists of helping clients use all of their resources. It also includes transforming traits that can be liabilities, such as stubbornness and compulsivity, into assets, such as determination and organization (Dinkmeyer & Losoncy, 1980).

Adlerians pay more attention to the subjective experiences of the client than they do to using techniques. They fit their techniques to the needs of each client. During this initial phase of counseling the main techniques are attending and listening, identifying and clarifying goals, and providing empathy. Attending implies engaging in behaviors such as maintaining eye contact and being psychologically available to the client. Listening entails grasping both the verbal and nonverbal messages of the client. Attending and listening both involve paying attention to the messages conveyed by the client's tone of voice, posture, facial expressions, gestures, and hesitations in speech. The counselor attempts to grasp the core of what the client is experiencing. Empathic understanding involves the therapist's ability to grasp the subjective world of clients and to communicate this understanding to them. If clients are deeply understood and accepted, they are likely to focus on what they want from therapy and thus establish goals.

The initial interview sets a foundation on which the relationship is created and maintained. Powers and Griffith (1987) provide many examples of the typical inquiries during the initial interview, such as the following:

- What brought you to see me?
- What have you done about your problem until now?
- How would your life be different if you did not have this problem? (Or what would you do if you were well?)
- What are your expectations of our work together?

## PHASE 2: EXPLORING THE INDIVIDUAL'S DYNAMICS

In the second phase the aim of clients is twofold: understanding their lifestyle and seeing how it affects their current functioning in all the tasks of life. The counselor begins the initial assessment by exploring how clients are functioning in the various aspects of their lives. As Mozdzierz and his associates (1984) point out, when clients enter therapy, their focus is often narrow and restricted. They feel overwhelmed by their struggles, their current relationships are strained, they feel stuck, and they feel alienated from their social system. At this stage the counselor's function is to provide a wide-angle perspective that will eventually help them view their world differently. Adlerians help their clients make connections between their past, present, and future behavior. In order to gain a sense of the client's lifestyle, counselors pay close attention to feelings, motives, beliefs, and goals. They explore feelings to understand motives, to develop empathy, and to enhance the quality of the therapeutic relationship. Adlerian therapists go beyond feelings to explore the beliefs underlying them. They then confront faulty beliefs so that clients can become freer.

Adlerians focus on the lifestyle assessment, which systematically deals with a thorough description of the members of the client's family of origin, their relationships, and their circumstances. Mozdzierz and his colleagues (1984) describe the counselor as a "lifestyle investigator" during this phase of therapy. Based on interviewing approaches developed by Adler and Dreikurs, the lifestyle assessment involves an investigation of the person's family constellation and early childhood history. Counselors also interpret the person's early memories. They seek to understand the whole person as he or she grew up in a social setting. They operate on the assumption that it is the interpretation that people develop about themselves, others, the world, and life that governs what they do. Lifestyle assessment aims at uncovering the private interpretations and private logic of the individual. For example, certain clients hold the mistaken notion that if they are not perfect, they are a failure. Through the assessment process they become aware of their negative thinking and how it results in restricted living.

The counselor explores how the client is functioning with reference to the life tasks of love, work, and friendship and community. Clients are expected to tell the counselor about these areas and also to set out what they want to improve or change. As a part of this assessment clients may be asked to rate their level of success in social relationships, work, intimacy, sexuality, and feelings about self. They are typically asked questions in each of the above areas. For example: "Do you find satisfaction in your relationships with other people? Do you feel belonging and acceptance? How are things for you in your work? Do you have any special concerns in relating to women or men? Do you typically feel good about yourself? How much fun do you have? How self-accepting are you?" Besides these questions, broad ones may be raised, such as: "What gives your life meaning? What are your goals? How well are you meeting your goals?" Adlerian counselors are especially interested in learning about the ways in which the individual meets the basic demands of life. As Mozdzierz and his colleagues (1984) observe, Adlerians function as "psychological explorers," for they invite their clients on a journey through what has been, what is, and what can be. They help clients explore their options for growth and the paths that lead to a more productive and constructive future.

THE FAMILY CONSTELLATION.   As noted earlier, Adlerian assessment relies heavily on the exploration of the client's family constellation, which includes evaluating the conditions that prevailed in the family when the person was a young child in the process of forming lifestyle convictions and basic assumptions. Both Powers and Griffith (1986) and Mosak and Shulman (1988) have developed lifestyle-assessment questionnaires that investigate what Adlerians consider to be influential factors in one's life. These include the child's psychological position in the family, birth order, and interactions between siblings and parents. Questions such as the following are explored: "Who was the favorite child? What was your father's relationship with the children? your mother's? Which child was most like the father? In what respects? Which was most like the mother? In what ways? What was your relationship with your mother? your father? Who among the siblings was most different from you? In what ways? Who was most like you? In what respects? What kind of child were you?" The counselor is also likely to ask why the person is seeking counseling and how satisfied he or she is with the way the basic tasks of life are being carried out. The questionnaire is far more comprehensive than these few questions, but this gives an idea of the type of information the counselor is seeking. The aim is to get a picture of clients' self-perception and of the experiences that have affected their development.

Once information on the family constellation has been collected, it is the counselor's task to make a brief summary of the material. The client's overall lifestyle assessment may also include separate summaries of his or her early recollections, dreams, and priorities.

EARLY RECOLLECTIONS.   Another assessment procedure used by Adlerians is asking clients to provide their earliest memories, including their age at the time of the remembered events and the feelings and thoughts that accompanied the reported incidents. Early recollections are one-time occurrences pictured by the client in clear detail. Adler reasoned that out of the millions of early memories we might have, we select those special memories that project the essential beliefs and even the basic mistakes of our lives.

To tap such recollections, the counselor may proceed as follows: "I would like to hear about your early memories. Think back to when you were very young, as early as you can remember, and tell me something that happened to you one time—something that you can envision quite clearly, not something that you were told about." Or: "I'd like to hear about a particular incident that you recall, as early as possible but certainly before the age of 9. Tell me what happened, what moment most stands out for you, and what you were feeling or thinking—your reaction—at that time." The number of early recollections that are elicited varies. Three memories are usually considered a minimum to assess a pattern, and some counselors ask for as many as a dozen memories.

Adlerians value these early recollections as an important clue to the understanding of an individual's lifestyle. They contend that people remember only those events that are consistent with their current views of themselves (Adler, 1958). Once people develop such views, they perceive only those things that fit their views. This limited perception strengthens people's private logic, which in turn helps them maintain their basic convictions. Early recollections thus provide a basic understanding of how we view and feel about ourselves, how we see the world, what our life goals are, what motivates us, what we believe in, and what we value. In interpreting these early recollections, Adlerians may consider questions such as the following: "Is the person an observer or a participant? What are the dominant themes and overall patterns of the memories? What are the typical responses of the person? Is the individual alone or with others? What feelings are expressed in the memories?"

DREAMS.    Dreams are projections of a client's current concerns and indications of his or her mood. Clients can learn to observe and understand their own internal dynamics by exploring their dreams (Peven & Shulman, 1986). Adlerians may ask about dreams as a part of the lifestyle assessment. In interpreting and discussing them, particular interest is given to childhood dreams, as well as recurrent and recent dreams. From the perspective of Individual Psychology, dreams are rehearsals for possible future courses of action. They serve as a weathervane for treatment, because they bring problems to the surface. In keeping with the Adlerian spirit, dreams are seen as purposeful and unique to the individual. Thus, there is no fixed symbolism in dreams; one cannot understand dreams without understanding the dreamer (Mosak, 1995).

PRIORITIES.    Adlerians believe that assessing clients' priorities is an important road to understanding interactional coping. An Israeli psychologist, Nera Kefir (1981), originally designated four priorities: superiority, control, comfort, and pleasing. Personality priorities are similar to what Adler called safeguarding tendencies. Unless challenged, people rely on a number-one priority, a first line of defense that they use as an immediate response to perceived stress or difficulty. Each priority involves a dominant behavior pattern with supporting convictions that an individual uses to cope. Priorities become a pathway for relating to others and for attaining a sense of significance. Kefir describes four behavioral patterns that reflect the four priorities:

1. People using *superiority* (significance) strive for significance through leadership or accomplishment or through any other avenue to make them feel superior. They seek to avoid meaninglessness in life but often complain of being overworked or overburdened.
2. People who *control* look for guarantees against ridicule. They feel a need for complete mastery of situations so that they will not be humiliated. They do not want to behave in a socially unsuccessful way.
3. People seeking *comfort* want to avoid stress or pain at all costs. They tend to delay dealing with problems and making decisions, and they do their best to avoid anything that implies stress or pain. Even routine tasks are avoided, because they are seen as stressful.
4. People who aim to *please* want to avoid rejection by seeking constant approval and acceptance. Out of their fear of not being liked, they go to great lengths to win approval.

A way for a counselor to pinpoint clients' highest priority is to ask them to describe in detail their typical day: what they do, how they feel, and what they think about. Typically, these descriptions reveal a consistent pattern. Clients' main priority can also be determined by discovering what they avoid at all costs and what feelings they consistently evoke in others.

It is *not* therapists' job to work toward changing a client's main priority. Instead, the goal is to enable clients to recognize the feelings they evoke in others and the price they pay for clinging to their number-one priority. Kefir (1981) asserts that in order to increase our self-awareness, we must learn what our priority, or condition for feeling significant, is. We also need to find alternative ways to gain significance by using a wider range of behaviors. (See Kefir, 1981, pp. 403–407 for a further discussion of working with priorities in counseling.)

INTEGRATION AND SUMMARY.  Once material has been gathered from the client's family constellation, early recollections, dreams, and priorities, separate summaries are done for each of these areas. Finally, based on the entire lifestyle-assessment questionnaire, this material is integrated, summarized, and interpreted. This lifestyle investigation reveals a pattern of basic mistakes, such as exaggerations, unfounded conclusions, faulty assumptions, absolutes, and rigid stances that make it difficult for the person to enjoy life. One of the counselor's major tasks is integrating and summarizing the information gathered about the client's family constellation, early recollections, and basic mistakes, as well as his or her assets. This summary is presented to the client and discussed in the session, with the client and counselor together refining specific points. Dinkmeyer, Dinkmeyer, and Sperry (1987) suggest that it is useful for the counselor to read the summary of the lifestyle in the presence of the client. In the following session the client reads the summary aloud. In this way clients have the chance to discuss specific topics and to raise questions. Also, the counselor can learn much about them from hearing them read and observing their nonverbal reactions.

The summary also contains an analysis of an individual's basic mistakes. Mosak (1995, p. 70) writes that the lifestyle can be conceived of as a personal mythology. People thus behave as if the myths were true, since for them they *are* true. Mosak lists five basic mistakes:

1. *Overgeneralizations:* "There is no fairness in the world."
2. *False or impossible goals:* "I must please everyone if I am to feel loved."
3. *Misperceptions of life and life's demands:* "Life is so very difficult for me."
4. *Denial of one's basic worth:* "I'm basically stupid, so why would anyone want anything to do with me?"
5. *Faulty values:* "I must get to the top, regardless of who gets hurt in the process."

As another example of a summary of basic mistakes, consider the following list of mistaken and self-defeating perceptions that are evident in Stan's auto-biography and that show up in his therapy (see Chapter 14):

- Don't get close to people, especially women, because they will suffocate and control you if they can (overgeneralization).
- I was not really wanted by my parents, and therefore it is best for me to become invisible (denial of one's basic worth).
- It is extremely important that people like me and approve of me; I'll bend over backward to do what people expect (false or impossible goals).

In order to get a clearer idea of the assessment procedures that Adlerians typically use, I suggest that you consult the appendix of *Understanding Life-Style: The Psycho-Clarity Process* (Powers & Griffith, 1987) for a detailed outline of the initial interview, guidelines for the lifestyle assessment, suggestions for making summaries, and notes for the course of therapy. *The Individual Psychology Client Workbook* (Powers & Griffith, 1986) contains a detailed and comprehensive initial-interview protocol and an excellent form for a lifestyle assessment. Also, the *Manual for Life Style Assessment* (Shulman & Mosak, 1988) presents a comprehensive guide for the initial interview and for establishing the lifestyle. The student manual that accompanies this textbook gives a concrete example of the lifestyle assessment as it is applied to the case of Stan. In *Case Approach to Counseling and Psychotherapy* (Corey, 1996) there is a detailed lifestyle assessment done on another hypothetical client, Ruth, which is based on the form by Powers and Griffith (1986). Consulting these references will help you get a concrete grasp of how Adlerian concepts come to life in practice.

THE ENCOURAGEMENT PROCESS.    After the lifestyle investigation is complete, clients can be encouraged to examine their mistaken perceptions, to begin to challenge their conclusions, and to take note of their assets, strengths, and talents. Encouragement is the most distinctive Adlerian procedure, and therefore it is essential that the overall assessment and interpretation include the client's positive qualities, not just a summary of deficits and mistakes. The encouragement process is basic to every phase of counseling. Adlerians seize every opportunity the client provides to introduce and reinforce this process (Powers & Griffith, 1987). Since clients often do not recognize or accept their positive qualities, one of the counselor's tasks is to help them do so. Through the encouragement process clients eventually begin to accept these strengths and assets.

Adlerians believe that discouragement is the basic condition that prevents people from functioning, and they see encouragement as the antidote. Encouragement takes many forms, depending on the phase of the counseling process. In the assessment phase, which is partially designed to illuminate personal strengths, clients are encouraged to recognize that they have the power to choose and to act differently based on their self-knowledge.

## PHASE 3: ENCOURAGING INSIGHT

Although Adlerian therapists are supportive, they are also confrontive. They challenge their clients to develop insights into mistaken goals and self-defeating behaviors. Insight into the hidden purposes and goals of behavior tends to emerge not only through encouragement and challenge but also through well-timed interpretations by the therapist that are stated as tentative hypotheses. Although insight is regarded by the Adlerians as a powerful adjunct to behavioral change, it is not seen as a prerequisite. Insight is viewed as a step toward change, but the emphasis is on translating this self-understanding into constructive action. People are able to make abrupt and significant changes in behavior without much insight.

Interpretation is a technique that facilitates the process of gaining insight. It is focused on here-and-now behavior and on the expectations and anticipations that arise from one's intentions. Adlerian interpretation is done in relationship to the lifestyle. It is concerned with creating awareness of one's direction in life, one's goals and purposes, one's private logic and how it works, and one's current behavior. Typically, interpretation is focused on behavior and its consequences, not on the causes of behavior. Adlerians operate on the assumption that no one knows the truth about another's world, so only guesses can be ventured. When they interpret another's world, therefore, they offer suggestions in the form of questions or qualified statements. Interpretations are presented tentatively in the form of open-ended sharings that can be explored in the sessions. They are hunches and guesses, and they are often stated thusly: "I have a hunch that I'd like to share with you." "It seems to me that . . ." "Could it be that . . . ?" "This is how it appears to me." Because interpretations are presented in this manner, clients are not led to defend themselves, and they feel free to discuss or argue over the counselor's hunches and impressions. Through this process clients eventually come to understand their own part in creating a problem, the ways in which they are now contributing to the problem, and what they can do to correct the situation.

Powers and Griffith (1987) maintain that learning how to make interpretations is more a matter of virtue than of technique. It is important that practitioners have the courage to extend themselves in empathic and intuitive guessing. These authors believe that as practitioners gain increased confidence in what they have to offer, they also become increasingly capable of empathy and develop more courage to make guesses. They add that it is crucial for counselors to have the humility to acknowledge wrong guesses when they are corrected or rejected by their clients.

## PHASE 4: HELPING WITH REORIENTATION

The final stage of the therapeutic process is the action-oriented phase known as reorientation and reeducation, or putting insights into practice. This phase focuses on helping people see new and more functional alternatives. Clients are both encouraged and challenged to develop the courage to take risks and make changes in their life.

During the reorientation phase of counseling, clients make decisions and modify their goals. They are encouraged to act *as if* they were the person they wanted to be, which can serve to challenge self-limiting assumptions. Clients are asked to catch themselves in the process of repeating old patterns that lead to ineffective behavior. Commitment is an essential part of this phase, for if clients hope to change, they must be willing to set tasks for themselves and do something specific about their problems. In this way they translate their new insights into concrete action.

This action-oriented phase is a time for solving problems and making decisions. This is a time when the counselor and the client consider possible alternatives and their consequences, evaluate how these alternatives will meet the client's goals, and decide on a specific course of action. Some of the major techniques that Adlerians often employ during the reorientation phase are described below; the material is adapted from Dinkmeyer, Dinkmeyer, and Sperry (1987) and Mosak (1995). The techniques described are immediacy, paradoxical intention, acting as if, spitting in the client's soup, catching oneself, push-button technique, avoiding the traps, task setting and commitment, and terminating and summarizing.

IMMEDIACY.    The technique known as immediacy involves dealing with what is going on in the present moment of the counseling session. It may help the client to see how what is occurring in the session is a sample of what goes on in everyday life. For example, assume that your client continually leans on you for advice, based on her conviction that she typically "messes things up" when she makes important decisions. If you make explicit how she is viewing you and treating you in this relationship and tell her how you are being affected by her expecting you to make decisions for her, you are using immediacy. You can show her how she is defeating herself by clinging to her mistaken belief that she is unable to make decisions, which sets her up for failure.

PARADOXICAL INTENTION.    Adler pioneered the paradoxical strategy as a way of changing behavior. This technique has also been called "prescribing the symptom" and "antisuggestion." It involves having clients consciously pay attention to and exaggerate debilitating thoughts and behaviors. As a result the symptoms become markedly out of proportion to the reality of the situation. The paradoxical strategy consists of seemingly self-contradictory and sometimes even absurd therapeutic interventions. The essence of the technique is that it joins the client's resistance rather than opposing it; it contains characteristics of empathy, encouragement, and humor and leads to increased social interest (Mozdzierz, Macchitelli, & Lisiecki, 1976). Adler used paradoxical interventions to treat a number of different problems. With people who complained of insomnia, for example, he might ask them to get up and stay awake as long as possible. He did not use this approach with all problems. In the case of depressed individuals, he cautioned, it is best to have someone watch them to determine if suicide is a possibility. For suicidal clients, hospitalization is recommended.

Paradoxical techniques are sometimes used for individuals who procrastinate. For example, such clients can be told to put off tasks even longer. A client who worries much of the time might be asked to schedule some time each day devoted exclusively to worrying about everything possible. The client who complains about being fearful of talking out in class is encouraged to sit in the back of the classroom and say nothing. In using this procedure, counselors might recommend exaggeration of a behavior pattern for a specific period of time so that clients can see what they might learn from the experiment. The rationale for paradoxical intention is that it assists people in becoming dramatically aware of how they are behaving in certain situations and how they are responsible for the consequences of their behavior. By going *with,* not against, the client's resistance, the therapist makes the behavior less attractive. The symptom is likely to appear foolish in the client's eyes. Further, when the client is confronted with a problem in a magnified way, he can then consider alternative ways of getting what he wants. Ethical issues are involved in the use of paradoxical procedures. Of course, therapists using them must be competent. Such techniques are usually employed after some of the more conventional techniques have failed to work in a given situation.

ACTING AS IF. The therapist can set up a role-playing situation in which clients imagine and act the way they would like to be. When clients say "If only I could . . . ," they can be encouraged to act out the role of their fantasy for at least a week, just to see what will happen. As an example of this technique, let's look at Stan's case. Assume that he says that he is troubled over his social inhibitions and that he would very much like to challenge his extreme fears of meeting and talking with women. His counselor may say:

> Stan, for the next week I'd like you to act as if you were very witty, attractive, and charming. Pretend that you have lots to offer and that women are missing out by not getting to know you. I suggest that you approach at least three women that you've been wanting to get to know.

By suggesting this task, the therapist is challenging Stan to take a risk and courageously do what he said he would like to do. By changing his expectations in positive ways, he may make his plan work. If he returns next week and says that he was rebuffed by the three women, he and his counselor can discuss what kept these experiences from being good ones.

SPITTING IN THE CLIENT'S SOUP. The counselor determines the purpose and payoff of some behavior and then spoils the game by reducing the usefulness of the behavior in front of the client's eyes. For example, a father may be getting some mileage out of continually telling his children how hard he works so that they can enjoy the finer things in life. The counselor may confront him on his martyr stance and show him how he is seeking appreciation from his children. It is not the counselor's role to persuade him to change his story to his children but, rather, to show him the price he is paying for this style. The client has the choice of continuing with the same behavior, but the payoff is likely to be spoiled because he is no longer as able to deceive himself.

CATCHING ONESELF.    In the process of catching oneself, a client becomes aware of some self-destructive behavior or irrational thought but does not engage in self-condemnation. Initially, clients may catch themselves too late, after they have gotten entangled in old patterns; eventually, with practice, they will learn to anticipate events and thus change their patterns. In the example given above, the father may decide that he wants to avoid using guilt as a way to get gratitude from his children. In spite of his good intentions to change, he may still catch himself reverting to his old patterns from time to time. At these times he can at least pause for a moment and consider other ways of responding to his children.

PUSH-BUTTON TECHNIQUE.    The push-button technique involves having clients picture alternately pleasant and unpleasant experiences and then pay attention to the feelings accompanying these experiences. The aim of the technique is to teach clients that they can create whatever feelings they wish by deciding on their thoughts (Mosak, 1995). In using the push-button technique, an Adlerian counselor will help a client recognize that she has chosen depression and that it is the result of her thinking. The counselor may use a visualization process, asking the client to recall a very pleasant incident, then turn to recall a very unpleasant incident, and then to imagine an incident that is turning out the way she would like it to. The client is asked to replay the last incident and to add the feeling that is created as an outcome of thinking. The counselor sends her home with two "buttons"—a depression button and a happy button—and suggests to her that she is in control of which button to push as future incidents are encountered.

AVOIDING TRAPS.    Clients bring with them to counseling some of the self-defeating patterns that they employ in daily life. They may cling to certain faulty assumptions because such biased perceptions do have a payoff. For example, some clients are convinced that nobody could really care about them, so they are likely to attempt to set up their counselor to eventually react to them as others have. Counselors need to be careful of falling into such traps and not to reinforce behaviors of clients that keep them stuck in old patterns. Instead, counselors are advised to encourage those behaviors that will lead to increased psychological maturity.

TASK SETTING AND COMMITMENT.    In taking concrete steps to resolve their problems, clients must set tasks and make a commitment to them. Plans should be designed for a limited period. In this way clients can succeed in accomplishing specific tasks, and they can then develop new plans with confidence. Such tasks must be realistic and attainable. If plans do not work out well, they can be discussed and revised at the next session. If clients do meet with success in dealing with their tasks, they can commit to some long-range goals that will help them move in the direction they desire. (You will see this procedure as a basic part of behavior therapy and reality therapy in later chapters.)

TERMINATING AND SUMMARIZING THE SESSION.   Setting limits for sessions, closing a session without stifling the client's willingness to continue exploring an issue, and summarizing the highlights of a session are all important skills for counselors to master. It is wise not to get into new material as a session is ending. Instead, the counselor can help the client review what was learned. This is a good time to discuss action-oriented "homework assignments" that the client can carry out during the week. In this way he or she is encouraged to apply new learning to everyday situations.

In addition to the techniques mentioned above, Adlerians are likely to draw from a wide range of procedures throughout the counseling process. Most of these techniques are also used by therapists of other orientations; Adlerians are pragmatic when it comes to using methods when they are appropriate (Manaster & Corsini, 1982). The following are a few of these techniques:

- *Advice.* Adlerians will sometimes give advice if they think a client is ready to hear it and to accept it.
- *Homework.* Clients are often asked to keep track of their behavior patterns, along with the feelings and thoughts that are associated with specific situations. For instance, a person may feel intimidated about returning defective merchandise. The assignment can consist of monitoring such situations and then recording what he does and what he is thinking. He can be encouraged to actually return a defective product to challenge his thinking that he does not have a right to complain.
- *Humor.* Therapeutic use of humor can result in a client's putting problems into perspective. At times, counselors can help clients learn to take themselves less seriously and even laugh at some of the foolishness of their behavior (Mosak, 1987).
- *Silence.* At times in the therapeutic process one of the best techniques a counselor can use is saying nothing. Giving advice too quickly or too often or rescuing clients when they are uncomfortable with silence can be counterproductive.

## AREAS OF APPLICATION

Individual Psychology, because it is based on a growth model, not a medical model, is applicable to such varied spheres of life as child-guidance centers, parent/child counseling, marital counseling, family therapy, group counseling, individual counseling with children and adolescents, cultural conflicts, correctional and rehabilitation counseling, and mental-health institutions. Its principles have been widely applied to substance-abuse programs, social problems to combat poverty and crime, problems of the aged, school systems, religion, and business.

APPLICATION TO EDUCATION.   Adler had a keen interest in applying his ideas to education, especially in finding ways to remedy faulty lifestyles of school-children. He initiated a process to work with students in groups and to educate parents and teachers. By providing teachers with ways to prevent and correct basic mistakes of children, he sought to promote social interest and mental health. Besides Adler, the main proponent of Individual Psychology as a foundation for the teaching/learning process was Dreikurs (1968, 1971).

APPLICATION TO PARENT EDUCATION.   The area of parent education has been one of the major Adlerian contributions. The goal is to improve the relationship between parent and child by promoting greater understanding and acceptance. Parents are taught simple Adlerian principles of behavior that can be applied in the home. Initial topics include understanding the purpose of a child's misbehavior, learning to listen, helping children accept the consequences of their behavior, holding family meetings, and using encouragement. The book considered to be the mainstay of many Adlerian parent-study groups is *Children: The Challenge,* by Dreikurs and Soltz (1964). Another book that presents Adlerian parent-education materials is *The Effective Parent* (Dinkmeyer, McKay, Dinkmeyer, & McKay, 1987).

APPLICATION TO MARRIAGE COUNSELING.   Adlerian marital therapy is designed to assess a couples' beliefs and behaviors while educating them in more effective ways to meet their goals. Dinkmeyer and Dinkmeyer (1982) outline four steps in the process of counseling couples, which correspond to the four stages of therapy described earlier:

1. The couple are asked what they expect from counseling, and the therapist discusses with them how their goals can be achieved.
2. The therapist then assesses both partners' lifestyles to determine the assumptions on which they operate, their basic mistaken perceptions, their assets, and their life goals. The lifestyle assessment is applied to marital therapy much as it is in individual counseling.
3. The therapist provides feedback to each partner on the themes and patterns emerging from the lifestyle assessment. The couple gain insight into their own dynamics and their marital system.
4. The couple are confronted by the therapist on their faulty beliefs about their relationship. This begins a reeducation process. The goal of the couple's reorientation is acquiring skills that they can use to carry out their new agreements.

The full range of techniques applicable to other forms of counseling can be used in working with couples. In marriage counseling and marriage education, couples are taught specific techniques that enhance communication and cooperation. Some of these techniques are listening, paraphrasing, giving feedback, having conferences, listing expectations, doing homework, and using paradoxical intention. Additional strategies in marriage counseling include psychodrama, bibliotherapy (recommending books that partners can read together and then discuss points of significance to them), storytelling and humor, and defining roles (Dinkmeyer, McKay, et al., 1987).

Adlerians will sometimes see married people as a couple, sometimes individually, and then alternatively as a couple and as individuals. Rather than looking for who is at fault in the relationship, the therapist considers the lifestyles of the partners and the interaction of the two lifestyles. Emphasis is given to helping them decide if they want to maintain their marriage and, if so, what changes they are willing to make. If you want more information on applying Adlerian principles to marriages, you can consult *Training in Marriage Enrichment* (Dinkmeyer & Carlson, 1984).

APPLICATION TO FAMILY COUNSELING.   Adlerian family therapy has its roots in the work of Adler and Dreikurs. With its emphasis on the family constellation, holism, and the freedom of the therapist to improvise, Adler's approach contributed to the foundation of the family-therapy perspective. Adlerians working with families focus on the family atmosphere, the family constellation, and the lifestyle of each member. The family atmosphere is the climate characterizing the relationship between the parents and their attitudes toward life, sex roles, decision making, competition, cooperation, dealing with conflict, responsibility, and so forth. This atmosphere, including the role models that the parents provide, influences the children as they grow up. The therapeutic process seeks to increase awareness of the interaction of the individual within the family system. Those who practice Adlerian family therapy strive to understand the goals, beliefs, and behaviors of each family member and the family as an entity in its own right. Because behavior has a social purpose, therapists focus on the relationships that characterize each family (Sherman & Dinkmeyer, 1987).

Adlerian family-therapy techniques are tied to the goals of therapy. Although specific goals are unique to each family, there are some general goals that provide direction (Sherman & Dinkmeyer, 1987):

- The interventions are designed to promote active and constructive movement.
- Family members are taught to accept personal responsibility.
- There is a joint effort between the therapist and each member of the family to evaluate goals and the means to achieve them.
- Family therapy has an educational purpose, for the therapist helps members learn ways to solve problems.
- Therapy is aimed at reorganizing family roles and relationships in a more effective and satisfying structure.

A number of techniques are available to family therapists to meet these goals. In addition to using many of the techniques described earlier in this chapter, they use other strategies: teaching communication skills, helping family members observe and interpret their transactions to differentiate between surface issues and real issues, offering encouragement, and confronting family members on their private logic and their purposes.

APPLICATION TO GROUP WORK.    Adler and his co-workers used a group approach in their child-guidance centers in Vienna as early as 1921 (Dreikurs, 1969). Dreikurs, a colleague, extended and popularized Adler's work with groups and used group psychotherapy in his private practice for over 40 years. Although he introduced group therapy into his psychiatric practice as a way to save time, he quickly discovered some unique characteristics of groups that made them an effective way of helping people change. Dreikurs's rationale for groups is as follows: "Since man's (sic) problems and conflicts are recognized in their social nature, the group is ideally suited not only to highlight and reveal the nature of a person's conflicts and maladjustments but to offer corrective influences" (1969, p. 43). Inferiority feelings can be challenged and counteracted effectively in groups, and the mistaken concepts and values that are at the root of social and emotional problems can be deeply influenced, because the group is a value-forming agent.

The group provides the social context in which members can develop a sense of belonging and a sense of community. Dinkmeyer (1975) writes that group participants come to see that many of their problems are interpersonal in nature, that their behavior has social meaning, and that their goals can best be understood in the framework of social purposes.

## ADLERIAN THERAPY APPLIED TO THE CASE OF STAN

The basic aims of an Adlerian therapist working with Stan are fourfold, corresponding to the four stages of counseling: (1) establishing and maintaining a good working relationship with him, (2) exploring his dynamics, (3) encouraging him to develop insight and understanding, and (4) helping him see new alternatives and make new choices.

The first goal is to develop mutual trust and respect. The therapist pays close attention to Stan's subjective experience and attempts to get a sense of how he has reacted to the turning points in his life. During the initial session, he reacts to his counselor as an expert who has the answers. In fact, he is convinced that he has made a mess of his life and that when he attempts to make decisions, he generally ends up regretting the results. Thus, he approaches his counselor out of desperation and almost pleads for a prescription for coping with his problems. Because his counselor views counseling as a relationship between equals, she initially focuses on his feeling of being unequal to most other people. A good place to begin is exploring his feelings of inferiority, which he says he feels in most situations. The goals of counseling are developed mutually, and the counselor avoids deciding for him what his goals should be. She also resists giving him the simple formula he is requesting.

The second stage of the counseling process deals with an analysis and assessment of Stan's lifestyle. This assessment is based on a questionnaire that taps information about his early years, especially his experiences in his family. (See the student manual for this text for a complete description of this lifestyle-assessment form as it is applied to Stan.) As mentioned earlier, this assessment includes a determination of whether he poses a danger to himself, since he did mention suicidal inclinations. During this assessment phase, which might take a few sessions, the Adlerian counselor explores his social relationships, his relationships with members of his family, his work responsibilities, his role as a man, and his feelings about himself. She places considerable emphasis on his goals in life and his priorities. She does not pay a great deal of attention to his past, except to show him the consistency between his past and present as he is moving toward the future.

Adlerian therapists assume that they can learn a great deal about the individual's dynamics from early recollections. Because Stan's counselor places value on exploring early recollections as a source of understanding his goals, motivations, and values, she asks him to report his earliest memories. He replies as follows:

> I was about 6. I went to school, and I was scared of the other kids and the teacher. When I came home, I cried and told my mother I didn't want to go back to school. She yelled at me and called me a baby. After that I felt horrible and even more scared.

Another of Stan's early recollections was at age 6½:

> My family was visiting my grandparents. I was playing outside, and some neighborhood kid hit me for no reason. We got in a big fight, and my mother came out and scolded me for being such a rough kid. She wouldn't believe me when I told her he had started the fight. I felt angry and hurt that she didn't believe me.

Based on these early recollections, Stan's counselor suggests that he sees life as frightening and unpredictably hostile and that he feels he cannot count on women; they are likely to be harsh, unbelieving, and uncaring.

Stan's counselor also encourages him to bring his dreams to the sessions, because she sees them as projections of his present concerns and possible rehearsals for living. He describes one of his childhood dreams: "I recall going to bed late at night and dreaming that the devil was at my window. It scared the hell out of me, and I remember burying myself under the covers to hide." Another dream, which Stan reports that he has often, goes as follows: "I'm alone in the desert, dying of thirst. I see people with water, but nobody seems to notice me, and nobody comes over to me to give me any water."

The counselor is interested in past dreams, recurring dreams, and recent dreams. In sharing with Stan her interpretation of his dreams, she suggests that he views life as basically frightening and that he cannot count on others to notice him or help him. Thus, he will do whatever he can to avoid confronting fearful situations.

During several therapy sessions Stan talks about his priorities. Initially he tentatively identifies one of his priorities as *superiority*. He tends to overstress the value of being competent, of accomplishing one feat after another, of winning, of being right at all costs, and of moving ahead in most situations. He tends to weigh himself down with the responsibility of constantly trying to prove himself, and he experiences a high level of stress in working so hard at being competent. Of course, his striving for superiority grows out of the pervasive feelings of inferiority that he has experienced for most of his life.

Eventually, Stan pinpoints *control* as his number-one priority. He often encounters situations that embarrass or humiliate him. He believes that if he can control his world, he can also control his painful feelings. Some of the methods that he uses to gain control over these feelings are escaping through alcohol, avoiding interpersonal situations that are threatening to him, keeping to himself, and deciding that he can't really count on others for psychological support. He is beginning to realize that although his style of seeking control apparently reduces his anxiety, he is paying a steep price for his behavior. The feelings he evokes in others are frustration and a lack of interest; for himself, the price he pays is distance from others and diminished spontaneity and creativity.

Having gathered the data based on the lifestyle assessment about his family constellation, his early recollections, his dreams, and his priorities, the therapist assists Stan in the process of summarizing and interpreting this information. Particular attention is given to identifying basic mistakes, which are faulty conclusions about life and self-defeating perceptions. In Stan's case some of the mistaken conclusions that form the core of his lifestyle are:

- "I must not get close to people, because they will surely hurt me."
- "Because my own parents didn't want me and didn't love me, I'll never be desired or loved by anybody."
- "If only I could become perfect, maybe people would acknowledge and accept me."
- "Being a man means not showing emotions."

The information that the counselor summarizes and interprets leads to insight and increased self-understanding on Stan's part. He becomes more aware of how he is functioning and how his *thinking* is contributing to his behavior and feelings. He learns that he is not "sick" and in need of being "cured"; rather, he is discouraged and needs to be encouraged to reorient his life. Through continued emphasis on his beliefs, goals, and intentions, he comes to see how his private logic is inaccurate. In his case the core of his style of life can be explained in this way: (1) "I am unloved, insignificant, and do not count"; (2) "the world is a threatening place to be, and life is unfair;" (3) "therefore, I must find ways to protect myself and keep safe." During this third phase of the process, his counselor makes interpretations centering on his lifestyle, his current direction, his goals and purposes, and how his private logic works. Of course, he is expected to carry out homework assignments that assist him in translating his insights into new behavior. In this way he is an active participant in his therapy.

In the final, or reorientation, phase of therapy Stan and his counselor work together to consider alternative attitudes, beliefs, and actions. By now he sees that he does not have to be locked into past patterns, feels encouraged, and realizes that he does have the power to change his life. He accepts that he will not change merely by gaining insights and knows that he will have to make use of these insights by carrying out an action-oriented plan. He begins to feel that he can create a new life for himself and not remain the victim of circumstances.

FOLLOW-UP: YOU CONTINUE AS STAN'S ADLERIAN THERAPIST.   Use these questions to help you think about how you would counsel Stan:

- What are some ways in which you would attempt to establish a relationship with Stan based on trust and respect? Can you imagine any difficulties you might have in developing this relationship?
- What aspects of Stan's lifestyle particularly interest you? In counseling him, how might these be explored?
- The Adlerian therapist identified four of Stan's mistaken conclusions. Can you identify with any of these basic mistakes? If so, do you think this would help or hinder your therapeutic effectiveness with him?
- Working from an Adlerian perspective, how might you assist Stan in discovering social interests and going beyond a preoccupation with his own problems?

# Summary and Evaluation

## SUMMARY

Adler was far ahead of his time, and most of the contemporary therapies have incorporated at least some of his ideas. His Individual Psychology assumes that people are motivated by social factors; are responsible for their own thoughts, feelings, and actions; are the creators of their own lives, as opposed to helpless victims; and are impelled by purposes and goals, looking more toward the future than to the past.

The basic goal of the Adlerian approach is to help clients identify and change their mistaken beliefs about life and thus participate more fully in a social world. Clients are not viewed as mentally sick but as discouraged. The therapeutic process helps them become aware of their patterns and make some basic changes in their beliefs and thinking, which lead to changes in the way they feel and behave. The role of the family in the development of the individual is emphasized. Therapy is a cooperative venture, structured by a contract and geared toward challenging clients to translate their insights into action in the real world.

Adlerian therapists are resourceful in drawing on many methods. The Adlerian viewpoint is applicable to a wide range of human relations, including but not limited to individual and group counseling, marital and family therapy, and the alleviation of social problems.

## CONTRIBUTIONS OF THE ADLERIAN APPROACH

The Adlerian approach gives practitioners a great deal of freedom in working with clients. Adlerian counselors are not bound to follow a specific procedure. Instead, they can use their clinical judgment in applying a wide range of techniques that they think will work best for a particular client.

The Adlerian concepts that I most draw on in my work with clients are (1) the importance of looking to one's life goals, including focusing on the direction they are leading one; (2) the focus on the individual's early experiences in the family, with special emphasis on their current impact; (3) the clinical use of early recollections; (4) the need to understand and confront basic mistakes; (5) the cognitive emphasis, which holds that emotions and behaviors are largely influenced by one's beliefs and thinking processes; (6) the idea of working out an action plan designed to help clients make changes; (7) the collaborative relationship, whereby the client and therapist work toward mutually agreed-on goals; and (8) the emphasis given to encouragement during the entire counseling process.

The Adlerian approach to social factors in personality lends itself exceptionally well to working with individuals in groups. Major Adlerian contributions have been made in the following areas: elementary education, consultation groups with teachers, parent-education groups, marriage counseling, and family counseling.

It is difficult to overestimate the contributions of Adler to contemporary therapeutic practice. His influence went beyond counseling individuals, extending into the community mental-health movement (Ansbacher, 1974). Abraham Maslow, Victor Frankl, Rollo May, and Albert Ellis have acknowledged their debt to Adler. Both Frankl and May see him as a forerunner of the existential movement because of his position that human beings are free to choose and are entirely responsible for what they make of themselves. This view makes him also a forerunner of the subjective approach to psychology, which focuses on the internal determinants of behavior: values, beliefs, attitudes, goals, interests, personal meanings, subjective perceptions of reality, and strivings toward self-realization.

In my opinion, one of Adler's most important contributions is his influence on other therapy systems. Many of his basic ideas have found their way into other psychological schools, such as family systems approaches, Gestalt therapy, learning theory, reality therapy, rational emotive behavior therapy, cognitive therapy, person-centered therapy, and logotherapy. All these approaches are based on a similar concept of the person as purposive and self-determining and as always striving for growth, value, and meaning in this world (Terner & Pew, 1978). In several important respects, Adler seems to have paved the way for the current developments in the cognitive therapies. Adlerians' basic premise is that if clients can change their thinking, then they can change their feelings and behavior.

CONTRIBUTIONS FROM A MULTICULTURAL PERSPECTIVE.    Although the Adlerian approach is called Individual Psychology, its focus is on the person in a social context. Adlerians' interest in helping others, in social interest, in belonging, and in the collective spirit fits well with the value systems of many ethnic groups. Those cultures that stress the welfare of the social group and that emphasize the role of the family will find the Adlerian focus on social interest to be congruent with their values. According to Mozdzierz and his colleagues (1984), Adlerians operate on the assumption that people are basically social, goal-seeking decision makers who live at their best when they cooperate, contribute to the common good, and face the demands of life. Therapists aim at increasing the individual's social interest and helping him or her contribute within an interpersonal framework.

Native American clients, for example, tend to value cooperation over competition. A client with an Indian cultural background told a story about a group of boys who were in a race. When one boy got ahead of the others, he would slow down and allow them to catch up, and they all made it to the finish line at the same time. Although the coach tried to explain that the point of the race was for an individual to finish first, these boys were socialized to work together cooperatively as a group. A counselor who would push individualistic and competitive values would be showing ignorance of socially oriented values in this case.

Clients who enter therapy are often locked into rigid ways of perceiving, interpreting, and behaving. It is likely that they have not questioned how their culture has influenced them. Thus, they may feel resigned to "the way things are." Mozdzierz and his colleagues (1984) characterize these clients as myopic and contend that one of the therapist's functions is to provide them with another pair of glasses that will allow them to see things more clearly. The Adlerian emphasis on the subjective fashion in which people view and interpret their world leads to a respect for clients' unique values and perceptions. Adlerian counselors use interpretations as an opportunity for clients to view things from a different perspective, yet it is up to the clients to decide whether to open their eyes and to use these glasses. Adlerians do not decide for clients what they should change or what their goals should be; rather, they work collaboratively with their clients in ways that enable them to reach their self-defined goals.

Not only is Adlerian theory congruent with the values of many cultural groups, but the approach offers flexibility in applying a range of cognitive and action-oriented techniques to helping clients explore their practical problems. As we have seen, Adlerian practitioners are not wedded to any particular set of procedures. Instead, they are conscious of the value of fitting their techniques to the needs of their clients. Although they utilize a diverse range of methods, most of them do conduct an assessment of each client's lifestyle. This assessment is heavily focused on the structure and dynamics within the client's family. Because of their cultural background, many clients have been conditioned to respect their family heritage and to appreciate the impact of their family on their own personal development. It is essential that counselors be sensitive to the conflicting feelings and struggles of their clients. If counselors demonstrate an understanding of these cultural values, it is likely that these clients will be receptive to an exploration of their lifestyle. Such an exploration will involve a detailed discussion of their own place within their family.

It should be noted that different authors give the term *culture* various meanings. Also, if culture is considered as a broad concept (to include age, roles, lifestyle, and gender differences), there can be cultural differences even within a family. The Adlerian approach emphasizes the value of subjectively understanding the unique world of an individual. Culture is one significant dimension for grasping the subjective and experiential perspective of an individual. Pedersen expresses this idea well: "Culture provides a metaphor to better understand the different perspectives within each of us as our different social roles compete, complement, and cooperate with one another in our decisions. It also provides an alternative for better understanding others whose culturally learned assumptions are different from our own" (1990, p. 94).

Adlerians view a client's cultural heritage in the same way that they address birth order. Indeed, both birth order and culture are vantage points, contexts from which one views self, others, and life. Vantage points can be generally described, but they are not the same for all individuals within them. In this sense, culture is an influence on each person within it, and it is expressed within each individual differently, according to the perception, evaluation, and interpretation of culture that the person holds.

Adlerian counselors seek to be sensitive to cultural and gender issues. Adler was one of the first psychologists at the turn of the century to advocate equality for women. He recognized that men and women were different in many ways, but he felt that the two genders were deserving of equal value and respect. This respect and appreciation for difference extends to culture as well as gender. Adlerians find in different cultures opportunities for viewing the self, others, and the world in multidimensional ways. Indeed, the strengths of one culture can often help correct the mistakes in another culture.

## LIMITATIONS AND CRITICISMS OF THE ADLERIAN APPROACH

Adler had to choose between devoting his time to formalizing his theory and teaching others the basic concepts of Individual Psychology. He placed practicing and teaching before organizing and presenting a well-defined and systematic theory. Thus, his writing style is often difficult to follow. Many of his ideas are somewhat loose and simplistic.

Although Individual Psychology has undergone further development and refinement, many of Adler's original formulations were stated in such a way that it would be difficult to empirically validate the basic hypotheses. Some of his basic concepts were global in nature and poorly defined, such as notions of the struggle for superiority, the creative power of the self, and the inferiority complex. He has been accused of basing most of his approach on a common-sense psychology and of oversimplifying complex concepts.

LIMITATIONS FROM A MULTICULTURAL PERSPECTIVE.  As is true of most Western models, the Adlerian approach tends to focus on the self as the locus of change and responsibility. Because other cultures have different conceptions, this primary emphasis on changing the autonomous self may be problematic for many clients.

Another limitation of Adlerian therapy involves its detailed explorations of one's early childhood, early memories, and dynamics within the family. Many clients who have pressing problems are likely to resent intrusions into areas of their lives that they may not see as connected to the struggles that bring them into therapy. For example, some clients may not see any point to going into the details of their lifestyle. Adlerians are aware that there are better ways of dealing with life problems than the ones the client is using, but they also know that there is no "one right way." Although therapists have expertise in the problems of living, they are not experts in solving other people's problems. Instead, they view it as their function to teach people alternative methods of coping with life concerns. However, the culture of some clients may contribute to their viewing the counselor as the "expert" and expecting that the counselor will provide them with the solutions to their problems.

# Where to Go from Here

If you find that your thinking is allied with the Adlerian approach, you might consider seeking training in Individual Psychology or becoming a member of the North American Society of Adlerian Psychology (NASAP). To obtain current information on the society, contact:

North American Society of Adlerian Psychology
65 East Wacker Place, Suite 400
Chicago, IL 60601
Telephone: (312) 629-8801

The society publishes a newsletter and a quarterly journal, and it maintains a list of training programs and workshops in Adlerian psychology. The quarterly *Individual Psychology: The Journal of Adlerian Theory, Research, and Practice* presents scholarly and professional research. Columns on counseling, education, and parent and family education are regular features. Information about subscriptions is available from NASAP.

If you are interested in pursuing a degree or obtaining training, postgraduate study, or continuing education, contact NASAP for a list of 58 Adlerian organizations and institutes. A few of these training institutes, some of which grant degrees, are listed below:

Adler School of Professional Psychology
65 East Wacker Place
Chicago, IL 60601
Telephone: (312) 201-5900

Adler-Dreikurs Institute of Human Relations
Room 0313, MLK Building
Bowie State University
Bowie, MD 20715
Telephone: (301) 464-7560

Alfred Adler Institute of Minnesota
1001 Highway 7, Suite 344
Hopkins, MN 55305
Telephone: (612) 933-9363

Alfred Adler Institute of New York
1780 Broadway, Suite 502
New York, NY 10019
Telephone: (212) 974-0431

Americas Institute of Adlerian Studies
Robert L. Powers and Jane Griffith
600 North McClurg Court, Suite 2502A
Chicago, IL 60611-3027
Telephone: (312) 337-5066

Americas Institute of Adlerian Studies
486 Hillway Drive
Vista, CA 92084
Telephone: (619) 758-4658

## Recommended Supplementary Readings

*Adlerian Counseling: A Practical Approach for a New Decade* (Sweeney, 1989) is the most comprehensive source on Adlerian counseling. It includes his life and work, an explanation of many key Adlerian concepts, and an overview of the counseling process as it is applied to individuals, couples, families, and groups.

*Understanding Life-Style: The Psycho-Clarity Process* (Powers & Griffith, 1987) is one of the best sources of information for doing a lifestyle assessment. This book comes alive with many good clinical examples. Separate chapters deal with interview techniques, lifestyle assessment, early recollections, the family constellation, and methods of summarizing and interpreting information.

*How You Feel Is Up to You* (McKay & Dinkmeyer, 1994) is a self-help book based on the assumption that our beliefs create our feelings. The authors deal with such topics as guilt, anger, depression, anxiety, and joy, focusing on the connection between thinking processes and feelings and actions.

*Psychopathology and Psychotherapy: From Diagnosis to Treatment* (Sperry & Carlson, 1993) is a complete Adlerian assessment of psychopathology coupled with therapeutic interventions.

## References and Suggested Readings*

ADLER, A. (1958). *What life should mean to you.* New York: Capricorn.

ADLER, A. (1964a). The Individual Psychology of Alfred Adler. In H. L. Ansbacher & R. R. Ansbacher (Eds.), *The Individual Psychology of Alfred Adler.* New York: Harper & Row (Torchbooks).

ADLER, A. (1964b). *Social interest: A challenge to mankind.* New York: Capricorn.

* ADLER, A. (1979). *Superiority and social interest: A collection of later writings* (3rd Rev. ed.) (H. L. Ansbacher & R. R. Ansbacher, Eds.). New York: Norton.

ALLEN, T. W. (1971). The Individual Psychology of Alfred Adler: An item of history and a promise of revolution. *The Counseling Psychologist, 3,* 3–24.

ANSBACHER, H. L. (1974). Goal-oriented individual psychology: Alfred Adler's theory. In A. Burton (Ed.), *Operational theories of personality.* New York: Brunner/Mazel.

* ANSBACHER, H. L. (1979). The increasing recognition of Adler. In A. Adler, *Superiority and social interest: A collection of later writings* (3rd Rev. ed). New York: Norton.

* ANSBACHER, H. L., & ANSBACHER, R. R. (Eds.). (1964). *The Individual Psychology of Alfred Adler.* New York: Harper & Row (Torchbooks).

COREY, G. (1995). *Theory and practice of group counseling* (4th ed.). Pacific Grove, CA: Brooks/Cole.

*Books and articles marked with an asterisk are suggested for further study.

* COREY, G. (1996). *Case approach to counseling and psychotherapy* (4th ed.). Pacific Grove, CA: Brooks/Cole.

CORSINI, R. J. (1990). Adlerian psychotherapy. In J. K. Zeig & W. M. Munion (Eds.), *What is psychotherapy? Contemporary perspectives* (pp. 50–53). San Francisco: Jossey-Bass.

DINKMEYER, D. (1975). Adlerian group psychotherapy. *International Journal of Group Psychotherapy, 25,* 219–226.

DINKMEYER, D. C. (1976). *Developing understanding of self and others* (D-2 Kit). Circle Pines, MN: American Guidance Service.

DINKMEYER, D., & CARLSON, J. (1984). *Training in marriage enrichment.* Circle Pines, MN: American Guidance Service.

* DINKMEYER, D. C., DINKMEYER, D. C., Jr., & SPERRY, L. (1987). *Adlerian counseling and psychotherapy* (2nd ed.). Columbus, OH: Merrill.

DINKMEYER, D., & DINKMEYER, J. (1982). Adlerian marriage therapy. *Individual Psychology, 38,* 115–122.

DINKMEYER, D., & DINKMEYER, R. (1963). *Encouraging children to learn: The encouragement process.* Englewood Cliffs, NJ: Prentice-Hall.

DINKMEYER, D., & ECKSTEIN, D. (1993). *Leadership by encouragement.* Dubuque, IA: Kendall/Hunt.

DINKMEYER, D., & LOSONCY, L. E. (1980). *The encouragement book: Becoming a positive person.* Englewood Cliffs, NJ: Prentice-Hall.

DINKMEYER, D., MCKAY, G., DINKMEYER, D., Jr., & MCKAY, J. (1987). *The effective parent.* Circle Pines, MN: American Guidance Service.

* DREIKURS, R. (1953). *Fundamentals of Adlerian psychology.* Chicago: Alfred Adler Institute.

DREIKURS, R. (1967). *Psychodynamics, psychotherapy, and counseling: Collected papers.* Chicago: Alfred Adler Institute.

DREIKURS, R. (1968). *Psychology in the classroom* (2nd ed.). New York: Harper & Row.

DREIKURS, R. (1969). Group psychotherapy from the point of view of Adlerian psychology. In H. M. Ruitenbeek (Ed.), *Group therapy today: Styles, methods, and techniques.* New York: Aldine-Atherton.

DREIKURS, R. (1971). *Social equality: The challenge of today.* Chicago: Regnery.

DREIKURS, R., & MOSAK, H. H. (1966). The tasks of life: I. Adler's three tasks. *The Individual Psychologist, 4,* 18–22.

DREIKURS, R., & MOSAK, H. H. (1967). The tasks of life: II. The fourth task. *The Individual Psychologist, 4,* 51–55.

DREIKURS, R., & SOLTZ, V. (1964). *Children: The challenge.* New York: Meridith Press.

ECKSTEIN, D., BARUTH, L., & MAHRER, D. (1992). *An introduction to life-style assessment.* Dubuque, IA: Kendall/Hunt.

* GRIFFITH, J., & POWERS, R. L. (1984). *An Adlerian lexicon.* Chicago: Americas Institute of Adlerian Studies.

GUSHURST, R. S. (1971). The technique, utility, and validity of life style analysis. *The Counseling Psychologist, 3,* 31–40.

KEFIR, N. (1981). Impasse/priority therapy. In R. J. Corsini (Ed.), *Handbook of innovative psychotherapies* (pp. 401–415). New York: Wiley.

LOWE, R. N. (1982). Adlerian/Dreikursian family counseling. In A. M. Horne & M. M. Ohlsen (Eds.), *Family counseling and therapy.* Itasca, IL: F. E. Peacock.

MANASTER, G. J. (1990). Adlerian psychotherapy. In J. K. Zeig & W. M. Munion (Eds.), *What is psychotherapy? Contemporary perspectives* (pp. 45–49). San Francisco: Jossey-Bass.

* MANASTER, G. J., & CORSINI, R. J. (1982). *Individual Psychology: Theory and practice.* Itasca, IL: F. E. Peacock.

MCKAY, G. D., & DINKMEYER, D. (1994). *How you feel is up to you.* San Luis Obispo, CA: Impact Publishers.

MOSAK, H. (1977) *On purpose.* Chicago: Alfred Adler Institute.

MOSAK, H. (1987). *Ha, ha, and aha.* Muncie, IN: Accelerated Development.

* MOSAK, H. (1995). Adlerian psychotherapy. In R. J. Corsini & D. Wedding (Eds.), *Current psychotherapies* (5th ed.) (pp. 51–94). Itasca, IL: F. E. Peacock.

* MOSAK, H., & SHULMAN, B. (1988). *Life style inventory.* Muncie, IN: Accelerated Development.

MOZDZIERZ, G. J., LISIECKI, J., BITTER, J. R., & WILLIAMS, A. L. (1984). *Role-functions for Adlerian therapists.* Unpublished paper.

MOZDZIERZ, G. J., MACCHITELLI, F. J., & LISIECKI, J. (1976). The paradox in psychotherapy: An Adlerian perspective. *Journal of Individual Psychology, 32*(2), 169–184.

PEDERSEN, P. (1990). The multicultural perspective as a fourth force in counseling. *Journal of Mental Health Counseling, 12*(1), 93–95.

PEVEN, D. E., & SHULMAN, B. H. (1986). Adlerian psychotherapy. In I. L. Kutash and A. Wolf (Eds.), *Psychotherapist's casebook* (pp. 101–123). San Francisco: Jossey-Bass.

* POWERS, R. L., & GRIFFITH, J. (1986). *The Individual Psychology client workbook.* Chicago: Americas Institute of Adlerian Studies.

* POWERS, R. L., & GRIFFITH, J. (1987). *Understanding life-style: The psycho-clarity process.* Chicago: Americas Institute of Adlerian Studies.

SCHULTZ, D., & SCHULTZ, S. E. (1994). *Theories of personality* (5th ed.). Pacific Grove, CA: Brooks/Cole.

SHERMAN, R., & DINKMEYER, D. (1987). *Systems of family therapy: An Adlerian integration.* New York: Brunner/Mazel.

* SHULMAN, B., & MOSAK, H. (1988). *Manual for life style assessment.* Muncie, IN: Accelerated Development.

* SPERRY, L., & CARLSON, J. (1993). *Psychopathology and psychotherapy: From diagnosis to treatment.* Muncie, IN: Accelerated Development.

* SWEENEY, T. J. (1989). *Adlerian counseling: A practical approach for a new decade* (3rd ed.). Muncie, IN: Accelerated Development.

TERNER, J., & PEW, W. L. (1978). *The courage to be imperfect: The life and work of Rudolf Dreikurs.* New York: Hawthorn Books.

# Existential Therapy

# VIKTOR FRANKL

VIKTOR FRANKL (b. 1905) was born and educated in Vienna. He founded the Youth Advisement Centers there in 1928 and directed them until 1938. He was also on the staff at several clinics and hospitals. From 1942 to 1945 Frankl was a prisoner in the Nazi concentration camps at Auschwitz and Dachau, where his parents, brother, wife, and children died. He vividly remembers his horrible experiences in these camps, yet he has been able to use them in a constructive way and has not allowed them to dampen his love and enthusiasm for life. In the late 1940s he married his present wife, Elleonara, with whom he lives in Austria. He has traveled all around the world and still gives lectures in Europe, Latin America, Southeast Asia, and the United States.

Frankl receive his M.D. in 1930 and his Ph.D. in 1949, both from the University of Vienna. Additionally, he holds honorary doctorates from more than 120 universities around the world. He became an associate professor at the University of Vienna and later was a distinguished speaker at the United States International University in San Diego. He has also been a visiting professor at Harvard, Stanford, and Southern Methodist universities. Frankl's works have been translated into more than 20 languages, and he continues to have a major impact on the development of existential therapy. His compelling book *Man's Search for Meaning* has been a best-seller around the world.

Although Frankl had begun to develop an existential approach to clinical practice before his grim years in the Nazi death camps, his experiences there confirmed his views. He observed and personally experienced the truths expressed by existential philosophers and writers, including the view that love is the highest goal to which humans can aspire and that our salvation is through love (1963, p. 59). That we have choices in every situation is another notion confirmed by his experiences in the concentration camps. Even in terrible situations, he believes, we can preserve a vestige of spiritual freedom and independence of mind. He learned experientially that everything could be taken from a person but one thing: "the last of human freedoms—to choose one's attitude in any given set of circumstances, to choose one's own way" (1963, p. 104). Frankl believes that the essence of being human lies in searching for meaning and purpose. We can discover this meaning through our actions and deeds, by experiencing a value (such as love or achievements through work), and by suffering.

As you will see, there was no single founder of the existential approach, because it had its roots in diverse movements. I have selected Frankl as one of its key figures because of the dramatic way in which his theories were tested by the tragedies of his life. His life is an illustration of his theory, for he lives what his theory espouses. Although others have written about existential concepts, they have not met with the popularity of Frankl.

# ROLLO MAY

ROLLO MAY (1909–1994) first lived in Ohio and then moved to Michigan as a young child with his five brothers and sister. He remembered his home life as being unhappy, a situation that had something to do with his interest in psychology and counseling. In his personal life May struggled with his own existential concerns and the failure of two marriages.

During his youth May spent some time studying ancient Greek civilization, which he believed gave him a perspective on human nature. He later traveled to Vienna and studied with Alfred Adler. While he was pursuing his doctoral program, he came down with tuberculosis, which resulted in a two-year stay in a sanitarium. During his recovery period he spent much time reading and learning firsthand about the nature of anxiety. This study resulted in his book *The Meaning of Anxiety* (1950), which he considered the watershed of his career (Rabinowitz et al., 1989). His popular book *Love and Will* (1969) reflects his own personal struggles with love and intimate relationships and mirrors Western society's questioning of its values pertaining to sex and marriage.

The greatest personal influence on May was the German philosopher Paul Tillich (author of *The Courage to Be,* 1952), who spent much time with him discussing philosophical, religious, and psychological topics. Most of May's writings reflect a concern with the nature of human experience, such as recognizing and dealing with power, accepting freedom and responsibility, and discovering one's identity. He draws from his rich knowledge based on the classics and his existential perspective.

May was one of the main proponents of humanistic approaches to psychotherapy, and he was the principal American spokesman of European existential thinking as it is applied to psychotherapy. His view is that psychotherapy should be aimed at helping people discover the meaning of their lives and should be concerned with the problems of *being* rather than with problem solving. Questions of being include learning to deal with issues such as sex and intimacy, growing old, and facing death. According to May, the real challenge is for people to be able to live in a world where they are alone and where they will eventually have to face death. He contends that our individualism should be balanced by what Adler refers to as social interest. May asserts that there is too much concern about the self and not enough concern about society and culture (Rabinowitz et al., 1989). Therapists need to help individuals find ways to contribute to the betterment of the society in which they live. He maintains that therapists should address the higher aspirations of the human race, including those values that make life worth living. If individuals in society were grounded on these higher values, therapists might well be out of business.

# Introduction

Existential therapy can best be described as a *philosophical approach* that influences a counselor's therapeutic practice. As such it is not a separate school of therapy or a neatly defined model with specific techniques. Thus, this chapter will focus on some of the existential ideas and themes that have significant implications for the existentially oriented practitioner.

The existential approach rejects the deterministic view of human nature espoused by orthodox psychoanalysis and radical behaviorism. Psychoanalysis sees freedom as restricted by unconscious forces, irrational drives, and past events; behaviorists see freedom as restricted by sociocultural conditioning. In contrast, existential therapists, while acknowledging some of these facts about the human situation, emphasize our freedom to choose what to make of our circumstances. This approach is grounded on the assumption that we are free and therefore responsible for our choices and actions. We are the author of our life, and we draw up the blueprints for its design.

A basic existential premise is that we are not the victim of circumstances, because to a large extent we are what we choose to be. A major aim of therapy is to encourage clients to reflect on life, to recognize their range of alternatives, and to decide among them. Once clients begin the process of recognizing the ways in which they have passively accepted circumstances and surrendered control, they can start on a path of consciously shaping their own lives.

Van Deurzen-Smith (1988) writes that existential counseling is not designed to *cure* people in the tradition of the medical model. Rather, clients are viewed as being sick of life or awkward at living. They need help in surveying the terrain and in deciding on the best route to take, so that they can ultimately discover their own way. Existential therapy is a process of searching for the value and meaning in life. The therapist's basic task is to encourage clients to explore their options for creating a meaningful existence. We can begin by recognizing that we do not have to remain the passive victim of our circumstances but instead can consciously become the architect of our life.*

## HISTORICAL BACKGROUND

There are many streams in the existential-therapy movement. It was not founded by any particular person or group. Rather, drawing from a major orientation in philosophy, it arose spontaneously in different parts of Europe and among different schools of psychology and psychiatry in the 1940s and 1950s. It grew out of an effort to help people resolve the dilemmas of contemporary life, such as isolation, alienation, and meaninglessness. Early writers focused on the individual's experience of being alone in the world and facing the anxiety of this situation. Rather than trying to develop sets of rules for therapy, they focused on understanding these deep human experiences (May & Yalom, 1995).

*I would like to thank Emmy van Deurzen-Smith and J. Michael Russell for their significant roles in the revision of this chapter.

Frankl, as the biographical sketch at the beginning of the chapter made clear, was a central figure in developing existential therapy. As a student of Freud, he began his career in psychiatry with a psychoanalytic orientation. Later he was influenced by the writings of existential philosophers, and he began developing his own existential philosophy and psychotherapy. He is fond of quoting Nietzsche: "He who has a *why* to live for can bear with almost any *how*" (1963, pp. 121, 164). Frankl contends that those words could be the motto for all psychotherapeutic practice. Another quotation from Nietzsche seems to capture the essence of his own experience and his writings: "That which does not kill me, makes me stronger" (1963, p. 130).

Frankl reacted against most of Freud's deterministic notions and built his theory and practice of psychotherapy on such basic concepts as freedom, responsibility, meaning, and the search for values. He developed *logotherapy*, which means "therapy through meaning." The central theme running through his works is the *will to meaning*. According to him, the modern person has the means to live but often has no meaning to live for. The malady of our time is meaninglessness, or the "existential vacuum" that is often experienced when people do not busy themselves with routine and with work. The therapeutic process is aimed at challenging individuals to find meaning and purpose through, among other things, suffering, work, and love (Frankl, 1965).

May, as we have also seen, was one of the key figures responsible for bringing existentialism from Europe to the United States and translating key concepts into psychotherapeutic practice. His writings have had a significant impact on existentially oriented practitioners. Of primary importance in introducing existential therapy to the United States was the book *Existence: A New Dimension in Psychiatry and Psychology* (May, Angel, & Ellenberger, 1958). According to May, it takes courage to "be," and our choices determine the kind of person we become. There is a constant struggle within us. Although we want to grow toward maturity and independence, we realize that expansion is often a painful process. Hence, the struggle is between the security of dependence and the delights and pains of growth.

Along with May, two other significant existential therapists in the United States are James Bugental and Irvin Yalom. Bugental, in his book *The Art of the Psychotherapist* (1987), describes a life-changing approach to therapy. He views therapy as a journey taken by the therapist and the client that delves deeply into the client's subjective world. He emphasizes that this quest demands the willingness of the therapist to be in contact with his or her own phenomenological world. According to Bugental, the central concern of therapy is to help clients examine how they have answered life's existential questions and to challenge them to revise their answers in order to begin living authentically.

Yalom acknowledges the contributions of both European and American psychologists and psychiatrists who have influenced the development of existential thinking and practice. Drawing on his clinical experience and on empirical research, philosophy, and literature, Yalom has developed an existential approach to therapy that focuses on four ultimate human concerns: death, freedom, existential isolation, and meaninglessness. His comprehensive textbook,

*Existential Psychotherapy* (1980), is considered a pioneering accomplishment. He acknowledges Frankl as an eminently pragmatic thinker who has had an impact on his writing and practice. Yalom believes that the vast majority of experienced therapists, regardless of their theoretical orientation, employ many of the existential themes that he discusses in his book. He contends that the four ultimate concerns, which constitute the heart of existential psychodynamics, have enormous relevance to clinical work.

# Key Concepts

## VIEW OF HUMAN NATURE

The crucial significance of the existential movement is that it reacts against the tendency to identify therapy with a set of techniques. Instead, it bases therapeutic practice on an understanding of what makes men and women *human* beings. The existential movement stands for respect for the person, for exploring new aspects of human behavior, and for divergent methods of understanding people. It uses numerous approaches to therapy based on its assumptions about human nature.

The existential tradition in Europe emphasizes the limitations and tragic dimensions of human existence. Existential philosophies provided the foundation for therapeutic approaches that focused on the alienated and fragmented individual who found no meaning in the family or in the social institutions of the time. These approaches grew out of a desire to help people address themes in contemporary life such as isolation, alienation, and meaninglessness. They addressed people who were experiencing difficulty in finding meaning and purpose in life and in maintaining their identity (Holt, 1986).

The current focus of the existential approach is on clients who feel alone in the world and are facing the anxiety of this isolation. Rather than trying to develop rules for therapy, existential practitioners strive to understand these deep human experiences (May & Yalom, 1995).

The existential view of human nature is captured, in part, by the notion that the significance of our existence is never fixed once and for all; rather, we continually re-create ourselves through our projects. Humans are in a constant state of transition, emerging, evolving, and becoming. Being a person implies that we are discovering and making sense of our existence. We continually question ourselves, others, and the world. Although the specific questions we raise vary in accordance with our developmental stage in life, the fundamental themes do not vary. We pose questions such as "Who am I? Who have I been? Whom can I become? Where am I going?" There are no preexisting designs and no meanings that are assigned or given to us (Fischer & Fischer, 1983).

The basic dimensions of the human condition, according to the existential approach, include (1) the capacity for self-awareness; (2) freedom and responsibility; (3) creating one's identity and establishing meaningful relationships with others; (4) the search for meaning, purpose, values, and goals; (5) anxiety as a condition of living; and (6) awareness of death and nonbeing. I develop these propositions below by summarizing themes that emerge in the writings of existential therapists, and I also discuss the implications for counseling practice of each of these propositions.

## PROPOSITION 1: THE CAPACITY FOR SELF-AWARENESS

As human beings we can reflect and make choices because we are capable of self-awareness. The greater our awareness, the greater our possibilities for freedom (see Proposition 2). Thus, to expand our awareness is to increase our capacity to live fully. We become aware that:

- We are finite, and we do not have an unlimited time to do what we want with our life.
- We have the potential to take action or not to act; inaction is a decision.
- We choose our actions, and therefore we can partially create our own destiny.
- Meaning is not automatically bestowed on us but is the product of our searching and of our discovering a unique purpose.
- Existential anxiety, which is basically a consciousness of our own freedom, is an essential part of living; as we increase our awareness of the choices available to us, we also increase our sense of responsibility for the consequences of these choices.
- We are subject to loneliness, meaninglessness, emptiness, guilt, and isolation.
- We are basically alone, yet we have an opportunity to relate to other beings.

Awareness can be conceptualized in the following way: Picture yourself walking down a long hallway with many doors on each side. Let yourself imagine that you can choose to open some of the doors, either a crack or fully, or to leave them closed. Perhaps if you opened one of the doors, you would not like what you saw—it might be fearsome or ugly. But you might also discover a room filled with beauty. You might debate with yourself whether to leave a door shut or attempt to pry it open.

We can choose either to expand or to restrict our consciousness. Because self-awareness is at the root of most other human capacities, the decision to expand it is fundamental to human growth. What follows is a list of some dawning awarenesses that individuals experience in the counseling process:

- They see how they are trading the security of dependence for the anxieties that accompany choosing for themselves.
- They begin to see that their identity is anchored in someone else's definition of them; that is, they are seeking approval and confirmation of their being in others instead of looking to themselves for affirmation.
- They learn that in many ways they are keeping themselves prisoner by some of their past decisions, and they realize that they can make new decisions.
- They learn that although they cannot change certain events in their lives, they can change the way they view and react to these events.

- They learn that they are not condemned to a future similar to the past, for they can learn from their past and thereby reshape their future.
- They realize that they are so preoccupied with death and dying that they are not appreciating living.
- They are able to accept their limitations yet still feel worthwhile, for they understand that they do not need to be perfect to feel worthy.
- They can come to realize that they are failing to live in the present moment because of preoccupation with the past, planning for the future, or trying to do too many things at once.

Increasing self-awareness, which includes awareness of alternatives, motivations, factors influencing the person, and personal goals, is an aim of all counseling. It is the therapist's task to indicate to the client that a price must be paid for increased awareness. As one becomes more aware, one finds it more difficult to "go home again." Ignorance of one's condition may have brought contentment along with a feeling of partial deadness, but as one opens the doors in one's world, one can expect more struggle as well as the potential for more fulfillment.

## PROPOSITION 2: FREEDOM AND RESPONSIBILITY

A characteristic theme of existential literature is that people are free to choose among alternatives and therefore have a large role in shaping their destinies. Even though we have no choice about being thrust into the world, the manner in which we live and what we become are the result of our choices. Because of the reality of this essential freedom, we must accept the responsibility for directing our lives. However, it is possible to avoid this reality by making excuses. In speaking about "bad faith," the existentialist philosopher Jean-Paul Sartre (1971) refers to the inauthenticity of not accepting personal responsibility. Examples of statements of bad faith are: "Since that's the way I'm made, I couldn't help what I did" or "Naturally I'm this way, because I grew up in an alcoholic family." For Sartre we are constantly confronted with the choice of what kind of person we are becoming, and to exist is never to be finished with this kind of choosing.

We are entirely responsible for our lives, for our actions, and for our failures to take action. From Sartre's perspective people are condemned to freedom. He calls for a *commitment* to choosing for ourselves. Existential guilt is being aware of having evaded a commitment, or having chosen not to choose. This is the guilt we experience when we do not live authentically. It results from allowing others to define us or to make our choices for us. Sartre said, "We are our choices." An inauthentic mode of existence consists of lacking awareness of personal responsibility for our lives and passively assuming that our existence is largely controlled by external forces. By contrast, living authentically implies being true to our own evaluation of what is a valuable existence for ourselves.

For existentialists, then, being free and being human are identical. Freedom and responsibility go hand in hand. We are the author of our life in the sense that we create our destiny, our life situation, and our problems (Russell, 1978).

Assuming responsibility is a basic condition for change. Clients who refuse to accept responsibility by persistently blaming others for their problems will not profit from therapy.

Frankl (1978) also links freedom with responsibility. He has suggested that the Statue of Liberty on the East Coast be supplemented by a Statue of Responsibility on the West Coast. His basic premise is that freedom is bound by certain limitations, because we are not free from conditions. But our freedom consists of taking a stand against such restrictions. Ultimately, these conditions are subject to our decisions. We are responsible.

Existential therapists continually focus on clients' responsibility for their situation. They will not allow clients to blame others, to blame external forces, or to blame heredity. If clients do not recognize and accept their responsibility for having created their situation, there is little motivation for them to commit themselves to personal change (May & Yalom, 1995; Yalom, 1980).

The therapist assists clients in discovering how they are avoiding freedom and encourages them to learn to risk using it. Not to do so is to cripple clients and make them neurotically dependent on the therapist. Therapists need to teach clients that they can explicitly accept that they have choices, even though they may have devoted most of their life to evading them.

People often come to counselors because they feel that they have lost control of how they are living. They may look to the counselor to direct them, give them advice, or produce magical cures. They may also need to be heard and understood. Two central tasks of the therapist are inviting clients to recognize how they have allowed others to decide for them and encouraging them to take steps toward autonomy. In challenging clients to explore other ways of being that are more fulfilling than their present restricted existence, some existential counselors ask, "Although you have lived in a certain pattern, now that you recognize the price of some of your ways, are you willing to consider creating new patterns?" Others may have a vested interest in keeping the client in an old pattern, so the initiative for changing it will have to come from the client.

## PROPOSITION 3: STRIVING FOR IDENTITY AND RELATIONSHIP TO OTHERS

People are concerned about preserving their uniqueness and centeredness, yet at the same time they have an interest in going outside of themselves to relate to other beings and to nature. Each of us would like to discover a self—that is, to find (or create) our personal identity. This is not an automatic process, and it takes courage. As relational beings, we also strive for a connectedness with others. We must give of ourselves to others and be concerned with them. Many existential writers discuss loneliness, uprootedness, and alienation, which can be seen as the failure to develop ties with others and with nature.

The trouble with so many of us is that we have sought directions, answers, values, and beliefs from the important people in our world. Rather than trusting ourselves to search within and find our own answers to the conflicts in our life, we sell out by becoming what others expect of us. Our being becomes rooted in their expectations, and we become strangers to ourselves.

THE COURAGE TO BE.    It does take courage to learn how to live from the inside (Tillich, 1952). We struggle to discover, to create, and to maintain the core deep within our being. One of the greatest fears of clients is that they will discover that there is no core, no self, no substance and that they are merely reflections of everyone's expectations of them. A client may say: "My fear is that I'll discover I'm nobody, that there really is nothing to me. I'll find out that I'm an empty shell, hollow inside, and nothing will exist if I shed my masks."

Existential therapists may begin by asking their clients to allow themselves to intensify the feeling that they are nothing more than the sum of others' expectations and that they are merely the introjects of parents and parent substitutes. How do they feel now? Are they condemned to stay this way forever? Is there a way out? Can they create a self if they find that they are without one? Where can they begin? Once clients have demonstrated the courage to simply recognize this fear, to put it into words and share it, it does not seem so overwhelming. I find that it is best to begin work by inviting clients to accept the ways in which they have lived outside themselves and to explore ways in which they are out of contact with themselves.

THE EXPERIENCE OF ALONENESS.    The existentialists postulate that part of the human condition is the experience of aloneness. But they add that we can derive strength from the experience of looking to ourselves and sensing our separation. The sense of isolation comes when we recognize that we cannot depend on anyone else for our own confirmation; that is, we alone must give a sense of meaning to our life, and we alone must decide how we will live. If we are unable to tolerate ourselves when we are alone, how can we expect anyone else to be enriched by our company? Before we can have any solid relationship with another, we must have a relationship with ourselves. We must learn to listen to ourselves. We have to be able to stand alone before we can truly stand beside another.

There is a paradox in the proposition that humans are existentially both alone and related, but this very paradox describes the human condition. To think that we can cure the condition, or that it should be cured, is a mistake. Ultimately we are alone.

THE EXPERIENCE OF RELATEDNESS.    We humans depend on relationships with others. We want to be significant in another's world, and we want to feel that another's presence is important in our world. When we are able to stand alone and dip within ourselves for our own strength, our relationships with others are based on our fulfillment, not our deprivation. If we feel personally deprived, however, we can expect little but a clinging, parasitic, symbiotic relationship with someone else.

Perhaps one of the functions of therapy is to help clients distinguish between a neurotically dependent attachment to another and a life-affirming relationship in which both persons are enhanced. The therapist can challenge clients to examine what they get from their relationships, how they avoid intimate contact, how they prevent themselves from having equal relationships, and how they might create therapeutic, healthy, and mature human relationships.

STRUGGLING WITH OUR IDENTITY.    The awareness of our ultimate aloneness can be frightening. Just as many shrink from accepting freedom and responsibility out of fear of the risks involved, some may attempt to avoid accepting their aloneness and isolation. Farha (1994) points out that because of our fear of dealing with our aloneness, some of us get caught up in ritualistic behavior patterns that cement us to an image or identity we acquired in early childhood. He writes that some of us become trapped in a *doing* mode to avoid the experience of *being*.

Part of the therapeutic journey consists of the therapist challenging clients to begin to examine the ways in which they have lost touch with their identity, especially by letting others design their life for them. The therapy process itself is often frightening for clients when they realize that they have surrendered their freedom to others and that in the therapy relationship they will have to assume back their freedom. By refusing to give easy solutions or answers, therapists thus confront clients with the reality that they alone must find their own answers.

## PROPOSITION 4: THE SEARCH FOR MEANING

A distinctly human characteristic is the struggle for a sense of significance and purpose in life. In my experience the underlying conflicts that bring people into counseling and therapy are centered in the existential questions "Why am I here? What do I want from life? What gives my life purpose? Where is the source of meaning for me in life?"

Existential therapy can provide the conceptual framework for helping the client challenge the meaning in his or her life. Questions that the therapist might ask are "Do you like the direction of your life? Are you pleased with what you now are and what you are becoming? If you are confused about who you are and what you want for yourself, what are you doing to get some clarity?"

THE PROBLEM OF DISCARDING OLD VALUES.    One of the problems in therapy is that clients may discard traditional values (and imposed values) without finding other, suitable ones to replace them. What does the therapist do when clients no longer cling to values that they never really challenged or internalized and now experience a vacuum? They report that they feel like a boat without a rudder. They seek new guidelines and values that are appropriate for newly discovered facets of themselves, and yet for a time they are without them. Perhaps the task of the therapeutic process is to help clients create a value system based on a way of living that is consistent with their way of being.

The therapist's job might well be to trust the capacity of clients to eventually discover an internally derived value system that does provide a meaningful life. They will no doubt flounder for a time and experience anxiety as a result of the absence of clear-cut values. The therapist's trust in them is important in teaching them to trust their own capacity to discover a new source of values.

MEANINGLESSNESS.    When the world they live in seems meaningless, clients may wonder whether it is worth it to continue struggling or even living. Faced with the prospect of our mortality, we might ask: "Is there any point to what I do now, since I will eventually die? Will what I do be forgotten once I am gone? Given the fact of mortality, why should I busy myself with anything?" A man in one of my groups captured precisely the idea of personal significance when he said, "I feel like another page in a book that has been turned quickly, and nobody bothered to read the page." For Frankl (1978) such a feeling of meaninglessness is the major existential neurosis of modern life.

Meaninglessness in life leads to emptiness and hollowness, or a condition that Frankl calls the existential vacuum. Because there is no preordained design for living, people are faced with the task of creating their own meaning. At times people who feel trapped by the emptiness of their life withdraw from the struggle of creating a life with purpose. The issues of experiencing meaninglessness and establishing values that are a part of a meaningful life may well be taken up in counseling.

Related to the concept of meaninglessness is what existential practitioners call existential guilt. This is a condition that grows out of a sense of incompleteness, or a realization that one is not what one might have become. It is the awareness that one's actions and choices express less than one's full range as a person. This guilt is not viewed as neurotic, nor is it seen as a symptom that needs to be cured. Instead, the existential therapist explores it to see what clients can learn about the ways in which they are living their life.

CREATING NEW MEANING.    Logotherapy is designed to help the person find a meaning in life. The therapist's function is not to tell clients what their particular meaning in life should be but to point out that they can discover meaning even in suffering (Frankl, 1978). This view does not share the pessimistic flavor that some people find in existential philosophy. It holds that human suffering (the tragic and negative aspects of life) can be turned into human achievement by the stand an individual takes in the face of it. Frankl also contends that people can face pain, guilt, despair, and death and, in the confrontation, challenge their despair and thus triumph. Yet meaning is not something that we can directly search for and obtain. Paradoxically, the more rationally we seek it, the more we are likely to miss it. Yalom (1980) and Frankl are in basic agreement on the point that, like pleasure, meaning must be pursued obliquely. Finding meaning in life is a by-product of *engagement,* which is a commitment to creating, loving, working, and building.

## PROPOSITION 5: ANXIETY AS A CONDITION OF LIVING

Anxiety, arising from one's personal strivings to survive and to maintain and assert one's being, must be confronted as an inevitable part of the human condition. Existential therapists differentiate between normal and neurotic anxiety, and they see anxiety as a potential source of growth. Normal anxiety is an appropriate response to an event being faced. Further, this kind of anxiety does not have to be repressed, and it can be used as a motivation to change. Neurotic anxiety, in contrast, is out of proportion to the situation. It is typically out of awareness, and it tends to immobilize the person. Because we could not survive without some anxiety, it is not the therapeutic task to eliminate normal anxiety.

Being psychologically healthy entails living with as little neurotic anxiety as possible while accepting and struggling with normal anxiety that is a part of living. Life cannot be lived, nor can death be faced, without anxiety (May & Yalom, 1995).

One constructive form of normal anxiety, existential anxiety, can be a stimulus for growth in that we experience it as we become increasingly aware of our freedom and the consequences of accepting or rejecting that freedom. In fact, when we make a decision that involves reconstruction of our life, the accompanying anxiety can be a signal that we are ready for personal change. If we learn to listen to the subtle messages of anxiety, we can dare to take steps necessary to change the direction of our lives.

Many clients who seek counseling want solutions that will enable them to eliminate anxiety. Although attempts to avoid anxiety by creating the illusion that there is security in life may help us cope with the unknown, we really know on some level that we are deceiving ourselves when we think we have found fixed security. We can blunt anxiety by constricting our life and thus reducing choices. Opening up to new life, however, means opening up to anxiety, and we pay a steep price when we short-circuit anxiety.

People who have the courage to face themselves are, nonetheless, frightened. I am convinced that those who are willing to live with their anxiety for a time are the ones who profit from personal therapy. Those who flee too quickly into comfortable patterns might experience a temporary relief but in the long run seem to experience the frustration of being stuck in their old ways.

According to May (1981), freedom and anxiety are two sides of the same coin; anxiety is associated with the excitement accompanying the birth of a new idea. Thus, we experience anxiety when we use our freedom to move out of the known into the realm of the unknown. Out of fear, many of us try to avoid taking such a leap into the unknown. As May puts it: "We can escape the anxiety only by not venturing—that is, by surrendering our freedom. I am convinced that many people never become aware of their most creative ideas since their inspirations are blocked off by this anxiety before the ideas even reach the level of consciousness" (1981, p. 191).

Existential therapy helps clients come to terms with the paradoxes of existence, such as life and death, success and failure, freedom and necessity, and certainty and doubt. As people recognize the realities of their confrontation with pain and suffering, their need to struggle for survival, and their basic fallibility, anxiety surfaces. Thus, existential anxiety, which is the dizziness of freedom (as the existential philosopher Søren Kierkegaard put it), is an indicator of the level of awareness that clients allow. Van Deurzen-Smith (1991) contends that an essential aim of existential therapy is not to make life seem easier or safer, but to encourage clients to recognize and deal with the sources of their insecurity and anxiety. Facing existential anxiety involves viewing life as an adventure, rather than hiding behind securities that seem to offer protection. As she puts it, "We need to question and scrape away at the easy answers and expose ourselves to some of the anxiety that can bring us back to life in a real and deep way" (1991, p 46).

It is essential that therapists recognize existential anxiety and guide clients in finding ways of dealing with it constructively. Existential therapy does not

aim at eliminating anxiety, for to do so would be to cut off a source of vitality. Counselors have the task of encouraging clients to develop the courage to face life squarely, largely by taking a stance, performing an action, or making a decision (van Deurzen-Smith, 1988).

As can be seen, if clients experience too little anxiety, their motivation for change will be low. Anxiety can be transformed into the energy needed for enduring the risks of experimenting with new behavior. Thus, the existential therapist can help the client recognize that learning how to tolerate ambiguity and uncertainty and how to live without props can be a necessary phase in the journey from dependency to autonomy. The therapist and client can explore the possibility that although breaking away from crippling patterns and building new lifestyles will be fraught with anxiety for a while, anxiety will diminish as the client experiences more satisfaction with newer ways of being. When clients become more self-confident, their anxiety that results from an expectation of catastrophe will decrease.

## PROPOSITION 6: AWARENESS OF DEATH AND NONBEING

The existentialist does not view death negatively but holds that awareness of death as a basic human condition gives significance to living. A distinguishing human characteristic is the ability to grasp the reality of the future and the inevitability of death. It is necessary to think about death if we are to think significantly about life. If we defend ourselves against the reality of our eventual death, life becomes insipid and meaningless. But if we realize that we are mortal, we know that we do not have an eternity to complete our projects and that each present moment is crucial. Our awareness of death is the source of zest for life and creativity. Death and life are interdependent, and though physical death destroys us, the idea of death saves us (Yalom, 1980).

The recognition of death plays a significant role in psychotherapy, for it can be the factor that helps us transform a stale mode of living into a more authentic one (Yalom, 1980). Thus, one focus in existential therapy is on exploring the degree to which clients are doing the things they value. Without being morbidly preoccupied by the ever-present threat of nonbeing, clients can develop a healthy awareness of death as a way to evaluate how well they are living and what changes they want to make in their lives. Those who fear death also fear life, as though they were saying, "I fear death because I have never really lived." If we affirm life and attempt to live in the present as fully as possible, however, we are not obsessed with the termination of life.

# The Therapeutic Process

## THERAPEUTIC GOALS

A basic goal of many therapeutic systems is enabling individuals to accept the awesome freedom and responsibility to act. Existential therapy is best considered as an invitation to clients to recognize the ways in which they are not living

fully authentic lives and to make choices that will lead to their becoming what they are capable of being. The existential orientation holds that there is no escape from freedom, in the sense that we can always be held responsible. We can relinquish our freedom, however, which is the ultimate inauthenticity.

Existential therapy seeks to take clients out of their rigid grooves and to challenge their narrow and compulsive trends, which are blocking their freedom. Although this process gives individuals a sense of release and increased autonomy, the new freedom does bring about anxiety. Freedom is a venture down new pathways, and there is no certainty about where these paths will lead. The "dizziness" and dread of freedom must be confronted if growth is to occur (May, 1981). Many fear the weight of being responsible for who they are now and what they are becoming. They must choose, for example, whether to cling to the known and the familiar or to risk opening themselves to a less certain and more challenging life. The lack of guarantees in life is precisely what generates anxiety. Thus, existential therapy also aims at helping clients face this anxiety and engage in action that is based on the authentic purpose of creating a worthy existence.

May contends that people come to therapy with the self-serving illusion that they are inwardly enslaved and that someone else (the therapist) can free them. Thus, "the purpose of psychotherapy is not to 'cure' the clients in the conventional sense, but to help them become aware of what they are doing and to get them out of the victim role" (1981, p. 210). The task of existential therapy is to teach clients to listen to what they already know about themselves, even though they may not be attending to what they know. Therapy is a process of bringing out the latent aliveness in the client (Bugental, 1986).

Bugental (1990) identifies three main tasks of therapy: (1) to assist clients in recognizing that they are not fully present in the therapy process itself and in seeing how this pattern may limit them outside of therapy; (2) to support clients in confronting the anxieties that they have so long sought to avoid; and (3) to help clients redefine themselves and their world in ways that foster greater genuineness of contact with life. In short, increased awareness is the central goal of existential therapy. According to Bugental, it allows clients to discover that alternative possibilities exist where none were recognized before and that they are able to make changes in their way of being in the world.

## THERAPIST'S FUNCTION AND ROLE

Existential therapists are primarily concerned with understanding the subjective world of the client in order to help that person come to new understandings and options. The focus is on the client's current life situation, not on helping clients recover a personal past (May & Yalom, 1995). Typically, existential therapists show wide latitude in the methods they employ, varying not only from client to client but also with the same client at different phases of the therapeutic process. On the one hand, they may make use of techniques such as desensitization, free association, or cognitive restructuring, and they may draw insights from therapists of other orientations. No set of techniques is specified

or essential (Fischer & Fischer, 1983). On the other hand, some existential therapists abhor techniques, seeing them as suggesting rigidity, routine, and manipulation. Throughout the therapeutic process, techniques are secondary to the
establishing of a relationship that will enable the counselor to effectively
challenge and understand the client. Existential therapists are especially concerned about the client's avoiding responsibility; they invite clients to accept
personal responsibility. When clients complain about the predicaments they are
in and blame others, the therapist is likely to ask them how they created the
situation.

Therapists with an existential orientation usually deal with people who have
what could be called a *restricted existence.* These clients have a limited awareness
of themselves and are often vague about the nature of their problems. They may
see few if any options to limited ways of dealing with life situations, and they
tend to feel trapped or helpless. A central task of the therapist is to confront
these clients with the ways they are living a restricted existence and to help them
become aware of their own part in creating this condition. The therapist may
hold up a mirror, so to speak, so that clients can gradually engage in self-
confrontation. In this way clients can see how they became the way they are
and how they might enlarge the way they live. Once they are aware of factors
in their past and of stifling modes of their present existence, they can begin to
accept responsibility for changing their future.

## CLIENT'S EXPERIENCE IN THERAPY

Clients in existential therapy are clearly encouraged to take seriously their own
subjective experience of their world. They are challenged to take responsibility
for how they *now* choose to be in their world. Effective therapy does not stop
with this awareness itself, for the therapist encourages clients to take action on
the basis of the insights they develop through the therapeutic process. Clients
are expected to go out into the world and decide *how* they will live differently.
Further, they must be active in the therapeutic process, for during the sessions
they must decide what fears, guilts, and anxieties they will explore. Merely
deciding to enter psychotherapy is itself often a scary prospect, as indicated by
the notes one of my clients kept for herself during the period of her therapy.
Sense the anxiety that she experienced as she chose to leave security and em-
bark on a search for herself:

> I started private therapy today. I was terrified, but I didn't know of what. Now
> I do. First of all, I was terrified of Jerry himself. He has the power to change
> me. I'm giving him that power, and I can't go back. That's what's really upset-
> ting me. I can't go back ever. . . . I'm sad and scared of this. I've sand-blasted
> security right out of my life, and I'm really frightened of who I'll become. I'm
> sad that I can't go back. I've opened the door into myself, and I'm terrified of
> what's there, of coping with a new me, of seeing and relating to people dif-
> ferently. I guess I have free-floating anxiety about everything, but most
> specifically I'm afraid of myself.

This experience of opening the doors to oneself is often frightening, exciting, joyful, depressing, or a combination of all of these. As clients wedge open the closed doors, they also begin to loosen the deterministic shackles that have kept them psychologically bound. Gradually, they become aware of what they have been and who they are now, and they are better able to decide what kind of future they want. Through the process of their therapy they can explore alternatives for making their visions become real.

When clients plead helplessness and attempt to convince themselves that they are powerless, May (1981) reminds them that their journey toward freedom begins by putting one foot in front of the other to get to his office. As minute as their range of freedom may be, they can begin building and augmenting that range by taking initial steps.

Another aspect of the experience of being a client in existential therapy is the confronting of ultimate concerns rather than coping with immediate problems. On this issue May writes: "The major experiences such as birth, death, love, anxiety, guilt are not problems to be solved, but paradoxes to be confronted and acknowledged. Thus in therapy we should talk of solving problems only as a way of making the paradoxes of life stand out more clearly" (1981, p. 67). Some major themes of the therapy sessions are anxiety, freedom and responsibility, isolation, alienation, death and its implications for living, and the continual search for meaning.

## RELATIONSHIP BETWEEN THERAPIST AND CLIENT

Existential therapists give central prominence to their relationship with the client. The relationship is important in itself, not because it promotes transference. The quality of this person-to-person encounter in the therapeutic situation is the stimulus for positive change. Therapists with this orientation believe that their basic attitudes toward the client and their own personal characteristics of honesty, integrity, and courage are what they have to offer. Therapy is a journey taken by therapist and client, a journey that delves deeply into the world as perceived and experienced by the client. But this type of quest demands that therapists also be in contact with their own phenomenological world. Buber's (1970) conception of the I/thou relationship has significant implications here. It is all too easy for counselors to smile and nod without really listening and attending. Many clients will sense this absence, or lack of presence, and it will negatively affect the relationship.

Therapists share their reactions to clients with genuine concern and empathy, as one way of deepening the therapeutic relationship. Bugental emphasizes the crucial role that the *presence* of the therapist plays in this relationship. In his view many therapists and therapeutic systems overlook its fundamental importance. He contends that therapists are too often so concerned with the content of what is being said that they are not aware of the distance between themselves and their clients. His view differs from the conception of the therapist as a skilled and objective director of the therapeutic venture: "The therapeutic alliance is the powerful joining of forces which energizes and supports the long, difficult, and frequently painful work of life-changing psychotherapy. The conception of the therapist here is not of a disinterested observer-technician but of a fully alive human companion for the client" (1987, p. 49).

May and Yalom (1995) also stress the crucial role of the therapist's capacity to *be there* for clients during the therapy hour, which includes being fully present and intensely involved. They caution that if therapists feel removed from their clients and look forward to the end of the hour, they are failing to achieve the authentic encounter that their clients so urgently require. The counselor guides the client toward engagement with others by first relating deeply with the client (Yalom, 1980).

The core of the therapeutic relationship is respect, which implies faith in clients' potential to cope authentically with their troubles and in their ability to discover alternative ways of being. Clients eventually come to view themselves as active and responsible for their existence, whereas before therapy they were likely to see themselves as helpless. They develop an increased ability to accept and confront the freedom they possess.

Therapists invite clients to grow by modeling authentic behavior. If they keep themselves hidden during the therapeutic session or if they engage in inauthentic behavior, clients will also remain guarded and persist in their inauthentic ways. Thus, therapists can help clients become less of a stranger to themselves by selectively disclosing their own responses at appropriate times. Of course, this disclosure does not mean an uncensored sharing of every fleeting feeling or thought. Rather, it entails a willingness to share persistent reactions with clients, especially when this sharing is likely to be facilitative.

# Application: Therapeutic Techniques and Procedures

As we have seen, the existential approach is unlike most other therapies in that it is not technique-oriented and does not have a well-defined set of techniques. The interventions that existential practitioners employ are based on philosophical views about the essential nature of human existence. Existential therapists are free to draw from techniques that flow from many other orientations. However, they do not employ an array of unintegrated techniques that are based on different assumptions about human change and development. They have a set of assumptions and attitudes that guides their interventions with clients.

In a discussion of therapeutic techniques, van Deurzen-Smith (1990a) points out that the existential approach is well known for its deemphasis of techniques. She stresses the importance of therapists reaching sufficient depth and openness in their own lives to allow them to venture into clients' murky waters without getting lost. She asserts that therapists who are fully available while their clients explore their deepest issues are implying that their own being is subject to change. Van Deurzen-Smith reminds us that existential therapy is a collaborative adventure in which both the client and the therapist will be transformed if they allow themselves to be touched by life.

The use of the therapist's self is the core of therapy (Baldwin, 1987). It is in the I/thou encounter, when the deepest self of the therapist meets the deepest part of the client, that the counseling process is at its best. Therapy is a creative, evolving process of discovery, which can be conceptualized in three general phases.

During the initial phase, counselors assist clients in identifying and clarifying their assumptions about the world. Clients are invited to define and question the ways in which they perceive and make sense of their existence. They examine their values, beliefs, and assumptions to determine their validity. For many clients this is a difficult task, because they may initially present their problems as resulting almost entirely from external causes. They may focus on what other people "make them feel" or on how others are largely responsible for their actions or inaction. The counselor teaches them how to reflect on their own existence and to examine their role in creating their problems in living.

During the middle phase of existential counseling, clients are encouraged to more fully examine the source and authority of their present value system. This process of self-exploration typically leads to new insights and some restructuring of their values and attitudes. Clients get a better idea of what kind of life they consider worthy to live. They develop a clearer sense of their internal valuing process.

The final phase of existential counseling focuses on helping clients take what they are learning about themselves and put it into action. The aim of therapy is to enable clients to find ways of implementing their examined and internalized values in a concrete way. Clients typically discover their strengths and find ways to put them to the service of living a purposeful existence.

## EXISTENTIAL THERAPY
## APPLIED TO THE CASE OF STAN

The counselor with an existential orientation approaches Stan with the view that he has the capacity to increase his self-awareness and decide for himself the future direction of his life. She wants him to realize more than anything else that he does not have to be the victim of his past conditioning but can be the architect in redesigning his future. He can free himself of his deterministic shackles and accept the responsibility that comes with directing his own life. This approach does not stress techniques but emphasizes the importance of the therapist's understanding of Stan's world, primarily by establishing an authentic relationship as a means to a fuller degree of self-understanding.

The therapist confronts Stan with the ways in which he is attempting to escape from his freedom through alcohol and drugs. He is demonstrating what Sartre would call "bad faith," which refers to his not accepting personal responsibility. Examples of his implicit statements of bad faith include: "Since my family never really cared for me, this is why I feel unworthy most of the time." "Since that's the way I am, I can't help what I do." "Naturally I'm a loser, because I've been rejected so many times." Eventually, his counselor confronts him with the passivity that is keeping him unfree. She reaffirms that he is now entirely responsible for his life, for his actions, and for his failure to take action. She does this in a kind manner, but she is still firm in challenging him.

The counselor does not see Stan's anxiety as something that needs to be cured; rather, he needs to learn that realistic anxiety is a vital part of living with uncertainty and freedom. Because there are no guarantees and because the individual is ultimately alone, he can expect to experience some degree of healthy anxiety, aloneness, guilt, and even despair. These conditions are not neurotic in themselves, but the way in which he orients himself to these conditions and how he copes with his anxiety are seen as critical.

Stan talks about feeling so low at times that he fantasizes about suicide. Certainly, the therapist investigates further to determine if he poses an immediate threat to himself. In addition to this assessment to determine lethality, the existential therapist may view his thoughts of "being better off dead" as symbolic. Could it be that he feels that he is dying as a person? Is he using his human potential? Is he choosing a dead way of merely existing instead of affirming life? Is he mainly trying to elicit sympathy from his family? The existentially oriented therapist confronts him with the issue of the meaning and purpose in his life. Is there any reason for him to want to continue living? What are some of the projects that enrich his life? What can he do to find a sense of purpose that will make him feel more significant and more alive?

Stan needs to accept the reality that he may at times feel alone, because choosing for oneself and living from one's own center accentuates the experience of aloneness. He is not, however, condemned to a life of isolation, alienation from others, and loneliness. The therapist helps him discover his own centeredness and live by the values he chooses and creates for himself. By doing so, he can become a more substantial person and learn to appreciate himself more. When he does, the chances are lessened that he will have a clinging need to secure approval from others, particularly his parents and parental substitutes. Instead of forming a dependent relationship, he could relate to others out of his strength. Only then would there be the possibility of overcoming his feelings of separateness and isolation.

FOLLOW-UP: YOU CONTINUE AS STAN'S EXISTENTIAL THERAPIST.   Use these questions to help you think about how you would counsel Stan:

- The existential therapist in this case confronted Stan with some of the ways in which he was attempting to escape from his freedom. If he resisted your attempts to help him see that he was responsible for the direction of his life, what interventions might you make?
- Stan experiences a great deal of anxiety. From an existential perspective, how do you view his anxiety? How might you work with his anxiety in creative ways?
- If Stan talks with you about suicide as a way out of despair and a life without meaning, how will you be inclined to work with him? Can you think of any ways in which he could find more meaning and purpose in his life?

# Summary and Evaluation

## SUMMARY

As humans, according to the existentialist view, we are capable of self-awareness, which is the distinctive capacity that allows us to reflect and to decide. With this awareness we become free beings who are responsible for choosing the way we live, and we thus influence our own destiny. This awareness of freedom and responsibility gives rise to existential anxiety, which is another basic human characteristic. Whether we like it or not, we are free, even though we may seek to avoid reflecting on this freedom. The knowledge that we must choose, even though the outcome is not certain, leads to anxiety. This anxiety is heightened when we reflect on the reality that we are mortal beings. Facing the inevitable prospect of eventual death gives the present moment significance, for we become aware that we do not have forever to accomplish our projects. Our task is to create a life that has meaning and purpose. As humans we are unique in that we strive toward fashioning purposes and values that give meaning to living. Whatever meaning our life has is developed through freedom and a commitment to make choices in the face of uncertainty.

Existential therapy places central prominence on the person-to-person relationship. It assumes that client growth occurs through this genuine encounter. It is not the techniques a therapist uses that make a therapeutic difference; rather, it is the quality of the client/therapist relationship that heals.

Because this approach is basically concerned with matters such as the goals of therapy, basic conditions of being human, and therapy as a shared journey, practitioners are not bound by specific techniques. Although they can apply techniques from other orientations, their interventions are guided by a philosophical framework about what it means to be human.

## CONTRIBUTIONS OF THE EXISTENTIAL APPROACH

The existential approach has helped bring the person back into central focus. It has concentrated on the central facts of human existence: self-consciousness and our consequent freedom. To the existentialist goes the credit for providing a new view of death as a positive force, not a morbid prospect to fear, for death gives life its meaning. The existentialist has contributed a new dimension to the understanding of anxiety, guilt, frustration, loneliness, and alienation.

In my judgment, one of the major contributions of the existential approach is its emphasis on the human quality of the therapeutic relationship. This aspect lessens the chances of dehumanizing psychotherapy by making it a mechanical process. I also find the philosophy underlying existential therapy exciting. I particularly like the emphasis on freedom and responsibility and the person's capacity to redesign his or her life by choosing with awareness. From my viewpoint this perspective provides a sound philosophical base on which to build a personal and unique therapeutic style, because it addresses itself to the core struggles of the contemporary person.

In my own work I've found that an existential view does provide the framework for understanding universal human concerns. These themes that come up in counseling sessions include wrestling with the problem of personal freedom, dealing with self-alienation and estrangement from others, facing the fear of death and nonbeing, finding the courage to live from within one's center, searching for a meaningful life, discovering a personal set of values, being able to deal constructively with anxiety and guilt, and making choices that lead to a fullness of personal expression. Although I have clear existential leanings, I employ a wide range of techniques drawn from systems such as Gestalt therapy and the cognitive-behavioral approaches.

AREAS OF APPLICATION.   What problems are most amenable to an existential approach? For which populations is existential therapy particularly useful? A strength of the perspective is its focus on available choices and pathways toward personal growth. Even for brief counseling, existential therapy can focus clients on significant areas such as assuming personal responsibility, making a commitment to deciding and acting, and expanding their awareness of their current situation. For clients who are struggling with developmental crises, existential therapy is especially appropriate (May & Yalom, 1995). Some examples of these critical turning points that mark passages from one stage of life into another are the struggle for identity in adolescence, coping with possible disappointments in middle age, adjusting to children leaving home, coping with failures in marriage and work, and dealing with increased physical limitations as one ages. These developmental challenges involve both dangers and opportunities. Uncertainty, anxiety, and struggling with decisions are all part of this process.

Van Deurzen-Smith (1990a) identifies the type of clients and range of problems that are most suited to an existential approach: This is a form of therapy for clients who are committed to dealing with their problems about living, rather than curing pathology or removing symptoms. The approach has particular relevance for people who feel alienated from the current expectations of society or for those who are searching for meaning in their lives. It tends to work well with people who are at a crossroads—for example, coping with changes of personal circumstances such as bereavement or loss of employment. Van Deurzen-Smith believes that existential therapy works better with individuals who question the state of affairs in the world and are willing to challenge the status quo. It can be useful for people who are on the edge of existence, such as those who are dying, who are working through a developmental or situational crisis, or who are starting a new phase of life.

Bugental and Bracke (1992) assert that the value and vitality of a psychotherapy approach depend on its ability to assist clients in dealing with the sources of pain and dissatisfaction in their lives. They contend that the existential orientation is particularly suited to individuals who are experiencing a lack of a sense of identity. The approach offers promise for individuals who are struggling to find meaning or who complain of feelings of emptiness. Cushman (1990) has written about the *empty self*—an emptiness that results from failing to listen to one's internal voice or from not trusting one's inner sense of direction. This inner emptiness is manifested in several ways: by restricting one's options, by depression, by lacking a purpose for life, by lacking clear priorities, by being addicted to food or drugs, and by other means of striving to fill the void. Many clients complain that even though they attempt to fill this emptiness of self, they are unsuccessful. This is probably because this emptiness serves as a defense against the fear that they are powerless to change the course of their lives. Unless they confront their fears and the sources that are blocking their ability to live fully, they are likely to continue to try in vain to numb the pain created by this inner void.

CONTRIBUTIONS TO THE INTEGRATION OF PSYCHOTHERAPIES.   According to May and Yalom (1995, p. 290), the main aim of the founders of existential therapy is that its key concepts and themes will become integrated into all therapeutic schools, rather than existential therapy's being a separate school. They think that this integration is clearly occurring. Although Bugental and Bracke (1992) are interested in the infusion of existential notions into other therapy approaches, they have some concerns. They call for a careful examination of areas of confluence and of divergence among the theoretical perspectives. In their concern that any integration be well thought out, they offer the following postulates for maintaining the integrity of the existential perspective as efforts toward integration proceed:

- The subjectivity of the client is a key focus in understanding significant life changes.
- A full presence and commitment of both the therapist and client are essential to life-changing therapy.
- The main aim of therapy is to help clients recognize the ways in which they are constricting their awareness and action.
- A key focus of therapy is on how clients actually use the opportunities in therapy for examining and changing their lives.
- As clients become more aware of the ways in which they define themselves and their world, they can also see new alternatives for choice and action.
- In situations involving transference and countertransference, therapists have an opportunity to model taking responsibility for themselves while inviting their clients to do the same.

Bugental and Bracke say that experienced clinicians of contrasting orientations often accept some existential concepts and thus operate implicitly within an existential framework. They accept the possibility of a creative integration of the conceptual propositions of existential therapy with psychodynamic or cognitive approaches. As to the future of psychotherapy, they write: "The inexorable uncertainty of the future calls on psychotherapists to respond with integrity, charity, and courage so that more of us can be helped in the lonely inner task of being alive and making our contributions to the general well-being" (1992, p. 32).

CONTRIBUTIONS FOR MULTICULTURAL COUNSELING.   At times clients may feel that their lives are out of control, and they may sense that they are being driven rather than doing the driving. There are always consequences of what people do or fail to do. Clients can be challenged to look at the price they are paying for the decisions they have made. Although it is true that some clients may not feel a sense of freedom, their freedom can be increased through their recognition of the social limits they are facing. Their freedom can be hindered by institutions and limited by their family. In fact, it may be difficult to separate individual freedom from the context of their family structure.

A client who is struggling with feeling limited by her family situation can be invited to look at her part in this process. For example, Meta, a Norwegian American, is working to attain a professional identity as a social worker, but her family thinks that she is being selfish and neglecting her primary duties. It is likely that as she moves from one culture to another she will experience culture shock. The family is likely to exert pressure on her to give up her personal interests in favor of what they feel is best for the welfare of the entire family. She may be convinced that she can take care of her family and at the same time satisfy her need for involvement in her profession. She may feel trapped in the situation and see no way out, unless she rejects what her family wants. In cases such as this, it is useful to explore the client's underlying values and to help her determine whether her values are working for her and for her family. Clients such as Meta who operate within two cultures have the challenge of weighing values and balancing behaviors based on their biculturality. Ultimately, it will be up to Meta to decide in what ways she might change her situation. But the basic clash is still between her feeling that there is almost nothing she can do to change her situation and the counselor's invitation to begin to explore what she *can* do. She can begin to reclaim her personal power by considering her own part in the difficulties she is having and in what direction she is inclined to move.

It is essential to respect the purpose that clients have in mind when they initiate therapy. If we pay careful attention to what our clients tell us about what they want, we can operate within an existential framework. Our task then becomes encouraging them to weigh the alternatives and to explore the consequences of what they are doing with their lives. We can help clients see that even though oppressive forces may be severely limiting the quality of their lives, they are not merely the victims of circumstances beyond their control. At the same time that these clients can be taught ways to change their external environments, they can also be challenged to look within themselves to recognize their own contribution to their plight. Through the therapy experience, they may be able to discover new courses of action that will lead to a change in their situation.

## LIMITATIONS AND CRITICISMS OF THE EXISTENTIAL APPROACH

A major criticism often aimed at this approach is that it lacks a systematic statement of the principles and practices of psychotherapy. It is also frequently accused of lacking rigorous methods. Some accuse it of mystical language and concepts, and some object to it as a fad based on a reaction against the scientific approach. Those who prefer a counseling practice based on research contend that the concepts should be empirically sound, that definitions should be operational, that the hypotheses should be testable, and that therapeutic practice should be based on the results of research into both the process and outcomes of counseling.

Some therapists who claim adherence to an existential orientation describe their therapeutic style in vague and global terms such as *self-actualization, dialogic encounter, authenticity,* and *being in the world.* This lack of precision causes confusion at times and makes it difficult to conduct research on the process or outcomes of existential therapy.

Another basic limitation that I see in the existential approach is that many of its concepts are quite abstract and difficult to apply in therapeutic practice. Both beginning and advanced practitioners who are not of a philosophical turn of mind tend to find many of the existential concepts lofty and elusive. And those counselors who do find themselves close to this philosophy are often at a loss when they attempt to apply it to practice. As we have seen, this approach places primary emphasis on understanding the world of clients. It is assumed that techniques follow understanding. The fact that few techniques are generated by this approach makes it essential for practitioners to develop their own innovative procedures or to borrow from other schools of therapy.

Philosophical insight may not be appropriate for some clients. For example, the existential approach may be ineffective in working with the seriously disturbed. And yet it should be noted that R. D. Laing (1965, 1967) has used an existential point of view in successfully treating schizophrenic patients. Laing's positive results suggest that existential practitioners may work well with all sorts of populations, treating people in humane ways that are in keeping with this approach while at the same time drawing on some of the more active and directive intervention methods to meet the unique needs of their clients. Also, van Deurzen-Smith says that much of her own work has been in psychiatric institutions with severely disturbed clients (personal communication, January 6, 1993). Her experience has taught her that even very withdrawn people often struggle with basic existential issues. For her, the art is to translate the complex philosophical notions into simple and fundamental ideas, which are present wherever people grapple with living.

LIMITATIONS FOR MULTICULTURAL COUNSELING.   There are some limitations of the existential approach as it is applied to multicultural populations. A common criticism of the existentialists is that they are excessively individualistic, seeming to suggest that all the changes can be made inside. Some ethnic-minority clients may operate on the assumption that they have very little choice. They often feel that their environmental circumstances severely restrict their ability to influence the direction of their lives. Even if they change internally, they see little hope that the external realities of racism, discrimination, and oppression will change. They are likely to experience a deep sense of frustration and feelings of powerlessness when it comes to making changes outside of themselves. This is especially true in an individualistic culture. Some multicultural experts maintain that therapeutic practice will be effective only to the extent that therapists intervene with some form of social action to change those factors that are creating the client's problem, rather than placing the responsibility on the client for his or her condition.

A good place to begin counseling is to explore the client's feelings of helplessness and hopelessness, eventually looking for ways to overcome certain limitations. It is critical that therapists listen carefully to their clients and enter their perceptual world. The therapeutic process is best guided by the particular goals and values of each client, not by what the therapist thinks is best.

Even accepting the fact of environmental limitations, some degree of freedom can still be exercised. Counselors with an existential orientation can take into account the sociocultural factors that do restrict choices, and at the same time they can challenge clients to recognize those steps they can take to change their situation. In working with people of color who come from the barrio or ghetto, for example, it is important to take up their survival issues. If a counselor consistently tells these clients that they have a choice in making their life better, they may feel patronized and misunderstood. These very real-life issues provide a good focus for counseling, assuming the therapist is willing to deal with them.

A limitation within existential theory is that it is highly focused on the philosophical assumption of self-determination, which does not take into account the complex social identities in which many racial and ethnic minorities find themselves embedded. For many cultures that do not subscribe to this assumption, it is not possible to talk about the self and self-determination apart from the context of the social network.

Another problem with this approach is the lack of direction that clients may get from the counselor. Clients are likely to approach counseling expecting answers and concrete solutions to immediate problems, or at least looking for expert advice. Although they may feel better if they have an opportunity to talk and to be understood, they are likely to expect the counselor to do something to bring about a change in their life situation. Many clients expect a structured and problem-oriented approach to counseling that is not found in the existential approach, which places the responsibility on the client for providing the direction of therapy. A major challenge facing the counselor is to provide enough concrete direction for these clients without taking the responsibility away from them. For a counselor to provide the structure that is often desired by some minority clients would be inconsistent with the existential approach. The counselor can still attempt to understand the client's world and at the same time help him or her to take action, even if it is only small steps toward change.

# Where to Go from Here

The Society for Existential Analysis is a professional organization devoted to exploring issues pertaining to an existential/phenomenological approach to counseling and therapy. Membership is open to anyone interested in this approach and includes students, trainees, psychotherapists, philosophers, psychiatrists, counselors, and psychologists. Members receive a regular newsletter and an annual copy of the *Journal of the Society for Existential Analysis.* The society provides a list of existentially oriented psychotherapists for referral purposes. The School of Psychotherapy and Counselling at Regent's College in London offers an advanced diploma in existential psychotherapy as well as short courses in the field. For information on any of the above contact:

Society for Existential Analysis
School of Psychotherapy and Counselling
Regent's College
Inner Circle, Regent's Park
London, England NW1 4NS

A videotaped interview and group therapy sessions with Irvin Yalom have been produced. The subjects of the interview are the existential approach to psychotherapy and Yalom's views on group therapy. The three-volume series entitled "Understanding Group Psychotherapy: Process and Practice," demonstrates Yalom's work with both outpatients and inpatients. These videotapes can be purchased from the University of California at Berkeley, Extension Center, telephone: (510) 642-1340.

## Recommended Supplementary Readings

*Existential Counselling in Practice* (van Deurzen-Smith, 1988), a very well written book, develops a practical method of counseling based on the application of concepts of existential philosophy. The author puts into clear perspective topics such as anxiety, authentic living, clarifying one's worldview, determining values, discovering meaning, and coming to terms with life. She draws upon her experience as an existential psychotherapist in describing numerous case illustrations.

*Existential Psychotherapy* (Yalom, 1980) is a superb treatment of ultimate human concerns of death, freedom, isolation, and meaninglessness as these issues relate to therapy. This book has depth and clarity, and it is rich with clinical examples that illustrate existential themes.

*The Art of the Psychotherapist* (Bugental, 1987) is an outstanding book that bridges the art and science of psychotherapy, making places for both. The author is an insightful and sensitive clinician who writes about the psychotherapist/client journey in depth therapy from an existential perspective.

*Psychotherapy and Process: The Fundamentals of an Existential-Humanistic Approach* (Bugental, 1978) is a concise and comprehensive overview. It is highly readable, and the clinical examples provide a sense of realness to the discussion of concepts. An excellent source.

*The Discovery of Being: Writings in Existential Psychology* (May, 1983) addresses fundamental human concerns that are central to existential therapy. The author writes about the cultural background of existential psychology and the contributions of the existential approach to therapy.

*Man's Search for Himself* (May, 1953) is a classic. It deals with key existential themes such as loneliness, anxiety, the experience of becoming a person, the struggle to be, freedom, choice, responsibility, and religion.

*I Never Knew I Had a Choice* (Corey & Corey, 1993) is a self-help book written from an existential perspective. It contains many exercises and activities that leaders can use for their group work and that they can suggest as "homework assignments" between sessions. The topics covered include our struggle to achieve autonomy; the roles that work, love, sexuality, intimacy, and solitude play in our lives; the meaning of loneliness, death, and loss; and the ways in which we choose our values and philosophies of life.

## References and Suggested Readings *

*BALDWIN, D. C., Jr. (1987). Some philosophical and psychological contributions to the use of self in therapy. In M. Baldwin & V. Satir (Eds.), *The use of self in therapy* (pp. 27–44). New York: Haworth Press.

BUBER, M. (1970). *I and thou* (W. Kaufmann, Trans.). New York: Scribner's.

BUGENTAL, J. F. T. (1976). *The search for existential identity: Patient-therapist dialogues in humanistic psychotherapy.* San Francisco: Jossey-Bass.

BUGENTAL, J. F. T. (1978). *Psychotherapy and process: The fundamentals of an existential-humanistic approach.* Reading, MA: Addison-Wesley.

BUGENTAL, J. F. T. (1981). *The search for authenticity: An existential-analytic approach to psychotherapy* (Rev. ed.). New York: Holt, Rinehart & Winston.

BUGENTAL, J. F. T. (1986). Existential-humanistic psychotherapy. In I. L. Kutash & A. Wolf (Eds.), *Psychotherapist's casebook* (pp. 222–236). San Francisco: Jossey-Bass.

*BUGENTAL, J. F. T. (1987). *The art of the psychotherapist.* New York: Norton.

BUGENTAL, J. F. T. (1990). Existential-humanistic psychotherapy. In J. K. Zeig & W. M. Munion (Eds.), *What is psychotherapy? Contemporary perspectives* (pp. 189–193). San Francisco: Jossey-Bass.

BUGENTAL, J. F. T., & BRACKE, P. E. (1992). The future of existential-humanistic psychotherapy. *Psychotherapy, 29*(1), 28–33.

COREY, G. (1995). *Theory and practice of group counseling* (4th ed.). Pacific Grove, CA: Brooks/Cole.

*COREY, G. (1996). *Case approach to counseling and psychotherapy* (4th ed.). Pacific Grove, CA: Brooks/Cole.

COREY, G. & COREY, M. (1993). *I never knew I had a choice* (5th ed.). Pacific Grove, CA: Brooks/Cole.

CUSHMAN, P. (1990). Why the self is empty: Toward a historically situated psychology. *American Psychologist, 45*(5), 599–611.

*DEURZEN-SMITH, E. VAN (1988). *Existential counselling in practice.* London: Sage.

*DEURZEN-SMITH, E. VAN (1990a). *Existential therapy.* London: Society for Existential Analysis Publications.

*DEURZEN-SMITH, E. VAN (1990b). What is existential analysis? *Journal of the Society for Existential Analysis, 1,* 6–14.

DEURZEN-SMITH, E. VAN (1991). Ontological insecurity revisited. *Journal of the Society for Existential Analysis, 2,* 38–48.

DEURZEN-SMITH, E. VAN (1992). Dialogue as therapy. *Journal of the Society for Existential Analysis, 3,* 15–23.

FARHA, B. (1994). Ontological awareness: An existential/cosmological epistemology. *The Person-Centered Periodical, 1*(1), 15–29.

FISCHER, C. T., & FISCHER, W. F. (1983). Phenomenological-existential psychotherapy. In M. Hensey, A. E. Kazdin, & A. S. Bellack (Eds.), *The clinical psychology handbook: Vol. 2.* New York: Pergamon Press.

*FRANKL, V. (1963). *Man's search for meaning.* Boston: Beacon.

*FRANKL, V. (1965). *The doctor and the soul.* New York: Bantam Books.

FRANKL, V. (1969). *The will to meaning: Foundations and applications of logotherapy.* New York: New American Library.

*Books and articles marked with an asterisk are suggested for further study.

FRANKL, V. (1978). *The unheard cry for meaning*. New York: Simon & Schuster (Touchstone).

\* GOULD, W. B. (1993). *Viktor E. Frankl: Life with meaning*. Pacific Grove, CA: Brooks/Cole.

HOLT, H. (1986). Existential analysis. In I. L. Kutash & A. Wolf (Eds.), *Psychotherapist's casebook* (pp. 177–194). San Francisco: Jossey-Bass.

KIERKEGAARD, S. (1944). *The concept of dread*. Princeton, NJ: Princeton University Press.

LAING, R. D. (1965). *The divided self*. Baltimore: Pelican.

LAING, R. D. (1967). *The politics of experience*. New York: Ballantine.

\* MAY, R. (1950). *The meaning of anxiety*. New York: Ronald Press.

MAY, R. (1953). *Man's search for himself*. New York: Dell (Delta).

MAY, R. (1958). The origins and significance of the existential movement in psychology. In R. May, E. Angel, & H. F. Ellenberger (Eds.), *Existence: A new dimension in psychiatry and psychology*. New York: Basic Books.

MAY, R. (Ed.). (1961). *Existential psychology*. New York: Random House.

MAY, R. (1969). *Love and will*. New York: Norton.

MAY, R. (1972). *Power and innocence: A search for the sources of violence*. New York: Norton.

MAY, R. (1975). *The courage to create*. New York: Norton.

MAY, R. (1981). *Freedom and destiny*. New York: Norton.

\* MAY, R. (1983). *The discovery of being: Writings in existential psychology*. New York: Norton.

MAY, R. (1985). *My quest for beauty*. New York: Norton.

MAY, R., ANGEL, E., & ELLENBERGER, H. F. (Eds.). (1958). *Existence: A new dimension in psychiatry and psychology*. New York: Basic Books.

\* MAY, R., & YALOM, I. (1995). Existential psychotherapy. In R. J. Corsini & D. Wedding (Eds.), *Current psychotherapies* (5th ed.) (pp. 262–292). Itasca, IL: F. E. Peacock.

\* RABINOWITZ, F. E., GOOD, G., & COZAD, L. (1989). Rollo May: A man of meaning and myth. *Journal of Counseling and Development, 67*(8), 436–441.

RUSSELL, J. M. (1978). Sartre, therapy, and expanding the concept of responsibility. *American Journal of Psychoanalysis, 38,* 259–269.

SARTRE, J.-P. (1971). *Being and nothingness*. New York: Bantam Books.

TILLICH, P. (1952). *The courage to be*. New Haven, CT: Yale University Press.

\* YALOM, I. D. (1980). *Existential psychotherapy*. New York: Basic Books.

YALOM, I. D. (1989). *Love's executioner: And other tales of psychotherapy*. New York: Harper Perennial.

YALOM, I. D. (1991). *When Nietzsche wept*. New York: Basic Books.

C H A P T E R   S E V E N

# Person-Centered Therapy

# CARL ROGERS

CARL ROGERS (1902–1987), as a major spokesman for humanistic psychology, led a life that reflected the ideas he developed for half a century. He showed a questioning stance, a deep openness to change, and a courage to forge into unknown territory, both as a person and as a professional. In writing about his early years, Rogers (1961) recalls his family atmosphere as characterized by close and warm relationships but also by strict religious standards. Play was discouraged, and the virtues of the Protestant ethic were extolled. His boyhood was a somewhat lonely one in which he pursued scholarly interests instead of social ones.

During his college years his interests and academic major changed from agriculture to history, then to religion, and finally to clinical psychology.

In 1964 Rogers joined the staff at the Western Behavioral Sciences Institute in La Jolla, California, where he worked with groups of people who were seeking to improve their abilities in human relations. Here he did much to foster the encounter-group movement in the 1960s. In 1968 he and his colleagues established the Center for the Studies of the Person in La Jolla.

In an interview Rogers was asked what he would want his parents to know about his contributions if he could communicate with them. He replied that he could not imagine talking to his mother about anything of significance, because he was sure she would have some negative judgment. Interestingly, a core theme in his theory is the necessity for nonjudgmental listening and acceptance if clients are to change (Heppner, Rogers, & Lee, 1984).

Rogers earned recognition around the world for originating and developing the humanistic movement in psychotherapy, pioneering in research, and influencing all fields related to psychology. During the last 15 years of his life he applied the person-centered approach to politics by training policymakers, leaders, and groups in conflict. Perhaps his greatest passion was directed toward the reduction of interracial tensions and the effort to achieve world peace, for which he was nominated for the Nobel Peace Prize shortly before he died. After a fall in 1987 that resulted in a fractured hip, he successfully underwent an operation. During the night following his surgery, however, his heart failed, and he died a few days later as he had hoped to— "with his boots on and, as always, looking forward" (Cain, 1987a). In writing some reflections, Rogers said that his life at 85 was better than anything he could have dreamed of or expected. He added: "I do not know when I will die, but I do know that I will have lived a full and exciting 85 years!" (1987b, p. 152).

In an assessment of Rogers's impact, Cain (1987b) writes that the therapist, author, and person were the same man. Rogers lived his life in accordance with his theory in his dealings with a wide variety of people in diverse settings. His faith in people deeply affected the development of his theories and the way that he related to all those with whom he came in contact. Rogers knew who he was, felt comfortable with his beliefs, and was without pretense. According to Cain, he embodied the characteristics of the fully functioning person. He was not afraid to take a strong position and challenge the status quo throughout his professional career.

# Introduction

## HISTORICAL BACKGROUND

The person-centered approach is based on concepts from humanistic psychology, and it can be classified as a branch of the existential perspective presented in the last chapter. Rogers's basic assumptions are that people are essentially trustworthy, that they have a vast potential for understanding themselves and resolving their own problems without direct intervention on the therapist's part, and that they are capable of self-directed growth if they are involved in a therapeutic relationship. From the beginning, he emphasized the attitudes and personal characteristics of the therapist and the quality of the client/therapist relationship as the prime determinants of the outcome of the therapeutic process. He consistently relegated to a secondary position matters such as the therapist's knowledge of theory and techniques.

In tracing the major turning points in Rogers's approach, Zimring and Raskin (1992) have identified four periods of development. The first period was during the 1940s, a time when he developed what was known as *nondirective counseling* as a reaction against the directive and traditional psychoanalytic approaches to individual therapy. His theory emphasized the counselor's creation of a permissive and nondirective climate. He caused a great furor when he challenged the basic assumption that "the counselor knows best." He also challenged the validity of commonly accepted therapeutic procedures such as advice, suggestion, direction, persuasion, teaching, diagnosis, and interpretation. Based on his conviction that diagnostic concepts and procedures were inadequate, prejudicial, and often misused, he omitted them from his approach. Nondirective counselors avoided sharing a great deal about themselves with clients and instead focused mainly on reflecting and clarifying the clients' verbal and nonverbal communications. During this period of initial development, the emphasis was on the counselor's acceptance of whatever feelings the client expressed. The central technique was the clarification of feelings with the aim of gaining insight into those feelings.

The second period was during the 1950s, when *Client-Centered Therapy* was published (Rogers, 1951). He renamed his approach *client-centered therapy* to reflect its focus on the client rather than on nondirective methods. During this phase, central importance was given to the phenomenological world of the client. Rogers assumed that the best vantage point for understanding how people behave was from their own internal frame of reference. He focused more explicitly on the actualizing tendency as the basic motivational force that leads to client change. Rogers (1957) also formulated his hypothesis of the necessary and sufficient conditions for change, which dealt with the core conditions promoting therapeutic progress. His contention was that if the therapist was able to offer a facilitative climate where congruence, acceptance, and empathy were present and the client perceived these conditions, therapeutic movement would occur (Thorne, 1992).

The third period, during the 1960s, began with the publication of *On Becoming a Person* (Rogers, 1961). The focus of the approach was on the nature of "becoming the self that one truly is." The process of "becoming one's experience" is characterized by an openness to experience, a trust in one's experience, an internal locus of evaluation, and the willingness to be a process. During the 1960s Rogers and his associates continued to test the underlying hypotheses of the client-centered approach by conducting extensive research on both the process and the outcomes of psychotherapy. He was interested in researching how people best learn in psychotherapy, and he studied the qualities of the client/therapist relationship as a catalyst leading to personality change. On the basis of this research the approach was further refined (Rogers, 1961). For example, client-centered philosophy was applied to education and was called student-centered teaching. It was also applied to encounter groups, which were led by laypersons in the 1960s (Rogers, 1970).

The fourth phase, during the 1970s and 1980s, was marked by considerable expansion to education, industry, groups, conflict resolution, and the search for world peace. Because of Rogers's ever-widening scope of influence, including his interest in how people obtain, possess, share, or surrender *power* and *control* over others and themselves, his theory became known as the *person-centered approach.* This shift in terms reflected the broadening of application of the approach. Although the person-centered approach has been applied mainly to individual and group counseling, important areas of further application include education, family life, leadership and administration, organizational development, health care, cross-cultural and interracial activity, and international relations. It was during the late 1970s and most of the 1980s that Rogers directed his efforts toward applying the person-centered approach toward politics, especially the achievement of world peace.

## EXISTENTIALISM AND HUMANISM

In the 1960s and 1970s there was a growing interest among counselors in a "third force" in therapy as an alternative to the psychoanalytical and behavioral approaches. Under this heading fall existential therapy, the person-centered approach, and Gestalt therapy, developed by Fritz Perls (the subject of Chapter 8). Both person-centered therapy and Gestalt therapy are experiential and relationship-oriented. They are humanistic approaches that grew out of the philosophical background of the existential tradition.

Partly because of this historical connection and partly because representatives of existentialist thinking and humanistic thinking have not always clearly sorted out their views, the connections between the terms *existentialism* and *humanism* have tended to be confusing for students and theorists alike. The two viewpoints have much in common, and yet there are also significant philosophical differences between them. They share a respect for the client's subjective experience and a trust in the capacity of the client to make positive and constructive conscious choices. They have in common an emphasis on concepts such as freedom, choice, values, personal responsibility, autonomy, purpose, and meaning. They differ in that existentialists take the position that we are faced with the anxiety of choosing to create an identity in a world that lacks intrinsic meaning. The humanists, in contrast, take the somewhat less anxiety-evoking position that each of us has within us by nature a potential that we can actualize and through which we can find meaning.

The underlying vision of humanistic philosophy is captured by the metaphor of how an acorn, if provided with the appropriate conditions, will *automatically* grow in positive ways, pushed naturally toward its actualization as an oak. In contrast, for the existentialist there is nothing that we "are," no internal "nature" we can count on, and we are faced at every moment with a choice about what to make of this condition. The humanistic philosophy on which the person-centered approach rests is expressed in attitudes and behaviors that create a growth-producing climate. According to Rogers (1986b), when this philosophy is lived, it helps people develop their capacities, and it stimulates constructive change in others. Individuals are empowered, and they are able to use this power for personal and social transformation.

As will become evident in this chapter, the existential and person-centered approaches have a number of parallel concepts, especially as they apply to the client/therapist relationship at the core of therapy. The phenomenology that is basic to the existentialist approach is also fundamental to the person-centered theory. Both approaches focus on the client's perceptions and call for the therapist to enter the client's subjective world.

# Key Concepts

## VIEW OF HUMAN NATURE

A common theme originating in Rogers's early writing and continuing to permeate all of his works is a basic sense of trust in the client's ability to move forward in a constructive manner if the appropriate conditions fostering growth are present. His professional experience taught him that if one is able to get to the core of an individual, one finds a trustworthy, positive center (Rogers, 1987c). He firmly maintains that people are trustworthy, resourceful, capable of self-understanding and self-direction, able to make constructive changes, and able to live effective and productive lives (Cain, 1987b). When therapists are able to experience and communicate their realness, caring, and nonjudgmental understanding, significant changes in the client are most likely to occur.

Rogers expresses little sympathy for approaches based on the assumption that the individual cannot be trusted and instead needs to be directed, motivated, instructed, punished, rewarded, controlled, and managed by others who are in a superior and "expert" position. He maintains that three therapist attributes create a growth-promoting climate in which individuals can move forward and become what they are capable of becoming. These attributes are (1) congruence (genuineness, or realness), (2) unconditional positive regard (acceptance and caring), and (3) accurate empathic understanding (an ability to deeply grasp the subject world of another person). According to Rogers, if these attitudes are communicated by the helper, those being helped will become less defensive and more open to themselves and their world, and they will behave in social and constructive ways. The basic drive to fulfillment implies that people will move toward health if the way seems open for them to do so. Thus, the goals of counseling are to set clients free and to create those conditions that will enable them to engage in meaningful self-exploration. When people are free, they will be able to find their own way (Combs, 1989).

In addition to Rogers, Abraham Maslow has been instrumental in developing the humanistic trend in psychology. Maslow (1968, 1970) focused much of his research on the nature of the self-actualizing person. Maslow writes of the "psychopathology of the average." So-called "normals" may never extend themselves to become what they are capable of becoming. Maslow argues that healthy people differ from normals in kind as well as in degree. He criticizes the Freudian preoccupation with the sick and crippled side of human nature. He contends that if we base our findings on a sick population, we will have a sick psychology. According to him, too much attention has been given to hostility, aggression, neuroses, and immaturities; likewise, too little attention has been given to love, creativity, joy, and "peak experiences."

This positive view of human nature has significant implications for the practice of therapy. Because of the belief that the individual has an inherent capacity to move away from maladjustment toward psychological health, the therapist places the primary responsibility on the client. The person-centered approach rejects the roles of the therapist as the authority who knows best and of the passive client who merely follows the dictates of the therapist. Therapy is thus rooted in the client's capacity for awareness and self-directed change in attitudes and behavior.

Seeing people in this light means that the therapist focuses on the constructive side of human nature, on what is right with the person, and on the assets that people bring with them to therapy. It focuses on how clients act in their world with others, how they can move forward in constructive directions, and how they can successfully encounter obstacles (both from within themselves and outside of themselves) that are blocking their growth. The implication is that therapy is more than "adjustment to norms," and this approach does not stop with merely solving problems. Instead, practitioners with a humanistic orientation aim at challenging their clients to make changes that will lead to living fully and authentically, with the realization that this kind of existence demands a continuing struggle. People never arrive at a final or a static state of being self-actualiz*ed*; rather, at best they are continually involved in the process of actualiz*ing* themselves.

## BASIC CHARACTERISTICS

Rogers did not present the person-centered theory as a fixed and completed approach to therapy. He hoped that others would view his theory as a set of tentative principles relating to how the therapy process develops, not as dogma. Rogers and Wood (1974, pp. 213–214) describe the characteristics that distinguish the person-centered approach from other models. An adaptation of this description follows.

The person-centered approach focuses on clients' responsibility and capacity to discover ways to more fully encounter reality. Clients, who know themselves best, are the ones to discover more appropriate behavior for themselves based on a growing self-awareness. The approach emphasizes the phenomenal world of the client. With an attempt to apprehend the client's internal frame of reference, therapists concern themselves mainly with the client's perception of self and of the world.

According to the person-centered approach, psychotherapy is only one example of a constructive personal relationship. People experience psychotherapeutic growth in and through a relationship with another person who is caring, understanding, and real. It is the relationship with a counselor who is congruent (matching external behavior and expression with internal feelings and thoughts), accepting, and empathic that facilitates therapeutic change for the client. Person-centered theory holds that the therapist's function is to be present and accessible to the client and to focus on the here-and-now experience.

This approach is perhaps best characterized as a way of being and as a shared journey in which therapist and client reveal their humanness and participate in a growth experience. The therapist can be a guide on this journey because he or she is usually more experienced and more psychologically mature than the client. However, it is important to realize that the therapeutic relationship involves two people, both of whom are fallible. Both of them can get better at what they are doing, yet they have limits. It is not realistic to expect that any therapist can be real, caring, understanding, and accepting all of the time with all clients—(Sanford, 1990).

# The Therapeutic Process

## THERAPEUTIC GOALS

The goals of person-centered therapy are different from those of traditional approaches. The person-centered approach aims toward a greater degree of independence and integration of the individual. Its focus is on the person, not on the person's presenting problem. In Rogers's view (1977) the aim of therapy is not merely to solve problems. Rather, it is to assist clients in their growth process, so that they can better cope with problems they are now facing and with future problems.

Rogers (1961) writes that people who enter psychotherapy are often asking: "How can I discover my real self? How can I become what I deeply wish to become? How can I get behind my facades and become myself?" The underlying aim of therapy is to provide a climate conducive to helping the individual become a fully functioning person. Before clients are able to work toward that goal, they must first get behind the masks they wear, which they develop through the process of socialization. Clients come to recognize that they have lost contact with themselves by using these facades. In a climate of safety in the therapeutic session, they also come to realize that there are other possibilities.

When the facades are worn away during the therapeutic process, what kind of person emerges from behind the pretenses? Rogers (1961) describes people who are becoming increasingly actualized as having (1) an openness to experience, (2) a trust in themselves, (3) an internal source of evaluation, and (4) a willingness to continue growing. Encouraging these characteristics is the basic goal of person-centered therapy.

These four characteristics provide a general framework for understanding the direction of therapeutic movement. The therapist does not choose specific goals for the client. The cornerstone of person-centered theory is the view that clients in a relationship with a facilitating therapist have the capacity to define and clarify their own goals. Many counselors, however, experience difficulty in allowing clients to decide for themselves their specific goals in therapy. Although it is easy to give lip service to the concept of clients' finding their own way, it takes considerable respect for clients and faith on the therapist's part to encourage clients to listen to themselves and follow their own directions— particularly when they make choices that are not what the therapist hoped for.

## THERAPIST'S FUNCTION AND ROLE

The role of person-centered therapists is rooted in their ways of being and attitudes, not in techniques designed to get the client to "do something." Research on person-centered therapy seems to indicate that the attitudes of therapists, rather than their knowledge, theories, or techniques, facilitate personality change in the client. Basically, therapists use themselves as an instrument of change. When they encounter the client on a person-to-person level, their "role" is to be without roles. Their function is to establish a therapeutic climate that helps the client grow.

The person-centered therapist thus creates a helping relationship in which clients experience the necessary freedom to explore areas of their life that are now either denied to awareness or distorted. They become less defensive and more open to possibilities within themselves and in the world. First and foremost, the therapist must be willing to be real in the relationship with a client. Instead of viewing clients in preconceived diagnostic categories, the therapist meets them on a moment-to-moment experiential basis and helps them by entering their world. Through the therapist's attitudes of genuine caring, respect, acceptance, and understanding, they are able to loosen their defenses and rigid perceptions and move to a higher level of personal functioning.

## CLIENT'S EXPERIENCE IN THERAPY

Therapeutic change depends on clients' perception both of their own experience in therapy and of the counselor's basic attitudes. If the counselor creates a climate conducive to self-exploration, clients have the opportunity to experience and explore the full range of their feelings. What follows is a general sketch of the experience of the client in therapy.

Clients come to the counselor in a state of incongruence; that is, a discrepancy exists between their self-perception and their experience in reality. For example, Leon, a college student, may see himself as a future physician, and yet his below-average grades might exclude him from medical school. The discrepancy between how he sees himself (self-concept) or how he would *like* to view himself (ideal self-concept) and the reality of his poor academic performance may result in anxiety and personal vulnerability, which can provide the necessary motivation to enter therapy. Leon must perceive that a problem exists or, at least, that he is uncomfortable enough with his present psychological adjustment to want to explore possibilities for change.

One of the reasons that clients seek therapy is a feeling of basic helplessness, powerlessness, and inability to make decisions or effectively direct their own life. They may hope to find "the way" through the guidance of the therapist. Within the person-centered framework, however, they soon learn that they can be responsible for themselves in the relationship and that they can learn to be freer by using the relationship to gain greater self-understanding.

As counseling progresses, clients are able to explore a wider range of their feelings (Rogers, 1987e). They can express their fears, anxiety, guilt, shame, hatred, anger, and other emotions that they had deemed too negative to accept and incorporate into their self-structure. With therapy, people constrict less, distort less, and move to a greater acceptance and integration of conflicting and confusing feelings. They increasingly discover aspects within themselves that had been kept hidden. As clients feel understood and accepted, their defensiveness is less necessary, and they become more open to their experience. Because they are not as threatened, feel safer, and are less vulnerable, they become more realistic, perceive others with greater accuracy, and become better able to understand and accept others. They come to appreciate themselves more as they are, and their behavior shows more flexibility and creativity. They become less oriented to meeting others' expectations, and thus they begin to behave in ways that are truer to themselves. These individuals empower themselves to direct their own lives, instead of looking outside of themselves for answers. They move in the direction of being more in contact with what they are experiencing at the present moment, less bound by the past, less determined, freer to make decisions, and increasingly trusting in themselves to manage their own lives. In short, their experience in therapy is like throwing off the self-imposed shackles that had kept them in a psychological prison. With increased freedom they tend to become more mature psychologically and more actualized.

## RELATIONSHIP BETWEEN THERAPIST AND CLIENT

The basic hypothesis of person-centered therapy is summarized in this sentence: "If I can provide a certain type of relationship, the other person will discover within himself or herself the capacity to use that relationship for growth and change, and personal development will occur" (Rogers, 1961, p. 33). Rogers hypothesizes further that "significant positive personality change does not occur except in a relationship" (1967, p. 73).

What are the characteristics of the therapeutic relationship that are conducive to creating a suitable psychological climate in which the client will experience the freedom necessary to initiate personality change? According to Rogers (1987e), the following six conditions are necessary and sufficient for personality changes to occur:

1. Two persons are in psychological contact.
2. The first, whom we shall term the client, is experiencing incongruency.
3. The second person, whom we shall term the therapist, is congruent or integrated in the relationship.
4. The therapist experiences unconditional positive regard or real caring and acceptance for the client.
5. The therapist experiences an empathic understanding of the client's internal frame of reference and endeavors to communicate this experience to the client.
6. The communication to the client of the therapist's empathic understanding and unconditional positive regard is to a minimal degree achieved [pp. 39–41].

Rogers hypothesizes that no other conditions are necessary. If the six conditions exist over some period of time, constructive personality change will occur. The conditions do not vary according to client type. Further, they are necessary and sufficient for all approaches to therapy and apply to all personal relationships, not just to psychotherapy. The therapist need not have any specialized knowledge. Accurate psychological diagnosis is not necessary and may more often than not interfere with effective therapy. Rogers admitted that his theory was striking and radical. His formulation has generated considerable controversy, for he asserts that many conditions that other therapists commonly regard as necessary for effective psychotherapy are nonessential.

From Rogers's perspective the client/therapist relationship is characterized by equality, for therapists do not keep their knowledge a secret or attempt to mystify the therapeutic process. The process of change in the client depends to a large degree on the quality of this equal relationship. As clients experience the therapist listening in an accepting way to them, they gradually learn how to listen acceptingly to themselves. As they find the therapist caring for and valuing them (even the aspects that have been hidden and regarded as negative), they begin to see worth and value in themselves. As they experience the realness of the therapist, they drop many of their pretenses and are real with both themselves and the therapist.

As we have noted, three personal characteristics, or attitudes, of the therapist form a central part of the therapeutic relationship: (1) congruence, or genuineness, (2) unconditional positive regard and acceptance, and (3) accurate empathic understanding.

CONGRUENCE, OR GENUINENESS. Of the three characteristics, congruence is the most important, according to Rogers's recent writings. Congruence implies that therapists are real; that is, they are genuine, integrated, and authentic during the therapy hour. They are without a false front, their inner experience and outer expression of that experience match, and they can openly express feelings and attitudes that are present in the relationship with the client.

Authentic therapists are spontaneously and openly *being* the feelings and attitudes, both negative and positive, that flow in them. By expressing (and accepting) any negative feelings, they can facilitate honest communication with the client.

Through authenticity therapists serve as a model of a human being struggling toward greater realness. Being congruent might necessitate the expression of anger, frustration, liking, attraction, concern, boredom, annoyance, and a range of other feelings in the relationship. This does not mean that therapists should impulsively share all feelings, for self-disclosure must also be appropriate. Nor does it imply that the client is the cause of the therapist's boredom or anger. A pitfall is that counselors can try too hard to be genuine. Sharing because one thinks it will be good for the client, without being genuinely moved to express something regarded as personal, can be incongruent. Therapists must, however, take responsibility for their own feelings and explore with the client *persistent* feelings that block their ability to be fully present with the client. The goal of counseling is not, of course, for therapists to continually discuss their own feelings with the client. Person-centered therapy also stresses that counseling will be inhibited if the counselor feels one way about the client but acts in a different way. Hence, if the counselor either dislikes or disapproves of the client but feigns acceptance, therapy will not work.

Rogers's concept of congruence does not imply that only a fully self-actualized therapist can be affective in counseling. Because therapists are human, they cannot be expected to be fully authentic. The person-centered model assumes that if therapists are congruent in the relationship with the client, the process of therapy will get under way. Congruence exists on a continuum rather than on an all-or-nothing basis, as is true of all three characteristics.

UNCONDITIONAL POSITIVE REGARD AND ACCEPTANCE.    The second attitude that therapists need to communicate to the client is a deep and genuine caring for him or her as a person. The caring is unconditional, in that is is not contaminated by evaluation or judgment of the client's feelings, thoughts, and behavior as good or bad. Therapists value and warmly accept the client without placing stipulations on the acceptance. It is not an attitude of "I'll accept you when . . ."; rather, it is one of "I'll accept you as you are." Therapists communicate through their behavior that they value the client as the client is and that he or she is free to have feelings and experiences without risking the loss of the therapist's acceptance. Acceptance is the recognition of the client's right to have feelings; it is not the approval of all behavior. All overt behavior need not be approved of or accepted.

It is important also that therapists' caring be nonpossessive. If the caring stems from their own need to be liked and appreciated, constructive change in the client is inhibited.

According to Rogers (1977), research indicates that the greater the degree of caring, prizing, accepting, and valuing the client in a nonpossessive way, the greater the chance that therapy will be successful. He also makes it clear that it is not possible for therapists to genuinely feel acceptance and unconditional caring at all times.

One implication of this emphasis on acceptance is that therapists who have little respect for their clients or an active dislike or disgust can anticipate that their work will not be fruitful. Clients will sense this lack of regard and become increasingly defensive.

ACCURATE EMPATHIC UNDERSTANDING.   One of the main tasks of the therapist is to understand clients' experience and feelings sensitively and accurately as they are revealed in the moment-to-moment interaction during the therapy session. The therapist strives to sense clients' subjective experience, particularly in the here and now. The aim is to encourage them to get closer to themselves, to feel more deeply and intensely, and to recognize and resolve the incongruity that exists within them.

Empathic understanding implies that the therapist will sense clients' feelings *as if* they were his or her own without becoming lost in those feelings. By moving freely in the world as experienced by clients, the therapist can not only communicate to them an understanding of what is already known to them but can also voice meanings of experience of which they are only dimly aware. It is important to understand that accurate empathy goes beyond recognition of obvious feelings to a sense of the less clearly experienced feelings of clients.

Empathy entails more than reflecting content to the client, and it is more than an artificial technique that the therapist routinely uses. It is not simply objective knowledge, which is an evaluative understanding *about* the client from the outside. Instead, empathy is a deep and subjective understanding *of* the client *with* the client. It is a sense of personal identification with the client's experience. Therapists are able to share the client's subjective world by tuning in to their own feelings that are like the client's feelings. Yet therapists must not lose their own separateness. Rogers asserts that when therapists can grasp the client's private world, as the client sees and feels it, without losing the separateness of their own identity, constructive change is likely to occur.

# Application: Therapeutic Techniques and Procedures

## EVOLUTION OF PERSON-CENTERED METHODS

Contemporary person-centered therapy is best considered as the result of an evolutionary process that continues to remain open to change and refinement. Certain trends go back more than 55 years. As you recall, Rogers's original emphasis was on methods of reflecting feelings. As his view of psychotherapy developed, its focus shifted away from therapeutic techniques toward the therapist's personal qualities, beliefs, and attitudes and toward the relationship with the client. Thorne points out that Rogers was committed to "the task of demystifying therapeutic relationships so that they could be studied and experienced as vibrant interactions between real human beings rather than as private, hermetic and essentially mysterious treatment processes between distressed patients and omniscient professionals" (1992, pp. 46–47).

The therapeutic relationship, as we have seen, is the critical variable, not what the therapist says or does. In the person-centered framework, the "techniques" are listening, accepting, respecting, understanding, and responding. A preoccupation with using techniques is seen as depersonalizing the relationship. The techniques must be an honest expression of the therapist; they cannot be used self-consciously, for then the counselor is not genuine. It is to be noted that although person-centered therapists subscribe to a set of basic beliefs about human beings and the desirable characteristics of a client/therapist relationship, they may differ widely in their therapeutic style or the manner in which they implement these beliefs in their counseling practice (Thorne, 1992).

As this approach has developed, counselors have been allowed greater freedom in participating more actively in the relationship. This change encourages the use of a wider variety of methods, rather than the traditional listening, reflecting, and communicating understanding.

## THE ROLE OF ASSESSMENT

Assessment is frequently viewed as a prerequisite to the treatment process. Many mental-health agencies utilize a variety of assessment procedures, including diagnostic screening, identification of clients' strengths and liabilities, and various tests. It may seem that assessment techniques are foreign to the spirit of the person-centered approach. What matters, however, is not how the counselor assesses the client but how the client assesses himself or herself. From a person-centered perspective, the best source of knowledge about individuals is not assessment devices but the individual client. For example, some clients may request certain tests as a part of the counseling process. What is important is for counselors to follow the client's lead in the therapeutic dance (Ward, 1994).

In the early development of nondirective therapy, Rogers (1942) recommended caution in using tests or in taking a complete case history at the outset of counseling. He believed that if a counseling relationship began with a battery of tests, clients could get the impression that the counselor would be providing the solutions to their problems. But he admitted that tests might have a place, especially if they were used toward the conclusion of counseling and if the client requested them.

At a time when assessment seems to be gaining in importance in short-term treatments in most counseling agencies, it is imperative that clients be involved in a collaborative process in making decisions that are central to their therapy. Thus, it may not be a question of whether to incorporate assessment into therapeutic practice but of how to involve clients as fully as possible in their assessment and treatment process.

## AREAS OF APPLICATION

As we have seen, the person-centered approach is used extensively in training professionals and paraprofessionals who work with people in a variety of settings.

This approach emphasizes staying with clients as opposed to getting ahead of them with interpretations. Hence, it is safer than models of therapy that put the therapist in the directive position of making interpretations, forming diagnoses, probing the unconscious, analyzing dreams, and working toward more radical personality changes. For a person with limited background in counseling psychology, personality dynamics, and psychopathology, the approach offers assurance that prospective clients will not be psychologically harmed.

People without advanced psychological education are able to benefit by translating the therapeutic conditions of genuineness, empathic understanding, and unconditional positive regard into both their personal and professional lives. The approach's basic concepts are straightforward and easy to comprehend, and they encourage locating power in the person, rather than fostering an authoritarian structure in which control and power are denied to the person. The core skills can be used by many people in the helping professions. These skills are also essential as a foundation for virtually all of the other therapy systems covered in this book. If counselors are lacking in these relationship and communication skills, they will not be effective in carrying out a treatment program for their clients.

An area where I see the person-centered approach as being especially applicable is crisis intervention. Many people in the helping professions (nursing, medicine, education, the ministry) are the first on the scene in a variety of crises. Consider specific life events that can lead to crises, such as an unwanted pregnancy, an illness, or the loss of a loved one. Even if the helping person is not a trained mental-health professional, he or she can do much if the basic attitudes described in this chapter are present. When people are in crisis, one of the first steps is to give them an opportunity to fully express themselves. Sensitive listening, hearing, and understanding are essential at this point. Although a person's crisis is not likely to be resolved by one or two contacts with a helper, such contacts can pave the way for an openness to receiving help later. If the person in crisis does not feel understood and accepted, the situation will probably become aggravated, so that the person may lose hope of "returning to normal" and may not seek help in the future. Genuine support, caring, and nonpossessive warmth can go a long way in building bridges that can motivate people to *do* something to work through and resolve a crisis. People in trouble do not need false reassurances that "everything will be all right." Yet the presence of and psychological contact with a caring person can do much to bring about healing.

## PERSON-CENTERED THERAPY APPLIED TO THE CASE OF STAN

Stan's autobiography indicates that he has a fairly clear idea of what he wants for his life. The person-centered therapist relies on his self-report of the way he views himself rather than on a formal assessment and a diagnosis. She is concerned with understanding him from his internal frame of reference. He has stated goals that are meaningful for him. He is motivated to change and seems to have sufficient anxiety to work toward these desired changes. The person-centered counselor thus has faith in his ability to find his own way and trusts that he has within himself the necessary resources for personal growth. She encourages him to speak freely about the discrepancy between the person he sees himself as being and the person he would like to become; about his feelings of being a failure, being inadequate, or being unmanly; about his fears and uncertainties; and about his hopelessness at times. She strives to create an atmosphere of freedom and security that will facilitate his exploring of threatening aspects of himself. To do this, the counselor does not merely reflect the content of his verbalizations. As he reveals his feelings to her, she listens intently not only to his words but also to the manner in which he delivers his message. She attempts to understand what it must be like to live in his world. As more than a mechanical technique, her authentic relationship with him is based on a concern, a deep understanding and appreciation of his feelings, a nonpossessive warmth and acceptance, and a willingness to allow him to explore any and all of his feelings during the therapeutic hour. She conveys to him the basic attitudes of understanding and accepting, and through this positive regard he may well be able to drop his pretenses and more fully and freely explore his personal concerns.

Stan has a low evaluation of his self-worth. Although he finds it difficult to believe that others really like him, he wants to feel loved ("I hope I can learn to love at least a few people, most of all, women"). He wants to feel equal to others and not have to apologize for his existence, yet most of the time he is keenly aware that he feels inferior. If his therapist can create a supportive, trusting, and encouraging atmosphere, he is likely to feel that she is genuinely interested in him. Basically, Stan can grow personally in the relationship with his therapist. He can use the relationship to learn to be more accepting of himself, with both his strengths and limitations. He has the opportunity to openly express his fears of women, of not being able to work with people, and of feeling inadequate and stupid. He can explore how he feels judged by his parents and by authorities. He has an opportunity to express his guilt—that is, his feelings that he has not lived up to his parents' expectations and that he has let them and himself down. He can also relate his feelings of hurt over not having ever felt loved and wanted. He can express the loneliness and isolation that he so often feels, as well as the need to dull these feelings with alcohol or drugs.

In relating his feelings, Stan is no longer totally alone, for he is taking the risk of letting his therapist into his private world. In doing so, how will he be helped? Through the relationship with her he gradually gets a sharper focus on his experiencing and is able to clarify his own feelings and attitudes. He is seen as having the capacity to muster his own strengths and make his own decisions. In short, the therapeutic relationship tends to free him from his self-defeating ways. Because of the caring and faith he experiences from his therapist, he is able to increase his own faith and confidence in his ability to resolve his difficulties and discover a new way of being.

Therapy will be successful if Stan comes to view himself in a more positive light. He will be more sensitive to listening to messages within himself and less dependent on confirmation from others around him. He will gradually discover that there is someone in his life whom he can depend on—himself.

FOLLOW-UP: YOU CONTINUE AS STAN'S PERSON-CENTERED THERAPIST.    Use these questions to help you think about how you would counsel Stan:

- Knowing what you do of Stan, how much faith do you have that he has the capacity to find his own way without active intervention on your part as a therapist?
- How would you describe Stan's deeper struggles? What is his world like, from his vantage point?
- In working with Stan from the person-centered perspective, how do you imagine you would function without relying on structured techniques?
- To what extent do you think that the relationship you could develop with Stan would help him move forward in a positive direction? What, if anything, might get in your way—either with him or in yourself—in establishing a therapeutic relationship?

# Summary and Evaluation

## SUMMARY

Person-centered therapy is based on a philosophy of human nature that postulates an innate striving for self-actualization. Further, Rogers's view of human nature is phenomenological; that is, we structure ourselves according to our perceptions of reality. We are motivated to actualize ourselves in the reality that we perceive.

Rogers's theory rests on the assumption that clients can understand the factors in their life that are causing them to be unhappy. They also have the capacity for self-direction and constructive personal change. Change will occur if a congruent therapist is able to establish with the client a relationship characterized by genuineness, acceptance, and accurate empathic understanding. Therapeutic counseling is based on an I/thou, or person-to-person, relationship in the safety and acceptance of which clients drop their rigid defenses and come to accept and integrate aspects that they have denied or distorted. The person-centered approach emphasizes this personal relationship between client and therapist; the therapist's attitudes are more critical than are knowledge, theory, or techniques. Clients are encouraged to use this relationship to unleash their growth potential and become more of the person they choose to become.

This approach places primary responsibility for the direction of therapy on the client. Clients are confronted with the opportunity to decide for themselves and come to terms with their own personal power. The general goals of therapy are becoming more open to experience, achieving self-trust, developing an internal source of evaluation, and being willing to continue growing. Specific goals are not imposed on clients; rather, clients choose their own values and goals. Current applications of the theory emphasize more active participation by the therapist or facilitator than was the case earlier. More latitude is given for them to express values, reactions, and feelings as they are appropriate to what is occurring in therapy. Counselors can be fully involved as persons in the relationship.

## CONTRIBUTIONS OF THE PERSON-CENTERED APPROACH

In assessing the merits and significance of the person-centered approach, Cain (1990a) points out that when Rogers founded nondirective counseling over 50 years ago, there were very few other therapeutic approaches. He notes: "At a point in time when there are well over 200 therapeutic approaches, it is worth noting that the client-centered approach continues to have a significant place and role among the major therapeutic systems" (p. 5). The longevity of this approach is certainly a factor to consider in assessing its influence.

Rogers had a major impact on the field of counseling and psychotherapy when he introduced his revolutionary ideas in the 1940s. Interestingly, there are few person-centered graduate programs in the United States today, although this approach is taught in most counseling programs. If one wants to study person-centered philosophy and practice, it appears that there are more opportunities to do so in several European countries, South America, and Japan.

Rogers consistently opposed the institutionalization of a client-centered "school." Likewise, he reacted negatively to the idea of the founding of institutes, the granting of certificates, and the setting of standards for membership. He viewed this institutionalization as leading to an increasingly narrow, rigid, and dogmatic perspective. Rogers warned that too much loyalty to a method, a school of thought, or a technique could have a counterproductive effect on the counseling process. The advice he often gave to students in training and followed in his own life was: "There is one *best* school of therapy. It is the school of therapy you develop for yourself based on a continuing critical examination of the effects of your way of being in the relationship" (1987c, p. 185).

To its credit, this approach allows for diversity and does not foster practitioners who become mere followers of a guru. Counselors can be person-centered and practice in a diversity of ways, so long as they demonstrate a belief in the core therapeutic conditions and so long as their practices do not undercut the capacity of clients to discover the best path for themselves.

EMPHASIS ON RESEARCH.  One of Rogers's contributions to the field of psychotherapy was his willingness to state his concepts as testable hypotheses and to submit them to research. He literally opened the field to research. He was truly a pioneer in his insistence on subjecting the transcripts of therapy sessions to critical examination and applying research technology to counselor/client dialogues (Combs, 1988). Even his critics give him credit for having conducted and inspired others to conduct extensive studies of counseling process and outcome. He presented a challenge to psychology to design new models of scientific investigation capable of dealing with the inner, subjective experiences of the person. His theories of therapy and personality change have had a tremendous heuristic effect, and though much controversy surrounds this approach, his work has challenged practitioners and theoreticians to examine their own therapeutic styles and beliefs.

Person-centered research has been conducted predominantly on the hypothesized necessary and sufficient conditions of therapeutic personality change

(Cain, 1986, 1987b). Most of the other counseling approaches covered in this book have incorporated the importance of the therapist's attitude and behavior in creating a therapeutic relationship that is conducive to the use of their techniques. For instance, the cognitive-behavioral approaches have developed a wide range of strategies designed to help clients deal with specific problems. These approaches are based on the assumption that a trusting and accepting client/therapist relationship is necessary for successful application of these procedures. Yet these practitioners contend that the working relationship is not sufficient to produce change. Active procedures are needed to bring it about.

From my own perspective, the therapeutic core conditions are necessary for therapy to succeed, yet I do not see them as being sufficient conditions for change for all clients at all times. I see these basic attitudes as being the foundation on which counselors must then build the *skills* of therapeutic intervention. Even though the appropriate use of techniques and the application of skills in counseling are important, I do think that there is a tendency to place too much emphasis on counseling skills to the neglect of the development of the personal characteristics and attitudes of the counselor.

CONTRIBUTIONS TO MULTICULTURAL COUNSELING.   Person-centered therapy has made significant contributions to the field of human relations and to practice in multicultural settings. In fact, this approach has been applied to bringing people of diverse cultures together to develop mutual understanding. Rogers (1987d) has elaborated on a theory of reducing tension among antagonistic groups that he began developing in 1948.

Rogers has had a global impact, for his work has reached over 30 countries, and his writings have been translated into 12 languages. Following are some examples of ways in which this approach has influenced various cultures:

• In several European countries, there has been a significant impact on the practice of counseling as well as on education, cross-cultural communication, and reduction of racial and political tensions. For instance, international encounter groups have provided participants with multicultural experiences.

• Japan, Australia, South America, and Mexico have all been receptive to person-centered concepts and have adapted practices to fit their cultures.

• In the 1970s Rogers and his associates began conducting workshops promoting cross-cultural communication. Well into his 80s he led large workshops in many parts of the world. He and his colleagues facilitated intensive groups in South Africa with equal numbers of black and white participants. He also facilitated a group from Belfast, Northern Ireland, composed of militant Protestants, militant Catholics, and English. He conducted similar workshops with different types of factions in Italy, Poland, France, Brazil, Japan, Mexico, the Philippines, and the United States.

• Shortly before his death Rogers conducted workshops in both Moscow and Tbilisi in the former Soviet Union. He reported that these intensive workshops with professionals had demonstrated that their concerns differed very little from the concerns felt by a similar professional group in the United States and that it was important to learn that the psychological climate that produced certain predictable results in other countries produced the same results in the Soviet Union (Rogers, 1987a).

Cain sums up the far-reaching extent of the person-centered approach to cultural diversity: "Our international family consists of millions of persons world-wide whose lives have been affected by Carl Rogers's writings and personal efforts as well as his many colleagues who have brought his and their own innovative thinking and programs to many corners of the earth" (1987c, p. 149).

## LIMITATIONS AND CRITICISMS OF THE PERSON-CENTERED APPROACH

Some students-in-training and practitioners with a person-centered orientation have a tendency to be very supportive of clients without being challenging. Out of their misunderstanding of the basic concepts of the approach, some have limited the range of their responses and counseling styles to reflections and empathic listening. Although there is value in really hearing a client and in reflecting and communicating understanding, counseling entails more than this. One limitation of the approach is the way some practitioners become "client centered" to the extent that they diminish the value of their own power as a person and thus lose the impact of their personality on the client.

More than any other quality, the therapist's genuineness determines the power of the therapeutic relationship. If therapists submerge their unique identity and style in a passive and nondirective way, they may not be harming many clients, but they may not be powerfully affecting clients. Therapist authenticity and congruence are so vital to this approach that those who practice within this framework must feel natural in doing so and must find a way to express their own reactions to clients. If not, a real possibility is that person-centered therapy will be reduced to a bland, safe, and ineffectual pabulum.

Cain (1988) organized a "roundtable" discussion on the issue "Why do you think there are so few person-centered practitioners or scholars considering that literally thousands of persons throughout the world attest to the enormous impact Carl Rogers has had on their personal and professional lives?" The responses of participants reflect some of the sources of criticisms of this approach. These responses include:

- Person-centered therapy is too simple.
- It is limited to techniques of attending and reflecting.
- The approach is ineffective and leads to undirected rambling by the client.
- Rather than emphasizing the counselor as a person, it would be better to focus on developing a variety of techniques that can be applied to solving specific problems.
- More emphasis should be placed on systematic training of counseling skills and less on the attitudes of the counselor.
- It is not necessarily true that individuals have within them a growth potential, or actualizing tendency.

- Not all clients have the capacity to trust their own inner directions and find their own answers.
- Counselors should not give up their role of authority and should advise and direct clients.

According to Combs (1988), one issue that needs increased attention is the teaching role of the counselor. Over the years, the person-centered approach has been somewhat resistant of the idea that the counselor should function as a teacher, seeing such a role as indicating that the counselor knows what is best for the client. Combs, in contrast, describes counseling as a process to help clients learn better and more satisfying ways of being in the world. He adds that counselors cannot help teaching and influencing their clients by their verbal and nonverbal behavior. He contends that they should recognize and accept their teaching role and use it to help clients attain their goals. I think that counselors can carry out both therapeutic and educative functions. They can teach clients, yet they can also encourage them to move toward independence.

CRITICISMS OF RESEARCH AND THEORY.   Although I have applauded person-centered therapists for their willingness to subject their hypotheses and procedures to empirical scrutiny, some researchers have been critical of methodological errors they see as being part of some of these studies. Some accusations of scientific shortcomings involve using control subjects who are not candidates for therapy; failing to use an untreated control group; failing to account for placebo effects; reliance on self-reports as a major way to assess the outcomes of therapy; and using inappropriate statistical procedures.

Rogers (1986a) saw that solid research would be essential to the future development of the person-centered approach. He acknowledged that there was relatively little new knowledge being developed in the field, and he expressed concern that the approach could become dogmatic and restrictive. For him, the way to avoid such regression was through "studies—simultaneously hardheaded and tender minded—which open new vistas, bring new insights, challenge our hypotheses, enrich our theory, expand our knowledge, and involve us more deeply in an understanding of the phenomena of human change" (Rogers, 1986a, p. 259).

Combs (1988) contends that the early momentum of person-centered research has flagged to the point where few therapists are engaging in any form of research. One reason for the decline of interest in research is that most practitioners interested in therapy are involved in private practice or in providing therapeutic services in community agencies. Combs asserts that without this firm research base, the practice of counseling is difficult to defend and the profession is deprived of a critical source of growth.

David Cain, the person-centered therapist who reviewed this chapter, comments that although Rogers valued research, neither he nor his colleagues have written much of significance in over 20 years. There has been little evolution of concepts or methods in person-centered theory since the 1960s. According to Cain (1993), the major reason that person-centered counseling is not now thriving is this lack of evolution. He contends that Rogers and the client-centered community in general have remained rather insulated from and unaffected by advances in the fields of human development, clinical psychology, psychiatry, psychopathology, and other approaches to counseling and psychotherapy. The potential of this approach is severely limited because of the relative paucity of information that is being incorporated. In addition, he argues, person-centered therapy is limited by a strong and conservative group committed to preserving the approach in its traditional form. Cain asserts that clients will not receive optimal help from traditional therapists who are practicing in limited and constricted ways. He concludes that the person-centered approach seems to be on the decline in the United States.

LIMITATIONS FOR MULTICULTURAL COUNSELING.  Although the person-centered approach has made significant contributions to the counseling of people with diverse social, political, and cultural backgrounds, there are some limitations to practicing exclusively within this framework. Many of the clients who come to a community mental-health clinic or who are involved in outpatient treatment tend to want more structure than is provided by this approach. Some ethnic-minority clients seek professional help to deal with a crisis, to alleviate psychosomatic symptoms, or to learn coping skills in dealing with everyday problems. When these clients do seek professional help, it may be as a last resort after their other resources have not worked. They expect a directive counselor and can be put off by one who does not provide some structuring.

A second limitation of the person-centered approach is that it is difficult to translate the core conditions into actual practice in certain cultures. The way in which counselors communicate these core conditions needs to be consistent with the client's cultural framework. Consider, for example, the expression of therapist congruence. Some clients may be accustomed to indirect communication and may therefore be uncomfortable with the openness and directness of the counselor. Chu and Sue (1984) provide a useful guideline: Practitioners must be sensitive to the cultural values of ethnic clients while at the same time avoiding stereotyping. Respect can be shown by recognizing and appreciating the rich diversity that exists within any group of people.

A third limitation in applying the person-centered approach with certain clients pertains to the fact that this approach extols the value of an internal locus of evaluation. Yet some ethnic groups value an external locus of evaluation. For example, they may look to traditional expectations for their direction. They are likely to be highly influenced by societal expectations and not simply motivated by their own personal preference. Also, the focus on the development of the individual is often at odds with the cultural value that stresses the common good. It may be viewed as selfish to think about one's personal growth rather than being primarily concerned with what is best for the group. Lupe, a Latina client, may well consider her role as a mother and a wife and the interests of her family before she focuses on what she wants for herself. Although it is possible that she might "lose her own identity" by being overly concerned with her role in taking care of others in the family to the exclusion of her personal interests, a counselor could make a mistake by pushing her to think about what she wants for herself apart from being a wife and a mother. The context of her cultural values and her level of commitment to these values must be considered in working with her. The counselor may well encourage Lupe to explore how well her values are working for her, but it would be inappropriate for the counselor to impose a vision of the kind of woman she should be.

Although there may be distinct limitations in working exclusively within a person-centered perspective with certain clients because of their cultural background, it should not be concluded that this approach is not suitable for these clients. There is great diversity among any group of people, and therefore, there is room for a variety of therapeutic styles. Although some clients prefer an active style on the counselor's part, other clients respond well to a less directive counselor.

I am convinced that the person-centered approach supplies an ideal foundation for establishing a solid relationship with ethnically diverse clients. Counselors are likely to find it necessary to utilize some structure, while maintaining a climate that fosters self-direction in their clients. If a counselor simply waits for clients to bring up their personal issues, they may become dissatisfied with counseling and quit. It seems to me that more activity and structuring may be called for than is usually the case in a person-centered framework. However, the potential positive impact of a counselor who responds empathically to a culturally different client cannot be underestimated. Often, a client has never met someone like the counselor who is able to truly listen and understand. However, counselors will certainly find it challenging to empathize with clients who have had a vastly different life experience.

# Where to Go from Here

As I hope you will do with all the approaches, consider going beyond the introduction that you have been given here. An excellent place to begin is by selecting at least one source from the annotated reading suggestions (especially one of Rogers's works). Then consider attending a workshop offered by a center or an institute. If you are interested in participating in such workshops, experiential groups, community meetings, or exchanges between individuals as ways of learning about person-centered therapy, contact:

> David Meador
> Center for Studies of the Person
> 1125 Torrey Pines Road
> La Jolla, CA 92037
> Telephone: (619) 459-3861

If you are interested in obtaining training and supervised experience in the person-centered approach, you might be interested in the Carl Rogers Institute of Psychotherapy Training and Supervision. The institute conducts four training programs a year, including a one-month intensive program. For more information contact:

Norman E. Chambers
Center for Studies of the Person
1125 Torrey Pines Road
La Jolla, CA 92037
Telephone: (619) 459-3861

An organization that you might consider joining is the Association for the Development of the Person-Centered Approach. The association is an interdisciplinary and international group with over 250 members. Membership includes a subscription to the *Person-Centered Journal,* the association's newsletter, a membership directory, and information about the annual meeting. It also provides information about continuing education and supervision and training in the approach. General membership is $45 a year; student membership is $20 a year. For more information contact:

David Cain
Person-Centered Association
7212 Plaza De La Costa
Carlsbad, CA 92009
Telephone: (619) 438-0684

## Recommended Supplementary Readings

One of the best primary sources for further reading is Rogers's *On Becoming a Person* (1961), a collection of his articles on the process of psychotherapy, its outcomes, the therapeutic relationship, education, family life, communication, and the nature of the healthy person.

*A Way of Being* (Rogers, 1980) contains a series of writings on Rogers's personal experiences and perspectives, as well as chapters on the foundations and applications of the person-centered approach. Especially useful are his chapters on new challenges to the helping professions and on the world of tomorrow and the person of tomorrow.

*A Theory of Therapy: Guidelines for Counseling Practice* (Combs, 1989) is a very important work based on a person-centered and humanistic philosophy. The author discusses topics such as the self in therapy, the nature of health and the goal of therapy, therapy as a learning process, the therapist as an instrument of change, and becoming a counselor.

*Carl Rogers* (Thorne, 1992) is a very informative book on the life and work of Rogers. The author focuses on his overall influence on the counseling field, his major contributions to both theory and practice, and criticisms of the person-centered approach. This book is highly recommended for a concise overview of Rogers's thinking.

*Three Psychologists: Perspectives from Freud, Skinner, and Rogers* (Nye, 1996) contains an excellent discussion of Rogers's humanistic phenomenology. The chapter clearly describes concepts such as the actualizing tendency, the core conditions for change, the fully functioning person, and the encounter-group movement.

# References and Suggested Readings*

BOZARTH, J. D. (1991a). Person-centered assessment. *Journal of Counseling and Development, 69*(5), 458–461.

BOZARTH, J. D. (1991b). Rejoinder: Perplexing perceptual ploys. *Journal of Counseling and Development, 69*(5), 466–468.

BOZARTH, J. D., & BRODLEY, B. T. (1986). Client-centered psychotherapy: A statement. *Person-Centered Review, 1*(3), 262–271.

* BRAATEN, L. J. (1986). Thirty years with Rogers' necessary and sufficient conditions of therapeutic personality change: A personal evaluation. *Person-Centered Review, 1*(1), 37–50.

CAIN, D. J. (1986). Editorial: A call for the "write stuff." *Person-Centered Review, 1*(2), 117–124.

CAIN, D. J. (1987a). Carl Rogers' life in review. *Person-Centered Review, 2*(4), 476–506.

* CAIN, D. J. (1987b). Carl R. Rogers: The man, his vision, his impact. *Person-Centered Review, 2*(3), 283–288.

CAIN, D. J. (Ed.). (1988). Roundtable discussion: Why do you think there are so few person-centered practitioners or scholars considering that literally thousands of persons throughout the world attest to the enormous impact Carl Rogers has had on their personal and professional lives? *Person-Centered Review, 3*(3), 353–390.

CAIN, D. J. (1990a). Fifty years of client-centered therapy and the person-centered approach. *Person-Centered Review, 5*(1), 3–7.

* CAIN, D. J. (1990b). Further thoughts about nondirectiveness and client-centered therapy. *Person-Centered Review, 5*(1), 89–99.

* CAIN, D. J. (1993). The uncertain future of client-centered counseling. *Journal of Humanistic Education and Development, 31*(3), 133–138.

CAIN, D. J., LIETAER, G., SACHSE, R., & THORNE, B. (1989). Proposals for the future of client-centered and experiential psychotherapy. *Person-Centered Review, 4*(1), 11–26.

CHU, J., & SUE, S. (1984). Asian/Pacific-Americans and group practice. In L. E. Davis (Ed.), *Ethnicity in social group work practice.* New York: Haworth Press.

COMBS, A. W. (1988). Some current issues for person-centered therapy. *Person-Centered Review, 3*(3), 263–276.

COMBS, A. W. (1989). *A theory of therapy: Guidelines for counseling practice.* Newbury Park, CA: Sage.

COREY, G. (1995). *Theory and practice of group counseling* (4th ed.). Pacific Grove, CA: Brooks/Cole.

* COREY, G. (1996). *Case approach to counseling and psychotherapy* (4th ed.). Pacific Grove, CA: Brooks/Cole.

GENDLIN, E. T. (1988). Carl Rogers (1902–1987). *American Psychologist, 43*(2), 127–128.

HEPPNER, P. P., ROGERS, M. E., & LEE, L. A. (1984). Carl Rogers: Reflections on his life. *Journal of Counseling and Development, 63*(1), 14–20.

LAMBERT, M. J. (1986). Future directions for research in client-centered psychotherapy. *Person-Centered Review, 1*(12), 185–200.

MASLOW, A. (1968). *Toward a psychology of being* (Rev. ed.). New York: Van Nostrand Reinhold.

MASLOW, A. (1970). *Motivation and personality* (Rev. ed.). New York: Harper & Row.

---

*Books and articles marked with an asterisk are suggested for further study.

MOKUAU, N. (1987). Social workers' perceptions of counseling effectiveness for Asian American clients. *Journal of the National Association of Social Workers, 32*(4), 331–335.

MURAYAMA, S., NOJIMA, K., & ABE, T. (1988). Person-centered groups in Japan: A selected review of the literature. *Person-Centered Review, 3*(4), 479–492.

NATIELLO, P. (1987). The person-centered approach: From theory to practice. *Person-Centered Review, 2*(2), 203–216.

NYE, R. D. (1996). *Three psychologies: Perspectives from Freud, Skinner, and Rogers* (5th ed.). Pacific Grove, CA: Brooks/Cole.

PROCHASKA, J. O., & NORCROSS, J. C. (1994). *Systems of psychotherapy: A transtheoretical analysis* (3rd ed.). Pacific Grove, CA: Brooks/Cole.

RICE, L. N., & GREENBERG, L. S. (1992). Humanistic approaches to psychotherapy. In D. K. Freedheim (Ed.), *History of psychotherapy: A century of change* (pp. 197–224). Washington, DC: American Psychological Association.

ROGERS, C. (1942). *Counseling and psychotherapy.* Boston: Houghton Mifflin.

ROGERS, C. (1951). *Client-centered therapy.* Boston: Houghton Mifflin.

* ROGERS, C. (1957). The necessary and sufficient conditions of therapeutic personality change. *Journal of Consulting Psychology, 21,* 95–103.

ROGERS, C. (1959). A theory of therapy, personality, and interpersonal relationships, as developed in the client-centered framework. In S. Koch (Ed.), *Psychology: A study of a science: Vol. 3.* New York: Basic Books.

* ROGERS, C. (1961). *On becoming a person.* Boston: Houghton Mifflin.

ROGERS, C. (1967). The conditions of change from a client-centered viewpoint. In B. Berenson & R. Carkhuff (Eds.), *Sources of gain in counseling and psychotherapy.* New York: Holt, Rinehart & Winston.

* ROGERS, C. (1970). *Carl Rogers on encounter groups.* New York: Harper & Row.

* ROGERS, C. (1977). *Carl Rogers on personal power: Inner strength and its revolutionary impact.* New York: Delacorte Press.

ROGERS, C. (1980). *A way of being.* Boston: Houghton Mifflin.

ROGERS, C. (1983). *Freedom to learn in the 80's.* Columbus, OH: Merrill.

ROGERS, C. (1984). One alternative to nuclear planetary suicide. In R. Levant & J. Shlien (Eds.), *Client-centered therapy and the person-centered approach: New directions in theory, research, and practice* (pp. 400–422). New York: Praeger.

ROGERS, C. (1986a). Carl Rogers on the development of the person-centered approach. *Person-Centered Review, 1*(3), 257–259.

* ROGERS, C. (1986b). Client-centered therapy. In I. L. Kutash & A. Wolf (Eds.), *Psychotherapist's casebook* (pp. 197–208). San Francisco: Jossey-Bass.

* ROGERS, C. R. (1987a). Inside the world of the Soviet professional. *Counseling and Values, 32*(1), 46–66.

ROGERS, C. R. (1987b). Our international family. *Person-Centered Review, 2*(2), 139–149.

ROGERS, C. R. (1987c). Rogers, Kohut, and Erickson: A personal perspective on some similarities and differences. In J. K. Zeig (Ed.), *The evolution of psychotherapy* (pp. 179–187). New York: Brunner/Mazel.

ROGERS, C. R. (1987d). Steps toward world peace, 1948–1986: Tension reduction in theory and practice. *Counseling and Values, 32*(1), 12–16.

ROGERS, C. R. (1987e). The underlying theory: Drawn from experiences with individuals and groups. *Counseling and Values, 32*(1), 38–45.

ROGERS, C. R., & MALCOLM, D. (1987). The potential contribution of the behavioral scientist to world peace. *Counseling and Values, 32*(1), 10–11.

ROGERS, C., & WOOD, J. (1974). Client-centered theory: Carl Rogers. In A. Burton (Ed.), *Operational theories of personality.* New York: Brunner/Mazel.

RYBACK, D. (1989). An interview with Carl Rogers. *Person-Centered Review, 4*(1), 99–112.

SANFORD, R. (1990). Client-centered psychotherapy. In J. K. Zeig & W. M. Munion (Eds.), *What is psychotherapy? Contemporary perspectives* (pp. 81–86). San Francisco: Jossey-Bass.

SMITH, D. (1982). Trends in counseling and psychotherapy. *American Psychologist, 37*(7), 802–809.

SUE, D. W., & SUE, D. (1990). *Counseling the culturally different: Theory and practice* (2nd ed.). New York: Wiley.

* THORNE, B. (1992). *Carl Rogers.* Newbury Park, CA: Sage.

WARD, F. L. (1994). Client-centered assessment. *The Person-Centered Periodical, 1*(1), 31–38.

ZIMRING, F. M., & RASKIN, N. J. (1992). Carl Rogers and client/person-centered therapy. In D. K. Freedheim (Ed.), *History of psychotherapy: A century of change* (pp. 629–656). Washington, DC: American Psychological Association.

# Gestalt Therapy

# FRITZ PERLS

FREDERICK S. ("FRITZ") PERLS (1893–1970) was the main originator and developer of Gestalt therapy. Born in Berlin in a lower-middle-class Jewish family, he later identified himself as a source of much trouble for his parents. Although he failed the seventh grade twice and was expelled from school because of difficulties with the authorities, he still managed to complete his schooling and receive an M.D. with a specialization in psychiatry. In 1916 he joined the German Army and served as a medic in World War I.

After the war Perls worked with Kurt Goldstein at the Goldstein Institute for Brain-Damaged Soldiers in Frankfurt. It was through this association that he came to see the importance of viewing humans as a whole rather than as a sum of discretely functioning parts. Later he moved to Vienna and began his psychoanalytic training. Perls was analyzed by Wilhelm Reich, a psychoanalyst who pioneered methods of self-understanding and personality change by working with the body. He was also supervised by several other key figures in the psychoanalytic movement, including Karen Horney.

Perls broke away from the psychoanalytic tradition around the time that he emigrated to the United States in 1946. He later established the New York Institute for Gestalt Therapy in 1952. Eventually, he settled in Big Sur, California, and gave workshops and seminars at the Esalen Institute, carving out his reputation as an innovator in psychotherapy. Here he had a great impact on people, partly through his professional writings but mainly through personal contact in his workshops.

Personally, Perls was both vital and perplexing. People typically either responded to him in awe or found him harshly confrontive and saw him as meeting his own needs through showmanship. He was viewed variously as insightful, witty, bright, provocative, manipulative, hostile, demanding, and inspirational. Unfortunately, some of the people who attended his workshops became followers of the "guru" and then went out to spread the gospel of Gestalt therapy. Even though Perls mentioned in one of his books his concerns over those who mechanically functioned as Gestalt therapists and promoted phoniness, it appeared to many that he did little to discourage this kind of cult.

Readers who want a firsthand account of the life of Perls should read his autobiography, *In and Out of the Garbage Pail* (1969b).

# Introduction

Gestalt therapy, developed by Fritz Perls and his wife, Laura, in the 1940s, is an existential/phenomenological approach based on the premise that people must find their own way in life and accept personal responsibility if they hope to achieve maturity. The basic, initial goal is for clients to gain *awareness* of what they are experiencing and doing. Through this awareness they gain self-understanding and the knowledge that they can change. Hence, they learn that they are *responsible* for what they are thinking, feeling, and doing. The approach is *phenomenological* as it focuses on the client's perceptions of reality. The approach is *existential* in that it is grounded on the here and now and emphasizes that each person is responsible for his or her own destiny. Being in the present moment involves a transition between one's past and one's future. Thus, clients are asked to bring any concerns about what was or will be into the present and directly experience these concerns. In this way Gestalt therapy is lively and promotes direct experiencing, rather than the abstractness of talking about situations. The approach is *experiential* in that clients come to grips with what and how they are thinking, feeling, and doing as they interact with another person, the therapist. Taking an I/thou approach to the client/therapist relationship, Gestalt counselors value being fully present during the therapeutic encounter. Growth occurs out of genuine contact between these two persons, not from the therapist's interpretations or techniques.

One of the therapist's roles is to devise *experiments* designed to increase clients' self-awareness of what they are doing and how they are doing it. Awareness includes insight, self-acceptance, knowledge of the environment, responsibility for choices, and the ability to make contact with others. It is based on a here-and-now experiencing that is always changing. Clients are expected to do their own seeing, feeling, sensing, and interpreting, as opposed to waiting passively for the therapist to give them insight and answers.

Fritz Perls was influenced by a number of intellectual trends of his time, including psychoanalysis, Gestalt psychology, psychodrama, and existentialism and phenomenology. Wilhelm Reich's influence on Gestalt therapy is found in the focus on experiencing one's body, such as working with one's breathing, one's level of energy, and blockages in certain areas of the body—for example, unexpressed pain being "trapped" in a tight chest. Although Perls was influenced by psychoanalytic concepts, he took issue with Freud's theory on a number of grounds. Whereas Freud's view of human beings is basically mechanistic, Perls stresses a holistic approach to personality. Freud focuses on repressed intrapsychic conflicts from one's early childhood; Perls values examining one's present situation. This approach focuses much more on process than on content. It emphasizes what is being presently experienced rather than the content of what clients reveal. Perls asserts that *how* individuals behave in the present moment is far more crucial to self-understanding than *why* they behave as they do.

# Key Concepts

## VIEW OF HUMAN NATURE

The Gestalt view of human nature, as we have seen, is rooted in existential philosophy and phenomenology. Genuine knowledge is the product of what is immediately evident in the experience of the perceiver. Therapy aims not at analysis but at integration of sometimes conflicting dimensions within the person. The process of "reowning" parts of oneself that have been disowned and the unification process proceed step by step until clients become strong enough to carry on with their own personal growth. By becoming aware, they become able to make informed choices and thus to live a meaningful existence.

A basic assumption of Gestalt therapy is that individuals can deal with their life problems themselves, especially if they are fully aware of what is happening in and around them. Because of certain problems in development, people find various ways to avoid problems and, therefore, reach impasses in their personal growth. Therapy provides the necessary intervention and challenge to help them proceed toward integration and a more authentic and vital existence.

The Gestalt theory of change posits that the more we attempt to be who or what we are not, the more we remain the same. According to Beisser's (1970) paradoxical theory of change, we change when we become aware of what we are, as opposed to trying to become what we are not. What is important is for clients to be as fully as possible in their current position, rather than striving to become what they "should be."

## THE NOW

For Perls nothing exists except the "now." Because the past is gone and the future has not yet arrived, only the present is significant. One of the main contributions of the Gestalt approach is its emphasis on learning to appreciate and fully experience the present moment. Focusing on the past can be a way to avoid coming to terms with the present.

In speaking of the "now ethos," E. Polster and Polster (1973) develop the thesis that "power is in the present." For many people the power of the present is lost; instead of being in the present moment, they invest their energies in bemoaning their past mistakes and ruminating about how life could and should have been different, or they engage in endless resolutions and plans for the future. As they direct their energy toward what was or what might have been, the power of the present diminishes. However, Erving Polster (1987a) points out that there is a danger in limiting the focus of therapy to the here and now. In his current thinking he stresses the importance of having clients flesh out their stories, which may include working with the past, present, and future.

To help the client make contact with the present moment, the Gestalt therapist asks "what" and "how" questions but rarely asks "why" questions. In order to promote "now" awareness, the therapist encourages a dialogue in the present tense by asking such questions as "What is happening now? What is going on now? What are you experiencing as you sit there and attempt to talk? What is your awareness at this moment? How are you experiencing your fear? How are you attempting to withdraw at this moment?" Perls (1969a) contends that without an intensification of feelings the person would speculate about *why* he or she was feeling this way. According to Perls, "why" questions lead only toward rationalizations and "self-deceptions" and away from the immediacy of experiencing. "Why" questions lead to an endless and heady rumination about the past that only serves to encourage resistance to present experience.

The questions and experiments used by the Gestalt therapist point up the specific methods the client is using to escape. Most people can stay in the present for only a short while. They are inclined to find ways of interrupting the flow of the present. Instead of experiencing their feelings in the here and now, they often *talk about* their feelings, almost as if their feelings were detached from their present experiencing. A Gestalt therapist's aim is to help people make contact with their experience with vividness and immediacy rather than merely talking about the experience. Thus, if a client begins to talk about sadness, pain, or confusion, the therapist makes every attempt to have the client experience that sadness, pain, or confusion *now*. Talking about problems can become an endless word game that leads to unproductive discussion and exploration of hidden meanings. It is one way of resisting growth and also a way of engaging in self-deception; clients attempt to trick themselves into believing that because they are facing their problems and talking about them, they are resolving them and growing as persons. To lessen the danger of this, attempts are made to intensify and exaggerate certain feelings. In a group setting, for example, the therapist may ask a client who reports how conscious he or she is of pleasing others and meeting others' expectations to choose several persons in the group and to strive at that very moment to please each one.

It is not accurate to say that Gestalt therapists have no interest in a person's past. When the past seems to have a significant bearing on one's present attitudes or behavior, it is dealt with by bringing it into the present as much as possible. Thus, when clients speak about their past, the therapist may ask them to reenact it as though they were living it now. The therapist directs clients to "bring the fantasy here" and strive to relive the feelings they experienced earlier. For example, rather than talking about a past childhood trauma with her father, a client *becomes* the hurt child and talks directly to her father in fantasy. Through this process there is a reliving of the hurt and a potential to change it to understanding and resolution.

## UNFINISHED BUSINESS

Another key concept is unfinished business, or unexpressed feelings such as resentment, rage, hatred, pain, anxiety, grief, guilt, and abandonment. Even though the feelings are unexpressed, they are associated with distinct memories and fantasies. Because the feelings are not fully experienced in awareness, they linger in the background and are carried into present life in ways that interfere with effective contact with oneself and others. Unfinished business persists until the individual faces and deals with the unexpressed feelings. In speaking of the effects of unfinished business, E. Polster and Polster (1973) maintain that "these incomplete directions *do seek* completion and when they get powerful enough, the individual is beset with preoccupation, compulsive behavior, wariness, oppressive energy and much self-defeating behavior" (p. 36). The effects of unfinished business often show up in some blockage within the body. Gestalt therapists emphasize paying attention to the bodily experience on the assumption that if feelings are unexpressed, they tend to result in some physical symptom.

Unacknowledged feelings create unnecessary emotional debris that clutters present-centered awareness. According to Perls (1969a), resentment is the most frequent and worst kind of unfinished business. When people are resentful, in his view, they become stuck, for they can neither let go nor engage in authentic communication until they express the resentment. Thus, he contends that it is imperative to express resentments. Unexpressed resentment frequently converts to guilt: "Whenever you feel guilty, find out what you are resenting and express it and make your demands explicit" (Perls, 1969a, p. 49).

An example of how unfinished business nags at one and manifests itself in current behavior can be seen in a man who never really felt loved and accepted by his mother. He developed resentment of her, for no matter how he sought her approval, he was always left feeling that he was not adequate. In an attempt to deflect the direction of this need for maternal approval in the present, he may look to women for his confirmation of worth as a man. In developing a variety of games to get women to approve of him, he reports that he is still not satisfied. The unfinished business is preventing him from authentic intimacy with women, because his need is that of a child rather than an adult. He needs to experience closure before he can experience real satisfaction; that is, he needs to return to the old business and express his unacknowledged feelings of disappointment and rage. In order to achieve this closure, he will have to tolerate the uncomfortable feelings that accompany recognizing and working through an impasse.

The impasse, or *stuck point,* is a situation in which individuals believe that they are unable to support themselves and thus seek external support. A frequent method of coping with this situation consists of manipulating others. Support from others, which is not a genuine source of nourishment for the self, becomes a replacement for self-support (Yontef, 1993). At the moment of impasse, clients attempt to maneuver their environment by playing roles of weakness, helplessness, stupidity, and foolishness. The therapist's task is to help them get through the impasse so that growth is possible. The counselor assists them by providing situations that encourage them to fully experience their condition of being stuck. By completely experiencing the impasse, they are able to get into contact with their frustrations. Clients will better be able to change if they accept whatever is, rather than wishing they were different. Gestalt therapy is based on the notion that individuals have a striving toward actualization and growth and that if they accept all aspects of themselves without judging these dimensions, they can begin to think, feel, and act differently.

## AVOIDANCE

A concept related to unfinished business is avoidance, which refers to the means people use to keep themselves from facing unfinished business and from experiencing the uncomfortable emotions associated with unfinished situations. Because we have a tendency to avoid confronting and fully experiencing our anxiety, grief, guilt, and other uncomfortable emotions, the emotions become a nagging undercurrent that prevents us from being fully alive. Perls (1969a) speaks of the catastrophic expectations that we conjure up and that keep us psychologically stuck: "If I express my pain fully, people will be embarrassed, and they won't have anything to do with me"; "If I were to express my anger to the significant people in my life, they would abandon me"; "If I ever allowed myself to mourn over my losses, I might sink so deep into depression that I'd never get out of that hole."

These fantasies keep us from living fully, because we use them to avoid taking the necessary risks that growth demands. Thus, the Gestalt therapist encourages expressing in the now of the therapeutic session intense feelings never directly expressed before. If a client says that she is afraid of getting in touch with her feelings of hatred and spite, she may be encouraged by the therapist to become her hateful and spiteful side and express these negative feelings. By experiencing the side of herself that she works so hard at disowning, she begins a process of integration and allows herself to get beyond the impasse that keeps her from growing. By going beyond our avoidances, we make it possible to dispose of unfinished business that interferes with our present life, and we move toward health and integration.

## LAYERS OF NEUROSIS

Perls (1970) likens the unfolding of adult personality to the peeling of an onion. In order for individuals to achieve psychological maturity, they must strip off five layers of neurosis. These superimposed growth disorders are (1) the phony, (2) the phobic, (3) the impasse, (4) the implosive, and (5) the explosive. The first layer we encounter, the *phony layer,* consists of reacting to others in stereotypical and inauthentic ways. This is the level where we play games and get lost in roles. By behaving *as if* we were a person that we are not, we are trying to live up to a fantasy that we or others have created. Once we become aware of the phoniness of game playing and become more honest, we experience unpleasantness and pain.

The next layer we encounter is the *phobic layer.* At this level we attempt to avoid the emotional pain that is associated with seeing aspects of ourselves that we would prefer to deny. At this point our resistances to accepting ourselves the way we actually are pop up. We have catastrophic fears that if we recognize who we really are and present that side of ourselves to others, they will surely reject us.

Beneath the phobic layer is the *impasse,* or the point where we are stuck in our own maturation. This is the point at which we are sure that we will not be able to survive, for we convince ourselves that we do not have the resources within ourselves to move beyond the stuck point without environmental support. Typically, this is the time when we attempt to manipulate the environment to do our seeing, hearing, feeling, thinking, and deciding for us. At the impasse we often feel a sense of deadness and feel that we are nothing. If we hope to feel alive, it is essential that we get through the impasse.

If we allow ourselves to fully experience our deadness, rather than denying it or running away, the *implosive level* comes into being. Perls (1970) writes that it is necessary to go through this implosive layer in order to get to the authentic self. By getting into contact with this layer, or our deadness and inauthentic ways, we expose our defenses and begin to make contact with our genuine self.

Perls contends that peeling back the implosive layer creates an explosive state. When we contact the *explosive layer,* we let go of phony roles and pretenses, and we release a tremendous amount of energy that we have been holding in by pretending to be who we are not. To become alive and authentic, it is necessary to achieve this explosion, which can be an explosion into pain and into joy.

## CONTACT AND RESISTANCES TO CONTACT

In Gestalt therapy, contact is necessary if change and growth are to occur. When we make contact with the environment, change is inevitable. Contact is made by seeing, hearing, smelling, touching, and moving. Effective contact means interacting with nature and with other people without losing one's sense of individuality. It is the continually renewed creative adjustment of individuals to their environment (M. Polster, 1987). Prerequisites for good contact are clear awareness, full energy, and the ability to express oneself (Zinker, 1978). Miriam Polster claims that contact is the lifeblood of growth. It entails zest, imagination, and creativity. There are only moments of this type of contact, so it is most accurate to think of levels of contact, rather than a final state to achieve. After a contact experience there is typically a withdrawal to integrate what has been learned.

The Gestalt therapist also focuses on resistances to contact. From a Gestalt perspective, resistance refers to defenses that we develop to prevent us from experiencing the present in a full and real way. The five layers of neurosis represent a person's style of keeping energy pent up in the service of maintaining pretenses. There are also ego-defense mechanisms that prevent people from being authentic. E. Polster and Polster (1973) describe five major channels of resistance that are challenged in Gestalt therapy: introjection, projection, retroflection, deflection, and confluence.

*Introjection* is the tendency to uncritically accept others' beliefs and standards without assimilating them to make them congruent with who we are. These introjects remain alien to us, because we have not analyzed and restructured

them. When we introject, we passively incorporate what the environment provides, spending little time on becoming clear about what we want or need. If
we remain in this stage, our energy is bound up in taking things as we find them.

*Projection* is the reverse of introjection. In projection we disown certain
aspects of ourselves by assigning them to the environment. When we are projecting, we have trouble distinguishing between the inside world and the outside world. Those attributes of our personality that are inconsistent with our
self-image are disowned and put onto other people. By seeing in others the very
qualities that we refuse to acknowledge in ourselves, we avoid taking responsibility for our own feelings and the person who we are, and this keeps us
powerless to initiate change.

*Retroflection* consists of turning back to ourselves what we would like to
do to someone else or doing to ourselves what we would like someone else
to do to us. If we lash out and injure ourselves, for example, we are often directing aggression inward that we are fearful of directing toward others. This process
seriously restricts engagement between the person and his or her environment.
Typically, these maladaptive styles of functioning are adopted out of our awareness; part of the process of Gestalt therapy is to help us discover a self-regulatory
system so that we can deal realistically with the world.

*Deflection* is the process of distraction so that it is difficult to maintain a
sustained sense of contact. People who deflect attempt to diffuse contact through
the overuse of humor, abstract generalizations, and questions rather than
statements (Frew, 1986). They engage their environment on an inconsistent basis,
which results in their feeling a sense of emotional depletion. Deflection involves
a diminished emotional experience. People who deflect speak through and for
others.

*Confluence* involves a blurring of the differentiation between the self and
the environment. For people who are oriented toward blending in, there is no
clear demarcation between internal experience and outer reality. Confluence
in relationships involves an absence of conflicts, or a belief that all parties experience the same feelings and thoughts. It is a style of contact characteristic
of clients who have a high need to be accepted and liked. It is a way of staying safe by going along with others and not expressing one's true feelings and
opinions. This condition makes genuine contact extremely difficult. A therapist
might assist clients who use this channel of resistance by asking questions such
as "What are you doing now? What are you experiencing at this moment? What
do you want right now?"

Introjection, projection, retroflection, deflection, and confluence represent
styles of resisting contact. The concern of Gestalt therapists is the interruption
of contact with the environment when the individual is unaware of this process. Terms such as *resistance to contact* or *boundary disturbance* refer to the
characteristic styles that people employ in their attempt to control their environment. The premise in Gestalt therapy is that contact is both normal and healthy.
Therefore, a discussion of these styles of resistance to contact focuses on the
degree to which these processes are in the individual's awareness. Clients in
Gestalt therapy are encouraged to become increasingly aware of their dominant
style of blocking contact.

## ENERGY AND BLOCKS TO ENERGY

In Gestalt therapy special attention is given to where energy is located, how it is used, and how it can be blocked. Blocked energy is another form of resistance. It can be manifested by tension in some part of the body, by posture, by keeping one's body tight and closed, by looking away from people when speaking as a way to avoid contact, and by speaking with a restricted voice, to mention only a few.

In commenting on the value of focusing on the client's energy in therapeutic work, Zinker (1978) writes that clients may not be aware of their energy or where it is located, and they may experience it in a negative way. From his perspective therapy at its best involves a dynamic relationship that awakens and nourishes the client without sapping the therapist of his or her own energy. He maintains that it is the therapist's job to help clients locate the ways in which they are blocking energy and transform this blocked energy into more adaptive behaviors. This process is best accomplished when resistance is not viewed as a client's refusal to cooperate and as something simply to be gotten around. Instead, therapists can learn to welcome resistance and use it as a way of deepening therapeutic work. Clients can be encouraged to recognize how their resistance is being expressed in their body, and rather than trying to rid themselves of certain bodily symptoms, they can actually delve fully into tension states. By allowing themselves to exaggerate their tight mouth and shaking legs, they can discover for themselves how they are diverting energy and keeping themselves from a full expression of aliveness.

# The Therapeutic Process

## THERAPEUTIC GOALS

The basic goal of Gestalt therapy, as mentioned, is attaining awareness and, with it, greater choice and responsibility. Awareness includes knowing the environment, knowing oneself, accepting oneself, and being able to make contact. Increased and enriched awareness, by itself, is seen as curative. Without awareness clients do not possess the tools for personality change. With awareness they have the capacity to face and accept denied parts as well as to fully experience their subjectivity. They can become unified and whole. When clients stay with their awareness, important unfinished business will always emerge so that it can be dealt with in therapy. The Gestalt approach helps clients note their own awareness process so that they can be responsible and can selectively and discriminatingly make choices. Awareness emerges within the context of a genuine meeting between the client and therapist, or within the context of I/thou relating (Jacobs, 1989; Yontef, 1993).

As we saw in Chapter 6, the existential view is that we are continually engaged in a process of remaking and discovering ourselves. We do not have a static identity but discover new facets of our being as we face new challenges. Gestalt therapy is basically an existential encounter out of which clients tend to move in certain directions. These directions are outlined by Zinker (1978). Through a creative involvement in Gestalt process, he expects, clients will:

- move toward increased awareness of themselves
- gradually assume ownership of their experience (as opposed to making others responsible for what they are thinking, feeling, and doing)
- develop skills and acquire values that will allow them to satisfy their needs without violating the rights of others
- become more aware of all of their senses
- learn to accept responsibility for what they do, including accepting the consequences of their actions
- move from outside support toward increasing internal support
- be able to ask for and get help from others and to give to others

In keeping with the humanistic spirit, Perls (1969a) contends that most of us use only a fraction of our potential. Our lives are patterned and stereotyped; we play the same roles again and again and find very few ways to reinvent our existence and make full use of the possibilities of the present moment. Perls contends that if we find out how we are preventing ourselves from realizing the full measure of our human potential, we can learn many ways to make life richer. This potential is based on the attitude of living each moment freshly. A major goal of therapy, therefore, is to help the client gain awareness, which allows for living a fuller life.

## THERAPIST'S FUNCTION AND ROLE

Earlier I made reference to Beisser's (1970) paradoxical theory of change, which contends that when we face and fully become what we *are,* rather than what we think we *should be,* we open rich possibilities for change. In this spirit, Gestalt therapists do not aim to change their clients. The therapist's function is, through engagement with clients, to assist them in developing their own awareness and experiencing how they *are* in the present moment. According to Perls, Hefferline, and Goodman (1951), the therapist's job is to invite clients into an active partnership where they can learn about themselves by adopting an experimental attitude toward life in which they try out new behaviors and notice what happens.

Gestalt therapists notice what is in both the foreground and the background. They focus on the client's feelings, awareness at the moment, body messages, energy, avoidance, and blocks to awareness. Gestalt therapy involves getting in touch with the obvious, according to Perls (1969a), who contends that neurotics do not see the obvious. They are unaware of their tightly clenched fist, of their controlled voice, or of not having responded to the therapist's suggestion. Thus, the therapist's job is to challenge them so that they learn to use their senses fully and get in touch with body messages. According to Yontef (1993), although the therapist functions as a guide and a catalyst, presents experiments, and shares observations, the basic work of therapy is done by the client. Yontef stresses that the therapist's job is to create a climate in which clients are likely to try out new ways of being. Gestalt therapists do not force change upon the client through confrontation. Instead, they work within a context of I/thou dialogue in a here-and-now framework.

An important function of the Gestalt therapist is paying attention to the client's body language. These nonverbal cues provide rich information, because they often betray feelings of which the client is unaware. Perls (1969a) writes that a client's posture, movements, gestures, voice, hesitations, and other cues tell the real story. He warns that verbal communication is usually a lie and that if therapists are content-oriented, they miss the essence of the person. Real communication is beyond words.

Thus, the therapist needs to be alert for gaps in attention and awareness and for incongruities between verbalizations and what clients are doing with their body. Clients demonstrate from moment to moment their lack of full contact with their present-centered actuality. Thus, a therapist might direct clients to speak for and become their gestures or body parts. Gestalt therapists often ask: "What do your eyes say?" "If your hands could speak at this moment, what would they say?" "Can you carry on a conversation between your right and left hands?" Clients may verbally express anger and at the same time smile. Or they may say that they are in pain and at the same time laugh. The therapist can ask clients to become aware of how they are using their laughter to mask feelings of anger or pain.

In addition to calling attention to a client's nonverbal language, the Gestalt counselor places emphasis on the relationship between language patterns and personality. This approach suggests that clients' speech patterns are often an expression of their feelings, thoughts, and attitudes. The Gestalt approach focuses on overt speaking habits as a way to increase clients' awareness of themselves, especially by asking them to notice whether their words are congruent with what they are experiencing or instead are distancing them from their emotions.

A function of the Gestalt counselor is to gently challenge clients by interventions that help them become aware of the effects of their language patterns. By focusing on language, clients are able to increase their awareness of what they are experiencing in the present moment and of how they are avoiding coming into contact with this here-and-now experience. Following are some examples of the aspects of language that the Gestalt therapist might focus on:

- *"It" talk.* When clients say "it" instead of "I," they are using depersonalizing language. The counselor may ask them to substitute personal pronouns for impersonal ones so that they will assume an increased sense of responsibility. For example, a client says, "It is difficult to make friends." She could be asked to restate this by making an "I" statement—"I have trouble making friends."
- *"You" talk.* The counselor will point out generalized use of "you" and ask the client to substitute "I" when this is what is meant. When a client says, "You feel sort of hurt when people don't accept you," he can be asked to look at how he is distancing himself from intense feelings by using a generalized "you." Again, he can be encouraged to change this impersonal "you" into an "I" statement such as "I feel hurt when I'm not accepted." He can be asked to notice the difference in his feelings when he makes each statement.

• *Questions.* Questions have a tendency to keep the questioner hidden, safe, and unknown. Gestalt counselors often ask clients to change their questions into statements. In making personal statements, clients begin to assume responsibility for what they say. They may become aware of how they are keeping themselves mysterious through a barrage of questions and how this serves to prevent them from making declarations that express themselves. For example, without stating their investment behind their question, group members often question one another by probing for information. If a member were to ask another member: "Why do you try so hard to get your father's approval when it seems so futile?" I would be likely to ask the questioning member: "Could you tell Judy what prompts you to ask her this question? Would you be willing to make a statement about yourself, rather than expecting her to answer your question?" Of course, not all questions are seen as resistances to change. Some questions are genuine requests for information.

• *Language that denies power.* Some clients have a tendency to deny their personal power by adding qualifiers or disclaimers to their statements. When a client says, "I want to stop feeling like a victim, but I feel powerless to change," she is adding to the powerlessness with the appendage of "but." Often what follows a "but" serves to discount the first part of the statement. The counselor may also point out to clients how certain qualifiers subtract from their effectiveness. In this way clients become aware of how qualifiers keep them ambivalent. Experimenting with omitting qualifiers such as "maybe," "perhaps," "sort of," "I guess," "possibly," and "I suppose" can help clients change ambivalent messages into clear and direct statements. Likewise, when clients say "I can't," they are really implying "I won't." Asking them to substitute "won't" for "can't" assists them in owning and accepting their power by taking responsibility for their decisions. Other words that deny power are the "shoulds" and "oughts" that some people habitually use. Clients can at least become aware of the frequency with which they tell themselves and others that they "should" or "ought to" do this or that. By changing these "I shoulds" to "I choose to" or "I want to," they can begin taking active steps that reduce the feeling of being driven and not in control of their life. The counselor must be careful in intervening so that clients do not feel that everything they say is subject to scrutiny. Rather than fostering a morbid kind of introspection, the counselor hopes to foster awareness of what is really being expressed through words.

• *Listening to a client's metaphors.* In his workshops, Erving Polster emphasizes the importance of a therapist learning how to listen to the metaphors of clients. By paying attention to metaphors, the therapist gets rich clues to a client's internal struggles. Examples of metaphors that can be amplified include client statements such as "It's hard for me to spill my guts in here." "At times I feel that I don't have a leg to stand on." "I need to be prepared in case someone blasts me." "I felt ripped to shreds after you confronted me last week." "After this session, I feel as though I've been put through a meat grinder." Beneath a metaphor may lie a suppressed internal dialogue that represents critical unfinished business or reactions to a present interaction. For example, to the client who says that she feels that she has been put through a meat grinder, the therapist could ask: "What is your experience of being ground meat?" or "Who is doing the grinding?" What is essential is to encourage this client to say more about what she is experiencing. The art of therapy consists of translating the meaning of these metaphors into manifest content so that they can be dealt with in therapy.

   • *Listening for language that uncovers a story.* Polster also teaches the value of what he calls "fleshing out a flash." He reports that clients often use language that is elusive yet give significant clues to a story that illustrates their life struggles. He suggests that therapists learn to pick out a small part of what someone says and then to focus on and develop this element. Clients are likely to slide over pregnant phrases, but the alert therapist can ask questions that will help them flesh out their story line. It is essential for therapists to pay attention to what is fascinating about the person who is sitting before them and get that person to tell a story.

   In one of Polster's workshops I observed his magnificent style in challenging a person (Joe) who had volunteered for a demonstration of an individual session. Although Joe had a fascinating story to reveal about a particular facet of his life, he was presenting himself in a lifeless manner, and the energy was going flat. Eventually, Polster asked him, "Are you keeping my interest right now?" He looked shocked, but he soon got the point. He accepted Polster's challenge to make sure that he not only kept the therapist interested but also presented himself in a way to keep those in the audience interested. It was clear that Polster was directing Joe's attention to a process of *how* he was expressing his feelings and life experiences, rather than being concerned with what he was talking about.

## CLIENT'S EXPERIENCE IN THERAPY

The general orientation of Gestalt therapy is toward clients' assumption of more and more responsibility for themselves—for their thoughts, feelings, and behavior. The therapist confronts them with the ways in which they are avoiding their personal responsibilities and asks them to make decisions about continuing therapy, about what they wish to learn from it, and about how they want to use their therapy time. Other issues that can become the focal point of therapy include the client/therapist relationship and the similarities in the ways clients relate to the therapist and to others in their environment. Clients in Gestalt therapy, then, are active participants who make their own interpretations and meanings. It is they who increase awareness and decide what they will or will not do with their personal meaning.

   Miriam Polster (1987) describes a three-stage integration sequence that characterizes client growth in therapy. The first part of this sequence consists of *discovery*. Clients are likely to reach a new realization about themselves or to acquire a novel view of an old situation, or they may take a new look at some significant person in their life. Such discoveries often come as a surprise to them.

   The second stage of the integration sequence is *accommodation*, which involves clients' recognizing that they have a choice. They are not bound tightly to one course, but there are alternative ways of behaving. Clients begin by trying out new behaviors in the supportive environment of the therapy office, and then they expand their awareness of the world. Making new choices is often done awkwardly, but with support clients can gain skills in coping with difficult situations. The therapeutic task is to mobilize the support system of the client and to encourage practice and experimentation with alternate ways of behaving. Clients are likely to carry out homework assignments that are aimed at achieving success.

The third stage of the integration sequence is *assimilation,* which involves clients' learning how to influence their environment. At this phase clients feel capable of dealing with the surprises they encounter in everyday living. They are now beginning to do more than passively accept the environment. Behavior at this stage may include a client's taking a stand on a critical issue. Eventually, clients develop confidence in their ability to improve and improvise. They are able to make choices that will result in getting what they want. The therapist points out that something has been accomplished and acknowledges the changes that have taken place within the client. At this phase clients have learned what they can do to maximize their chances of getting what is needed from their environment.

## RELATIONSHIP BETWEEN THERAPIST AND CLIENT

As an existential brand of therapy, Gestalt practice involves a person-to-person relationship between the therapist and the client. Therapists are responsible for the quality of their presence, for knowing themselves and the client, and for remaining open to the client. They are also responsible for establishing and maintaining a therapeutic atmosphere that will foster a spirit of work on the client's part. The therapist's experiences, awareness, and perceptions provide the background of the therapy process, and the client's awareness and reactions constitute the foreground. It is important that therapists allow themselves to be affected by their clients and that they actively share their own present perceptions and experiences as they encounter clients in the here and now.

Gestalt therapists not only allow their clients to be who they are but also remain themselves and do not get lost in a role. They are willing to express their reactions and observations, they share their personal experience in appropriate ways, and they do not manipulate clients. Further, they give feedback, particularly on what clients are doing with their body. Feedback allows clients to develop an awareness of what they are actually doing. The therapist must encounter clients with honest and immediate reactions and explore with them their fears, catastrophic expectations, blockages, and resistances.

A number of writers have given central importance to the I/thou relationship and the quality of the therapist's presence, as opposed to technical skills. They warn of the dangers of becoming technique-bound and losing sight of their own being as they engage the client. Techniques are not the issue; rather, the therapist's attitudes and behavior and the relationship that is established are what really count (Jacobs, 1989; E. Polster, 1987a, 1987b; M. Polster, 1987; Yontef,

1993). These writers point out that current Gestalt therapy has moved beyond earlier therapeutic practices. Many contemporary therapists place increasing emphasis on factors such as presence, authentic dialogue, gentleness, more direct self-expression by the therapist, decreased use of stereotypic exercises, and a greater trust in the client's experiencing.

E. Polster and Polster (1973) emphasize the importance of therapists knowing themselves and being a therapeutic instrument. Like artists who need to be in touch with what they are painting, therapists are artistic participants in the creation of new life. The Polsters implore therapists to use their own experiences as essential ingredients in the therapy process. According to them, therapists are more than mere responders or catalysts. If they are to function effectively, they must be in tune with the clients before them, and they must be in tune with themselves. Thus, therapy is a two-way engagement on a genuine I/thou basis. Not only does the client change, but so does the therapist. If therapists are not sensitively tuned to their own qualities of tenderness, toughness, and compassion and to their reactions to the client, they become technicians.

In a seminal article, "Dialogue in Gestalt Theory and Therapy," Jacobs (1989) explores the role of the therapeutic relationship as a factor in healing and the extent to which the client/therapist relationship is the focus of therapy. She shows how Martin Buber's philosophy of dialogue, which involves a genuine and loving meeting, is congruent with Gestalt concepts of contact, awareness, and the paradoxical theory of change. Jacobs asserts that a current trend in Gestalt practice is toward greater emphasis on the client/therapist relationship rather than on techniques divorced from the context of this encounter. She believes that a therapist who operates from this orientation establishes a present-centered, nonjudgmental dialogue that allows the client to deepen awareness and to find contact with another person. Therapy that takes place within a dialogic relationship affords clients the chance to meet others and to come to know themselves. The techniques that therapists employ evolve out of this process. Certainly, techniques are still important in Gestalt practice, yet they must always be a phenomenological part of the therapeutic process. The experiments that we consider later in this chapter are aimed at awareness, not at simple solutions to a client's problem. Jacobs maintains that if therapists use experiments when they are frustrated with a client and want to change the person, they are misusing the experiments and will probably thwart the client's growth, rather than fostering growth and change.

# Application: Therapeutic Techniques and Procedures

## THE EXPERIMENT IN GESTALT THERAPY

Although the Gestalt approach is concerned with the obvious, its simplicity should not be taken to mean that the therapist's job is easy. Developing a variety of Gestalt gimmicks is simple, but employing the techniques in a mechanical fashion allows the clients to continue inauthentic living. If clients are to become authentic, they need contact with an authentic therapist. In *Creative Process in Gestalt Therapy* Zinker (1978) emphasizes the role of the therapist as a creative agent of change, an inventor, and a compassionate and caring human being. Zinker, although borrowing from Perls, has carried Gestalt therapy beyond the Perlsian style.

Before discussing the variety of Gestalt methods that you could include in your repertoire of counseling procedures, I think it is helpful to differentiate between exercises and experiments, as does Zinker (1978). *Exercises* are ready-made techniques that are sometimes used to evoke certain emotions (such as the expression of anger) in clients. *Experiments,* in contrast, grow out of the interaction between client and therapist. They can be considered the very cornerstone of experiential learning. Zinker sees therapy sessions as a series of experiments, which are the avenues for clients to learn experientially. What is learned from an experiment is a surprise to both the client and the counselor. Gestalt experiments are a creative adventure and a way in which clients can express themselves behaviorally. As Yontef (1993) says, experimentation, rather than being a Gestalt *technique,* is an attitude inherent in all Gestalt therapy. Although the therapist sets up experiments, this is a collaborative process with full participation of the client.

Miriam Polster (1987) says that an experiment is a way to bring out some kind of internal conflict by making this struggle an actual process. It is aimed at facilitating a client's ability to work through the stuck points of his or her life. Experiments encourage spontaneity and inventiveness by bringing the possibilities for action directly into the therapy session. By dramatizing or playing out problem situations or relationships in the relative safety of the therapy context, clients increase their range of flexibility of behavior. According to Polster, Gestalt experiments can take many forms: imagining a threatening future encounter; setting up a dialogue between a client and some significant person in his or her life; dramatizing the memory of a painful event; reliving a particularly profound early experience in the present; assuming the identity of one's mother or father through role playing; focusing on gestures, posture, and other nonverbal signs of inner expression; or carrying on a dialogue between two conflicting aspects within the person. Through these experiments, clients actually experience the feelings associated with their conflicts, as opposed to merely talking about their problems in a detached fashion. The main point is that experiments bring struggles to life by inviting clients to enact them in the present. It is crucial that experiments be tailored to each individual and used in a timely manner; they also need to be carried out in a context that offers a balance between support and risk. The Polsters call for sensitivity and careful attention on the therapist's part so that clients are "neither blasted into experiences that are too threatening nor allowed to stay in safe but infertile territory" (M. Polster & Polster, 1990, p. 104).

## PREPARING FOR GESTALT EXPERIMENTS

Sometimes I hear students maintain that Gestalt therapy relies too much on techniques and that they would be afraid to introduce many of these methods into a counseling session for fear that their clients would perceive them as being slightly odd. Unless these techniques are experienced, they may seem strange. After all, who would talk to an empty chair? Moreover, who would expect the chair to answer back? Asking clients to "become" an object in one of their dreams, for instance, can seem silly and pointless to some. It is a good practice for counselors to be familiar with the experiments they introduce (or the kinds of experiment they create and suggest). It is important for counselors to *personally* experience the power of Gestalt experiments and to feel comfortable suggesting them to clients.

It is also essential that counselors establish a relationship with their clients, so that the clients will feel trusting enough to participate in the learning that can result from Gestalt experiments. Clients will get more from Gestalt experiments if they are oriented and prepared for them. Through a trusting relationship with the therapist, clients are likely to challenge their resistance and allow themselves to participate in these experiments.

If clients are to cooperate, counselors must avoid directing them in a commanding fashion to carry out an experiment. Typically, I ask people if they are willing to try out an experiment to see what they might learn from it, and I take care to emphasize that no specific result is expected. I also tell clients that they can stop when they choose to, so the power is with them. Clients at times say that they feel silly or self-conscious or that the task feels artificial or unreal. At such times I am likely to respond with something like: "Oh, why not go ahead and be silly? Will the roof cave in if you act foolish? Are you willing to give it a try and see what happens?" I cannot overemphasize the power of the therapeutic relationship and the necessity for trust as the foundation for implementing any technique. If I meet with resistance, I tend to be interested in exploring the client's reluctance. It is helpful to know the reason that the client is stopping. The reluctance to become emotionally involved often is a function of the client's cultural background. Some clients have been conditioned to work hard to maintain emotional control. They may have reservations about expressing intense feelings openly, even if they are in an emotional state. This can well be due to their socialization and to cultural norms that they abide by. In some cultures it is considered rude to express emotions openly. And there are certain cultural injunctions against showing one's vulnerability or psychological pain. If clients have had a long history of containing their feelings, it is understandable that they will be reluctant to participate in exercises that are designed to bring their emotions to the surface. Of course, many men have been socialized not to express intense feelings. Their reluctance to allow themselves to be emotional needs to be dealt with in a respectful manner.

Other clients may resist becoming emotionally involved because of their fear, lack of trust, concern over being foolish, or some other concern. The *way* in which the client resists doing an experiment reveals a great deal about the client's personality and his or her way of being in the world. Therefore, resistance does not have to be met with therapist defensiveness. I find that when I respect resistance and go with it, some of these defenses melt away. I attempt to show clients that I am willing to go as far as they are and that I will not push them to do what they say they do not want to do. Further, I hope that they can discover for themselves the meaning of their patterns of behavior through the experiment or through their resistance to it.

It is well to remember that the techniques of Gestalt therapy are designed to expand the client's awareness and to help him or her experiment with new modes of behavior. These techniques are only means to the end of helping people change, not ends in themselves. The following guidelines, largely taken from Passons (1975) and Zinker (1978), are suggestions I find useful both in preparing clients for Gestalt experiments and in carrying them out in the course of therapy:

- It is important for counselors to be sensitive enough to know when to leave the client alone.
- To derive maximum benefit from Gestalt experiments, the counselor must be sensitive to introducing them at the right time.
- The nature of the experiment depends on the individual's problems, what the person is experiencing, and the life experiences that both the client and the therapist bring to the session.
- Experiments require the client's active role in self-exploration.
- Gestalt experiments work best when the therapist is respectful of the client's cultural background and is in good contact with the person.
- If counselors meet with hesitation, it is a good idea to explore its meaning for the client.
- It is important that counselors be flexible in using techniques, paying particular attention to how the client is responding.
- Counselors should be ready to scale down tasks so that clients have a good chance to succeed in their efforts. It is not helpful to suggest experiments that are too advanced for a client.
- It is helpful for counselors to learn which experiments can best be practiced in the session itself and which can best be performed outside.

## THE ROLE OF CONFRONTATION

I have found that students are sometimes put off by Gestalt therapy because of their perception that a Gestalt counselor's style is direct and confrontational. They base this perception on the few quotations I have given them from Perls or what they have read about his ideas and style. I tell my students that it is a mistake to equate the practice of any theory with its founder. Therefore, it is possible to subscribe to many Gestalt concepts and principles without incorporating the way that Perls practiced therapy.

The contemporary practice of Gestalt therapy has progressed beyond the style exhibited by Perls. Yontef (1993) refers to the Perlsian style as a "boom-boom-boom therapy" that was characterized by theatrics, abrasive confrontation, and intense catharsis. He implies that the charismatic style of Perls probably met more of his own narcissistic needs than the needs of his clients. Yontef is critical of the antiintellectual, individualistic, dramatic, and confrontive flavor that characterized Gestalt therapy in the "anything goes environment" of the 1960s.

Although there is now less emphasis on confrontation in Gestalt practice, this should not be taken to mean that confrontation is absent. A solid therapeutic relationship allows the therapist to suggest challenging experiments that invite clients to face some of their deeper fears. Most of the Gestalt techniques that I describe *are* confrontational. Counselors who use these methods must be willing to be active and at times challenging. Clients must also be willing to take risks and challenge themselves, and in that sense self-confrontation becomes crucial. I agree with Passons (1975) that some people tend to ascribe too much power to Gestalt techniques. He views these experiments as designed to enhance awareness, with no power of their own; the power lies in the person who uses the techniques. If they are used in a caring and appropriate manner, they can heighten the experiencing of clients. The skill comes in challenging clients to push beyond their usual level of resistance and avoidance without fostering increased defensiveness.

Confrontation is a part of many Gestalt techniques, yet it does not have to be viewed as a harsh attack. Confrontation can be done in such a way that clients cooperate, especially when they are *invited* to examine their behaviors, attitudes, and thoughts. Counselors can encourage clients to look at certain incongruities, especially gaps between their verbal expression and nonverbal expression. If a client is speaking of a painful event yet smiling at the same time, calling attention to the lack of congruence can be confrontational to the extent that she may become aware of her attempt to avoid feeling the intensity of her pain. Further, confrontation does not have to be aimed at weaknesses or negative traits; clients can be challenged to recognize the ways in which they are blocking their strengths and are not living as fully as they might. In this sense confrontation can and should be a genuine expression of caring that results in positive changes in a client.

Perhaps one of the most essential ingredients in effective confrontation is respect for the client. Counselors who care enough to make demands on their clients are telling them, in effect, that they could be in fuller contact with themselves and others. Ultimately, however, clients must decide for themselves if they want to accept this invitation to learn more about themselves. This caveat needs to be kept in mind with all of the techniques that are to be described.

## TECHNIQUES OF GESTALT THERAPY

Techniques can be useful tools to help the client gain fuller awareness, experience internal conflicts, resolve inconsistencies and dichotomies, and work through an impasse that is preventing completion of unfinished business.

Levitsky and Perls provide a brief description of a number of techniques, including (1) the dialogue exercise, (2) making the rounds, (3) unfinished business, (4) "I take responsibility," (5) "I have a secret," (6) playing the projection, (7) reversals, (8) the rhythm of contact and withdrawal, (9) "rehearsal," (10) "exaggeration," (11) "May I feed you a sentence?" (12) marriage-counseling games, and (13) "Can you stay with this feeling?" (1970, pp. 144–149). The following discussion is based on some of the exercises described by Levitsky and Perls, although I have modified the material and added suggestions for implementing these techniques.

THE DIALOGUE EXERCISE.   As we saw earlier, a goal of Gestalt therapy is to bring about integrated functioning and the acceptance of aspects of one's personality that have been disowned and denied. Gestalt therapists pay close attention to splits in personality function. A main division is between the "top dog" and the "underdog." Often therapy focuses on the war between the two.

The top dog is righteous, authoritarian, moralistic, demanding, bossy, and manipulative. This is the "critical parent" that badgers with "shoulds" and "oughts" and manipulates with threats of catastrophe. The underdog manipulates by playing the role of victim; by being defensive, apologetic, helpless, and weak; and by feigning powerlessness. This is the passive side, the one without responsibility, and the one that finds excuses. The top dog and the underdog are engaged in a constant struggle for control. The struggle helps to explain why one's resolutions and promises often go unfulfilled and why one's procrastination persists. The tyrannical top dog demands that one be thus-and-so, whereas the underdog defiantly plays the role of disobedient child. As a result of this struggle for control, the individual becomes fragmented into controller and controlled. The civil war between the two sides continues, with both sides fighting for their existence.

The conflict between the two opposing poles in the personality is rooted in the mechanism of introjection, which involves incorporating aspects of others, usually parents, into one's ego system. Perls implies that the taking in of values and traits is both inevitable and desirable; the danger is in the uncritical and wholesale acceptance of another's values as one's own, which makes becoming an autonomous person difficult. It is essential that one become aware of one's introjects, especially the toxic introjects that poison the system and prevent personality integration.

The empty-chair technique is one way of getting the client to externalize the introject. In this technique two chairs are used. The therapist asks the client to sit in one chair and be fully the top dog and then shift to the other chair and become the underdog. The dialogue can continue between both sides of the client. Essentially, this is a role-playing technique in which all the parts are played by the client. In this way the introjects can surface, and the client can experience the conflict more fully. The conflict can be resolved by the client's acceptance and integration of both sides. This technique helps clients get in touch with a feeling or a side of themselves that they may be denying; rather than merely talking about a conflicted feeling, they intensify the feeling and experience it fully. Further, by helping clients realize that the feeling is a very real part of themselves, the technique discourages them from disassociating the feeling. The technique can help clients identify distasteful parental introjects.

The dialogues between opposing tendencies have as their aim the promotion of a higher level of integration between the polarities and conflicts that exist in everyone. The aim is not to rid oneself of certain traits but to learn to accept and live with the polarities. Many common conflicts lend themselves to the game of dialogue. Some that I find applicable include (1) the parent inside versus the child inside, (2) the responsible one versus the impulsive one, (3) the puritanical side versus the sexual side, (4) the "good boy" versus the "bad boy," (5) the aggressive self versus the passive self, (6) the autonomous side versus the resentful side, and (7) the hard worker versus the goof-off.

Let me describe one example of a common conflict between the top dog and underdog that I have found to be a powerful agent in helping a client become more intensely aware of the internal split and of which side would become dominant. The client, in this case a woman, plays the weak, helpless, dependent game of "poor me." She complains that she is miserable and that she hates and resents her husband, yet she fears that if he leaves her, she will disintegrate. She uses him as the excuse for her impotence. She continually puts herself down, always saying: "I can't." "I don't know how." "I am not capable." If she decided that she was miserable enough to want to change her dependent style, I would probably ask her to sit in one chair in the center of the room and become fully the underdog martyr and to exaggerate this side of herself. Eventually, if she got disgusted with this side, I would ask her to be the other side—that is, the top-dog side that puts her down—and talk to the "poor me." Then I might ask her to pretend that she were powerful, strong, and independent and to act as if she were not helpless. I might ask, "What would happen if you were strong and independent and if you gave up your clinging dependency?" That technique can often energize clients into really experiencing the roles they continue to play, the result frequently being the reinvention of the autonomous aspects of self.

MAKING THE ROUNDS.   Making the rounds is a Gestalt exercise that involves asking a person in a group to go up to others in the group and either speak to or do something with each. The purpose is to confront, to risk, to disclose the self, to experiment with new behavior, and to grow and change. I have employed the technique when I sensed that a participant needed to face each person in the group with some theme. For example, a group member might say: "I've been sitting here for a long time wanting to participate but holding back because I'm afraid of trusting people in here. And besides, I don't think I'm worth the time of the group anyway." I might counter with "Are you willing to do something right now to get yourself more invested and to begin to work on gaining trust and self-confidence?" If the person answers affirmatively, my suggestion could well be "Go around to each person and finish this sentence: 'I don't trust you because . . .'" Any number of exercises could be invented to help individuals involve themselves and choose to work on the things that keep them frozen in fear.

Some other related illustrations and examples that I find appropriate for the making-the-rounds technique are reflected in clients' comments such as these: "I would like to reach out to people more often." "I'm bored by what's going on in this group." "Nobody in here seems to care very much." "I'd like to make contact with you, but I'm afraid of being rejected [or accepted]." "It's hard for me to accept good stuff; I always discount good things people say to me." "It's hard for me to say negative things to people; I always want to be nice." "I'd like to feel more comfortable in touching and getting close." If it is appropriate, group members can be asked to respond.

"I TAKE RESPONSIBILITY FOR . . ."   The therapist may ask the client to make a statement and then add, "and I take responsibility for it." Some examples: "I'm feeling bored, and I take responsibility for my boredom." "I'm feeling excluded and lonely, and I take responsibility for my feelings of exclusion." "I don't know what to say now, and I take responsibility for my not knowing." This technique is designed to help clients recognize and accept their feelings instead of projecting them onto others. Although this technique may sound mechanical, it can be very meaningful.

PLAYING THE PROJECTION.   The dynamics of projection consist of one's seeing clearly in others the very things one does not want to see and accept within oneself. A client can invest much energy in denying feelings and imputing motives to others. Often, the statements an individual makes toward and about others are in fact projections of attributes he or she possesses.

In the playing-the-projection game the therapist asks the person who says "I can't trust you" to play the role of the untrustworthy person—that is, to become the other—in order to discover the degree to which the distrust is an inner conflict. In other words, the therapist asks the person to "try on for size" certain statements he or she makes about others.

THE REVERSAL TECHNIQUE.   Certain symptoms and behavior often represent reversals of underlying or latent impulses. Thus, the therapist could ask a person who claims to suffer from severe inhibitions and excessive timidity to play the role of an exhibitionist. I remember a client in one of our groups who had difficulty in being anything but sugary sweet. I asked her to reverse her typical style and be as negative as she could be. The reversal worked well; soon she was playing her part with real gusto and later was able to recognize and accept her "negative side" as well as her "positive side."

The theory underlying the reversal technique is that clients take the plunge into the very thing that is fraught with anxiety and make contact with those parts of themselves that have been submerged and denied. This technique can thus help clients begin to accept certain personal attributes that they have tried to deny.

THE REHEARSAL EXERCISE.   According to Perls, much of our thinking is rehearsing. We rehearse in fantasy for the role we think we are expected to play in society. When it comes to the performance, we experience stage fright, or anxiety, because we fear that we will not play our role well. Internal rehearsal consumes much energy and frequently inhibits our spontaneity and willingness to experiment with new behavior.

When clients share their rehearsals out loud with a therapist, they become more aware of the many preparatory means they use in bolstering their social roles. They also become increasingly aware of how they try to meet the expectations of others, of the degree to which they want to be approved, accepted, and liked, and of the extent to which they go to attain acceptance.

THE EXAGGERATION EXERCISE.   One aim of Gestalt therapy is for clients to become more aware of the subtle signals and cues they are sending through body language. Movements, postures, and gestures may communicate significant meanings, yet the cues may be incomplete. The person is asked to exaggerate the movement or gesture repeatedly, which usually intensifies the feeling attached to the behavior and makes the inner meaning clearer.

Some examples of behavior that lends itself to the exaggeration technique are trembling (shaking hands, legs), slouched posture and bent shoulders, clenched fists, tight frowning, facial grimacing, crossed arms, and so forth. If a client reports that his or her legs are shaking, for instance, the therapist may ask the client to stand up and exaggerate the shaking. Then the therapist may ask the client to put words to the shaking limbs.

As a variation, verbal behavior also lends itself to the exaggeration exercise. The therapist can ask a client to repeat a statement that he or she had glossed over and to repeat it each time louder and louder. Frequently, the effect is that clients begin to really listen to and hear themselves.

STAYING WITH THE FEELING.   At key moments when a client refers to a feeling or a mood that is unpleasant and from which he or she has a great urge to flee, the therapist urges the client to stay with, or retain, the feeling.

Most clients desire to escape from fearful stimuli and to avoid unpleasant feelings. The therapist may ask clients to remain with whatever fear or pain they are experiencing at present and encourage them to go deeper into the feeling and behavior they wish to avoid. Facing, confronting, and experiencing feelings not only take courage but also are a mark of a willingness to endure the pain necessary for unblocking and making way for newer levels of growth.

THE GESTALT APPROACH TO DREAM WORK.   In psychoanalysis, dreams are interpreted, intellectual insight is stressed, and free association is used as one method of exploring the unconscious meanings of dreams. The Gestalt approach does not interpret and analyze a dream. Instead, the intent is to bring the dream back to life and relive it as though it were happening now. The dream is not told as a past event but is acted out in the present, and the dreamer becomes a part of his or her dream. The suggested format for working with dreams includes making a list of all the details of the dream, remembering each person, event, and mood in it, and then becoming each of these parts by transforming oneself, acting as fully as possible and inventing dialogue. Because each part of the dream is assumed to be a projection of oneself, one creates scripts for encounters between various characters or parts. All of the different parts of a dream are expressions of one's own contradictory and inconsistent sides. Thus, by engaging in a dialogue between these opposing sides, one gradually becomes more aware of the range of one's own feelings.

Perls's concept of projection is central in his theory of dream formation. According to him, every person and every object in the dream represent a projected aspect of the dreamer. Perls (1969a) suggests that "we start with the impossible assumption that whatever we believe we see in another person or in the world is nothing but a projection" (p. 67). He writes that the recognition of the senses and the understanding of projections go hand in hand. Thus, he did not interpret dreams, play intellectual guessing games, or tell clients the meaning of their dreams. Clients do not think about or analyze the dream but use it as a script and experiment with the dialogue among the various parts of the dream. Because clients can act out a fight between opposing sides, eventually they can appreciate and accept their inner differences and integrate the opposing forces. Whereas Freud calls the dream the royal road to the unconscious, to Perls it is the "royal road to integration" (1969a, p. 66).

According to Perls, the dream is the most spontaneous expression of the existence of the human being. It represents an unfinished situation, but it is more than an uncompleted situation or an unfulfilled wish. Every dream contains an existential message of oneself and one's current struggle. Everything is to be found in dreams if all the parts are understood and assimilated. Each piece of work done on a dream leads to some assimilation. Perls asserts that if dreams are properly worked with, the existential message becomes clearer. According to him, dreams serve as an excellent way to discover personality voids by revealing missing parts and the client's methods of avoidance. If people do not remember dreams, they are refusing to face what is wrong with their life. At the very least, the Gestalt counselor asks clients to talk to their missing dreams. For example, as directed by her therapist, a client reported the following dream in the present tense, as though she were still dreaming:

> I have three monkeys in a cage. One big monkey and two little ones! I feel very attached to these monkeys, although they are creating a lot of chaos in a cage that is divided into three separate spaces. They are fighting with one another—the big monkey is fighting with the little monkey. They are getting out of the cage, and they are clinging onto me. I feel like pushing them away from me. I feel totally overwhelmed by the chaos that they are creating around me. I turn to my mother and tell her that I need help, that I can no longer handle these monkeys because they are driving me crazy. I feel very sad and very tired, and I feel discouraged. I am walking away from the cage, thinking that I really love these monkeys, yet I have to get rid of them. I am telling myself that I am like everybody else. I get pets, and then when things get rough, I want to get rid of them. I am trying very hard to find a solution to keeping these monkeys and not allowing them to have such a terrible effect on me. Before I wake up from my dream, I am making the decision to put each monkey in a separate cage, and maybe that is the way to keep them.

The therapist then asked his client, Brenda, to "become" different parts of her dream. Thus, she became the cage, and she became and had a dialogue with each monkey, and then she became her mother, and so forth. One of the most powerful aspects of this technique was Brenda's reporting her dream as though it were still happening. She quickly perceived that her dream expressed a struggle that she was having with her husband and her two children. From her dialogue work, she discovered that she both appreciated and resented her family. She learned that she needed to let them know about her feelings and that together they might work on improving an intensely difficult lifestyle. She did not need an interpretation from her therapist to understand the clear message of her dream.

## GESTALT THERAPY APPLIED TO THE CASE OF STAN

The Gestalt-oriented therapist will focus on the unfinished business that Stan has with his parents, siblings, and ex-wife. It appears that this unfinished business consists mainly of feelings of resentment, yet he turns this resentment inward toward himself. His present life situation will be spotlighted, but he may also need to reexperience past feelings that could be interfering with his present attempts to develop intimacy with others.

Although the focus is on Stan's present behavior, his therapist is likely to guide him toward becoming aware of how he is carrying old baggage around and how it interferes with his life today. Her task is to assist him in recreating the context in which he made earlier decisions that are no longer serving him well. Essentially, he needs to learn that his decision about the way he had to be in order to survive during his childhood years may no longer be appropriate. One of his cardinal decisions was: "I'm stupid, and it would be better if I were not here. I'm a loser."

Stan has been influenced by cultural messages that he has accepted. His counselor is interested in exploring his cultural background, including his values and the values characteristic of his culture. With this focus, it is likely that he may identify some of the following cultural injunctions: "Don't talk about your family with strangers, and don't hang out your dirty linen in public." "Don't confront your parents, because they deserve respect." "Don't be too concerned about yourself." "Don't show your vulnerabilities; hide your feelings and weaknesses." Although his counselor respects the cultural context in which he grew up, she still challenges him to examine those injunctions that are no longer functional. Although he can decide to retain those aspects of his cultural background that he prizes, he is also in a position to modify certain cultural expectations.

Stan's therapist is likely to proceed by designing experiments that will enable him to explore the many ways in which he continues to be affected by unfinished business from his past. In typical Gestalt fashion, he deals with his present struggles within the context of the relationship with his therapist, not simply by talking about his past or by analyzing his insights. She may ask him to "become" some of those individuals who told him how to think, feel, and behave as a child. He can then become the child that he was and respond to them from the place where he feels the most confusion or pain. He experiences in new ways the feelings that accompany his beliefs about himself, and he comes to a deeper appreciation of how his feelings and thoughts influence what he is doing today.

From his cultural conditioning, Stan has learned to hide his emotions rather than to reveal them. Understanding this about him, his counselor explores his hesitations and concerns about "getting into feelings." She recognizes that he is hesitant in expressing his emotions and thus helps him assess whether he would like to experience them more fully and express them more freely.

When Stan decides that he does want to experience his emotions rather than to deny them, the therapist does not merely ask him to talk about past experiences. Instead, she asks him to imagine himself in earlier scenes with his ex-wife, as though the painful situation were occurring in the here and now. He symbolically relives and reexperiences the situation, perhaps by talking "directly" to his wife. He tells her of his resentments and hurts and eventually completes his unfinished business with her. It is also important that he speak with his older brother and sister, toward whom he feels resentment because they were always seen as the "perfect" children in the family. More important than speaking to them in reality, however, is his willingness to talk to them symbolically as a part of a therapy session. He also needs to talk symbolically with his mother and father, as though he were a child again. The therapist uses the empty-chair technique to "bring" a sibling or parent into therapy. Stan is encouraged to "say" to them what he has never told them before. The therapist asks: "What are your resentments toward each of these people? What did you want from them that you never received? How would you have liked to be treated by them? What do you need to tell them now so that you can keep from being destroyed by your resentments?"

Through awareness of what he is now doing and how he keeps himself locked into his past, Stan can increasingly assume personal responsibility for his own life. In working toward this end, he engages in a "game of dialogue" in which his "top-dog" side talks with his "underdog" side. These dimensions within himself are struggling for control. He plays both parts for himself, and again, the empty-chair technique is used. Through this procedure he can become aware of the self-torture game he is continuing to play with himself. He also maintains that he has difficulty in feeling like a man, especially in relationships with strong women. He becomes the little boy in exaggerated fashion and talks to a powerful woman (in the empty chair), and then he becomes the threatening woman and talks back to his little-boy side. The main point is that he is facing his fears and engaging in a dialogue between the polarities that exist within him. The aim is not to extract his feelings but to learn to live with his polarities.

Most of the Gestalt exercises serve one main function for Stan: helping him gain a fuller sense of what he is doing in the present to keep significant figures alive and powerful within himself. As he gains more complete awareness of his dependency, he also finds an internal capacity to strive for his own wishes, rather than remaining controlled by the expectations of others.

FOLLOW-UP: YOU CONTINUE AS STAN'S GESTALT THERAPIST. Use these questions to help you think about how to counsel Stan:

- What unfinished business can you identify in Stan's case? Does any of his experience of being stuck, his avoidance, or his unfinished business remind you of aspects within yourself? As his Gestalt therapist, how might you work with him if he did bring up your own unfinished business?
- Identify what you consider to be Stan's impasse. What kind of avoidance patterns do you notice in him?
- In the example above of the Gestalt therapist's work with Stan, she used several techniques to facilitate bringing his work into the here and now. Assuming that he identified some problems that he wanted to explore with his parents, what Gestalt techniques might you employ? What would you hope to accomplish in using these techniques?
- What are some polarities that you see in Stan? How might you work with them?
- How might you work with Stan's cultural messages? Would you be able to respect his cultural values and still encourage him to make an assessment of some of the ways in which his culture is affecting him today?

# Summary and Evaluation

## SUMMARY

Gestalt counseling is an experiential therapy stressing here-and-now awareness. The major focus is on the *what* and *how* of behavior and the role of unfinished business from the past that prevents effective functioning in the present. Some of the key goals of the approach are accepting personal responsibility, living in the immediate moment, and direct experiencing as opposed to abstract talking about experiences. The approach helps clients deal with avoidance, unfinished business, and impasses.

A central therapeutic aim is to challenge the client to move more fully into self-support. Expansion of awareness, which is viewed as curative of itself, is a basic goal. With awareness clients are able to reconcile polarities and dichotomies within themselves and thus proceed toward the reintegration of all aspects of themselves.

In this approach the therapist assists clients to experience all feelings more fully, and this enables them to make their own interpretations. The therapist avoids making interpretations and instead focuses on how clients are behaving. Clients identify their own unfinished business, and they work through the blockages impeding their growth. They do this largely by reexperiencing past situations as though they were happening in the present. Therapists have many techniques at their disposal, all of which have two things in common: They are designed to intensify direct experiencing and to integrate conflicting feelings.

## CONTRIBUTIONS OF GESTALT THERAPY

I make frequent use of Gestalt methods. I am impressed with the action approach, which brings conflicts and human struggles to life. Through such techniques, I have found, people actually experience their struggles, as opposed to merely talking about problems endlessly in a detached manner. In doing so, they are able to increase their awareness of what they are experiencing in the present moment. I especially like the range of experiments and exercises that a therapist can suggest to help clients discover new facets of themselves.

Another of Gestalt therapy's contributions is the exciting way in which the past is dealt with in a lively manner by bringing relevant aspects into the present. Practitioners challenge clients in creative ways to become aware of and work with issues that are obstructing current functioning. Further, paying attention to the obvious verbal and nonverbal leads provided by the client is a useful way to approach a counseling session. Through the skillful and sensitive use of Gestalt approaches, practitioners can assist people in heightening their present-centered awareness of what they are thinking and feeling as well as what they are doing. Through this awareness they are enabled to assume an increased share of personal responsibility for what they are experiencing.

I especially value the compassionate confrontational aspect of this approach in refusing to accept helplessness as an excuse for not changing. The client is provided with a wide range of tools, in the form of Gestalt experiments, for making decisions about changing the course of living.

The Gestalt approach to working with dreams is a unique pathway for people to increase their awareness of key themes in their life. By seeing each aspect of a dream as a projection of themselves, clients are able to bring the dream to life, to interpret its personal meaning, and to assume responsibility for it.

The Gestalt approach is a perspective on growth and enhancement, not merely a system of techniques to treat disorders. With the emphasis given to the existential relationship between client and therapist, there is a creative spirit of suggesting, inventing, and carrying out experiments aimed at increasing awareness. Of all the approaches, Gestalt therapy has the greatest potential for creativity.

CONTRIBUTIONS TO MULTICULTURAL COUNSELING.    There are opportunities to sensitively and creatively use Gestalt methods, if they are timed appropriately, with culturally diverse populations. One of the advantages of drawing on Gestalt experiments is that they can be tailored to fit the unique way in which an individual perceives and interprets his or her culture. Furthermore, Gestalt methods can allow the client and the therapist to break down certain cross-cultural barriers between them. One of my colleagues goes to Japan almost every year for three months and teaches a combination of body work, Rolfing (or structural integration, as developed by Ida Rolf), and Gestalt therapy. He finds the Japanese he teaches to be very receptive to Gestalt methods, for many of the principles are grounded on Eastern notions.

Gestalt therapy is particularly effective in helping people integrate the polarities within themselves. Many bicultural clients experiences an ongoing struggle in reconciling what appear to be diverse aspects of the two cultures in which they live. In one of my weeklong groups a dynamic piece of work was done by a woman with European roots. Her struggle consisted of integrating her American side with her experiences in Germany as a child. I asked her to "bring her family into this group" by talking to selected members in the group as though they were members of her family. She was asked to imagine that she was 8 years old and that she could now say to her parents and siblings things that she had never expressed. I asked her to speak in German (since this was her primary language as a child). The combined factors of her trust in the group, her willingness to recreate an early scene by reliving it in the present moment, and her symbolic work with fantasy helped her achieve a significant breakthrough. She was able to put a new ending to an old and unfinished situation through her participation in this Gestalt experiment.

There are many opportunities to apply Gestalt exercises in creative ways with diverse client populations. Various cultures give attention to expressing oneself nonverbally, rather than emphasizing the content of verbal communication. Some clients may express themselves nonverbally more expressively than they do with words. For example, therapists may ask clients to focus on their gestures, facial expressions, and what they are experiencing within their own body. One of the advantages of drawing on Gestalt experiments is that they can be tailored to fit the unique way in which an individual perceives and interprets his or her culture. Of course, before Gestalt techniques are introduced, it is essential that clients have been adequately prepared for such methods.

Sue and Sue (1990) suggest that Gestalt approaches of focusing on the here and now appear to be congruent with Native American values. There are other aspects of Gestalt work that can be useful in understanding Native Americans. For example, paying attention to nonverbal behavior, without stereotyping the client, often provides significant leads. Following the client's lead in regard to nonverbal behavior helps prevent misunderstandings and increases rapport. However, the Sues caution that many Gestalt techniques, because they are confrontational, may be embarrassing to Native American clients.

## LIMITATIONS AND CRITICISMS OF GESTALT THERAPY

A chief criticism of the Perlsian style of Gestalt therapy involves its deemphasis of the cognitive factors of personality. Perls did discourage thinking about one's experience, and many Gestaltists have stressed becoming aware of and expressing feelings to the neglect of examining thoughts. Some practitioners view an intellectual process, or even attempting to bring cognitive structuring to something they experience in therapy, as a defense against feeling and fully experiencing in the here and now. To some degree, however, this one-sidedness is changing, with many therapists integrating cognitive work. It appears that more attention is being given to theoretical instruction, theoretical exposition, and cognitive factors in general (Yontef, 1993).

Although Gestalt therapy discourages interrupting the process of immediate experiencing and integration by focusing on cognitive explanations, clients do clarify their thinking, explore beliefs, and put meaning to experiences they are reliving in therapy. Gestalt therapy also discourages the therapist from *teaching* clients, as opposed to *facilitating* the clients' own process of self-discovery and learning. It seems to me, however, that clients can engage in self-discovery and at the same time benefit from appropriate teaching by the therapist. Why should therapy exclude giving information, making suggestions, cognitive processing, explanations, interpretations, and coaching on the therapist's part? As you will see, I favor blending the emotional and experiential work of Gestalt therapy with theoretical concepts and techniques of the cognitive and behavioral approaches (especially behavior therapy, rational emotive behavior therapy, and reality therapy). This type of integration of approaches would answer my major criticism of Gestalt therapy as it is often practiced.

Current Gestalt practice places a high value on the contact and dialogue between the therapist and client. For Gestalt therapy to be effective, I think, the therapist must have a high level of personal development. Being aware of one's own needs and seeing that they do not interfere with the client's process, being present in the moment, and being willing to be nondefensive and self-revealing all demand a lot of the therapist. There is a danger that power-hungry therapists who are inadequately trained will be primarily concerned with impressing and manipulating clients.

CAUTIONS ABOUT TECHNIQUES. As exciting and dynamic as Gestalt methods are, they are not for all clients. According to Shepherd (1970), the appropriate application of Gestalt techniques hinges on questions of "When?" "With whom?" and "In what situation?" She indicates that, in general, Gestalt therapy is most effective with overly socialized, constricted individuals, often described as neurotic, phobic, perfectionistic, ineffective, and depressed. On the other hand, Gestalt work with less organized, more severely disturbed, or psychotic individuals is more problematic and requires caution, sensitivity, and patience.

A major concern I have about Gestalt therapy is the potential danger for abusing techniques. Typically, Gestalt therapists are highly active and directive, and if they do not have the characteristics mentioned by Zinker (1978)—sensitivity, timing, inventiveness, empathy, and respect for the client—their experiments can easily boomerang.

With an approach that can have powerful effects on clients, either constructive or destructive, ethical practice depends on the level of training and supervision of its therapists. The most immediate limitation of Gestalt, or any other therapy, is the skill, training, experience, and judgment of the therapist. Probably the most effective application of Gestalt techniques comes from personal therapeutic experiences gained in professional training workshops and work with competent therapists and supervisors (Shepherd, 1970).

The Gestalt approach can be dangerous, because of the therapist's power to manipulate the client with techniques. An ethical issue is raised by inept therapists who use powerful techniques to stir up feelings and open up problems that clients have kept from full awareness, only to abandon the clients once they have managed to have a dramatic catharsis. Such a failure to stay with clients, by helping them work through what they have experienced and bring some closure to the experience, can be detrimental.

LIMITATIONS FOR MULTICULTURAL COUNSELING.    To a greater extent than is true of most other approaches, there are definite hazards in too quickly utilizing some Gestalt techniques with ethnic-minority clients. As is evident from this chapter, Gestalt techniques tend to produce a high level of intense feelings. This focus on affect has some clear limitations with those clients who have been culturally conditioned to be emotionally reserved. As mentioned earlier, some clients believe that expressing feelings openly is a sign of weakness and a display of one's vulnerability. Counselors who operate on the assumption that catharsis is necessary for any change to occur are likely to find certain clients becoming increasingly resistant, and such clients may prematurely terminate counseling. Other clients have strong cultural injunctions prohibiting them from directly expressing their emotions to their parents (such as "Never show your parents that you are angry at them" or "Strive for peace and harmony, and avoid conflicts"). For instance, I recall a client from India who was asked by his counselor to "bring your father into the room." The client was very reluctant to even symbolically tell his father of his disappointment with their relationship. In his culture the accepted way to deal with his father was to use his uncle as a go-between, and it was considered highly inappropriate to express any negative feelings toward one's father. The client later said that he would have felt terrible guilt if he had symbolically told his father what he sometimes thought and felt.

Gestalt therapists who have truly integrated their approach are sensitive enough to practice in a flexible way. They consider the client's cultural framework and are thus able to adapt techniques that are likely to be well received. They strive to help clients experience themselves as fully as possible in the present, yet they are not rigidly bound by dictates, nor do they routinely intervene whenever clients stray from the present. Sensitively staying in contact with a client's flow of experiencing entails the ability to focus on the person and not on the mechanical use of techniques for a certain effect.

# Where to Go from Here

If you have become excited about including Gestalt techniques in your counseling style, I encourage you to attend a workshop led by a competent professional. I have real concerns about practitioners who employ Gestalt techniques if they have not experienced them personally. Although reading is surely of value, it is not sufficient to produce skillful clinicians. In addition to personally experiencing Gestalt experiments, it is crucial to have careful supervision, to learn the theoretical framework underlying these techniques, and to be well aware of the boundaries of one's competence.

There are a number of training centers in the United States, Canada, Belgium, England, France, Italy, Spain, Chile, and Israel. Since no national Gestalt therapy organization exists, each of the institutes establishes its own standards and criteria for membership and training. The Center for Gestalt Development offers an international guide listing practitioners of Gestalt therapy and institutes and centers providing training in Gestalt therapy. You can obtain a single copy of *The Gestalt Directory* by contacting:

Center for Gestalt Development, Inc.
P.O. Box 990
Highland, NY 12528
Telephone: (914) 691-7192

This organization is also the place to contact if you are interested in becoming a member of the Association for the Advancement of Gestalt Therapy (AAGT) or if you want to subscribe to the *Gestalt Journal,* which is devoted to the theory and practice of Gestalt therapy. Published twice yearly, it offers articles, reviews, and commentaries of interest to the practitioner, theoretician, academician, and student; the subscription fee is $30. The AAGT also offers a newsletter and a price list of books, audio tapes, and videotapes dealing with Gestalt practice.

A few resources for training in Gestalt therapy are:

Gestalt Institute of Cleveland
1588 Hazel Drive
Cleveland, OH 44106
Telephone: (216) 421-0468

Gestalt Training Center in San Diego
P.O. Box 2189
La Jolla, CA 92038
Telephone: (619) 454-9139

Gestalt Therapy Institute of Los Angeles
1460 7th Street, Suite 301
Santa Monica, CA 90401
Telephone: (310) 458-9747

## Recommended Supplementary Readings

*Gestalt Therapy Verbatim* (Perls, 1969a) is one of the best places to get a firsthand account of the style in which Perls worked. If you like that book and want to know more about Perls as a person, I recommend *In and Out of the Garbage Pail* (Perls, 1969b).

*Gestalt Approaches in Counseling* (Passons, 1975) is one of the books about Gestalt therapy that I most highly recommend, as it deals with the practical applications of Gestalt concepts in a wide variety of counseling situations. It is an excellent resource for techniques, and it stresses the importance of preparing clients for these techniques.

*Gestalt Therapy Integrated: Contours of Theory and Practice* (E. Polster & Polster, 1973) is a superb source for those who want a more advanced and theoretical treatment of this model.

*Creative Process in Gestalt Therapy* (Zinker, 1978) is a beautifully written book that is a delight to read. Zinker captures the essence of Gestalt therapy as a combination of phenomenology and behavior modification by showing how the therapist functions much like an artist in creating experiments that encourage clients to expand their boundaries. His concepts are fleshed out with rich clinical examples. The book shows how Gestalt can be practiced in a creative, eclectic, and integrative style.

*Fritz Perls* (Clarkson & Mackewn, 1993) provides a detailed overview of Perls's life and his contributions to the theory and practice of Gestalt therapy. The authors have excellent chapters on the criticisms and rebuttals of this approach and an assessment of his overall influence.

*Body Process: Working with the Body in Psychotherapy* (Kepner, 1993) is a well-written book that deals with many basic principles of Gestalt therapy, emphasizing the role of the body as an integral part of Gestalt practice.

*Awareness, Dialogue and Process: Essays on Gestalt Therapy* (Yontef, 1993) is an excellent collection that develops the message that much of Gestalt therapy theory and practice consists of dialogue. This book brings the reader up to date with some current trends in the practice of Gestalt counseling.

## References and Suggested Readings*

ATKINSON, D. R., MORTEN, G., & SUE, D. W. (1993). *Counseling American minorities: A cross-cultural perspective* (4th ed.). Madison, WI: Brown & Benchmark.

BEISSER, A. R. (1970). The paradoxical theory of change. In J. Fagan & I. L. Shepherd (Eds.), *Gestalt therapy now* (pp. 77–80). New York: Harper & Row (Colophon).

* CLARKSON, P., & MACKEWN, J. (1993). *Fritz Perls*. London: Sage.

COREY, G. (1995). *Theory and practice of group counseling* (4th ed.). Pacific Grove, CA: Brooks/Cole.

COREY, G. (1996). *Case approach to counseling and psychotherapy* (4th ed.). Pacific Grove, CA: Brooks/Cole.

DOWNING, J., & MARMORSTEIN, R. (Eds.). (1973). *Dreams and nightmares: A book of Gestalt therapy sessions*. New York: Harper & Row.

*Books and articles marked with an asterisk are suggested for further study.

FREW, J. E. (1986). The functions and patterns of occurrence of individual contact styles during the development phase of the Gestalt group. *The Gestalt Journal, 9*(1), 55–70.

GOULDING, M., & GOULDING, R. (1979). *Changing lives through redecision therapy.* New York: Brunner/Mazel.

*JACOBS, L. (1989). Dialogue in Gestalt theory and therapy. *The Gestalt Journal, 12*(1), 25–67.

*JAMES, M., & JONGEWARD, D. (1971). *Born to win: Transactional analysis with Gestalt experiments.* Reading, MA: Addison-Wesley.

*KEPNER, J. I. (1993). *Body process: Working with the body in psychotherapy.* San Francisco: Jossey-Bass.

LEVITSKY, A., & PERLS, F. (1970). The rules and games of Gestalt therapy. In J. Fagan & I. Shepherd (Eds.), *Gestalt therapy now* (pp. 140–149). New York: Harper & Row (Colophon).

*PASSONS, W. R. (1975). *Gestalt approaches in counseling.* New York: Holt, Rinehart & Winston.

*PERLS, F. (1969a). *Gestalt therapy verbatim.* Moab, UT: Real People Press.

PERLS, F. (1969b). *In and out of the garbage pail.* Moab, UT: Real People Press.

PERLS, F. (1970). Four lectures. In J. Fagan & I. Shepherd (Eds.), *Gestalt therapy now* (pp. 14–38). New York: Harper & Row (Colophon).

*PERLS, F. (1973). *The Gestalt approach and eye witness to therapy.* New York: Bantam Books.

PERLS, F., HEFFERLINE, R., & GOODMAN, P. (1951). *Gestalt therapy integrated: Excitement and growth in the human personality.* New York: Dell.

PERLS, L. (1970). One Gestalt therapist's approach. In J. Fagan & I. Shepherd (Eds.), *Gestalt therapy now* (pp. 125–129). New York: Harper & Row (Colophon).

POLSTER, E. (1987a). Escape from the present: Transition and storyline. In J. K. Zeig (Ed.), *The evolution of psychotherapy* (pp. 326–340). New York: Brunner/Mazel.

POLSTER, E. (1987b). *Every person's life is worth a novel.* New York: Norton.

*POLSTER, E., & POLSTER, M. (1973). *Gestalt therapy integrated: Contours of theory and practice.* New York: Brunner/Mazel.

POLSTER, M. (1987). Gestalt therapy: Evolution and application. In J. K. Zeig (Ed.), *The evolution of psychotherapy* (pp. 312–325). New York: Brunner/Mazel.

POLSTER, M., & POLSTER, E. (1990). Gestalt therapy. In J. K. Zeig & W. M. Munion (Eds.), *What is psychotherapy? Contemporary perspectives* (pp. 103–107). San Francisco: Jossey-Bass.

*RAINWATER, J. (1979). *You're in charge! A guide to becoming your own therapist.* Los Angeles: Guild of Tutors Press.

RICE, L. N., & GREENBERG, L. S. (1992). Humanistic approaches to psychotherapy. In D. K. Freedheim (Ed.), *History of psychotherapy: A century of change* (pp. 197–224). Washington, DC: American Psychological Association.

SHEPHERD, I. (1970). Limitations and cautions in the Gestalt approach. In J. Fagan & I. Shepherd (Eds.), *Gestalt therapy now* (pp. 234–238). New York: Harper & Row (Colophon).

*SIEGEL, B. S. (1988). *Love, medicine, and miracles.* New York: Harper & Row (Perennial Library).

STEVENS, J. O. (1971). *Awareness: Exploring, experimenting, experiencing.* Moab, UT: Real People Press.

STOEHR, T. (1994). *Here now next: Paul Goodman and the origins of Gestalt therapy.* San Francisco: Jossey-Bass.

SUE, D. W., & SUE, D. (1990). *Counseling the culturally different: Theory and practice* (2nd ed.). New York: Wiley.

THOMASON, T. C. (1991). Counseling Native Americans: An introduction for non–Native American counselors. *Journal of Counseling and Development, 69*(4), 321–327.

* YONTEF, G. M. (1993). *Awareness, dialogue and process: Essays on Gestalt therapy.* Highland, NY: Gestalt Journal Press.

ZEIG, J. K., & MUNION, W. M. (Eds.). (1990). *What is psychotherapy? Contemporary perspectives.* San Francisco: Jossey-Bass.

ZINKER, J. (1971). Dream work as theater: An innovation in Gestalt therapy. *Voices, 7*(2).

* ZINKER, J. (1978). *Creative process in Gestalt therapy.* New York: Random House (Vintage).

* ZINKER, J. (1994). *In search of good form: Gestalt therapy with couples and families.* San Francisco: Jossey-Bass.

CHAPTER NINE

# Reality Therapy

# WILLIAM GLASSER

WILLIAM GLASSER (b. 1925) was educated in Cleveland and finished medical school at Case Western Reserve University in 1953. He became a chemical engineer at 19 and a physician at 28. He then took his psychiatric training at the Veterans Administration Center in West Los Angeles and did his final year at the University of California at Los Angeles in 1957. During his training he began to be more and more aware that there was a vast difference between what he was being taught to do (follow the Freudian model) and what seemed to him to work.

In 1956 Glasser became a consulting psychiatrist at the Ventura School for Girls, a California state facility for the treatment of delinquent adolescents. This experience convinced him even further of the futility of classical psychoanalytic concepts and techniques, so he began to develop and experiment with a different therapeutic approach that in many ways was antithetical to Freudian psychoanalysis. In 1961 Glasser published his first book, *Mental Health or Mental Illness?*, which laid the foundation for reality therapy.

By 1965, when he published *Reality Therapy,* he was able to state his fundamental beliefs, which are that we are all responsible for what we choose to do with our lives and that in a warm, accepting, nonpunitive therapeutic environment we are willing to learn more effective choices, or more responsible ways to live our lives.

During the 1960s Glasser worked as a consultant in public education, where he put into practice his basic concepts of reality therapy. This work was the beginning of his efforts to apply these powerful ideas to systems rather than to individuals, and the result was his first major book on education, *Schools without Failure* (1969). At this time he turned his professional interests to how teachers and students interacted with each other, how learning in schools could be connected to the lives of the learners, how schools often contributed to a "failure identity," and how they could be changed to make learning come alive. He continued to flesh out his ideas, and by 1972, when he published *The Identity Society,* he had already begun to lay the groundwork for what would be his acceptance and support of *control theory,* which explains not only how we function as individuals, both psychologically and physiologically, but also how we function as groups and even as societies. Although the ideas of control theory are not original with Glasser, he has applied them to systems in *Control Theory* (1985); to school administration in *The Quality School* (1990); and to management in *The Control Theory Manager* (1994).

Glasser established the Institute for Control Theory, Reality Therapy, and Quality Management, through which these ideas are taught throughout the world. He frequently gives lectures and workshops, both nationally and internationally, on the practical applications of control theory and reality therapy.

# Introduction

In many ways, control theory/reality therapy (CT/RT) parallels existential therapy, person-centered therapy, and Gestalt therapy. Like these three theories, reality therapy is concerned with the phenomenological world of the client and stresses the subjective way in which clients perceive and react to their world from an internal locus of evaluation. Glasser (1985) maintains that we perceive the world in the context of five basic, genetic needs and do not perceive the world as it really is. Clients live both in the external world (or real world) and their own internal world (or perceived world). Glasser stresses that it is not the way the real world exists that influences our behavior, but the way we perceive it to exist. So our behavior is always our best attempt to control our perceptions of the external world so they fit our internal, need-satisfying pictures.

Again, like all three previous theories, reality therapy emphasizes that people have freedom, can make choices, and must wrestle with the subsequent responsibilities that flow out of their choices. We can take more effective control of our life if we are willing to make the effort to shape our destiny, because all our behavior is generated from within to meet our five basic needs. Thus, by putting the principles of control theory into practice, people can prevent many potential problems that could lead them into therapy.

Reality therapy differs from the existential, person-centered, and Gestalt approaches in that Glasser teaches that behavior is total; that is, it involves the four components of doing, thinking, feeling, and physiology. This means that clients are responsible for choosing not only what they are doing but also what they are thinking, feeling, and experiencing physically.

In common with the existential approach, CT/RT is based on the assumption that we do not have to be a victim of our past or our present unless we choose to be. Nor are we at the mercy of unconscious motivations. We have more control over life than most of us believe. The more effectively we exercise our control, the more fulfilled we will be (Glasser, 1989). In short, we are almost never the victims of circumstances outside of us, for the capacity to change is within ourselves.

The general aim of this therapeutic system, then, is to provide conditions that will help clients develop the psychological strength to evaluate their present total behavior—specifically, its doing, thinking, feeling, and physiological components. If it does not meet their needs, the clients are assisted in developing more effective total behavior. This learning process is facilitated by the application of the basic principles of reality therapy and the various counseling procedures developed by Glasser. As in person-centered therapy, a warm and accepting counseling environment is fundamental to the practice of reality therapy. Once therapists establish a therapeutic involvement with their clients, they encourage them to make an assessment of their current style of living. This assessment enables them to determine how well their chosen behaviors are working for them. Individuals can improve the quality of their life through a process of honest self-evaluation. Clients are taught about the functioning of their basic needs and are asked to identify the wants (or specific desires, goals, and directions) that lead to satisfying one or more of those needs. If they determine that they want to make certain changes, they are expected to formulate an action plan, to commit themselves to the plan, and to follow through with their commitment.

It will become apparent when reading the following two chapters, which cover behavior therapy and cognitive-behavior therapy, that reality therapy shares some common denominators with both of those approaches. For one thing, reality therapists focus clients on what they are doing and, to a lesser degree, on what they are thinking. They work collaboratively with clients in formulating specific and workable action plans for change. Although reality therapy is grounded on existential and phenomenological principles, it makes use of both cognitive and behavioral techniques. So in some ways, this approach could be broadly classified as a cognitive-behavioral therapy, because its focus is on what individuals are doing and thinking in order to change how they are feeling what they are experiencing physically.

Reality therapy was selected for inclusion in this book for several reasons. First, this approach provides a good contrast to most of the other counseling approaches we explore. It raises questions and issues that you will want to examine, especially those dealing with the role of the therapist in challenging clients to evaluate what they are doing. Second, reality therapy continues to be popular among school counselors, teachers, principals, rehabilitation workers, and those who counsel in community agencies. The principles of control theory need not be restricted to psychotherapists; rather, they can be used by parents, ministers, doctors, husbands, and wives in working on interpersonal relationships. Third, it presents many of the basic issues in counseling, such as: What motivates people to behave? How can clients be challenged to make an honest self-assessment? If the therapist focuses clients on what they are doing, will this tend to influence what they are thinking and how they are feeling? What is the role of values in counseling? And finally, should therapists teach their clients? Reality therapy stresses a much more directive and educative role of the therapist than do the experiential therapies that were covered in Chapters 6–8. As you read this chapter, keep these questions in mind and compare reality therapy with the other therapeutic approaches you have studied.

# Key Concepts

## VIEW OF HUMAN NATURE

Control theory, as we have seen, rests on the notion that human behavior is purposeful and originates completely from within the individual rather than from external forces. Although environmental factors have an influence on our decisions, our behavior is not caused by them. All our internally motivated behavior is geared toward getting things we want that satisfy one or more of our basic human needs. Glasser (1985, 1989) identifies these as the four psychological needs for *belonging, power, freedom,* and *fun* and the physiological need for *survival.* Control theory explains that our brain functions as a control system to get us what we want to satisfy these needs. When we choose behaviors that fail to provide us what we want, our psychological needs are thwarted, and the chosen behaviors feel painful. Consequently, we are not satisfied with life. When we choose behaviors that *do* provide us what we want and meet our needs in a responsible way, we develop an identity characterized by success and self-esteem, and the behaviors we use feel good.

Although we all possess the same five needs, each of us fulfills them in unique ways. We develop an inner "picture album" of specific wants, also called a "quality world," which contains precise images of how we would best like to fulfill our needs. A major goal of reality therapy is to teach people better and more effective ways of attaining what they want in life.

Clearly, then, control theory challenges the deterministic philosophy of human nature. In a democratic society, if people wish to make the effort, they can change and live more effectively. They can behave for a purpose: to mold their environment, as a sculptor molds clay, to match their own inner pictures of what they want. These goals are achievable only through hard work (Wubbolding, 1988b). When people make choices that infringe on others' freedom, their behavior is irresponsible. Through the practice of reality therapy, people learn how to achieve freedom so that others do not suffer in the process.

## A CONTROL-THEORY EXPLANATION OF BEHAVIOR

In his workshops Glasser frequently explains the concept of *total behavior* by comparing how we function to how a car functions. Just as the four wheels guide a car, so do the four components of our total behavior influence our direction in life. These components of total behavior are *doing* (or active behaviors such as getting up and going to work); *thinking* (generating thoughts and self-statements); *feeling* (such as anger, joy, pain, depression, anxiety); and *physiology* (such as sweating or developing psychosomatic symptoms). Although these behavioral components always blend to make a whole, or total, behavior, they can be distinguished from one another, and one of them is usually more prominent than the others (W. Glasser, 1989).

When explaining the concept of total behavior, Glasser (1992) gives emphasis to the "two front wheels" (doing and thinking), which steer us, just as the front wheels steer the direction of a car. It is difficult to directly change how we are feeling, separately from what we are doing or thinking. However, we have an almost complete ability to change what we are doing and thinking, in spite of how we might be feeling:

> In reality therapy, we focus on helping other people to choose or change the only parts they can change, which are their actions and thoughts. It is not that we ignore or deny feelings and/or physiology; it is that we do not dwell upon what no one can change directly [Glasser, 1992, p. 7].

To summarize, then, control theory asserts that all we ever do from birth to death is behave, and every total behavior is always our best attempt to get what we want to satisfy our needs. In this context behavior is purposeful because it is designed to close the gap between what we want and what we perceive that we are getting. Specific behaviors are always generated from this discrepancy.

Wubbolding (1988b) writes that we are all sculptors of our behavior as we strive to change the world outside of us to match our internal pictures of what we want. Our behaviors come from the inside, and thus we are choosing our destiny.

Glasser says that to speak of being depressed, having a headache, being angry, or being anxious implies passivity and lack of personal responsibility, and it is inaccurate. It is more accurate to think of these as parts of total behaviors and to use the verb forms *depressing, headaching, angering,* and *anxietying* to describe them. He speaks of people depressing or angering themselves, rather than being depressed or being angry. When people choose misery by developing a range of "paining" behaviors, it is because these are the best behaviors that they are able to devise at the time, and these behaviors often get them what they want. But why does it make sense to choose misery? Glasser (1985) gives three reasons: (1) to keep anger under control, (2) to control ourselves or others, (3) to indirectly ask others to help us, and (4) to excuse our unwillingness to do something more effective. From this perspective, depression can be explained as an active choice that we make to attain one or more of these four things. This process of "depressing" keeps anger in check, and it also allows us to ask for help. Glasser contends that as long as we cling to the notion that we are victims of depression and that misery is something that happens to us, we will not change for the better. When people begin to say, "I am choosing to depress," fewer people will make this choice.

## CHARACTERISTICS OF REALITY THERAPY

Control theory provides the conceptual framework for reality therapy. This theory underlies the principles and practices that a counselor applies to helping people change. A few of the distinguishing characteristics of reality therapy are described below.

REJECTION OF THE MEDICAL MODEL.    Discarding the orthodox concept of mental illness, including neurotic and psychotic disorders, has been a driving force of reality therapy since its origin. Formulations such as "schizophrenic" and "depressive psychosis" are based on the notion that these illnesses are reactions to external events. Reality therapists contend that "neurotic" or "psychotic" behavior is not something that merely happens to us; rather, it is behavior that we choose as a way of attempting to control our world. Even though certain behaviors (such as psychosomatic disorders and addictions to drugs and alcohol) may be both painful and ineffective, they work for us to some extent, or we would not use them. It is Glasser's contention (1984a, 1985) that we choose most of these unsatisfactory behaviors as a way of closing the gap between what we want and what we have. Thus, external factors that we call "stressful" are identified as such because we are not able to control them satisfactorily with the behaviors we choose. Glasser maintains that stress is a subjective phenomenon. What is stressful to some is joyful to others—for example, parachute jumping. Our reactions to the environment are unique, and we can control almost all stressful situations.

SUCCESS IDENTITY AND POSITIVE ADDICTION. The concept of *success identity* is helpful in understanding reality therapy. People who possess a success identity see themselves as being able to give and receive love, feel that they are significant to others, feel powerful, possess a sense of self-worth, and meet their needs in ways that are not at the expense of others. Those people with a success identity possess *strength,* which helps them create a satisfying life. Glasser (1976a) also develops the idea of *positive addiction* as a major source of psychological strength in our life. Two ways of developing positive addiction are running and meditation.

EMPHASIS ON RESPONSIBILITY. Reality therapy has consistently emphasized responsibility, which Glasser (1984a, 1984b, 1985, 1992) defines as behavior that satisfies one's needs in ways that do not interfere with others' fulfilling their needs. Responsible people are autonomous in the sense that they know what they want from life and make plans for meeting their needs and goals. In short, responsibility means that people have learned to take effective control of their lives. Glasser emphasizes avoiding criticism, either from the therapist or from ourselves. We can learn to live and behave responsibly without becoming harshly self-critical. Searching for our faults and criticizing ourselves certainly does not help us.

DEEMPHASIS ON TRANSFERENCE. Rejecting the idea of transference as a misleading concept, Glasser (1984a) contends that conventional therapists are putting ideas into the client's head by imposing that notion. Reality therapy sees transference as a way for the therapist to remain hidden as a person. Glasser calls for therapists to be themselves and not to think or teach that they are playing the role of the client's mother or father. The reality therapist deals with whatever perceptions clients have, and there is no attempt to teach clients that their reactions and views are other than what they state. Since the inception of reality therapy, Glasser has taught that clients do not look to repeat unsuccessful involvements in their past but, rather, seek a satisfying human involvement with a person in their present existence. Instead of dwelling on a client's past failures, reality therapists look to the past for evidences of the client's ability to successfully control the world, and they help clients deal with situations that are directly related to their present lives.

# The Therapeutic Process

## THERAPEUTIC GOALS

The overall goal of reality therapy is to help individuals find more effective ways of meeting their needs for belonging, power, freedom, and fun. At his workshops, Glasser stresses that counseling consists of assisting clients in learning ways to regain control of their lives and to live more effectively. This includes encouraging them to examine what they are doing, thinking, and feeling to find out whether there is a better way for them to function.

Reality therapy focuses on what clients are conscious of and then helps them increase their level of awareness. As clients become aware of the ineffective behaviors they are using to control the world, they are more open to learning alternative ways of behaving. Unlike many other approaches, reality therapy is concerned with teaching people these more effective ways to deal with the world. The core of reality therapy is to help clients evaluate whether their wants are realistic and whether their behavior is helping them. It is clients who decide if what they are doing is ineffective in getting what they want; they determine what changes in behavior, if any, they are willing to make. After they make this assessment, they are assisted by the counselor in designing a plan for change as a way of translating talk into action. Glasser (1989, 1992) emphasizes that we can control only our own behavior. Since we cannot control anyone else's behavior, the best way to control events around us is through what *we* do.

## THERAPIST'S FUNCTION AND ROLE

The reality therapist's job is to get involved with clients and to develop a relationship with them that will lay the groundwork for the rest of the counseling process. The counselor functions as an instructor by teaching them control theory, offering them behavioral choices, and being active in the sessions (see N. Glasser, 1989).

Therapists challenge clients with the basic question of reality therapy: "Is what you are choosing to do getting you what you want?" If clients make the judgment that what they are doing is not working, therapists may suggest an alternative course of action (W. Glasser, 1989). The counselor also teaches clients how they can create a success identity by accepting accountability for their own chosen behaviors (Glasser, 1986c). This role requires counselors to perform several functions:

- establishing a structure and limits for the sessions
- establishing rapport based on care and respect
- focusing on the individual's strengths and potentials that can lead to success
- actively promoting discussion of the client's current behavior and actively discouraging excuses for irresponsible or ineffective behavior
- introducing and fostering the process of evaluating realistically attainable wants
- teaching clients to formulate and carry out plans to change their behaviors
- helping clients find ways to meet their needs and encouraging them not to give up easily, even if they become discouraged

## CLIENT'S EXPERIENCE IN THERAPY

People who come for counseling are typically behaving in ineffective ways. Their behavior is an attempt to meet their needs, yet what they are doing is not working well. Therefore, clients who initiate counseling with the presenting complaint of depression are doing what they can to close the gap between what they want and what they have.

In his workshops, Glasser often relates the case of a man (Melvyn) who is depressing after his wife has left him. Melvyn wants his wife back, and he wants to feel loved and accepted. He complains that he is depressed, that he is not going to work, that he is unable to sleep, and that he wants to know how to get his wife to return. He is focused on her, and he sees few options for changing his misery. The balance has been tipped, and he is striving to regain control of his life.

From a reality-therapy perspective, Melvyn is *choosing* to depress. By making this choice, he is attempting to control both his wife and himself. In his case, the therapist will focus on helping him choose more effective ways to act and think because he has much more control over these components (the front wheels) of his total behavior than he has over his feelings and physiology (the rear wheels). If he learns to steer the front wheels in a more responsible direction, his emotional upsets and physical symptoms will decrease.

## RELATIONSHIP BETWEEN THERAPIST AND CLIENT

Before effective therapy can occur, an involvement between the client and the counselor must be established. Clients need to know that the helping person cares enough about them to accept them and to help them fulfill their needs in the real world. Reality therapy emphasizes an understanding and supportive relationship. An important factor is the willingness of counselors to develop their own individual therapeutic style. Sincerity and being comfortable with one's style are crucial traits in being able to carry out therapeutic functions.

For this involvement between the therapist and the client to occur, the counselor must have certain personal qualities, including warmth, understanding, acceptance, concern, respect for the client, openness, and the willingness to be challenged by others. One of the best ways to develop this goodwill and therapeutic friendship is simply by listening to clients. Involvement is also promoted by talking about a wide range of topics that have relevance for the client. Once involvement has been established, the counselor confronts clients with the reality and consequences of their current behavior.

# Application: Therapeutic Techniques and Procedures

## THE PRACTICE OF REALITY THERAPY

The practice of reality therapy can best be conceptualized as the *cycle of counseling,* which consists of two major components: (1) the counseling environment and (2) specific procedures that lead to changes in behavior. The art of counseling is to weave these components together in ways that lead clients to evaluate their lives and decide to move in more effective directions.

How do these components blend in the counseling process? The cycle of counseling begins, as we have seen, with establishing a working relationship with clients. The process proceeds through an exploration of their wants, needs, and perceptions. Clients then explore their total behavior and make their own evaluation of how effective they are in getting what they want. If clients decide to try new behavior, they make plans that will lead to change, and they commit themselves to their plan. During this process counselors do not accept excuses for failing to follow through with plans, do not criticize clients, and do not easily give up on them. The cycle of counseling includes following up on how well clients are doing and offering further consultation as needed.

It is important to keep in mind that although the concepts discussed below may seem simple as they are presented, being able to translate them into actual therapeutic practice takes considerable skill and creativity. Although the principles will be the same when used by any counselor who is certified in reality therapy, the manner in which they are applied does vary depending on the counselor's style and personal characteristics. Just because the principles are applied in a progressive manner, they should not be thought of as discrete and rigid categories. Glasser (1986c) stresses that the art of practicing reality therapy involves far more than following procedures in a step-by-step, or "cookbook," fashion.

The discussion that follows is best considered as an aid for teaching reality therapy, but it should not be thought of as a replacement for the extensive training that is needed to counsel effectively. It is an integrated summary and adaptation of material from various sources (Glasser, 1965, 1969, 1976b, 1980, 1981, 1984a, 1984b, 1985, 1986a, 1986b, 1986c, 1992; Glasser & Wubbolding, 1995; Wubbolding, 1988b, 1991).

## THE COUNSELING ENVIRONMENT

PERSONAL INVOLVEMENT WITH THE CLIENT. The practice of reality therapy begins with the counselor's efforts to create a supportive environment within which clients can begin to make changes in their lives. To create this therapeutic climate, counselors must become involved in their clients' lives and establish rapport. This involvement occurs through a combined process of listening to the client's story and skillfully questioning. One of the most effective ways of building this relationship is for the counselor to explore the pictures in the client's mind as well as his or her wants, needs, and perceptions.

COUNSELOR ATTITUDES AND BEHAVIORS THAT PROMOTE CHANGE. Counselors consistently attempt to focus clients on what they are *doing now.* They also avoid discussing clients' feelings or physiology as though these were separate from their total behavior. Counselors help their clients see connections between what they are feeling and their concurrent actions and thoughts. Although reality therapists focus on the actions and thoughts of clients (the front wheels that drive the car), they consider it quite legitimate to talk about feelings and physiology. When people begin to act differently, they will also begin to feel differently.

Counselors hope to teach their clients to value the attitude of accepting responsibility for their total behavior. Thus, they accept no excuses for irresponsible behavior, even though they recognize that ineffective behavior is still the clients' best attempt to get what they want. If clients do not follow through with their agreed-on plans for change, counselors are likely to help them reassess the situation, yet they are firm in their refusal to accept excuses. Reality therapists show clients that excuses are a form of self-deception that may offer temporary relief but ultimately leads to failure and to the cementing of a failure identity. By refusing to accept excuses, counselors convey their belief in the client's ability to regain control.

Reality therapy holds that punishment is not a useful means of changing behavior. This principle is especially useful in applying reality therapy to parenting or management. Specific punishments that are avoided include chastising individuals for what they have failed to do and making deprecating remarks to them. Instead of being punished, individuals can learn to accept the *reasonable consequences* that flow from their actions. By not making critical comments, by refusing to accept excuses, and by remaining nonjudgmental, counselors are in a position to ask clients if they are really interested in changing.

It is important that counselors not easily give up their belief in the client's ability to find a more responsible life, even if the client makes little effort to follow through. If the counselor gives up, it tends to confirm the client's belief that no one cares enough to help (Glasser, 1986a, 1986c). Those with a failure identity *expect* others to give up on them. Such people are rarely helped if the counselor acts on the assumption that they will never change or that they are hopeless.

In addition to the counselor's attitudes mentioned above that create an environment conducive to client change, Wubbolding (1988b) emphasizes the importance of practitioners' being willing to seek consultation with someone else who is trained in reality therapy. Regardless of how well a person practices reality therapy, Wubbolding contends, there is room for improvement. It can be achieved both by consultation and by developing an ongoing plan for professional development.

## PROCEDURES THAT LEAD TO CHANGE: THE "WDEP" SYSTEM

According to Glasser (1992), the procedures that lead to change are based on the assumption that human beings are motivated to change when (1) they are convinced that their present behavior is not getting them what they want, and (2) they believe that they can choose other behaviors that will get them closer to what they want.

Glasser and Wubbolding (1995) and Wubbolding (1991, 1994) use an acronym, WDEP, to describe key procedures that can be used in the practice of reality therapy. Each of the letters refers to a cluster of strategies, as follows: W = wants; D = direction and doing; E = evaluation; and P = planning. These strategies, designed to promote change, are discussed in the sections below.

WANTS (EXPLORING WANTS, NEEDS, AND PERCEPTIONS). Reality therapists ask, "What do you want?" Through the therapist's skillful questioning, clients are encouraged to recognize, define, and refine how they wish to meet their needs. Part of counseling consists of exploring their "picture album" and the ways in which their behavior is aimed at moving their perception of the external world closer to their inner world of wants.

The skill of reality therapy involves counseling in a noncritical and accepting way, so that clients will reveal what is in their special world. Clients are given the opportunity to explore every facet of their lives, including what they want from their family, friends, and work. Furthermore, it is useful for them to define what they expect and want from the counselor and from themselves (Wubbolding, 1988b, 1991, 1994). This exploration of wants, needs, and perceptions should continue throughout the counseling process, because the client's pictures change.

Some useful questions to help clients pinpoint what they want include: "If you were the person that you wish you were, what kind of person would you be?" "What would your family be like if your wants and their wants matched?" "What would you be doing if you were living as you want to?" "Do you really want to change your life?" "What is it you want that you don't seem to be getting from life?" "What do you think stops you from making the changes you would like?" This line of questioning sets the stage for applying other procedures in reality therapy.

DIRECTION AND DOING.    Reality therapy stresses current behavior and is concerned with past events only insofar as they influence how the client is behaving now. The focus on the present is characterized by the question so often asked by the reality therapist: "What are you doing?" Even though problems may be rooted in the past, clients need to learn how to deal with them in the present by learning better ways of getting what they want. Glasser (1989, 1992) contends that no matter how frustrating the past was, there is no way that either the client or the therapist can undo these frustrations. What can be done now is to help clients make more need-satisfying choices.

The past may be discussed if doing so will help clients plan for a better tomorrow. If an adult client was sexually abused as a child, for example, Glasser stresses the value of working on the problem that this client has now. If it becomes necessary to working through her present problems, she can explore her childhood abuse. Glasser is distrustful of going back too far in childhood. For him the task of the counselor consists of steering this client into dealing with her present situation. She needs to learn how to live her life despite what happened to her earlier.

Early in counseling it is essential to discuss with clients the overall direction of their lives, including where they are going and where their behavior is taking them. This exploration is preliminary to the subsequent evaluation of whether it is a desirable direction. The therapist functions by holding a mirror before the client and asking "What do you see for yourself now and in the future?" For this reflection to become clear to clients, some time is necessary for them to be able to verbally express their perceptions (Wubbolding, 1988b).

Reality therapy concentrates on changing current total behavior, not merely attitudes and feelings. Questions such as the following are likely to be asked: "What are you doing now?" "What did you actually do this past week?" "What did you want to do differently this past week?" "What stopped you from doing what you say you want to do?" "What will you do tomorrow?"

Listening to clients talk about feelings can be productive, but only if it is linked to what they are doing. When an emergency light on the car dashboard lights up, the driver is alerted that something is wrong and that immediate action is necessary to remedy a problem. In a similar way, when clients talk about problematic feelings, the counselor, rather than focusing on these feelings, needs to encourage them to take action by changing what they are doing and thinking. According to Glasser (1980, 1981, 1985, 1989, 1992), what we are doing is easy to see and impossible to deny, and thus it serves as the proper focus in therapy. Discussions centering on feelings, without strongly relating them to what people are doing, are counterproductive (Glasser, 1980). Briefly, then, the focus of reality therapy is on gaining awareness of current total behavior, because this process contributes to helping a person get what he or she wants and to developing a positive self-image.

EVALUATION.　The core of reality therapy, as we have seen, is to ask clients to make the following evaluation: "Does your present behavior have a reasonable chance of getting you what you want now, and will it take you in the direction you want to go?" (Glasser, 1986a, 1986c). Through skillful questioning the counselor helps clients evaluate their behavior. These questions include "Is what you are doing helping or hurting you?" "Is what you are doing now what you want to be doing?" "Is your behavior working for you?" "Is what you are doing against the rules?" "Is what you want realistic or attainable?" "Does it help you to look at it that way?" "How committed are you to the therapeutic process and to changing your life?" (Wubbolding, 1988b). It is the counselor's task to confront clients with the consequences of their behavior and to get *them* to judge the quality of their actions. Without this self-assessment clients will not change.

Asking clients to evaluate each component of their total behavior is a major task in reality therapy. When therapists ask a depressing client if this behavior is helping in the long run, they introduce the idea of choice to the client. The process of evaluation of the doing, thinking, feeling, and physiological components of total behavior is within the scope of the client's responsibility.

From the reality therapist's perspective it is acceptable to be directive with certain clients at the beginning of treatment. This is done to help them recognize that some behaviors are not effective. In working with clients who are in crisis, for example, it is sometimes necessary to suggest straightforwardly what will work and what will not. Other clients, such as alcoholics and children of alcoholics, need direction early in the course of treatment, for they often do not have the thinking behaviors in their control system to be able to make consistent evaluations of when their lives are seriously out of effective control. These clients are likely to have blurred pictures and, at times, to be unaware of what they want or whether their wants are realistic. As they grow and continually interact with the counselor, they learn to make the evaluations with less help from the counselor (Wubbolding, 1988b).

PLANNING AND COMMITMENT.　Once clients determine what they want to change, they are generally ready to explore other possible behaviors and formulate an action plan. When plans have been formulated by a joint effort between the counselor and the client, a commitment must be made to carry them out.

Much of the significant work of the counseling process involves helping clients identify specific ways to fulfill their wants and needs. The process of creating and carrying out plans enables people to gain effective control over their lives. Glasser (1992) says that once clients commit to solving their problems, they need to make a plan. If the plan does not work, for whatever reason, the counselor and client work together to devise a different one. Throughout this planning phase the counselor continually urges clients to assume responsibility for their own choices and actions. This is done by reminding them that no one in the world will do things for them or live their life for them.

Wubbolding (1988b, 1991) discusses the central role of planning and commitment. The culmination of the cycle of counseling rests with a plan of action. He uses the acronym SAMIC³ to capture the essence of a good plan, which is simple, attainable, measurable, immediate, involved, controlled by the planner, committed to, and continuously done. He writes that clients gain more effective control over their lives with plans that have the following characteristics:

- The plan should be within the limits of the motivation and capacities of each client. Skillful counselors help members identify plans that involve greater need-fulfilling payoffs. A client may be asked, "What plans could you make now that would result in a more satisfying life?"
- Good plans are simple and easy to understand. Although they need to be specific, concrete, and measurable, they should be flexible and open to modification as clients gain a deeper understanding of the specific behaviors that they want to change. It is important to realize that there is no perfect plan, which means that plans are subject to revision.
- The plan should involve a positive course of action, and it should be stated in terms of what the client is willing to do. Counselors can help clients recognize that even small plans can help them take significant steps toward their desired changes.
- Counselors should encourage clients to develop plans that they can carry out independently of what others do. Plans that are contingent on others lead clients to sense that they are not steering their own ship but are at the mercy of the ocean.
- Effective plans are repetitive and, ideally, are performed daily.
- Plans should be carried out as soon as possible. Counselors can ask questions such as "What are you willing to do today to begin to change your life?" "You say you would like to stop depressing. What are you going to do now to attain this goal?"
- Effective planning involves process-centered activities. For example, clients may plan to do any of the following: apply for a job, write a letter to a friend, take a yoga class, substitute nutritious food for junk food, devote two hours a week to volunteer work, and take a vacation that they have been wanting.
- Before clients carry out their plan, it is a good idea for them to evaluate it with their therapist to determine if it is realistic and attainable and if

it relates to what they need and want. After the plan has been carried out in real life, it is useful to evaluate it again. The counselor needs to ask "Is your plan helpful?" If a plan does not work, it can reevaluated, and alternatives can be considered.

• In order for clients to commit themselves to their plan, it is useful for them to firm it up in writing.

Resolutions and plans are empty unless there is a commitment to carry them out. It is up to each client to determine ways of taking these plans outside the restrictedworld of therapy and into the everyday world. Effective therapy can be the catalyst that leads to self-directed, responsible living.

## APPLICATIONS OF REALITY THERAPY

Reality therapy is applicable to counseling, social work, education, crisis intervention, corrections and rehabilitation, institutional management, and community development. It is a popular approach in schools, correctional institutions, general hospitals, state mental hospitals, halfway houses, and substance-abuse centers. Most of the military clinics that treat drug and alcohol abusers use reality therapy as their preferred therapeutic approach.

Glasser (1984a) maintains that reality therapy is applicable to people "with any sort of psychological problem, from mild emotional upset to complete psychotic withdrawal." It is used with children, adolescents, adults, and the aged. According to Glasser, the only factor limiting its applicability is the technical skill of the therapist.

*What Are You Doing?* (N. Glasser, 1980) demonstrates how more than two dozen reality therapists worked with a variety of clients. Examples of cases include dealing with the problems of a divorced parent, therapy with depressed clients, helping an alcoholic find a new life, helping suicidal adolescents develop a sense of purpose, working with people with severe handicaps, and providing teachers and school counselors with ways of helping children. The therapists who worked with these cases took the basic tools provided in reality therapy and found an individualistic way of using them effectively to help the clients look at their life and design constructive behavioral alternatives.

In her more recent book, *Control Theory in the Practice of Reality Therapy: Case Studies,* the late Naomi Glasser (1989), who was Glasser's wife and colleague, provides illustrations of how reality therapy can be applied to diverse populations, including children and adolescents, survivors of incest, abused children, prisoners, and people with eating disorders.

## REALITY THERAPY APPLIED TO THE CASE OF STAN

The reality therapist is guided by the key concepts of control theory to identify Stan's behavioral dynamics, to provide a direction for him to work toward, and to teach him about better alternatives for getting what he wants. Although he is aware that he is suffering when he initially comes to therapy, he is convinced that he is the victim of past events over which he has no control. The reality therapist shows him that he does not have to be a victim of his past unless he chooses to be. Although she has compassion for his suffering and the difficulties he continues to face, she wants him to realize that if he decides to change, he has many options. She has a hunch that he wants to focus on talking about his past because that is easier than facing the present, which will involve considerable work. She grants that all of his behavior is his best attempt to get what he wants, yet she also helps him see that what he is doing is not working very well. As counseling progresses, he learns that even though most of his problems did indeed begin in childhood, there is little he can now do to undo what happened. He eventually realizes that he has little control over changing others but has a great deal of control over what he can do now.

Initially, Stan wants to tell his counselor how miserable he feels. He does this by attempting to focus on his major symptoms: depression, anxiety, inability to sleep, and other psychosomatic symptoms, He very much needs someone who is willing to listen to him and not criticize him for what he says. Most of his life he has had people criticize him, so now as he presents his story, he expects criticism and invites it from his counselor. During the early phase of counseling, the therapist listens to him and continues to reinforce the idea that she will not criticize him. She works at establishing involvement with him to provide a good foundation on which to support future therapy. Although she listens, she also challenges him, especially as he focuses on his misery and his symptoms. She explains to him that he has an ideal picture of what he wants his life to be, yet he does not possess effective behaviors for meeting his needs. The counselor talks to him about his needs and how this type of therapy will teach him to satisfy them in effective ways. She also explains that his total behavior is made up of acting, thinking, feeling, and physiology. Even though he says he hates feeling anxious most of the time, he learns that much of what he is doing and thinking is directly leading to his unwanted feelings and physiological reactions. When he complains of feeling depressed much of the time, anxious at night, and overcome by panic attacks, she lets him know that she is more interested in what he is doing and thinking, since these components can be directly changed more easily than what he is feeling. She teaches him that instead of being depressed, he is, on some level, actually choosing to be depressed; that is, he is *depressing*.

In his therapy Stan tells his counselor about the pictures in his head, a few of which are becoming a counselor, acting confident in meeting people, thinking of himself as a worthwhile person, and enjoying life. Through therapy he makes the evaluation that much of what he is doing is not getting him closer to the pictures in his head or getting him what he wants. After he decides that he is willing to work on himself to be different, the majority of time in the sessions is devoted to making plans and discussing their implementation. Together he and the therapist focus on many steps that he can take right now to bring about the changes he would like. Instead of waiting for others to initiate contacts, he practices seeking out those people he would like to get to know better. He might get involved in volunteer work with young people at a community agency, especially since this is the kind of activity that he finds meaningful. The point is that he is encouraged to actually do more of the things he wants to do, rather than focusing on what he perceives to be his deficits. As he continues to carry out plans in the real world, he gradually begins to experience success. When he does backslide, his counselor does not put him down but helps him do better. Together they develop a new plan that they feel more confident about. She is not willing to give up on him, which is a source of real inspiration for him to keep working on himself.

FOLLOW-UP: YOU CONTINUE AS STAN'S REALITY THERAPIST.   Use these questions to help you think about how to counsel Stan:

- If Stan complains of feeling depressed most of the time and wants you to "cure" him, how might you proceed as a reality therapist?
- If Stan persists, telling you that his mood is getting the best of him and that he wants you to work with his physician in getting him on an anti-depressant drug, what might you say or do?
- What are some of Stan's basic needs that are not being met? What action plans can you think of in helping him find better ways of getting what he wants?
- In working with Stan as a reality therapist, what are some interventions that you might make to help him explore his total behavior?

# Summary and Evaluation

## SUMMARY

The reality therapist functions as a teacher and a model, confronting clients in ways that help them evaluate what they are doing and whether their behavior is fulfilling their basic needs without harming themselves or others. The heart of reality therapy is accepting personal responsibility and gaining more effective control. People take charge of their life rather than being the victims of circumstances beyond their control. Thus, practitioners of reality therapy focus on what clients are *able and willing to do* in the *present* to change their behavior.

The practice of reality therapy weaves together two components, the counseling environment and specific procedures that lead to changes in behavior. This process enables clients to move in the direction of getting what they want.

## CONTRIBUTIONS OF REALITY THERAPY

Among the advantages of reality therapy are its relatively short-term focus and the fact that it deals with conscious behavioral problems. Insight and awareness are not enough; the client's self-evaluation, a plan of action, and a commitment to following through are the core of the therapeutic process. I like the focus on strongly encouraging clients to evaluate their life situation, to decide if what they are doing is working, and to commit themselves to make changes.

Reality therapy provides a structure in which both clients and therapists can measure the degree and nature of changes. The contract approach is one such method that can lead to specificity and accountability. I like the idea of not accepting excuses for violating contracts and the avoidance of punishment and blaming that is basic to reality therapy. If clients do not carry out their plans, it is important to frankly explore with them the implications of this situation and to make a new plan.

VIEW OF PSYCHOSIS.    In contemporary reality therapy, mental health is equated with the responsible fulfilling of one's needs or drives, and mental illness is what occurs when people are unable to control the world to satisfy their needs. However, their behavior is still their best attempt to deal with reality at that particular time. On this point Glasser (1985) has written that reality therapists believe that psychosis can be directly related to unfulfilled needs. Psychotic persons may have been unable to figure out satisfying behavior and therefore have turned to living with distortions. In their perceived world they have created unrealistic (psychotic) ways of reducing the pain they experience in attempting to cope with reality.

In many respects I am in agreement with reality therapy's view of mental health and mental illness. I certainly think that we choose the way we behave to a large extent, and thus we also choose how we feel and how we think. In my view the disease concept can easily be an excuse for not accepting the consequences of our behavior. It seems almost fashionable to have a disease label attached to most forms of human misery. Although it may be easier for people to convince themselves that they are the victims of a disease (such as depression or some type of addiction), this conviction renders them passive and powerless to change their situation. By accepting their own role in creating situations, individuals empower themselves to discover more effective ways of living. The reality of psychiatric disease does exist, however, and not all mental and emotional disturbance can be reduced to a "cop-out." As therapists we need to distinguish between psychiatric disorders and irresponsible actions. Indeed, there is increasing evidence of a biological or biochemical basis for some disorders.

CONTRIBUTIONS TO MULTICULTURAL COUNSELING.    The core principles of reality therapy have much to offer in the area of multicultural counseling. In cross-cultural therapy it is essential that counselors respect the differences in worldview between themselves and their clients. Counselors demonstrate their respect for the cultural values of their clients by helping them explore how satisfying their current behavior is both to themselves and to others. Once clients make this assessment, they can formulate realistic plans that are consistent with their cultural values. It is a further sign of respect that the counselor refrains from deciding what behavior should be changed. Through skillful questioning on the counselor's part, ethnic-minority clients can be helped to determine the degree to which they have acculturated into the dominant society. It is possible for them to find a balance, retaining their ethnic identity and values while integrating some of the values and practices of the dominant group. Again, the counselor does not determine this balance for clients but challenges them to arrive at their own answer. With this focus on acting and thinking rather than on identifying and exploring feelings, many clients are less likely to display resistance to counseling.

Wubbolding (1990b) has expanded the practice of reality therapy into multicultural situations. He believes that the approach needs to be modified to fit the cultural context of people other than North Americans. Wubbolding's experience in conducting reality-therapy workshops in Japan, Taiwan, Hong Kong, Singapore, Korea, India, and countries in Europe has taught him about the difficulty in making generalizations about other cultures. Based on these multicultural experiences, he has adapted the cycle of counseling to working with Japanese clients. He points to some basic language differences between the Japanese and Western cultures. North Americans are inclined to say what they mean, to be assertive, and to be clear and direct in asking for what they want. In Japanese culture, assertive language is not appropriate between a child and a parent or between an employee and a supervisor. Ways of communicating are more indirect. Because of this style, some of the following specific adaptations are needed to make the practice of reality therapy relevant to Japanese clients:

- The reality therapist's tendency to ask direct questions may need to be softened, with questions being raised more elaborately and indirectly. Confrontation may be avoided in working with Japanese clients.
- There is no exact Japanese translation for the word *plan,* nor is there an exact word for the term *accountability,* yet both of these are key dimensions in the practice of reality therapy.
- In asking clients to make plans and commit to them, Western counselors do not settle for a response of "I'll try." Instead, they tend to push for an explicit pledge to follow through. In the Japanese culture, however, the counselor is likely to accept an "I'll try" as a firm commitment.

These are but a few illustrations of ways in which reality therapy might be adapted to non-Western clients. Although this approach assumes that all people have the same basic needs (survival, belonging, power, fun, and freedom), the way these needs are expressed depends largely on the cultural context. What is essential is that in working with culturally diverse clients, the therapist allows latitude for a wide range of acceptable behaviors to satisfy these needs. As with other theories and the techniques that flow from them, flexibility is a foremost requirement.

To its credit, this approach provides clients with tools to make the desired changes. This is especially true during the planning phase, which is so central to the process of reality therapy. The focus is on positive steps that can be taken, not on what cannot be done. Clients identify those problems that are causing them difficulty, and these problems become the targets for change. This type of specificity and the direction that is provided by an effective plan are certainly assets in working with diverse client populations.

## LIMITATIONS AND CRITICISMS OF REALITY THERAPY

In my estimation one of the main limitations of reality therapy is that it does not give adequate emphasis to the role of these aspects of the counseling process:

the unconscious, the power of the past and the effect of traumatic experiences in early childhood, the therapeutic value of dreams, and the place of transference. It seems to me that reality therapy focuses almost exclusively on consciousness and, by doing so, does not take into account factors such as repressed conflicts and the power of the unconscious in influencing how we think, feel, behave, and choose.

From my vantage point dreams are powerful tools in helping people recognize their internal conflicts. Yet the analysis of dreams is not part of the reality therapist's repertoire. From Glasser's (1984a) standpoint there is virtually no evidence to indicate that working with dreams is of any therapeutic value, and he holds that such work can be used as a defense to avoid talking about one's behavior. My colleagues and I continue to be impressed by the richness of an individual's dream, which can be a shorthand message of his or her central struggles, hopes, and visions of the future. Asking clients to recall, report, share, and relive their dreams in the here and now of the therapeutic session has helped unblock them and has paved the way for taking a different course of action.

Similarly, I have a difficult time accepting Glasser's view of transference as a misleading concept, for I find that clients are able to learn that significant people in their life have a present influence on how they perceive and react to others. True, a focus on transference can be an avoidance on both the therapist's and the client's part, yet to rule out an exploration of this special type of projection that distorts accurate perception of others seems narrow.

Reality therapy is vulnerable to the practitioner who assumes the role of an expert in deciding for others such questions as how life should be lived, what is realistic or unrealistic, what is right or wrong behavior, and what constitutes responsible behavior. Thus, counselors who are unaware of their own needs to "straighten people out" can stunt a client's growth and autonomy by becoming overly moralistic and by strongly influencing the client to accept their view of reality. If counselors do this, however, they are perverting the basic concepts inherent in reality therapy, for the approach calls on clients to make their own evaluation of their behavior.

LIMITATIONS FOR MULTICULTURAL COUNSELING.   One of the shortcomings in working with ethnic-minority clients is that they may not feel that this approach takes into account some very real environmental forces that operate against them in their everyday lives. Discrimination and racism are unfortunate realities, and these forces do limit many minority clients in getting what they want from life. If counselors do not accept these environmental restrictions, such clients are likely to feel misunderstood. There is a danger that some reality therapists will too quickly or too forcefully stress the ability of these clients to take charge of their lives.

Another problem that needs to be taken into account is that some clients are very reluctant to say what they need. Their culture has not reinforced them in assertively asking for what they want, and in fact, they may be socialized to think more of what is good for the social group than of their individual wants. In working with people with these values, counselors must "soften" reality therapy somewhat. Such clients should not be pushed to assertively declare their wants. If this method is not applied sensitively, these clients are likely to leave therapy, because they will perceive what is being asked of them as foreign to them. Reality therapy needs to be used artfully and not blindly. Many of its principles and concepts can be incorporated in a dynamic and personal way into the style of counselors, and there is a basis for integrating them with most of the other therapeutic approaches covered in this book.

If reality therapy is to be effectively used with clients from cultures other than North American, the procedures need to be adapted to the life experiences and values of members from various cultures (Glasser & Wubbolding, 1995).

# Where to Go from Here

The programs offered by the Institute for Control Theory, Reality Therapy, and Quality Management are designed to teach the concepts of control theory and the practice of reality therapy. The institute offers a certification process involving a one-week intensive basic seminar, in which participants take part in discussions, demonstrations, and role playing, followed by a supervised practicum designed specifically to best meet the needs of each individual trainee. A second intensive week and a second practicum follow. The basic and advanced practicums each entail a minimum of 30 hours over at least a six-month period. For further information about these training programs contact either of these two organizations:

> Institute for Control Theory, Reality Therapy, and Quality
>    Management
> 7301 Medical Center Drive, Suite 104
> Canoga Park, CA 91307
> Telephone: (818) 888-0688

> Center for Reality Therapy
> 7777 Montgomery Road
> Cincinnati, OH 45236
> Telephone: (513) 561-1911

The *Journal of Reality Therapy* publishes manuscripts concerning research, theory development, and specific descriptions of the successful application of reality therapy in field settings. If you are interested in subscribing, contact:

> Dr. Lawrence Litwack, Editor
> *Journal of Reality Therapy*
> 203 Lake Hall, Boston-Bouve College
> Northeastern University
> 360 Huntington Avenue
> Boston, MA 02115

## *Recommended Supplementary Readings*

*Control Theory: A New Explanation of How We Control Our Lives* (Glasser, 1985) gets my top recommendation. In this popular and easy-to-read book, Glasser discusses how we can choose to change our actions and thus gain better control of our thoughts and feelings and live healthier and more productive lives. He shows how our behavior makes sense in light of our attempt to meet our basic needs, which are the powerful forces that drive us. Other interesting topics that are explored include choosing misery, craziness and responsibility, psychosomatic illness as a creative process, addictive drugs, taking control of our health, and how to start using control theory.

*Control Theory in the Practice of Reality Therapy: Case Studies* (N. Glasser, 1989) shows how control theory is applied to the practice of reality therapy with a diverse range of clients. It brings the concepts of the approach up to date by illustrating how therapists integrate the concepts of control theory into their practice. These cases demonstrate how the key ideas of control theory actually work in helping clients to ask themselves the question "Is what I am choosing to do now getting me what I want?"

*Using Reality Therapy* (Wubbolding, 1988b) extends the principles of reality therapy by presenting case studies that can be applied to marital and family counseling as well as individual counseling. This book is clearly written, with practical guidelines. There are excellent questions and brief examples that clarify ways of using reality-therapy concepts. The author has extended the scope of practicing reality therapy by describing other procedures such as paradoxical techniques, humor, skillful questioning, supervision, and self-help. He presents reality therapy as a philosophy of life rather than a doctrinaire theory or set of prescriptions.

## References and Suggested Readings*

COREY, G. (1995). *Theory and practice of group counseling* (4th ed.). Pacific Grove, CA: Brooks/Cole.

*COREY, G. (1996). *Case approach to counseling and psychotherapy* (4th ed.). Pacific Grove, CA: Brooks/Cole.

GLASSER, N. (Ed.). (1980). *What are you doing? How people are helped through reality therapy.* New York: Harper & Row.

*GLASSER, N. (Ed.). (1989). *Control theory in the practice of reality therapy: Case studies.* New York: Harper & Row.

GLASSER, W. (1961). *Mental health or mental illness?* New York: Harper & Row.

GLASSER, W. (1965). *Reality therapy: A new approach to psychiatry.* New York: Harper & Row.

GLASSER, W. (1969). *Schools without failure.* New York: Harper & Row.

GLASSER, W. (1972). *The identity society.* New York: Harper & Row.

GLASSER, W. (1976a). *Positive addiction.* New York: Harper & Row.

GLASSER, W. (1976b). Reality therapy. In V. Binder & B. Rimland (Eds.), *Modern therapies.* Englewood Cliffs, NJ: Prentice-Hall.

GLASSER, W. (1980). Reality therapy. An explanation of the steps of reality therapy. In N. Glasser (Ed.), *What are you doing? How people are helped through reality therapy.* New York: Harper & Row.

GLASSER, W. (1981). *Stations of the mind.* New York: Harper & Row.

GLASSER, W. (1984a). Reality therapy. In R. Corsini (Ed.), *Current psychotherapies* (3rd ed.) (pp. 320–353). Itasca, IL: F. E. Peacock.

GLASSER, W. (1984b). *Take effective control of your life.* New York: Harper & Row.

*GLASSER, W. (1985). *Control theory: A new explanation of how we control our lives.* New York: Harper & Row (Perennial Paperback).

*GLASSER, W. (1986a). *The basic concepts of reality therapy* (chart). Canoga Park, CA: Institute for Control Theory, Reality Therapy, and Quality Management.

*Books and articles marked with an asterisk are suggested for further study.

GLASSER, W. (1986b). *Control theory in the classroom.* New York: Harper & Row (Perennial Paperback).

*GLASSER, W. (1986c). *The control theory–reality therapy workbook.* Canoga Park, CA: Institute for Control Theory, Reality Therapy, and Quality Management.

*GLASSER, W. (1989). Control theory in the practice of reality therapy. In N. Glasser (Ed.), *Control theory in the practice of reality therapy: Case studies* (pp. 1–15). New York: Harper & Row.

GLASSER, W. (1990). *The quality school.* New York: Harper & Row.

*GLASSER, W. (1992). Reality therapy. *New York State Journal for Counseling and Development,* 7(1), 5–13.

GLASSER, W. (1994). *The control theory manager.* New York: Harper & Row.

GLASSER, W., & WUBBOLDING, R. (1995). Reality therapy. In R. Corsini & D. Wedding (Eds.), *Current psychotherapies* (5th ed.) (pp. 293–321). Itasca, IL: F. E. Peacock.

WUBBOLDING, R. E. (1988a). Professional ethics: Intervention in suiciding behaviors. *Journal of Reality Therapy,* 7(2), 13–17.

*WUBBOLDING, R. E. (1988b). *Using reality therapy.* New York: Harper & Row (Perennial Library).

WUBBOLDING, R. E. (1990a). *Evaluation: The cornerstone in the practice of reality therapy.* Alexandria, Egypt: Omar Center for Psychological and Academic Consultations, Studies, and Services.

WUBBOLDING, R. E. (1990b). *Expanding reality therapy: Group counseling and multicultural dimensions.* Cincinnati, OH: Real World Publications.

*WUBBOLDING, R. E. (1991). *Understanding reality therapy.* New York: Harper & Row (Perennial Library).

*WUBBOLDING, R. E. (1994). *Cycle of managing, supervising, counseling and coaching using reality therapy (chart)* (8th revision). Cincinnati, OH: Center for Reality Therapy.

CHAPTER TEN

# Behavior Therapy

# ARNOLD LAZARUS

ARNOLD A. LAZARUS (b. 1932) was born and educated in Johannesburg, South Africa. The youngest of four children (his sisters were 17 and 14 when he was born, and his brother was 9), he grew up in a neighborhood where there were very few children, and he remembers being lonely and frightened. He learned to play the piano at an early age and performed on Saturday mornings at a movie theater during intermission, for which he received the equivalent of $1 ("a small fortune for a 7-year-old when 8 cents got you into a movie, and an ice cream cone cost 1 cent"). "When I was 7," he says, "I used to play like a talented 12-year-old, but when I turned 14 and still played like a 12-year-old, I decided to quit!" At that time his interests changed to body-building, weight lifting, boxing, and wrestling. "I was a pathetically skinny kid, often beaten up and bullied, so I started training rather frantically." Through sheer determination he ended up winning boxing and weight-lifting competitions and planned to own and operate a gym or health center.

Although Lazarus grew up in South Africa, he strongly identified with the United States. "I loved to read Superman and Batman Comics, and these heroes espoused liberty, justice, and the American (not South African) way." At an early age he felt that racism and discrimination were totally unacceptable. These views got him into lots of fights, which was another reason he took up boxing and weight lifting.

He entered college intending to major in English with a view to journalism as a career, "but the English professors were stodgy and boring, so I switched my majors to psychology and sociology, where the subject matter soon intrigued me and where there were three or four inspiring teachers." He obtained a master's degree in experimental psychology in 1957 and a Ph.D. in clinical psychology in 1960, and then he went into full-time private practice in Johannesburg. In 1963 he was invited by Albert Bandura to teach at Stanford University. "So my wife, Daphne, my 4-year-old daughter, Linda, my 2-year-old son, Cliff, and I set out for California." Although Lazarus found his year at Stanford "amazingly stimulating," he was extremely homesick, so he returned to Johannesburg and went back into full-time private practice. But he had tasted America and Academia and found life in South Africa "politically untenable," so in 1966 he returned to California with his wife and children to head the Behavior Therapy Institute.

In 1967 he was appointed a full professor at Temple University Medical School in Philadelphia, where he worked with Dr. Joseph Wolpe, who had been his mentor. When Lazarus criticized Wolpe for being too rigid and narrow in his outlook, they parted company. In 1970 Lazarus went to Yale University as Director of Clinical Training, and in 1972 he received the rank of Distinguished Professor at Rutgers University, where he teaches in the Graduate School of Applied and Professional Psychology. He has a private practice in Princeton, New Jersey.

"What sets me apart from most of my colleagues," Lazarus says, "is that they seem to live for their work, whereas I work in order to live. My wife and kids have always come first, followed by the cultivation of really meaningful friendships, and the pursuit of fun."

# Introduction

Behavior therapy offers various action-oriented methods to help people change what they are doing and thinking. Many techniques, particularly those developed within the last two decades, emphasize cognitive processes. Writers in the field often make the case that because this orientation is so diverse, it is difficult to clearly agree upon a definition of behavior therapy. Recent definitions focus on the application of principles broadly derived from psychological research, the rejection of a traditional intrapsychic or medical model of behavior, and the empirical evaluation of treatment effectiveness (Glass & Arnkoff, 1992).

## HISTORICAL BACKGROUND

The behavioral approach had its origin in the 1950s and early 1960s as a radical departure from the dominant psychoanalytic perspective. At this time the behavior-therapy movement differed from other therapeutic approaches in its application of principles of classical and operant conditioning (which will be explained shortly) to the treatment of a variety of problem behaviors. Today, behavior therapy can no longer be defined so simply. The summary of key developments below is based on Spiegler and Guevremont's (1993) description of the approach's historical roots.

Contemporary behavior therapy arose simultaneously in the United States, South Africa, and Great Britain in the 1950s. In spite of harsh criticism and resistance from traditional psychotherapists, the approach was able to survive. Its focus was on demonstrating that behavioral conditioning techniques were effective and were a viable alternative to traditional psychotherapy.

In the 1960s Albert Bandura developed social-learning theory, which combined classical and operant conditioning with observational learning. He made cognition, which had been ruled out by B. F. Skinner's radical behaviorism, a legitimate focus for behavior therapy. During the 1960s a number of cognitive-behavioral approaches sprang up, and they still have a significant impact on therapeutic practice. Albert Ellis created rational-emotive therapy, Aaron Beck developed cognitive therapy, and Donald Meichenbaum devised treatments such as stress inoculation and self-instructional training. The cognitive-behavioral approaches—which are covered in the next chapter—focus on changing clients' cognitions that maintain psychological disorders.

It was during the 1970s that behavior therapy emerged as a major force in psychology and made a significant impact on education, psychotherapy, psychiatry, and social work. Behavioral techniques were developed and expanded, and they were also applied to fields such as business, industry, and child rearing. This approach was now viewed as the treatment of choice for certain psychological problems.

The 1980s were characterized by a search for new horizons in concepts and methods that went beyond traditional learning theory. Behavior therapists continued to subject their methods to empirical scrutiny and to consider the impact of the practice of therapy on both their clients and the larger society.

Increased attention was given to the role of affect in therapeutic change, as well as to the role of biological factors in psychological disorders. Two of the most significant developments in the field were (1) the continued emergence of cognitive-behavior therapy as a major force and (2) the application of behavioral techniques to the prevention and treatment of medical disorders.

By the 1990s the Association for Advancement of Behavior Therapy was claiming a membership of about 4000. More than 20 major journals were now devoted to the theory and practice of this approach. Behavior therapy today is marked by a diversity of views and procedures. The central characteristics that unite this heterogeneous movement are an orientation toward treatment, a focus on behavior, an emphasis on learning, and rigorous assessment and evaluation (Kazdin, 1994). Lazarus is considered one of the pioneers of clinical behavior therapy, for he has contributed to broadening its conceptual bases and introducing innovative clinical techniques (Wilson, 1995, p. 244).

## THREE AREAS OF DEVELOPMENT

Contemporary behavior therapy can be understood by considering three major areas of development: classical conditioning, operant conditioning, and cognitive therapy. First is the approach of *classical conditioning,* in which certain respondent behaviors, such as knee jerks and salivation, are elicited from a passive organism. In the 1950s Wolpe and Lazarus of South Africa and Hans Eysenck of England began using the findings of experimental research with animals to help treat phobias in clinical settings. They based their work on Hullian learning theory and Pavlovian (or classical) conditioning. An underlying characteristic of the work of these pioneers was the focus on experimental analysis and evaluation of therapeutic procedures. Wolpe's contribution to the development of the technique of systematic desensitization, which is described later in this chapter, is based on the classical-conditioning model, and it illustrates how principles of learning derived from the experimental laboratory can be applied clinically.

Second is the approach of *operant conditioning.* Operant behavior consists of actions that operate on the environment to produce consequences. Examples of operant behaviors include reading, writing, driving a car, and eating with utensils. Such behaviors include most of the significant responses we make in everyday life. If the environmental changes brought about by the behavior are reinforcing (if they provide some reward to the organism or eliminate aversive stimuli), the chances are strengthened that the behavior will occur again. If the environmental changes produce no reinforcement, the chances are lessened that the behavior will recur.

At the same time that Wolpe, Lazarus, and Eysenck were carrying out their experiments in the 1950s, Skinner was studying the use of the principles of operant conditioning with psychotic patients in the United States. Skinner's view of controlling behavior is based on the principles of operant conditioning, which rest on the assumption that changes in behavior are brought about when that behavior is followed by a particular kind of consequence. Skinner contends that learning cannot occur in the absence of some kind of reinforcement, either positive or negative. For him actions that are reinforced tend to be repeated, and those that are discouraged tend to be extinguished. His general writings apply concepts of operant conditioning to society. His model is based on re-inforcement principles and has the goal of identifying and controlling en-vironmental factors that lead to behavioral change.

Positive reinforcement is a procedure in which a response is followed by the presentation of a stimulus. It involves the addition of something (such as praise or money) as a consequence of certain behavior. The stimulus is a positive reinforcer, which is something the organism seeks, such as food. For example, a child may whine when she wants candy. If her father gives her the candy each time she whines, to quiet her, her whining has become positively reinforced. Negative reinforcement involves the removal of unpleasant stimuli from a situation once a certain behavior has occurred. Negative reinforcers are generally unpleasant, so that the individual is motivated to exhibit a desired behavior in order to avoid the unpleasant condition. For example, I will eventually go to the woodpile and bring in logs for the stove, because I have learned that if I don't, my wife will tell me how lazy I am or the house will get cold. I have learned to interrupt my work long enough to fetch wood, because if I don't, there are some unpleasant consequences.

Third is the *cognitive trend* in behavior therapy. The behaviorists of both the classical-conditioning and operant-conditioning models excluded any reference to mediational concepts (such as the role of thinking processes, at-titudes, and values), perhaps as a reaction against the insight-oriented psycho-dynamic approaches. Since the early 1970s, as we have seen, the behavioral movement has conceded a legitimate place to thinking, even to the extent of giving cognitive factors a central role in understanding and treating behavioral problems (see Bandura, 1969, 1986; Beck, 1976; Beck & Weishaar, 1995; Goldfried & Davison, 1976; Lazarus, 1989; London, 1986; Mahoney, 1977, 1979, 1991; Meichenbaum, 1977, 1985).

The future of behavior therapy looks bright, and even greater expansion of its methods can be expected. With the rising costs of health care, the emer-gence of national health programs, and the increasing involvement of psy-chologists in health issues, there will be a need for even greater integration of behavioral self-help, coping-skills training, relaxation training, and self-management programs into health care (Glass & Arnkoff, 1992). Furthermore, it has been predicted that the importance of cognitive and affective processes in behavior change will attract increasing attention. Treatment procedures may well be refined and applied to an ever-broader range of psychiatric disorders and health problems (Wilson & Agras, 1992). In a slightly dissenting view, Prochaska and Norcross (1994) forecast that behavior therapy, after more than 30 years of significant development, will consolidate its gains, experiment with its self-identity, and expand more slowly.

In this chapter I will describe some of the basic behavior-therapy principles and will clarify important characteristics of the therapeutic process. The bulk of the material describes the application of therapeutic techniques to many different populations. Chapter 11 will be devoted to the cognitive-behavioral approaches of Ellis, Beck, and Meichenbaum.

# Key Concepts

## VIEW OF HUMAN NATURE

Modern behavior therapy is grounded on a scientific view of human behavior that implies a systematic and structured approach to counseling. This view does not rest on a deterministic assumption that humans are a mere product of their sociocultural conditioning. Rather, the current view is that the person is the producer *and* the product of his or environment (Bandura, 1974, 1977, 1986).

Whereas the radical behaviorists such as Skinner (1948, 1971) rule out the possibility of self-determination and freedom, the current trend is toward developing procedures that actually give control to clients and thus increase their range of freedom. Behavior modification aims to increase people's skills so that they have more options for responding. By overcoming debilitating behaviors that restrict choices, people are freer to select from possibilities that were not available earlier. Thus, as behavior modification is typically applied, it will increase rather than stifle individual freedom (Kazdin, 1978).

Philosophically, the behavioristic and the humanistic approaches have often been viewed as polar opposites. The writings of contemporary behavior therapists suggest that bridges are being built, allowing the possibility of a fruitful synthesis. The strict environmental view of human nature that is based on a stimulus/response model of behavior has been criticized by the pioneer of social-learning theory, Bandura (1974, 1977, 1986). He rejects the mechanistic and deterministic model of human behavior because of its exclusive reliance on environmental determinants. He contends that this view, which holds that we are passive agents subjected to the influences of our surroundings, does indeed fail to take into account our capacity to actually affect our environment.

Other writers have made a case for using behavioristic methods to attain humanistic ends (Kazdin, 1994; Mahoney & Thoresen, 1974; Meichenbaum, 1977; Thoresen & Coates, 1980; Watson & Tharp, 1993). According to Thoreson and Coates, greater attention is being given to the emerging similarities among theories. They identify three interrelated themes that characterize this convergence. First is the focus on therapy as an action-oriented approach. Clients are being asked to act rather than to reflect passively and introspect at length on their problems. They are being helped to take specific actions to change their life. Second is the increasing concern of behavior therapists with how stimulus events are mediated by cognitive processes and private or subjective meanings. Third is the increasing emphasis on the role of responsibility for one's behavior. Given the techniques and skills of self-change, people have the capacity to improve their life by altering one or more of the various factors influencing their behavior. These three converging themes provide a conceptual framework for a bridge between the behavioral and humanistic approaches.

## BASIC CHARACTERISTICS AND ASSUMPTIONS

Spiegler and Guevremont (1993) list the following six recurrent themes as characterizing behavior therapy:

1. Behavior therapy is based on the principles and procedures of the scientific method. Experimentally derived principles of learning are systematically applied to help people change their maladaptive behaviors. Conclusions are based on what has been observed rather than on personal beliefs. The distinguishing characteristic of behavioral practitioners is their systematic adherence to specification and measurement. They state treatment goals in concrete and objective terms in order to make replication of their interventions possible. Throughout the course of therapy, they assess problem behaviors and the conditions that are maintaining them. Research methods are used to evaluate the effectiveness of both assessment and treatment procedures. Thus, behavioral concepts and procedures are stated explicitly, tested empirically, and revised continually.

2. Behavior therapy deals with the client's current problems and the factors influencing them, as opposed to historical determinants. Counselors assume that a client's problems are influenced by present conditions. They then use behavioral techniques to change the relevant current factors that are influencing the client's behaviors.

3. In behavior therapy, clients are expected to engage in specific actions to deal with their problems. Rather than simply talking about their condition, they do something to bring about change. They monitor their behaviors both during and outside the therapy sessions, learn and practice coping skills, and role-play new behavior. This is an action-oriented approach.

4. Behavior therapy is generally carried out in the client's natural environment, as much as possible. The approach is largely educational. It emphasizes teaching clients skills of self-management, with the expectation that they will be responsible for transferring what they learn in the therapist's office to their everyday lives. Homework assignments are an integral part of behavior therapy.

5. Behavioral procedures are tailored to fit the unique needs of each client. Several therapy techniques may be used to treat a client's problems. An important question that serves as a guide for this choice is "*What* treatment, by *whom*, is the most effective for *this* individual with *that* specific problem and under *which* set of circumstances?" (Paul, 1967, p. 111).

6. The practice of behavior therapy is based on a collaborative partnership between the therapist and client in two major respects. First, every attempt is made to inform clients about the nature and course of treatment. Second, clients are often trained to initiate, conduct, and evaluate their own treatment under the guidance of the therapist.

These assumptions represent a basis for unity within the heterogeneity of the behavioral approaches. The basic assumption is that disorders commonly treated in therapy are best understood from the perspective of experimental psychology (Wilson, 1978). The principles that are derived from a variety of psychological experiments can be applied in clinical practice toward the goal of changing behavior.

# The Therapeutic Process

## THERAPEUTIC GOALS

Goals occupy a place of central importance in behavior therapy. The general goal is to create new conditions for learning, on the assumption that learning can ameliorate problem behaviors. The client usually formulates the goals, which are specifically defined at the outset of the therapeutic process. Continual assessment throughout therapy determines the degree to which these goals are being met. Assessment and treatment occur together.

Contemporary behavior therapy stresses clients' active roles in deciding about their treatment. The therapist assists clients in formulating goals that are specific, unambiguous, and measurable. A number of characteristics of behavior therapy ensure that the rights of clients are protected. These include the detailed specification of goals and target behaviors, a reliance on empirically tested procedures, the brief nature of treatment, and the collaborative relationship between the client and therapist (Spiegler & Guevremont, 1993). The goals of therapy must be refined to the point that they are clear, concrete, understood, and agreed on by the client and the counselor. This process of determining therapeutic goals entails a negotiation between the client and the counselor, which results in a contract that guides the course of therapy. Behavior therapists and clients alter goals throughout the therapeutic process as needed.

The sequence of selecting and defining goals is described by Cormier and Cormier (1991, pp. 218–226). This process demonstrates the essential nature of a collaborative relationship:

- The counselor explains the purpose of goals.
- The client specifies the positive changes that he or she wants from counseling.
- The client and counselor determine whether the stated goals are changes "owned" by the client.
- Together they explore whether the goals are realistic.
- They discuss the possible advantages and disadvantages of the goals.
- They make one of the following decisions: to continue seeking the stated goals, to reconsider the client's goals, or to seek a referral.

Once goals have been agreed to, a process of defining them begins. The counselor and client discuss the behaviors associated with the goals, the circumstances required for change, the nature of subgoals, and a plan of action to work toward these goals.

A case can be made for the use of behavioral technology as a means for accomplishing societal goals as well as the individual's goals. As previously noted, behavioral techniques do not threaten to eliminate or reduce freedom of choice. For example, behavior-modification programs in hospitals and other institutions have established goals endorsed by society. These aims include returning an individual to the community, fostering self-help, increasing social skills, and alleviating bizarre behaviors. The general goals of behavior therapy are to increase personal choice and effective living. Relieving people from behaviors that interfere with living fully is consistent with the democratic value that individuals should be able to pursue their own goals freely as long as these goals are consistent with the general social good (Kazdin, 1978, 1994).

## THERAPIST'S FUNCTION AND ROLE

Behaviorally oriented practitioners function in some ways as other clinicians do. They pay attention to the clues given by clients, and they are willing to follow their clinical hunches. They use techniques such as summarizing, reflection, clarification, and open-ended questioning. But there are two functions that distinguish behavioral clinicians: They focus on specifics, and they systematically attempt to get information about situational antecedents, the dimensions of the problem behavior, and the consequences of the problem (Goldfried & Davison, 1976).

As an example of how a behavior therapist might perform these functions, assume that a client comes to therapy to reduce her anxiety, which is preventing her from leaving the house. The therapist is likely to begin with a specific analysis of the nature of her anxiety. The therapist will ask how she experiences the anxiety of leaving her house, including what she actually *does* in these situations. Systematically, the therapist gathers information about this anxiety. When did it begin? In what situation(s) does it arise? What does she do at these times? What are her feelings and thoughts in these situations? How do her present fears interfere with living effectively? What are the consequences of her behaviors in threatening situations? After this assessment, specific behavioral goals will be developed, and strategies will be designed to help the client reduce her anxiety to a manageable level. The therapist will get a commitment from her to work toward the specified goals, and the two of them will evaluate her progress toward meeting these goals throughout the duration of therapy.

Another important function of the therapist is role modeling for the client. Bandura (1969, 1971a, 1971b, 1977, 1986) maintains that most of the learning that occurs through direct experiences can also be acquired through observation of others' behavior. One of the fundamental processes by which clients learn new behavior is through imitation. The therapist, as a person, becomes a significant model. Because clients often view the therapist as worthy of emulation, they pattern attitudes, values, beliefs, and behavior after him or her. Thus, therapists should be aware of the crucial role that they play. To be unaware of the power they have in influencing the client's way of thinking and behaving is to deny the central importance of their own personhood in the therapeutic process.

## CLIENT'S EXPERIENCE IN THERAPY

One of the unique contributions of behavior therapy is that it provides the therapist with a well-defined system of procedures to employ with the context of a well-defined role. It also provides the client with a clear role, and it stresses the importance of client awareness and participation in the therapeutic process. Clients must be motivated to change and must be willing to cooperate in carrying out therapeutic activities, both during therapy sessions and in their life. If they are not involved in this way, the chances are slim that therapy will be successful.

Clients are encouraged to experiment for the purpose of enlarging their repertoire of adaptive behaviors. They are helped to generalize and to transfer the learning acquired within the therapeutic situation to situations outside therapy. Counseling is not complete unless actions follow verbalizations. Indeed, it is only when the transfer of changes is made from the sessions to everyday life and when the effects of therapy are extended beyond termination that treatment can be considered successful (Granvold & Wodarski, 1994). It is clear that clients are expected to do more than merely gather insights; they need to be willing to make changes and continue implementing new behavior once formal treatment has ended.

The treatment goals are stated in concrete and measurable terms, as we have seen, which provides clients with a frame of reference for assessing their progress in accomplishing their goals. Clients are as aware as the therapist when the goals have been accomplished and when it is appropriate to terminate treatment. After successful behavior therapy, clients experience an increase of options for behaving, which broadens their range of personal freedom (Spiegler & Guevremont, 1993).

## RELATIONSHIP BETWEEN THERAPIST AND CLIENT

Some clinical and research evidence suggests that a therapeutic relationship, even in the context of a behavioral orientation, can contribute significantly to the process of behavior change (Granvold & Wodarski, 1994). A good therapeutic relationship increases the chances that the client will be receptive to therapy. Not only is it important that the client cooperate with the therapeutic procedures, but the client's positive expectations about the effectiveness of therapy often contribute to successful outcomes. The skilled behavior therapist is one who can conceptualize problems behaviorally and make use of the client/therapist relationship in facilitating change.

As you will recall, the experiential therapies (existential therapy, person-centered therapy, and Gestalt therapy) place primary emphasis on the nature of the engagement between the counselor and client. In psychoanalysis the transference relationship serves as the stage on which therapy is played. In contrast, most behavioral practitioners do not assign an all-important role to relationship variables. Instead, they contend that factors such as warmth, empathy, authenticity, permissiveness, and acceptance are considered necessary, but not sufficient, for behavior change to occur. It is not a matter of the importance of the relationship per se but, rather, the role of the relationship as a foundation on which therapeutic strategies are built to help clients change in the direction they wish. Lazarus (1989) maintains that unless clients respect their therapist, it will be difficult to develop the trust necessary for them to engage in significant self-disclosure. Yet he adds that counselors need an array of clinical skills and techniques to employ once an effective client/therapist relationship has been established.

It is clear that behavior therapy demands a high level of skills and sensitivity and an ability to form a working relationship with clients. In the section that follows, on behavioral techniques, keep in mind that all the procedures described depend on a combination of the therapist's level of skill and rapport with the client. Behavior therapists tend to be active and directive and to function as consultants and problem solvers. Because they use a coping model in instigating behavioral change in the client's natural environment, it is important that they be personally supportive.

# Application: Therapeutic Techniques and Procedures

One of the major strengths of the behavioral approaches to counseling and psychotherapy is the development of specific therapeutic procedures that lend themselves to refinement through the scientific method. As we have seen, behavioral techniques must be shown to be effective through objective means, and there is a constant effort to improve them. Although behavior therapists may make mistakes in analysis or in applying therapeutic procedures, the results of their mistakes are obvious to them, for they receive continual direct response from their clients. The main finding produced by research into the behavioral therapies is that treatment outcomes are multifaceted. Changes are not all or nothing. Improvements are likely to occur in some areas but not in others, all improvements do not emerge at one time, and gains in some areas may be associated with problems emerging in other areas (see Kazdin, 1982; Voltz & Evans, 1982).

In the contemporary behavior therapies any technique that can be demonstrated to change behavior may be incorporated into a treatment plan. Lazarus (1989, 1992b) advocates the use of diverse techniques, regardless of their theoretical origin. He outlines a wide range of techniques that he has used in his clinical practice to supplement behavioral methods. In his view the more extensive the range of therapy techniques, the more potentially effective the therapist is. It is clear that behavior therapists do not have to restrict themselves strictly to methods derived from learning theory. Likewise, behavioral techniques can be incorporated into other approaches.

The therapeutic procedures used by behavior therapists are specifically appropriate for a particular client, rather than being randomly selected from a "bag of techniques." Therapists are often quite creative in their design of interventions.

In the following sections I will describe a range of behavioral techniques available to the practitioner: relaxation training, systematic desensitization, modeling methods, assertion-training programs, self-management programs, and multi-modal therapy. I want to emphasize that these techniques do not encompass the full spectrum of behavioral procedures. In a brief overview it is difficult to capture the diversity and scope of the field, which is continually developing.

## RELAXATION TRAINING AND RELATED METHODS

Relaxation training has become increasingly popular as a method of teaching people to cope with the stresses produced by daily living. It is aimed at achieving muscle and mental relaxation and is easily learned. After clients learn the basics of relaxation procedures, it is essential that they practice these exercises daily in order to obtain maximum results.

Jacobson (1938) is credited with initially developing the progressive-relaxation procedure. It has since been refined and modified, and relaxation procedures are frequently used in combination with a number of other behavioral techniques. These include imaginal-desensitization procedures, systematic desensitization, assertion training, self-management programs, tape-recorded instruction, biofeedback-induced relaxation, hypnosis, meditation, and autogenic training—teaching control of bodily and imaginal functions through auto-suggestion.

Relaxation training involves several components that typically require from four to eight hours of instruction. Clients are given a set of instructions that asks them to relax. They assume a passive and relaxed position in a quiet environment while alternately contracting and relaxing muscles. Deep and regular breathing is also associated with producing relaxation. At the same time, clients learn to mentally "let go," perhaps by focusing on pleasant thoughts or images. Relaxation becomes a well-learned response, which can become a habitual pattern if practiced daily for 20 or 25 minutes. During these exercises it helps clients to actually feel and experience the tension building up, to notice their muscles getting tighter and study this tension, and to hold and fully experience the tension. Also, it is useful to experience the difference between a tense and a relaxed state.

Until the last few years relaxation training was primarily used as a part of systematic-desensitization procedures (which will be described next). Recently, relaxation procedures have been applied to a variety of clinical problems, either as a separate technique or in conjunction with related methods. The most common use has been with problems related to stress and anxiety, which are often manifested in psychosomatic symptoms. Other ailments for which relaxation training is helpful include high blood pressure and other cardiovascular problems, migraine headaches, asthma, and insomnia.

## SYSTEMATIC DESENSITIZATION

Systematic desensitization, which is based on the principle of classical conditioning, is one of the most widely employed and empirically researched behavior-therapy procedures. The basic assumption underlying this technique is that an anxiety response is learned, or conditioned, and can be inhibited by substituting an activity that is antagonistic to it. The procedure is used primarily for anxiety and avoidance reactions. It involves, first, a behavioral analysis of stimuli that evoke anxiety and the constructing of a hierarchy of anxiety-producing situations; then relaxation procedures are taught and are paired with imagined scenes. Situations are presented in a series that moves from the least to the most threatening. Anxiety-producing stimuli are repeatedly paired with relaxation training until the connection between those stimuli and the response of anxiety is eliminated (Wolpe, 1958, 1990).

Before desensitization begins, the therapist conducts an initial interview to identify specific information about the anxiety and to gather relevant background information about the client. This interview, which may last several sessions, gives the therapist a good understanding of who the client is. The therapist questions the client about the particular circumstances that elicit the conditioned fears. For instance, under what circumstances does the client feel anxious? If the client is anxious in social situations, does the anxiety vary with the number of people present? Is the client more anxious with people of the same sex or the other sex? The client is asked to begin a self-monitoring process consisting of observing and recording situations during the week that elicit anxiety responses. Some therapists also administer a questionnaire to gather additional data about situations leading to anxiety.

If the decision is made to use the desensitization procedure, the therapist gives the client a rationale for the procedure and briefly describes what is involved. Morris (1986) outlines three steps in the use of systematic desensitization: (1) relaxation training, (2) development of the anxiety hierarchy, and (3) systematic desensitization proper:

1. During the first few sessions the client is taught how to relax. The steps in this relaxation training are based on a modified version of the technique developed by Jacobson (1938) and described in detail by Wolpe (1990). The therapist uses a very quiet, soft, and pleasant voice to teach progressive muscular relaxation. The client is induced to create imagery of previously relaxing situations, such as sitting by a lake or wandering through a beautiful field. It is important that the client reach a state of calm and peacefulness. The client is then taught how to relax all the muscles while visualizing the various parts of the body, with emphasis on the facial muscles. The arm muscles are relaxed first, followed by the head, the neck and shoulders, the back, abdomen, and thorax, and then the lower limbs. The client is instructed to practice relaxation outside the session for about 30 minutes each day.

2. After completing the initial interview and during the relaxation-training phase, the therapist works with the client to develop an anxiety hierarchy for each of the identified areas. Stimuli that elicit anxiety in a particular area, such as rejection, jealousy, criticism, disapproval, or any phobia, are analyzed. The therapist constructs a ranked list of situations that elicit increasing degrees of anxiety or avoidance. The hierarchy is arranged in order from the worst situation that the client can imagine down to the situation that evokes the least anxiety. If it has been determined that the client has anxiety related to fear of

rejection, for example, the highest-anxiety-producing situation might be rejection by the spouse, next rejection by a close friend, and then rejection by a co-worker. The least disturbing situation might be a stranger's indifference toward the client at a party.

3. Desensitization does not begin until several sessions after the initial interview has been completed. Enough time is allowed for clients to learn relaxation in the office, to practice it at home, and to construct the anxiety hierarchy. The desensitization process begins with the client's reaching compete relaxation with eyes closed. A neutral scene is presented, and the client is asked to imagine it. If the client remains relaxed, he or she is asked to imagine the least-anxiety-arousing scene on the hierarchy of situations that has been developed. The therapist moves progressively up the hierarchy until the client signals that he or she is experiencing anxiety, at which time the scene is terminated. Relaxation is then induced again, and the client continues up the hierarchy. Treatment ends when the client is able to remain in a relaxed state while imagining the scene that was formerly the most disturbing and anxiety producing.

Homework and follow-up are essential components of successful desensitization (Cormier & Cormier, 1991). Clients can practice selected relaxation procedures daily, at which time they visualize scenes completed in the previous session. Gradually, they also expose themselves to real-life situations as a further way to manage their anxieties.

Systematic desensitization is an appropriate technique for treating phobias, but it is a misconception that it can be applied only to the treatment of anxiety. It has also been used effectively in dealing with nightmares, anorexia nervosa, obsessions, compulsions, stuttering, and depression. Cormier and Cormier (1991) indicate that historically, desensitization probably has the longest track record of any behavioral technique in dealing with fears, and its results have been frequently documented.

## MODELING METHODS

The terms *modeling, observational learning, imitation, social learning,* and *vicarious learning* have been used interchangeably. All refer to the process by which the behavior of an individual or a group (the model) acts as a stimulus for similar thoughts, attitudes, and behaviors on the part of observers. Through the process of observational learning, clients can learn to perform desired acts themselves without trial-and-error learning. Bandura (1969, 1971a, 1971b, 1977, 1986) has emphasized the role of modeling in the development and the modification of much of human behavior. For example, he has suggested that most fears are developed through social transmission rather than through direct experience with aversive stimuli.

EFFECTS OF MODELING. Bandura outlines three major effects of modeling, each of which has significant implications for clinical practice. First is the acquisition of new responses or skills and the performance of them. This observational-learning effect refers to integrating new patterns of behavior based on watching a model or models. Examples include learning skills in sports, learning language patterns, training autistic children to speak through the use of models, learning social skills, and teaching hospital patients coping skills necessary for their return to the community.

The second effect of modeling is an inhibition of fear responses, which occurs when the observers' behaviors are inhibited in some way. In this case the model who performs an inhibited fear response either does not suffer negative consequences or, in fact, meets with positive consequences. Examples include models who handle snakes and are not bitten, models who perform daring feats and do not get hurt, and models who perform prohibited acts. An example of the latter is the worker who walks off the job and strikes. If the person does not lose his or her job, fellow workers may follow suit.

The third effect of modeling is a facilitation of responses, in which a model provides cues for others to emulate. The effect is to increase behaviors that the individual has already learned and for which there are no inhibitions. Examples include models such as attractive teenagers who talk on a television commercial about a brand of jeans. Other youths who see the ad may follow the fad. Another model who channels or influences behavior is the person who is the first one to leave a social gathering. Typically, others soon follow this action.

TYPES OF MODEL.   Several types of model can be used in therapeutic situations. A *live model* can teach clients appropriate behavior, influence attitudes and values, and teach social skills. For example, therapists can model the very characteristic that they hope the clients will acquire. Through their actual behavior during sessions, therapists can best teach self-disclosure, risk taking, openness, honesty, compassion, and the like. Therapists are constantly serving as a live model for their clients—for better or for worse! In addition to modeling desired behaviors and attitudes, therapists can also adversely influence their clients by modeling rigidity, lack of regard and respect, fear, rudeness, coldness, and aloofness.

Behavior therapists also use *symbolic models*. A model's behaviors are shown on films, videotapes, and other recording devices. In reviewing the research evidence, Bandura (1969) writes that symbolic models have been used successfully in a variety of situations. One example is clients who experience fears. By observing a model or models who successfully encounter certain fearful situations without negative consequences, such clients can decrease or eliminate certain fears.

*Multiple models* are especially relevant in group therapy. The observer can change attitudes and learn new skills through observation of successful peers in the group (or through observing co-leaders). An advantage of multiple models is that observers learn some alternative ways of behaving, for they see a variety of appropriate and successful styles of behavior.

What are the characteristics of effective models? Reviews of research (Bandura, 1969) indicate that a model who is similar to the observer with respect to age, sex, race, and attitudes is more likely to be imitated than a model who is unlike the observer. Models who have a degree of prestige and status are more likely to be imitated than those who have a low level of prestige. However, the status level of the model should not be so high that the observer sees the model's behavior as unrealistic. Further, models who are competent in their performances and who exhibit warmth tend to facilitate modeling effects.

CLINICAL USES OF MODELING METHODS.  Perry and Furukawa (1986) present a comprehensive survey of the uses of modeling with a variety of special populations and problem areas. Clinical applications include treating snake phobias and helping to alleviate fears of children facing surgery. Modeling is used to teach new behaviors to socially disturbed children in the classroom, basic survival skills to retarded individuals, and verbal and motor skills to autistic children. Psychotic adults are taught the social skills they will need on returning to their community, and drug addicts and alcoholics learn interpersonal skills.

Modeling is also used in teaching counseling skills to staff members in clinical settings. It appears that counselor trainees can learn to increase their empathic level of responding to clients through a combination of modeling with other behavioral methods such as role playing, feedback, and reinforcement.

Modeling is part of other treatments, particularly those involving role playing, in which the therapist may rehearse and enact alternative behaviors. However, modeling by itself in the manner that Bandura has described is not typically used in clinical situations. Perry and Furukawa (1986) write that a review of recent studies, in comparison with earlier ones, reveals a trend toward treatment packages in which modeling is one component.

## ASSERTION TRAINING

A behavioral approach that has gained popularity is assertion training, which is one form of social-skills training. At each developmental stage in life important social skills must be mastered. Children need to learn how to make friends, adolescents need to learn how to interact with the opposite sex, and adults must learn how to effectively relate to mates, peers, and supervisors. People who lack social skills frequently experience interpersonal difficulties at home, at work, at school, and during leisure time. Behavioral methods have been designed to teach such individuals ways of interacting successfully. Many people have difficulty in feeling that it is appropriate or right to assert themselves. Assertion training can be useful for the following people: (1) those who cannot express anger or irritation, (2) those who have difficulty in saying no, (3) those who are overly polite and who allow others to take advantage of them, (4) those who find it difficult to express affection and other positive responses, and (5) those who feel that they do not have a right to express their thoughts, beliefs, and feelings.

The basic assumption underlying assertion training is that people have the right (but not the obligation) to express themselves. One goal of assertion training is to increase people's behavioral repertoire so that they can make the *choice* of whether to behave assertively in certain situations. Another goal is teaching people to express themselves in a way that reflects sensitivity to the feelings and rights of others. Assertion does not mean aggression; thus, truly assertive people do not stand up for their rights at all costs, ignoring the feelings of others.

Many assertion-training methods are based on principles of the cognitive-behavioral therapies, which will be covered in the next chapter. For now, it is sufficient to say that most assertion-training programs focus on a client's negative self-statements, self-defeating beliefs, and faulty thinking. People often behave in unassertive ways because they think that they do not have a right to state a viewpoint or ask for what they want or deserve. Thus, their thinking leads to passive behavior. Effective assertion-training programs do more than merely giving people skills and techniques for dealing with difficult situations. Such programs challenge people's beliefs that accompany their lack of assertiveness and teach them to make constructive self-statements and to adopt a new set of beliefs that will result in assertive behavior.

Assertion training is not a panacea, but it is a treatment of choice for most clients with interpersonal difficulties. Although counselors can adapt assertion-training procedures to suit their own style, it is important to include behavioral rehearsal and continual assessment as basic aspects of the program. According to Alberti and Emmons (1995a), there are many advantages to conducting assertiveness training in a group setting. The group provides a laboratory for members to work on common problems and goals. It offers the support and guidance that is necessary to experiment with new behaviors. There are also diverse perspectives for feedback on interpersonal issues. Because the assertion-training group focuses on social situations that involve anxiety, it offers a realistic opportunity for people to face and challenge their difficulties in a structured and safe environment. As members are learning new skills, they have the advantage of social reinforcement. Alberti and Emmons indicate that assertiveness-training groups are not appropriate for all people. They therefore recommend an assessment of individual clients before assigning them to a group. Furthermore, they recommend that members be prepared for the group experience. They stress the importance of a trusting atmosphere in order for productive work to occur. If you are interested in learning more about the issues involved in assertion training and how to set up such a program, I suggest you consult *Your Perfect Right: A Guide to Assertive Behavior* (Alberti & Emmons, 1995a).

## SELF-MANAGEMENT PROGRAMS AND SELF-DIRECTED BEHAVIOR

There is a growing trend toward integrating cognitive and behavioral methods to help clients manage their own problems (Kanfer & Goldstein, 1986). A related trend, toward "giving psychology away," involves psychologists' sharing their knowledge so that "consumers" can increasingly lead self-directed lives and not be dependent on experts to deal with their problems. Psychologists who share this perspective are primarily concerned with teaching people the skills they will need to manage their own lives effectively.

Self-management is a relatively recent phenomenon in counseling and therapy, and reports of clinical applications have burgeoned since 1970. Self-management strategies include, but are not limited to, self-monitoring, self-reward, self-contracting, and stimulus control. Self-management strategies have been applied to many populations and many problems, such as anxiety, depression, and pain.

The basic idea of self-management assessments and interventions is that change can be brought about by teaching people to use coping skills in problematic situations. Generalization and maintenance of the outcomes are enhanced by encouraging clients to accept the responsibility for carrying out these strategies in daily life.

In self-management programs people make decisions concerning specific behaviors they want to control or change. Some common examples include control of smoking, drinking, and drugs; learning study and time-management skills; and dealing with obesity and overeating. People frequently discover that a major reason that they do not attain their goals is the lack of certain skills. It is in such areas that a self-directed approach can provide the guidelines for change and a plan that will lead to change.

Five characteristics of an effective self-management program are identified by Cormier and Cormier (1991, p. 519):

1. A combination of self-management strategies is usually more useful than a single strategy.
2. Consistent use of strategies is essential. If self-management efforts are not employed regularly over a sustained period, their effectiveness may be too limited to produce any significant change.
3. It is necessary to set realistic goals and then evaluate the degree to which they are being met.
4. The use of self-reinforcement is an important component of self-management programs.
5. Environmental support is necessary to maintain changes that result from a self-management program.

Watson and Tharp offer a model designed for self-directed change. The following four stages of the model are based on material drawn from several sources, including Watson and Tharp (1993), Cormier and Cormier (1991), Kanfer and Gaelick (1986), and Kazdin (1994).

1. *Selecting goals.* The initial stage begins with specifying what changes are desired. Goals should be established one at a time, and they should be measurable, attainable, positive, and significant for the person. This last requirement is extremely important, for if the individual develops a self-change program based on goals determined by someone else, the program has a real possibility of failing.

2. *Translating goals into target behaviors.* Next, the goals selected in the initial stage are translated into target behaviors. To that effect, questions such as the following are relevant: "What specific behaviors do I want to increase or decrease? What chain of actions will produce my goal?"

3. *Self-monitoring.* A major first step in self-directed change is the process of self-monitoring, which consists of deliberately and systematically observing one's own behavior (Kazdin, 1994). This monitoring presumably leads to aware-

ness, focused on concrete and observable behaviors rather than on historical events or feeling experiences. A *behavioral diary* is one of the simplest methods for observing one's behavior. The occurrence of a particular behavior is recorded, along with comments about the relevant antecedent cues and consequences. If you want to change your eating habits, for example, the behavioral diary will contain entries of what you eat, events and situations before eating or snacking, meal frequency, types of food eaten, and so forth. Total counts can also be transferred at the end of each day or week to a chart, providing a visual illustration of progress (or the lack of it) toward self-selected goals. Cormier and Cormier (1991) maintain that self-monitoring is indispensable as a measuring device to define problems and to collect evaluative data. They add that although it is necessary and useful for many clients, it is often not sufficient unless it is used in conjunction with other self-management procedures, such as stimulus control, self-reward and self-punishment, and self-contracting (see below).

4. *Working out a plan for change.* This stage begins with a comparison between the information obtained from self-monitoring and the individual's standards for a specific behavior. After clients make the evaluation of behavioral changes they want to acquire, they need to devise an action program to bring about actual change. Plans help to gradually replace an unwanted action with a desirable one or to increase a desirable action. Such a plan of action entails some type of self-reinforcement system and the negotiating of a working contract.

A basic part of the plan for change is *self-reinforcement,* such as participating in pleasant activities. Self-praise can be a useful reinforcer, because it can be easily applied after a target behavior occurs. The use of reinforcement to change behavior is the cornerstone of modern behavior therapy. It is important to choose appropriate self-rewards, ones that are personally motivating. Watson and Tharp suggest that the purpose of self-reinforcement is to make desired behavior so successful that the natural consequences of daily life will sustain it. In other words, self-reinforcement is a temporary strategy to be used until people can implement new behaviors in everyday life.

*Self-contracting* is another facet of a plan for change. It is a strategy that involves determining in advance the external and internal consequences that will follow the execution of the desired or undesired action. Such contracts can help clients keep their commitment to carry out their action plan with some degree of consistency.

*Evaluating the plan for change* is essential to determine the degree to which clients are achieving their goals. After the plan of action is set forth, it must be readjusted and revised as clients learn other ways to meet their goals. Evaluation is an ongoing process rather than a one-time occurrence. Watson and Tharp (1993, p. 258) point out that a perfect plan for a problem does not exist. But they list these characteristics of successful plans:

- rules that state which behaviors and techniques for change will be used in various situations
- explicit goals and subgoals

- a system of getting feedback on one's progress, derived largely from self-observation
- a comparison of feedback with one's goals and subgoals to measure progress
- adjustments in the plan as conditions change

Counselors who encourage their clients to utilize self-management programs need to ensure that the plan developed and selected meets the above characteristics to a large degree. The value of such programs lies in learning responsibility for one's own actions. Furthermore, as Watson and Tharp say, self-direction is a lifelong practice.

## MULTIMODAL THERAPY

Multimodal therapy is a comprehensive, systematic, holistic approach to behavior therapy developed by Lazarus (1971, 1986, 1987b, 1989, 1992a, 1992b, 1995). It is an open system and encourages a *technical eclecticism*. New techniques are constantly being introduced, and existing techniques are refined, but they are never used in a shotgun manner. Multimodal therapists ask the question "Who or what is best for this particular person?" Thus, they take great pains not to try to fit the client to a predetermined treatment. Instead, they make a careful attempt to determine precisely what relationship and what treatment strategies will work best with each client and under which particular circumstances. The underlying assumption of this approach is that because individuals are troubled by a variety of specific problems, it is appropriate that a multitude of treatment strategies be used in bringing about change. Multimodal therapists are constantly adjusting their procedures to achieve the client's goals in therapy (Lazarus, 1995).

Most of the techniques listed by Lazarus (1989) are standard behavioral procedures. His multimodal schema serves as an example of how behavior therapists can draw on methods from the three major thrusts of the behavioral approach, the classical, operant, and cognitive.

THE BASIC I.D.   The essence of Lazarus's multimodal approach is the premise that human beings' complex personality can be divided into seven major areas of functioning: B – behavior; A = affective responses; S = sensations; I = images; C = cognitions; I = interpersonal relationships; and D = drugs, biological functions, nutrition, and exercise (Lazarus, 1989, 1992a, 1992b, 1995). Although these modalities are interactive, they can be considered discrete functions.

The multimodal therapist takes the view that a complete assessment and treatment program must account for each modality of the BASIC I.D. Thus, the BASIC I.D. is the cognitive map that ensures that each aspect of personality receives explicit and systematic attention. Thus, comprehensive therapy entails the correction of irrational beliefs, deviant behaviors, unpleasant feelings, bothersome images, stressful relationships, negative sensations, and possible biochemical imbalances. Multimodal therapists believe that the more clients learn in therapy, the less likely it is that old problems will reoccur. They view enduring change as a function of combined strategies and modalities.

Lazarus (1992a, 1992b) lists the following five principles that embody the essence of the multimodal perspective: (1) Humans act and interact across the seven areas of the BASIC I.D.; (2) these modalities are interconnected and must be onsidered as an interactive system; (3) accurate evaluation is best accomplished by systematically assessing each of the seven modalities and the interaction among them; (4) a comprehensive approach to treatment involves the specific correction of significant problems across the BASIC I.D.; and (5) psychological disturbance is a product of factors such as conflicting feelings, misinformation, lack of interpersonal skills, external stressors, and existential concerns.

Multimodal therapy begins with a comprehensive assessment of the seven modalities of human functioning. Clients are asked questions pertaining to the BASIC I.D. What follows is a modification of this assessment process based on questions that Lazarus typically asks (1989, 1992a, 1992b, 1995):

1. *Behavior.* This modality refers primarily to overt behaviors, including acts, habits, and reactions that are observable and measurable. Some questions asked are "What would you like to change?" "How active are you?" "How much of a doer are you?" "What would you like to start doing?" What would you like to stop doing?" "What are some of your main strengths?" "What specific behaviors keep you from getting what you want?"

2. *Affect.* This modality refers to emotions, moods, and strong feelings. Questions sometimes asked include "How emotional are you?" "What emotions do you experience most often?" "What makes you laugh?" "What makes you cry?" "What makes you sad, mad, glad, scared?" "What emotions are problematic for you?"

3. *Sensation.* This area refers to the five basic senses of touch, taste, smell, sight, and hearing. Examples of questions asked are "Do you suffer from unpleasant sensations, such as pains, aches, dizziness, and so forth?" "How much do you focus on sensations?" "What do you particularly like or dislike in the way of seeing, smelling, hearing, touching, and tasting?"

4. *Imagery.* This modality pertains to ways in which we picture ourselves, and it includes memories, dreams, and fantasies. Some questions asked are "What are some bothersome recurring dreams and vivid memories?" "Do you engage in fantasy and daydreaming?" "Do you have a vivid imagination?" "How do you view your body?" "How do you see yourself now?" "How would you like to be able to see yourself in the future?"

5. *Cognition.* This modality refers to insights, philosophies, ideas, opinions, self-talk, and judgments that constitute one's fundamental values, attitudes, and beliefs. Questions include "How much of a thinker are you?" "What are some ways in which you meet your intellectual needs?" "How do your thoughts affect your emotions?" "What are the values and beliefs you most cherish?" "What are some negative things that you say to yourself?" "What are some of your central irrational beliefs?" "What

are the main 'shoulds,' 'oughts,' and 'musts' in your life? How do they get in the way of effective living?"

6. *Interpersonal relationships.* This modality refers to interactions with other people. Examples of questions include "How much of a social being are you?" "To what degree do you desire intimacy with others?" "What do you expect from the significant people in your life?" "What do they expect from you?" "Are there any relationships with others that you would hope to change?" "If so, what kinds of changes do you want?

7. *Drugs/biology.* This modality includes more than drugs; it takes into consideration one's nutritional habits and exercise patterns. Some questions asked are "Are you healthy and health conscious?" "Do you have any concerns about your health?" "Do you take any prescribed drugs?" "What are your habits pertaining to diet, exercise, and physical fitness?"

You should not think that the above list is a complete representation of the BASIC I.D., but a preliminary investigation brings out some central and significant themes that can be productively explored. The preliminary questioning is followed by a detailed life-history questionnaire. (See Lazarus & Lazarus, 1991, for the multimodal life-history inventory.) Once the main profile of a person's BASIC I.D. has been established, the next step consists of an examination of the interactions among the different modalities. This second phase of work intensifies specific facets of the client's problem areas and allows the therapist to understand the person more fully as well as to devise effective coping and treatment strategies.

TECHNICAL ECLECTICISM.  As mentioned earlier, multimodal therapists are aware that people have unique and diverse needs and expectations and that they therefore require a wide range of therapeutic styles. Based on the assumption that many clients come to therapy needing to learn skills, therapists are willing to teach, coach, train, model, and direct their clients. They typically function directively by providing information, instruction, and reactions. They challenge self-defeating beliefs, offer constructive feedback, provide positive reinforcement, and are appropriately self-disclosing. It is essential that therapists start where the client is and then move into other productive areas for exploration. Failure to apprehend the client's situation can easily lead the client to feel alienated and misunderstood (Lazarus, 1995).

Multimodal therapists borrow techniques from many other therapy systems. Some of these principal techniques that they employ in individual psychotherapy are anxiety-management training, behavior rehearsal, bibliotherapy, biofeedback, communication training, contingency contracting, hypnosis, meditation, modeling, paradoxical strategies, positive imagery, positive reinforcement, relaxation training, self-instruction training, sensate-focus training, social-skills and assertiveness training, the empty chair, time projection, and thought stopping. (See Lazarus, 1987a for a detailed description of these methods.)

Multimodal therapists must have technical eclecticism; that is, they should be able to employ any techniques that have been demonstrated to be effective in dealing with specific problems (Roberts, Jackson, & Phelps, 1980). The kind of eclecticism that Lazarus (1987b) favors is scientific and has three other qualities: breadth, depth, and specificity. In espousing technical (or systematic) eclecticism, he is not arguing in favor of a theoretical eclecticism, because blending bits and pieces of different theories is likely to obfuscate matters. By remaining both theoretically consistent and technically eclectic, however, practitioners can spell out precisely what interventions they will employ with various clients, as well as the means by which they select these procedures. Systematic eclecticism borrows techniques from diverse sources without necessarily subscribing to the theories that spawned them (Lazarus, 1986, 1987b, 1992b, 1995; Lazarus & Beutler, 1993; Lazarus, Beutler, & Norcross, 1992).

Lazarus, Beutler, and Norcross make it clear that the purpose of technical eclecticism is not to produce another separate school of therapy. Instead, they believe "that it will engender an open system of empirically grounded clinical practice, an interdisciplinary and collaborative cadre of researchers building on each other's work" (1992, p. 17). They hope that in the future therapists will think and practice eclectically and integratively, but critically.

## BEHAVIOR THERAPY APPLIED TO THE CASE OF STAN

Working with Stan from a behavioral perspective, the therapist begins with a comprehensive assessment utilizing the categories that are a part of the multi-modal approach. In Stan's case many specific and interrelated problems can be identified by using the following BASIC I.D. diagnosis:

*Behavior*
- is defensive, avoids eye contact, speaks hesitantly
- uses alcohol excessively
- has gotten into trouble with the law because of his drinking
- has a poor sleep pattern
- pounds his leg with his fist, turning his anger inward
- displays various avoidance behaviors

*Affect*
- feels anxiety
- panics (especially at night when trying to sleep)
- experiences depression
- fears criticism and rejection
- feels worthless
- feels stupid
- feels isolated and alienated
- has resentment toward his siblings

*Sensation*
- feels dizziness
- suffers from impotence
- has palpitations
- gets headaches

*Imagery*
- receives ongoing negative parental messages
- has an unfavorable body image and poor self-image
- sees himself as a failure in life
- has suicidal fantasies at times
- views himself in an inferior light in the presence of women
- sees himself as homely
- fantasizes himself as being shunned by others

*Cognition*
- asks self-identity questions ("Who and what am I?")
- has worrying thoughts (death and dying)
- questions his right to succeed in his projects
- has many self-defeating thoughts and beliefs
- is governed by categorical imperatives ("shoulds," "oughts," "musts")
- seeks new values
- compares himself with others
- engages in fatalistic thinking

*Interpersonal characteristics*
- is unassertive
- has an unsatisfactory relationship with his parents
- has very few friends
- is afraid of contact with women and fears intimacy
- feels like an outcast
- feels socially inferior

*Drugs and biological factors*
- abuses alcohol
- has used illegal drugs
- lacks an exercise program
- has various physical complaints
- shows no organic pathology

After completing this assessment of Stan, his therapist focuses on helping him define the specific areas where he would like to make changes. They then talk about how the therapy sessions (and his work outside of them) can help him reach his goals. Early during treatment she helps him translate some of his general goals into concrete and measurable ones. Thus, when he says, "I want to feel better about myself," she helps him define more specific goals. When he says, "I want to get rid of my inferiority complex," she replies: "What are some situations in which you feel inferior?" "What do you actually do that leads to feelings of inferiority?" In his case some concrete aims include his desire to function without drugs or alcohol. She asks him to keep a record of when he drinks and what events lead up to his drinking.

Stan indicates that he does not want to feel apologetic for his existence. His therapist asks him to engage in some assertiveness-training exercises. Because he has trouble talking with his boss or co-workers, for example, she demonstrates how to approach them more directly and confidently. This procedure includes modeling, role playing, and behavior rehearsal. He then tries more effective behaviors with his therapist, who plays the role of the boss and then gives feedback on how strong or apologetic he seemed.

Stan's anxiety about women can also be explored by behavior-rehearsal methods. The therapist plays the role of a woman whom Stan wants to date. He practices being the way he would like to be with his date and says the things to his therapist that he might be afraid to say to his date. He can thus explore his fears, get feedback on the effects of his behavior, and experiment with more assertive behavior.

Systematic desensitization is appropriate in working with Stan's fear of failing. He first learns relaxation procedures during the sessions and then practices them daily at home. Next he lists his specific fears relating to failure. Stan identifies his greatest fear as sexual impotence with a woman. The least fearful situation he identifies is being with a female student for whom he does not feel an attraction. He then imagines a pleasant scene and begins a desensitization process beginning with his lesser fears and working up to the anxiety associated with his greatest fear.

Therapy focuses on modifying the behavior that results in Stan's feelings of guilt and anxiety. This approach does not place importance on his past except to the extent necessary to modify his faulty learning. The therapist does not explore his childhood experiences but works directly with the present behaviors that are causing his difficulties. Insight is not seen as important, nor is having him experience or reexperience his feelings. The assumption is that if he can learn more appropriate coping behaviors, eliminate unrealistic anxiety and guilt, and acquire more adaptive responses, his presenting symptoms will decrease, and he will report a greater degree of satisfaction.

FOLLOW-UP: YOU CONTINUE AS STAN'S BEHAVIOR THERAPIST. Use these questions to help you think about how to counsel Stan:

- What is your impression of Stan's characteristics from the multimodal perspective described above? What are some areas that you might be inclined to pursue?
- How would you collaboratively work with Stan in identifying specific behavioral goals to give a direction to your therapy?
- As a behavior therapist, you would be far more interested in Stan's current struggles than in his early childhood issues. How might you deal with him if he indicated that he wanted to talk about what happened to him as a child?
- What are some behavioral techniques that might be most appropriate in helping Stan with his problems?
- Stan indicates that he does not want to feel apologetic for his existence. How might you help him translate this wish into a specific behavioral goal? What behavioral techniques might you draw upon in helping him in this area?
- What homework assignments are you likely to suggest for Stan?

# Summary and Evaluation

## SUMMARY

Contemporary behavior therapy (unlike traditional behaviorism and radical behaviorism) places emphasis on the interplay between the individual and the environment. Cognitive factors and the subjective reactions of people to the environment now have a place in the practice of behavior therapy. Thus, behavioral technology can be used to attain humanistic ends. It is clear that bridges can connect the humanistic and the behavioristic therapies, especially with the current focus of attention on self-directed approaches and multimodal therapy.

Behavior therapy is diverse with respect not only to basic concepts but also to techniques that can be applied in coping with specific problems. The behavioral movement includes three major areas of development: classical conditioning, operant conditioning, and increasing attention to the cognitive factors influencing behavior (the subject of the next chapter). A unique characteristic of behavior therapy is its strict reliance on the principles of the scientific method. Concepts and procedures are stated explicitly, tested empirically, and revised continually. Treatment and assessment are interrelated, for they occur simultaneously. Research is considered to be a basic aspect of the approach, so that therapeutic techniques can be continually refined.

A hallmark of behavior therapy is the identification of specific goals at the outset of the therapeutic process. In helping clients achieve their goals, behavior therapists typically assume an active and directive role. Although the client generally determines *what* behavior will be changed, the therapist typically determines *how* this behavior can best be modified. In designing a treatment plan, behavior therapists employ techniques and procedures that are specifically appropriate for a particular client. In selecting these strategies, therapists have a wide range of options, a few of which are relaxation training, systematic desensitization, modeling methods, assertion-training programs, and self-management programs. The approach of multimodal therapy provides a context in which therapists can borrow techniques from a variety of therapeutic systems and apply them to the unique needs of each client. Such an approach provides for the therapeutic flexibility and versatility required to effectively achieve a diverse range of goals.

## CONTRIBUTIONS OF BEHAVIOR THERAPY

Behavioral practitioners have contributed to the counseling field with their focus on specifics and their systematic way of applying therapeutic techniques. They challenge us to reconsider our global approach to counseling. Although we may assume that we know what a client means by the statement "I feel unloved; life has no meaning," behavior therapists will work with the client in defining what he or she means so that therapy can proceed. Whereas a humanist might nod in acceptance to such a statement, the behaviorist might retort: "Who specifically

is not loving you? What is going on in your life to bring about this meaninglessness? What are some specific things that you might be doing that contribute to the state you are in? What would you most like to change?"

Another contribution is the wide variety of specific behavioral techniques
at the disposal of the therapist. Because behavior therapy stresses *doing,* as opposed to merely talking about problems and gathering insights, practitioners
have many behavioral strategies that assist clients in formulating a plan of action for changing behavior. These methods have been employed to treat a wide
array of problems. Behavioral techniques have been extended to more areas of
human functioning than have any of the other therapeutic approaches (Kazdin,
1994). Behavior therapy is deeply enmeshed in medicine, geriatrics, pediatrics,
rehabilitation programs, and stress management. This approach has made significant contributions to health psychology, especially in the areas of helping people
maintain a healthy lifestyle and also in the management of illnesses.

An extensive study by a task force under the aegis of the Division of Clinical
Psychology, American Psychological Association, demonstrated that, to date,
behavioral methods were the only examples of *well-established empirically-
validated psychological treatments* for chronic pain, panic disorder, generalized
anxiety disorder, phobias, obsessive-compulsive disorder, tension headache, ir-
ritable bowel syndrome, female orgasmic dysfunction, male erectile dysfunction, and several other conditions (see Chambless, 1995).

What follows is a summary of other selected problem areas for which behavior therapy appears to be an effective treatment, as discussed by Wilson (1995):

- *Anxiety disorders.* Studies have demonstrated the success of behavior
  therapy in treating phobias, such as fear of open places.
- *Depression.* The combination of cognitive and behavioral procedures has
  yielded promising results in the treatment of depression.
- *Sexual disorders.* Behavior therapy is the preferred treatment for sexual
  problems such as impotence, premature ejaculation, orgasmic dysfunction, and vaginismus.
- *Prevention and treatment of cardiovascular disease.* Certain behavior
  patterns and lifestyles have been associated with an increased risk of
  premature cardiovascular disease, and modification of these behaviors is
  likely to produce a reduction of the disease. Behavioral methods have
  been effectively used in combating cigarette smoking, overeating, and
  overdrinking. They are of value in helping people stick to an exercise plan
  and in managing stress and hypertension. In fact, behavioral medicine,
  the wellness movement, and approaches to holistic health incorporate
  behavioral strategies as a part of their practice.

Another major contribution of behavior therapy is its emphasis on research
into and assessment of treatment outcomes. It is up to practitioners to demonstrate that therapy is working. If progress is not being made, they take a careful
look at the original analysis and the treatment plan that was formulated. Of all
the therapies presented in this book, no other approach and its techniques
have been subjected to the degree of empirical research that behavior therapy
has. This scrutiny may account for the fact that this model has changed so

dramatically since its origin. Behavior therapists now raise more specific research questions. In the early years of research, investigators framed questions in terms of global outcomes. Now they ask, "Which type of client, meeting with which type of counselor, using which type of treatment, will yield what outcome?" It is recognized that some techniques and therapists are appropriate for certain clients but not for others. Furthermore, almost no procedure can be expected to lead to behavior change in all clients or to correct all the problems of any client (Kanfer & Goldstein, 1986). This kind of focused research is more characteristic of behavior therapy than of any other approach, and it provides a framework for studies that could be used to evaluate techniques that flow from other schools.

A contribution of behavior therapists is their willingness to examine the effectiveness of their procedures in terms of the generalizability, meaningfulness, and durability of change. Most studies show that behavior-therapy methods are more effective than no treatment. Moreover, a number of behavioral procedures are currently the best treatment strategies available for a range of specific problems. Compared with alternative approaches, behavioral techniques have generally been shown to be at least as effective and frequently more effective in changing target behaviors (Spiegler & Guevremont, 1993).

CONTRIBUTIONS TO ETHICAL PRACTICE.   A related strength is ethical accountability. Spiegler and Guevremont (1993) write that behavior therapy is ethically neutral in that it does not dictate whose behavior or what behavior should be changed. At least in cases of voluntary counseling, the behavioral practitioner only specifies *how* to change those behaviors that the client targets as targets for change. Thus, in deciding *what* the goals of therapy will be, clients actually have a good deal of control and freedom.

Behavior therapists, in general, have been particularly concerned with the ethical aspects of practice. Although they have powerful means of modifying behavior at their disposal, their willingness to involve clients in the various stages of the therapy process seems to serve as a good safeguard. At the outset of therapy, clients learn about the nature of counseling, the procedures that may be employed, and the benefits and risks. With this information, they become informed, fully enfranchised partners in the therapeutic venture.

CONTRIBUTIONS TO MULTICULTURAL COUNSELING.   Behavior therapy has some clear advantages over many other theories in working with multicultural populations. Because of their cultural and ethnic backgrounds, some clients hold values that are contrary to the free expression of feelings and the sharing of personal concerns. Behavioral counseling does not place emphasis on experiencing catharsis but, rather, stresses changing specific behaviors and developing problem-solving skills. Clients who are looking for action plans and behavioral change are likely to cooperate with this approach, for they can see that it offers them concrete methods for dealing with their problems of living. Behavior therapy has appeal for multicultural counseling because it goes beyond intrapsychic factors and focuses on environmental conditions that contribute to a client's problems. Social and political influences play a significant role in the lives of people of color. Some of these are discriminatory practices and economic problems that are inconsistent with the person's cultural values or background.

Thus, a strength of behavioral procedures is that they take into consideration the social and cultural dimensions of the client's life. Kanfer and Goldstein (1986) assert that simply having a catalog of available techniques is not sufficient preparation for competent therapeutic practice. They emphasize the need to give careful consideration to the client's life setting, personal values, and biological and sociopsychological characteristics. They also point out that various sociocultural developments contribute to psychological problems and to violence and abuse in personal relationships. It seems clear that the behavioral approach has moved beyond treating clients for a specific symptom or behavioral problem. Instead, it stresses a thorough evaluation of the person's life circumstances, to ascertain not only whether the target behavior is amenable to change but also whether such a change is likely to lead to a significant improvement in the client's total life situation. In designing a change program for clients, effective behavioral practitioners conduct a functional analysis of the problem situation. This assessment includes the cultural context in which the problem behavior occurs, the consequences both to the client and to the client's sociocultural environment, the resources within the environment that can promote change, and the impact that change is likely to have on others in the client's surroundings (Kanfer & Goldstein, 1986). Tanaka-Matsumi and Higginbotham (1994) write that the foundation of behavior therapy is the assessment of a functional relationship between the individual's behavior and the environment. In their discussion of the clinical applications of behavior therapy across ethnic and cultural boundaries, they stress that practitioners need to adapt behavior therapy to the cultural context if it is to be accepted by the client.

## LIMITATIONS AND CRITICISMS OF BEHAVIOR THERAPY

Behavior therapists need to listen very carefully to their clients and to allow them to express and explore their feelings *before* implementing a treatment plan. The basic therapeutic conditions that are stressed by the person-centered therapist— such as active listening, accurate empathy, positive regard, genuineness, respect, and immediacy—can be integrated into a behavioral framework. However, too often counselors are so anxious to work toward resolving problems that they are not fully present with their clients. A mistake some counselors make is focusing on the presenting issue instead of listening to the client's deeper message.

FIVE CRITICISMS.   Below are some common criticisms and misconceptions that people often have about behavior therapy, together with my reactions:

*Criticism 1: Behavior therapy may change behaviors, but it does not change feelings.*   Some critics argue that feelings must change before behavior can change. Behavioral practitioners generally contend that if clients can change their behavior, they are likely to change their feelings also. They hold that empirical evidence has not borne out the criticism that feelings must be changed first. Although they do not focus primarily on feelings, behavioral clinicians do in actual practice deal with feelings as an overall part of the treatment process.

I do not think that behavior therapy deals with emotional processes as fully or as adequately as do the experiential therapies. A general criticism of both the behavioral and the cognitive approaches is that clients are not encouraged to experience their emotions. In concentrating on how clients are behaving or thinking, counselors play down the working through of emotional issues. Generally, I favor initially focusing on what clients are feeling and then working with the behavioral and cognitive dimensions.

*Criticism 2: Behavior therapy ignores the important relational factors in therapy.* The charge is often made that the importance of the relationship between the client and the therapist is discounted in behavior therapy. Although it appears to be true that behavior therapists do not place primary weight on the relationship variable, this does not mean that the approach is condemned to a mechanical and nonhumanistic level of functioning. As we have seen, behavior therapists contend that a good working relationship with their clients is a basic foundation necessary for the effective use of techniques. As Lazarus and Fay (1984) write, "The relationship is the soil that enables the techniques to take root" (p. 493).

Research has not shown that the behavioral therapies are any different from other therapeutic orientations in the relationship variables that emerge (Sloane, Staples, Cristol, Yorkston, & Whipple, 1975). It may be true that some therapists are attracted to behavior therapy because they can be directive, can play the role of expert, or can avoid the anxieties and ambiguities of establishing a more personal relationship. This is not an intrinsic characteristic of the approach, however, and I think that many behavior therapists are more humanistic in practice than some of the therapists are who profess to practice humanistic therapy.

*Criticism 3: Behavior therapy does not provide insight.* If this assertion is indeed true, behavior-modification theorists would probably respond that insight isn't necessary. They would maintain that they do not focus on insight because of the absence of clear evidence that insight is critical to outcome. Behavior is changed directly. If the goal of achieving insight is an eventual change of behavior, then behavior therapy, which has proven results, has the same effect. Moreover, a change in behavior often leads to a change in understanding; it is a two-way street. Nevertheless, many people want not just to change their behavior but also to gain an understanding of why they behave the way they do. The answers are often buried deep in past learning and in historical events. Although it is possible for behavior therapists to give explanations in this realm, in fact they usually do not.

*Criticism 4: Behavior therapy treats symptoms rather than causes.* The psychoanalytic assumption is that early traumatic events are at the root of present dysfunction. The progression is from discovering original causes to reliving past situations in the therapeutic relationship and to facilitating insight. This process is thought to lead to changing present behavior. Behavior therapists may acknowledge that deviant responses have historical origins, but they contend that history is seldom important in the maintenance of current problems. Thus, behavior therapy focuses on providing the client with opportunities to acquire the new learning needed for effectively coping with problem situations.

Related to this criticism is the notion that unless historical causes of present behavior are therapeutically explored, new symptoms will soon take the place of those that were "cured." Behaviorists rebut this assertion on both theoretical and empirical grounds. They do not accept the assumption that symptoms are manifestations of underlying intrapsychic conflicts. Furthermore, they assert that there is no empirical evidence that symptom substitution occurs after behavior therapy has successfully eliminated unwanted behavior (Kazdin & Wilson, 1978; Sloane et al., 1975; Spiegler & Guevremont, 1993).

*Criticism 5: Behavior therapy involves control and manipulation by the therapist.* Some writers in behavior therapy clearly acknowledge that therapists *do* have control, but they contend that this capacity to manipulate relevant variables is not necessarily undesirable or unethical. Kazdin (1994) believes that no inherent issues of control and manipulation are associated with behavioral strategies that are not also raised by other therapeutic approaches. He maintains that behavior therapy does not embrace particular goals or argue for a particular lifestyle, nor does it have an agenda for changing society. Surely, in all therapeutic approaches there is control by the therapist, who hopes to change behavior in some way. This does not mean, however, that clients are helpless victims at the mercy of the whims and values of the therapist. Contemporary behavior therapists employ techniques aimed at increased self-direction and self-control, which are skills that clients actually learn in the therapy process.

LIMITATIONS IN MULTICULTURAL COUNSELING.   Perhaps a major limitation of behavioral counseling rests more with certain practitioners than with the approach itself. There is a tendency for some behavioral counselors to focus on using a variety of techniques in narrowly treating a specific behavioral problem. Instead of viewing clients in the context of their sociocultural environment, these practitioners concentrate too much on problems within the individual, and in doing so they may overlook significant issues in the lives of clients. Such practitioners are not likely to bring about beneficial changes for ethnic clients.

The fact that behavioral interventions often work well raises an interesting issue in multicultural counseling. When clients make significant personal changes, it is very likely that others in their environment will react to these people differently. Before deciding too quickly on goals for therapy, the counselor and client need to discuss the advantages and disadvantages of change. It is essential for therapists to conduct a thorough assessment of the interpersonal and cultural dimensions of the problem. Clients should be helped in assessing the possible consequences of some of their newly acquired social skills. Once goals are determined and therapy is under way, they should have opportunities to talk about the problems they encounter as they become different people in their home and work settings. For example, a client may want to become more assertive with her husband and children and may strive for increased independence. It is conceivable that as she becomes more assertive and independent, divorce may result. Her culture may place a premium on compliance with tradition, and being assertive can lead to problems if she decides to stay within that culture.

As a divorced woman she could find herself without any support from relatives and friends, and she might eventually regret having made the changes she did.

# Where to Go from Here

Because the literature in this field is so extensive and diverse, it is not possible in one brief survey chapter to present a comprehensive and in-depth discussion of behavioral techniques. I hope you will be challenged to examine any misconceptions you may hold about behavior therapy and be stimulated to do some further reading of selected sources.

If you have an interest in further training in behavior therapy, the Association for Advancement of Behavior Therapy (AABT) is an excellent source. The AABT is a professional organization of over 4300 mental-health professionals and students who are interested in behavior therapy, cognitive-behavior therapy, behavioral assessment, and applied behavioral analysis. If you are interesting in becoming a member of this organization, contact:

Association for Advancement of Behavior Therapy
305 Seventh Avenue
New York, NY 10001
Telephone: (800) 685-AABT

Regular and associate member dues are $95, and student dues are $25. Membership includes a subscription to *The Behavior Therapist,* a newsletter that contains news of the field, feature articles, book and audiovisual reviews, information about training programs, and practical articles of use to mental-health professionals. Members also receive a copy of the membership directory. Membership includes reduced registration and continuing-education course fees for the annual AABT convention, which features workshops and special sessions, institutes, and professional seminars. Members receive discounts on all AABT publications, some of which are listed below:

- *Directory of Graduate Training in Behavior Therapy,* an excellent source for students and job seekers who want information on programs with an emphasis on behavioral training
- *Directory of Psychology Internships: Programs Offering Behavioral Training,* which lists training programs having a behavioral component
- *Behavior Therapy,* an international journal focusing on articles dealing with original experimental and clinical research on theory and practice
- *Cognitive and Behavioral Practice,* a new journal primarily for practitioners that is aimed at the integration of behavior-therapy principles and clinical practices

You can keep up with this ever-expanding field by consulting other journals devoted exclusively to behavior therapy: *Advances in Behaviour Research and Therapy, Behaviour Research and Therapy, Behavioural Assessment, Behavior*

*Modification, Behavioural Psychotherapy, Journal of Behavior Therapy and Experimental Psychiatry, Child and Family Behavior Therapy, Journal of Applied Behavior Analysis,* and *Cognitive Therapy and Research.*

*The Cognitive Behaviorist* is another valuable source for keeping abreast in this field. For information on getting this newsletter, contact:

E. Thomas Dowd
Counseling Psychology Program
130 Bancroft Hall
University of Nebraska
Lincoln, NE 68588

## Recommended Supplementary Readings

The literature in the field of behavior therapy is vast. One excellent starting place is a comprehensive textbook, such as the two listed just below:

*Contemporary Behavior Therapy* (Spiegler & Guevremont, 1993) is a comprehensive and up-to-date treatment of basic principles and applications of the behavior therapies, as well as a fine discussion of ethical issues. Specific chapters deal with procedures that can be usefully applied to a range of client populations: behavioral assessment, modeling therapy, systematic desensitization, cognitive restructuring, and cognitive coping skills.

*Interviewing Strategies for Helpers: Fundamental Skills and Cognitive Behavioral Interventions* (Cormier & Cormier, 1991) is a comprehensive and clearly written textbook dealing with training experiences and skill development. Its excellent documentation offers practitioners a wealth of material on a variety of topics, such as assessment procedures, selection of goals, development of appropriate treatment programs, and methods of evaluating outcomes.

*The Practice of Multimodal Therapy* (Lazarus, 1989) is an excellent source of techniques and procedures that can be applied to working with diverse client populations in various settings. It represents an attempt to deal with the whole person by developing assessments and treatment interventions for all the modalities of human experience.

*Self-Directed Behavior: Self-Modification for Personal Adjustment* (Watson & Tharp, 1993) provides readers with specific steps for carrying out self-modification programs. The authors deal with topics of selecting a goal, developing a plan, keeping progress notes, and recognizing and coping with obstacles to following through with a self-directed program.

*Behavior Modification in Applied Settings* (Kazdin, 1994) provides a good overview of behavioral principles such as operant conditioning, positive and negative reinforcement, punishment, and extinction. It also deals with identifying and assessing goals, self-control techniques, cognitively based treatment, transfer of training, applications of behavioral techniques, ethical and legal issues in the practice of behavior therapy, and future directions.

## References and Suggested Readings *

* ALBERTI, R. E., & EMMONS, M. L. (1995a). *Your perfect right: A guide to assertive behavior* (6th ed.). San Luis Obispo, CA: Impact.
* ALBERTI, R. E., & EMMONS, M. L. (1995b). *Your perfect right: A manual for assertiveness trainers.* San Luis Obispo, CA: Impact.

*Books and articles marked with an asterisk are suggested for further study.

BANDURA, A. (1969). *Principles of behavior modification.* New York: Holt, Rinehart & Winston.

BANDURA, A. (Ed.). (1971a). *Psychological modeling: Conflicting theories.* Chicago: Aldine-Atherton.

BANDURA, A. (1971b). Psychotherapy based upon modeling principles. In A. E. Bergin & S. L. Garfield (Eds.), *Handbook of psychotherapy and behavior change.* New York: Wiley.

BANDURA, A. (1974). Behavior therapy and the models of man. *American Psychologist, 29,* 859–869.

BANDURA, A. (1977). *Social learning theory.* Englewood Cliffs, NJ: Prentice-Hall.

BANDURA, A. (1986). *Social foundations of thought and action: A social cognitive theory.* Englewood Cliffs, NJ: Prentice-Hall.

* BECK, A. T. (1976). *Cognitive therapy and emotional disorders.* New York: New American Library.

BECK, A. T., & WEISHAAR, M. E. (1995). Cognitive therapy. In R. J. Corsini & D. Wedding (Eds.), *Current psychotherapies* (4th ed.) (pp. 285–320). Itasca, IL: F. E. Peacock.

CHAMBLESS, D. L. (1995). Training in and dissemination of empirically-validated psychological treatments: Report and recommendations. *The Clinical Psychologist, 48,* 3–24.

COREY, G. (1995). *Theory and practice of group counseling* (4th ed.). Pacific Grove, CA: Brooks/Cole.

* COREY, G. (1996). *Case approach to counseling and psychotherapy* (4th ed.). Pacific Grove, CA: Brooks/Cole.

* CORMIER, W. H., & CORMIER, L. S. (1991). *Interviewing strategies for helpers: Fundamental skills and cognitive behavioral interventions* (3rd ed.). Pacific Grove, CA: Brooks/Cole.

* GLASS, C. R., & ARNKOFF, D. B. (1992). Behavior therapy. In D. K. Freedheim (Ed.), *History of psychotherapy: A century of change* (pp. 587–628). Washington, DC: American Psychological Association.

* GOLDFRIED, M. R., & DAVISON, G. C. (1976). *Clinical behavior therapy.* New York: Holt, Rinehart & Winston.

* GRANVOLD, D. K., & WODARSKI, J. S. (1994). Cognitive and behavioral treatment: Clinical issues, transfer of training, and relapse prevention. In D. K. Granvold (Ed.), *Cognitive and behavioral treatment: Method and applications* (pp. 353–375). Pacific Grove, CA: Brooks/Cole.

JACOBSON, E. (1938). *Progressive relaxation.* Chicago: University of Chicago Press.

KANFER, F. H., & GAELICK, L. (1986). Self-management methods. In F. H. Kanfer & A. P. Goldstein (Eds.), *Helping people change: A textbook of methods* (3rd ed.) (pp. 283–345). New York: Pergamon Press.

KANFER, F. H., & GOLDSTEIN, A. P. (1986). Introduction. In F. H. Kanfer & A. P. Goldstein (Eds.), *Helping people change: A textbook of methods* (3rd ed.) (pp. 1–18). New York: Pergamon Press.

KAZDIN, A. E. (1978). *History of behavior modification: Experimental foundations of contemporary research.* Baltimore: University Park Press.

KAZDIN, A. E. (1982). Symptom substitution, generalization, and response covariation: Implications for psychotherapy outcome. *Psychological Bulletin, 91,* 349–365.

* KAZDIN, A. E. (1994). *Behavior modification in applied settings* (5th ed.). Pacific Grove, CA: Brooks/Cole.

KAZDIN, A. E., & WILSON, G. T. (1978). *Evaluation of behavior therapy: Issues, evidence, and research strategies.* Cambridge, MA: Ballinger.

KUEHNEL, J. M., & LIBERMAN, R. P. (1986). Behavior modification. In I. L. Kutash & A. Wolf (Eds.), *Psychotherapist's casebook* (pp. 240–262). San Francisco: Jossey-Bass.

LAZARUS, A. A. (1971). *Behavior therapy and beyond.* New York: McGraw-Hill.

LAZARUS, A. A. (1986). Multimodal therapy. In J. C. Norcross (Ed.), *Handbook of eclectic psychotherapy* (pp. 65–93). New York: Brunner/Mazel.

LAZARUS, A. A. (1987a). The multimodal approach with adult outpatients. In N. S. Jacobson (Ed.), *Psychotherapists in clinical practice.* New York: Guilford Press.

LAZARUS, A. A. (1987b). The need for technical eclecticism: Science, breadth, depth, and specificity. In J. K. Zeig (Ed.), *The evolution of psychotherapy* (pp. 164–178). New York: Brunner/Mazel.

LAZARUS, A. A. (Ed.). (1988). *Casebook of multimodal therapy.* New York: Guilford Press.

* LAZARUS, A. A. (1989). *The practice of multimodal therapy.* Baltimore: John Hopkins University Press.

LAZARUS, A. A. (1990). Multimodal therapy. In J. K. Zeig & W. M. Munion (Eds.), *What is psychotherapy? Contemporary perspectives* (pp. 221–225). San Francisco: Jossey-Bass.

LAZARUS, A. A. (1992a). The multimodal approach to the treatment of minor depression. *American Journal of Psychotherapy, 46*(1), 50–57.

* LAZARUS, A. A. (1992b). Multimodal therapy: Technical eclecticism with minimal integration. In J. C. Norcross & M. R. Goldfried (Eds.), *Handbook of psychotherapy integration* (pp. 231–263). New York: Basic Books.

LAZARUS, A. A. (1995). Multimodal therapy. In R. Corsini & D. Wedding (Eds.), *Current psychotherapies* (5th ed.) (pp. 322–355). Itasca, IL: F. E. Peacock.

LAZARUS, A. A., & BEUTLER, L. E. (1993). On technical eclecticism. *Journal of Counseling and Development, 71*(4), 381–385.

LAZARUS, A. A., BEUTLER, L. E., & NORCROSS, J. C. (1992). The future of technical eclecticism. *Psychotherapy, 29*(1), 11–20.

LAZARUS, A. A., & FAY, A. (1984). Behavior therapy. In T. B. Karasu (Ed.), *The psychiatric therapies* (pp. 483–538). Washington, DC: American Psychiatric Association.

LAZARUS, A. A., & LAZARUS, C. N. (1991). *Multimodal life-history inventory.* Champaign, IL: Research Press.

LAZARUS, A. A., & MAYNE, T. J. (1990). Relaxation: Some proposed limitations, side effects, and proposed solutions. *Psychotherapy, 27*(2), 261–266.

LONDON, P. (1986). *The modes and morals of psychotherapy* (2nd ed.). Washington, DC: Hemisphere.

MAHONEY, M. J. (1977). Reflections on the cognitive-learning trend in psychotherapy. *American Psychologist, 32,* 5–13.

MAHONEY, M. J. (1979). *Self-change: Strategies for solving personal problems.* New York: Norton.

* MAHONEY, M. J. (1991). *Human change processes: The scientific foundations of psychotherapy.* New York: Basic Books.

MAHONEY, M. J., & THORESEN, C. E. (1974). *Self-control: Power to the person.* Pacific Grove, CA: Brooks/Cole.

* MEICHENBAUM, D. (1977). *Cognitive behavior modification: An integrative approach.* New York: Plenum.

MEICHENBAUM, D. (1985). *Stress inoculation training.* New York: Pergamon Press.

MORRIS, R. J. (1986). Fear reduction methods. In F. H. Kanfer & A. P. Goldstein (Eds.), *Helping people change: A textbook of methods* (3rd ed.) (pp. 145–190). New York: Pergamon Press.

PAUL, G. L. (1967). Outcome research in psychotherapy. *Journal of Consulting Psychology, 31,* 109–188.

PERRY, M. A., & FURUKAWA, M. J. (1986). Modeling methods. In F. H. Kanfer & A. P. Goldstein (Eds.), *Helping people change: A textbook of methods* (3rd ed.) (pp. 66–110). New York: Pergamon Press.

PROCHASKA, J. O., & NORCROSS, J. C. (1994). *Systems of psychotherapy: A trans-theoretical analysis* (3rd ed.). Pacific Grove, CA: Brooks/Cole.

REHM, L. P., & ROKKE, P. (1988). Self-management therapies. In K. S. Dobson (Ed.), *Handbook of cognitive-behavioral therapies* (pp. 136–166). New York: Guilford Press.

ROBERTS, T. K., JACKSON, L. J., & PHELPS, R. (1980). Lazarus's multimodal therapy model applied in an institutional setting. *Professional Psychology, 11,* 150–156.

SKINNER, B. F. (1948). *Walden II.* New York: Macmillan.

SKINNER, B. F. (1971). *Beyond freedom and dignity.* New York: Knopf.

SLOANE, R. B., STAPLES, F. R., CRISTOL, A. H., YORKSTON, N. J., & WHIPPLE, K. (1975). *Psychotherapy versus behavior therapy.* Cambridge, MA: Harvard University Press.

* SPIEGLER, M. D., & GUEVREMONT, D. C. (1993). *Contemporary behavior therapy* (2nd ed.). Pacific Grove, CA: Brooks/Cole.

TANAKA-MATSUMI, J., & HIGGINBOTHAM, H. N. (1994). Clinical application of behavior therapy across ethnic and cultural boundaries. *The Behavior Therapist, 17*(6), 123–126.

THORESEN, C. E., & COATES, T. J. (1980). What does it mean to be a behavior therapist? In C. E. Thoresen (Ed.), *The behavior therapist.* Pacific Grove, CA: Brooks/Cole.

VOLTZ, L. M., & EVANS, I. M. (1982). The assessment of behavioral interrelationships in child behavior therapy. *Behavioral Assessment, 4,* 131–165.

* WATSON, D. L., & THARP, R. G. (1993). *Self-directed behavior: Self-modification for personal adjustment* (6th ed.). Pacific Grove, CA: Brooks/Cole.

WILSON, G. T. (1978). Cognitive behavior therapy: Paradigm shift or passing phase? In J. P. Foreyt & D. P. Rathjen (Eds.), *Cognitive behavior therapy: Research and applications.* New York: Plenum.

WILSON, G. T. (1995). Behavior therapy. In R. J. Corsini & D. Wedding (Eds.), *Current psychotherapies* (5th ed.) (pp. 197–228). Itasca, IL: F. E. Peacock.

WILSON, G. T., & AGRAS, W. S. (1992). The future of behavior therapy. *Psychotherapy, 29*(1), 39–43.

WOLPE, J. (1958). *Psychotherapy by reciprocal inhibition.* Stanford, CA: Stanford University Press.

WOLPE, J. (1990). *The practice of behavior therapy* (4th ed.). Elmsford, NY: Pergamon Press.

# Cognitive-Behavior Therapy

# ALBERT ELLIS

ALBERT ELLIS (b. 1913) was born in Pittsburgh but escaped to the wilds of New York at the age of 4 and has lived there (except for a year in New Jersey) ever since. He was hospitalized nine times as a child, mainly with nephritis, and developed renal glycosuria at the age of 19 and diabetes at the age of 40. But by rigorously taking care of his health and stubbornly refusing to make himself miserable about it, he has lived an unusually robust and energetic life.

Realizing that he could counsel people skillfully and that he greatly enjoyed doing so, Ellis decided to become a psychologist. Eight years after he had graduated from college, he matriculated in the clinical psychology program at Teachers College, Columbia. He began practicing in the areas of marriage, family, and sex therapy. Ellis, believing psychoanalysis to be the deepest form of psychotherapy, was analyzed and supervised by a training analyst of the Karen Horney school. From 1947 to 1953 he practiced classical analysis and analytically oriented psychotherapy.

After coming to the conclusion that psychoanalysis was a relatively superficial and unscientific form of treatment, he experimented with several other systems.

Early in 1955 he combined humanistic, philosophical, and behavioral therapy to form rational-emotive therapy (now known as rational emotive behavior therapy, or REBT). Ellis is rightly known as the grandfather of cognitive-behavior therapy.

To some extent Ellis developed his approach as a method of dealing with his own problems during his youth. At one point in his life, for example, he had exaggerated fears of speaking in public. During his adolescence he was extremely shy around girls. At age 19 he forced himself to talk to 100 women in the Bronx Botanical Gardens over a period of one month. Although he never managed to get a date from these brief encounters, he does report that he desensitized himself to his fear of rejection by women. By applying cognitive-behavioral methods, he has managed to conquer some of his worst blocks (Ellis, 1979c, 1994). Moreover, he has learned to actually *enjoy* public speaking and other activities about which he was once highly anxious.

People who hear Ellis lecture often comment about his abrasive, humorous, and flamboyant style (Dryden, 1989). He does see himself as more abrasive than most in his workshops, and he also considers himself humorous and startling in some ways. In his workshops it seems that he takes delight in giving vent to his eccentric side. He enjoys his work, which is his primary commitment in life.

Ellis is a highly energetic and productive person and is surely one of the most prolific writers in the field of counseling and psychotherapy. In his busy professional life he sees as many as 80 clients a week for individual sessions, conducts five group-therapy sessions weekly, and gives about 200 talks and workshops to professionals and the public each year. He has published over 50 books and more than 700 articles, mostly on the theory and applications of REBT.

# Introduction

Arnkoff and Glass (1992) provide a brief historical sketch of the development of cognitive approaches to therapy. These treatment approaches were initiated at a time when behavior therapy was in its prime. In the 1950s Ellis developed what was known as rational therapy, which he soon changed to rational-emotive therapy (RET). He announced in 1993 that he had changed the name once again, to *rational emotive behavior therapy* (REBT), because the approach had always stressed the reciprocal interactions among cognition, emotion, and behavior. The approach has always favored *in vivo* desensitization, and many REBT procedures are highly behavioral. Like the multimodal therapy of Arnold Lazarus, which was discussed in the previous chapter, the approach has pioneered a large number of thinking, feeling, and activity-oriented methods. As is true of behavior therapy, the cognitive-behavioral approaches are quite diverse, and although they share common denominators, they cannot be accurately lumped together as a unified theory.

Rational emotive behavior therapy departs radically from several of the other systems presented in this book—namely, the psychoanalytic, person-centered, and Gestalt approaches. I have selected it for inclusion because it is a challenging perspective on many of the basic issues of counseling and psychotherapy. REBT has more in common with the therapies that are oriented toward cognition and behavior in that it stresses thinking, judging, deciding, analyzing, and doing. Over the course of its development, it has always been characterized by being highly rational, persuasive, interpretative, directive, and philosophical. This approach is based on the assumption that cognitions, emotions, and behaviors interact significantly and have a reciprocal cause-and-effect relationship. REBT has consistently emphasized all three of these modalities and their interactions, thus qualifying it as a multimodal and integrative approach (Ellis, 1979a, 1979c, 1979e, 1987a, 1994, 1995).

As was mentioned in the previous chapter, behavior therapy began to broaden in the 1960s to include cognitions as legitimate behavior that could be learned and modified. Mahoney (1977) coined the term *cognitive revolution* to describe the new perspective, which recognized private events and interpersonal factors along with the importance of environmental variables. This revolution included a number of therapeutic models and techniques that incorporated the concept of cognition in behavioral clinical psychology. Although these attempts at integrating a cognitive perspective within behavior therapy were resisted by some behavior therapists, applications of the role of cognition continued to take root (Dobson, 1988b).

As REBT became more widely accepted and practiced, behavior therapists developed their own views of the cognitive dimensions of an individual's problems and devised techniques to modify cognitions. The basic assumption of this approach is that people contribute to their own psychological problems, as well as specific symptoms, by the way they interpret events and situations in their life. To a large degree cognitive-behavior therapy is based on the assumption that a reorganization of one's self-statements will result in a corresponding reorganization of one's behavior. Meichenbaum (1977) writes that within a learning-theory framework the client's cognitions are explicit behaviors that can be modified in their own right, just as are overt behaviors that can be directly observed. Thus, the behavioral techniques that have been used to modify overt behaviors, such as operant conditioning, modeling, and behavioral rehearsal (practicing a skill in a therapy session in preparation for an anticipated situation), can also be applied to the more covert and subjective processes of thinking and internal dialogue. All of the cognitive-behavioral approaches include a variety of behavioral strategies as a part of their integrative repertoire.

Although this chapter is entitled "Cognitive-Behavior Therapy," it features Ellis's rational emotive behavior therapy, largely because "REBT is regarded by many as one of the premiere examples of the cognitive-behavioral approach" (Dobson & Block, 1988). Later in this chapter I will give an overview of two other cognitive-behavioral approaches, Aaron T. Beck's *cognitive therapy* and Donald Meichenbaum's *cognitive behavior modification*.

Although there are theoretical and methodological differences among these three approaches, they share the following attributes: (1) a collaborative relationship between the client and therapist, (2) the premise that psychological distress is largely a function of disturbances in cognitive processes, (3) a focus on changing cognitions in order to produce desired changes in affect and behavior, and (4) a generally time-limited and educational treatment focusing on specific and structured target problems (Arnkoff & Glass, 1992; Dobson & Block, 1988; Weishaar, 1993). All of the cognitive-behavioral approaches are based on a structured psychoeducational model, and they all emphasize the role of homework, place responsibility on the client to assume an active role both during and outside of the therapy sessions, and draw from a variety of cognitive and behavioral strategies to bring about change.

## DEVELOPMENT OF RATIONAL EMOTIVE BEHAVIOR THERAPY

Ellis developed rational emotive behavior therapy after finding that his training as a psychoanalyst was inadequate in dealing with his clients. He argues that the psychoanalytic approach is more than inefficient, because people often seem to get worse instead of better (Ellis, 1988). Out of this conviction he began to persuade and encourage his clients to *do* the very things they were most afraid of doing, such as risking rejection by significant others. Gradually, he became much more eclectic and more active and directive as a therapist.

REBT became a general school of psychotherapy aimed at providing clients with the tools to restructure their philosophic and behavioral styles (Ellis & Yeager, 1989). Although it is generally conceded to be the parent of today's cognitive-behavioral approaches, it was preceded by earlier schools of thought. The interrelationship among cognitions, emotions, and behaviors was noted by several ancient Eastern and Western philosophers (Ellis, 1984b). Ellis acknowledges his debt to the ancient Greeks, especially the Stoic philosopher Epictetus, who is quoted as having said, in the first century A.D., "People are disturbed not by things, but by the view which they take of them" (Ellis, 1995). Horney's (1950) ideas on the "tyranny of the shoulds" are apparent in the conceptual framework of REBT. Ellis also gives credit to Adler as an influential precursor. As you will recall, Adler writes that our emotional reactions and lifestyle are associated with our basic beliefs and are therefore cognitively created. Like the Adlerian approach, REBT emphasizes the role of social interest in determining psychological health. There are other Adlerian influences on REBT, such as the importance of goals, purposes, values, and meanings in human existence; the focus on active teaching; the use of persuasive methods; and the giving of live demonstrations before an audience (Dryden & Ellis, 1988).

REBT's basic hypothesis, then, is that our emotions stem mainly from our beliefs, evaluations, interpretations, and reactions to life situations. Through the therapeutic process, clients learn skills that give them the tools to identify and dispute irrational beliefs that have been learned and self-constructed and are now maintained by self-indoctrination. They learn how to replace such ineffective ways of thinking with effective and rational cognitions, and as a result they change their emotional reactions to situations. The therapeutic process allows clients to apply REBT principles of change not only to a particular presenting problem but also to many other problems in life or future ones they might encounter. Several therapeutic implications flow from these assumptions: The focus in on working with *thinking* and *acting* rather than primarily with expressing feelings. Therapy is seen as an *educational* process. The therapist functions in many ways like a teacher, especially in collaborating with a client on homework assignments and in teaching strategies for straight thinking; and the client is a learner, who practices the skills that are being discussed in therapy in everyday life.

The concepts of cognitive-behavior therapy raise several key questions that you would do well to keep in mind as you read this chapter: Is psychotherapy essentially a process of reeducation? Is it appropriate for therapists to use persuasion and highly directive methods? How effective is it to attempt to help clients reduce their faulty thinking by using questions, logic, advice, information, and interpretations? Will changing one's thoughts often lead to changing how one feels and acts? What are the advantages of a collaborative client/therapist relationship?

# Key Concepts

## VIEW OF HUMAN NATURE

Rational emotive behavior therapy is based on the assumption that human beings are born with a potential for both rational, or straight, thinking and irrational, or crooked, thinking. People have predispositions for self-preservation, happiness, thinking and verbalizing, loving, communion with others, and growth and self-actualization. They also have propensities for self-destruction, avoidance of thought, procrastination, endless repetition of mistakes, superstition, intolerance, perfectionism and self-blame, and avoidance of actualizing growth potentials. Taking for granted that humans are fallible, REBT attempts to help them accept themselves as creatures who will continue to make mistakes yet at the same time learn to live more at peace with themselves.

Ellis has concluded that humans are *self-talking, self-evaluating,* and *self-sustaining.* They develop emotional and behavioral difficulties when they take *simple preferences* (desires for love, approval, success) and make the mistake of thinking of them as dire needs. Ellis also affirms that humans have inborn tendencies toward growth and actualization, yet they often sabotage their movement toward growth as a result of their inborn tendency toward crooked thinking and also the self-defeating patterns they have learned (Ellis, 1991a, 1991b, 1991c; Ellis & Dryden, 1987).

## VIEW OF EMOTIONAL DISTURBANCE

We originally learn irrational beliefs from significant others during our childhood. Additionally, we create irrational dogmas and superstitions by ourselves. Then we actively reinstill self-defeating beliefs by the processes of autosuggestion and self-repetition and by behaving as if they are useful. Hence, it is largely our own repetition of early-indoctrinated irrational thoughts, rather than a parent's repetition, that keeps dysfunctional attitudes alive and operative within us.

REBT insists that blame is the core of most emotional disturbances. Therefore, if we are to recover from a neurosis or a personality disorder, we had better stop blaming ourselves and others. Instead, it is important that we learn to accept ourselves despite our imperfections. Ellis (1987b) hypothesizes that virtually all people are born with the ability to think rationally; however, we also have strong tendencies to escalate our desires and preferences into dogmatic, absolutistic "shoulds," "musts," "oughts," demands, and commands. If we stay with preferences and rational beliefs, we will not become inappropriately depressed, hostile, and self-pitying. It is when we live by demands that we disturb ourselves. Our unrealistic and illogical ideas create disruptive feelings and also create dysfunctional behaviors (Ellis, 1987b).

Ellis (1988) contends that because we largely create our own disturbed thoughts and feelings, we have the power to control our emotional destiny. He suggests that when we are upset, it is a good idea to look to our hidden dogmatic "musts" and absolutistic "shoulds." Absolutistic cognitions are at the core of human misery, because most of the time these beliefs impede and obstruct people in their pursuit of their goals and purposes. Practically all human self-destructiveness and serious neurotic turmoil are unnecessary. We create, both consciously and unconsciously, the ways we think and, hence, the ways we feel in a variety of situations. Because we have the capacity for self-awareness, we can observe and evaluate our goals and purposes and, thus, can change them. We are able to creatively decide to feel differently about a situation and therefore stubbornly refuse to make ourselves severely anxious or depressed about anything (Ellis, 1988).

REBT contends that people do not *need* to be accepted and loved, even though it may be highly desirable. The therapist teaches clients how to feel undepressed even when they are unaccepted and unloved by significant others. Although REBT encourages people to experience sadness over being unaccepted, it attempts to help them find ways of overcoming depression, anxiety, hurt, loss of self-worth, and hatred.

Here are some irrational ideas that we internalize and that inevitably lead to self-defeat (Dryden & Ellis, 1988; Ellis, 1987b, 1988):

- "I *must* have love or approval from all the significant people in my life."
- "I *must* perform important tasks competently and perfectly well."
- "Because I strongly desire that people treat me considerately and fairly, they *absolutely must* do so!"
- "If I don't get what I want, it's terrible, and I can't stand it."
- "It's easier to avoid facing life's difficulties and responsibilities than to undertake more rewarding forms of self-discipline."

Most humans have a strong tendency to make and keep themselves emotionally disturbed by internalizing self-defeating beliefs such as the ones listed above. Therefore, they find it virtually impossible to achieve and maintain good mental health (Ellis, 1987b).

## A-B-C THEORY OF PERSONALITY

As we have seen, the basic tenet of REBT is that emotional disturbances (as distinguished from feelings of sorrow, regret, and frustration) are largely the product of irrational, self-defeating thinking. The irrational quality comes from *demanding* that the universe *should, ought to,* and *must* be different. From the REBT perspective, many therapists err by focusing on past history and activating events, as if anything could be done to change the client's early childhood. Other therapists make the mistake of overemphasizing the effort to have clients recognize, express, and ventilate feelings. Some urge clients to relive early events and feelings in the present. Ellis would say that this tactic is not too productive, because emotional consequences will not vanish merely because feelings have been intensified and expressed. Instead, the client and the therapist work together to dispute the irrational beliefs that are causing disturbed emotional consequences. They work toward transforming an unrealistic, immature, demanding, and absolutist style of thinking into a realistic, mature, logical, and empirical approach to thinking and behaving. This results in more appropriate feeling reactions to life's situations.

The following diagram will clarify the interaction of the various components being discussed:

A (activating event) ⟵— B (belief) —⟶ C (emotional and behavioral consequence)

⟰

D (disputing intervention) —⟶ E (effect) —⟶ F (new feeling)

The A-B-C theory of personality is central to REBT theory and practice. A is the existence of a fact, an event, or the behavior or attitude of an individual. C is the emotional and behavioral consequence or reaction of the individual; the reaction can be either appropriate or inappropriate. A (the activating event) does not cause C (the emotional consequence). Instead, B, which is the person's belief about A, largely causes C, the emotional reaction. For example, if a person experiences depression after a divorce, it may not be the divorce itself that causes the depressive reaction but the person's *beliefs* about being a failure, being rejected, or losing a mate. Ellis would maintain that the beliefs about the rejection and failure (at point B) are what mainly cause the depression (at point C), not the actual event of the divorce (at point A). Thus, human beings are largely responsible for creating their own emotional reactions and disturbances. Showing people how they can change the irrational beliefs that directly "cause" their disturbed emotional consequences is the heart of REBT (Ellis, 1979b).

How is an emotional disturbance fostered? It is fed by the illogical sentences that the person continually repeats to himself or herself, such as "I am totally to blame for the divorce," "I am a miserable failure, and everything I did was wrong," "I am a worthless person." Ellis repeatedly makes the point that "you mainly feel the way you think." Disturbed emotional reactions such as depression and anxiety are initiated and perpetuated by the self-defeating belief system, which is based on irrational ideas that one has incorporated and invented.

After A, B, and C comes D, disputing. Essentially, D is the application of the scientific method to help clients challenge their irrational beliefs. Because the principles of logic can be taught, they can be used to destroy any unrealistic, unverifiable hypothesis. Ellis and Bernard (1986) describe three components of this disputing process: detecting, debating, and discriminating. First, clients learn how to *detect* their irrational beliefs, particularly their absolutistic "shoulds" and "musts," their "awfulizing," and their "self-downing." Then clients *debate* their dysfunctional beliefs by learning how to logically and empirically question them and to vigorously argue themselves out of and act against believing them. Finally, clients learn to *discriminate* irrational (self-defeating) beliefs from rational (self-helping) beliefs.

Although REBT uses many other cognitive, emotive, and behavioral methods to help clients minimize their irrational beliefs, it stresses this process of disputing both during the therapy sessions and in outside life. Eventually clients arrive at E, an effective philosophy, which has a practical side. A new and effective rational philosophy consists of replacing inappropriate thoughts with appropriate ones. If we are successful in doing this, we also create F, or a new set of feelings. Instead of feeling seriously anxious or depressed, we feel appropriately in accord with a situation. The best way to begin to feel better is to develop an effective and rational philosophy. Thus, instead of berating oneself and punishing oneself with depression over the divorce, one would reach a rational and empirically based conclusion: "Well, I'm genuinely sorry that our marriage didn't work out and that we divorced. Although I wish we could have worked things out, we didn't, and that isn't the end of the world. Because our marriage failed doesn't mean that I'm a failure in life, and it's foolish for me to continue blaming myself and making myself wholly responsible for the breakup." According to REBT theory, the ultimate effect is the minimizing of feelings of depression and self-condemnation.

In sum, philosophical restructuring to change our dysfunctional personality involves the following steps: (1) fully acknowledging that we are largely responsible for creating our own emotional problems; (2) accepting the notion that we have the ability to change these disturbances significantly; (3) recognizing that our emotional problems largely stem from irrational beliefs; (4) clearly perceiving these beliefs; (5) seeing the value of disputing such foolish beliefs, using rigorous methods; (6) accepting the fact that if we expect to change, we had better work hard in emotive and behavioral ways to counteract our beliefs and the dysfunctional feelings and actions that follow; and (7) practicing REBT methods of uprooting or changing disturbed consequences for the rest of our life (Ellis, 1979d, 1988).

# The Therapeutic Process

## THERAPEUTIC GOALS

The many roads taken in rational emotive behavior therapy lead toward the one destination of clients minimizing their emotional disturbances and self-defeating behaviors by acquiring a more realistic and workable philosophy of life. Other important therapeutic goals include reducing a tendency for blaming oneself or others for what goes wrong in life and learning ways to deal with future difficulties.

REBT strives for a thorough philosophical reevaluation based on the assumption that human problems are philosophically rooted. Thus, it is not aimed primarily at removing symptoms. It is mainly designed to induce people to examine and change some of their most basic values that keep them disturbed. If a client's fear is of failing in her marriage, the aim is not merely to reduce that specific fear; instead, the therapist attempts to work with her exaggerated fears of failing in general.

Following are specific goals toward which REBT therapists work with their clients: self-interest, social interest, self-direction, tolerance, flexibility, acceptance of uncertainty, commitment, scientific thinking, self-acceptance, risk taking, high tolerance of frustration, and self-responsibility for disturbance (Ellis, 1979c, 1991a; Ellis & Bernard, 1986; Ellis & Dryden, 1987).

## THERAPIST'S FUNCTION AND ROLE

To achieve the aims just detailed, the therapist has specific tasks. One of the first steps is to show clients that they have incorporated many irrational "shoulds," "oughts," and "musts." Clients learn to separate their rational beliefs from their irrational ones. To foster this awareness, the therapist serves the function of a scientist who challenges the self-defeating idea that the client originally accepted or invented without question as truth. The therapist encourages, persuades, and at times even directs the client to engage in activities that will counter this propaganda.

A second step in the therapeutic process takes clients beyond the stage of awareness. It demonstrates that they are keeping their emotional disturbances active by continuing to think illogically and by repeating self-defeating meanings and philosophies. In other words, because clients keep reindoctrinating themselves, they are largely responsible for their own neuroses. That the therapist merely shows clients that they have illogical processes is not enough, for a client is likely to say: "Now I understand that I have fears of failing and that these fears are exaggerated and unrealistic. But I'm still afraid of failing!"

To get beyond client's mere recognition of irrational thoughts and feelings, the therapist takes a third step: helping them modify their thinking and abandon their irrational ideas. REBT assumes that their self-defeating beliefs are so deeply ingrained that clients will not normally change them by themselves. The therapist therefore assists them in understanding the vicious circle of the self-blaming process.

The fourth step in the therapeutic process is to challenge clients to develop a rational philosophy of life so that in the future they can avoid becoming the victim of other irrational beliefs. Tackling only specific problems or symptoms can give no assurance that new illogical fears will not emerge. What is desirable, then, is for the therapist to dispute the core of the irrational thinking and to teach clients how to substitute rational beliefs and attitudes for the irrational ones; the more scientific and tolerant clients become, Ellis contends, the less disturbed they will be.

A therapist who works within this framework functions differently from most other practitioners. Because REBT is essentially a cognitive and directive behavioral process, it often minimizes the intense relationship between the therapist and the client. The therapist mainly employs a persuasive methodology that emphasizes education. Ellis outlines what the REBT practitioner does (1991a, 1991c, 1992b, 1994, 1995; Ellis & Velten, 1992):

- encourages clients to discover a few basic irrational ideas that motivate much disturbed behavior
- challenges clients to validate their ideas
- demonstrates to clients the illogical nature of their thinking
- uses absurdity and humor to confront the irrationality of clients' thinking
- uses a logical analysis to minimize these irrational beliefs
- shows how these beliefs are inoperative and how they will lead to future emotional and behavioral disturbances
- explains how these ideas can be replaced with more rational ideas that are empirically grounded
- teaches clients how to apply the scientific approach to thinking so that they can observe and minimize present or future irrational ideas and illogical deductions that foster self-destructive ways of feeling and behaving
- uses several cognitive, emotive, and behavioral methods to help clients work directly on their feelings and to act against their disturbances

Wessler and Wessler (1980) describe the evolution of a typical REBT case. During the critical first session the focus is on building rapport and creating the kind of client/therapist relationship that will encourage the client to talk freely. Once a collaborative and therapeutic alliance is formed, the relationship aspect is given less emphasis. Therapy proceeds by identifying those problems that will be targeted for exploration. Goal setting is a major task during the early phase of therapy. Clients identify beliefs, feelings, and actions that they would like to acquire or increase as well as merely listing ones they want to reduce or eliminate. A therapist might ask, "In what ways would you like to think, feel, and act differently than you do now?"

Clients are then oriented to the basic principles and practices of REBT. Therapists take the mystery out of the therapeutic process. They teach clients about the cognitive hypothesis of disturbance, showing how irrational beliefs lead to negative consequences. When clients understand that certain irrational beliefs lead to dysfunctional emotions and behaviors, the therapist challenges them to examine why they are clinging to the old misconceptions instead of letting go of them.

Homework is carefully designed and agreed upon, aimed at getting clients to carry out positive actions and induce emotional and attitudinal change. These assignments are checked in later sessions, and clients learn effective ways to dispute self-defeating thinking. Toward the end of therapy, clients review their progress, make plans, and identify strategies for dealing with continuing or potential problems.

In summary, REBT therapists actively *teach* clients that self-condemnation is one of the main causes of emotional disturbance; that it is possible to stop *rating* themselves on their performances; and that by hard work and by carrying out behavioral homework assignments, they can minimize irrational thinking that leads to disturbances in feeling and behaving.

REBT differs from many other therapeutic approaches in that it does not place much value on free association, working with dreams, focusing on the client's past history, endlessly expressing and exploring feelings, and dealing with transference phenomena. Ellis (1995) believes that devoting any length of time to these factors is "indulgence therapy," which might result in clients' *feeling* better but will rarely aid them in *getting* better.

## CLIENT'S EXPERIENCE IN THERAPY

Once clients begin to accept that their beliefs are the primary cause of their emotions and behaviors, they are able to participate effectively in the cognitive-restructuring process (Ellis & Yeager, 1989). Thus, to a large measure, the client's role in REBT is that of a learner. Psychotherapy is viewed as a reeducative process whereby the client learns how to apply logical thought to problem solving and emotional change.

The therapeutic process focuses on the client's experience in the present. Like the person-centered and existential approaches to therapy, REBT mainly emphasizes here-and-now experiences and clients' present ability to change the patterns of thinking and emoting that they constructed earlier. The therapist does not devote much time to exploring client's early history and making connections between their past and present behavior. Nor does the therapist usually explore in depth their early relationships with their parents or siblings. Instead, the therapeutic process stresses that regardless of clients' basic, irrational philosophies of life, they are presently disturbed because they still believe in their self-defeating view of themselves and their world. Questions of where, why, or how they acquired their irrational philosophy are of secondary importance. The central issue is how clients can become aware of their self-defeating tacit philosophies and can challenge and act against them.

According to REBT theory, superficial insight alone does not typically lead to personality change, for at best it teaches people that they have problems and that there are factors antecedent to these disturbances. Even when insight is correct, it does not automatically make a situation better. Insight can help us see how we are continuing to sabotage ourselves and what we can do to change.

Ellis (1979e, 1988) describes three main levels of insight in REBT. The first level refers to the fact that we choose to disturb ourselves about events in our lives. We largely upset ourselves at point C (consequences) and do not merely get upset by the events at point A (activating events). We upset ourselves by accepting and inventing irrational beliefs. The second level of insight pertains to the ways in which we acquired our irrational beliefs originally and how we are choosing to maintain them. How, when, or why we originally became emotionally disturbed is not important; rather, we remain this way today because we keep reindoctrinating ourselves with our absolutistic beliefs. Our self-conditioning is more important than our early conditioning by others. The third level of insight involves the recognition that there are no magical ways for us to change our personality and our tendencies to upset ourselves. We can usually change only if we are willing to work and practice. Mere acceptance that a belief is irrational is generally not enough to bring about change. No matter how clearly we see that we are upsetting ourselves and making ourselves miserable, we will rarely improve unless we actively change our disturbance-creating beliefs and act against them.

## RELATIONSHIP BETWEEN THERAPIST AND CLIENT

The issue of the personal relationship between the therapist and the client takes on a different meaning in REBT than it has in most other forms of therapy. In close agreement with the person-centered concept of unconditional positive regard is REBT's concept of *full acceptance,* or *tolerance.* The basic idea here is to help clients avoid self-condemnation. Although they may evaluate their behavior, the goal is for them to refuse to rate themselves as persons, no matter how ineffectual some of their behavior is. Therapists show their full acceptance by refusing to evaluate their clients as persons while at the same time being willing to honestly confront clients' nonsensical thinking and self-destructive behaviors. Unlike the relationship-oriented therapies, REBT does not place a premium on personal warmth and empathic understanding, on the assumption that too much warmth and understanding can be counterproductive by fostering a sense of dependence for approval from the therapist. In fact, REBT therapists can accept their clients as imperfect beings without giving personal warmth, instead using a variety of impersonal techniques such as teaching, bibliotherapy, and behavior modification (Ellis, 1995), but always modeling as well as teaching unconditional full acceptance. Some REBT practitioners, however, give more emphasis to the importance of building rapport and a collaborative relationship than does Ellis.

Rational emotive behavior therapists are often open and direct in disclosing their own beliefs and values. Some are willing to share their own imperfections as a way of disputing the client's unrealistic notion that therapists are "completely put together" persons. Along this line, transference is not encouraged, and when it does occur, the therapist is likely to attack it. The therapist wants to show that a transference relationship is based on the irrational belief that the client must be liked and loved by the therapist (or parent figure) (Ellis, 1995).

# Application: Therapeutic Techniques and Procedures

## THE PRACTICE OF RATIONAL EMOTIVE BEHAVIOR THERAPY

Rational emotive behavior therapists are multimodal and integrative and use a variety of cognitive, affective, and behavioral techniques, tailoring them to individual clients. These techniques are applied to the treatment of a range of common clinical problems such as anxiety, depression, anger, marital difficulties, poor interpersonal skills, parenting failures, personality disorders, obsessive/compulsive disorders, eating disorders, psychosomatic disorders, addictions, and psychotic disorders (Warren & McLellarn, 1987). What follows is a brief summary of the major cognitive, emotive, and behavioral techniques Ellis describes (Dryden & Ellis, 1988; Ellis, 1979a, 1986a; Ellis & Dryden, 1987; Ellis & Yeager, 1989; Ellis & Velten, 1992).

COGNITIVE METHODS.    REBT practitioners usually incorporate into the therapeutic process a forceful cognitive methodology. They demonstrate to clients in a quick and direct manner what it is that they are continuing to tell themselves. Then they teach them how to deal with these self-statements so that they no longer believe them, encouraging them to acquire a philosophy based on reality. REBT relies heavily on thinking, disputing, debating, challenging, interpreting, explaining, and teaching. A few of these cognitive techniques that are available to the therapist are:

• *Disputing irrational beliefs.* The most common cognitive method of REBT consists of the therapist's actively disputing clients' irrational beliefs and teaching them how to do this challenging on their own. The therapist quickly challenges irrational beliefs by asking questions such as "Where is the evidence for your beliefs? Why is it *terrible* and *horrible* if life is not the way you want it to be? Where is it written that you *cannot stand* a situation? Why do you assume that you are a *rotten person* because of the way you behave? Would it really be catastrophic if your worst fantasies were to come true? Through a series of refutations, therapists are instrumental in raising the consciousness of their clients to a more rational (self-helping) level. Clients work on a major irrationality (especially an absolutistic "must") in a systematic way on a daily basis. They go over a particular "must," "should," or "ought" until they no longer hold that irrational belief, or at least until it is diminished in strength. Some examples of questions or statements that clients learn to tell themselves are "Why *must* people treat me fairly?" "Where did I learn that I will be a total flop if I don't succeed in everything I try?" "If I don't get the job I want, it may be disappointing, but I can certainly stand it." "If life doesn't always go the way I would like it to, it isn't *awful*, just inconvenient."

• *Cognitive homework.* REBT clients are expected to make lists of their problems, look for their absolutistic beliefs, and dispute these beliefs. They agree upon given homework assignments, which is a way of tracking down the absolutistic "shoulds" and "musts" that are a part of their internalized self-messages. Part of homework consists of applying the A-B-C theory to many of the problems they encounter in daily life. They often fill out the REBT Self-Help Form (which is reproduced in the student manual of this text). Clients are encouraged to put themselves in risk-taking situations that will allow them to challenge their self-limiting beliefs. For example, a person with a talent for acting who is afraid to act in front of an audience because of fear of failure may be asked to take a small part in a stage play. The person is instructed to replace negative self-statements such as "I will fail," "I will look foolish," or "No one will like me" with more positive messages such as "Even if I do behave foolishly at times, this does not make me a foolish *person*. I can act. I will do the best I can. It's nice to be liked, but not everybody will like me, and that isn't the end of the world." The theory behind this and similar assignments is that people often create a negative, self-fulfilling prophecy and actually fail because they told themselves in advance that they would. Clients are encouraged to carry out specific assignments during the sessions and, especially, in everyday situations between sessions. In this way they gradually learn to deal with anxiety and challenge basic irrational thinking. Because therapy is seen as an educational process, clients are also encouraged to read REBT self-help books, such as Ellis's *How to Stubbornly Refuse to Make Yourself Miserable about Anything—Yes, Anything!* (1988). They also listen to and criticize tapes of their own therapy sessions. Making changes is hard work, and doing work outside of the sessions is of real value in revising one's thinking, feeling, and behaving.

• *Changing one's language.* REBT contends that imprecise language is one of the causes of distorted thinking processes. Practitioners pay particular attention to the language patterns of their clients on the grounds that language shapes thinking and that thinking shapes language. Clients learn that "musts," "oughts," and "shoulds," can be replaced by *preferences*. Instead of saying, "It would be absolutely awful if . . ." they can learn to say "It would be inconvenient if . . ." Clients who use language patterns that reflect helplessness and self-condemnation can learn to employ new self-statements. They can assume personal power by replacing their "shoulds" and "musts" with nonabsolutistic preferences. Through the process of changing their language patterns and making new self-statements, clients come to think and behave differently. As a consequence they also begin to feel differently.

• *Use of humor.* A survey has revealed that humor is one of the most popular techniques of REBT practitioners (Warren & McLellarn, 1987). Ellis himself tends to use a good deal of humor as a way to combat exaggerated thinking that leads clients into trouble (1986a). REBT contends that emotional disturbances often result from taking oneself too seriously and losing one's sense of perspective and humor over the events of life. Consequently, counselors employ humor to counterattack the overserious side of individuals and to assist them in disputing their *must*urbatory philosophy of life. In his workshops and therapy sessions Ellis typically uses humorous songs, and he encourages people to sing to themselves or in groups when they feel depressed or anxious (Ellis & Yeager, 1989). He believes that humor shows the absurdity of certain ideas that clients steadfastly maintain. It is one approach that can be of value in helping clients take themselves much less seriously.

EMOTIVE TECHNIQUES.    Emotively, REBT practitioners use a variety of procedures, including unconditional acceptance, rational-emotive role playing, modeling, rational-emotive imagery, and shame-attacking exercises. Clients are taught the value of unconditional acceptance. Even though their behavior may be difficult to accept, they can decide to see themselves as worthwhile persons. They are taught how destructive it is to engage in "putting oneself down" for perceived deficiencies. One of the main techniques that therapists employ to teach clients how to accept themselves is modeling. Therapists are able to be themselves in the sessions; they avoid seeking the approval of their clients, do not live by "shoulds" and "musts," and are willing to risk themselves as they continue to challenge their clients. They also model or display full acceptance of difficult clients.

It should be noted that regardless of the client's presenting problem, REBT practitioners do not necessarily focus on all its details, nor do they attempt to get the client to extensively express feelings surrounding the problem. Although REBT employs a variety of emotive and forceful therapeutic strategies, it does so in a selective and discriminating manner. These strategies are used both during the therapy sessions and as homework assignments in daily life. Their purpose is not simply to provide a cathartic experience but to help clients *change* some of their thoughts, emotions, and behavior (Ellis & Yeager, 1989). These evocative and emotive therapeutic techniques include the following:

• *Rational-emotive imagery.* This technique is a form of intense mental practice designed to establish new emotional patterns. Clients imagine themselves thinking, feeling, and behaving exactly the way they would like to think, feel, and behave in real life (Maultsby, 1984). They can also be shown how to imagine one of the worst things that could happen to them, how to feel inappropriately upset about this situation, how to intensely experience their feelings, and then how to change the experience to an appropriate feeling (Ellis & Yeager, 1989). Once they are able to change their feelings to appropriate ones, they stand a better chance of changing their behavior in the situation. Such a technique can be usefully applied to interpersonal and other situations that are problematic for the individual. Ellis (1988) maintains that if we keep practicing rational-emotive imagery several times a week for a few weeks, we will reach the point that we no longer feel upset over such events. (If you are interested in an illustration of rational-emotive imagery, see Ellis, 1979a; see also Ellis's therapeutic work with a hypothetical patient, Ruth, in Corey, 1996).

• *Role playing.* There are both emotional and behavioral components in role playing. The therapist often interrupts to show clients what they are telling themselves to create their disturbances and what they can do to change their inappropriate feelings to appropriate ones. Clients can rehearse certain behaviors to bring out what they feel in a situation. The focus is on working through the underlying irrational beliefs that are related to unpleasant feelings. For example, a woman may put off applying to a graduate school because of her fears of not being accepted. Just the thought of not being accepted to the school of her choice brings out her feelings of "being stupid." She role-plays an interview with the dean of graduate students, notes her anxiety and the irrational beliefs leading to it, and challenges the irrational thoughts that she absolutely *must* be accepted and that not gaining such acceptance means that she is a stupid and incompetent person.

• *Shame-attacking exercises.* Ellis (1988) has developed exercises to help people reduce irrational shame over behaving in certain ways. He thinks that we can stubbornly refuse to feel ashamed by telling ourselves that it is not catastrophic if someone thinks we are foolish. The main point of these exercises is that clients work to feel unashamed even when others clearly disapprove of them. This procedure typically involves both emotive and behavioral components. Clients may accept a homework assignment to take the risk of doing something that they are ordinarily afraid to do because of what others might think. Minor infractions of social conventions often serve as useful catalysts. For example, clients may shout out the stops on a bus or a train, wear "loud" clothes designed to attract attention, sing at the top of their lungs, ask a silly question at a lecture, ask for a left-handed monkey wrench in a grocery store, or refuse to tip a waitress or waiter who gives them poor service. By carrying out such assignments, clients are likely to find out that other people are not really that interested in their behavior. They work on themselves so that they do not feel ashamed or humiliated. They continue practicing these exercises until they realize that their feelings of shame are self-created and until they are able to behave in less inhibited ways. Clients eventually learn that they often have no reason for continuing to let others' reactions or possible disapproval stop them from doing the things they would like to do.

• *Use of force and vigor.* Ellis has suggested the use of force and energy as a way to help clients go from intellectual to emotional insight. Clients are also shown how to conduct forceful dialogues with themselves in which they express their irrational beliefs and then powerfully dispute them. Sometimes the therapist will engage in reverse role playing by strongly clinging to the client's self-defeating philosophy; the client is asked to vigorously debate with the therapist in an attempt to persuade him or her to give up these dysfunctional ideas. Force and energy are a basic part of the shame-attacking exercises described above.

BEHAVIORAL TECHNIQUES. REBT practitioners use most of the regular behavior-therapy procedures, especially operant conditioning, self-management principles, systematic desensitization, relaxation techniques, and modeling. Behavioral homework assignments to be carried out in real-life situations are particularly important. These assignments are done systematically and are recorded and analyzed on a form. Many involve desensitization, skill training, and assertiveness training. REBT clients are encouraged to desensitize themselves gradually and also, at times, to perform the very things they dread doing. For example, a person with a fear of elevators may decrease his or her fears by going up and down in one 20 or 30 times in a day. Clients actually *do* new and difficult things, and in this way they put their insights to use in the form of concrete action. By acting differently, they also tend to change their irrational beliefs, such as "I'll always fail because I have failed so many times up to now."

## APPLICATIONS OF REBT TO CLIENT POPULATIONS

REBT has been widely applied to the treatment of anxiety, hostility, character disorders, psychotic disorders, and depression; to problems of sex, love, and marriage; to child rearing and adolescence; and to social-skills training and self-management (Ellis, 1979b). However, Ellis does not assert that all clients can be helped through logical analysis and philosophical reconstruction. Some of the main areas of application are (1) individual therapy, (2) group therapy, (3) brief therapy, (4) marital therapy, and (5) family therapy (Ellis, 1995).

1. APPLICATION TO INDIVIDUAL THERAPY.   In one-to-one work REBT tends to be focused on a specific problem. Ellis (1994) writes that most clients who are seen individually have 1 session weekly for anywhere from 5 to 50 sessions. He recommends that clients with severe emotional disturbances continue individual therapy for up to a year so that they can practice what they are learning.

2. APPLICATION TO GROUP THERAPY.   REBT is very suitable for group therapy, because the members are taught to apply its principles to one another in the group setting. They get an opportunity to practice new behaviors that involve taking risks, and they have abundant chances to do homework assignments. Members can also experience assertiveness training, role playing, and a variety of risk-taking activities. They can learn social skills and practice interacting with others in after-group sessions. Both other group members and the leader can observe their behavior and give feedback. In a group setting clients are able to engage in contacts designed to foster a radical philosophical change. Ellis recommends that most REBT clients experience group as well as individual therapy at some point.

3. BRIEF THERAPY.   By design, REBT is appropriate as a brief therapy. The A-B-C approach to changing basic disturbance-creating attitudes can be learned in from one to ten sessions. People with specific problems—such as coping with the loss of a job or dealing with retirement—are taught how to apply REBT principles to treat themselves, often with supplementary didactic materials (books, tapes, self-help forms, and the like). A useful device is for clients to tape their

therapy sessions and then listen frequently to the entire tape on their own time (Ellis, 1992b).

For both professional mental-health workers and paraprofessionals, REBT offers a useful perspective and tools for helping people who are experiencing a crisis. In most crises our cognitive perspective has a lot to do with how a particular event affects us. It is not simply the crisis itself that leads to disturbance, but how we interpret and react to the event. For example, consider a middle-aged man (Sam) who is suddenly told by his wife that she is leaving him, that she has been having a long-standing affair, and that she has never really felt love for him. Sam approaches a therapist feeling absolutely devastated, saying over and over that this proves that he is basically an "unlovable creep who will never be able to have a relationship with any woman!" In working with him, it would be useful to think of an analogy to a computer program. How can he process this new information? If for years he has viewed his wife as a person who loves and appreciates him and who will be eternally faithful to him, accepting what is happening to him will be most difficult. The therapist can work with his expectations, as well as with the self-damning things he is saying to himself. Although he may feel appropriately hurt, sad, and shocked, he can learn not to feel totally immobilized and devastated by his wife's actions. By using the tools of REBT, he can challenge his limiting view that no woman would want anything to do with him. If he eventually wants a relationship with a woman, he can challenge himself by doing what is necessary to go out and meet women. He might take a critical look at the ways he elevated his wife and the power he gave to her. In a relatively brief time Sam could begin to successfully cope with his emotional upsets by working on his thinking and self-verbalizations and by actually doing something differently.

4. MARITAL THERAPY.  REBT practitioners typically see couples together (Ellis, Sichel, Yeager, DiMattia, & DiGuiseppe, 1989). The therapist listens to each person's complaints but soon attempts to minimize guilt, depression, and hostility. The partners are taught the principles of REBT so that they can work out their differences or at least become less disturbed about them. The couple decide whether they want to work on the relationship. If they are committed to dealing with some of their basic conflicts, they make contracts, discuss compromises, and learn how to speak directly and rationally with each other. The concern is with each person as an individual, not in keeping the relationship together at all costs. As each person applies REBT principles individually, the relationship often improves (Ellis & Dryden, 1987).

5. APPLICATION TO FAMILY THERAPY.  Members of a family are helped to see that they are responsible for disturbing themselves by taking the actions of other members too seriously. They are encouraged to consider letting go of the demand that others in the family behave in ways they would like them to. Instead, REBT teaches family members that they are primarily responsible for their own actions and for changing their own reactions to the family situation. The rational emotive behavioral perspective is that one family member actually has

little power to directly change another person in the family. The family is shown that each member has the power to control his or her individual thinking and feeling patterns. Thus, each person is in control of modifying his or her behavior, which may have a real effect on the family as a unit (Ellis, 1992d).

## RESEARCH EFFORTS IN REBT

REBT is characterized by a growing collection of therapeutic strategies for assisting people in changing their maladaptive cognitions. Therapists typically use a combination of cognitive, emotive, and behavioral methods within a single session with a given client. If a particular technique does not seem to be producing results, the therapist is likely to switch to another. This technical eclecticism and therapeutic flexibility make controlled research difficult (Wessler, 1986). As enthusiastic as he is about cognitive-behavior therapy, Ellis admits that practically all REBT studies are flawed (personal communication, July 7, 1994). According to him, these studies mainly test how people *feel* and how they have changed their *thinking,* but not how they actually *behave* after therapy. He says that most of the studies focus on cognitive, not emotive and behavioral, methods.

In one of his articles, Ellis (1979c) deals with a review of research literature that supports cognitive-behavior therapy in general as well as REBT in particular. He concludes that REBT and other cognitive-behavioral approaches have "immense—indeed, almost awesome—research backing" (p. 103). In a review of outcome studies from 1977 to 1989, McGovern and Silverman (1986) and Silverman, McCarthy, & McGovern (1992) report general findings that are supportive of the efficacy of REBT. Of the 47 studies reviewed, 31 had significant findings in favor of the REBT position. In the remaining studies, the REBT treatment groups showed improvement, and in no study was another treatment technique significantly superior to REBT. The authors concluded that the efficacy of REBT had been upheld, with no significant results against the position. Other recent reviews have also shown that REBT has clinical effectiveness (Engels & Diekstra, 1987; Haaga & Davison, 1989; Jorm, 1987; Lyons & Woods, 1991).

## REBT APPLIED TO THE CASE OF STAN

The rational emotive behavior therapist has as her broad objective minimizing Stan's self-defeating attitudes and helping him acquire a more realistic outlook on life. In essence, the goal is to teach him how to identify those thoughts that result in his feeling upset and how to make functional self-statements. To begin with, she teaches him that he is keeping alive some of his irrational ideas by reindoctrinating himself in an unthinking manner and that he can learn to challenge the source of his difficulties. If he learns how to think more rationally, he may begin to feel better.

Although the role of insight is not a central concept in REBT, three levels of awareness can contribute to Stan's improvement, provided he is willing to put his insights into action. He tells his therapist that he would like to work on his fear of women and would hope to feel far less intimidated by them. He reports that he feels threatened by most women, but especially by women he perceives as powerful. In the first level of insight, he becomes aware that there is some antecedent cause of his fear of women. This cause is not that his mother tried, for example, to dominate him. Rather, it is his self-defeating beliefs that she should not have tried to dominate him and that it was, and still is, awful that she did try and that other women may dominate him, too.

On the second level of insight, Stan recognizes that he is still threatened by women and feels uncomfortable in their presence because he still believes in, and keeps repeating endlessly to himself, the faulty beliefs that he once accepted. He sees that he keeps himself in a state of panic with women because he continues to tell himself: "Women can castrate me!" or "They'll expect me to be a superman!" or some other dysfunctional notion.

The third level of insight consists of Stan's acceptance that he will not improve unless he works diligently and practices changing his self-defeating beliefs by actively disputing them and engaging in behavior that allows him to confront his fears. Once he clearly identifies some of his self-defeating beliefs, he is in a position to examine them in his therapy sessions. What follows are some of the steps his therapist might employ to assist him in changing his beliefs and also in incorporating a new set of behaviors.

First, the therapist challenges Stan to examine the many "shoulds," "oughts," and "musts" that he has blindly accepted. She confronts him on the issue of his continued repetition of specific illogical sentences and irrational beliefs, which in his case are "I always have to be strong, tough, and perfect. I'm not a man if I show any signs of weakness. If everyone didn't love me and approve of me, things would be catastrophic. If a woman rejected me, I really would be diminished to a 'nothing.' If I fail, I'm a rotten person. I'm apologetic for my existence, because I don't feel equal to others."

Second, the therapist asks Stan to evaluate the ways in which he keeps reindoctrinating himself with those self-defeating sentences. She does not only attack specific problems but also confronts the core of his irrational thinking with ideas such as the following:

> You're not your father, and you don't need to continue telling yourself that you're just like him. You no longer need to accept without question your parents' value judgments about your worth. You say that you're such a failure and that you feel inferior. Do your present activities support this? Why do you continue to be so hard on yourself? Does having been the scapegoat in your family mean that you need to continue making yourself the scapegoat?

Third, once Stan has understood the nature of his self-defeating beliefs and has become aware of how he is maintaining faulty notions about himself, the therapist urges him to work diligently at attacking them by engaging in counterpropaganda. He continues to work and practice on looking for evidence to support some of his conclusions. The counselor gives him specific homework assignments to help him deal with his fears. At one point, for instance, she asks him to explore his fears of powerful women and his reasons for continuing to tell himself: "They can castrate me. They expect me to be strong and perfect.

If I'm not careful, they'll dominate me." His homework includes approaching a woman for a date. If he succeeds in getting the date, he can challenge his catastrophic expectations of what might happen. What would be so terrible if she did not like him or if she refused the date? Why does he have to get all his confirmation from one woman? Stan tells himself over and over that he must be *approved of* by women and that if any woman rebuffs him, the consequences are more than he can bear. With awareness of the unrealistic demands he is accepting, he eventually begins to tell himself that although he prefers acceptance to rejection, it is not the end of the world if he does not get what he wants. He learns to substitute preferences and desires for "musts" and "shoulds."

In addition to using homework assignments, the therapist may employ many other behavioral techniques, such as role playing, humor, modeling, behavior rehearsal, and desensitization. She asks Stan to read some cognitive-behavioral self-help books. He can use the ideas he learns from them as he works and practices on changing. Basically, she works in an active, directive manner and focuses on cognitive and behavioral dimensions. She pays little attention to Stan's past. Instead, she highlights his present functioning and his illogical thinking and teaches him to rethink and reverbalize in a more logical and constructive way. Thus, he can learn how to be different by telling himself a new set of statements, which might include: "I can be lovable. I'm able to succeed as well as fail at times. I need not make all women into my mother. I don't have to punish myself by making myself feel guilty over past failures, because it is not essential to always be perfect."

Stan can benefit from the range of cognitive-behavioral procedures aimed at helping him learn to make constructive self-statements. He can profit from cognitive restructuring, which proceeds as follows: First, the therapist assists him in learning ways to observe his own behavior in various situations. This can best be accomplished by his completing a written rational self-analysis. He can do this by completing the REBT Self-Help Form, and it would be a good idea for him to bring the form to his therapy session. During the week he can take a particular situation that is problematic for him, paying particular attention to his automatic thoughts and internal dialogue. What is he telling himself as he approaches a difficult situation? How is he setting himself up for failure with his self-talk? Second, as he learns to attend to his maladaptive behaviors, he begins to see that what he tells himself has as much impact as others' statements about him. He also sees the connections between his thinking and his behavioral problems. With this awareness he is in an ideal place to begin to learn a new, more rational internal dialogue. Third, he can also learn new coping skills, which he can practice first in the sessions and then in real-life situations. It will not be enough for him to merely say new things to himself, for to become proficient in new cognitive and behavioral coping skills he needs to apply them in various daily situations. As he experiences success with his assignments, these tasks can become increasingly demanding.

FOLLOW-UP: YOU CONTINUE AS STAN'S COGNITIVE-BEHAVIOR THERA-PIST. Use these questions to help you think about how to counsel Stan:

- What are some of Stan's most prominent faulty beliefs that are getting in the way of his living fully? What cognitive, emotive, and behavioral techniques might you use in helping him examine his dysfunctional thinking?
- Stan lives by many "shoulds" and "oughts." What are some techniques you would use to work with him in examining the basis of accepting these imperatives?
- If Stan rigidly held to his beliefs, saying that they seemed perfectly logical to him, how might you proceed if you were convinced that his thinking was dysfunctional?

# Beck's Cognitive Therapy

## INTRODUCTION

Aaron T. Beck, like Ellis, was trained in psychoanalysis, and he also found Freud's approach lacking as he reexamined it in the early 1960s. The approach he developed, known as *cognitive therapy* (*CT*), has a number of basic similarities to rational emotive behavior therapy. It shares with REBT an active, directive, time-limited, present-centered, and structured approach (Beck, Rush, Shaw, & Emery, 1979). It is an insight-focused therapy that emphasizes recognizing and changing negative thoughts and maladaptive beliefs, otherwise referred to as schemata. Beck's approach is based on the theoretical rationale that the way people feel and behave is determined by how they perceive and structure their experience. He developed his theory independently of Ellis, but their approaches have the same goal of assisting clients in recognizing and discarding self-defeating cognitions. Beck and Ellis exchanged ideas, and Beck credits Ellis with introducing the fundamental concept that people's beliefs are accessible and with attracting even skeptics to the value of focusing on cognitive factors as a route to changing feelings and behaviors. Ellis sees Beck as an extremely clear thinker who has made major contributions to psychotherapy through his research (Weishaar, 1993). He credits Beck and his students with having done an unusually fine job of gathering valuable research data on dysfunctional beliefs and on how changing them leads to therapeutic progress (personal communication, July 7, 1994).

The basic theory of CT holds that in order to understand the nature of an emotional episode or disturbance, it is essential to focus on the cognitive content of an individual's reaction to the upsetting event or stream of thoughts (DeRubeis & Beck, 1988). The goal is to change the way clients think by using their automatic thoughts to reach the core schemata and begin to introduce the idea of schema restructuring. This is done by encouraging clients to gather and weigh the evidence in support of their beliefs. Clinical studies indicate the value of cognitive therapy in a wide variety of disorders, particularly depression and the anxiety disorders (Beck, 1991). It has been successfully applied in treating phobias, psychosomatic disorders, eating disorders, anger, panic disorders, substance abuse (Beck, Wright, Newman, & Liese, 1993), and chronic pain (Beck, 1987) and in crisis intervention (Dattilio & Freeman, 1994).

## BASIC PRINCIPLES

Beck, as a practicing psychoanalytic therapist for many years, grew interested in his clients' "automatic thoughts" (personalized notions that are triggered by particular stimuli that lead to emotional responses). As a part of his psychoanalytic study, he was looking in the dream content of depressed clients for anger that they were turning back on themselves. He began to notice that more than such retroflected anger, as Freud theorized, there was a bias in their interpretation or thinking. He asked them to observe negative automatic thoughts that persisted even though they were contrary to objective evidence.

Beck contends that people with emotional difficulties tend to commit "characteristic logical errors" that tilt objective reality in the direction of self-deprecation. Cognitive therapy perceives psychological problems as stemming from commonplace processes such as faulty thinking, making incorrect inferences on the basis of inadequate or incorrect information, and failing to distinguish between fantasy and reality. The following are systematic errors in reasoning that lead to such faulty assumptions and misconceptions, which are termed *cognitive distortions* (Beck et al., 1979; Beck & Weishaar, 1995; Dattilio & Freeman, 1992):

- *Arbitrary inferences* refer to making conclusions without supporting and relevant evidence. This includes "catastrophizing," or thinking of the absolute worst scenario and outcomes for most situations. You might begin your first job as a counselor with the conviction that you will not be liked or valued by either your colleagues or your clients. You are convinced that you fooled your professors and somehow just managed to get your degree, but now people will certainly see through you!
- *Selective abstraction* consists of forming conclusions based on an isolated detail of an event. In this process other information is ignored, and the significance of the total context is missed. The assumption is that the events that matter are those dealing with failure and deprivation. As a counselor, you might measure your worth by your errors and weaknesses, not by your successes.
- *Overgeneralization* is a process of holding extreme beliefs on the basis of a single incident and applying them inappropriately to dissimilar events or settings. If you have difficulty in working with one adolescent, for example, you might conclude that you will not be effective in counseling any adolescents. You might also conclude that you will not be effective in working with *any* clients!
- *Magnification and minimization* consist of perceiving a case or situation in a greater or lesser light than it truly deserves. You might make this cognitive error by assuming that by even minor mistakes in counseling a client could easily create a crisis for the individual and might even result in psychological damage.
- *Personalization* is a tendency for individuals to relate external events to themselves, even when there is no basis for making this connection. If a client does not return for a second counseling session, you might be

absolutely convinced that this absence is due to your terrible performance during the initial session. You might tell yourself, "This situation proves that I really let that client down, and now she may never seek help again!"

- *Labeling and mislabeling* involve portraying one's identity on the basis of imperfections and mistakes made in the past and allowing them to define one's true identity. Thus, if you are not able to live up to all of a client's expectations, you might say to yourself, "I'm totally worthless and should turn my professional license in right away!"
- *Polarized thinking* involves thinking and interpreting in all-or-nothing terms, or categorizing experiences in either/or extremes. With such dichotomous thinking, events are labeled in black or white terms. You might give yourself no latitude for being an imperfect person and imperfect counselor. You might view yourself as either being the perfectly competent counselor (which means you always succeed with all clients) or as a total flop if you are not fully competent (which means there is no room for any mistakes).

Beck (1976) writes that, in the broadest sense, "cognitive therapy consists of all of the approaches that alleviate psychological distress through the medium of correcting faulty conceptions and self-signals" (p. 214). For him the most direct way to change dysfunctional emotions and behaviors is to modify inaccurate and dysfunctional thinking. The cognitive therapist teaches clients how to identify these distorted and dysfunctional cognitions through a process of evaluation. Through a collaborative effort, clients learn to discriminate between their own thoughts and events that occur in reality. They learn the influence that cognition has on their feelings and behaviors and even on environmental events. Clients are taught to recognize, observe, and monitor their own thoughts and assumptions, especially their negative automatic thoughts.

After they have gained insight into how their unrealistically negative thoughts are affecting them, clients are trained to test these automatic thoughts against reality, by examining and weighing the evidence for and against them. This process involves empirically testing their beliefs by actively participating in a variety of methods, such as engaging in a Socratic dialogue with the therapist, carrying out homework assignments, gathering data on assumptions they make, keeping a record of activities, and forming alternative interpretations (Freeman & Dattilio, 1994). Clients form hypotheses about their behavior and eventually learn to employ specific problem-solving and coping skills. Through a process of guided discovery, they acquire insight about the connection between their thinking and the ways they feel and act.

SOME DIFFERENCES BETWEEN CT AND REBT.   In both Beck's cognitive therapy and REBT, the reality testing is highly organized. Clients come to realize on an experiential level that they have misconstrued situations. Yet there are some important differences between REBT and CT, especially with respect to therapeutic methods and style.

As is clear by now, REBT is often highly directive, persuasive, and confrontive; it also focuses on the teaching role of the therapist. In contrast, Beck uses a Socratic dialogue by posing open-ended questions to clients with the aim of getting them to reflect on personal issues and arrive at their own conclusions. He places more emphasis on helping clients discover their misconceptions for themselves, and he generally applies more structure than REBT. Through this reflective questioning process, he attempts to collaborate with them in testing the validity of their cognitions (a process that he terms *collaborative empiricism*). Therapeutic change is the result of clients confronting faulty beliefs with contradictory evidence that they have gathered and evaluated.

Ellis works to persuade clients that certain of their beliefs are irrational; he shows them that such beliefs simply won't work, largely through a process of rational disputation. REBT aims at deliberately getting clients to seek out their dogmatism and absolutistic thinking and to vigorously and repetitively minimize it.

Beck takes exception to REBT's concept of irrational beliefs, asserting that telling clients that they are "thinking irrationally" can be detrimental, for many clients believe that they are "seeing things as they really are" (1976, p. 246). He views dysfunctional beliefs as being problematic because they interfere with normal cognitive processing, not because they are irrational (Beck & Weishaar, 1995). He takes a more functional view of biased beliefs as opposed to seeing them as philosophically incongruent with reality, as does REBT (Weishaar, 1993). Instead, he stresses the idiosyncratic nature of thoughts, assumptions, and inaccurate conclusions. The cognitive therapist helps clients look for the evidence that supports or contradicts their views and hypotheses. Beck maintains that certain ideas are not irrational but, rather, too absolute, broad, and extreme. For him, people live by *rules* (premises or formulas); they get into trouble when they label, interpret, and evaluate by a set of rules that is unrealistic or when they use the rules inappropriately or excessively. If clients make the determination that they are living by rules that are likely to lead to misery, the therapist may *suggest* alternative rules for them to consider, without indoctrinating them. Although cognitive therapy often begins by recognizing the client's frame of reference, the therapist continues to ask for evidence for a belief system. "Where is the evidence for . . .?" is a question often posed to the client.

## THE CLIENT/THERAPIST RELATIONSHIP

One of the main ways in which the practice of cognitive therapy differs from the practice of rational emotive behavior therapy is its emphasis on the therapeutic relationship. As you will recall, Ellis views the therapist largely as a teacher and does not think that a warm personal relationship with a client is essential, though it may have advantages. In contrast, Beck (1987) emphasizes that the quality of the therapeutic relationship is basic to the application of cognitive therapy. Successful counseling rests upon a number of desirable characteristics of therapists, such as genuine warmth, accurate empathy, nonjudgmental acceptance, and the ability to establish trust and rapport with clients. The core therapeutic conditions described by Rogers in his person-centered approach are viewed by cognitive therapists as being necessary, but not sufficient, to produce optimum therapeutic effect. Therapists must also have a cognitive conceptualization of cases, be creative and active, be able to engage clients through a process of Socratic questioning, and be knowledgeable and skilled in the use of cognitive and behavioral strategies aimed at guiding clients in significant self-discoveries that will lead to change (Weishaar, 1993). The therapist functions as a catalyst and a guide who helps clients understand how their beliefs and attitudes influence the way they feel and act. Therapists promote corrective experiences that lead to cognitive change and the acquiring of new skills (Beck et al., 1979; Beck & Weishaar, 1995).

In CT, techniques are most effectively applied in the context of a working alliance, or therapeutic collaboration, between the therapist and client. This position is consistent with the theoretical assumptions that (1) people's internal communication is accessible to introspection, (2) clients' beliefs have highly personal meanings, and (3) these meanings can be discovered by the client rather than taught or interpreted by the therapist (Weishaar, 1993). Cognitive therapists are continuously active and deliberately interactive with clients; they also strive to engage the clients' active participation and collaboration throughout all phases of therapy. The therapist and client work together to frame the client's conclusions in the form of a testable hypothesis. Beck conceptualizes a partnership to devise personally meaningful evaluations of the client's negative assumptions, as opposed to the therapist directly suggesting alternative cognitions (Beck & Haaga, 1992). The assumption is that lasting changes in the client's thinking and behavior will be most likely to occur with the client's initiative, understanding, awareness, and effort (Beck et al., 1979; Weishaar, 1993). This makes cognitive therapy, like REBT, an integrative form of psychotherapy.

## CLINICAL PROCEDURES

The basic procedural sequence of cognitive therapy is (1) preparing the client by providing a cognitive rationale for treatment and demystifying treatment; (2) applying the client to monitor thoughts that accompany distress; (3) implementing behavioral and cognitive techniques; (4) identifying and challenging cognitions through the process of being in problematic situations that evoke such thoughts; (5) examining beliefs and assumptions by testing them in reality; and (6) preparing clients by teaching them coping skills that will work against relapse (Beck et al., 1979).

Cognitive therapists employ a range of treatment strategies designed to assist clients in testing the validity of their cognitions. They use both cognitive and behavioral techniques, many of which are used by rational emotive behavior therapists and behavior therapists as well.

COGNITIVE TECHNIQUES. Many of the cognitive techniques that are a part of REBT are also employed in cognitive therapy, such as challenging clients to come up with evidence for the beliefs they hold. In addition, cognitive therapists assist clients in exploring their cognitive distortions. They help clients replace negative imagery with more positive and successful coping scenes. Clients frequently participate in cognitive rehearsal.

BEHAVIORAL TECHNIQUES.    Like REBT, cognitive therapy borrows heavily from the behavioral approaches. Eventually, clients learn to substitute realistic and accurate interpretations for their biased cognitions. They also learn to modify the dysfunctional beliefs and assumptions that predispose them to distort their experience (Beck et al., 1979). Some of these techniques are assertiveness training, behavioral rehearsal, graded task assignments, relaxation methods, social-skills training, shame-attacking exercises, homework, and bibliotherapy.

Cognitive therapists typically use homework that is tailored to the client's specific problem and arises out of the collaborative therapeutic relationship. Generally, the therapist takes a directive role during the early sessions. As we have seen, homework is used in many therapeutic approaches. The purpose of homework in cognitive therapy is not merely to teach clients new skills but also to enable them to test their beliefs in real-life situations. The emphasis is placed on self-help assignments that serve as a continuation of issues addressed in a therapy session.

As part of homework assignments, clients can be asked to complete readings dealing with the philosophy of cognitive therapy. According to Dattilio and Freeman (1992), these readings are assigned as an adjunct to therapy and are designed to enhance the therapeutic process by providing an educational focus. Some of the popular books that are often recommended are *Love Is Never Enough* (Beck, 1988); *Feeling Good* (Burns, 1988); *The Feeling Good Handbook* (Burns, 1989); *Own Your Own Life* (Emery, 1984); and *Woulda, Coulda, Shoulda* (Freeman & DeWolf, 1990). Through self-help books such as these, cognitive therapy became known to the general public. These books also give people practical knowledge that they can use in dealing with some of their difficulties.

To a large degree, cognitive therapy is a psychoeducational model, for it emphasizes therapy as a learning process, including acquiring and practicing new skills, learning new ways of thinking, and acquiring more effective ways of dealing with problematic situations. This educational focus lasts throughout treatment. Toward the end of the therapy process, clients learn information that will enable them to cope effectively with any relapse. They review what they have learned, both cognitively and behaviorally, and through role-playing methods and homework, they increase the chances of maintaining the new skills they have acquired so that they can prevent slipping into old and ineffective patterns.

## APPLICATIONS OF COGNITIVE THERAPY

Cognitive therapy initially gained recognition as an approach to treating depression and has also devoted extensive research to the study and treatment of anxiety disorders. According to Dattilio and Freeman (1992), cognitive therapy is effective in treating a broad range of disorders commonly encountered in the mental-health field. One advantage of a cognitive approach is that there is a specific limit on the number of therapy sessions. The authors report that studies have demonstrated a reduction of symptoms by the end of 12 to 20 sessions for a number of specific disorders.

Cognitive-behavioral methods have been applied to children and families, parent training, child abusers, individuals recovering from substance abuse, marital distress, divorce counseling, anxiety disorders, skill training, stress management, and health-care problems (see Granvold, 1994; Reineke, Dattilio, & Freeman, 1995).

In their edited books, Freeman and Dattilio (1992) and Dattilio and Freeman (1994) illustrate the scope of treating clinical problems with cognitive therapy. These conditions include generalized anxiety disorder, performance anxiety, social phobia, panic attacks, chronic pain, posttraumatic stress disorder, adjustment disorder, suicidal behavior, eating disorders, borderline personality disorders, narcissistic personality disorders, marital and family dysfunction, and schizophrenic disorders. Clearly, cognitive-behavioral programs have been designed for all ages and for a variety of client populations.

AN EXAMPLE OF APPLYING COGNITIVE TECHNIQUES.  Regardless of the nature of the specific problem, the cognitive therapist is mainly interested in applying procedures that will assist individuals in making alternative interpretations of events in their daily living. In the following example, I recommend that you think about how you might apply the principles of CT to yourself in a classroom situation, thus changing your feelings surrounding the situation (Beck, 1976).

The *situation* is that your professor does not call on you during a particular class session. Your *feelings* include depression. *Cognitively,* you are telling yourself: "My professor thinks that I'm stupid and that I really don't have much of value to offer the class. Furthermore, he's right, because everyone else is brighter and more articulate than I am. It's been this way most of my life!" Some possible *alternative interpretations* are that the professor wants to include others in the discussion, that he is short on time and wants to move ahead, that he already knows your views, or that you are self-conscious about being singled out or called upon.

As can be readily seen from this example, Beck would have you become aware of the distortions in your thinking patterns. He would ask you to look at your inferences, which may be faulty, and then trace them back to earlier experiences in your life. Then he would help you see how you sometimes come to a conclusion (your decision that you are stupid, with little of value to offer) when evidence for such a conclusion is either lacking or based on distorted information from the past.

As a client in cognitive therapy, you would also learn about the process of magnification or minimization of thinking, which involves either exaggerating the meaning of an event (you believe that the professor thinks you are stupid because he did not acknowledge you on this one occasion) or minimizing it (you are belittling your value as a student in the class). Beck would assist you in learning about how you disregard important aspects of a situation, engage in overly simplified and rigid thinking, and generalize from a single incident of failure. Can you think of other situations where you could apply CT procedures?

TREATMENT OF DEPRESSION. Beck, as we have seen, challenges the notion that depression results from anger turned inward. Instead, he focuses on the content of the depressive's negative thinking and biased interpretation of events (DeRubeis & Beck, 1988). In an earlier study that provided much of the backbone of his theory, he even found cognitive errors in the dream content of depressed clients (Beck, 1963).

Beck (1987) writes about the *cognitive triad* as a pattern that triggers depression. In the first component of the triad, clients hold a negative view of *themselves.* They blame their setbacks on personal inadequacies without considering circumstantial explanations. They are convinced that they lack the qualities that are essential to bring them happiness. The second component of the triad consists of the tendency to interpret *experiences* in a negative manner. It almost seems as if depressed people select certain facts that conform to their negative conclusions, a process Beck refers to as selective abstraction. The third component of the triad pertains to depressed clients' gloomy vision and projections about the *future.* They expect their present difficulties to continue, and they anticipate only failure in the future.

Depression-prone people often set rigid, perfectionistic goals for themselves that are impossible to attain. Their negative expectations are so strong that even if they experience success in specific tasks, they anticipate failure the next time. They screen out successful experiences that are not consistent with their negative self-concept. The thought content of depressed individuals centers on a sense of irreversible loss, which results in emotional states of sadness, disappointment, and apathy.

The Beck Depression Inventory (BDI) was designed as a standardized device to assess the depth of depression. The items are based on observations of the symptoms and basic beliefs of depressed people. The inventory contains the following 21 areas of symptoms and attitudes: (1) sadness, (2) pessimism, (3) sense of failure, (4) dissatisfaction, (5) guilt, (6) sense of punishment, (7) self-dislike, (8) self-accusations, (9) suicidal ideation, (10) crying spells, (11) irritability, (12) social withdrawal, (13) indecision, (14) distorted body image, (15) work inhibition, (16) sleep disturbance, (17) tendency to become fatigued, (18) loss of appetite, (19) weight loss, (20) somatic preoccupations, and (21) loss of libido (Beck, 1967).

Applied to treating depressed clients, Beck's therapeutic approach focuses on specific problem areas and the reasons clients give for such symptoms. Some of the behavioral symptoms of depression are inactivity, withdrawal, and avoidance. Clients report that they are too tired to do anything, that they will feel even worse if they become active, and that they will fail at anything they try. The therapist is likely to probe with Socratic questioning such as: "What would be lost by trying? Will you feel worse if you are passive? How do you know that it is pointless to try?" Therapy procedures include setting up an activity schedule, with graded tasks to be completed. Clients are asked to complete easy tasks first, so that they will meet with some success and become slightly more optimistic. The point is to enlist the client's cooperation with the therapist, on the assumption that *doing something* will lead to feeling better than *doing nothing.*

Some depressed clients may harbor suicidal wishes. Behind these symptoms the following attitudes are often expressed: "I'm a burden to others. I can't cope with my problems. There's no point to going on. Since I'm so miserable, I need to escape." Cognitive-therapy strategies may include exposing the client's ambivalence, generating alternatives, and reducing problems to manageable proportions. For example, the therapist may ask the client to list the reasons for living and for dying. Further, if the client can develop alternative views of a problem, then alternative courses of action can be developed. This can result in a client's not only feeling better but also behaving in more effective ways.

A central characteristic of most depressive people is self-criticism. Underneath the person's self-hate are attitudes of weakness, inadequacy, and lack of responsibility. A number of therapeutic strategies can be used. Clients can be asked to identify and provide reasons for their excessively self-critical behavior. The therapist may ask the client, "If I were to make a mistake the way you do, would you despise me as much as you do yourself?" A skillful therapist may play the role of the depressed client, portraying himself or herself as inadequate, inept, and weak. This technique can be effective in demonstrating the client's cognitive distortions and arbitrary inferences. The therapist can then discuss with the client how the "tyranny of shoulds" can lead to self-hate and depression.

Depressed clients typically experience painful emotions. They may say that they cannot stand the pain or that nothing can make them feel better. One procedure to counteract painful affect is humor. A therapist can demonstrate the ironical aspects of a situation. If clients can even briefly experience some lightheartedness, it can serve as an antidote to their sadness. Such a shift in their cognitive set is simply not compatible with their self-critical attitude.

Another specific characteristic of depressed people is an exaggeration of external demands, problems, and pressures. Such people often exclaim that they feel overwhelmed and that there is so much to accomplish that they can never do it. A cognitive therapist might ask the client to list things that need to be done, set priorities, check off tasks that have been accomplished, and break down an external problem into manageable units. When problems are discussed, clients often become aware of how they are magnifying the importance of these difficulties. Through rational exploration, they are able to regain a perspective on defining and accomplishing tasks.

The therapist typically has to take the lead in helping clients make a list of their responsibilities, set priorities, and develop a realistic plan of action. Because carrying out such a plan is often inhibited by self-defeating thoughts, it is well for therapists to use cognitive-rehearsal techniques in both identifying and changing negative thoughts. If clients can learn to combat their self-doubts in the therapy session, they may be able to apply their newly acquired cognitive and behavioral skills in real-life situations.

## CONSTRUCTIVISM AS A TREND IN COGNITIVE THERAPY

In recent years, cognitive therapy has increasingly viewed the subjective framework and interpretations of the client as more important than the objective bases of faulty beliefs. The constructivist's perspective focuses on the capacity of humans for creative and imaginative thought. Constructivism stresses the client's reality without disputing whether it is accurate or rational (Weishaar, 1993). One of the advantages of this constructivist viewpoint is that there is less danger of therapists imposing their values on clients. Lindsley (1994) emphasizes that therapists can encourage their clients to reconsider absolutistic judgments by moving toward seeing both "good" and "bad" elements in situations. By using a constructivist perspective, therapists can enable clients to modify painful beliefs, values, and interpretations without imposing their value system and interpretations.

The constructivist approach provides a philosophical context in which therapy is done more than prescribing a set of techniques. At the core of constructivist theory is a view of people as active agents who are able to derive meaning out of their experiential world. Thus, the process of change can be facilitated, but not directed, by a therapist. Like cognitive therapists, constructivist practitioners work with clients collaboratively by helping them construct more coherent and comprehensive stories that they live by (Neimeyer, 1993a).

Because constructivist philosophy serves as an overarching framework for understanding human knowing and change, it shows promise as a force contributing to a systematic integration of divergent therapeutic approaches (Neimeyer, 1993b; Neimeyer & Lyddon, 1993). Constructivism has begun to permeate numerous fields of contemporary psychology. Family therapy is one of the areas in which it has had a profound impact, a topic that is considered in more detail in Chapter 12.

# Meichenbaum's Cognitive Behavior Modification

## INTRODUCTION

Another major alternative to rational emotive behavior therapy is Donald Meichenbaum's cognitive behavior modification (CBM). His self-instructional therapy, which is basically a form of cognitive restructuring, focuses on changing the client's self-verbalizations. According to Meichenbaum (1977), self-statements affect a person's behavior in much the same way as statements made by another person. A basic premise of CBM is that clients, as a prerequisite to behavior change, must notice how they think, feel, and behave and the impact they have on others. For change to occur, clients need to interrupt the scripted nature of their behavior so that they can evaluate their behavior in various situations (Meichenbaum, 1986).

This approach shares with REBT and Beck's cognitive therapy the assumption that distressing emotions are typically the result of maladaptive thoughts. There are differences, however. Whereas REBT is more direct and confrontational in uncovering and disputing irrational thoughts, Meichenbaum's self-instructional therapy focuses more on helping clients become aware of their self-talk. The therapeutic process consists of training clients to modify the instructions they give to themselves so that they can cope more effectively with the problems they encounter. The emphasis is on acquiring practical coping skills for problematic situations such as impulsive and aggressive behavior, fear of taking tests, and fear of public speaking.

Cognitive restructuring plays a central role in Meichenbaum's approach. He describes *cognitive structure* as the organizing aspect of thinking, which seems to monitor and direct the choice of thoughts (1977). Cognitive structure implies an "executive processor," which "holds the blueprints of thinking" that determine when to continue, interrupt, or change thinking.

## HOW BEHAVIOR CHANGES

Meichenbaum proposes that "behavior change occurs through a sequence of mediating processes involving the interaction of inner speech, cognitive structures, and behaviors and their resultant outcomes" (1977, p. 218). He describes a three-phase process of change in which those three aspects are interwoven. According to him, focusing on only one aspect will probably prove insufficient.

*Phase 1: self-observation.* The beginning step in the change process consists of clients learning how to observe their own behavior. When they begin therapy, their internal dialogue is characterized by negative self-statements and imagery. A critical factor is their willingness and ability to *listen* to themselves. This process involves an increased sensitivity to their thoughts, feelings, actions, physiological reactions, and ways of reacting to others. If depressed clients hope to make constructive changes, for example, they must first realize that they are not a "victim" of negative thoughts and feelings. Rather, they are actually contributing to their depression through the things they tell themselves. Although self-observation is seen as a necessary process if change is to occur, it is not sufficient, per se, for change. As therapy progresses, clients acquire new cognitive structures that enable them to view their problems in a new light. This reconceptualization process comes about through a collaborative effort between the client and therapist.

*Phase 2: starting a new internal dialogue.* As a result of the early client/ therapist contacts, clients learn to notice their maladaptive behaviors, and they begin to see opportunities for adaptive behavioral alternatives. If clients hope to change, what they say to themselves must initiate a new behavioral chain, one that is incompatible with their maladaptive behaviors. Clients learn to change their internal dialogue through therapy. Their new internal dialogue serves as a guide to new behavior. In turn, this process has an impact on the client's cognitive structures.

*Phase 3: learning new skills.* The third phase of the modification process consists of teaching clients more effective coping skills, which are practiced in real-life situations. (For example, clients who can't cope with failure may avoid appealing activities for fear of not succeeding at them. Cognitive restructuring can help them change their negative view, thus making them more willing to engage in desired activities.) At the same time, clients continue to focus on telling themselves new sentences and observing and assessing the outcomes. As they behave differently in situations, they typically get different reactions from others. The stability of what they learn is greatly influenced by what they say to themselves about their newly acquired behavior and its consequences.

## COPING-SKILLS PROGRAMS

The rationale for coping-skills programs is that we can acquire more effective strategies in dealing with stressful situations by learning how to modify our cognitive "set." The following procedures are designed to teach coping skills:

- exposing clients to anxiety-provoking situations by means of role playing and imagery
- requiring clients to evaluate their anxiety level
- teaching clients to become aware of the anxiety-provoking cognitions they experience in stressful situations
- helping clients examine these thoughts by reevaluating their self-statements
- having clients note the level of anxiety following this reevaluation

Research studies have demonstrated the success of coping-skills programs when applied to problems such as speech anxiety, test anxiety, phobias, anger, social incompetence, addictions, alcoholism, sexual dysfunctions, and social withdrawal in children (Meichenbaum, 1977, 1986).

A particular application of a coping-skills program is teaching clients stress-management techniques by way of a strategy known as *stress inoculation.* Using cognitive techniques, Meichenbaum (1985) has developed stress-inoculation procedures that are a psychological and behavioral analog to immunization on a biological level. Individuals are given opportunities to deal with relatively mild stress stimuli in successful ways, so that they gradually develop a tolerance for stronger stimuli. This training is based on the assumption that we can affect our ability to cope with stress by modifying our beliefs and self-statements about our performance in stressful situations. Meichenbaum's stress-inoculation training is concerned with more than merely teaching people specific coping skills. His program is designed to prepare clients for intervention and motivate them to change, and it deals with issues such as resistance and relapse. Stress-inoculation training (SIT) consists of a combination of information giving, Socratic discussion, cognitive restructuring, problem solving, relaxation training, behavioral rehearsals, self-monitoring, self-instruction, self-reinforcement, and modifying environmental situations. This approach is designed to teach coping skills that can be applied to both present problems and future difficulties.

Meichenbaum (1985) has designed a three-stage model for stress-inoculation training: (1) the conceptual phase, (2) the skills-acquisition and rehearsal phase, and (3) the application and follow-through phase.

During the initial stage of SIT—the *conceptual phase*—the primary focus is on creating a working relationship with clients. This is mainly done by helping them gain a better understanding of the nature of stress and reconceptualizing it in social-interactive terms. The therapist enlists the client's collaboration during this early phase. Together the two rethink the nature of the problem(s). Initially, clients are provided with a conceptual framework in simple terms designed to help them understand the ways in which they are responding to a variety of stressful situations. They learn about the role that cognitions and emotions play in creating and maintaining stress. They are taught this by didactic presentations, through Socratic questioning, and by a process of guided self-discovery.

Clients often begin treatment feeling that they are the victims of external circumstances, thoughts, feelings, and behaviors over which they have no control. Training includes teaching them to become aware of their own role in creating their stress. They acquire this awareness by systematically observing the statements they make internally as well as monitoring the maladaptive behaviors that flow from this inner dialogue. Such self-monitoring continues throughout all the phases. As is true in cognitive therapy, clients typically keep an open-ended diary in which they systematically record their specific thoughts, feelings, and behaviors. In teaching these coping skills, therapists strive to be flexible in their use of techniques and to be sensitive to the individual, cultural, and situational circumstances of their clients.

The second stage of SIT—the *skills-acquisition and rehearsal phase*— focuses on giving clients a variety of behavioral and cognitive coping techniques to apply to stressful situations. This phase involves direct actions, such as gathering information about their fears, learning specifically what situations bring about stress, arranging for ways to lessen the stress by doing something different, and learning methods of physical and psychological relaxation. The training involves cognitive coping; clients are taught that adaptive and maladaptive behaviors are linked to their inner dialogue. They acquire and rehearse a new set of self-statements. Meichenbaum (1986) provides some examples of coping statements that are rehearsed in this phase of SIT:

- "How can I prepare for a stressor?" ("What do I have to do? Can I develop a plan to deal with the stress?")
- "How can I confront and deal with what is stressing me?" ("What are some ways I can handle a stressor? How can I meet this challenge?")
- "How can I cope with feeling overwhelmed?" ("What can I do right now? How can I keep my fears in check?")
- "How can I make reinforcing self-statements?" ("How can I give myself credit?")

As a part of the stress-management program, clients are also exposed to various behavioral interventions, some of which are relaxation training, social-skills training, time-management instruction, and self-instructional training. They are helped to make lifestyle changes such as reevaluating priorities, developing support systems, and taking direct action to alter stressful situations. Clients are introduced to a variety of methods of relaxation and are taught to use these skills to decrease arousal due to stress. Through teaching, demonstration, and guided practice, clients learn the skills of progressive relaxation, which are to be practiced regularly. Other approaches that are recommended for learning to relax include meditation, yoga, tensing and relaxing muscle groups, and breath-control techniques. Relaxation also includes activities such as walking, jogging, gardening, knitting, or other physical activities. Meichenbaum stresses that relaxation is as much a state of mind as it is a physical state.

In the third phase of SIT—the *application and follow-through phase*—the focus is on carefully arranging for transfer and maintenance of change from the therapeutic situation to the real world. It is clear that teaching coping skills is a complex procedure that relies on varied treatment programs. For clients to merely say new things to themselves is generally not sufficient to produce change. They need to practice these self-statements and apply their new skills in real-life situations. Once they have become proficient in cognitive and behavioral coping skills, they practice behavioral assignments, which become increasingly demanding. Clients are asked to write down the homework assignments that they are willing to complete. The outcomes of these assignments are carefully checked at subsequent meetings, and if clients do not follow through with them, the trainer and the client collaboratively consider the reasons for the failure. Follow-up and booster sessions typically take place at 3-, 6-, and 12-month periods as an incentive for clients to continue practicing and refining their coping skills. SIT can be considered part of an ongoing stress-management program that extends the benefits of training into the future.

Stress-management training has potentially useful applications for a wide variety of problems and clients, both for remediation and prevention. Some of these applications include anger control, anxiety management, assertion training, improving creative thinking, treating depression, and dealing with health problems. The approach has also been used in treating obese people, hyperactive children, social isolates, and schizophrenics (Meichenbaum, 1977, 1985).

# Summary and Evaluation

## SUMMARY

REBT is a form of cognitively oriented behavioral therapy. It has evolved into a comprehensive and integrative approach that emphasizes thinking, judging, deciding, and doing. The approach retains Ellis's highly didactic and directive quality, and REBT is as much concerned with the cognitive dimensions as with feelings. It starts with clients' disturbed emotions and behaviors and reveals and disputes the thoughts that directly create them.

In order to block the self-defeating beliefs that are reinforced by a process of self-indoctrination, REBT therapists employ active and directive techniques such as teaching, suggestion, persuasion, and homework assignments, and they challenge clients to substitute a rational belief system for an irrational one. They do this by continually urging clients to validate their observations and ideas and showing them how to do this type of refutation themselves. They demonstrate how and why irrational beliefs lead to negative emotional and behavioral results. They teach clients how to think scientifically and how to annihilate new self-defeating ideas and behaviors that might occur in the future.

It is crucial that therapists demonstrate full acceptance and tolerance. They do so by refusing to judge the person while at the same time confronting self-destructive behaviors. Also given primary importance is the therapist's ability and willingness to challenge, confront, probe, and convince the client to practice activities (both inside and outside of therapy) that will lead to constructive changes in thinking and behaving. REBT stresses action—doing something about the insights one gains in therapy. Change comes about mainly by a commitment to consistently practice new behaviors that replace old and ineffective ones.

Rational emotive behavior therapists are typically eclectic in selecting therapeutic strategies. They draw heavily on cognitive and behavioral techniques that are geared to uprooting the irrational beliefs that lead to self-defeating feelings and behaviors and to teaching clients how to replace this negative process with a rational philosophy of life. Therapists have the latitude to develop their own personal style and to exercise creativity; they are not bound by fixed techniques for particular problems. As long as they stay within the spirit of rational emotive behavior theory, therapists have the freedom to bring themselves into their therapeutic work in inventive ways.

As we have seen, REBT is the forerunner of other cognitive-behavioral approaches. Two therapies that are considered modifications and, in some ways, extensions of REBT are Beck's *cognitive therapy* and Meichenbaum's *cognitive behavior modification*. These therapies stress the importance of cognitive processes as determinants of behavior. They maintain that how people *feel* and what they actually *do* is largely influenced by their subjective assessment of situations. Because this appraisal of life situations is influenced by beliefs, attitudes, assumptions, and internal dialogue, such cognitions become the major focus of therapy.

## CONTRIBUTIONS OF THE COGNITIVE-BEHAVIORAL APPROACHES

Most of the therapies discussed in this book can be considered "cognitive," in a general sense, because they have the aim of changing clients' subjective views of themselves and the world. But the cognitive-behavioral approaches explored in this chapter are different in their major focus on both undermining faulty assumptions and beliefs and teaching clients the coping skills needed to deal with their problems.

ELLIS'S REBT.   I find aspects of REBT very valuable in my work. I believe that significant others in our past contributed to the shaping of our current lifestyle, but in strong agreement with Ellis, I contend that we are responsible for maintaining self-destructive ideas and attitudes that influence our daily transactions. I see value in confronting clients with questions such as: "What are your assumptions and basic beliefs? Have you really examined some of the core ideas that you live by to determine if they are your own values or merely introjects?" REBT has built on the Adlerian notion that events themselves do not have the power to determine us; rather, it is our interpretation of these events that is crucial. The

A-B-C model simply and clearly illustrates how human disturbances occur and the ways in which problematic behavior can be changed. Rather than focusing on events themselves, therapy stresses how clients interpret and react to what happens to them.

Another contribution of the cognitive-behavioral approaches in general, and especially REBT, is the emphasis on putting newly acquired insights into action. Homework assignments are well suited to enabling clients to practice new behaviors and assisting them in the process of their reconditioning. Adlerian therapy, reality therapy, and behavior therapy all share with the cognitive-behavioral approaches this action orientation.

One of the strengths of REBT is the focus on teaching clients ways to carry on their own therapy without the direct intervention of a therapist. I particularly like the emphasis that REBT puts on supplementary approaches such as listening to tapes, reading self-help books, keeping a record of what they are doing and thinking, and attending workshops. In this way clients can further the process of change in themselves without becoming excessively dependent on a therapist.

A major contribution of REBT is its emphasis on a comprehensive and eclectic therapeutic practice. Numerous cognitive, emotive, and behavioral techniques can be employed in changing one's emotions and behaviors by changing the structure of one's cognitions. Further, REBT is open to using therapeutic procedures derived from other schools, especially from behavior therapy.

BECK'S COGNITIVE THERAPY.   Beck's key concepts are very similar to Ellis's, though there are some differences in underlying philosophy and the process by which therapy proceeds. Beck made pioneering efforts in the treatment of anxiety, phobias, and depression. He developed specific cognitive procedures that are useful in challenging a depressive client's assumptions and beliefs and in providing a new cognitive perspective that can lead to optimism and changed behavior. His approach has received a great deal of attention from clinical researchers, and a number of experiments support its efficacy for depressed clients (Haaga & Davison, 1986). The effects of cognitive therapy on depression and hopelessness seem to be maintained for at least one year after treatment.

Weishaar (1993) writes that when Beck developed cognitive therapy, it served as a bridge between psychoanalytic therapy and behavior therapy. Cognitive therapy provided a structured, focused, active approach that focused on the client's inner world. Further, according to Weishaar, Beck demonstrated that a structured therapy that is present-centered and problem-oriented can be very effective in treating depression and anxiety in a relatively short time.

One of the contributions of cognitive therapy is that from the outset, it focuses on developing a detailed case conceptualization as a way to understand how clients view their world. Thus, cognitive therapy shares the phenomenological perspective with the Adlerian, existential, person-centered, and Gestalt approaches. According to Weishaar (1993), one of Beck's major theoretical contributions has been bringing private experience back into the realm of legitimate scientific inquiry.

In commenting on current and future trends in cognitive therapy, Beck (1993) cites its application to a range of disorders such as chronic pain, social phobia, HIV-related distress, guilt, and shame. In appraising the value of his approach, he writes:

> I conclude that cognitive therapy has fulfilled the criteria of a system of psychotherapy by providing a coherent, testable theory of personality, psycho-pathology, and therapeutic change; a teachable, testable set of therapeutic prin-ciples, strategies, and techniques that articulate with the theory; and a body of clinical and empirical data that support the theory and efficacy of the theory [p. 194].

In writing about the future of cognitive therapy, Beck (1991b) says that during the early years of its development it was pitted against the giants in the field, psychoanalysis and behavior therapy. It is now one of the more popular ap-proaches. "At this point in time," he comments, "cognitive therapy is no longer a fledgling and has demonstrated its capacity to fly under its own power. How far it will fly remains to be seen" (p. 374).

MEICHENBAUM'S COGNITIVE BEHAVIOR MODIFICATION.   As we have seen, Meichenbaum is one of the leading figures in cognitive-behavior therapy. His work in self-instruction therapy and stress-inoculation training has been applied successfully to a variety of client populations and specific problems. Of special note is his contribution to understanding how stress is largely self-induced through inner dialogue. He has gone beyond simply adding a few cognitive techniques to behavior therapy and has actually broadened its theoretical base through his demonstration of the importance of self-talk (Patterson, 1986). Meichenbaum (1986) cautions cognitive-behavioral practitioners against the tendency to become overly preoccupied with techniques. Instead, he suggests that if progress is to be made, cognitive-behavior therapy must develop a testable theory of behavior change. He reports that some attempts have been made to formulate a cognitive social-learning theory that will explain behavior change and specify the best methods of intervention.

A major contribution made by both Beck and Meichenbaum is the demysti-fication of the therapy process. Both of these cognitive-behavioral approaches are based on an educational model that stresses a working alliance between the therapist and client. The models encourage self-help, they provide for continuous feedback from the client on how well treatment strategies are working, and they provide a structure and direction to the therapy process that allows for evaluation of outcomes. Clients are active, informed, and responsible for the direction of therapy, because they are partners in the enterprise. The cognitive-behavioral approaches may well be the treatment of choice in the current managed-care environment.

CONTRIBUTIONS OF COGNITIVE-BEHAVIOR THERAPY FROM A MULTICUL-TURAL PERSPECTIVE.   The cognitive-behavioral approaches have certain ad-vantages in multicultural counseling situations. Some clients, because of their social and cultural conditioning, will experience difficulty if they are confronted in therapy. If they are not challenged too quickly, however, they can be effectively invited to examine the premises upon which they base their behavior. Consider an Asian-American client, Sung, from a culture that stresses values such as doing one's best, cooperation, interdependence, and working hard. It is likely that Sung is struggling with feelings of shame and guilt if she perceives that she is not living up to the expectations and standards set for her by her family and her community. She may feel that she is bringing shame to her family if she is going through a divorce.

If a counselor confronts Sung too quickly on living by the expectations of others, or on her "dependency," the results are likely to be counterproductive. In fact, she may leave counseling because she feels misunderstood. A sensitive cognitive-behavioral practitioner may, however, encourage her to begin to question how she might have uncritically accepted all of the messages from her cultural background. Without encouraging her to abandon respect for her cultural heritage, the therapist can still invite her to examine the consequences of basing her behavior on her belief system. If Sung maintains that she worries about letting her parents down and that she feels as though she is a failure because she failed in her marriage, it is not wise to label her basic values dysfunctional. If her therapist understands the cultural context in which she interprets a divorce as being shameful, she can be helped to clarify which values she wants to guide her decisions. Also, she can gradually begin to understand some of the consequences of trying as hard as she does to live up to both her own standards and those of her family. It is important that the therapist also respect some of her core values, which include interdependence, her sense of concern for her family, her wanting to maintain ties with her support system, and the concept of shame. As is the case for many ethnic- and cultural-minority clients, she is likely to be torn between the two cultures. So it is crucial for the counselor to help her explore her values and to gain a full awareness of her conflicting feelings. The counselor can point out that Sung may retain many facets of her culture even though she chooses to make modifications in her beliefs and practices.

Because counselors with a cognitive-behavioral orientation function as teachers, the client's focus is on learning skills to deal with the problems of living. In speaking with colleagues who work with culturally diverse populations, I have learned that their clients tend to appreciate the emphasis on cognition and action, as well as the stress on relationship issues. Beck's collaborative approach offers clients the structure they often feel they need, yet the therapist still makes every effort to enlist their active cooperation and participation.

The constructivist dimension of cognitive therapy provides clients with a framework to think about their thinking, in order to determine the impact that their beliefs have upon what they do. Within the framework of their cultural values and worldview, clients can explore their beliefs and can provide their own reinterpretations of significant life events. The cognitive-behavioral practitioner can guide clients in a manner that respects their underlying values. This dimension is especially important in those cases where counselors are from a different cultural background or do not share the same worldview as their clients.

# LIMITATIONS AND CRITICISMS
# OF THE COGNITIVE-BEHAVIORAL APPROACHES

ELLIS'S REBT.   My major criticisms of REBT involve aspects of the client's life that it ignores or does not give adequate attention to. As you will recall, rational emotive behavior therapists do not encourage clients to recount "long tales of woes." They make little use of unconscious dynamics, free association, dream work, and the transference relationship, whereas I value the therapeutic power of these tools. Although most REBT practitioners emphasize the building of rapport and a collaborative relationship between the therapist and the client, Ellis maintains that dimensions such as personal warmth, liking for the client, empathy, and a personal interest or caring are not essential ingredients for effective therapy. As is clear by now, I view the client/therapist relationship as the central factor accounting for client change. It seems hard for me to imagine effective therapy taking place in the absence of empathy, understanding, and caring. Therapy is more than simply challenging and modifying an individual's faulty thinking.

When transference appears, Ellis attacks it on the ground that the client is inventing a false connection between the therapist and some significant other in the client's past. I think that such feelings can teach clients about areas in their life that they still need to explore and resolve. Attacking such feelings hardly helps the client work therapeutically with them.

My view of therapeutic practice places value on paying attention to a client's past without getting lost in this past and without assuming a fatalistic stance about earlier traumatic experiences. I question the view of most cognitive-behavioral therapists that exploring the past is ineffective in helping clients change faulty thinking and behavior. In some cases not enough emphasis is given to encouraging clients to express and explore their feelings. I believe that the cognitive-behavioral approaches can work best once clients have expressed their feelings, which often occurs when they relive and work through earlier emotional issues.

A criticism that I have of all the cognitive-behavioral approaches, including REBT, is that they are less concerned with unconscious factors and ego defenses than I would like. I question the assumption of these approaches that most problems can be resolved without exploring repressed unconscious material. The psychoanalytic analogy of consciousness as only the tip of the iceberg makes sense to me, for I do not see how clients can truly choose or make changes without awareness of influential factors in their development. Likewise, past unfinished business and childhood experiences have a great deal of therapeutic power if they are connected to our present functioning. From my perspective, some painful early experiences need to be recognized, *felt fully,* reexperienced, and worked through in therapy before people can free themselves of restrictive influences.

REBT is a confrontational therapy, which provides both advantages and disadvantages. Some clients will have trouble with a confrontive therapist before he or she has earned their respect and trust. If they feel that they are not being listened to and cared about, there is a good chance that they will terminate therapy.

A concern I have about REBT as it is sometimes practiced is that therapists can misuse their power by imposing their ideas of what constitutes rational thinking. Due to the directive nature of this approach, it is particularly important for practitioners to know themselves well and to take care not to impose their own philosophy of life on their clients. Because the therapist has a large degree of power by virtue of persuasion, psychological harm is more possible in REBT than in less directive approaches. The therapist's level of training, knowledge, skill, perceptiveness, and judgment is particularly important. It is essential that the therapist be aware of when and how much to confront clients. There is a danger that an untrained therapist who uses REBT might view therapy as wearing down a client's resistance with persuasion, indoctrination, logic, and advice. Thus, a practitioner can misuse REBT by reducing it to dispensing quick-cure procedures—that is, by telling clients what is wrong with them and how they can best change.

It is well to underscore that REBT can be done by many people in a style different from Ellis's. Because he has so much visibility, it is worth distinguishing between the principles and techniques of REBT and his very confrontational tactics. Indeed, a therapist can be soft-spoken and gentle and still use REBT concepts and methods. At times inexperienced REBT practitioners may assume that they must follow the fast pace of Ellis. Therapists who employ REBT techniques can use different degrees of directiveness, can vary the amount of activity, and can be themselves by developing a style that is consistent with their own personality.

BECK'S COGNITIVE THERAPY.    Some of the criticisms of Beck's cognitive therapy are summarized by Freeman and Dattilio (1992b) and Weishaar (1993). Cognitive therapy has been criticized as focusing too much on the power of positive thinking; as being too superficial and simplistic; as denying the importance of the client's past; as being too technique-oriented; as failing to use the therapeutic relationship; as working only on eliminating symptoms, but failing to explore the underlying causes of difficulties; as ignoring the role of unconscious factors; and as neglecting the role of feelings.

Freeman and Dattilio (1992b, 1994) do a good job of debunking the myths and misconceptions about cognitive therapy, and Weishaar (1993) concisely addresses a number of criticisms leveled at the approach. Although the cognitive therapist is straightforward and looks for simple rather than complex solutions, this does not imply that the practice of cognitive therapy is simple. Further, cognitive therapists do not put weight on exploring the unconscious or underlying conflicts. Instead, they work with clients in the present to bring about schematic changes. Although it is true that cognitive therapists do not focus on the past or devote much time in therapy to exploring the roots of a client's problems, they do recognize that the client's current problems are often a product of earlier life experiences. However, they dispute the value of asking clients to relive traumatic events; instead, they help clients examine in the present the ways in which their cognitions are influencing how they feel and act. A criticism of cognitive therapy, like REBT, is that emotions are played down in treatment. Both approaches draw on emotional techniques, along with cognitive and behavioral strategies, to bring about client change. However, neither encourages emotional ventilation or emotionally reexperiencing painful events. In my view, this criticism of underplaying the role of emotions in therapy has validity for all the cognitive-behavioral therapies. One way of minimizing this shortcoming would be for practitioners to incorporate techniques from Gestalt therapy into their repertoire. If you are interested in a further discussion of criticisms and rebuttals of cognitive therapy, consult Weishaar (1993) and Freeman and Dattilio (1992b).

MEICHENBAUM'S COGNITIVE BEHAVIOR MODIFICATION.   In his critique of Meichenbaum's approach, Patterson (1986) raises some excellent questions that can apply to most cognitive-behavioral approaches. The basic issue is discovering the best way to change a client's internal dialogue. Is directly teaching the client the most effective approach? Is the client's failure to think rationally or logically always due to a lack of understanding of reasoning or problem solving? Is learning by self-discovery more effective and longer lasting than being taught by a therapist?

LIMITATIONS OF THE COGNITIVE-BEHAVIORAL APPROACHES FROM A MULTI-CULTURAL PERSPECTIVE.   Since exploring values plays such an important role in all of the cognitive-behavioral approaches, it is crucial for therapists to have some understanding of the cultural background of clients and to be sensitive to their struggles. Therapists would do well to use caution in challenging clients about their beliefs and behaviors until they clearly understand their cultural context.

With regard to the application of cognitive-behavior therapy to diverse cultures, one of the shortcomings pertains to the hesitation of some clients to question their basic cultural values. Dattilio notes that some Mediterranean and Middle Eastern cultures have strict rules with regard to religion, marriage and family, and child-rearing practices (personal communication, September 12, 1994). They often do not adhere well to the cognitive-behavioral suggestions of disputation. For example, a therapist might suggest to a woman that she question her husband's motive. Clearly, in some Middle-Eastern or other Asian cultures, such questioning is forbidden. Thus, modifications in a therapist's style need to be made.

One limitation of REBT in multicultural settings stems from its negative view of dependency. Many cultures view interdependence as necessary to good mental health. According to Ellis (1994), REBT is aimed at inducing people to examine and change some of their most basic values. Clients with certain long-cherished cultural values pertaining to interdependence are not likely to respond favorably to forceful methods of persuasion.

A potential limitation of the cognitive-behavioral approaches is that culturally different clients could become dependent upon the counselor to make decisions about what constitutes rationality and about the appropriate ways to solve problems. If the therapist were not well qualified, it would be easy for him or her to assume a highly directive stance that kept the client in a dependent position. Cognitive-behavior therapists walk a fine line between being directive and promoting dependence. Such practitioners may be directive, yet it is important that they teach their clients to question and to assume an active role in the therapeutic process.

# Where to Go from Here

The *Journal of Rational-Emotive and Cognitive-Behavior Therapy* is published by Human Sciences Press, 72 Fifth Avenue, New York, NY 10011-8004. This quarterly journal is an excellent way to keep informed of the developments of REBT. Subscriptions are $34 a year for individuals.

The Institute for Rational-Emotive Therapy in New York City offers a variety of professional training involving a primary certificate, an advanced certificate, an associate fellowship, and a fellowship program. Each of these programs has requirements in the areas of clinical experience, supervision, and personal experience in therapy. Several affiliated branches of REBT around the world offer official programs of study. You can get a catalog describing REBT workshops, books, cassette tapes, films, self-help forms, software items, and an order form for publications from:

Institute for Rational-Emotive Therapy
45 East 65th Street
New York, NY 10021-6593
Telephone: (212) 535-0822

The institute and many affiliated centers throughout the country provide official training programs that qualify for the institute's Primary Training Certificate in REBT for professionals. Some of the places where this training is available are Riverside, California; Denver, Colorado; Tampa, Florida; Jamesville, Iowa; Beachwood, Ohio; Lake Oswego, Oregon; Wilkes-Barre, Pennsylvania; Austin, Texas; and Charlottesville, Virginia. For information regarding international affiliated training centers and for a list of training institutes in the United States, contact the institute. Training outside the United States is available through the affiliated centers in Australia, England, Germany, India, Israel, Italy, Mexico, and the Netherlands.

As a way of keeping up with the theory, practice, and research in cognitive therapy, consult the *Journal of Cognitive Psychotherapy,* which is edited by E. Thomas Dowd, 405 White Hall, Kent State University, Kent, OH 44242.

Back issues of the *International Cognitive Therapy Newsletter* are available, along with a resource and referral list of Cognitive Therapy Centers, many of which provide training, from:

Center for Cognitive Therapy
1101 Dove Street, Suite 240
Newport Beach, CA 92660-2803
Telephone: (714) 964-7312

For more information about a one-year, full-time postdoctoral fellowship and for shorter-term clinical institutes, contact:

Beck Institute for Cognitive Therapy and Research
GSB Building
City Line and Belmont Avenues, Suite 700
Bala Cynwyd, PA 19004-1610
Telephone: (610) 664-3020

For information regarding ongoing training and supervision in cognitive therapy, contact:

Center for Integrative Psychotherapy
1251 South Cedar Crest Boulevard, Suite 211-D
Allentown, PA 18103
Telephone: (610) 432-5066

## Recommended Supplementary Readings

*Handbook of Cognitive-Behavioral Therapies* (Dobson, 1988a) is a well-balanced collection of chapters on problem-solving therapies, self-management therapies, cognitive-behavioral methods with children, REBT, cognitive therapy, and an overview of the current status and future of the cognitive-behavioral approaches.

*Cognitive Therapy of Depression* (Beck et al., 1979) describes techniques used with depressed clients. The wide range of cognitive techniques is a useful handbook for practitioners.

*Comprehensive Casebook of Cognitive Therapy* (Freeman & Dattilio, 1992b) provides a good introduction to cognitive therapy. This edited book presents an array of treatment approaches for specific clinical problems. The epilogue contains an excellent discussion of cognitive therapy in the year 2000.

*New Directions in Cognitive Therapy: A Casebook* (Emery, Holland, & Bedrosian, 1981) emphasizes the clinical application of cognitive therapy in working with a variety of special populations. It also describes treatment of a range of specific clinical problems and the use of special techniques.

*Cognitive Behavior Modification: An Integrative Approach* (Meichenbaum, 1977) integrates the techniques of behavior therapy with the clinical concerns of the cognitive approaches. The author summarizes both empirical studies and clinical techniques and offers a number of innovative procedures, such as self-instructional training and stress-inoculation training.

*Stress Inoculation Training* (Meichenbaum, 1985) provides a framework for understanding ways to reduce and prevent maladaptive stress reactions. The author clearly describes specific stages and techniques of his model for helping clients cope with stress.

## References and Suggested Readings *

* ARNKOFF, D. B., & GLASS, C. R. (1992). Cognitive therapy and psychotherapy integration. In D. K. Freedheim (Ed.), *History of psychotherapy: A century of change* (pp. 657–694). Washington, DC: American Psychological Association.

*Books and articles marked with an asterisk are suggested for further study.

BECK, A. T. (1963). Thinking and depression: Idiosyncratic content and cognitive distortions. *Archives of General Psychiatry, 9*, 324–333.

BECK, A. T. (1967). *Depression: Clinical, experimental, and theoretical aspects.* New York: Harper & Row. (Republished as *Depression: Causes and treatment.* Philadelphia: University of Pennsylvania Press, 1972.)

* BECK, A. T. (1976). *Cognitive therapy and emotional disorders.* New York: International Universities Press.

BECK, A. T. (1987). Cognitive therapy. In J. K. Zeig (Ed.), *The evolution of psychotherapy* (pp. 149–178). New York: Brunner/Mazel.

BECK, A. T. (1988). *Love is never enough.* New York: Harper & Row.

BECK, A. T. (1991a). Cognitive therapy as the integrative therapy: A reply to Alford and Norcross [Commentary]. *Journal of Psychotherapy Integration, 1*(3), 191–198.

BECK, A. T. (1991b). Cognitive therapy: A 30-year retrospective. *American Psychologist, 46*(4), 368–375.

BECK, A. T. (1993). Cognitive therapy: Past, present, and future. *Journal of Consulting and Clinical Psychology, 61*(2), 194–198.

BECK, A. T., & EMERY, G. (1985). *Anxiety disorders and phobias: A cognitive perspective.* New York: Basic Books.

BECK, A. T., & HAAGA, D. A. F. (1992). The future of cognitive therapy. *Psychotherapy, 29*(1), 34–38.

* BECK, A. T., RUSH, A., SHAW, B., & EMERY, G. (1979). *Cognitive therapy of depression.* New York: Guilford Press.

BECK, A. T., & STEER, R. A. (1987). *Manual for the revised Beck Depression Inventory.* San Antonio, TX: Psychological Corporation.

BECK, A. T., & WEISHAAR, M. E. (1995). In R. J. Corsini & D. Wedding (Eds.), *Current psychotherapies* (5th ed.) (pp. 229–261). Itasca, IL: F. E. Peacock.

BECK, A., WRIGHT, F. D., NEWMAN, C. F., & LIESE, B. (1993). *Cognitive therapy of substance abuse.* New York: Guilford Press.

BERNARD, M. E. (Ed.). (1991). *Using rational-emotive therapy effectively: A practitioner's guide.* New York: Plenum.

BERNARD, M. E. (1992). *Staying rational in an irrational world.* New York: Carol Publishing.

BURNS, D. (1988). *Feeling good: The new mood therapy.* New York: Signet.

* BURNS, D. (1989). *The feeling good handbook.* New York: Morrow.

COREY, G. (1995). *Theory and practice of group counseling* (4th ed.). Pacific Grove, CA: Brooks/Cole.

* COREY, G. (1996). *Case approach to counseling and psychotherapy* (4th ed.). Pacific Grove, CA: Brooks/Cole.

* DATTILIO, F. M., & FREEMAN, A. (1992). Introduction to cognitive therapy. In A. Freeman & F. M. Dattilio (Eds.), *Comprehensive casebook of cognitive therapy* (pp. 3–11). New York: Plenum.

DATTILIO, F. M., & FREEMAN, A. (Eds.). (1994). *Cognitive behavioral strategies in crisis intervention.* New York: Guilford Press.

* DATTILIO, F. M., & PADESKY, C. A. (1990). *Cognitive therapy with couples.* Sarasota, FL: Professional Resources Exchange.

* DERUBEIS, R. J., & BECK, A. T. (1988). Cognitive therapy. In K. S. Dobson (Ed.), *Handbook of cognitive-behavioral therapies* (pp. 273–306). New York: Guilford Press.

DIGIUSEPPE, R. A., MILLER, N. J., & TEXLER, L. D. (1979). A review of rational-emotive psychotherapy outcome studies. In A. Ellis & J. M. Whiteley (Eds.), *Theoretical and empirical foundations of rational-emotive therapy* (pp. 218–235). Pacific Grove, CA: Brooks/Cole.

*DOBSON, K. S. (Ed.) (1988a). *Handbook of cognitive-behavioral therapies*. New York: Guilford Press.

DOBSON, K. S. (1988b). The present and future of the cognitive-behavioral therapies. In K. S. Dobson (Ed.), *Handbook of cognitive-behavioral therapies* (pp. 387–414). New York: Guilford Press.

*DOBSON, K. S., & BLOCK, L. (1988). Historical and philosophical bases of the cognitive-behavioral therapies. In K. S. Dobson (Ed.), *Handbook of cognitive-behavioral therapies* (pp. 3–38). New York: Guilford Press.

DRYDEN, W. (1986). Vivid methods in rational-emotive therapy. In A. Ellis & R. Grieger (Eds.), *Handbook of rational-emotive therapy: Vol. 2* (pp. 221–245). New York: Springer.

DRYDEN, W. (1989). Albert Ellis: An efficient and passionate life. *Journal of Counseling and Development, 67*(10), 539–546.

*DRYDEN, W., & ELLIS, A. (1988). Rational-emotive therapy. In K. S. Dobson (Ed.), *Handbook of cognitive-behavioral therapies* (pp. 214–272). New York: Guilford Press.

*DRYDEN, W., & HILL, L. K. (1993). *Innovations in rational-emotive therapy*. Newbury Park, CA: Sage.

*ELLIS, A. (1973). *Humanistic psychotherapy: The rational-emotive approach*. New York: Julian Press.

ELLIS, A. (1979a). The practice of rational-emotive therapy. In A. Ellis & J. Whiteley (Eds.), *Theoretical and empirical foundations of rational-emotive therapy* (pp. 61–100). Pacific Grove, CA: Brooks/Cole.

ELLIS, A. (1979b). Rational-emotive therapy. In A. Ellis & J. M. Whiteley (Eds.), *Theoretical and empirical foundations of rational-emotive therapy* (pp. 1–6). Pacific Grove, CA: Brooks/Cole.

ELLIS, A. (1979c). Rational-emotive therapy: Research data that support the clinical and personality hypotheses of RET and other modes of cognitive-behavior therapy. In A. Ellis & J. M. Whiteley (Eds.), *Theoretical and empirical foundations of rational-emotive therapy* (pp. 101–173). Pacific Grove, CA: Brooks/Cole.

ELLIS, A. (1979d). The theory of rational-emotive therapy. In A. Ellis & J. Whiteley (Eds.), *Theoretical and empirical foundations of rational-emotive therapy* (pp. 33–60). Pacific Grove, CA: Brooks/Cole.

ELLIS, A. (1979e). Toward a new theory of personality. In A. Ellis & J. Whiteley (Eds.), *Theoretical and empirical foundations of rational-emotive therapy* (pp. 7–32). Pacific Grove, CA: Brooks/Cole.

*ELLIS, A. (1980). Overview of the clinical theory of rational-emotive therapy. In R. Grieger & J. Boyd (Eds.), *Rational-emotive therapy: A skills-based approach* (pp. 1–31). New York: Van Nostrand Reinhold.

ELLIS, A. (1984a). Is the unified-interaction approach to a cognitive behavior modification a reinvention of the wheel? *Clinical Psychology Review, 4*, 215–217.

ELLIS, A. (1984b). Maintenance and generalization in rational-emotive therapy. *The Cognitive Behaviorist, 6*(1), 2–4.

*ELLIS, A. (1985). *Overcoming resistance: Rational-emotive therapy with difficult clients*. New York: Springer.

ELLIS, A. (1986a). Rational-emotive therapy. In I. L. Kutash & A. Wolf (Eds.), *Psychotherapist's casebook* (pp. 277–287). San Francisco: Jossey-Bass.

ELLIS, A. (1986b). Rational-emotive therapy and cognitive behavior therapy: Similarities and differences. In A. Ellis & R. Grieger (Eds.), *Handbook of rational-emotive therapy: Vol. 2* (pp. 31–45). New York: Springer.

ELLIS, A. (1987a). The evolution of rational-emotive therapy (RET) and cognitive behavior therapy (CBT). In J. K. Zeig (Ed)., *The evolution of psychotherapy* (pp. 107–132). New York: Brunner/Mazel.

ELLIS, A. (1987b). The impossibility of achieving consistently good mental health. *American Psychologist, 42*(4), 364–375.

* ELLIS, A. (1988). *How to stubbornly refuse to make yourself miserable about anything— Yes, anything!* Secaucus, NJ: Lyle Stuart.

ELLIS, A. (1990). Rational-emotive therapy. In J. K. Zeig & W. M. Munion (Eds.), *What is psychotherapy? Contemporary perspectives* (pp. 146–151). San Francisco: Jossey-Bass.

ELLIS, A. (1991a). Achieving self-actualization. In A. Jones & R. Crandall (Eds.), *Handbook of self-actualization.* Corte Madera, CA: Select Press.

ELLIS, A. (1991b). The revised ABC's of rational-emotive therapy. In J. Zeig (Ed.), *The evolution of psychotherapy: The second conference.* New York: Brunner/Mazel. (Expanded version: *Journal of Rational-Emotive and Cognitive-Behavior Therapy, 9,* 139–172.)

ELLIS, A. (1991c). Using RET effectively: Reflections and interview. In M. E. Bernard (Ed.), *Using rational-emotive therapy effectively* (pp. 1–33). New York: Plenum.

ELLIS, A. (1992a). Brief therapy: The rational-emotive method. In S. H. Budman, M. F. Hoyt, & S. Friedman (Eds.), *The first session in brief therapy* (pp. 36–58). New York: Guilford Press.

ELLIS, A. (1992b). Group rational-emotive and cognitive-behavioral therapy. *International Journal of Group Psychotherapy, 42,* 63–80.

ELLIS, A. (1992c). Rational-emotive approaches to peace. *Journal of Cognitive Psychotherapy, 6,* 79–104.

ELLIS, A. (1992d). Rational-emotive family therapy. In A. M. Horne & J. L. Passmore (Eds.), *Family counseling and therapy* (2nd ed.). Itasca, IL: F. E. Peacock.

ELLIS, A. (1993). Fundamentals of rational-emotive therapy. In W. Dryden & L. K. Hill (Eds.), *Innovations in rational-emotive therapy* (pp. 1–32). Newbury Park, CA: Sage.

* ELLIS, A. (1994). *Reason and emotion in psychotherapy revised.* New York: Carol Publishing.

* ELLIS, A. (1995). Rational emotive behavior therapy. In R. J. Corsini & D. Wedding (Eds.), *Current psychotherapies* (5th ed.) (pp. 162–196.). Itasca, IL: F. E. Peacock.

ELLIS, A., ABRAMS, M., & DENGELEGI, L. (1992). *The art and science of rational eating.* New Jersey: Barricade Books.

* ELLIS, A., & BERNARD, M. E. (1986). What is rational-emotive therapy (RET)? In A. Ellis & R. Grieger (Eds.), *Handbook of rational-emotive therapy: Vol. 2* (pp. 3–30). New York: Springer.

* ELLIS, A., & DRYDEN, W. (1987). *The practice of rational-emotive therapy.* New York: Springer.

ELLIS, A., & DRYDEN, W. (1990). *The essential Albert Ellis.* New York: Springer.

ELLIS, A., & DRYDEN, W. (1991). *A dialogue with Albert Ellis: Against dogma.* Milton Keynes, England: Open University Press.

ELLIS, A., & GRIEGER, R. (1977). *Handbook of rational-emotive therapy: Vol. 1.* New York: Springer.

* ELLIS, A., & GRIEGER, R. (1986). *Handbook of rational-emotive therapy: Vol. 2.* New York: Springer.

ELLIS, A., & HARPER, R. (1975). *A new guide to rational living* (Rev. ed). Hollywood, CA: Wilshire Books.

ELLIS, A., SICHEL, J. L., YEAGER, R. J., DIMATTIA, D. J., & DIGIUSEPPE, R. (1989). *Rational-emotive couples therapy: Psychological practitioner's guidebook.* New York: Pergamon Press.

ELLIS, A., & VELTEN, E. (1992). *When AA doesn't work: Rational steps for quitting alcohol.* New York: Barricade Books.

ELLIS, A., & WHITELEY, J. M. (Eds). (1979). *Theoretical and empirical foundations of rational-emotive therapy.* Pacific Grove, CA: Brooks/Cole.

ELLIS, A., & YEAGER, R. J. (1989). *Why some therapies don't work.* Buffalo, NY: Prometheus Books.

EMERY, G. (1981). *A new beginning: How you can change your life through cognitive therapy.* New York: Simon & Schuster (Touchstone).

EMERY, G. (1984). *Own your own life.* New York: Signet.

EMERY, G., HOLLAND, S. D., & BEDROSIAN, R. C. (1981). *New directions in cognitive therapy: A casebook.* New York: Guilford Press.

ENGELS, G., & DIEKSTRA, R. (1987). *Efficacy of rational-emotive therapy: A quantitative review.* Unpublished manuscript, University of Leiden.

*FREEMAN, A., & DATTILIO, F. M. (1992a). Cognitive therapy in the year 2000. In A. Freeman & F. M. Dattilio (Eds.), *Comprehensive casebook of cognitive therapy* (pp. 375–379). New York: Plenum.

*FREEMAN, A., & DATTILIO, F. M. (Eds.). (1992b). *Comprehensive casebook of cognitive therapy.* New York: Plenum.

FREEMAN, A., & DATTILIO, F. M. (1994). Cognitive therapy: An overview of theory and techniques for practitioners. In J. Ronch, W. Van Ornum, & N. Stilwell, (Eds), *The Counseling Sourcebook* (pp. 61–71). New York: Continuum Press.

FREEMAN, A., & DEWOLF, R. (1990). *Woulda, coulda, shoulda.* New York: Morrow.

*GRANVOLD, D. K. (Ed.). *Cognitive and behavioral treatment: Method and applications.* Pacific Grove, CA: Brooks/Cole.

GRIEGER, R., & BOYD, J. (1980). *Rational-emotive therapy.* New York: Van Nostrand Reinhold.

HAAGA, D. A., & DAVISON, G. C. (1986). Cognitive change methods. In F. H. Kanfer & A. P. Goldstein (Eds.), *Helping people change: A textbook of methods* (3rd ed.) (pp. 236–282). New York: Pergamon Press.

HAAGA, D. A., & DAVISON, G. C. (1989). Outcome studies of rational-emotive therapy. In M. E. Bernard & R. DiGiuseppe (Eds.), *Inside rational-emotive therapy.* San Diego: Academic Press.

HORNEY, K. (1950). *Neurosis and human growth.* New York: Norton.

JORM, A. P. (1987). *Modifiability of a personality trait which is a risk factor for neurosis.* Paper presented at the meeting of the World Psychiatric Association, Reykjavik, Iceland.

LINDSLEY, J. R. (1994). Rationalist therapy in a constructivistic frame. *The Behavior Therapist, 17*(7), 160–162.

LYONS, L. C., & WOODS, P. J. (1991). The efficacy of rational-emotive therapy: A quantitative review of the outcome research. *Clinical Psychology Review, 11,* 357–369.

MAHONEY, M. J. (1974). *Cognition and behavior modification.* Cambridge, MA: Ballingcr.

MAHONEY, M. J. (1977). Reflections on the cognitive-learning trend in psychotherapy. *American Psychologist, 32,* 5–13.

MAHONEY, M. J. (1990). Developmental cognitive therapy. In J. K. Zeig & W. M. Munion (Eds.), *What is psychotherapy? Contemporary perspectives* (pp. 164–168). San Francisco: Jossey-Bass.

MAHONEY, M. J. (1991). *Human change processes: The scientific foundations of psychotherapy.* New York: Basic Books.

MAULTSBY, M. C. (1984). *Rational behavior therapy.* Englewood Cliffs, NJ: Prentice-Hall.

McGOVERN, T. E., & SILVERMAN, M. (1986). A review of outcome studies of rational-emotive therapy from 1977 to 1982. In A. Ellis & R. Grieger (Eds.), *Handbook of rational-emotive therapy: Vol. 2* (pp. 81–102). New York: Springer.

McMULLIN, R. E. (1986). *Handbook of cognitive therapy techniques.* New York: Norton.

McMULLIN, R. E., & CASEY, B. (1975). *Talk sense to yourself: A guide to cognitive restructuring therapy.* New York: Counseling Research Press.

\* MEICHENBAUM, D. (1977). *Cognitive behavior modification: An integrative approach.* New York: Plenum.

\* MEICHENBAUM, D. (1985). *Stress inoculation training.* New York: Pergamon Press.

MEICHENBAUM, D. (1986). Cognitive behavior modification. In F. H. Kanfer & A. P. Goldstein (Eds.), *Helping people change: A textbook of methods* (pp. 346–380). New York: Pergamon Press.

NEIMEYER, R. A. (1990). Personal construct therapy. In J. K. Zeig & W. M. Munion (Eds.), *What is psychotherapy? Contemporary perspectives* (pp. 159–164). San Francisco: Jossey-Bass.

\* NEIMEYER, R. A. (1993a). An appraisal of constructivist psychotherapies. *Journal of Consulting and Clinical Psychology, 61*(2), 221–234.

\* NEIMEYER, R. A. (1993b). Constructivism and the cognitive psychotherapies: Some conceptual and strategic contrasts. *Journal of Cognitive Psychotherapy, 7*(3), 159–171.

NEIMEYER, R. A., & LYDDON, W. J. (1993). Constructivist psychotherapy: Principles into practice. *Journal of Cognitive Psychotherapy, 7*(3), 155–157.

PATTERSON, C. H. (1986). *Theories of counseling and psychotherapy* (4th ed.). New York: Harper & Row.

REHM, L. P., & ROKKE, P. (1988). Self-management therapies. In K. S. Dobson (Ed.). *Handbook of cognitive-behavioral therapies* (pp. 136–166). New York: Guilford Press.

REINEKE, M., DATTILIO, F. M., & FREEMAN, A. (Eds.). (1995). *Casebook of cognitive-behavior therapy with children and adolescents.* New York: Guilford Press.

SHANNON, C. (1994). Stress management. In D. K. Granvold (Ed.), *Cognitive and behavioral treatment: Method and applications* (pp. 339–352). Pacific Grove, CA: Brooks/Cole.

SILVERMAN, M. S., MCCARTHY, M., & MCGOVERN, T. (1992). A review of outcome studies of rational-emotive therapy from 1982–1989. *Journal of Rational-Emotive and Cognitive Behavior Therapy, 10*(3), 111–181.

\* WALEN, S., DIGIUSEPPE, R., & DRYDEN, W. (1992). *A practitioner's guide to rational-emotive therapy.* New York: Oxford University Press.

WARREN, R., & MCLELLARN, R. W. (1987). What do RET therapists think they are doing? An international survey. *Journal of Rational-Emotive Therapy, 5*(2), 92–107.

\* WEISHAAR, M. E. (1993). *Aaron T. Beck.* London: Sage Publications.

\* WESSLER, R. L. (1986). Varieties of cognitions in the cognitively oriented psychotherapies. In A. Ellis & R. Grieger (Eds.), *Handbook of rational-emotive therapy: Vol. 2* (pp. 46–58). New York: Springer.

\* WESSLER, R. A., & WESSLER, R. L. (1980). *The principles and practice of rational-emotive therapy.* San Francisco: Jossey-Bass.

# Family Systems Therapy

Co-authored by James Robert Bitter and Gerald Corey

# Introduction

You will discover as you read this chapter that family systems therapy is a complex and developing field, which includes many approaches to understanding and working with families. My (Jerry Corey's) own training did not include a systemic perspective, and thus I have had to rely on reading and attending workshops to learn about this vast field. I invited a friend and colleague, Jim Bitter, who is a professor and chairperson of Human Development and Learning at East Tennessee State University, to co-author this chapter. He has had training in family therapy and teaches courses in its theory and practice. His scholarly activities include publications in the areas of family mapping and family constellation, couples counseling, and family reconstruction.

## THE FAMILY SYSTEMS PERSPECTIVE

Although Adler started working with families and systems in Vienna in the 1920s (Dreikurs, 1957), the seeds of a North American family therapy movement were not planted until the 1940s. By the 1950s, systemic family therapy began to take root, but it was still considered a revolutionary approach to treatment. In the 1960s and 1970s, psychodynamic, behavioral, and humanistic approaches (called the first, second, and third force, respectively) dominated counseling and psychotherapy. Today, the various approaches to family systems represent a paradigm shift that we might even call the "fourth force." They are becoming the major theoretical orientations of many practitioners. Young (1992) found that 10% of counselors and counselor educators identified with a family systems orientation. The prediction was that this figure would rise to 23% within five years.

The family systems perspective holds that individuals are best understood through assessing the interactions within an entire family. Symptoms are often viewed as an expression of a dysfunction within a family; these dysfunctional patterns are thought to be passed across several generations. It is revolutionary to conclude that the identified client's problem might be a symptom of how the system functions, not just a symptom of the individual's maladjustment, history, and psychosocial development. This perspective is grounded on the assumptions that a client's problematic behavior may (1) serve a function or purpose for the family, (2) be a function of the family's inability to operate productively, especially during developmental transitions, or (3) be a symptom of dysfunctional patterns handed down across generations. All these assumptions challenge the more traditional intrapsychic frameworks for conceptualizing human problems and their formation.

The one central principle agreed upon by family therapy practitioners, regardless of their particular approach, is that the client is connected to living systems and that change in one part of the unit reverberates throughout other parts. Therefore, a treatment approach that comprehensively addresses the other family members and the larger context as well as an "identified" client is required. Because a family is an interactional unit, it has its own set of unique traits. It is not possible to accurately assess an individual's concerns without observing the interaction of the other family members, as well as the broader contexts in which the person and the family live. To focus primarily on studying the internal dynamics of an individual without adequately considering interpersonal dynamics yields an incomplete picture. Because the focus is on interpersonal relationships, Becvar and Becvar (1996) maintain that *family therapy* is a misnomer and that *relationship therapy* is a more appropriate label.

The family therapy perspective calls for a conceptual shift, for the family is viewed as a functioning unit that is more than the sum of the roles of its various members. The family provides a primary context for understanding how individuals function in relationship to others and how they behave. Actions by any individual family member will influence all the others in the family, and their reactions will have a reciprocal effect on the individual. Goldenberg and Goldenberg (1996) point to the need for therapists to view all behavior, including the symptoms expressed by the individual, within the context of the family and society. They add that a systems orientation does not preclude dealing with the dynamics within the individual but that this approach broadens the traditional emphasis.

## DIFFERENCES BETWEEN SYSTEMIC AND INDIVIDUAL APPROACHES

There are significant differences between individual therapeutic approaches and systemic approaches. A case may help to illustrate these differences. Ann, age 22, sees a counselor because she is suffering from a depression that has lasted for more than two years and has impaired her ability to maintain friendships and work productively. She wants to feel better, but she is pessimistic about her chances. How will a therapist choose to help her?

Both the individual therapist and the systemic therapist are interested in Ann's current living situation and life experiences. Both discover that she is still living at home with her parents, who are in their 60s. They note that she has a very successful older sister, who is a prominent lawyer in the small town in which the two live. The therapists are impressed by Ann's loss of friends who have married and left town over the years while she stayed behind, often lonely and isolated. Finally, both therapists note that Ann's depression affects others as well as herself. It is here, however, that the similarities tend to end:

| *The individual therapist may:* | *The systemic therapist may:* |
|---|---|
| focus on obtaining an accurate diagnosis, perhaps using the DSM-IV | explore the system for family process and rules, perhaps using a genogram |
| begin therapy with Ann immediately | invite Ann's mother, father, and sister into therapy with her |
| focus on the causes, purposes, and cognitive, emotional, and behavioral processes involved in Ann's depression and coping | focus on the family relationships within which the continuation of Ann's depression "makes sense" |

| *The individual therapist may:* | *The systemic therapist may:* |
|---|---|
| be concerned with Ann's individual experiences and perspectives | be concerned with transgenerational meanings, rules, cultural and gender perspectives within the system, and even community and larger systems affecting the family |
| intervene in ways designed to help Ann cope | intervene in ways designed to help change the context |

Systemic therapists do not deny the importance of the individual in the family system, but they believe that an individual's systemic affiliations and interactions have more power in the person's life than a single therapist could ever hope to have. By working with the whole family—or even community—system, the therapist has a chance to observe how the individual acts within and serves the system's needs; how the system influences (and is influenced by) the individual; and what interventions might lead to changes that help the couple, family, or larger system as well as the individual expressing pain.

In Ann's case, her depression may have organic, genetic, or hormonal causes. It may be the result of cognitive, experiential, or behavioral patterns that interfere with effective coping. Even if her depression can be explained in this manner, however, the systemic therapist will be very interested in how her depression affects the family and is perhaps integrated into family functioning. Indeed, many family systems approaches would investigate how the depression serves other family members; distracts from problems in the intimate relationships of others; or reflects her need to adjust to family rules, to cultural injunctions, or to processes influenced by gender or family-life-cycle development. Rather than losing sight of the individual, family therapists understand the person as specifically embedded in larger systems.

From the systemic perspective, an individual may carry a symptom for the entire family. An individual's level of functioning is a manifestation of the way in which the family is functioning. For example, a young girl who develops ulcers may be signaling not only her own pain but also the unexpressed pain of the family. Thus, if individual change is a goal of therapy with the daughter, it is essential to understand how the family has a continuing influence on her and how any changes she makes are likely to affect the other members of her family. It should be noted that an individual can have a symptom or disorder that exists independently of the family structure. As noted, Ann's clinical depression could have been caused by a biochemical imbalance rather than some family dynamic. However, a symptom always has ramifications for members of the family. Even if Ann's depression is biochemical, her family will have to react to it and make systemic adjustments to the problem.

In Part Two of this textbook you have examined eight contemporary theories of individual counseling and psychotherapy, most of which have made some contributions to the development of family systems thinking and practice. Yet all of these theoretical approaches to individual counseling have some major differences from family systems therapy. The main goal of most of these orientations is to bring about changes within an individual in the realms of thinking, feeling, and behaving. It is true that these changes often have repercussions on the system of which the client is part. Yet the therapies that we've discussed up to this point generally do not aim at changing that system.

In contrast, the goal of most approaches to family therapy is change in the system, which is assumed to produce change in the individual members. Family, or relationship, therapy is aimed at helping family members change the dysfunctional patterns of relations and create functional ways of interacting. From a pure family systems perspective, families have a tendency to remain static and to resist change. Even in clearly dysfunctional families, members tend to prefer known and practiced patterns to new and unknown processes. Family therapists are all too familiar with abusive systems in which victims of violence return to what is painfully "known" rather than risk a potentially healthier but "thoroughly unknown" change in living. The process of systemic change may be slow, requiring patience, understanding, and often carefully planned interventions. The family therapist may function as a teacher, a coach, a model, or a director. When therapy is successful, the family may learn about patterns that have been transmitted from generation to generation or learn ways to detect and solve problems that keep members stuck in dysfunctional relational patterns.

## OVERVIEW OF THIS CHAPTER

Guerin and Chabot (1992) make a critical point: "Forty years into its life-cycle, the family therapy movement has not yet developed a single comprehensive integrated theory" (p. 257). Some practitioners would not consider such an integration of approaches an appropriate goal anyway, noting that it has been 100 years since the birth of modern psychotherapy and there is still no comprehensive model for counseling individuals or groups. Indeed, we are entering a period in the helping professions when multiple perspectives are needed and valued. It is easy to see that it would not be possible in one chapter to integrate the diverse therapy perspectives that fall under the family systems umbrella. Rather than covering most of the approaches to family therapy, this chapter presents a brief overview of the major systemic theories and describes some of their common denominators. Let us warn you that this is the longest chapter in this textbook; there is no way that a short chapter can do justice to this ever-growing field.

Several excellent survey books deal with the major systems of contemporary family therapy: *Family Therapy: An Overview* (Goldenberg & Goldenberg, 1996); *The Practice of Family Therapy: Key Elements across Models* (Hanna & Brown, 1995); *Family Therapy: Concepts and Methods* (Nichols & Schwartz, 1995); *Family Therapy: A Systemic Integration* (Becvar & Becvar, 1996); *Family Counseling and Therapy* (Horne & Passmore, 1991); *The Family Interpreted: Feminist Theory in Clinical Practice* (Luepnitz, 1988); and *Ethnicity and Family Therapy* (McGoldrick, Pearce, & Giordano, 1982). If you are interested in gaining a more in-depth understanding of the theory and practice of family therapy, we highly recommend that you begin by reading one or more of these books. In addition to these survey books, separate textbooks have been written on each of the following theoretical viewpoints: multigenerational family therapy, experiential/symbolic family therapy, conjoint family therapy, structural family therapy, strategic family therapy, social construction in family therapy, feminist therapy with families, and culture and family therapy. Some primary sources are listed in the References and Suggested Readings section at the end of this chapter.

Because of our space restrictions, this chapter deals with six of the major models of family therapy: (1) the multigenerational family systems model of Murray Bowen; (2) the human validation process model of Virginia Satir; (3) the experiential/symbolic approach of Carl Whitaker; (4) the structural approach of Salvador Minuchin; (5) the strategic approach of Jay Haley and Cloé Madanes; and (6) the recent innovations in family therapy, such as social constructionism. A systemic therapist of the 1990s may practice by utilizing any one of the above approaches or may creatively employ various perspectives when dealing with a particular case. These approaches are briefly compared in Table 12-1.

Because there is no unified theory of family therapy, this chapter deviates from the usual format for the preceding theory chapters. Each of the first five models of family therapy is described by attending to a set of common themes: (1) key concepts, (2) therapy goals, (3) the therapist's role and function, and (4) techniques. The recent developments in family therapy are then sketched, with particular attention given to social constructionism. Following this relatively brief overview, we discuss the trend toward integration of approaches to family therapy. As with the preceding chapters, the case of Stan illustrates how a family systems therapist might work with his presenting problems.

# Multigenerational Family Therapy

## INTRODUCTION

Murray Bowen was one of the original developers of mainstream family therapy. His family systems theory, which is a theoretical/clinical model that evolved from psychoanalytic principles and practices, is sometimes referred to as multigenerational (or transgenerational or intergenerational) family therapy. In fairness, Bowen would have seen his approach as a departure from psychoanalytic therapy. His approach operates on the premise that a family can best be understood when it is analyzed from at least a three-generation perspective, because a predictable pattern of interpersonal relationships connects the functioning of family members across generations. According to Bowen, the cause of an individual's problems can be understood only by viewing the role of the family as an emotional unit. A basic assumption of Bowenian family therapy is that unresolved emotional fusion to one's family must be addressed if one hopes to achieve a mature and unique personality.

## KEY CONCEPTS

Bowen emphasizes the role of theory as a guide in practicing family therapy. For him a well-articulated theory is essential in remaining emotionally detached as a family therapist. Bowen (1976) believed that the absence of a clearly articulated

TABLE 12-1
A Comparison of Six Theoretical Viewpoints in Family Therapy

| | MULTIGENERA-TIONAL FAMILY THERAPY | HUMAN VALIDA-TION PROCESS MODEL | EXPERIENTIAL/ SYMBOLIC FAMILY THERAPY | STRUCTURAL FAMILY THERAPY | STRATEGIC FAMILY THERAPY | SOCIAL CON-STRUCTIONISM |
|---|---|---|---|---|---|---|
| *Key figures* | Murray Bowen | Virginia Satir | Carl Whitaker | Salvador Minuchin | Jay Haley and Cloé Madanes | Tom Andersen, Michael White, and others |
| *Time focus* | Present and past; family of origin; three generations | Here and now | Present | Present and past | Present and future | Present and future |
| *Therapy goals* | Differentiate the self; change the individual within the context of the system; decrease anxiety. | Promote growth, self-esteem, and connection; help family reach congruent communication and interaction. | Promote sponta-neity, creativity, autonomy, and ability to play. | Restructure fam-ily organization; change dysfunc-tional transac-tional patterns. | Eliminate pre-senting prob-lem; change dysfunctional patterns; inter-rupt sequence. | Deconstruct problem nar-ratives; co-construct new life story. |

TABLE 12-1 (continued)

| | MULTIGENERATIONAL FAMILY THERAPY | HUMAN VALIDATION PROCESS MODEL | EXPERIENTIAL/ SYMBOLIC FAMILY THERAPY | STRUCTURAL FAMILY THERAPY | STRATEGIC FAMILY THERAPY | SOCIAL CONSTRUCTIONISM |
|---|---|---|---|---|---|---|
| *Role and function of the therapist* | Guide, objective researcher, teacher; monitor of own reactivity | Active facilitator; resource person; detective; model for congruence | Family coach; challenger; model for change through play | "Friendly uncle"; stage manager; promoter of change in family structure | Active director of change; problem solver | Listener and questioner; collaborator; solution finder |
| *Process of change* | Questions and cognitive processes lead to differentiation and understanding of family of origin. | Family is helped to move from status quo through chaos to new possibilities and new integration. | Awareness and seeds of change are planted in therapy confrontations. | Therapist joins the family in a leadership role; changes structure; sets boundaries. | Change occurs through action-oriented directives and paradoxical interventions. | Stories are elicited; life stories are reauthored. |
| *Techniques and innovations* | Genograms; questions; dealing with family-of-origin issues; detriangulating relationships | Empathy; touch, communication stances and sculpting; role playing; humor; family-life chronology | Co-therapy; self-disclosure; confrontation; use of self as change agent | Joining and accommodating; unbalancing; tracking; boundary making; enactments | Reframing; directives and paradox; amplifying; pretending; enactments | Empathy; "not-knowing" position; externalizing; unique events; reauthoring |

theory had resulted in an unstructured state of chaos in family therapy. According to Becvar and Becvar (1996), Bowenian therapeutic practice is built on a solid theoretical base, and the practices are consistent with that conceptual foundation. This approach offers a method for organizing data, explaining past events, and predicting future events. It contributes to an understanding of both the causes and control of events.

Bowen's theory and practice of family therapy grew out of his work with schizophrenic individuals in families. He was much more interested in developing a theory of family systems therapy than in designing techniques for working with families. In two major articles, Bowen (1966, 1976) identifies eight key concepts as being central to his theory: differentiation of the self, triangulation; the nuclear-family emotional system; the family-projection process; emotional cutoff; the multigenerational transmission process; sibling position; and societal regression. Of these, the major contributions of Bowen's theory are the core concepts of differentiation of the self and triangulation. In this section we also deal with the importance of self-awareness on the part of the family therapist, especially with reference to understanding how experiences in the family of origin are likely to affect clinical practice.

DIFFERENTIATION OF THE SELF.    The cornerstone of Bowen's theory is differentiation of the self, which involves both the psychological separation of intellect and emotion and independence of the self from others. Differentiated individuals are able to choose between being guided by their feelings or by their thoughts. Undifferentiated people have difficulty in separating themselves from others and tend to fuse with dominant emotional patterns in the family. These people have a low degree of autonomy, they react emotionally, and they are unable to take a clear position on issues. People who are fused to their family of origin tend to marry others to whom they can become fused. Two undifferentiated individuals seek and find each other and become a couple. Unproductive family dynamics of the previous generation are transmitted from one generation to the next through such a marriage (Becvar & Becvar, 1996). In family systems theory, the key to being a healthy person encompasses both a sense of belonging to one's family and a sense of separateness and individuality.

Similar to psychoanalytic theory, the process of *individuation* involves a differentiation whereby individuals acquire a sense of self-identity. This differentiation from the family of origin allows one to accept personal responsibility for one's thoughts, feelings, perceptions, and actions. Simply leaving one's family of origin, however, does not imply that one has differentiated. Individuation, or psychological maturity, is not a fixed destination that is reached once and for all; rather, it is a lifelong developmental process that is achieved relative to the family of origin through reexamination and resolution of conflicts within the individual and relational contexts.

The distinction between emotional reactivity and thinking can be difficult to discern at times. Those who are not emotionally reactive experience themselves as having a choice of possible responses; their reactions are not automatic but involve a reasoned and balanced assessment of self and others. Emotional reactivity, in contrast, is easily seen in clients who present themselves as paranoid, intensely anxious, panic stricken, or even "head over heels in love." In these cases feelings have overwhelmed thinking and reason, and people experience themselves as being unable to choose a different reaction. Clarity of response, in Bowen's theory, is marked by a broad perspective, a focus on facts and knowledge, an appreciation of complexity, and a recognition of feelings, rather than being dominated by them (Papero, 1991).

TRIANGULATION.   Bowen (1976) notes that anxiety can easily develop within intimate relationships. Under stressful situations, two people may recruit a third person into the relationship to reduce the anxiety and gain stability. This is called triangulation. Although triangulation may lessen the emotional tension between the two people, the underlying conflict is not addressed, and in the long run the situation worsens. If a couple have unresolved and intense conflicts, for instance, they may focus their attention on a problematic son. Instead of fighting with each other, they are temporarily distracted by riveting their attention on their son. Yet their basic conflict remains unsolved. Once the child's problem is resolved or he leaves home, they no longer have him to balance their system. The couple often resume fighting and may even file for divorce, because their differences and conflicts were never resolved. Because the family is not a static entity, a change in one part of the system affects the actions of all others involved.

   In his therapy, Bowen sometimes worked with both members of a conflictual dyad (the couple). He did not require that every family member be involved in the therapy sessions. Bowen tended to work from the inside out: Starting with the spousal relationship, he helped the two adults establish their own differentiation. He often worked with individuals while the rest of the family was present, coaching each person through his or her conflictual relationships. As a therapist, he attempted to maintain a stance of neutrality. From his vantage point, if the therapist becomes emotionally entangled with any one family member, he or she loses effectiveness and becomes part of a triangulated relationship. Bowen maintains that to be effective, family therapists have to have a very high level of differentiation. If therapists still have unresolved family issues and are emotionally reactive, they are likely to revisit those difficulties in every family they see.

## THERAPY GOALS

Although all family therapists are interested in resolving problems presented by a family and decreasing symptoms, Bowenians are mainly interested in changing the individuals within the context of the system. They contend that problems that are manifest in one's current family will not significantly change until relationship patterns in one's family of origin are understood and directly challenged. Emotional problems will be transmitted from generation to generation until unresolved emotional attachments are dealt with effectively. Change must occur with other family members and cannot be done by an individual in a counseling room.

   The practice of Bowenian family therapy is governed by the following two goals: (1) lessening of anxiety and symptom relief and (2) an increase in each family member's level of differentiation of the self (Kerr & Bowen, 1988). To bring about significant change in a family system, it is necessary to open closed family ties and to engage actively in a detriangulation process. Although problems are seen as residing in the system rather than in the individual, the route to changing oneself is through changing in relationship to others in the family of origin (Nichols & Schwartz, 1995).

## THERAPIST'S ROLE AND FUNCTION

Bowen viewed himself as an objective researcher who aimed to help individuals in the family assess and understand their relational styles within the family system. Bowenian therapists function as teachers, coaches, and neutral observers who are responsible for establishing the tone of family therapy. Bowen taught individuals or couples about triangulation and then expected them to go back to their family of origin to emotionally extricate themselves from these triangular patterns. The purpose of going home again is not to confront family members or even to establish peace and harmony but to encourage clients to come to know others in their family as they are (Bowen, 1976).

Let us say that an adult only child of aging parents returns home to help her parents decide whether to sell the home they have had for 35 years. The minute that Alice walks in the door, her parents begin to bicker about little things. This is a pattern that she knows all too well, and in the past it has left her stomach in knots. Today, however, she is prepared. Rather than getting caught up in the content of their arguments, she carefully observes how they handle their disagreements. She notices that her parents seem to argue about things that don't really matter, and she wonders if it helps them avoid the bigger issue of possibly leaving their home. When Alice's father turns to her and says, "You're a banker; will you please tell your mother that we can't be wasting money all the time?" she does not take the bait this time. Rather, she says: "Mom. Dad. Please sit down. I want you to know that I love you both. I know a decision about moving is a very big decision, and that's why I want to be here to support you. But it's your decision to make, not mine. The two of you have been working things out together a long time, and you can work this out too. I want to be here with you, but I won't be part of the decision-making team."

In his role as expert, Bowen helped individuals or couples gather information, and he coached or guided them into new behaviors by demonstrating ways in which individuals might change their relationships with their parents, siblings, and extended family members. He instructed them how to be better observers and also taught them how to move from emotional reactivity to increased objectivity. He did not tell clients what to do but asked a series of questions that were designed to help them figure out their own role in their family emotional process. Although he provided guidance for how they could free themselves from fused emotional relationships, he saw it as their responsibility to take the steps necessary to bring about self-differentiation. According to Bowenians, this occurs through a rational understanding of the nuclear-family emotional system, the family-projection process, and the transmission process over several generations. Bowenians maintain that therapy sessions can be viewed as rehearsals for becoming differentiated; the main therapeutic work is relating to members of their family in new ways. Clients learn through the work they do outside the therapy session. It should be mentioned that extended family systems work cannot be completed in a few visits to one's family, for it is an ongoing process.

THERAPIST SELF-AWARENESS.   As a prerequisite to practicing effectively with families, therapists must be aware of how they have been influenced by their own family of origin. If a family therapist overly identifies with one family member in the therapeutic encounter, it is likely that his or her own childhood issues will be triggered. Without self-awareness, perceptions will be colored and distorted by one's personal history. The therapist will probably not be objective or open to understanding certain clients. It is inevitable that we will encounter aspects of our family in the families with whom we work. The premise underlying the significance of understanding our family of origin is that the patterns of interpersonal behavior we learned in our family of origin will be repeated with clients.

IMPLICATIONS FOR TRAINING OF FAMILY THERAPISTS.   Bowen (1972) developed a method for training family therapists that is aimed at helping them differentiate themselves from others in their family of origin and that will reduce their inclination to become involved in triangulated relationships. There are four steps in Bowen's training method:

1. Trainees are encouraged to construct comprehensive family diagrams (called genograms) in order to identify key turning points in their family. It is essential that trainees learn information about their family relational system.
2. Trainees are given the task of making visits to their family of origin for the purpose of becoming a keen observer of their family's process. During this time it is crucial that they learn how to identify and control their own emotional reactivity to members in their family.
3. Bowenians encourage trainees to visit their family in times of high tension, such as a serious illness or imminent death of a family member, for it is at these times when change is most likely. Their task is to keep free from entering into old triangular patterns. In essence, they are to detriangulate themselves from emotionally reactive situations.
4. Instead of getting trapped into old patterns of emotional reactivity, they are expected to develop person-to-person relationships with as many family members as possible. The members should strive to relate to one another, rather than to talk about others.

Lawson and Gaushell (1991) suggest that training programs consider family-of-origin work for students as a part of growth-group experiences. Trainees can benefit from an exploration of their family dynamics because it enables them to relate more effectively to the families they will meet in their clinical practice. Lawson and Gaushell cite literature revealing some of the following intergenerational family characteristics of counselor trainees:

- Those clinicians who have resolved negative family experiences are better able to assist their clients, especially those with whom they have issues in common.
- It is essential that trainees be given assistance in identifying and addressing their own problematic family issues to enhance their psychological functioning and their clinical effectiveness.
- Unmet needs in early family experiences later manifest themselves in intense and conflicting ties with these family members.
- Helpers who took on roles in their family as peacemakers may later experience ambivalence regarding intimacy with significant others.
- Counselor trainees' problematic experiences in their own family of origin may lead to difficulties in their current relationships.

## TECHNIQUES

Bowen's theory describes how individuals function within a family system, how they develop dysfunctional patterns, and how they can repair and enhance their relationships with members of their family. The transgenerational approach focuses on emotional sequences with one's family of origin, spouse, and children. Bowenians believe that understanding how a family system operates is far more important than using a particular technique. They tend to use interventions such as questions, tracking sequences, teaching, and directives to a family. They value information about past relationships as a significant context from which they design interventions in the present.

GENOGRAM WORK.   Bowen assumes that multigenerational patterns and influences are central in understanding present nuclear-family functioning. What occurs in one generation will probably occur in the next, because key unresolved emotional issues tend to be played out over generations. He devised a "family diagram," or *genogram,* as a way of collecting and organizing important data over at least three generations. A family genogram consists of a pictorial layout of each partner's three-generational extended family. It is a tool for both the therapist and family members to understand critical turning points in the family's emotional processes and to note dates of births, deaths, marriages, and divorces. The genogram also gives information about some of these characteristics of a family: cultural and ethnic origins, religious affiliation, socioeconomic status, type of contact among family members, and proximity of family members. By providing an evolutionary picture of the nuclear family, a genogram becomes a tool for assessing each partner's degree of fusion to extended families and to each other. Bowen also integrates the perspective of Walter Toman (1994) on birth order and family constellation, so that these family maps would have a structural consistency. Unlike Adlerians, who approach the family constellation more phenomenologically, Toman and Bowen tend to present birth order as fixed and ordinal with more or less constant characteristics. Thus, siblings are presented in genograms horizontally, oldest to youngest, each with more of a relationship to the parents than to one another. It should be noted that genograms are used by family therapists of various orientations, not simply Bowenians, and many adaptations in form have been made. For a comprehensive guide to working with genograms, see McGoldrick and Gerson's (1985) book, *Genograms in Family Assessment*.

ASKING QUESTIONS.   Another Bowenian technique consists of asking questions that are designed to get clients to think about the role they play in relating with members of their family. Bowen's style tended to be controlled, somewhat detached, and cerebral. In working with a couple, for example, he expected each partner to talk to him rather than to talk directly to each other in the session. His calm style of questioning was aimed at helping each partner think about particular issues that are problematic with their family of origin. The attempt is to resolve the fusion that exists between the partners and to maximize each person's self-differentiation both from the family of origin and the nuclear-family system.

A Bowenian therapist is more concerned with managing his or her own neutrality than with having the "right" question at the right time. Still, questions that emphasize personal choice are very important. A therapist attempting to help a woman who has been divorced by her husband may ask:

- "Do you want to continue to react to him in ways that keep the conflict going, or would you rather feel more in charge of your life?"
- "What other ways could you consider responding if the present way isn't very satisfying to you and is not changing him?"
- "Given what has happened recently, how do you want to react when you're with your children and the subject of their father comes up?"

Notice that these questions are all asked of the person as part of a relational unit. This type of questioning is called *circular*, or is said to have *circularity*, because the focus of change is in relation to others who are recognized as having an effect on the person's functioning.

## CONCLUDING COMMENTS

Bowen's approach to family therapy can be characterized as the application of rational thinking in emotionally saturated systems. His emphasis on the separation of thought and feeling as well as therapeutic detachment has been criticized by some feminists as another case of elevating "rationality" and "autonomy" over connectedness, integration, and interdependence (Luepnitz, 1988). And indeed Bowen's model, while claiming to support personal presence and involvement, tends to put greater emphasis on emotional neutrality and objective observation than on personal connection and conjoint family process. The current feminist emphasis on collaboration, involvement, and connection places most feminist therapists at the opposite end of the continuum from Bowen's detachment theory.

If you are interested in a more in-depth study of this approach, we recommend the following sources: Papero (1991), Kerr and Bowen (1988), and Bowen

(1966, 1972, 1976, 1978). In addition to Bowen, James Framo (1992) has made significant contributions to multigenerational family therapy, integrating perspectives from object-relations theory.

# Human Validation Process Model

## INTRODUCTION

At the same time that Bowen was developing his approach, Virginia Satir (1983) began emphasizing family connection in a model called conjoint family therapy. The human validation process model (Satir & Baldwin, 1983; Satir & Bitter, 1991) grew out of her mission to release the potential that she saw in every family. Her approach emphasizes communication as well as emotional experiencing. She was highly intuitive and believed that spontaneity, creativity, self-disclosure, and risk taking were central to family therapy. In her view, techniques are secondary to the relationship that the therapist is able to establish with the family. It is not techniques but, rather, the personal involvement of the therapist with a family that makes a difference.

## KEY CONCEPTS

Satir's human validation process stresses enhancement and validation of self-esteem, family rules, congruence versus defensive communication patterns, sculpting, nurturing triads and family mapping, and family life-fact chronologies. It emphasizes factors such as making contact, metaphor, reframing, emotional honesty, clear communication, creating new possibilities, drama, humor, and personal touch in the therapy process. Like Bowen, Satir believed in looking at three generations of family life. Unlike him, she worked to bring those patterns to life *in the present,* either by having families develop maps (her word for genograms) and life-fact chronologies or by creating a group process in which family patterns and experiences could be simulated in a reconstruction.

FAMILY LIFE.   Children always enter the world as part of preexisting systems, with the family being the most common and central one. Their early experience is a constant transition from what is known and familiar to what is unknown and unfamiliar, the movement from the womb to the outside world being but the first of many such transitions. These transitions often leave children with feelings of fear, helplessness, and even anger as they struggle for competence and security in a challenging and often difficult new environment. Children enter families that are already loaded with rules, and as they grow, more rules are developed to help the system function and prosper. Rules can pertain to any part of human living and interaction, but the most important rules, according to Satir, are the ones that govern communication: who says what to whom under what conditions. Rules may be spoken or unspoken, embedded in the behavioral responses and interactions of the system. These rules, which are often couched in terms of "shoulds" or "should nots," become strong messages that govern interactions within a family. When parents feel worried or helpless, they tend to set rules in an attempt to control a situation. These family rules may initially assist children in handling anger, helplessness, and fear. They are intended to provide a safety net as children venture into the world (Satir, Bitter, & Krestensen, 1988).

It is impossible for children to escape growing up without such rules. Unfortunately, they often receive these rules in forms that quickly lose their effectiveness; that is, the rules are perceived to be *absolute* and too often *impossible.* Examples are: "Never be angry with your father." "Always keep a smile on your face." "Don't bring attention to yourself." "Never let people see your weaknesses; show neither affection nor anger." "Don't confront your parents; always try to please them." "Don't talk to outsiders about your family." "Children are to be seen but not heard." "Have fun only when all the work is finished." "Don't be different from other family members." Children have to make early decisions about these rules, whether to accept them or to fight against them.

As children, we learn rules by observing the behavior of our parents. When rules are presented without choice and as absolutes, they typically pose problems for us. As small children, we may have decided to accept a rule and live by it for reasons of both physical and psychological survival. When we carry such a pattern into our adult interactions, it can become self-defeating and dysfunctional.

Rather than trying to get people to give up these survival rules in their lives, Satir would assist them in transforming those that were extreme into something useful and functional. For example, if she were working with a person's rule "You must never get angry!" she would broaden the range of choice and transform the impossibility of living up to "always" and "never" standards. To make the element of choice more salient, she would ask clients to think of three times that they could imagine getting angry and list these situations. Through this process, a dysfunctional survival rule can be transformed rather than being attacked (Satir & Baldwin, 1983).

In healthy families, rules are few and are consistently applied. They are humanly possible, relevant, and flexible depending on changing situations (Bitter, 1987). According to Satir and Baldwin (1983), the most important family rules are the ones that govern individuation (being unique) and the sharing of information (communication). These rules influence the ability of a family to function openly, allowing all members the possibility to change. Satir notes that many people develop a range of styles as a means for coping with the stress that results from such change and the inability of family rules to meet the demands of change.

FUNCTIONAL VERSUS DYSFUNCTIONAL COMMUNICATION IN FAMILIES.   Satir's approach to family therapy distinguishes between functional and dysfunctional communication patterns. Bitter (1987) contrasts a functional family structure with one that is dysfunctional. In families that are functioning relatively well, each member is allowed to have a separate life as well as a shared life with the family group. Different relationships are allowed and are nurtured. Change is expected and invited, not viewed as a threat. When differentness leads to disagreements, the situation is viewed as an opportunity for growth rather than an attack on the family system. The structure of this family system is characterized by freedom and flexibility and by open communication. All the members within the family have a voice and can speak for themselves. In this atmosphere, individuals feel support for taking risks and venturing into the world. A healthy family encourages the sharing of experiences; the members are secure enough to be themselves and to allow others to be who they are.

By contrast, a dysfunctional family is characterized by closed communication, by poor self-esteem of one or both parents, and by rigid patterns. This kind of family resists awareness and blunts responsiveness. There is little support for individuality, and relationships are strained. In a family that exhibits dysfunctional patterns, the members are incapable of autonomy or genuine intimacy. Rules serve the function of masking fears over differences. Rules are rigid, many, and frequently inappropriate in meeting given situations. The members are expected to think, feel, and act in the same way. Parents attempt to control the family by using fear, punishment, guilt, or dominance. Eventually, the system breaks down because the rules are no longer able to keep the family structure intact.

DEFENSIVE STANCES IN COPING WITH STRESS.   When stress increases, threatening a breakdown of the family system, members tend to resort to defensive stances. Satir (1983, 1988) and Satir and Baldwin (1983) identify four universal communication patterns that express these defensive postures, or stress positions: placating, blaming, being super-reasonable, and being irrelevant.

1. Family members who use *placating* behaviors as a style for dealing with stress pay the price of sacrificing themselves in their attempt to please others. They are weak, tentative, and self-effacing. Because they do not feel an inner sense of value, and because they feel helpless without others, such people say and do what they think others expect of them. Out of their fear of being rejected, they strive to be too many things to too many significant others.

2. People who adopt a *blaming* posture will sacrifice others to maintain their view of themselves. They assume a dominating style and find fault with others. As they point the finger of blame at others, they avoid responsibility for mistaken actions and the perceived loss of self-worth and meaning. They frequently say, "If it weren't for you . . ." They attribute responsibility to others for the way they are.

3. People who become *super-reasonable* tend to function much like a computer. They strive for complete control over themselves, others, and their environment by living a life governed by principle. In their attempt to avoid humiliation and embarrassment, they keep their emotions tightly in check. Of course, the price they pay for being overly controlled and rigid is distance and isolation from others.

4. *Irrelevant behavior* is manifested by a pattern of distractions in the mistaken hope that hurt, pain, or stress will diminish. The irrelevant person is unable to relate to what is going on. He or she appears to be in constant motion,

with everything going in different directions at the same time. Because people who rely on this style of behavior are frightened of stress, they avoid taking a clear position, lest they offend others.

Is there an alternative to dealing with family life other than taking one of the four defensive postures described above? How does a healthy person deal with the stress of meeting family rules? Satir and Bitter (1991) describe how congruent people cope with this stress. They do not sacrifice themselves to a singular style in dealing with it. Instead, they transform it into a challenge that is met in a useful way. Such people are centered, and they avoid changing their colors like a chameleon. Their words match their inner experience, and they are able to make direct and clear statements: They are congruent. They face stress with confidence and courage, because they know that they have the inner resources to cope effectively and to make sound choices. The congruent communicator is alert, balanced, sensitive, and real and sends clear messages.

It is a mistake to assume that once decisions have been made, they are cemented forever. Even as children, people are not completely helpless with respect to how they will respond to the messages that are sent to them. If there are two children in a family, for example, each may react very differently to the same message of working hard that is modeled by their parents. The son decides to have more fun in his life than his parents and places little value on work. The daughter decides to outdo her parents and work even harder, becoming a workaholic. Children are not passively programmed, although they frequently develop patterns in reaction to what they see their parents doing. On some level, children cooperate in making the early decisions that direct their lives, which means that they have the capacity to make new decisions that are appropriate to changing life circumstances.

FAMILY ROLES AND FAMILY TRIADS.   Various members also assume roles that influence family interactions. For instance, a youngest brother assumed the role of victim, whereby he typically felt picked on and was constantly seeking protection. His sister assumed the role of keeping peace within the family. Even at an early age, other members looked to her as their counselor or expected her to take care of family difficulties. Her father took on the role of the stern taskmaster and disciplinarian, and her mother assumed a hard-working caregiver role. In this family, each member learned a role that characterized his or her behavior.

The roles that the parents play in relation to each child is especially important, because children always see their parents as essential to their survival. Like Bowen, Satir acknowledges that a child can be brought into the parents' relationship and that the resulting triadic process will be dysfunctional for everyone involved. Unlike Bowen, however, Satir also sees the possibility of parents forming a *nurturing triad* with each of the children. In such a triad, roles become flexible and open to change. Children are encouraged to make a place for themselves that fits the various situations they are in; they are supported, allowed to make mistakes, and engaged in congruent communication; most importantly, each child's self-esteem is tended and enhanced. They are heard, acknowledged, appreciated, allowed to complain, and given the information they need to handle life both within and outside of the family.

## THERAPY GOALS

The key goals of Satir's approach to family therapy are clear communication, expanding of awareness, enhancing potentials for growth, especially in self-esteem, and coping with the demands and process of change. Satir says that families, like all systems, tend to establish a relatively constant state that she calls the *status quo*. Each family's status quo is familiar and known; as such, it will be maintained by the family even if there are problems, because it is less threatening than what is unknown and unfamiliar. When a *foreign element*, or outside stressor, is introduced into the system, change is required, and the family system is thrown into *chaos* while the members try to adapt. To the extent that the family can be helped to identify *new possibilities* and practice them, it is possible for it to change and *integrate the change* in a new way to engage in family process (family life). This model of family therapy is concerned with the growth of individuals and the family, rather than merely stabilizing the family. The aim is for individual members of the family to become more sensitive to one another, to share their experiences, and to interact in new and genuine ways. The task of therapy is to transform defenses and dysfunctional rules, opening people to new possibilities and an integration of nurturing family-life experiences.

The general goal, and process, of therapy is the facilitation of desired change in the family system. The specific goals, which are related to this change process, are:

- generating hope and courage in the family members to formulate new options
- accessing, strengthening, enhancing, or generating coping skills in family members
- encouraging members to exercise options that will result in health as opposed to the mere elimination of symptoms (Satir & Bitter, 1991)

Satir (1988) identifies three goals of family therapy: (1) each individual within a family should be able to report honestly about what he or she sees, hears, feels, and thinks; (2) decisions in a family are best made through exploring individual needs and negotiating, rather than through power; and (3) differences should be openly acknowledged and used for growth within the family.

## THERAPIST'S ROLE AND FUNCTION

The therapist's role and function are to guide family members through the change process. Who the therapist is as a person is far more important than specific intervention techniques. Therapists are best conceived of as facilitators in charge of the therapeutic process; they do not have the task of making change happen or curing individuals. The therapist's faith in the ability of family members to move toward growth and actualization is central to this approach. This attitude infuses the therapy experience with nurturance, support, safety, and human validation (Satir & Bitter, 1991).

Satir (1983) views the therapist as a resource person who has a special advantage in being able to observe the family situation. She uses the analogy of a camera with a wide-angle lens, which allows the counselor to see things from each person's vantage point. As an official observer, the therapist is able to report on what the family cannot see. Satir (1983) describes many roles and techniques that family therapists employ in helping a family achieve its goals. Several of these are listed below. The therapist:

- creates a setting in which people can risk looking clearly and objectively at themselves and their actions
- assists family members in building self-esteem
- helps clients identify their assets
- takes the family's history and notes past achievements
- decreases threats by setting boundaries and reducing the need for defenses
- shows that pain and the forbidden are acceptable to explore
- uses certain techniques for restoring the client's feeling of accountability
- helps family members see how past models influence their expectations and behavior, and looks for change in these expectations
- delineates roles and functions
- completes gaps in communication and interprets messages
- points out significant discrepancies in communication
- identifies nonverbal communication

Although Satir's therapeutic style is quite different from Carl Whitaker's approach, which we will examine next, both emphasize the role of the therapist as a person. Whereas Whitaker developed his methods out of existential and psychoanalytic roots, Satir was influenced by the thinking of Carl Rogers and studied with him. Along with Rogers, she based her practice on the notion that we have an inner striving toward fulfillment and that we have the resources to reach our full potential. As you will remember from the person-centered perspective, it is the quality of the relationship between the therapist and client that stimulates growth and change in the client. In Satir's view, the therapist is a model of effective communication and a resource person for developing it in a family. Regardless of the counselor's theoretical orientation of the therapist, it is possible to utilize many of the concepts of Satir's model in working with families.

## TECHNIQUES

Change occurs in the session and healing occurs in the family's relationships, largely as a function of the relationship and climate created by the therapist. It is the individual family member, not the therapist, who is responsible for change. Within the therapy session, the focus of techniques is on emotional honesty, congruence, and systemic understanding. Although Satir developed a number of techniques aimed at facilitating the change process, most of her interventions grew out of her intuitions about what a given family or member needed. Some of the techniques for assessment and intervention that she developed or employed in a special way are family maps (similar to genograms), family life-fact chronology (a listing of a family's three-generation history), family sculpting, drama, reframing, humor, touch, "parts parties," and family reconstruction (Satir & Bitter, 1991). Techniques from approaches such as Gestalt therapy, psychodrama, and person-centered therapy are often incorporated into her work with a family.

FAMILY SCULPTING.   One of Satir's techniques is known as family sculpting, which may be used to increase members' awareness of how they function and how they are viewed by others in the system. Satir would actually physically position each family member in relation to the whole, often using her communication stances when she wanted to emphasize how members were coping. Through the use of this technique the family process, boundaries, and interactions became evident, yielding significant information about each member. Family sculpting gives members an opportunity to express how they view one another in the family struture and also to express how they would like relationships to be different.

FAMILY RECONSTRUCTION.   As a form of psychodramatic reenactment, family reconstruction enables clients to explore significant events in three generations of family life. This technique guides clients in unlocking dysfunctional patterns that stem from their family of origin. Family reconstruction, which takes members through different stages of their lives, has three goals: (1) to enable family members to identify the roots of old learning, (2) to help them formulate a more realistic picture of their parents, and (3) to assist them in discovering their unique personality (Satir & Baldwin, 1983; Satir, Bitter, & Kiestensen, 1988).

   Although Satir would occasionally use reconstruction with whole families who were stuck in a closed system, the real advantage of this approach is for individuals who have family issues but little or no access to their family of origin. By using a group to simulate three generations of family life, clients are able to make sense out of past experiences that would otherwise continue to mystify them. Satir tended to build family reconstructions around the person's family maps, family life-fact chronology, wheel of influence (a spatial diagram of all the significant people in one's life), or some combination of the three. The experience of reenacting and observing significant life events in a focused group process often gives the protagonist a new starting point and the opportunity to interrupt old and entrenched family patterns in favor of more useful processes.

PARTS PARTIES.   Satir sees each person as a system of parts, both positive and negative. She says that people often distort, deny, or disown parts that are less useful in adolescent and adult life but that served the younger child's need for survival. A parts party is a psychodramatic process, often used in groups, to help individuals acknowledge and integrate multiple aspects of the self. Used with couples or families, it is a means of showing members what is happening when they interact (Bitter, 1993; Satir & Baldwin, 1983). A simple parts party with couples might invite each partner to list six characteristics (represented in the form of well-known public figures). One partner might choose Abraham Lincoln (to represent integrity); Robert Redford (sexiness); Meryl Streep (talent); Hillary

Clinton (leadership); Charles Manson (evil); and Roseanne Barr (bossiness). The other partner might pick Ralph Nader (activism); Robin Williams (humor); Maya Angelou (creativity); Martin Luther King, Jr. (strength); Archie Bunker (grouchiness); and Jane Alexander (intelligence). One way to show the couple why they have difficulty communicating at home some nights and not others would be to put the two sets of parts (played by group members) on either side of a sheet, partition, or wall. As one part for each partner comes out randomly from behind the wall, it is possible that the "Robert Redford" character will run into "Archie Bunker," and the couple won't get very far. On the other hand, "Meryl Streep" and "Jane Alexander" might do very well.

## CONCLUDING COMMENTS

For many years, Satir was the only woman to have developed a complete model of family therapy. To be sure, much of her approach and emphasis on relationship will be welcomed by people who sense too much detachment or use of power in other systems of family therapy. Although feminists have often acknowledged Satir's courageous stand in favor of nurturance, connection, personal involvement, and even touch in therapy, they also recognized that Satir was not primarily a feminist in her approach. Satir was concerned with the *personhood* of everyone—men, women, and children alike. She tended to play down the importance of political struggles and believed that change started within, extended to relationships, and would eventually change the world (Satir & Baldwin, 1983).

Satir devoted a great deal of time to giving workshops and conducting training for family therapists. To her credit, she demonstrated her work with families before large audiences of mental-health workers. It was in these public demonstrations that her concepts came alive and that her practice was validated. During her career she worked with over 5000 families, representing a wide range of diversity. She developed a group known as the Avanta Network for implementing her approach to family therapy. The network is made up of mental-health professionals from various disciplines who have worked and trained with her. Information about the training programs that are offered through this group is available by contacting the Avanta Network, 310 Third Avenue, N.E., Suite 126, Issaquah, WA 98027.

If you are interested in a more in-depth study of this approach, we recommend the following sources: Satir and Bitter (1991); Satir (1983, 1988); Bitter (1987); and Satir and Baldwin (1983).

# Experiential Family Therapy

## INTRODUCTION

Experiential family therapy, sometimes known as the experiential/symbolic approach, has a strong relationship to other existential, humanistic, and phenomenological orientations. The experiential approach stresses choice, freedom, self-determination, growth, and actualization. It is an interactive process involving a family with a therapist who is willing to be real. The focus is on here-and-now interaction between the family and the therapist, rather than on exploring past experiences.

Carl Whitaker, who died in April 1995, was the best known exponent of this freewheeling, intuitive approach. His aim was to unmask pretense and create new meaning while liberating family members to be themselves. As in the other existential approaches, techniques are secondary to the relationship that the therapist is able to establish with the family. Whitaker does not propose a set of methods; rather, it is the personal involvement of the therapist with a family that makes a difference. When techniques are employed, they arise from the therapist's intuitive and spontaneous reactions to the present situation and are designed to increase clients' awareness of their inner potential and to open up channels of family interaction.

## KEY CONCEPTS

SUBJECTIVE FOCUS.    Experiential family therapists focus on the subjective needs of the individual in the family as they attempt to facilitate family interaction that will result in the individuality of each member (Hanna & Brown, 1995). They operate on the assumption that all members have the right to be themselves but that the needs of the family may suppress this individuation and self-expression.

ATHEORETICAL STANCE.    Whitaker's approach to family therapy is pragmatic and atheoretical, to the point of being antitheoretical. He believes that theory can be a hindrance to clinical practice (Whitaker, 1976). He maintains that clinicians may use their theory to create distance in the name of being objective or that unseasoned therapists may use theory as a way of controlling their anxiety over dealing with a family (Guerin & Chabot, 1992). His highly intuitive form of therapy is aimed at intensifying present experiencing. Indeed, his personal style is unconventional and provocative, and he values his capacity for "craziness," which is the ability to reach into his own unconscious to understand what is going on in the family. Through his own spontaneous reactions, he is able to tap material that a family keeps secret. Although the family members may view secret material as crazy, it is the process of keeping secrets that drives family members crazy.

## THERAPY GOALS

In Whitaker's view, the goal of family therapy is to promote the feeling dimension: spontaneity, creativity, the ability to play, and the willingness to be "crazy." Keith and Whitaker (1991) write that "we seek to increase the creativity (what we call craziness or right-brained living) of the family and of the individual members" (p. 118). The central goal is to facilitate individual autonomy *and* a sense of belonging in the family. Experiential family therapists operate on the assumption that if individual members increase their awareness and capacity for experiencing, more genuine intimacy will result within the family circle. According to Keith and Whitaker, it is experience, not education, that changes families. They assume that most of human experience occurs on the unconscious level, which can best be reached symbolically. For Keith and Whitaker, "symbolic" refers to finding multiple meanings for the same process.

A central tenet of Whitaker's approach is that therapists need to be aware of their own responses to families in order to be therapeutic. The therapist functions best as an instigator of family openness, realness, and spontaneity. Experiential therapists place value on their own responses as a measure of healthy interaction. Furthermore, their personal experience determines their work in family therapy. Whitaker sees experiential therapy as a way for therapists to be actively engaged in their own personal development. Thus, therapy is a process that helps the therapist as much as the family.

## THERAPIST'S ROLE AND FUNCTION

Experiential therapists tend to create family turmoil and then coach the members through the experience. They are primarily interested in the interaction between themselves and the family. The therapist's role requires immediacy, a willingness to be oneself, vitality, a degree of transparency, and a willingness to use personal reactions during the family sessions. Although these therapists are willing to act as temporary experts and issue directives to the family, they are just as likely to maintain long periods of silence to augment the members' anxiety. Whitaker likes to think of himself as a coach or a surrogate grandparent. His enactment of these roles requires structure, discipline, creativity, and presence (Keith & Whitaker, 1991). The relationship between the active and vital therapist and the family is the catalyst for growth and movement.

Therapeutic interventions are aimed at intensifying what is going on in the here and now of the family session. The focus of therapy is on the process of what is unfolding during the session, a time when the seeds of change are planted. Instead of giving interpretations, the therapist provides an opportunity for the family members to be themselves by freely expressing what they are thinking and feeling. Whitaker does not tell a family what it should do or be. He does not treat families. Instead, he sees his role as creating, with the family, a context in which change can occur through a process of reorganization and reintegration (Becvar & Becvar, 1996).

As a therapist, Whitaker strives to grasp the complex world of a family by focusing on impulses and symbols. He is interested in going beyond the surface level of interactions by dealing with symbolic meanings of what evolves between the family and himself. In his sometimes outrageous style, he gives voice to his own impulses and fantasies, and in doing so he encourages family members to become more accepting of their moment-by-moment experiencing (Goldenberg & Goldenberg, 1996).

Whitaker contends that family therapy occurs in three phases, engagement, involvement, and disentanglement. According to Keith and Whitaker (1991), the counselor's role changes throughout therapy. During the early phase, the therapist assumes an all-powerful position. Initially, the therapist increases the anxiety a family is experiencing so that members are challenged to recognize interactional patterns. In this context, families are almost forced to come up with alternative ways of operating. At different times in therapy the counselor shifts from being a dominant and parental figure to being an adviser and a resource person. Eventually, family members are expected to assume responsibility for their own living and changing. As the family assumes more independence, the co-therapists generally become more personal and less involved in the family system. The therapy team respects the family's initiative as it moves toward termination.

Because this approach emphasizes the counselor's personal characteristics over the use of techniques, therapy for the therapist is viewed as being essential. This therapy may include marital and family counseling as well as personal counseling to increase the therapist's access to his or her own creativity. The reason behind recommending family therapy for therapists—coupled with the study of their own family—is not only to assist them in the process of individuating from their family but also to help them establish a greater sense of belongingness to their family (Keith & Whitaker, 1991).

## TECHNIQUES

In Whitaker's model, change must be experienced rather than understood or designed. Families will tend to stay the same unless the therapist can disturb or frustrate family process. Keith and Whitaker (1991) put this notion as follows: "Whether they change or not has to do with their level of desperation, which must outweigh the pressure for homeostasis, or remaining the same" (p. 122). Within the experiential therapy session, the focus of techniques is on expressing blocked affect.

Whitaker believes that the person of the therapist is the main therapeutic factor that facilitates change within a family. He does not use planned techniques or structured exercises but places emphasis on *being with* a family. His interventions are aimed at challenging the symbolic meaning that people give to events. In his view, the ability to be caring, vital, firm, and unpredictable is a more effective therapeutic instrument than any technical strategies (Nichols & Schwartz, 1995).

Whitaker likes to be part of a co-therapy team. He feels that having a co-therapist frees him to act in whatever manner seems to fit the situation; he knows that his co-therapists will be available to help the family deal with what has happened. Over the years, Whitaker has teamed with some of the most sensitive and innovative family therapists in the field, including Thomas Malone, Gus Napier, and David Keith. This co-therapy arrangement allows for a sharing of the emotional involvement of the therapeutic process. Furthermore, the practice affords both therapists opportunities to have fun together, to disagree, to embellish upon each other's interventions, and to model creative and productive interaction (Goldenberg & Goldenberg, 1996).

Keith and Whitaker (1991) maintain that practicing family therapy stirs up emotional reactions in the therapist. Because countertransference tends to be unconscious, the use of a co-therapist lessens the danger of acting out such feelings with a family. Each therapist can use his or her subjectivity more freely, for the colleague can function as a counterbalancing force. For example, Napier and Whitaker (1978) would express their thoughts and consult about the family during the therapy session.

## CONCLUDING COMMENTS

In some ways, Whitaker's experiential approach to family therapy is not unlike other approaches that focus on the therapist/client relationship. As you recall, individual approaches such as existential therapy, person-centered therapy, and Gestalt therapy all assign a central role to the importance of the therapist as a person and view the quality of the therapeutic relationship as significantly affecting the process and outcomes of therapy. Experiential family therapy applies many of the processes of these relationship-oriented therapies to working with families. Relying on empathy, interactions, joining, enactments, and experiments, the experiential therapist attempts to understand the family's dynamics and create experiences that will lead to family vitality and change. It is clear that this approach places primary value on therapist self-awareness and the full use of the therapist's self in encountering a family.

Whitaker's insistence on "nontheory" foreshadows the efforts of social constructionists to confront the dominant culture and change standardized and fixed approaches to functionality. Indeed, feminists see in Whitaker someone willing to "play with patriarchy" (Luepnitz, 1988, p. 88), to change role patterns and role definitions so completely that meanings are turned upside down and inside out. Whitaker confronts men in therapy more than almost any other therapist, and he is also able to get to their vulnerability better than most. He has been known to tell men that they are hopeless, that they cannot stand their own envy of women who give birth, and that women are constantly struggling to bring them alive. In a film from the Philadelphia Child Guidance Clinic, he tells a client who has said that he could never accept his mother's nurturance, "I know; that's what makes your wife's job so gruesome."

If you are interested in a more in-depth study of this approach, we recommend the following sources: Keith and Whitaker (1991); Napier and Whitaker (1978); Whitaker (1976); and Whitaker and Malone (1981).

# Structural Family Therapy

## INTRODUCTION

The origins of structural family therapy can be traced back to the early 1960s when Salvador Minuchin was conducting therapy, training, and research with delinquent boys from poor families at the Wiltwyck School in New York. This approach to family therapy flourished in the 1970s, when Minuchin and his colleagues at the Philadelphia Child Guidance Clinic more fully developed the theory and practice of structural therapy. In his book *Families and Family Therapy,* Minuchin (1974) focuses on the interactions of family members as a way of understanding the *structure,* or organization, of a family. Structural family therapists concentrate on how, when, and to whom family members relate. Through this information the structure of a family and the problems that bring the family into therapy can be assessed.

This orientation is based, then, on the notion that most symptoms are a by-product of structural failings within the family organization (Guerin & Chabot, 1992). Therapeutic change consists of helping the family modify its stereotyped patterns and redefine relationships (Colapinto, 1991). Minuchin's central idea is that an individual's symptoms are best understood from the vantage point of interactional patterns within a family and that structural changes must occur in a family before an individual's symptoms can be reduced or eliminated.

Structural family therapy views the individual in a social context. The distinctive features of this approach are its emphasis on structural change as the primary goal of therapy and the therapist's active role as the agent in the process of restructuring the family (Colapinto, 1991). Minuchin (1974) writes: "Therapy based on this framework is directed toward changing the organization of the family. When the structure of the family group is transformed, the positions of members in that group are altered accordingly. As a result, each individual's experience changes" (p. 2).

## KEY CONCEPTS

Structural family therapy is an approach to understanding the nature of the family, the presenting problem, and the process of change. In this perspective the key concepts are family structure, family subsystems, and boundaries, each of which is briefly described below.

FAMILY STRUCTURE.    According to Minuchin (1974), a family's structure is the invisible set of functional demands or rules that organize the way family members relate to one another. The structure that governs a family's transactions can be understood by observing the family in action or by seeing interactions unfold among family members in the therapy sessions. To understand a family's structure, it is useful to pay attention to who says what to whom and in what way with what result. By noting family process, rather than listening for mere content, the therapist can detect problematic transactions. Repeated sequences that emerge in a therapy session reveal the structural patterns of a family. Of particular interest is the appropriateness of hierarchical structure in the family.

For example, if every time a woman complains about her husband, he hangs his head and says nothing, the theme of the process is the *avoidance of conflict.* If a father's expression of anger leads almost inevitably to an asthma attack in his daughter, the sequence is *complementary* (an exchange of opposite kinds of behaviors) and reveals problems in the power structure between parent and child. In violent families, therapists often find a *symmetrical* sequence (an exchange of similar behaviors) in which each person assumes absolute positions in an argument from which neither can withdraw. Each part of the symmetrical sequence happens at once, leading to an almost automatic escalation of the fight (Fishman, 1993). An example of such an argument is:

*Husband:*  Where are you going?

*Wife:*  Out.

*Husband:*  Did I say you could go out?!

*Wife:*  You don't tell me what to do!

*Husband* [shouting]:  The hell I don't!

*Wife* [shouting back]:  The hell you *do*!

FAMILY SUBSYSTEMS.    The family is considered a basic human system, which is composed of a variety of subsystems. The term *subsystems* encompasses various categories: *spousal* (wife and husband), *parental* (mother and father), *sibling* (children), and *extended* (grandparents, other relatives, and even reaching into the church and school). Members who join together do so to perform tasks that are essential for the functioning of the subsystems as well as the overall family system. Determining that the parent subsystem is appropriately separate from the child subsystem is central to structural therapy. It is important to note that each family member plays roles in different subgroups. For example, Tom is a father in the parental subsystem, a husband in the spousal subsystem, and the third brother in the sibling subsystem of his own family of origin. Ann is the daughter of Tom, but she is also the sister of Julie in her sibling subsystem, the wife of Hank in her spousal subsystem, and a member of her church choir in her extended community subsystem. Subsystems are typically determined by factors such as gender, age, common interests, and role function. These subsystems are also defined by rules and boundaries.

   In structural family therapy, subsystems have appropriate tasks and functions. When family members of another subsystem take over or intrude on one in which they do not belong, the result is usually some form of structural difficulty. For example, the sex life of the adults in the family belongs to the spousal subsystem; when children are allowed to witness, comment on, or investigate their parents' sexual activity, they are inappropriately involved in the spousal subsystem. This extreme example may be easier to understand than noting that parents ought to allow their children to form their own relationships. This second example, however, is just as important; working out brother and sister relationships is a task for the sibling subsystem, not the parental subsystem. Parents have their own activities and functions to address.

BOUNDARIES.    The emotional barriers that protect and enhance the integrity of individuals, subsystems, and families are referred to as boundaries. The demarcation of boundaries governs the amount of contact with others. These interpersonal boundaries can best be conceptualized on a continuum ranging from rigid boundaries (*disengagement*) to diffuse boundaries (*enmeshment*).

   Rigid boundaries lead to impermeable barriers between subsystems and with subsystems outside the family. In some cases, because of a generational gap, parent and child may be unable to understand or relate to each other. In this process of disengagement, individuals or subsystems become isolated, and relationships suffer or even deteriorate. Family members become isolated not only from one another but also from systems in the community. In a case where a teacher notified the police that a student in her sixth-grade class had been missing for several days and that she had been unable to contact his parents in spite of repeated tries, police officers went to the house to investigate. Finding the father at home and engaged in personal projects, they asked him about his son. They discovered that both parents were unaware that the boy had also been missing from home for three days. Again, this is an extreme form of disengagement that illustrates a physical as well as emotional cutoff.

At the other end of the spectrum are diffuse interpersonal boundaries, which are blurred to the extent that others can intrude into them. A diffuse boundary leads to enmeshment, which is characterized by family members' overinvolvement in one another's lives. There is an extreme of giving support, and there is too much accommodation. Although overly concerned parents invest a great deal of interest in their children, they often tend to foster dependency and make it difficult for the children to form relationships with people outside of the family. This results in a loss of independence for both the children and the parents.

Minuchin in working with a psychosomatic family once demonstrated enmeshment in the therapy session by pinching a 12-year-old diabetic daughter and asking the father if he felt the pain of the pinch. The father responded that he did. When Minuchin asked the same question of the mother, she said that she did not feel the pain but that she had "poor circulation" (Fishman, 1993, p. 43).

In the middle of the continuum between rigid and diffuse boundaries are clear or healthy boundaries, which consist of an appropriate blending of rigid and diffuse characteristics. These help individuals attain a sense of their own identity yet allow for a sense of belongingness within the overall family system. In healthy families there is an ability to cope effectively with the various stresses of living by maintaining a sense of family unity, and at the same time there is the flexibility that allows for restructuring of the family and meeting the individual developmental needs of its members.

## THERAPY GOALS

The goals of structural family therapy are twofold: to reduce symptoms of dysfunction and to bring about structural change within the system by modifying the family's transactional rules and developing more appropriate boundaries. Colapinto (1991) points out that by releasing family members from their stereotyped roles and functions, the system is able to mobilize its resources and to improve its ability to cope with stress and conflict.

In general, the goal for families is the creation of an effective hierarchical structure. Parents are in charge of their children and give them increasing independence and freedom as they mature. The family attempts to change the rules governing interactional patterns so that individual members have clear boundaries. A healthy family is characterized by a system that supports the growth of the members and at the same time encourages the growth of the family unit. In working with enmeshed families, the aim is to assist individuals in achieving greater individuation. In the case of disengaged families, the goal is to increase interaction between members by loosening up rigid boundaries and moving toward clear ones.

Structural therapists do not limit their interventions to families alone; they are interested in the role that the community has in relation to the family. In their book *Institutionalizing Madness: Families, Therapy, and Society,* Elizur & Minuchin (1989) develop the idea that because the larger social structure affects the organization of a family, it is essential that the influence of the community on the family be considered.

Fishman (1993) reports a case that demonstrates the impact of family and community systems working together:

> A mildly retarded 19-year-old woman was living in a system that was organized to provide for her every need. The society provided an abundance of helping services, and between the family and the outside helpers the young woman was prevented from becoming more independent. After a cautious suicide attempt, she confided to a therapist that she desperately wanted to try to get a job in a horticultural nursery, make a life away from home, and manage her own money [p. 44].

The daughter's desires were both attainable and useful, but the societal services that had been set up to help her were actually holding her back. Further investigation revealed that these same community resources supported the parents' overprotectiveness, so that two major subsystems seemed to create a structural system from which it was practically impossible to escape. The daughter's "cautious suicide attempt" made it possible for her to enlist the support of the therapist in a needed change.

## THERAPIST'S ROLE AND FUNCTION

Minuchin (1974) identifies three interactive functions of the therapist: (1) joining the family in a position of leadership, (2) mapping its underlying structure, and (3) intervening in ways designed to transform an ineffective structure. Structural therapists assume that individual change will result from modifying a family's organization and from changing its transactional patterns. The therapist's basic task is to actively engage the family as a unit for the purpose of initiating a restructuring process.

Structural therapists are active in challenging rigid transactional patterns that characterize certain families as they attempt to organize themselves to cope with stressful situations. The therapeutic endeavor involves pushing for clearer boundaries, increasing the degree of flexibility in family interactions, and modifying a dysfunctional family structure (Goldenberg & Goldenberg, 1996). It is the job of structural therapists to join with the family, to block stereotyped interactional patterns, and to facilitate the development of more flexible transactions.

Colapinto (1991) writes that structural therapists play a number of different roles with families, depending on the phase of therapy. From the initial session, therapists are engaged in a dance with the family. Soon after this dance they become stage directors who create scenarios in which problems are played out according to different scripts. Therapists lay the groundwork for a particular situation, create a scenario, assign roles and tasks to a family, and issue directives to members. Then they sit back as a spectator and observe the family in action. Therapists must offer a combination of support and challenge. They need to sustain certain patterns and undermine other patterns. They must learn the appropriate balance between accommodating and negotiating with a family.

## TECHNIQUES

It should be mentioned that more than being a set of techniques, structural family therapy provides a context for viewing a family, offering a clear description of how a healthy family should operate. Minuchin's approach is a therapy of action, rather than insight. Action changes behavior without the need for insight. It also provides opportunities that lead to new experiences and to a transformed family organization. Family therapy aims to modify the present organization of a family, not to explore and interpret the past. Therapists join the family system they are helping, and they make interventions designed to transform the organization of that family. *Joining* is the process of building and maintaining a therapeutic alliance. As the family accepts the leadership of the therapist, it becomes possible for him or her to intervene actively. The therapist joins the family for the purpose of modifying its functioning, not to solve the family's problem. In order for the therapist to become a part of the family system, it is critical that he or she establish rapport by being sensitive to each of the members. Through the process of joining, the family learns that the therapist understands the members and is working with and for each of them. The family and the therapist form a therapeutic partnership to achieve a common goal: "to free the family symptom bearer of symptoms, to reduce conflict and stress for the whole family, and to learn new ways of coping" (Minuchin & Fishman, 1981, p. 29). By joining the family and accommodating to its style, the therapist gains a picture of how members cope with problems and with one another. The aim is to change dysfunctional patterns while they occur in the session; there is a focus on realigning faulty hierarchies and correcting family structure.

In their book *Family Therapy Techniques,* Minuchin and Fishman (1981) emphasize the importance of the therapist's use of self. They believe that therapists need to be comfortable with different levels of involvement. A wide range of techniques may be employed, depending on what fits the situation, the family, and the therapist. At times, therapists may want to disengage from a family by prescribing a course of action. At other times, they may engage and operate as a coach. And yet at other times, they may align with one member of the family, a process called *unbalancing,* which involves the therapist lending his or her authority and weight to break a stalemate maintained by the family system.

Minuchin's techniques are active, directive, and well thought out. His style is typically assertive and even blunt. At times he manipulates the system toward the end of changing inappropriate structures. For example, he may ask the children in the family to solve a sibling problem by discussing it without the parents interfering. A therapist can use whatever strategy is appropriate for meeting a therapeutic goal. These therapeutic techniques need to be suited to the personal characteristics of the therapist and the characteristics of the family. Minuchin draws from many other approaches and combines strategies. Although his basic theory has remained relatively constant, he has moved toward eclecticism in techniques (Nichols & Schwartz, 1995). Techniques include joining, accommodation, working with family interactions, tracking sequences, enactments, intensifying, boundary making, restructuring (strengthening diffuse boundaries and softening rigid ones), reframing, issuing directives, and family mapping. Three of these will be briefly outlined.

FAMILY MAPPING.   Minuchin (1974) employs a method for mapping the structure of the family. In drawing a family map, the therapist identifies boundaries as rigid, diffuse, or clear; transactional styles are identified as enmeshed or disengaged. A variety of maps can highlight the functioning and nature of interpersonal relationships within the family and can be used fruitfully in the therapy sessions. Most of Minuchin's mapping processes are incorporated in McGoldrick and Gerson's (1985) book on genograms.

ENACTMENTS.   In enactments, the therapist asks family members to act out some conflict situation that would happen at home. This allows the therapist to observe how family members interact and to draw conclusions about the structure of the family. The therapist also blocks existing patterns, determines the family's ability to accommodate to different rules, and encourages members to experiment with more functional rules. Change occurs as a result of enacting and dealing with problems, rather than merely talking about these problems (Colapinto, 1991).

REFRAMING.   When the therapist "reframes," he or she casts a new light and provides a different interpretation to a problem situation in a family. The presenting problem can be explored in ways that allow the family to understand an original complaint from many angles. Through reframing it becomes possible to grasp the underlying family structure that is contributing to an individual's problem. In this way, one member does not bear the full burden of blame for a problem or the total responsibility for solving it.

In a session at the Boston Family Institute, Minuchin demonstrated reframing, boundary setting, and enactment with a family including an anorexic 12-year-old girl. After suggesting that the girl's problem was not anorexia but stubbornness and a desire to be the youngest, the baby of the family, Minuchin asked the siblings to discuss how they would handle the girl's temper tantrums and stubbornness. He watched this enactment very carefully in an effort to discern the hierarchy that existed among the children. Occasionally, he used his hands in a gesture designed to stop the mother from interfering with the children's discussion, setting an appropriate boundary for the directed task.

## CONCLUDING COMMENTS

The basic processes of structural family therapy have been delineated by Becvar and Becvar (1996). The focus is on the structure, or organization, within a family. Therapists observe transactions and patterns and are involved in joining, accepting, and respecting the family in its efforts to reorganize and to achieve its goals. A structural map is formed, which provides the therapist with a basis for intervening firmly and directly so that the family will move toward health. Family members are both supported and challenged as they try new behaviors in the session.

Although feminists would join Minuchin in his consideration of larger systems affecting the family, he has not been favorably disposed to feminist interventions designed to save the woman at the expense of the family unit. Feminists, in turn, note that he will often join with the father in the family structure, reinforcing the patriarchy and male authority in the system. Indeed, the process of unbalancing, whether used by Bowenian, structural, strategic, or other therapists, has all too often been used in favor of men and at the expense of women, even in potentially abusive and dangerous situations.

Minuchin's extension of systemic process into larger systems is to be applauded. He was one of the first to work actively with poor families in slums, and he has applied his approach to homosexual couples with the same equanimity as heterosexual couples, seeing no difference in the processes observed. Because of his ability to join successfully with fathers in family systems, his approach is particularly well suited for cultures that place a high value on the authority of the father.

If you are interested in a more in-depth study of this approach, we recommend the following sources: Minuchin (1974); Minuchin and Fishman (1981); Colapinto (1991); and Fishman (1993).

# Strategic Family Therapy

## INTRODUCTION

Strategic therapy—called that because the therapist designs strategies for change—has its foundation in communications theory. The key contributors to the communication model included Gregory Bateson, Don Jackson, Paul Watzlawick, and Jay Haley, all of whom were associated with the Mental Research Institute (MRI) in Palo Alto, California. Satir was associated with the MRI in its early stages of development, but she eventually left to develop her own approach. Bateson in the 1960s first proposed a blending of general systems theory with metaphor. At the same time, Milton Erickson was carving out a professional reputation for being particularly skilled at dealing with resistance through unconventional techniques such as hypnosis and paradoxical directives. Strategic family therapy received its impetus from his therapy (Haley, 1973). Haley, a key strategic therapist, was affiliated during his development with the MRI communications group, with Erickson, and with Minuchin's structural therapy. He was influenced by all of these approaches, and because he was a prolific writer, he was able to have a significant impact on the development of strategic family therapy.

While Watzlawick (1978), Segal (1991), and others stayed with the MRI and developed a similar strategic approach called brief family therapy, Haley left to work with Minuchin at the Philadelphia Child Guidance Clinic. In the 1970s he and Cloé Madanes (who was his wife at the time) established their own Family Institute in Washington, D.C. They focused on working with hierarchy, power, and strategic interventions; they contributed to the development of this approach through their therapy practice, writings, and training of family therapists. At that time, structural family therapy enjoyed the status of being the most popular therapeutic approach; during the 1980s, the strategic approach (or a blend of strategic and structural) was clearly receiving top billing in the field of family therapy.

## KEY CONCEPTS

In strategic family therapy, the problem is *not* addressed as a symptom of some other systemic dysfunction (as in Bowenian or structural family therapy). The problem brought by the family is treated as "real" and is solved. This is a pragmatic approach based on the notion that change occurs through a family carrying out a therapist's directives and changing its transactions. Understanding and insight are not required or sought. No value is placed on therapist interpretation. The focus of therapy is not on growth or resolving issues from the past; rather, it is on solving problems in the present. Therapy tends to be brief, focused on process rather than content, and solution-oriented. The process orientation deals with who is doing what to whom under what conditions. The presenting problem is seen as both the real problem and a metaphor for the system functioning. Considerable emphasis is given to power, control, and hierarchies in families and in the therapy sessions.

In a court-ordered referral of a teenager who attempted suicide, for example, the strategic family therapist assumes that the court is now operating in executive control of the family, because the potential suicide indicates that the family is not handling the problem adequately. Based on an understanding of structural requirements in functional families, the therapist works immediately to join the family and assist in putting the parents back in charge, reestablishing the appropriate hierarchy. The therapist seeks to engage the parents in a discussion about their concern for this suicidal situation, rather than attempting to establish rules or consequences for behavior. Why would this teenager in this family be taking such a desperate measure? This frames the problem as a system problem that is real and must be solved. The therapist does not let the session end without a plan that will guarantee the child's safety. It is possible that the therapist will help the family hospitalize the adolescent or establish a 24-hour watch that involves responsible adult members of the family.

Haley and Madanes are far more interested in the practical applications of strategic interventions to ameliorate a family's problems than they are in formulating a theory of therapy. Strategic family therapy stresses some of the same key concepts as the structural approach to family therapy. In addition, Haley and Madanes maintain a primary concern with how power is distributed in a family, how members communicate with one another, and how the family is organized.

## THERAPY GOALS

The goals of strategic therapy are to resolve a presenting problem by focusing on behavioral sequences. Being rather behavioral at heart, Haley has little use for insight as a goal of therapy. He is concerned about getting people to behave differently, and he is unconcerned with helping people figure out why they act as they do. It is his view that behavior change is the main goal of therapy, for if there is a change in behavior, feelings will change as a result. He hopes to prevent the repetition of maladaptive sequences and attempts to introduce a greater number of alternatives. The intent of strategic interventions is to shift the family organization so that a presenting problem is no longer functional. Strategic therapists have short-range goals that guide their interventions.

During the initial interview, Haley (1976) suggests, therapy tends to be characterized by a number of stages:

- At the *social stage,* the goal is to make the family feel comfortable. The therapist attempts to get all members involved in the therapy session.
- At the *problem stage,* the goal is to find out why the family is seeking help. All members are asked to share their perception of the problem. The therapist poses questions such as: "What do we most need to work on?" "Why are you coming to my office at this time?" "What would you need to change for you to see and feel differently about your family?" "What is each of you willing to do to make the changes you want?"
- The *family-interaction stage* involves family members talking among themselves about their problem in the therapist's presence. The therapist pays particular attention to sequential patterns of behavior, power struggles, hierarchies, communication patterns, and subgroupings. The therapist's goal is to identify possible therapeutic strategies to use in future sessions.
- During the *goal-setting stage,* the therapist and the family work together to identify the specific nature of the problem. In this final phase of the initial family session, a contract is often formulated that spells out treatment goals and ways in which participants can continually assess their progress in meeting these goals.

Strategic family therapists assume that people often develop problems during transitions from one developmental stage to the next; therapy moves the family forward to the appropriate stage of family life. Haley (1973) identifies these phases of family life as (1) the courtship period, (2) the early years of marriage, (3) childbirth and rearing of children, (4) the middle years of marriage, (5) weaning parents from children, and (6) retirement and old age.

## THERAPIST'S ROLE AND FUNCTION

The therapist's role is that of a consultant, an expert, and a stage director. Clearly, the therapist is in charge of the session. There is very little focus on the client/therapist relationship; instead, the therapist is directive and authoritarian. Because Haley (1976) believes that direct educational methods are of little value, he tends to be unwilling to explain himself to his clients; instead, he operates covertly. The therapist is primarily interested in control of power within the therapy relationship. Haley believes that the responsibility for initiating change rests with the therapist, not with the client. Because he views his task as assuming the responsibility for changing the organization of a family and resolving the problems that it brings to therapy, he operates directively, giving the members specific directives on what they are to do, both inside and outside of the therapy sessions. These instructions are aimed at changing the manner in which clients behave with other family members and with the therapist. The way in which people respond to directives reveals valuable information to the therapist and guides both overt and covert interventions that may follow.

A basic feature of Haley's approach is that it is the therapist's responsibility to plan a strategy for solving the client's problems (Haley, 1973). At the initial phase of therapy, clear goals are established, a plan is developed, and specific therapeutic strategies are carefully designed to address problems. Because therapy focuses on the social context of human dilemmas, the therapist's task is to design interventions aimed at the client's social situation (Madanes, 1981).

It is not uncommon these days for divorce to lead to single-parent households in which the mother is having to adjust socially, economically, and emotionally. When such a parent becomes overwhelmed, the hierarchy needed in the family may break down. If there are two children, it is likely that one will overfunction, perhaps becoming parental in the process, and the other will underfunction, becoming the family's reason for referral. In a case where a young boy began missing school while his divorced mother worked and his older sister attempted to get him to behave, the therapist realized that the children were inappropriately in charge of the family. By joining with the mother, the therapist was able to devise a plan to help her regain a sense of competence. She was asked to win the support of a truant officer for the plan. Because she left for work early in the morning, her daughter was asked to merely see that the son had left for school. If the son was not leaving at the appointed time, the daughter was to call the mother, who in turn would call the truant officer, and the boy would be taken to school. Although this plan temporarily left the daughter in a dual parent/child role, it did reduce her involvement with her brother and signal that she was really referring the problem to her mother, the appropriate person to be in charge. The plan was presented to the mother first; she then presented it to the daughter alone and then the son, thereby reinforcing a functional hierarchy for the family (Schilson, 1991).

## TECHNIQUES

Like structural family therapists, strategic therapists tend to track sequences, use reframing techniques, and issue directives. Key techniques are paradoxical interventions, joining, reframing, amplifying, pretending, asking about attempted solutions, and enactments. Haley and Madanes developed ordeal therapy, which is a clinical method for working strategically with marital or family dysfunction (Haley, 1984). Strategic ordeals provide rituals of penance and absolution, and they facilitate a bonding among family members who go through the ordeal together. Madanes (1991) applied this approach to families in which an older child had sexually molested a younger one; she required the family to insist that the perpetrator kneel down in front of the molested child, confess the crime, and beg for forgiveness. The ordeal was not complete unless the confession and begging were sincerely enacted.

The strategic therapy that is taught and practiced by Haley and Madanes views symptoms as some form of communication aimed at gaining control over other family members. For instance, a child's acting-out behavior may symbolize a way to communicate his or her fear of an impending divorce. Madanes and Haley are likely to use indirect methods of provoking the parents and the child to interact and communicate in a way that would make the symptoms unnecessary.

In writing about the elements of strategic family therapy, Madanes (1981) describes the employing of strategic interventions. Each problem is defined as involving at least two people. It is the therapist's job to figure out who is involved in the problem and in what way. The therapist then decides on what interventions will most effectively reorganize the family so that the presenting problem will no longer serve the same function. Interventions are designed to involve certain family members with one another or to disengage other members of a family.

USE OF DIRECTIVES.   Interventions usually take the form of a directive, which may be either straightforward or paradoxical. Straightforward directives include giving advice, making suggestions, coaching, and giving ordeal-therapy assignments (Haley, 1984). The clearer the formulation of the problem and the goals of therapy, the easier it becomes to design and implement directives. Therapists intervene to change a dysfunctional family structure by assigning homework. Directives may be simple, in that they involve one or two people, or complex, involving an entire family. For example, when Haley (1976) discovers that a father is indirectly siding with his daughter (who was wetting her bed) against his wife, he directs the father "to wash the sheets when the daughter wets the bed. The task will tend to disengage daughter and father or cure the bedwetting" (p. 60). This is a simple, straightforward directive designed to change the system and end the problem.

PARADOXICAL INTERVENTIONS.    Strategic therapists rely upon paradoxical interventions to cut through a client's resistance and to bring about change. They devote a great deal of effort to devising paradoxical assignments that fit a problem situation or an individual's symptom. Haley (1976) assumes that families who seek his help will typically resist help from a therapist, often resulting in a power play between family members and the therapist. By using indirect procedures such as paradox, the counselor can deal with an individual's resistance to change creatively and therapeutically. Haley believes that paradoxical strategies force the family to change. In taking control, the therapist upsets the power balance in the family.

Paradoxical techniques place clients in a double bind, so that therapeutic change occurs regardless of the paradoxical directives. Clients may be asked to exaggerate and even perfect a problematic behavior; these directives are designed to move the person and a family relationship in the direction of a solution. For example, a mother who is overly involved with her daughter, watching everything that she does, may be asked to increase this activity and "hover" over the daughter every waking minute. The paradoxical intervention is designed to get the mother to protest that the daughter is not taking enough responsibility for herself.

Similarly, a client who complains that he or she cannot sleep is directed to stay awake. A client who is depressed is told: "Maybe you should not give up this symptom too quickly. It gets you the attention that you say you want. If you got rid of your depression, your family might not notice you." By accepting the therapist's directives and thus maintaining the symptom, the client demonstrates control over it and is no longer helpless to change it. On the other hand, if clients choose to resist the directives and let go of a particular symptom, the problem is not merely controlled but eliminated. For a more detailed review of current schools of paradoxical interventions and a compilation of paradoxical techniques, see Weeks and L'Abate (1982).

Strategic therapists monitor the outcomes of their directives. If a strategy is not working after a short time, they will design a new one. In working with a family, they freely borrow any technique from another approach if it proves to be useful in dealing with a presenting problem.

Haley maintains that his methods, including the use of paradoxical interventions, are not overly manipulative, because all forms of therapy utilize interpersonal influence and depend on the therapist's expertise in solving a family problem. It should be pointed out that all forms of paradoxical intervention do not have to rely so heavily on the power base, authority, and confrontational style of the therapist. For example, Madanes (1981, 1984) has designed techniques for working with a family that are less confrontational than Haley's. Her approach tends to be gentler; she uses humor, fantasy, and playfulness, all of which are a part of her "pretend" techniques. She might ask a child to pretend to have symptoms and the family to pretend to help the child. Madanes views the problem from a metaphorical standpoint. Her goal is to open up possibilities for creating more adaptive behavioral patterns and for the families to abandon dysfunctional or symptomatic patterns of behaving.

REFRAMING.   At times, problematic behavior patterns become entrenched. Reframing consists of reinterpreting such problematic behavior. If a husband devotes most of his time to work and if his preoccupation interferes with the family's functioning, his behavior can be given a new interpretation. Rather than labeling him a "workaholic," the therapist interprets his behavior as his way of showing his concern for his family. The underlying assumption is that giving new meaning to a behavior pattern may produce new behaviors that fit the interpretation. Not only does reframing change the meaning, but frequently it results in understanding other levels of meaning that exist in a transaction. The ultimate objective of a reframing technique is to help family members view problematic behaviors from a different vantage point. From the new vantage point, an intractable problem may become solvable.

## CONCLUDING COMMENTS

Strategic family therapy gained much of its popularity from focusing on problems and solutions. By accepting that the presenting problem really was the problem, it avoided the appearance of ignoring the problem in favor of system correction. And by concentrating on solutions, strategic therapists were able to use the same planning and measurement of effectiveness that are inherent in behavioral models. It is, however, the refusal of most strategic therapists to address insight or even an understanding of family processes that generates the most criticism.

Without insight and understanding, strategic interventions fall easily into "the ends justify the means" approaches to therapy. Although strategic therapists would say that "common sense" is required in designing interventions, common sense is always common sense *to someone or some group* and may not reach the level of universal acceptance (Luepnitz, 1988). There are plenty of examples in the strategic reports of the 1970s and early 1980s of interventions that maintained sexism within families. A depressed man was congratulated for getting his wife to have sex with him the way he desired "by demanding what you have coming to you" (Madanes, 1981, p. 192). To be fair, other strategic interventions involve empowerment of women and broadening men's useful participation in the family, but there is nothing in strategic therapy that requires or seeks the integration of an ethical, social, or political value system.

It is interesting to note that practitioners and students of strategic therapy often have more insight into the cases that are presented than the people or families involved. Haley would argue that just as a person does not need a degree in auto mechanics to get a car fixed at a service station and moving down the road, a family in order to change does not need to understand the metaphor expressed by a symptom, the family organizational pattern that maintains a problem, or the way in which an intervention works. There is a large difference, however, between seeking a one-time service for an object (as from an auto mechanic for your car) and seeking guidance for a significant, ongoing change in family functioning. If discovering the use and purpose of a symptom or a problematic organizational problem helps the therapist make a difference, why would this information not be useful for the family members too? Would such information not reduce confusion? Is the mother, above, who was directed paradoxically to "hover over her daughter" going to use this technique with all of her other children? Or does the family have to return to the therapeutic mechanic for a new prescription each time a problem develops? It is difficult to see how even a focus on "brief" therapy would be harmed by a session devoted to "debriefing" the therapeutic process and an understanding of what processes made a real difference.

If you are interested in a more in-depth study of this approach, we recommend the following sources: Schilson (1991), Haley (1963, 1973, 1976, 1984), Madanes (1981, 1984, 1991); and Watzlawick, Weakland, and Fisch (1974).

# Recent Innovations in Family Therapy

## INTRODUCTION TO SOCIAL CONSTRUCTIONISM

What most of the family therapy approaches we have studied so far have in common is a belief in some essential function(s) of family systems. Each has a claim to its own version of "reality." Bowen emphasizes the need for differentiation of self, the power of families to transmit problems over generations, and the difficulties caused by triangulation. Satir stresses congruent communication, nurturance, connection, and support through the process of change. Even Whitaker's atheoretical approach consistently aims at enlarging a family's ability to experience by creating interpersonal stress and coaching members in alternative ways of relating. Both Minuchin and Haley believe to varying degrees in the foundational nature of family structure and the use of problems within family systems to maintain structure as well as more or less fixed family processes. Each of these approaches to family therapy rests on the assumption that there is something essential about a system (expressed in processes, structures, or rules) that can be discovered and, if discovered, will reveal the universal principles that explain all human behavior in the system. In this sense, most of American family therapy shares with medicine, economics, the sciences, and even religion the search for universal truth that we associate with a modernist perspective. The simultaneous existence of multiple and often antithetic "truths" has led to increasing skepticism in the possibility that a singular, universal truth will one day explain human beings and the systems in which they live. This skepticism is growing in many fields as paradigm shifts create whole new ways of looking at the world: Einstein's theory of relativity shook the very foundation of Newton's physics, and tomorrow it is possible that the work of Stephen Hawkings (1988) will challenge even Einstein's beliefs. The global village is a reality, with television exposing us more and more to multiple cultures, multiple political systems, and multiple ways of understanding human life and the world in which we all live. We have entered into a postmodern world in which truth and reality are understood as conceptualizations, points of view bound by history and context.

To differentiate a modern from a postmodern perspective, it is helpful to look at their differing views of reality. Modernists believe in objective reality that can be observed and systematically known. They further believe that reality exists independently of any attempt to observe it. A modernist believes that people seek therapy for a problem when they have deviated too far from some objective norm. For example, clients are depressed when the range of their mood is below that of what we would consider normal, everyday blues. Postmodernists, in contrast, believe in subjective realities that cannot exist independently of the observational processes used. To postmodern constructivists, reality is based on the use of language and is largely a function of the situations in which people live. In this sense, a problem exists when people agree there is a problem that needs to be addressed: A person is depressed when he or she has internalized a definition of self as depressed. Once a definition of self is internalized, it is hard to recognize behaviors that are counter to the definition; that is, it is hard for someone who is suffering from depression to notice a good mood even when he or she is in it. Similarly, it is hard for a family to recognize when "the bad kid" is being good or when the critical parent is trying to be kind.

In all fields of study some approaches, or knowledge-positions, gain more power than others. For a given period in history these positions are presented as "the truth," and people who support that truth develop processes and "proofs" that are designed to maintain the knowledge-position against all others. The French philosopher Michel Foucault (1970) investigated knowledge-positions in many fields, seeing them not as different truths but as "stories" about life. He noted that currently popular and widely accepted stories become or act as a "dominant culture"; these stories are designed for self-perpetuation and the minimization of alternative stories.

In postmodern thinking, language and the use of language in stories create meaning. There may be as many stories of meaning as there are people to tell the stories, and each of these stories is true for the person telling it. Further, every person involved in a situation has a perspective on the "reality" of that situation. Assuming that each perspective has validity, if only subjective validity, the concept of *universe* (single reality) evolves to that of a *multiverse* (multiple realities). When Kenneth Gergen (1985, 1991), among others, began to emphasize the ways in which people make meaning in social relationships, the field of *social constructionism* was born, signaling a shift in emphasis in both individual and family therapy. Although social constructionists would not primarily identify themselves with either systemic perspectives or even marital and family therapy (they often see only individuals as clients), their focus on social interaction is vital to a new reconsideration of family therapy. In social constructionism, points of view about families are pluralistic (Breunlin, Schwartz, & Mac Kune-Karrer, 1992). Gender awareness, cultural outlooks, developmental processes, and even an interest in the impact of mental illness on families are all entertained as important perspectives in understanding how individuals and families construct their lives. In social construction, the therapist disavows the role of expert, preferring a more collaborative or consultative stance. Empathy and therapeutic process are more important than assessment or technique. Narratives and language processes (linguistics) have become the focus for both understanding families and helping them construct desired change.

At a time when strategic and structural therapists, with their emphasis on brief therapy and therapist-directed change, were the dominant culture in family therapy, another group of counselors in Milan began to design multiple-therapist interventions based on the work of Bateson and Haley, but with a twist. Their process of circular, or relational, questioning was embedded in long interviews involving both hypothesizing and neutrality (Selvini Palazzoli, Boscolo, Cecchin, & Prata, 1980) that explored the family history and the meaning attached to events and problems. The therapists ask questions that allow the family members to verify or modify a hypothesis about the nature of the clients' problems. The stance of the therapists had to be experienced by family members as both neutral and nonblaming. Milan therapists brought to their process a determination that family members could decide what to change if enough questions and discovery led to new or clearer meanings in their lives. They softened greatly the rather aggressive stance that North American strategic therapists took in relation to families and change. They activated an appreciation for the belief systems that supported observed behaviors in families. In this sense, the Milan group became a bridge between modern and postmodern approaches to family therapy (Nichols & Schwartz, 1995). We will now examine five of these newer approaches.

THE REFLECTING TEAM: TOM ANDERSEN.   In northern Norway, there are two months each winter in which the 24-hour day is mostly dark and two months each summer in which the day is mostly light. Most Norwegians live in the southern part of the country, which is more closely related to the rest of Europe. In the north, however, the communities are fewer and farther apart. It is in the north that Tom Andersen (1987, 1991) practices family therapy.

Andersen is a psychiatrist who has both pioneered community-based mental-health programs and initiated a "reflecting team" approach to systemic family therapy in Norway. Norwegian health programs have been nationalized, and everyone has equal access to both physical- and mental-health services. When Andersen started to visit the smaller communities of the north, he immediately recognized that "help" would often include work with extended families. Starting in the mid-1970s, he and his colleagues began to study the structural and strategic approaches used in the United States, incorporating some of the behind-the-mirror processes that Haley had popularized. This process involved a therapist who interviewed a family in one room while a team of consulting therapists watched through a two-way mirror in another room. Occasionally, strategic interventions were sent into the therapy session from the observing team. In the early 1980s, the use of circular questions and longer interviews replaced much of the strategic interventions the team had used for some time. Still, the therapy team remained detached from the family, continuing to work behind the observation mirrors as they had for many years.

In a curious way, their therapy process paralleled the Norwegian environment: The family spent long periods in the light of the therapy room while being kept in equally extended darkness about what the therapy team was thinking and doing. Andersen (1991) reports that it was a family mired in misery that pulled the therapy team out of the darkness and into the light. One day when the team was getting nowhere with its interventions, a therapist knocked on the door of the interview room and asked the family members if they would like to watch and listen to the team's conversation about the family. When the family agreed, the lights in the observation room were turned on, and the family and their interviewer listened to the team process their session. This was the birth of the *reflecting team,* an approach that has quickly gained wide acceptance in family therapy.

Over time, an interviewing process that Andersen (1991) calls "dialogues and dialogues about the dialogues" has been developed to facilitate the use of a reflecting team. An initial interview with a family involves the development of an extensive picture of the clients, the therapist, and "the history of the idea of coming for therapy" (pp. 131–133). A second level of dialogue is about the family's stories of how their family picture and history came to be; each person in the family may have a different story. A third level of dialogue is about the future, about how the family members would like the picture of themselves to change and what alternative stories about their lives might be developed.

When the reflecting team responds to the family, the team members are expected to let their imaginations flow, subject only to a respect for the system and a sensitivity about what the family can handle. Reflections are most often offered as tentative ideas directly connected to the verbal and nonverbal information in the preceding dialogue. The team remains positive in reflecting, reframing stories and parts of stories, looking for alternative stories, and wondering out loud about the possibility and impact of implementing these alternative stories. The family and the initial interviewer listen, and the interviewer notes family reactions, looking for ways in which the reflecting team may be expanding the family's ideas. The session ends with the initial interviewer seeking the family members' reactions to what they have experienced (Becvar & Becvar, 1996).

Andersen (1992) clearly places his reflecting-team approach in the environment of social construction:

> The open conversations that constitute "the Reflecting Process" have brought
> clients and professionals toward more egalitarian relationships. . . . The listener
> is not only a receiver of a story but also, by being present, an encouragement
> to the act of making the story. And that act is the act of constituting one's self
> [p. 66].

THE LINGUISTIC APPROACH: HARLENE ANDERSON AND HAROLD GOOLISHIAN.   A less structured social-constructionist dialogue has been suggested by Harlene Anderson and the late Harold Goolishian (1992) of the Houston Galveston Institute. Rejecting the more therapist-controlled and theory-based interventions of North American family therapy, Anderson and Goolishian developed a therapy of *caring* and *being with* the client. Informed by and contributing to the field of social constructionism, they came to believe that human life is constructed in personal and family narratives that maintain both process and meaning in people's lives. These narratives are constructed in social interaction over time, and the sociocultural systems in which people live are a product of social interaction, not the other way around. In this sense, therapy is also a systemic process created in the therapeutic conversations of the client and the listener/facilitator.

When people or families come for therapy, they are often "stuck" in a dialogic system that has a unique language, meaning, and process related to "the problem." Therapy is another conversational system that becomes therapeutic through its "problem-organizing, problem-dis-solving" nature (Anderson & Goolishian, 1992, p. 27). It is the therapist's willingness to enter the therapeutic conversation from a "not-knowing" position that facilitates this caring relationship with clients. In the *not-knowing position,* therapists still retain all of the knowledge and personal, experiential capacities they have gained over years of living, but they allow themselves to enter the conversation in *curiosity* and with intense interest in discovery. From this position, clients become the experts who are informing and sharing with the therapist the significant narratives of their lives. The not-knowing position is empathic and is most often characterized by questions that "come from an honest, continuous therapeutic posture of not understanding too quickly" (Anderson, 1993, p. 331).

In this model, the questions the therapist asks are always informed by the answers the client/expert has provided. The therapist enters the session with some sense from referral or intake of what the client or family wishes to address. The initial question reflects an interest in hearing the story that clients want to tell. Their answers provide information that stimulates the interest of the therapist, still in a posture of inquiry, and another question proceeds from each answer given. The process is similar to the Socratic method without any preconceived idea about how or in which direction the development of the stories should go. The intent of the conversation is not to confront or challenge the narrative of the clients but to facilitate the telling and retelling of the story until opportunities for new meaning and new stories develop: "Telling one's story is a representation of experience; it is constructing history in the present" (Anderson & Goolishian, 1992, p. 37). By staying with the story, the therapist/client conversation evolves into dialogues of new meaning, constructing new narrative possibilities.

THE NARRATIVE APPROACH: MICHAEL WHITE AND DAVID EPSTON.    Of all the social constructionists, Michael White and David Epston (1990) most reflect the influence of Michel Foucault (1979, 1980) in their use of narrative in therapy. Foucault asserts that those perspectives that become dominant culture narratives have to be challenged at every level and every opportunity, because their function is, in part, to minimize or eliminate alternative knowledge-positions and alternative narratives. Because of the power of dominant culture narratives, individuals and families tend to integrate these positions as if they are the only possible ones to take—even if those positions are not useful to the individual or the family. Like those who identify themselves with feminist therapy, White (1992) believes that a dominant culture is designed to perpetuate viewpoints, processes, and stories that serve those who benefit from that culture but that may work against the freedom and functionality of the individual and the family.

Societal narratives in most countries perpetuate a strong preference for men, often discriminate against diversity, and may be designed to exclude gay men and lesbians from being full members of a given community. These narratives are so strong that even the people who suffer within these stories believe them. Hence, many women *accept* their inequality with men; members of minority cultures discriminate against one another and against other cultures; and gay men and lesbians, like the heterosexual community, may also be homophobic, if to a lesser extent.

Families, too, incorporate the dominant culture narratives about what a family "should" be, and to the extent that problems can be met and handled within that narrative structure, life seems to go smoothly. When the dominant story loses its power to meet the needs and demands of family life, the family has a problem. Within the family, narratives are maintained that allow each individual as well as the system to construct meaning in the lives and relationships of the members. These stories become dominant culture narratives for a given family unit and are given the same power that a societal narrative often has.

According to White, individuals construct the meaning of life in interpretive stories, which are then treated as "truth." The construction of meaning can happen monologically (by oneself) or dialogically (with others), with the latter having the greater power in our lives because we are social beings. In this sense, an individual is most often a socially constructed narrative system. The process of *living our story* is not simply metaphorical; it is very "real," with real effects and real consequences in family and societal systems. Families are microsystems, small social systems, with communal narratives that express their values and meanings; they are embedded in larger macrosystems, such as culture and society. Because people are systems within systems within still other systems, they can easily lose freedom. Therapy is, in part, a reestablishment of individual and family freedom from the oppression of external problems and the dominant stories of larger systems.

Like Anderson and Goolishian, White and Epston (1990) have developed a therapeutic process based on questions. Their questions, however, are purposeful and politically organized to deconstruct oppressive narratives. Their therapy starts with an exploration of the family in relation to the presenting problem. It is not uncommon for clients to present initial stories in which they and the problem are fused, as if one and the same. White uses externalizing questions to separate the problem from the people affected by the problem. These questions, sometimes called "relative influence questioning" (p. 42), assist the clients in charting the influence of the problem in their life as well as charting their own influence in the life of the problem. This shift in language already begins the deconstruction of the original narrative in which the people and the problem were fused; now the problem is objectified as external to them.

Jim starts by saying that he gets angry far too much, especially when he feels that his wife is criticizing him unjustly: "I just flare! I pop off, get upset, fight back. Later, I wish I hadn't, but it's too late. I've messed up again." Although questions about how his anger occurs, complete with specific examples and events, will help chart the influence of the problem, it is really the following kinds of questions that *externalize* the problem: "What is the mission of the anger, and how does it recruit you into this mission?" "How does the anger get you, and what are you doing to let it become so powerful?" "What does the anger require of you, and what happens to you when you meet its requirements?"

In this narrative approach, externalizing questions are followed by questions searching for unique outcomes: "Was there ever a time in which anger wanted to take you over, and you resisted? What was that like for you? How did you do it?" Unique outcomes can often be found in the past or present, but they can also be hypothesized for the future: "What form would taking a stand against your anger take?" It is within the account of unique events that alternative narratives are facilitated and developed.

Following a description of a unique event, White (1992) suggests questions that lead to more clearly declared narratives:

What do you think this tells me about what you have wanted for your life, and about what you have been trying for in your life?
How do you think that knowing this has affected my view of you as a person?
Of all those people who have known you, who would be least surprised that you have been able to take this step in challenging the problem's influence in your life? [p. 133].

The development of unique outcome stories into solution stories is facilitated by what Epston and White (1992) call "circulation questions":

Now that you have reached this point in life, who else should know about it?
I guess there are a number of people who have an outdated view of who you are as a person. What ideas do you have about updating these views?
If other people seek therapy for the same reasons that you did, can I share with them any of the important discoveries that you have made? [p. 23].

One of the people we will study in the next section is William O'Hanlon. In a review of White and Epston's work, O'Hanlon (1994) describes their narrative therapeutic process in the following steps:

- The collaboration with the person or the family begins with coming up with a mutually acceptable name for the problem;
- Personifying the problem and attributing oppressive intentions and tactics to it;
- Investigating how the problem has been disrupting, dominating, or discouraging the person and the family;
- Discovering moments when the clients haven't been dominated or discouraged by the problem or their lives have not been disrupted by the problem;
- Finding historical evidence to bolster a new view of the person as competent enough to have stood up to, defeated, or escaped from the dominance or oppression of the problem;
- Evoking speculation from the person and the family about what kind of future is to be expected from the strong, competent person that has emerged from the interview so far;
- Finding or creating an audience for perceiving the new identity and new story [pp. 25–26].

Epston has developed a special facility for carrying on therapeutic dialogues between sessions through the use of letters (White & Epston, 1990). His letters may be long—chronicling the process of the interview and the agreements reached—or short—highlighting a meaning or understanding reached in the session and asking a question that has occurred to him since the end of the previous therapy visit. These letters are also used to encourage clients, by noting their strengths and accomplishments in relation to handling problems, or to note the meaning of accomplishments for others in their community:

> [This] re-authoring therapy intends to assist persons to resolve problems by: (1) enabling them to separate their lives and relationships from knowledges/stories that are impoverishing; (2) assisting them to challenge practices of self and relationship that are subjugating; and (3) encouraging persons to re-author their lives according to alternative knowledge/stories and practices of self and relationship that have preferred outcomes [Epston, White, & Murray, 1992, p. 108].

SOLUTION-ORIENTED THERAPY: WILLIAM O'HANLON, MICHELLE WEINER-DAVIS, AND STEVE DE SHAZER.   Similar in many ways to White's reauthoring process, but growing out of the strategic therapy orientation at the Mental Research Institute, solution-oriented therapy finds its place in social constructionism by shifting the MRI focus on problem solving to a complete focus on solutions. Steve de Shazer (with Insoo Berg) initiated this shift at the Brief Therapy Center in Milwaukee in the late 1970s. He had trained with the MRI people but had grown dissatisfied with the constraints of their strategic model. In the 1980s, he collaborated with a number of therapists, including Michelle Weiner-Davis, who started her own solution-focused center. Weiner-Davis later joined O'Hanlon, who had been trained by Milton Erickson, and together they have expanded the foundation originated by de Shazer (Nichols & Schwartz, 1995).

Solution-oriented therapy differs from both strategic models and traditional therapies by eschewing the past—and even the present—in favor of the future. It is so focused on what is possible that it has little or no interest in or understanding of the problem. De Shazer (1991), who is often the most radical of the group, has suggested that therapists do not need to know a problem in order to solve it and that there is no necessary relationship between problems and their solutions. If knowing and understanding problems is unimportant, so is searching for "right" solutions. O'Hanlon and Weiner-Davis (1989) believe that there are multiple solutions that any person or family might consider and that what is right for one person or family may not be for others. Unlike the MRI strategic-therapy approach, in this model clients choose the goals they wish to accomplish in therapy.

Because clients often come to therapy in a "problem-oriented" state, even the few solutions they have considered are wrapped in the power of the problem orientation. Solution-oriented therapists counter this client presentation with optimistic conversations that highlight their belief in achievable, usable goals that are just around the corner. These goals are developed by using what de Shazer (1985, 1988) calls the *miracle question:* Essentially, if a miracle happened and the problem you have was solved overnight, how would you know it was solved, and *what would be different*? Clients are then encouraged to enact "what would be different" in spite of perceived problems. This process reflects O'Hanlon and Weiner-Davis's (1989) belief that changing the *doing* and *viewing* of the perceived problem changes the problem.

Similar to White's process of eliciting "unique events," solution-oriented therapists ask *exception questions* that direct clients to times in their lives when the problem didn't exist. This exploration reminds clients that problems are not all-powerful and have not existed forever; it also provides a field of opportunity for evoking resources, engaging strengths, and positing possible solutions. Solution-oriented therapists focus on small, achievable changes that may lead to additional positive outcomes. Their language joins with the client's, using similar words, pacing, and tone, but also involves questions that presuppose change, posit multiple answers, and remain goal-directed and future-oriented.

Solution-oriented therapists also use *scaling questions* when change is required in human experiences not easily observed, such as feelings, moods, or communication. For example, a woman reporting feelings of panic or anxiety might be asked: "On a scale of zero to ten, with zero being how you felt when you first came to therapy and ten being how you feel the day after your miracle occurs and your problem is gone, how would you rate your anxiety right now?" Even if the client has only moved away from zero to one, she has improved. How did she do that? What does she need to do to move another number up the scale?

Individuals and families bring narratives to therapy. Some are used to justify their belief that life can't be changed or, worse, that life is moving them further and further away from their goals. De Shazer (1991) prefers to engage clients in conversations that lead to progressive narratives whereby people create situations in which they can make steady gains toward their goals—for example: "Tell me about times when you feel good, when things are going your way, and when you enjoy your family and friends." It is in these stories of life worth living that the power of problems is deconstructed and new solutions are manifest and made possible. Like other social constructionists, solution-oriented therapists believe that nothing is ever the same. Life is *change,* and change is inevitable. Solution-oriented therapists seek only to guide the changer and the changed in a self-chosen direction.

FEMINIST PSYCHOTHERAPY WITH FAMILIES. Feminist therapists integrate many theoretical orientations in their work with families. Some use object-relations theory (reconsidered and reconstituted to empower women) as a therapeutic model, and others employ Adlerian, existential, Gestalt, or cognitive principles. Still others have adopted the systemic approaches of Bowen, Satir, Whitaker, Minuchin, and even the strategic therapists. The professions that most affect the family are being transformed by women like Betty Bardige, Mary Field Belenky, Blythe McVicker Clinchy, Carol Gilligan, Nancy Rule Goldberger, Jill Mattuck Tarule, Jill McLean Taylor, and Janie Victoria Ward in human development; Michele Bograd, Paula J. Caplan, Phyllis Chesler, Barbara Ehrenreich, Bell Hooks, Dell Martin, Jean Baker Miller, and Lenore Walker in sociology and psychology; and Carol M. Anderson, Marianne Ault-Riche, Judith Myers Avis, Pauline Boss, Lois Braverman, Annette M. Brodsky, Betty Carter, Nancy Chodorow, Dorothy Dinnerstein, Virginia Goldner, Thelma Jean Goodrich, Rachel T. Hare-Mustin, Molly Layton, Harriet Goldhor Lerner, Deborah Anna Luepnitz, Monica McGoldrick, Peggy Papp, Sallyann Roth, Olga Silverstein, J. Pamela Weiner, Dorothy Wheeler, Barre Thorne, Froma Walsh, and Marianne Walters, to name a few, in family systems therapy. Feminists come from all cultures and may be conservative, "liberal, Marxist, Zionist, Christian, radical, and lesbian separatist" (Luepnitz, 1988, p. 14). In short, they interact with and incorporate psychological, social, cultural, and political positions that span the spectrum of human life.

As such, it is impossible to point to a singular, unified "feminist family therapy." What feminists do share in common is (1) a belief that patriarchy is *alive and sick* in sociopolitical life and the life of the family; (2) a realization that "the normal family" has not been so "normal" or wonderful for mothers and clearly reflects the discrimination against women evident in world systems beyond the family; (3) a commitment to reforming family and society in ways that fully empower and enfranchise women economically, socially, and politically; and (4) therapeutic processes that include a positive attitude toward women, social analysis, explicit consideration of gender issues, and treating the *personal as political* (Avis, 1986).

Given the wide diversity of feminist therapeutic practice, why have we included feminist psychotherapy in the larger context of social constructionism? To be sure, there are some differences between the two conceptualizations. The radical social constructionists (such as Gergen) do not believe that a person "has a self," unified and somewhat consistent throughout life; many feminists do believe this. Some social constructionists are willing to look at all stories, personal narratives, and dialogues as neutral (or equal in value) and as unique to those people involved in a given socially constructed event; feminists would profoundly disagree. Still, there are many areas of common ground, enough to place feminist psychotherapy with families at the center of recent innovations in family therapy.

Feminists share a belief, similar to the position of Michael White, that dominant culture positions are designed to maintain themselves and to advance views that benefit the powerful and disenfranchise all "others." Indeed, feminists see patriarchy as the oldest and most universal dominant culture position in the world, extending across cultures, religions, nations, and history. For many years, major schools of family therapy ignored patriarchy or treated it as unimportant or even nonexistent, noting that fathers were often absent from families, physically and emotionally. Indeed, some schools of family therapy suggested that mothers "ran" families and that, if anything, fathers needed to have more influence, not less. Both Ferguson (1983) and Luepnitz (1988) have noted, however, that the personal patriarchy of former centuries has been replaced by the "public patriarchy" of the 20th century. "While under earlier forms of patriarchy it was a male *person* who limited women's expenditures, freedom to work, and sexual activity, in the case of public patriarchy, it is the state, the welfare agency, and the media that control these things" (Luepnitz, 1988, p. 16). It is not difficult to notice that most of the "founding masters" of family therapy have been men and that their systems have all too often joined the dominant culture in conveying to women what "good mothering and femininity" are. The dominant culture of patriarchy functions even in the absence of fathers and is passed along in our descriptions and investigations of the normal family.

Many researchers have noted the ways in which family life is configured in favor of men and to the detriment of women (Bernard, 1972; Degler, 1980; Durkheim, 1951; Luepnitz, 1988). From Durkheim's work on suicide in families at the turn of the last century to Bernard's thesis that married men are happier than single men and single women are happier than married women, marriage and family have not boded well for women. Perhaps the most significant study of normal families has been the Timberlawn research (Gurman & Kniskern, 1981; Lewis, Beaver, Gossett, & Phillips, 1976; Walsh, 1993). Luepnitz (1988) summarizes the findings as follows:

> Women in the "adequate" (also called normal) families were "overwhelmed with responsibility," "obese," "psychosomatically ill," and "sexually dissatisfied." The men in these same families were "functioning well" and were not sexually dissatisfied. Thus . . . an adequate family consists of a husband and children who are functioning adequately and a wife who is not [pp. 10–11].

Taking a stand against a society or culture that defines the pathologizing and subservice of women as "normal" is a primary objective when feminists engage in psychotherapy with families. Just as other social constructionists see dominant positions asserted and maintained in narratives, even narratives about research, feminists know that patriarchy will be expressed in narratives, too. Like Foucault, whom we mentioned earlier, feminists use a careful examination of history to generate alternative stories, to contextualize current human experience, and to deconstruct the power and mythology maintained in a patriarchal system.

When it is suggested that families were better when a woman stayed home to raise "her" children, feminists note that women have always had outside help *from other women* while they worked in the fields or the factories. Neither work outside the home nor day care are occurrences of the last 50 years. Neither is it true that women who work outside the home have poorer health. Indeed, working women have been getting healthier for the last few decades (studies cited in Luepnitz, 1988). It is true that women still maintain the primary responsibility for child and home care. Until men take a more equal and committed role in family life and experience a more connected relationship to their children as normal, women who work will continue to do double duty.

Patriarchy infuses not only our stories about what constitutes a *normal family* but also most narratives about *normal human development*. Carol Gilligan (1982) began to change all of that. She noted that developmental psychologists ranging from Freud and Erikson to Piaget and Kohlberg had based their theories on male populations, assuming either that women's growth was similar to that of men or that women were insignificant exceptions to the male norm. Gilligan and her associates conducted thousands of hours of interviews with adolescent and young adult women (Belenky, Clinchy, Goldberger, & Tarule, 1986; Gilligan, 1982; Gilligan, Ward, & Taylor, 1988). These studies produced significant new data and are important to social constructionists both for their findings and for the methods used to develop the findings.

Taken together, the studies noted above demonstrate that women and men develop different moral outlooks, become human knowers in different ways, and solve problems in manners that seek different ends. Women tend to see life in the development of intimate connections; men tend to see life from a detached perspective and become protective of individual rights. Women employ a code of care and "no harm" in relationships, whereas men are more concerned with rules and rights. Women tend to grow from what may literally be a silenced self into increasingly considering their own voice and participation in what is valued in their lives. Men, on the other hand, are quick to gain voice. Their participation in the human experience is never in doubt. Their moral growth is characterized by the attainment of justice and an application of principles that enact this justice. In that sense, women's development is grounded on empathy, concern, and care, the qualities that nurture and promote connection in families and community; men's development seeks good judgment.

Understanding these different developmental narratives allows us to value processes of growth fundamental to women rather than treating women as inadequately developed men. The long interviews that led to this new knowledge incorporated many of the therapeutic processes encouraged by social constructionists: The interviewee was treated as the expert, and the interviewer was a collaborator in the discovery of knowledge; the information was approached from a not-knowing position; and the use of reflection as a means of clarifying ideas was constant. These postmodern researchers, like the other social-constructionist therapists we have studied, saw themselves as participants/observers engaged in the co-construction of new, alternative positions.

Although the diversity of feminist therapy with families makes it impossible to delineate a singular process or a set of techniques employed by all, feminist counseling does tend to have some commonalities. First of all, it is conducted with conscious purpose, including (1) a positive attitude toward women, (2) valuing that which is considered "feminine" or "nurturing" in society and social interactions, (3) a willingness to confront patriarchal process and reinvolve fathers in family life, and (4) empowering women while supporting egalitarian families. Helping women give voice to the meanings in their lives, demonstrating interest in and empathy for women's stories, and contextualizing as well as validating women's experiences are all processes associated with feminist therapy, and they developed in many ways from the early experiences that women had in consciousness-raising groups.

In addition, Judith Myers Avis (1986) lists six ways in which gender issues might be introduced into therapy with families:

1. defining the problem in such a way as to include the dimensions of power and gender;
2. introducing and discussing in therapy gender issues such as money, power, equity, flexibility, options, housekeeping, and childcare;
3. making connections for the family between gender issues in the family and those in the wider social system;
4. challenging stereotypic behaviors, attitudes, and expectations;

5. discussing the differing impact of divorce on women and on men; and

6. raising gender issues in relation to family of origin [p. 226].

Feminist consciousness of alternative and diverse perspectives has infused family therapy with some of its most significant issues. In addition to helping families address issues of power and to reconsider and change gender-based roles and rules, feminists have called upon the profession of family therapy to stop ignoring the social problems of family violence, cultural discrimination, ageism, poverty, race, and class as well as discrimination against gay men and lesbians (Nichols & Schwartz, 1995). Feminist research and therapeutic practice continually work to enlarge the focus and consciousness of family therapists, calling on us to participate in the largest social reconstruction of all.

The five social-constructionist approaches to family therapy that we have considered are compared in Table 12-2.

## KEY CONCEPTS

COLLABORATION AND EMPOWERMENT.   In social-constructionist theory, the therapist as expert is replaced by the client as expert. The therapist enters into dialogues in an effort to elicit the perspectives, resources, and the unique experiences of the client(s). A heavy emphasis is placed on the use of questions, often relational in nature, that empower the people in families to speak, to give voice to their diverse positions, and to own their capabilities in the presence of others. The past is history and sometimes provides a foundation for understanding and discovering differences that will make a difference. But it is the present and the future in which life will be lived. The therapist supplies the optimism and sometimes a process, but the client generates what is possible and contributes the movement that actualizes it.

STORIED LIVES AND NARRATIVES.   Social constructionists believe that real people live in families and that each person is living the "story of his or her life"; each person contributes to the "story of family life"; and all of the stories are in constant co-construction. Human beings "make meaning" expressed in language and narratives; in this sense, families are meaningful systems. When the narratives of meaning become saturated with problems and overwhelming to those who live with and through them, social constructionists enter the personal and familial searches for alternative stories.

## THERAPY GOALS

Social constructionists, although somewhat different from therapist to therapist, share an interest in the generation of new meaning in the lives of the people and families they serve. They seek to enlarge perspective and focus, facilitate the discovery or creation of new options, and co-develop solutions that are

T A B L E  12-2
A Comparison of Five Approaches to Social Construction in Family Therapy

| | THE REFLECTING TEAM | THE LINGUISTIC APPROACH | THE NARRATIVE APPROACH | SOLUTION-ORIENTED THERAPY | FEMINIST THERAPY WITH FAMILIES |
|---|---|---|---|---|---|
| *Key figures* | Tom Andersen | Harlene Anderson and Harold Goolishian | Michael White and David Epston | William O'Hanlon, Michelle Weiner-Davis, and Steve de Shazer | See names on pages 413 and 414 |
| *Therapy goals* | Share reflections; create new life stories for family. | Create alternative narratives. | Deconstruct dominant narratives; reauthor lives. | Stop problem focus; co-create new solutions and life stories. | Deconstruct male-dominated culture; achieve women-supported egalitarian families. |
| *Role and function of the therapist* | Actively facilitates; investigates life stories of family; reflects and conducts dialogue | Reflects empathic responses; co-evolves new alternative stories; displays compassion and "not-knowing" | Questions clients to develop life narrative; facilitates deconstruction and reauthoring | Co-develops new solutions with family | Supports and develops women's position in family; collaborates |
| *Process of change* | Develop family life story; use reflecting team dialogue; help family reflect. | Adopt not-knowing position; follow stories; evolve alternative stories. | Develop narrative; deconstruct story; reauthor new narrative. | Focus on the positive; develop solutions; support progress; celebrate change. | Listen carefully; honor women; challenge stereotypes; support equality. |
| *Techniques and innovations* | Reflections and dialogues; open teams | Listening from a not-knowing position | Externalization and developing unique events | Miracle questions; exception questions; scaling questions | Focus on women and families as political |

unique to the people and families they see. Social constructionism almost always includes an awareness of the impact of various aspects of dominant culture on human life, and therapists in this model seek to develop alternative ways of being, acting, knowing, and living.

## THERAPIST ROLE AND FUNCTION

Therapists in the social-constructionist model are active facilitators. The concepts of care, interest, empathy, contact, and even fascination that are essential to the person-centered therapists, the existentialists, the Gestalt therapists, and other humanists reemerge here as a relational necessity. The not-knowing position, which allows therapists to follow, affirm, and be guided by the stories of their client(s), creates participant/observer and process-facilitator roles for the therapist and integrates therapy with a postmodern science of human inquiry. Collaboration, compassion, reflection, and discovery characterize the interactions of therapist and client in a social-constructionist model.

## TECHNIQUES

LISTENING WITH AN OPEN MIND.   Whether the therapist is part of a reflecting team or is a single interviewer, all social-constructionist theories place a strong emphasis on listening to clients without judgment or blame, affirming and valuing them, and creating meaning and new possibilities out of the stories they share rather than out of a preconceived and ultimately imposed theory of importance and value.

QUESTIONS THAT MAKE A DIFFERENCE.   Depending on the approach, the questions therapists ask may seem embedded in a unique conversation, part of a dialogue about earlier dialogues, a discovery of unique events, a search for miracle solutions, or an exploration of dominant culture processes and imperatives. Whatever the purpose, the questions are often circular, or relational, and they seek to empower clients and families in new ways. To use Bateson's famous phrase, they are questions in search of a difference that will make a difference.

DECONSTRUCTION AND EXTERNALIZATION.   Human beings and families come to therapy when their lives are overwhelmed by the problems they face. Both people and systems of people express their concerns in problem-saturated stories to which they are fused. Social constructionists differ from many early family therapists in believing that it is neither the person nor the family that is the problem. Living life means coping with problems, not being fused with them. Problems and problem-saturated stories have real impacts on real people and dominate living in extremely negative ways. Externalization is one process for deconstructing the power of a narrative and separating the person or family from identifying with the problem. The separation facilitates hope by allowing clients to take a stand against that which is not useful in their storied lives. In a different way, feminists deconstruct the power of patriarchy by holding "commonly held" views up to the light of history and alternative data that refute the dominant culture position. Both deconstructions seek to empower the person and the family as competent to handle the problems faced.

ALTERNATIVE STORIES AND RE-AUTHORING.    Whether involved in a free-flowing conversation or engaged in a series of questions in a relatively consistent process, social constructionists seek to elicit new possibilities and embed them in the life narratives and processes of the people they serve. White and Epston's inquiry into unique events is similar to the exception questions of solution-oriented therapists. Both seek to build upon the competence already present in the person or the family. The development of alternative stories, or narratives, is an enactment of ultimate hope: Today is the first day of the rest of your life.


## CONCLUDING COMMENTS

A mere hundred years ago, Freud, Adler, and Jung were part of a major paradigm shift that transformed psychology as well as philosophy, science, medicine, and even the arts. Now we prepare for another dramatic turning point as we approach the 21st century. Postmodern constructions of alternative knowledge sources seem to be one of the paradigm shifts most likely to affect family counseling and psychotherapy in the immediate future. The creation of the self, which so dominated the modernist search for human essence and truth, is being replaced with the concept of *storied lives.* Diversity, multiple frameworks, and an integration/collaboration of the knower with the known are all part of this new social movement to enlarge perspectives and options. For some social constructionists, the process of "knowing" includes a distrust of the dominant culture positions that permeate families and society today. For these people, change starts with deconstructing the power of cultural narratives and then proceeds to the co-construction of a new life of meaning.

   If you are interested in a more in-depth study of the newer approaches to family therapy, we recommend the following sources: Andersen (1991); White and Epston (1990); O'Hanlon and Weiner-Davis (1989); de Shazer (1991); Luepnitz (1988); McNamee and Gergen (1992); Becvar and Becvar (1996); and Nichols and Schwartz (1995, Chapter 11).

# Integration of Family-Therapy Models

Satir (1983) suggests that although most family therapists agree on some basic points about how family systems operate, they have wide differences regarding the best ways of modifying these systems. She calls for family practitioners to be open to drawing from the best of what the schools of family therapy offer. Contending that the last word has yet to be spoken, Satir writes: "It behooves all of us to continue being students. My recommendation is that we free ourselves to look anywhere and to use what seems to fit. This makes each of us a continually growing entity" (p. ix).

In predicting the future of marital and family therapy, Gurman and Kniskern (1992) say that the field will be characterized by less purity of therapy methods. They predict a loosening of boundaries both among the various orientations within the field and between family therapy and other therapies. Today there is a flexible combining of treatment techniques and strategies from seemingly incompatible systems of family therapy. Gurman and Kniskern emphasize the importance of a basic theoretical foundation to serve as a guide for integrating concepts and techniques from the various approaches, which will lead to improved practice. As you will see in Chapter 13, there is a similar trend toward the integration of individual counseling models.

Hanna and Brown (1995) assert that rigidly adhering to a theoretical orientation is likely to limit therapeutic effectiveness. They acknowledge that the majority of family therapists do not limit themselves to a single approach; rather, they integrate their own blend of methods based on their training, personality, and the population of families they serve. They believe that the integrative approach, which can begin at an early stage of training, is developed by focusing on similarities among approaches and identifying common elements of how families change. These elements include the role of the therapist and theories explaining how change comes about in a family. Hanna and Brown maintain that the practice of family therapy can be based on a synthesis of key principles across multiple models. They raise two pivotal questions about the integration of concepts and methods from various models: (1) What knowledge do family therapists need to practice effectively? and (2) What specific skills and attitudes are common to the practice of family therapy? (For a concise discussion of this trend toward integrated practice of family therapy, see Hanna and Brown, 1995, Chapter 2.)

Nichols and Schwartz (1995) also maintain that family therapy is moving toward integration. They put this trend toward convergence nicely: "Today it no longer makes sense to study one and only one model and to neglect the insights of others. Family therapists are not only cross-fertilizing across models of family therapy, they are also adding concepts and methods from psychology and individual psychotherapy" (p. 536). In their recommendations to students about how to select a theoretical position, they make these points:

- During training it is a good idea to concentrate on learning one approach well by becoming immersed in that particular model.
- Because the therapy techniques are never separate from the person using them, it makes sense to choose an approach that is congruent with one's style as a person.
- The ability to integrate various theoretical orientations with one's personal style involves a knowledge of the major approaches to family therapy and a thorough background of training and supervision in some form of family therapy.
- Ultimately, experienced family therapists will be able to integrate their knowledge and skills with their personal style.

For a comparative analysis of the major models of family therapy and an excellent discussion of an integrative perspective, see Nichols and Schwartz, 1995, Chapter 12.

# Family Therapy Applied to the Case of Stan

Although it is impossible to provide an example of each family systems approach to the case of Stan, we will offer two pictures of how a family session might go. In the first example, we use processes and interventions from the first five systemic approaches presented above. We want to demonstrate at various points in the session the uses of genograms, engaging a multigenerational family, joining, reframing, congruent communication, boundary setting in therapy, and creating new possibilities. Although we have tried to provide an integrative example, we want to emphasize that this is not *the* way to do family therapy. In the second example, we use a narrative approach from social-construction theory to demonstrate how change based on relational questioning can happen even when there is only one client.

## AN INTEGRATED SYSTEMS APPROACH

A therapist with a family systems orientation begins working with Stan by conducting an assessment of his family of origin (see Figure 12-1). In addition to assessing relationships with his parents, grandparents, and siblings, a systemic therapist is interested in finding out about his interactions at his school, place of work, church, and any friendship networks. The assumption is that his problems cannot be fully understood or fruitfully explored in therapy without considering his relationships to his family and other key systems of which he is a part. Many of his presenting complaints are best understood as symptoms of power struggles and dysfunctional communication patterns within his family of origin. The family therapist approaches him as part of an ongoing, living unit. As we will see, most of his problems have familial roots, and he is still very much engaged with his parents and siblings, no matter how difficult their relationships may be.

Stan's genogram is really a family picture, or map of his family-of-origin system. In this genogram, he is the index person (IP) whose problems are the purpose for the family session. The index person is indicated on the genogram with either a double square (for a man or boy) or a double circle (for a woman or girl). All other men are designated with a single square, and women with a single circle. In each square or circle, the name of the person is noted along with the year the person was born. In Stan's family, his grandparents tend to have fairly long lives. One grandparent (Joseph) died at the age of 69; the rest are still alive in their 70s. Death in a genogram is indicated by an **X** through a person's name and square or circle. Next to the person we indicate the year and cause of death. Stan's uncle Seth died in Vietnam in 1968 at 26 years of age. He wanted to be a career soldier, but his career was all too short. Stan's paternal grandfather died of cancer in 1976.

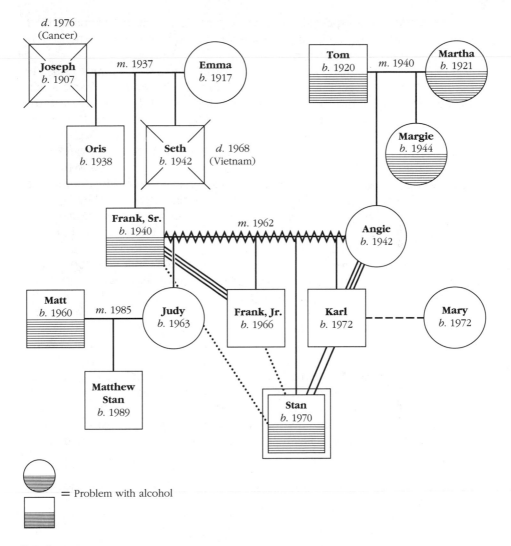

F I G U R E   12-1
Three-Generation Genogram of Stan's Family

Stan's maternal grandparents are both alive. The shaded lower half of their square and circle indicates that each had some problem with alcohol. In the case of Tom, Stan reports that he was an admitted alcoholic who recommitted himself to Christ and found help through Alcoholics Anonymous. Stan's maternal grandmother always drank a little socially and with her husband, but she never considered herself to have a problem. In her later years, however, she seems to sneak alcohol more and more, and it is a source of distress in her marriage. Stan also knows that Margie drinks a lot, because he has been drinking with his aunt for years. She is the one who gave him his first drink.

Angie, Stan's mother, married Frank, Sr., after he had stopped drinking, also with the help of AA. He still goes to meetings. Angie is suspicious of all men around alcohol. She is especially upset with Stan and with Judy's husband, Matt, who "also drinks too much." The genogram makes it easy to see the pattern of alcohol problems in this family.

Solid lines between people indicate a formal and direct relationship. The solid lines between Joseph and Emma; Tom and Martha; Frank, Sr., and Angie; and Matt and Judy all indicate a marriage, and the year of the marriage is above the line. The dashes between Karl and Mary indicate a relationship that is not formalized. They are living together but are not married. The jagged lines /\/\/\ between Frank, Sr., and Angie indicate conflict in the relationship. The three solid lines ═══════ between Frank, Sr., and Frank, Jr., and between Angie and Karl indicate a very close or even fused relationship. The double lines ═══════ between Karl and Stan are used to note a close relationship only. As we will see, Karl actually looks up to Stan in this family. The dotted lines . . . . . . . between Frank, Sr., and Stan and between Frank, Jr., and Stan indicate a distant or even disengaged relationship.

It is interesting to note that Frank, Sr., was a middle child who took orders and was criticized by his mother, a very strong woman. He married an oldest child, who was also a strong, critical woman. Although Angie has never had a personal problem with alcohol, it has been an issue in her family life for three generations now. She is surrounded by people who have problems or have had problems with drinking. In Stan's family of origin, there are two oldest children (the oldest girl, Judy, and the oldest boy, Frankie); both are very good kids. Stan is a middle child who never quite lives up to his parents' expectations, and Karl is the baby who was spoiled when he was young and now gets to do things his own way. This is the beginning picture of Stan's family system. This genogram serves as a map to guide the family therapist through the initial interviews.

The family therapist starts by helping Stan invite his family into the therapeutic process:

*Therapist:*   What will it be like for you to invite your parents, your brothers, and your sister into therapy with you?

*Stan:*   It will be very difficult. I don't really think that my dad and mom will come.

*Therapist:*   Who do you think will come? Whom in your family genogram here can you really count on?

*Stan:*   I think my sister Judy would come, and my brother Karl. We haven't been all that close—any of us—but I think they would want to help if they could.

*Therapist:*   And would either Judy or Karl or both be able to help you get your parents and Frank, Jr., in?

*Stan:*   I don't know. Maybe. Maybe not.

*Therapist:*   Maybe I should call everyone and see what I could do.

*Stan:*   That might have to happen. I'd like to try it myself, though, first. Maybe Judy and Karl will help me get the rest in.

*Therapist:*   OK, then. What about grandparents?

To a family therapist, Stan is part of a system that is part of still larger systems. Whereas counselors and therapists who see individuals may already have enough information to begin work with him, the family therapist wants to work with the whole system or as much of it as Stan can get into therapy. The family of origin is essential in his case, because he still lives much of his life in relation to these people. His extended family is also important, because these members can help him understand familial patterns over many generations, find new resources in the system, and perhaps even humanize his parents. Realizing that his family has lived in the same community for many years, it may even be important for the therapist to encourage him to consider including people from his work, his school, or his neighborhood.

Stan may have many difficulties, but at the moment his difficulty with alcohol is the primary focus. Alcohol is a negative part of his life, and as such it has systemic meaning. It may have started out as a symptom of other problems, but now the alcohol is a problem in itself. From a systemic perspective, the question is "How does this problem affect the family?" or "Is the family using this problem to serve some other purpose?"

*Therapist* [to Frank, Sr.]:   I know this time was an inconvenience for you, but I want you to know how appreciative I am that you came. Can you tell me what it's like for you to be here?

*Frank, Sr.:*   Well, I have to tell you that I don't like it much. [pause] Things are a lot different today than they used to be. We didn't have counseling 20 years ago. I had a problem with drinking at one point, but I got over it. I just quit—on my own. That's what Stan needs to do. He just needs to stop.

*Therapist:*   So I'm hearing that life is better for you without alcohol, and you would like Stan's life to be better, too.

*Frank, Sr.:*   Yeah. I'd like his life to be better in a lot of different ways.

*Therapist:*   Angie, what about you? What is it like for you to be here?

*Angie:*   It's heartbreaking. It's always heartbreaking. He makes it sound as if he just summoned up his own personal power and quit drinking through his own strength of character. That's a laugh. I threatened to leave him. That's what really happened. I was ready to get a divorce! And we're Catholic. We don't get divorced.

*Therapist:*   So you've been through this before.

*Angie:*   Oh my, yes. My father and mother drank. Dad still does. My sister won't admit it, but she drinks too much. She gets crazy with it. Judy's husband has a problem. I'm surrounded. I get so angry. I wish they would all just die or go away.

*Therapist:*   So this is something the whole family has been dealing with for a long time.

*Angie:*   Not everyone. I don't drink. Frankie and Judy don't drink. And Karl doesn't seem to have a problem.

*Therapist:*   Is that how the family gets divided: those who drink and those who don't?

*Judy:*   Drinking isn't the only problem we have. It's probably not even the most important.

*Therapist:*   Say more about that.

*Judy:*   Stan has always had it hard. I feel sorry for him. Frankie is clearly Dad's favorite [Frank, Sr., protests, saying he doesn't have favorites.] and things have always come easily for me. And Karl, he gets whatever he wants. He's Mom's favorite. Mom and Dad have fought a lot over the years. None of us have been all that happy, but Stan seems to have gotten the worst of it.

*Frank, Jr.:*   As I remember it, Stan gave Dad and Mom a lot to fight about. He was always messing up in one way or another.

*Therapist:*   Frankie, when your father was talking earlier, I sensed he had some disappointment about Stan too, but he also wanted to see things work out better for him. Is that true for you too?

*Frank, Jr.:*   Yes. I would like his life to be better.

The initial part of this counseling session has been devoted to meeting the family, joining with various family members, and reframing Stan's problem into a family problem in which everyone has a stake. Although there is a long way to go, the seeds of change have already been planted. There is evidence in these early interactions that Stan's problem has a multigenerational context; if this context is explored, family processes that support and maintain alcohol as a problem may be identified. It is possible to track the interactions of the family members and to transform communication patterns into more useful possibilities. Alliances and resources in this family might be explored as a means of creating new possibilities in the life of the family. If the therapist were just listening to Stan, only one point of view would be evident. In this family session, multiple perspectives and the entire interactive process become clear in a very short time.

As the family interview proceeds, a number of possibilities are presented for consideration. The therapist considers and may structure therapy around any or all of the following possibilities:

1. Stan's parents have not functioned as a team in a long time, and both their spousal relationship and their parenting have suffered.
2. The siblings need a new opportunity to function together without the influence and distractions continually imposed by the parents.
3. If Stan can find a new place, a new way of relating, within the family and tap the strengths he has personally and as a part of this system, he might cope with the problem of alcohol more effectively.

From the family systems perspective, one goal of therapy is to assist Stan in individuating from his parents and helping everyone in the family establish clearer boundaries and more useful interactions. In the early part of therapy, he reveals how much resentment he feels toward his mother, the emotional distance he experiences from his father, and his tendency to compare himself unfavorably with his older sister and brother. One intervention used by the therapist to help change the family's interactive process with him is to ask the siblings to talk among themselves without the interference of their parents. The parents are asked to just listen.

*Therapist:*    Would the four of you who have been the children in this family talk about what it has been like to grow up together? I'd like your parents to hear this but not to get involved otherwise.

*Frank, Jr.:*    Growing up, I knew that Judy was older than me, but I was the oldest boy, and that seemed important. The thing was that Judy and I were good at different things, but we were both good, and we knew it.

*Judy:*    It's not as if Frankie and I were a team. We had our own friends and our own interests, and I knew Mom approved of me, of us both. But Stan . . . you just amazed me all the time. You would do anything. You seemed to look for trouble, and trouble always found you.

*Angie* [leaning toward Stan]:    You could never . . .

*Therapist* [holding up a hand toward her and interrupting]:    No, this is for the kids. Just listen.

*Judy:*    I felt sorry for you, Stan.

*Therapist* [to Judy]:    I'm wondering if you also admired him in some way. I thought I heard admiration in your voice.

*Judy:*    You know, I did admire you. I still do. You aren't weak. You take chances. You make a lot of mistakes, but you don't seem to be as rule-bound as I am. When you were younger, you tried things that scared me, but at least you lived.

*Therapist:*    What is it like for you to hear that, Stan?

*Stan:*    It's wonderful! I feel Judy cares about me. I just wish I could hear something like that from my mother or father.

*Therapist:*    Isn't it interesting? People in this family can't stand to stay with just one process or one interaction at a time. You always want to bring someone else in or get involved in someone else's business. Let's just stay with what was happening between you and Judy and your brothers. How did you see Judy, Stan, when you were younger? How do you see her now?

*Stan:*    I looked up to her. I always have. She seemed to be the one who knew how to handle things, how to get along with others. She never seemed afraid.

*Judy:*    Are you kidding? I was worried all the time. I worried about how I was doing at school, whether I was a good enough friend, what was going to happen with Mom and Dad . . . everything.

*Stan* [after a pause, to Judy]:    Maybe we had more in common than I thought.

*Karl:*    You know, Stan, you were the one I looked up to. I looked up to Frankie too, but I thought you knew how to do a lot of things, and I wanted to do everything you did.

*Angie:*    Over my dead . . .

*Therapist:*    Not yet. Your turn is coming.

Setting boundaries in therapy can take vigilance and tenacity. Here, the therapist senses that a new relationship might emerge between the siblings, including a new way for them to see themselves in relation to others, if the parents, especially Angie, can be kept out of the discussion. In this case, the therapist positions herself as a leader of the process and provides the children with an opportunity to create new relationships. Much more may happen in these sessions; many relationships still need attention. Some family therapists might decide what the clients need to do to address Stan's presenting problem and intervene with directives designed to make a difference. What is clear, however, is that *this* therapist views his presenting problem as a crack in the family vase. By working to strengthen the vase (the coping mechanisms and interactive processes of everyone involved), she hopes to transform the system and activate solutions that the family designs.

## A NARRATIVE APPROACH

In the above example, the problem is *not* seen as the problem; the family's coping and interactive processes are seen as the problem. In contrast to this systems approach, the narrative approach of White and Epston accepts Stan's drinking as the problem. The therapist works to help him deconstruct his alcohol-saturated life story and reauthor a new life altogether. Below are excerpts from an interview with Stan designed to use narrative process in creating a therapeutic outcome.

*Naming the problem*

*Therapist:*    There's a lot going on in your life. A lot of issues and a lot of feelings about those issues. I'm wondering what's most important to you? What problem is taking the most unfair advantage in your life?

*Stan:*    I'd have to say it's the alcohol. That's why I'm here: I drink, I drive, and I get thrown in jail. I mess everything up.

*Therapist:*    Alcohol has been around you a long time.

*Stan:*    Yeah, I'm kind of on a first-name basis with it.

*Therapist:*    Yes, well, what name do you call this alcohol?

*Stan:*    My grandfather, my mom's dad, used to call it demon rum. It doesn't much matter what kind it is. It's all demon rum.

*Therapist:*    So you know it to be demonic. Straight from hell. What are its demonic powers?

*Personifying the problem and attributing oppressive intentions and tactics to it*

*Stan:*    The same as all demons, I guess; it lures me into feeling good, and then it disappoints and hurts me.

*Therapist:*    So demon rum lies to you. How does it succeed in fooling you? How does it trick you into believing life will be better while it tries to kill you?

*Stan:*    You see, that's it. I'm not going to die. If I died, I wouldn't feel bad anymore, and neither would anyone who knows me. But I'm not dying, so I drink.

*Therapist:*    So this demon tells you "You're not dying" while it tries to kill you and anyone in your path? How does it get you to believe that you're not going to die?

*Stan:*    Well, I know I'm going to die. Just not soon enough.

*Therapist:*    So this demon wants to kill you and can't do it fast enough by itself and has recruited you into helping it. How does demon rum recruit you as a perpetrator in your own murder?

*Stan:*    It tells me I can't bear living. It wants my soul in hell.

*Investigating how the problem has been disrupting, dominating, or discouraging the person and the family*

*Therapist:*    What does the demon tell you to make you believe that you can't bear living? How does it assault your determination?

*Stan:*    It tells me that I'm weak, that I've been a mistake from the beginning. It says I should never have been born. It promises me I won't feel any pain until this life is over.

*Therapist:*    How does it get you to ignore people who love you, all that you have accomplished, getting and keeping a job, going to school—how does it get you to ignore all that and believe such lies?

*Stan:*    The demon tells me that loved ones don't exist, that nothing counts, but that's not true. Some things, some people, do count.

*Discovering moments when the client hasn't been dominated or discouraged by the problem or when life has not been disrupted by the problem*

*Therapist:*    So there are times when you know it's lying to you, when you resist joining it in hell?

*Stan:*    Yes.

*Therapist:*    What's happening when you see the lie clearly? What are you doing to catch it at its evil game? How do you rise up against the demon and slay it?

*Stan:*    It's like when my sister's birthday came up. I knew Matt—that's her husband—was trying to quit drinking for her. I knew my family would be at the party, but I thought Matt needed me to be sober with him. It was a gift we could do together for Judy.

*Therapist:*   It was a gift! A kind of enormous generosity of your spirit in support of both Matt and Judy. Was it that the demon just didn't exist that night, couldn't lie to you?

*Stan:*   Oh, no, it existed. It was at its lying best. Especially when my parents arrived.

*Therapist:*   But you knew it was a lie. How did you get the better of it?

*Stan:*   I stood by Matt all night. We laughed. We told old stories to each other. We danced with my sister.

*Therapist:*   You lived right in the face of death.

*Finding historical evidence to bolster a new view of the person as competent enough to have stood up to, defeated, and escaped from the dominance of the problem*

*Stan:*   Yes. It was wonderful. I went home, and the next day I enrolled for another quarter in college.

*Therapist:*   How did you carry it over to the next day? You didn't even have Matt or Judy with you then. How did you keep this defiance of death going?

*Stan:*   I just kept thinking about all that I wanted to accomplish, about the difference I had made.

*Therapist:*   So you think of yourself as a person who can make a difference?

*Stan:*   Yes. I'm in construction. I often think about what I'm building and how it will make a difference in people's lives.

*Therapist:*   Besides Judy and Matt, who else has always known that you were a person who could make a difference?

*Stan:*   I had a teacher in the ninth grade who liked what I did in shop. He always said that great things would come from my hands.

*Evoking speculation from the person about what kind of future is to be expected from the strong, competent person who has emerged from the interview so far*

*Therapist:*   What was that teacher's name?

*Stan:*   Mr. Johnston.

*Therapist:*   What would Mr. Johnston and you think a person with your capabilities might accomplish? What kind of difference would the two of you see in store for you in the near future?

*Stan:*   I think we would expect me to make real progress in completing school. When I finish school, it will be like not being a loser anymore.

*Therapist:*   What will you be?

*Stan:*   I'll be a graduate who has made it.

*Therapist:*   A graduate in what?

*Stan:*   In human services, with a minor in history.

*Finding or creating an audience for perceiving the new identity and new story*

*Therapist:*   Does Mr. Johnston know that you're about to be a human services major who considers his history minor?

*Stan* [chuckles]:   No.

*Therapist:*   What would it be like to catch him up on this heroic life after all these years? Would it be OK to give him the opportunity to say: "I knew it. I told you back in the ninth grade this would happen"?

FOLLOW-UP: YOU CONTINUE AS STAN'S FAMILY THERAPIST.   Use these questions to help you think about how you would counsel Stan:

- What unique values do you see in working with Stan from a systemic perspective, as opposed to doing individual therapy?
- If you were Stan's therapist and he resisted the idea of family therapy, what direction might you take with him?
- Assuming that Stan was successful in getting at least some of his family members to another session, where would you want to begin? How do you expect that you'd get everyone involved in the sessions?
- What are some specific ways in which you might keep a systemic focus, even if you were seeing Stan individually?

# Summary and Evaluation

## SUMMARY

This section reviews the themes that unite the many schools of family therapy and also looks at some of the variations among these theoretical orientations.

VIEW OF THE FAMILY.   If we hope to work therapeutically with an individual, it is critical to consider him or her within the system. An individual's dysfunctional behavior grows out of the interactional unit of the family as well as the larger community and societal systems. With the exception of some social-constructionist perspectives, virtually all other orientations accept the notion that families are systems.

FOCUS OF FAMILY THERAPY.   Most of the family therapies tend to be brief, because families who seek professional help typically want resolution of some problematic symptom. In addition to being short-term, solution-focused, and action-oriented, family therapy tends to deal with present interactions. One way in which it differs from many individual therapies is its emphasis on how current family relationships contribute to the development and maintenance of symptoms.

Almost all of the family therapies are concerned with here-and-now interactions in the family system. The role of history is handled in different ways. Some approaches assume that family history is crucial in understanding present functioning, whereas other models do not make this assumption. With his multi-generational approach, Bowen gives high priority to both current history and early history as a means of helping clients differentiate themselves from their family of origin. In a different way, Satir considers the past as a way to help members of a family realize that problems are the result of decisions that have been made by the family unit. Experiential therapists generally deal with past unresolved conflicts by treating their expression in current interactions.

Both strategic and structural family therapists tend to be less concerned about gathering family history. They are more concerned with what maintains the current problem and how to solve it in the present. The past does have a bearing from a developmental perspective on the structural problems within a family. Haley's strategic therapy, however, deals mainly with here-and-now power struggles and control issues in a family, and it does not attempt to educate clients about the origin or development of these problems.

Another focus that characterizes family therapy is the attention it pays to communication. Basically, all orientations emphasize both verbal and nonverbal communication. Structural and strategic therapy, both of which are derivatives of the communications model, focus on various aspects of how family members communicate. Structural therapists focus on the family organization as it is expressed in repeated patterns of communication. They identify the underlying organization of a family by noting who speaks to whom and in what manner with what results. Strategic therapy, as practiced by Haley and Madanes, assumes that the central aim of communication is attaining power in interpersonal relationships. Symptoms are seen as ways of communicating with the aim of controlling other family members. For instance, a child's fears of going to school may be expressing his or her insecurity in dealing with the world alone. In this case, strategic therapists will not generally attempt to teach the parents what the child's symptoms mean but will try to provoke them to communicate with the child in a different way, which would make the symptom unnecessary (Nichols & Schwartz, 1995).

Satir's approach is an example of a humanistically oriented communications model of family therapy. This model strives to teach all the members of a family how to express what they want for themselves and with others. Satir (1983) holds that communication is a process of giving and getting information. In conducting family sessions, the therapist attends to both the verbal and nonverbal process of making requests. People who communicate in a functional way are able to be firm in their position, yet they can ask for feedback and be open to it when they get it. People who communicate dysfunctionally leave others guessing what is in their heart or head.

ROLE OF THE THERAPIST.   In most of the models considered, the therapist functions as a teacher, model, or coach. These approaches have in common a commitment to helping family members learn new and more effective ways of interacting. Bowenians block triangulation and encourage members of a family to move toward differentiation; structural therapists realign psychological boundaries and strengthen hierarchical organization; strategic therapists identify interactional sequences that maintain a problem; and experiential therapists attempt to reduce defensiveness and facilitate open and honest expression of feelings and thoughts (Nichols & Schwartz, 1995).

GOALS OF FAMILY THERAPY.   There are some general goals that most family therapists adhere to, and some of the specific goals are determined by the practitioner's orientation or by a collaborative process between the family and the therapist. Global goals include intervening in ways that enable individuals and a family to change in order to relieve their distress. Tied to the question of what goals should guide a therapist's interventions is the question of the therapist's values. As you have seen, each of the six theories of family therapy is grounded on a set of values and theoretical assumptions. Ultimately, every intervention a therapist makes is an expression of a value judgment. It is critical for therapists, regardless of their theoretical orientations, to be aware of their values and monitor how these values influence their practice with families.

HOW FAMILIES CHANGE.   An integrative approach to the practice of family therapy must include guiding principles that help the therapist organize goals, interactions, observations, and ways to promote change. In reviewing the theories of family therapy, it is evident that they can be grouped into two categories: (1) those that focus on change within the therapy sessions and (2) those that deal with the occurrence of change outside of the therapeutic context, in the natural world (Hanna & Brown, 1995). Some theories focus on perceptual and cognitive change, others deal mainly with changing feelings, and other theories emphasize behavioral change. Change needs to happen relationally, not just intrapsychically, in all family therapy models.

TECHNIQUES OF FAMILY THERAPY.   There is a diversity of techniques, depending on the therapist's theoretical orientation. Yet the intervention strategies that therapists employ are best considered in conjunction with their personal characteristics. Writers such as Goldenberg and Goldenberg (1996) and Nichols and Schwartz (1995) emphasize that techniques are tools for achieving therapeutic goals but that these intervention strategies do not make a family therapist. Personal characteristics such as respect for clients, compassion, empathy, and sensitivity are human qualities that influence the manner in which techniques are delivered. It is also essential to have a rationale for the techniques that are used, with some sense of the expected outcomes. Faced with meeting the demands of clinical practice, practitioners will need to be flexible in selecting intervention strategies. The central consideration is what is in the best interests of the family. Many therapy procedures can be borrowed from various models, depending on what is likely to work best with a given family. As we have seen, there is a great deal of overlap among the techniques used by family therapists, irrespective of their theoretical base.

## CONTRIBUTIONS OF FAMILY SYSTEMS APPROACHES

One of the key contributions of most systemic approaches is that neither the individual nor the family is blamed for a particular dysfunction. The family is empowered through the process of identifying and exploring interactional patterns. If change is to come about in a family or with individual members of a family, there is a need to be aware of as many of the systems of influence as possible.

Most of the individual therapies that have been considered in this textbook have not given a primary focus to the role of systemic factors in influencing the individual. All of the contemporary approaches to family therapy give major emphasis to understanding the individual in their systems, which sheds an entirely different perspective on assessment and treatment of individuals and of families. An advantage to this viewpoint is that an individual is not scapegoated as the "bad person" in the family. Rather than blaming either an individual "identified patient" or a family, the entire family has an opportunity to examine the interactional patterns that characterize the unit and participate in finding solutions.

CONTRIBUTIONS TO MULTICULTURAL COUNSELING.    One of the contributions of the systemic perspective in working from a multicultural framework is that many ethnic and cultural groups place great value on the extended family. If therapists are working with an individual from a cultural background that gives special value to including grandparents, aunts, and uncles in the treatment, it is easy to see that family approaches have a distinct advantage over individual therapy. Family therapists can do some excellent networking with members of the extended family.

In many ways, family therapists are like systems anthropologists. They approach each family as a unique culture whose particular characteristics must be understood. Like larger cultural systems, families have a unique language that governs behavior, communication, and even how to feel about and experience life. Families have celebrations and rituals that mark transitions, protect them against outside interference, and connect them to their past as well as a projected future.

Although each family has a discrete culture, it is also connected to the larger culture from which it emanates. Culture and ethnicity are so interrelated with family that it is hard to know one without the other. The larger experience of culture and ethnicity has been in families so long that it permeates relationships stretching back generations, often to other lands and other periods of time and history. Our children may ask us why we always throw rice on the bride and groom when they leave a wedding, and we are so far removed from the origin of the ritual that we can only say: "I don't know. We've always done it, that's why." Yet even without understanding the ritual, we feel compelled to do it.

Just as differentiation means coming to understand our family well enough to both be a part of it—to belong—and to be separate and our own person, understanding cultures allows therapists and the families they serve to appreciate diversity and to contextualize family experiences in relation to the larger cultures. As fundamental as culture is to family life, it has only been in the last 15 years that the field of family therapy has significantly addressed this relationship. McGoldrick, Pearce, and Giordano (1982) are largely responsible for elevating an awareness of and sensitivity to culture in family systems therapy. In their groundbreaking work *Ethnicity and Family Therapy,* McGoldrick says:

Even the definition of "family" differs greatly from group to group. The dominant American (WASP) definition focuses on the intact nuclear family. Black families focus on a wide network of kin and community. For Italians there is no such thing as the "nuclear" family. To them family means a strong, tightly knit three- or four-generation family, which also includes godparents and old friends. The Chinese go beyond this and include in their definition of family all their ancestors and all their descendants [p. 10].

Today, family therapists explore both the individual culture of the family and the larger culture to which the family belongs. They look for ways in which culture can both inform and modify family work. Interventions are no longer applied universally, regardless of the culture(s) involved, but rather are adapted and even designed to join with the cultural systems. Just as society can exact standards and practices from families that may not fit the needs of a given system, however, so can cultural imperatives. Sensitivity to culture in family therapy means knowing when cultural meaning can enlarge and contextualize family experience and when it needs to be faced as an external stress on the system.

## LIMITATIONS AND CRITICISMS
## OF FAMILY SYSTEMS APPROACHES

In the early days of family therapy, it appeared that people all too often got lost in the consideration of system. In adopting the language of systems, therapists began to describe and think of families as being made up of "dyads" and "triads"; as being "functional" or "dysfunctional," "stuck" or "unstuck," and "enmeshed" or "disengaged"; and as displaying "positive" and "negative" outcomes and "feedback loops." It was as if the family was a well-oiled machine or perhaps a computer that occasionally broke down. Just as it was easy to fix a machine without an emotional consideration of the parts involved, some therapists approached family systems work with little concern for the individuals as long as the "whole" of the family "functioned" better. Feminists were perhaps the first, but not the only, group to lament the loss of a personal perspective within a systemic framework. As the field moves now toward an integration of individual and systemic frameworks, it is important to reinvest the language of therapy with human emotional terminology that honors the place real people have always held in families.

ETHICAL ISSUES IN USING PARADOXICAL TECHNIQUES.    With some forms of family therapy, manipulation of the client, use of indirect therapy techniques, and inappropriate use of paradoxical interventions raise ethical issues. Weeks and L'Abate (1982) contend that there are still many problems in learning how and when to employ paradoxical interventions. They add that paradoxical therapy has no underlying theory to guide its development and practice. Because this approach is powerful and risky, certain factors need to be carefully considered in employing it. Paradox appears to be especially well suited for resistant clients with specific behaviorally defined problems. Weeks and L'Abate contend that practitioners who overuse these methods with every client are intervening irrelevantly. They further suggest that paradox is best applied in selected cases and usually in combination with a variety of other techniques. When used appropriately, what looks paradoxical from the outside actually makes sense in another context.

Ethical practice dictates that we know when paradoxical interventions should be avoided. The use of these techniques is obviously neither clinically indicated nor ethical in those situations where harmful consequences to the client are likely. Paradoxical intervention is inadvisable in situations that involve crisis, potential suicide or homicide, violence, abuse, or excessive drinking. Paradox in these situations is most likely to be unhelpful and irresponsible (Weeks & L'Abate, 1982).

It appears that there is much to learn about how paradox works, when and where to use these methods, whether therapeutic gains carry over into a client's "real world," and how effective treatment is in the long term. The use of these techniques is best learned in supervised practice under an experienced therapist. There is agreement in the literature that much more research is necessary in order to understand and evaluate paradoxical strategies (Huddleston & Engels, 1986).

LIMITATIONS FOR MULTICULTURAL COUNSELING.   Some approaches to family therapy are heavily loaded with value orientations that are not congruent with the value system of clients from certain ethnic and cultural backgrounds. It should be kept in mind that the notions of independence, autonomy, and self-determination mirror Western values and that not all cultures pay homage to such values. Other cultures, such as Asian-American, Native American, and Latino may be in conflict with these concepts and how they are addressed in family therapy. The Western emphasis on the nuclear family and independence tends to reduce the importance of the family of origin. For example, Sue and Sue (1991) note that in Chinese-American families the notion of filial piety is a strong determinant of how children behave, even as they move to adulthood. Obedience, respect, obligation to parents, and duty leave little room for self-determination. Allegiance to one's parents is expected from a man even after he marries and has his own family. The concept of separation from his family can easily lead to conflicts in his family relationships.

The process of differentiation occurs in most cultures, but it takes on a different shape because of cultural norms. For instance, a young person may become separate from her parents yet not move out of the house. When many ethnic-minority families immigrate to North America, their children often adapt to a Western concept of differentiation. In such cases, the intergenerational process of therapy is appropriate if the therapist is sensitive to the family of origin's cultural roots. Bowen believes that when one determines one's direction in life, there needs to be a balance between what is beneficial for the individual and what is beneficial for the group (system or family). Although his theory addresses the notion of togetherness and individuality from a balanced perspective, many non-Western cultures would not embrace a theory that valued individuality above loyalty to family in any form.

# Where to Go from Here

A good place to begin is by doing some of the supplementary reading listed in the next section. It is also a good idea to join the American Association for Marriage and Family Therapy, which has a student membership category. You must obtain an official application, including the names of at least two Clinical Members from whom the association can request official endorsements. You also need a statement signed by the coordinator or director of a graduate program in marital and family therapy in a regionally accredited educational institution, verifying your current enrollment. Student membership may be held until receipt of a qualifying graduate degree or for a maximum of five years. Members receive the *Journal of Marital and Family Therapy,* which is published four times a year, and a subscription to six issues yearly of *The Family Therapy Networker.* For a copy of the AAMFT Code of Ethics, membership applications, and further information, write to:

American Association for Marriage and Family Therapy
1133 15th Street, NW, Suite 300
Washington, DC 20005-2710
Telephone: (202) 452-0109

Another option is for students to join the International Association of Marital and Family Counselors (IAMFC), which is a division of the ACA. Student membership to the ACA is $59.50 per year, plus IAMFC dues of $6.00. Dues include a subscription to the *Journal of Counseling and Development, The Family Journal,* and the *IAMFC Newsletter* as well as the monthly *Counseling Today.* For a copy of the ACA Code of Ethics and Standards of Practice, membership applications, and further information, write to:

ACA Membership Division
5999 Stevenson Avenue
Alexandria, VA 22304
Telephone: (800) 347-6647

## Recommended Supplementary Readings

*Family Therapy: Concepts and Methods* (Nichols & Schwartz, 1995) is an excellent text that is written in a clear manner. The authors provide a historical and conceptual context of family therapy as well as covering seven of the major contemporary systems. Their final chapter, on a comparative analysis of the various theoretical orientations, is a superb integration of key themes among the diverse approaches to family therapy.

*Family Counseling and Therapy* (Horne & Passmore, 1991) is a comprehensive overview of the major models of family therapy, each written by an expert in the field. The format of the book allows for comparisons among the models.

*Family Therapy: A Systemic Integration* (Becvar & Becvar, 1996) provides a clear and comprehensive discussion of the contemporary models of family therapy. Chapter 1 consists of a useful discussion of the different world views in the frameworks of individual and family therapies. In Chapter 2 the authors do a fine job of tracing the history of family therapy. They also have a chapter on the evolving therapeutic models (social constructionism, solution-focused therapy, and the narrative approach).

*The Practice of Family Therapy: Key Elements across Models* (Hanna & Brown, 1995) focuses on the diversity of family therapy and integrating common elements of the field. It also deals with family therapy assessment skills and treatment skills.

*The Family Interpreted: Feminist Theory in Clinical Practice* (Luepnitz, 1988) provides the reader with an introduction to feminist perspective in general as well as a comprehensive evaluation of systemic models. Luepnitz also offers her own integration of feminist theory and object-relations therapy as a foundation for considering seminal issues in family therapy.

*Ethnicity and Family Therapy* (McGoldrick, Pearce, & Giordano, 1982) is the seminal work on culture in family therapy. The authors review the importance of cultural considerations in relation to family therapy and provide chapters on the background, research, and therapy issues of more than 15 cultures.

*Family Therapy: An Overview* (Goldenberg & Goldenberg, 1996) provides an excellent basic overview of these contemporary perspectives on family therapy: psychodynamic approaches, experiential/humanistic approaches, Bowenian family systems, structural family therapy, communications and strategic family therapy, and behavioral approaches. The authors also do a fine job of presenting issues in training and professional practice.

*Family Evaluation* (Kerr & Bowen, 1988) presents a comprehensive examination and discussion of Bowen's family system theory. It focuses on the integration of theory and practice.

*Family-of-Origin Therapy: An Intergenerational Approach* (Framo, 1992) presents one of the more comprehensive approaches to multigenerational family systems work. Framo integrates Bowenian family therapy with the psychoanalytic family therapy he developed with Ivan Boszormenyi-Nagy at the Eastern Pennsylvania Psychiatric Institute.

*Genograms in Family Assessment* (McGoldrick & Gerson, 1985) is a reference guide for those interested in constructing genograms. It provides a standard format for genogram symbols. The book describes various methods for developing underlying assumptions and for interpreting data.

*Conjoint Family Therapy* (Satir, 1983) is one of the best books dealing with humanistic family therapy. Satir describes family theory and communication theory and applies them to the practice of working with families. Her book is sprinkled with many fine examples and illustrations.

*The New Peoplemaking* (Satir, 1988) is a book for families that deals with family process. The author does a clear job of presenting topics such as styles of communicating, family rules, open versus closed systems, family mapping, the family blueprint, and the extended family. The original book was a best-seller, published in 1972 and eventually translated into 27 languages.

*Satir: Step by Step* (Satir & Baldwin, 1983) is divided into two parts. The first part is a complete family therapy session (with session drawings) and commentary by Satir on what she is doing with the family. The second part is a complete description of the various aspects of her theory and practice.

*The Family Crucible* (Napier & Whitaker, 1978) is an easy-to-read and interesting account of the experiential approach to family therapy using the co-therapy model.

*Families and Family Therapy* (Minuchin, 1974) is considered to be the most important book describing structural family therapy. Minuchin explores the dynamics of change, examining the variety of restructuring operations that can be employed to challenge a family and to change its basic patterns. The first chapter presents some of the key elements of structural family therapy.

*Family Therapy Techniques* (Minuchin & Fishman, 1981) is a practical book and a companion to Minuchin's earlier book. In this volume the authors discuss the main concepts of the structural approach: understanding the family, joining the family, and treating the family. Specific chapters deal with techniques such as reframing, enactment, restructuring, boundaries, and paradoxes.

*Strategic Family Therapy* (Madanes, 1981) is a useful guide to the theory and practice of strategic family therapy. Madanes describes intervention strategies that can be employed to correct power imbalances and change destructive patterns of interaction among family members. Chapter 1 presents the dimensions of various schools of family therapy; Chapter 2 is a good description of the elements of strategic family therapy.

*Ordeal Therapy: Unusual Ways to Change Behavior* (Haley, 1984) presents detailed case studies with various client problems. He explains how ordeals can promote change with difficult clients.

*Therapy as Social Construction* (McNamee & Gergen, 1992) is a complete overview of social-construction theory and practice. It includes contributions by Tom Andersen, Harlene Anderson and Harold Goolishian, Michael White and David Epston, and William O'Hanlon.

*Narrative Means to Therapeutic Ends* (White & Epston, 1990) is a detailed account of narrative therapy. The book offers an overview of the philosophical underpinnings and theoretical perspectives that have informed the practice of narrative therapy as well as many examples of the process, questions, and letters used in therapy.

*Case Approach to Counseling and Psychotherapy* (Corey, 1996) contains a chapter giving a detailed example of working with a hypothetical client, Ruth, from a cognitive-behavioral, family systems perspective and also from an integrative perspective (by combining elements of Bowenian and structural approaches). These examples, as well as two other cases, provide concrete illustrations of many of the concepts and techniques used in family systems approaches.

## References and Suggested Readings*

ANDERSEN, T. (1987). The reflecting team: Dialogue and metadialogue in clinical work. *Family Process, 26*(4), 415–428.

* ANDERSEN, T. (1991). *The reflecting team: Dialogues and dialogues about the dialogues.* New York: Norton.

ANDERSEN, T. (1992). Reflections on reflecting with families. In S. McNamee & K. J. Gergen (Eds.), *Therapy as social construction* (pp. 54–68). Newbury Park, CA: Sage.

ANDERSON, H. (1993). On a roller coaster: A collaborative language system approach to therapy. In S. Friedman (Ed.), *The new language of change* (pp. 323–344). New York: Guilford Press.

ANDERSON, H., & GOOLISHIAN, H. (1992). The client is the expert: A not-knowing approach to therapy. In S. McNamee & K. J. Gergen (Eds.), *Therapy as social construction* (pp. 25–39). Newbury Park, CA: Sage.

AVIS, J. M. (1986). Feminist issues in family therapy. In F. P. Piercy, D. H. Sprenkle, & Associates (Eds.), *Family therapy sourcebook* (pp. 213–242). New York: Guilford Press.

BECVAR, D. S., & BECVAR, R. J. (1996). *Family therapy: A systemic integration* (3rd ed.). Needham Heights, MA: Allyn & Bacon.

*Books and articles marked with an asterisk are suggested for further study.

BELENKY, M. F., CLINCHY, B. MC., GOLDBERGER, N. R., & TARULE, J. M. (1986). *Women's ways of knowing: The development of self, voice, and mind.* New York: Basic Books.

BERNARD, J. (1972). *The future of marriage.* New York: Bantam Books.

BITTER, J. R. (1987). Communication and meaning: Satir in Adlerian context. In R. Sherman & D. Dinkmeyer (Eds.), *Systems of family therapy: An Adlerian integration* (pp. 109–142). New York: Brunner/Mazel.

BITTER, J. R. (1993). Satir's parts party with couples. In T. S. Nelson & T. S. Trepper (Eds.), *101 interventions in family therapy* (pp. 132–136). New York: Haworth Press.

BOWEN, M. (1966). The use of family theory in clinical practice. *Comprehensive Psychiatry, 7,* 345–374.

* BOWEN, M. (1972). On the differentiation of self. In J. Framo (Ed.), *Family interaction: A dialogue between family researchers and family therapists* (pp. 111–173). New York: Springer.

* BOWEN, M. (1976). Theory in the practice of psychotherapy. In P. J. Guerin, Jr. (Ed.), *Family therapy: Theory and practice* (pp. 42–90). New York: Gardner Press.

* BOWEN, M. (1978). *Family therapy in clinical practice.* New York: Aronson.

BREUNLIN, D. C., SCHWARTZ, R. C., & MAC KUNE-KARRER, B. (1992). *Metaframeworks: Transcending the models of family therapy.* San Francisco: Jossey-Bass.

BROWN, J. H., & CHRISTENSEN, D. N. (1986). *Family therapy: Theory and practice.* Pacific Grove, CA: Brooks/Cole.

BROWN, L. S., & BRODSKY, A. M. (1992). The future of feminist therapy. *Psychotherapy, 29*(1), 51–57.

CARTER, B., & MCGOLDRICK, M. (1989). *The changing family life cycle: A framework for family therapy.* Needham Heights, MA: Allyn & Bacon.

CHANEY, R. (1991). Evolving Milan approaches to family therapy. In A. M. Horne & J. L. Passmore (Eds.), *Family counseling and therapy* (2nd ed.) (pp. 235–261). Itasca, IL: F. E. Peacock.

COLAPINTO, J. (1991). Structural family therapy. In A. M. Horne & J. L. Passmore (Eds.), *Family counseling and therapy* (2nd ed.) (pp. 77–106). Itasca, IL: F. E. Peacock.

COREY, G. (1996). *Case approach to counseling and psychotherapy* (4th ed.). Pacific Grove, CA: Brooks/Cole.

DEGLER, C. (1980). *At odds: Women and the family in America from the revolution to the present.* New York: Oxford University Press.

DE SHAZER, S. (1985). *Keys to solutions in brief therapy.* New York: Norton.

DE SHAZER, S. (1988). *Clues: Investigating solutions in brief therapy.* New York: Norton.

DE SHAZER, S. (1990). Brief therapy. In J. K. Zeig & W. M. Munion (Eds.), *What is psychotherapy? Contemporary perspectives* (pp. 278–282). San Francisco: Jossey-Bass.

DE SHAZER, S. (1991). *Putting difference to work.* New York: Norton.

DREIKURS, R. (1957). *Our child guidance clinics in Chicago. Collected papers of Rudolf Dreikurs.* Eugene: University of Oregon Press.

DURKHEIM, E. (1951). *Suicide: A study in sociology* (J. A. Spaulding & G. Simpson, Trans.). Glencoe, IL: Free Press.

ELIZUR, J., & MINUCHIN, S. (1989). *Institutionalizing madness: Families, therapy, and society.* New York: Basic Books.

ENNS, C. Z. (1993). Twenty years of feminist counseling and therapy. *The Counseling Psychologist, 21*(1), 3–87.

EPSTON, D., & WHITE, M. (1992). Consulting your consultants: The documentation of alternative knowledges. In *Experience, contradiction, narrative, and imagination: Selected papers of David Epston and Michael White, 1989–1991* (pp. 11–26). Adelaide, South Australia: Dulwich Centre Publications.

EPSTON, D., WHITE, M., & MURRAY, K. (1992). A proposal for reauthoring therapy: Rose's revisioning of her life and a commentary. In S. McNamee & K. J. Gergen (Eds.), *Therapy as social construction* (pp. 96–115). Newbury Park, CA: Sage.

FERGUSON, A. (1983). On conceiving motherhood and sexuality: A feminist materialist approach. In H. Trebilcot (Ed.), *Mothering: Essays in feminist theory* (pp. 153–184). Totowa, NJ: Rowman & Littlefield.

FISHMAN, H. C. (1993). *Intensive structural therapy: Treating families in their social context.* New York: Basic Books.

FOUCAULT, M. (1970). *The order of things: An archaeology of the human sciences.* New York: Random House.

FOUCAULT, M. (1979). *Discipline and punishment: The birth of the prison.* Middlesex: Peregrine Books.

FOUCAULT, M. (1980). *Power/knowledge: Selected interviews and other writings.* New York: Pantheon Books.

FRAMO, J. L. (1990). Intergenerational family therapy. In J. K. Zeig & W. M. Munion (Eds.), *What is psychotherapy? Contemporary perspectives* (pp. 253–261). San Francisco: Jossey-Bass.

* FRAMO, J. L. (1992). *Family-of-origin therapy: An intergenerational approach.* New York: Brunner/Mazel.

GERGEN, K. (1985). The social constructionist movement in modern psychology. *American Psychologist, 40,* 266–275.

GERGEN, K. (1991). *The saturated self.* New York: Basic Books.

GILLIGAN, C. (1982). *In a different voice.* Cambridge, MA: Harvard University Press.

GILLIGAN, C., WARD, J. V., & TAYLOR, J. (Eds.). (1988). *Mapping the moral domain.* Cambridge, MA: Harvard University Press.

GOLDENBERG, H., & GOLDENBERG, I. (1994). *Counseling today's families* (2nd ed.). Pacific Grove, CA: Brooks/Cole.

* GOLDENBERG, I., & GOLDENBERG, H. (1996). *Family therapy: An overview* (4th ed.). Pacific Grove, CA: Brooks/Cole.

* GUERIN, P. J., & CHABOT, D. R. (1992). Development of family systems theory. In D. K. Freedheim (Ed.), *History of psychotherapy: A century of change* (pp. 225–260). Washington, DC: American Psychological Association.

GURMAN, A. S., & KNISKERN, D. P. (1981). *Handbook of family therapy.* New York: Brunner/Mazel.

GURMAN, A. S., & KNISKERN, D. P. (1992). The future of marital and family therapy. *Psychotherapy, 29*(1), 65–71.

HALEY, J. (1963). *Strategies of psychotherapy.* New York: Grune & Stratton.

HALEY, J. (1973). *Uncommon therapy: The psychiatric techniques of Milton H. Erickson, M.D.* New York: Norton.

* HALEY, J. (1976). *Problem-solving therapy: New strategies for effective family therapy.* San Francisco: Jossey-Bass.

* HALEY, J. (1984). *Ordeal therapy: Unusual ways to change behavior.* San Francisco: Jossey-Bass.

* HANNA, S. M., & BROWN, J. H. (1995). *The practice of family therapy: Key elements across models.* Pacific Grove, CA: Brooks/Cole.

HAWKINGS, S. (1988). *A brief history of time: From big bang to black holes.* New York: Bantam Books.

* HORNE, A. M., & PASSMORE, J. L. (1991). *Family counseling and therapy* (2nd ed.). Itasca, IL: F. E. Peacock.

HUDDLESTON, J. E., & ENGELS, D. W. (1986). Issues related to the use of paradoxical techniques in counseling. *Journal of Counseling and Human Service Professions, 1*(1), 127–133.

\* KEITH, D. V., & WHITAKER, C. A. (1991). Experiential/symbolic family therapy. In A. M. Horne & J. Passmore (Eds.), *Family counseling and therapy* (2nd ed.) (pp. 107–140). Itasca, IL: F. E. Peacock.

\* KERR, M. E., & BOWEN, M. (1988). *Family evaluation*. New York: Norton.

LAWSON, D. M., & GAUSHELL, H. (1991). Intergenerational family characteristics of counselor trainees. *Counselor Education and Supervision, 30*(4), 309–321.

LEWIS, J. M., BEAVER, W. R., GOSSETT, J. T., & PHILLIPS, V. A. (1976). *No single thread: Psychological health in family systems*. New York: Brunner/Mazel.

\* LUEPNITZ, D. A. (1988). *The family interpreted: Feminist theory in clinical practice*. New York: Basic Books.

\* MADANES, C. (1981). *Strategic family therapy*. San Francisco: Jossey-Bass.

\* MADANES, C. (1984). *Behind the one-way mirror: Advances in the practice of strategic therapy*. San Francisco: Jossey-Bass.

MADANES, C. (1991). *Sex, love, and violence: Strategies for transformation*. New York: Norton.

\* McGOLDRICK, M. (1982). Ethnicity and family therapy: An overview. In M. McGoldrick, J. K. Pearce, & J. Giordano (Eds.), *Ethnicity and family therapy* (pp. 3–30). New York: Guilford Press.

\* McGOLDRICK, M., & GERSON, R. (1985). *Genograms in family assessment*. New York: Norton.

\* McGOLDRICK, M., PEARCE, J. K., & GIORDANO, J. (Eds.). (1982). *Ethnicity and family therapy*. New York: Guilford Press.

\* McNAMEE, S., & GERGEN, K. J. (Eds.). (1992). *Therapy as social construction*. Newbury Park, CA: Sage Publications.

\* MINUCHIN, S. (1974). *Families and family therapy*. Cambridge, MA: Harvard University Press.

\* MINUCHIN, S., & FISHMAN, H. C. (1981). *Family therapy techniques*. Cambridge, MA: Harvard University Press.

\* NAPIER, A. Y., & WHITAKER, C. A. (1978). *The family crucible*. New York: Harper & Row.

\* NICOLS, M. P., & SCHWARTZ, R. C. (1995). *Family therapy: Concepts and methods* (3rd ed.). Boston: Allyn & Bacon.

O'HANLON, W. H. (1994). The third wave: The promise of narrative. *The Family Therapy Networker, 18*(6), 18–29.

O'HANLON, W. H., & WEINER-DAVIS, M. (1989). *In search of solutions: A new direction in psychotherapy*. New York: Norton.

PAPERO, D. V. (1991). The Bowen theory. In A. M. Horne & J. L. Passmore (Eds.), *Family counseling and therapy* (2nd ed.) (pp. 47–75). Itasca, IL: F. E. Peacock.

\* SATIR, V. (1983). *Conjoint family therapy* (3rd ed.). Palo Alto, CA: Science and Behavior Books.

\* SATIR, V. (1988). *The new peoplemaking*. Palo Alto, CA: Science and Behavior Books.

SATIR, V., & BALDWIN, M. (1983). *Satir: Step by step*. Palo Alto, CA: Science and Behavior Books.

SATIR, V. M., & BITTER, J. R. (1991). The therapist and family therapy: Satir's human validation process model. In A. M. Horne & J. L. Passmore (Eds.), *Family counseling and therapy* (2nd ed.) (pp. 13–45). Itasca, IL: F. E. Peacock.

SATIR, V., BITTER, J. R., & KRESTENSEN, K. K. (1988). Family reconstruction: The family within—a group experience. *Journal for Specialists in Group Work, 13*(4), 200–208.

SCHILSON, E. A. (1991). Strategic therapy. In A. M. Horne & J. L. Passmore (Eds.), *Family counseling and therapy* (2nd ed.) (pp. 141–178). Itasca, IL: F. E. Peacock.

SEGAL, L. (1991). Brief family therapy. In A. M. Horne & J. L. Passmore (Eds.), *Family counseling and therapy* (2nd ed.) (pp. 179–205). Itasca, IL: F. E. Peacock.

SELVINI PALAZZOLI, M., BOSCOLO, L., CECCHIN, F. G., & PRATA, G. (1980). Hypothesizing-circularity-neutrality: Three guidelines for the conductor of the session. *Family Process, 19*(1), 3–12.

SUE, D., & SUE, D. W. (1991). Counseling strategies for Chinese Americans. In C. C. Lee & B. L. Richardson (Eds.), *Multicultural issues in counseling: New approaches to diversity* (pp. 79–90). Alexandria, VA: American Counseling Association.

TOMAN, W. (1994). *Family constellation: Its effects on personality and social behavior* (4th ed.). Northvale, NJ: Aronson.

WALSH, F. (1993). *Normal family processes* (2nd ed.). New York: Basic Books.

WATZLAWICK, P. (1978). *The language of change.* New York: Basic Books.

* WATZLAWICK, P., WEAKLAND, J. H., & FISCH, R. (1974). *Change: Principles of problem formation and problem resolution.* New York: Norton.

WEEKS, G. R., & L'ABATE, L. (1982). *Paradoxical psychotherapy: Theory and practice with individuals, couples, and families.* New York: Brunner/Mazel.

WHITAKER, C. A. (1976). The hindrance of theory in clinical work. In P. J. Guerin, Jr. (Ed.)., *Family therapy: Theory and practice.* New York: Gardner Press.

WHITAKER, C. A., & MALONE, T. P. (1981). *The roots of psychotherapy.* New York: Brunner/Mazel.

WHITE, M. (1992). Deconstruction and therapy. In *Experience, contradiction, narrative, and imagination: Selected papers of David Epston and Michael White, 1989–1991* (pp. 109–151). Adelaide, South Australia: Dulwich Centre Publications.

* WHITE, M., & EPSTON, D. (1990). *Narrative means to therapeutic ends.* New York: Norton.

WORDEN, M. (1994). *Family therapy basics.* Pacific Grove, CA: Brooks/Cole.

* WORRELL, J., & REMER, P. (1992). *Feminist perspectives in therapy: An empowerment model for women.* New York: Wiley.

YOUNG, M. E. (1992). *Counseling methods and techniques: An eclectic approach.* New York: Macmillan.

# INTEGRATION AND APPLICATION

# An Integrative Perspective

# Introduction

This chapter will help you think about areas of convergence and divergence among the nine therapeutic systems. Although the approaches all have at least some of the same goals, they have many differences when it comes to the best route to achieve these aims. Some therapies call for an active and directive stance on the therapist's part, and others place value on the client's being the active agent. Some therapies focus on bringing out feelings, whereas others stress identifying cognitive patterns, and still others concentrate on actual behavior. The key challenge is for you to find ways to integrate certain features of each of these therapies so that you can work with clients on all three levels of human experience.

Although we have examined only nine theoretical orientations in this book, the field of psychotherapy is characterized by a diverse range of specialized models. Corsini (1981) lists over 240 forms of psychotherapy, Herink (1980) describes more than 250, and Karasu (1986) puts the number at over 400. With all the diversity in systems of counseling, is there any hope that a practitioner can develop skills in all of the existing techniques? How does a student decide which theories are most relevant to practice? In addressing these questions, it is well to consider the competitive strife and theoretical "cold war" that dominated the field of counseling and psychotherapy for decades. The rivalry among theoretical orientations, dating back to Freud, has been characterized by various systems battling over who has the "best" way to bring about personality change. According to Norcross (1986a), the proliferation of therapy systems has been accompanied by a deafening cacophony of rival claims. He pleads for networks of practitioners who are willing to work toward rapprochement and integration. Although we certainly do not need to develop any additional theories of counseling, models that integrate existing approaches would be useful.

There are clear indications that since the early 1980s psychotherapy has been characterized by a rapidly developing movement toward integration and eclecticism. This movement is based on combining the best of differing orientations so that more complete theoretical models can be articulated and more efficient treatments developed (Goldfried & Castonguay, 1992). The Society for the Exploration of Psychotherapy Integration is an international organization that was formed in 1983. Its members are professionals who are working toward the development of therapeutic approaches that transcend single theoretical orientations.

In this chapter I consider the advantages of developing an integrated perspective on counseling and deal briefly with some of the potential problems. I also present a framework for helping you begin to integrate concepts and techniques from various approaches. As you read, attempt to formulate your personal perspective of counseling and how it best proceeds. Rather than merely reviewing the basic issues, look for a basis to begin synthesizing what sometimes appear to be diverse elements of different theoretical perspectives. As much as possible, be alert to ways in which these systems can function in harmony.

# The Trend toward Psychotherapy Integration

Integrative counseling and psychotherapy is the process of selecting concepts and methods from a variety of systems. Surveys of clinical and counseling psychologists consistently reveal that 30% to 50% of the respondents consider themselves to be eclectic or integrative in their therapeutic practice (Norcross & Newman, 1992). Practitioners of all persuasions are increasingly seeking a rapprochement among various systems and an integration of therapeutic techniques. Psychologists generally believe that the best hope for a truly comprehensive therapeutic approach lies with eclecticism (Norcross & Prochaska, 1988; K. R. Kelly, 1991; Smith, 1982). It should be mentioned, however, that the trend toward integrating perspectives has both promises and pitfalls. Goldfried and Safran (1986) caution that if this trend is carried to its extreme, there is a danger of constructing too many eclectic models. They are concerned that the growing interest in integration could result in competition to determine who can formulate the best eclectic system.

Although a large number of therapists identify themselves as "eclectic," this category covers a broad range of practice. Perhaps at its worst, eclectic practice consists of a haphazard picking of techniques without any overall theoretical rationale. This is known as *syncretism,* a practice by which the practitioner grabs for anything that seems to work, often making no attempt to determine whether the therapeutic procedures are indeed effective. This unsystematic approach is eclecticism "by default," in which its practitioners lack the knowledge and skill to select interventions meaningfully (Norcross, 1986a). Such a hodgepodge is no better than a narrow and dogmatic orthodoxy (Lazarus, 1986; Lazarus, Beutler, & Norcross, 1992).

Psychotherapy integration is best characterized by attempts to look beyond and across the confines of single-school approaches in order to see what can be learned from—and how clients can benefit from—other perspectives (Arkowitz, 1992). There are multiple pathways to achieving this integration, two of the most common being technical eclecticism and theoretical integration. *Technical eclecticism* tends to focus on differences, chooses from many approaches, and is a collection of techniques. This path calls for using techniques from different schools, without necessarily subscribing to the theoretical positions that spawned them. In contrast, *theoretical integration* refers to a conceptual or theoretical creation beyond a mere blending of techniques. This path has the goal of producing a conceptual framework that synthesizes the best of two or more theoretical approaches under the assumption that the outcome will be richer than either of the theories alone (Norcross & Newman, 1992).

Norcross and Prochaska (1988) found that 40% of the respondents in their study favored the term *integrative* and 25% favored *eclectic.* They also found three central themes for defining eclecticism: (1) pragmatically selecting whichever method best fits for a particular client or problem (34% of the sample), (2) combining a couple of theories in therapy practice (18%), and (3) integrating a number of therapies (21%). They write that relying on a single theory and a few techniques may be a product of inexperience; experience seems to result in diversity and resourcefulness.

Norcross and Newman (1992) identify the following eight interacting and mutually reinforcing motives that have fostered the trend toward psychotherapy integration:

1. a proliferation of therapies
2. the inadequacy of a single theory that is relevant to all clients and all problems
3. external socioeconomic realities, such as restrictions for insurance reimbursement and the prospect of national health insurance
4. the growing popularity of short-term, prescriptive, and problem-focused therapies
5. opportunities to observe and experiment with various therapies
6. a paucity of differential effectiveness among therapies
7. recognition that therapeutic commonalities play major roles in determining therapy outcome
8. development of professional societies aimed at the integration of psychotherapies

One reason for the trend toward psychotherapy integration is the recognition that no single theory is comprehensive enough to account for the complexities of human behavior, especially when the range of client types and their specific problems are taken into consideration. Because no one theory has a patent on the truth, and because no single set of counseling techniques is always effective in working with diverse client populations, K. R. Kelly (1988/1991) does not think it makes sense to follow a single theory. Instead, he calls for theoretical integration as the basis for future counseling practice. Practitioners who are open to an integrative perspective may find that several theories play a crucial role in their personal counseling approach. Each theory has its unique contributions and its own domain of expertise. By accepting that each theory has strengths and weaknesses and is, by definition, "different" from the others, practitioners have some basis to begin developing a theory that fits for them. Developing an integrative perspective is a lifelong endeavor that is refined with experience.

In a study done by Young, Feiler, and Witmer (1989), counselor educators and mental-health counselors were surveyed to determine their primary theoretical orientation. The results, in alphabetical order, are as follows:

| *Theoretical orientation* | *Percent* | *Counselor educators* | *Mental-health counselors* |
|---|---|---|---|
| Adlerian | 2% | 1.5% | 1% |
| Behavior modification | 3% | 3% | 3% |
| Cognitive-behavioral | 6% | 8% | 4% |
| Eclectic | 32% | 30% | 30% |
| Ericksonian hypnosis | 2% | — | 3% |

*(continued)*

| Theoretical orientation | Percent | Counselor educators | Mental-health counselors |
|---|---|---|---|
| Existential | 0.8% | — | 1% |
| Family systems | 10% | 5% | 14% |
| Gestalt | 2% | 1.5% | 1% |
| Multimodal | 3% | 3% | 3% |
| Person-centered | 22% | 32% | 10% |
| Psychoanalytic | 5% | — | 10% |
| Psychoeducational | 3% | 5% | 1% |
| Rational-emotive | 2% | — | 3% |
| Reality | 4% | 8% | 4% |
| Other | 9% | 5% | 9% |
| *N =* | | 66 | 69 |

# THE FUTURE OF PSYCHOTHERAPY: SOME PREDICTIONS

In discussing the future of psychotherapy, Norcross and Freedheim (1992) draw on several studies in which experts forecast which theoretical orientations are likely to flourish or decline. The approaches predicted to gain are family systems therapy, technical eclecticism, cognitive therapy, theoretical integration, psychobiological therapy, behavior therapy, and feminist therapy. Predicted to wane are transactional analysis, psychoanalytic therapy, neurolinguistic programming, existential therapy, person-centered therapy, psychodynamic therapy, and humanistic therapy. The experts forecast that psychotherapy practice will become more short-term, directive, educational, present-centered, structured, prescriptive, and problem-focused. Therapies that are relatively long-term, unstructured, and focused on the past are viewed as on the decline.

The nine systems discussed in this book have evolved in the direction of broadening their theoretical and practical bases, becoming less restrictive in their focus. Thus, many practitioners who claim allegiance to a particular system of therapy are expanding their theoretical outlook and developing a wider range of therapeutic techniques to fit a more diverse population of clients. Lazarus and his colleagues (1992) predict that "technical eclecticism will represent the psychotherapeutic *Zeitgeist* well into the 21st century" (p. 13). They also suggest a trend toward matching clients not only to specific treatment techniques but also to therapists' interpersonal styles. What this means is that we will be better able to prescribe therapeutic relationships of choice for individual clients. Prochaska and Norcross (1994) agree with this prediction and also foresee enormous pressure toward intertheoretical cooperation, convergence, integration, and cost-effective treatments.

Goldfried and Castonguay (1992) identify several future directions in the field of psychotherapy: a greater consolidation of the more traditional orientations, an increased focus on treating more specific problems, the incorporation of concepts from the cognitive sciences, and the combination of psychotherapeutic and psychobiological approaches. They write: "Indeed, it would not surprise us if we saw future generations of therapists choosing to be trained in one particular orientation, while at the same time showing a greater openness toward the theoretical, clinical, and empirical contributions of other approaches" (p. 5). Goldfried, Castonguay, and Safran (1992) predict that although the traditional theoretical orientations are likely to continue in the future, these systems will increasingly incorporate contributions from other approaches. They express concerns about delineating "integrative psychotherapy" as yet another system, because there is no consensus on what should be integrated.

## INTEGRATION OF MULTICULTURAL AND SPIRITUAL CONCERNS IN PSYCHOTHERAPY

As I survey the literature, it seems clear that during the latter half of the 1990s we will see a continuation of the trend toward convergence. Furthermore, due to the increased diversity of client problems and client populations, I predict that psychotherapy integration will focus on including cultural factors in the assessment and treatment process. Multiculturalism is a reality that cannot be ignored by practitioners if they hope to meet the needs of their diverse client groups. There is a growing movement toward creating a separate multicultural theory of counseling and therapy (see Sue, Ivey, & Pedersen, 1996). I maintain that current theories can be expanded to incorporate a multicultural component. If current theories are not modified, they will have limited applicability in dealing with the complexity of a culturally diverse population. An integrative perspective favors broadening the base of the contemporary theories to encompass a social, spiritual, and political dimension. Existing counseling theories can also be expanded to include a focus on gender issues, cultural differences, spiritual concerns, and family and systemic concerns. According to Pate and Bondi (1992), religious beliefs and practices are an aspect of clients' cultural background that should be considered a central part of a counselor's multicultural awareness. Thus, the education of counselors needs to incorporate specific training in dealing with issues pertaining to multiculturalism, gender, and spirituality.

From my perspective, spirituality entails the belief in a higher power than ourselves, and it involves an attempt to align our life toward this higher power. Whatever one's particular view of spirituality, it is a force that can help the individual make sense of the universe and to find a purpose (or purposes) for living. For some, spirituality entails embracing a religion, which can have many different meanings. Others value spirituality, yet do not have any ties to a formal religion. There are many paths toward fulfilling spiritual needs, and it is not the therapist's task to prescribe any particular pathway. However, it is therapists' responsibility to be aware that spirituality is a significant force for many of their clients. It is especially important to pursue spiritual concerns if the client initiates them. Therapists inquire about their clients' general physical health and their attitudes and practices about their physical health. In a like manner, it is in the realm of duty for therapists to inquire about their clients' values, beliefs, and the sources from which they have attempted to find meaning in life. As a part of the assessment process, it is good practice to ask about clients' beliefs and values that have been influenced by their culture and possibly their religion. If clients give an indication that they are concerned about any of their beliefs or practices, this is a useful focal point for exploration. The key here is that the therapist remain finely tuned to the client's story and to the purpose for which he or she sought therapy.

Within the coming decade, I think, there will be an increased emphasis on integrating a spiritual perspective into counseling practice. There is already widespread interest in the topic of spiritual and religious beliefs—both the therapist's and the client's—and how such beliefs might be incorporated into therapeutic practice. According to Bergin (1988), it is timely to add a spiritual keystone to the building blocks provided by the therapeutic approaches, because such an orientation contributes to an understanding of techniques and provides a moral frame of reference for values that influence a client's behavior. Miller (1988) advocates the value of including clients' spiritual perspectives in cognitive-behavior therapy. He endorses a collaborative approach that respects the integrity of the individual's belief system. Miller suggests that once clients clarify their basic assumptions, it is the therapist's task to help them examine the consequences of their beliefs.

Grimm (1994) takes the position that a therapist's spiritual and religious values influence the course of psychotherapy, both directly and indirectly. Although he believes it is essential for mental-health professionals to be aware of their spiritual and religious values, he cautions them to avoid any attempts to indoctrinate their clients with their own values. At a recent symposium of the American Psychological Association, Elkins (1994) called for the movement toward a "soulful psychology." He contends that contrary to the myth that psychologists have little interest in spiritual matters, it is now clear that the majority of clinicians are paying more attention to the spiritual dimensions of the human being. Suggesting that many clients are hungry for therapeutic experiences that offer them help with the spiritual and existential issues of life, he concludes that psychotherapy ought to be considered a journey of the soul in search of its own healing.

Mattson (1994), who writes that our society is placing more emphasis on religious issues, maintains that a client's spiritual beliefs need not be feared in a counseling setting but should be used to the client's benefit. He identifies some excellent practical suggestions in working with clients' religious concerns. Faiver and O'Brien (1993) write that religion may be a source of spiritual strength or a source of conflict and guilt. They have devised a form to assess the religious beliefs of clients, which they use for diagnostic, treatment, and referral purposes.

In spite of the position of these writers, it appears that counselor-education programs have a long way to go in training future practitioners to deal with religious and spiritual issues. In a national survey of such programs, E. W. Kelly (1994) found that religious and spiritual issues were being dealt with as a course component in fewer than 25% of the programs. What may be more surprising is his finding that only about half the counselor educators who participated in the study believed that religious and spiritual issues were either "very important" or "important" in the education and training of counselors. Clearly, if counselors are to meet the challenge of addressing the role of spirituality in counseling, they not only need training in this area in both their coursework and in their fieldwork experiences but also need inspiration and leadership from their teachers.

If you are interested in the issue of the possibilities of integrating a spiritual orientation into counseling, I recommend the following sources: Bergin (1988), Elkins (1994), Faiver and O'Brien (1993), Georgia (1994), Grimm (1994), Hinterkopf (1994), Ingersoll (1994), E. W. Kelly (1994), Mattson (1994), Miller (1988), Miller and Martin (1988), Pate and Bondi (1992), and Peck (1978).

# THE CHALLENGE OF
# DEVELOPING AN INTEGRATIVE PERSPECTIVE

In addressing the proper degree of integration to introduce into counseling practice, Messer (1986, 1992) concludes that the debate will continue between adherents of a single theoretical system and those who favor moving toward some form of integration. A survey of approaches to counseling and psychotherapy reveals that no common philosophy unifies them. Many of the theories have different basic philosophies and views of human nature (see Tables 13-1 and 13-2, pp. 463–466). Your philosophical assumptions are important because they influence which "reality" you perceive, and they direct your attention to the variables that you are "set" to see. A word of caution, then: Beware of subscribing exclusively to any one view of human nature; remain open and selectively incorporate a framework for counseling that is consistent with your own personality and your belief system.

Despite the divergences in the various theories, there are possibilities for a creative synthesis among some models. Thus, an existential orientation does not necessarily preclude using techniques drawn from behavior therapy or from some of the cognitive theories. That all these theories represent different vantage points from which to look at human behavior does not mean that one theorist has "the truth" and the others are in error. Each point of view can offer you a perspective for helping clients in their search for self. I encourage you to study all the major theories, to resist being converted to any single point of view, and to remain open to what you might take from the various orientations as a basis for an integrative perspective that will guide your practice.

In developing a personal integrative perspective, however, it is important to be alert to the problem of attempting to mix theories with incompatible underlying assumptions. As Lazarus (1986) has noted, for therapists to choose their theories and techniques primarily on the basis of subjective appeal can lead to confusion. In working toward the goal of integration, you need to be aware of irreconcilable differences among the systems that make rapprochement impossible. The basic philosophies of classical psychoanalysis and radical behaviorism, for example, do not easily lend themselves to a merger. Furthermore, many of the concepts of the psychoanalytic approach are fundamentally different from those of reality therapy.

According to Lazarus (1986, 1989, 1992), who is an advocate of technical eclecticism, therapists who hope to be effective with a wide range of problems and with different client populations must be flexible and versatile. The basic questions they ask are: What works for whom under which particular circumstances? Why are some procedures helpful and others unhelpful? What can be done to ensure long-term success and positive follow-ups? Lazarus emphasizes that technical eclecticism draws on many effective techniques without necessarily subscribing to the theories that give rise to them. He notes that some clients respond to warm, informal counselors but that others want more formal counselors. Whereas some clients work well with therapists who are quiet and nonforceful, others work best with directive and outgoing therapists. Further, the same client may respond favorably to various therapeutic techniques and styles at different times. (For a review of multimodal procedures and their rationale, refer to Chapter 10, "Behavior Therapy.")

An integrative perspective at its best entails a *systematic integration* of underlying principles and methods common to a range of therapeutic approaches. In order for you to develop this kind of integration, you will eventually need to be thoroughly conversant with a number of theories, to be open to the idea that these theories can be unified in some ways, and to be willing to continually test your hypotheses to determine how well they are working. An integrative perspective is the product of a great deal of study, clinical practice, research, and theorizing.

If you are interested in developing an eclectic approach or in the movement toward the integration of psychotherapies, a great deal has been written: Beutler (1983), Beutler and Clarkin (1990), Beutler and Consoli (1992), Brammer, Shostrom, and Abrego (1989), Feldman and Powell, (1992), Garfield (1980, 1986, 1992a), Goldfried and Castonguay (1992), Goldfried et al. (1992), Goldfried and Newman (1992), K. R. Kelly (1988, 1991), Lazarus (1986, 1989, 1992), Lazarus and Beutler (1993), Lazarus et al., (1992), Messer (1986, 1992), McBride and Martin (1990), Murray (1986), Norcross (1986a, 1986b), Norcross and Freedheim (1992), Norcross and Newman (1992), Norcross and Prochaska (1988), Prochaska and DiClemente (1992), Prochaska and Norcross (1994), Saltzman and Norcross (1990), Simon (1989, 1991), Smith (1982), Young (1992), and Young et al. (1989).

# Issues Related to the Therapeutic Process

## THERAPEUTIC GOALS

The goals of counseling are almost as diverse as are the theoretical approaches. Goals include restructuring the personality, uncovering the unconscious, creating social interest, finding meaning in life, curing an emotional disturbance, examining old decisions and making new ones, developing trust in oneself, becoming more self-actualizating, reducing anxiety, shedding maladaptive behavior and learning adaptive patterns, and gaining more effective control of one's life (see Table 13-3, pp. 466–467). Is there a common denominator in this range of goals?

This diversity can be simplified by considering the degree of generality or specificity of goals. Goals exist on a continuum from specific, concrete, and short term, on one end, to general, global, and long term, on the other. The cognitive-behavioral approaches stress the former; the relationship-oriented therapies tend to stress the latter. The goals at opposite ends of the continuum are not necessarily contradictory; it is a matter of how specifically they are defined.

## THERAPIST'S FUNCTION AND ROLE

Just as the various theories are guided by different goals, so, too, do the therapist's functions vary among the models. In working toward an integrative perspective, we need to address a number of questions about the counselor's behaviors: How do the counselor's functions change depending on the stage of the counseling process? Does the therapist maintain a basic role, or does this role vary in accordance with the characteristics of the client? How does the counselor determine how active and directive to be? How is structuring handled as the course of therapy progresses? What is the optimum balance of responsibility in the client/therapist relationship? When and how much does the counselor self-disclose?

CONTROL OF CLIENT BEHAVIOR.   As you saw through your study of the nine therapeutic approaches, a central issue of each system is the degree to which the therapist exercises control over the client's behavior both during and outside the session. Cognitive-behavior therapists and reality therapists, for example, operate within a directive and didactic structure. They frequently suggest homework assignments that are designed to get clients to practice new behavior outside therapy sessions. By contrast, person-centered therapists operate with a much looser and less defined structure.

Structuring depends on the particular client and the specific circumstances he or she brings to the therapy situation. From my perspective, clear structure is most essential during the early phase of counseling. It helps encourage clients to talk about the problems that led them to seek therapy. In a collaborative way, it is useful for both the counselor and the client to make some initial assessment that can provide a focus for the therapy process. As soon as possible, it is useful for clients to be given a significant share of the responsibility of deciding on the content of the sessions. From early in the therapy process, clients can be empowered if the counselor expects that they will become an active participant in the process.

## CLIENT'S EXPERIENCE IN THERAPY

What expectations do clients have as they approach therapy? What are their responsibilities in the process? Is therapy only for the "disturbed"? Can the relatively healthy person benefit from it? Are there any commonalities among the grand diversity of clients?

Most clients share some degree of suffering, pain, or at least discontent. There is a discrepancy between how they would like to be and how they are. Some initiate therapy because they hope to cure a specific symptom or set of symptoms: They want to get rid of migraine headaches, free themselves of chronic anxiety attacks, lose weight, or get relief from depression. They may have conflicting feelings and reactions, may struggle with low self-esteem, or may have limited information and skills. Many seek to resolve conflicts with a marital partner. Increasingly, people are entering therapy with existential problems; their complaints are less defined but relate to the experiences of emptiness, meaninglessness in life, boredom, dead personal relationships, a lack of intense feelings, and a loss of their sense of self.

The initial expectations of many clients are expert help and a fast result. They often have great hope for major changes in their lives with little effort on their part. As therapy progresses, they discover that they must be active in the process; they need to select their own goals and work for them, both in the sessions and in daily living.

In thinking about your integrative perspective on counseling practice, consider the characteristics of each client who seeks your help. Some clients can benefit from recognizing and expressing pent-up feelings, others will need to examine their beliefs and thoughts, others will most need to begin behaving in different ways, and others will benefit from talking with you about their relationships with the significant people in their lives. In deciding what interventions are most likely to be helpful, take into account the client's cultural, ethnic, and socioeconomic background. Moreover, the focus of counseling may change with each of these clients at different phases in the counseling process. Although some clients initially feel a need to be listened to and allowed to express deep feelings, they can profit later from examining the thought patterns that are contributing to their psychological pain. And certainly, at some point in therapy it is essential that clients translate what they are learning about themselves into concrete action. The client's given situation in the environment provides a framework for selecting interventions that are most appropriate.

## RELATIONSHIP BETWEEN THERAPIST AND CLIENT

Most approaches share common ground in accepting the importance of the therapeutic relationship. The existential, person-centered, and Gestalt views are based on the personal relationship as the crucial determinant of treatment outcomes. It is clear that some other approaches—such as rational emotive behavior therapy, cognitive-behavior therapy, and behavior therapy—do not ignore the relationship factor, even though they do not give it a place of central importance (see Table 13-4, pp. 467–468).

Counseling is a personal matter that involves a personal relationship, and evidence indicates that honesty, sincerity, acceptance, understanding, and spontaneity are basic ingredients of successful outcomes. Therapists' degree of caring, their interest and ability in helping their clients, and their genuineness are factors that influence the relationship. Lazarus (1986) describes what he considers to be the common characteristics of "highly successful therapists": a genuine respect for people, flexibility, a nonjudgmental attitude, a good sense of humor, warmth, authenticity, and the willingness to recognize and reveal their shortcomings. Lazarus (1992) views the client/therapist relationship as the soil that enables the therapist's techniques to take root. Within the context of a warm, caring, therapeutic relationship, it is also necessary to remedy faulty cognitions and maladaptive behaviors. To bring about these changes, effective therapy often requires that therapists teach clients a range of coping skills that they can use in solving their problems. Clients also contribute to the relationship with variables such as their motivation, cooperation, interest, concern, and expectations.

As you think about developing your personal counseling perspective, give consideration to the issue of the match between client and counselor. I certainly do not advocate changing your personality to fit your perception of what each client is expecting; it is important that you *be yourself* as you meet clients. You also need to consider the reality that you will probably not work effectively with every client, because results are not determined solely by your knowledge and your technical competence. Some clients will work better with counselors who have another type of personal and therapeutic style than yours. Thus, I recommend sensitivity in assessing what your clients need, along with good judgment about the appropriateness of the match between you and a potential client.

Although you do not have to be like your clients or have experienced the same problems to be effective with them, it is critical that you be able to understand their world and respect them. The matter of matching client and therapist has interesting implications for multicultural counseling. You might ask yourself how well prepared you feel to counsel clients from a different cultural background. To what degree do you think you can successfully establish a therapeutic relationship with a client of a different race? ethnic group? gender? age? sexual orientation? socioeconomic group? Do you see any potential barriers in yourself that would make it difficult to form a working relationship with certain clients? (This would be a good time to review the discussion of the culturally skilled counselor in Chapter 2 and to consult Tables 13-9 and 13-10, pp. 475–478.)

# The Place of Techniques and Evaluation in Counseling

## DRAWING ON TECHNIQUES FROM VARIOUS APPROACHES

As I've mentioned, I see it as needlessly restrictive for you to apply only a few techniques from a single theory to most clients. Instead, incorporate a wide range of procedures into your therapeutic style. Indeed, it would get boring if you were to play one or two notes on the piano instead of using the full range of keys available. At times, reflection of feeling and simply listening to a client's verbal and nonverbal messages are appropriate, but to limit yourself to these procedures exclusively is to hamper your effectiveness.

It is often beneficial to confront clients with their evasions of reality or their illogical thinking, but again, to focus primarily on this behavior is to restrict yourself unnecessarily. At times you may need to be interpretive, and at other times you may invite clients to interpret for themselves the meaning of their behavior. Sometimes it is appropriate to be very directive and structured, and at other times it is better to flow without a clear structure. So much depends on the purpose of therapy, the setting, the personality and style of the therapist, the qualities of the particular client, and the problems selected for intervention.

Beutler (1983) addresses the question "What therapy activities are most appropriate for what type of problem, by which therapist, for what kind of client?" Regardless of what model you may be working with, you must decide *what* techniques, procedures, or intervention methods to use, *when* to use them, and with *which clients*. This would be a good time to review the charts on the therapeutic relationship, therapeutic techniques, and application of techniques (Tables 13-4–13-6, pp. 467–472). It is critical to be aware of how clients' cultural backgrounds contribute to their perceptions of their problems.

As we have seen, each of the nine therapeutic approaches has both strengths and limitations when applying its techniques to culturally diverse client populations (see Tables 13-9 and 13-10, pp. 475–478). Although it is unwise to stereotype clients because of their cultural heritage, it is useful to assess how the cultural context has a bearing on their concerns. Some techniques are contraindicated because of a client's socialization. Thus, the client's responsiveness (or lack of it) to certain techniques is a critical barometer in judging the effectiveness of these methods.

I see it as a mistake to equate counselor effectiveness simply with proficiency in a single technique or even a set of techniques. For example, some counselors become specialists in confrontational techniques. They develop a style of relating to clients geared to provoking them, goading them to "get their anger expressed," or merely focusing on techniques to deal with anger. These therapists derive a sense of power from becoming "confrontation specialists." For a different set of motives, other counselors limit themselves to techniques of reflection and clarification. Perhaps they are fearful of getting involved with clients on more than the empathic and supportive level; thus, they continue to reflect because there are few risks involved.

By reviewing the models presented in this book and the techniques that flow from them, it is possible to learn that effective counseling involves proficiency in a *combination* of cognitive, affective, and behavioral techniques. Such a combination is necessary to help clients *think* about their beliefs and assumptions, to experience on a *feeling* level their conflicts and struggles, and to actually translate their insights into *action* programs by behaving in new ways in day-to-day living.

At this point I suggest that you review the charts on the applications, contributions, and limitations of the various therapeutic approaches (Tables 13-6–13-8, pp. 470–475). These charts should help you identify elements from the various approaches that you may want to incorporate into your own counseling perspective.

## EVALUATING THE EFFECTIVENESS
## OF COUNSELING AND THERAPY

Research in psychotherapy gained little momentum until the 1950s. Since the late 1950s and the early 1960s it has mainly addressed the process and outcomes of therapy. Its central purpose is to gain a clearer understanding of what constitutes therapeutic change and how it comes about, so that more effective counseling methods can be developed (Strupp, 1986; VandenBos, 1986).

The acceleration of public funding for all types of human-services programs during the 1960s also stirred a keen interest in evaluation research. In essence, if government funds were to continue to be allocated to human-services agencies, the burden of proof rested on researchers and practitioners to demonstrate the effectiveness of psychotherapy by using scientific methods. The central question raised was: Of what value is psychotherapy to the individual and society? (Strupp, 1986). Mental-health providers are still faced with accountability. In the era of managed care, it becomes even more essential for practitioners to demonstrate the degree to which their interventions are both clinically sound and cost-effective.

This brief section examines issues pertaining to the effectiveness of counseling and psychotherapy in achieving the goals of personality and behavior change. Questions that can be asked are: Does therapy make a significant difference? Are people substantially better after therapy than they were without it? Can therapy actually be more harmful than helpful? Because a thorough discussion of these questions is beyond the scope of this book, I will not review the vast literature related to therapy outcomes. Instead, I will address a few basic issues related to evaluating the effectiveness of counseling.

If you are interested in such a review and other articles on psychotherapy research, I suggest the following sources: Bergin and Lambert (1978); Cohen, Sargent, and Sechrest (1986); Garfield (1987, 1992b); Gendlin (1986); Imber, Glanz, Elkin, Sotsky, Boyer, & Leber (1986); Lambert (1992); Lambert and Bergin (1992); Morrow-Bradley and Elliott (1986); Smith, Glass, and Miller (1980); Stiles, Shapiro, and Elliott (1986); Strupp (1986); Strupp and Howard (1992); and VandenBos (1986).

There are problems in lumping together many research efforts to answer the general question "Does psychotherapy work?" A basic difficulty is that each of the multitude of therapeutic systems is applied by a practitioner with individual characteristics that are difficult to measure. Further, clients themselves have much to do with therapeutic outcomes. If they choose to engage in activities that are self-destructive, this behavior will cancel out the positive effects of therapy. To add to the problem, effects resulting from unexpected and uncontrollable events in the environment can destroy gains that are made in psychotherapy. As Garfield (1992b) has pointed out, the basic variables that influence therapy research are extremely difficult to control and evaluate. Clinical research cannot exert the degree of control that is true for controlled laboratory experiments but can only strive for approximations. It should be clear that evaluating how well psychotherapy works is far from simple.

One of the first issues is how much outcome research has been conducted on the therapeutic approaches presented in this book. Most of the studies have been done by two divergent groups: (1) the behavior and cognitive therapists, who have based their therapeutic practice on empirical studies, and (2) the person-centered researchers, who have made significant contributions to the understanding of both process and outcome variables. To a lesser extent, REBT and short-term psychodynamic therapy have also been subjected to research to support their main hypotheses. The other models covered in this book have not produced significant empirical research dealing with how well their therapy works.

By about 1980 a consensus had emerged that psychotherapy was demonstrably more effective than no treatment (VandenBos, 1986). Smith et al. (1980) presented a meta-analysis of psychotherapy outcome literature and concluded that psychotherapy was highly effective. In spite of this general support of the value of psychotherapy, if we are looking for hard data to support the concepts and procedures of most of the therapeutic approaches discussed in this book, we will be disappointed. One reason is that one approach's "cure" is another approach's "resistance." In other words, because each approach works toward different outcomes, it is almost impossible to compare them. Despite the wide range of purportedly distinct psychotherapeutic treatments, most reviews of outcome research show little differential effectiveness of the tested psychotherapies (Stiles et al., 1986). Factors other than scientific data must be considered if we are to determine the validity and usefulness of most of the therapeutic approaches.

Lambert (1992) writes that because of the wide variability of techniques employed by integrative practitioners, it is extremely difficult to assess the effectiveness of standard eclectic approaches. Although his discussion of the implications of therapy-outcome research for integrative therapists is quite involved, below are four of his salient points:

1. A substantial number of outpatients improve without formal psychotherapy. One implication for eclectic therapists is to draw upon the natural helping systems in the client's environment.

2. In general, psychological treatments are beneficial. However, considering the many different therapeutic approaches, each containing its own rationale and specific set of techniques, there is little evidence to support the superiority of one school or technique over another.

3. Various factors—interpersonal, social, and affective—that are common across therapy systems account for a substantial degree of the improvement found in clients. They include *support factors* (therapist warmth, respect, empathy, acceptance, feedback, and other factors associated with a positive relationship); *learning factors* (insight, cognitive learning, and self-acceptance); and *action factors* (expectations for improvement, facing

one's fears, reality testing, modeling, practice, and working through). Research suggests that these common factors may be more important than specific techniques as a catalyst for facilitating positive changes in clients.

4. Specific techniques can be selected for dealing with specific problems on the basis of their effectiveness. This provides a framework to assess the direction and outcomes of therapy.

One of Lambert's key points is the lack of clear research evidence to support the therapeutic value of many eclectic practices. He concludes that until empirical investigations are conducted, integrative therapists would do well to be more modest in their claims of being superior to the single-school models.

The general question "Does psychotherapy work?" is often raised. Such a global question is very difficult to answer meaningfully (Strupp & Howard, 1992). Garfield (1980) argues that the question is "Is psychotherapy effective?" is a poor one destined to receive poor answers. He makes the point that psychotherapy is not a clearly defined and uniform process and that there is thus no basis for any objective answer to the question. As VandenBos (1986) concludes, it appears that outcome research aimed at proving the efficacy of therapy should be a thing of the past. He contends that future research should be focused on exploring the relative advantages and disadvantages of alternative treatment strategies for clients with different psychological and behavioral problems. Included in this research should be factors such as the relative cost, the length of time necessary to effect change, and the nature and extent of change. Whatever form it takes, research will apparently play an increasingly important role in determining the future of psychotherapy (Strupp, 1986).

A guideline for improving on this global question is provided by Paul (1967) with the following question: *"What* treatment, by *whom,* is the most effective for *this* individual with *that* specific problem, and under what set of circumstances?" It is clear that greater precision and specificity are needed in research (Stiles et al., 1986). Thus, the question of the effectiveness of psychotherapy needs to be narrowed down to a specific type of therapy and usually narrowed further to a certain technique. Moreover, practitioners who adhere to the same approach are likely to use techniques in various ways and relate to clients in diverse fashions. They may function differently depending on the type of client and the clinical setting.

# Summary and Review Charts

As we have seen, creating an integrative stance is truly a challenge, for it does not simply mean picking bits and pieces from theories in a random and fragmented manner. In forming an integrated perspective, it is important to ask: Which theories provide a basis for understanding the *cognitive* dimensions? What about the *feeling* aspects? And how about the *behavioral* dimension? Most of the nine therapeutic orientations focus on one of these dimensions of human experience. Although the other dimensions are not necessarily ignored, they are often given short shrift.

Developing an integrated theoretical perspective requires much reading, thinking, and actual counseling experience. Unless you have an accurate, in-depth knowledge of these theories, you cannot formulate a true synthesis. Simply put, you cannot integrate what you do not know (Norcross & Newman, 1992). A central message of this book has been to remain open to each theory, to do further reading, and to reflect on how the key concepts of each approach fit your personality. Building your personalized theory of counseling, which is based on what you consider to be the best features of several theories, is a long-term venture.

Besides considering your own personality, think about what concepts and techniques work best with a range of clients. It requires knowledge, skill, art, and experience to be able to determine what techniques are suitable for particular problems. It is also an art to know when and how to use a particular therapeutic intervention. Although reflecting on your personal preferences is important, I would hope that you also balance your preferences with scientific evidence. Developing a personal approach to counseling practice does not imply that anything goes. Indeed, in this era of managed care and cost-effectiveness, your personal preferences may not always be the sole determinant of your psychotherapy practice. In counseling clients with certain problems, specific techniques have demonstrated their effectiveness. For instance, behavior therapy, cognitive therapy, interpersonal therapy, and short-term psychodynamic therapy have repeatedly proved successful in treating depression. Although I am not suggesting that you adopt a theory with which you are uncomfortable, ethical practice implies that you employ efficacious procedures in dealing with certain clients or problems. You might examine the following questions: "Under what circumstances is it appropriate, or ethical, for me to bypass a scientifically proved treatment for a treatment that I personally prefer?" "What relative weight do I give to my personal preferences and to scientific evidence?"

At this point it would be useful for you to identify the major insights you have gained so far in reading this book. Most of all, think about which theories seem to have the most practical application in helping you understand your present life situation. Consider what changes you are interested in making and which approaches could provide you with strategies to modify specific thoughts, feelings, and behaviors. This is a good time to review what you may have learned about your ability to establish effective relationships with other people. Especially important is a review of any personal characteristics that could either help or hinder you in developing solid working relationships with clients. Some questions you might ask yourself are: "What have I learned about my personal needs and how they are likely to operate in a counseling relationship?" "What did I learn about my values and how my attitudes and beliefs could work either for or against establishing effective relationships with clients?" "What steps can I take now to increase the chances of becoming an effective person and counselor?"

After you make this review of significant personal learning, I suggest that you ponder what you have learned about the counseling process. It could help to identify a particular theory that you might adopt as a foundation for establishing your own perspective on counseling theory and practice. As you review the following charts summarizing the nine theories, consider from which therapies you would be most inclined to draw (1) underlying assumptions, (2) major concepts, (3) therapeutic goals, (4) therapeutic relationship, and (5) techniques and procedures. Also consider the major applications of each of the therapies, as well as their basic limitations and major contributions.

T A B L E   13-1
The Basic Philosophies

| | |
|---|---|
| *Psychoanalytic therapy* | Human beings are basically determined by psychic energy and by early experiences. Unconscious motives and conflicts are central in present behavior. Irrational forces are strong; the person is driven by sexual and aggressive impulses. Early development is of critical importance, because later personality problems have their roots in repressed childhood conflicts. |
| *Adlerian therapy* | A positive view of human nature is stressed. Humans are motivated by social interest, by striving toward goals, and by dealing with the tasks of life. People are in control of their fate, not victims of it. Each person at an early age creates a unique style of life, which tends to remain relatively constant throughout life. |
| *Existential therapy* | The central focus is on the nature of the human condition, which includes capacity for self-awareness, freedom of choice to decide one's fate, responsibility, anxiety as a basic element, the search for a unique meaning in a meaningless world, being alone and being in relation with others, and finiteness and death. |
| *Person-centered therapy* | The view of humans is positive; humans have an inclination toward becoming fully functioning. In the context of the therapeutic relationship, the client experiences feelings that were previously denied to awareness. The client actualizes potential and moves toward increased awareness, spontaneity, trust in self, and inner directedness. |
| *Gestalt therapy* | The person strives for wholeness and integration of thinking, feeling, and behaving. The view is antideterministic, in that the person is viewed as having the capacity to recognize how earlier influences are related to present difficulties. Growth involves moving from environmental support to self-support. |
| *Reality therapy* | Based on the assumption that people are ultimately self-determining and in charge of their life, the approach is both antideterministic and positive. The model describes how people attempt to control the world around them. It teaches them ways to more effectively satisfy their needs. |

*(continued)*

T A B L E    13-1
The Basic Philosophies *(continued)*

| | |
|---|---|
| *Behavior therapy* | Behavior is the product of learning. We are both the product and the producer of the environment. We are both the product and the producer of the environment. No set of unifying assumptions about behavior can incorporate all the existing procedures in the behavioral field. |
| *Cognitive-behavior therapy* | Individuals tend to incorporate faulty thinking, which leads to emotional and behavioral disturbances. Cognitions are the major determinants of how we feel and act. Therapy is primarily oriented toward cognition and behavior, and it stresses the role of thinking, deciding, questioning, doing, and redeciding. This is a psychoeducational model, which emphasizes therapy as a learning process, including acquiring and practicing new skills, learning new ways of thinking, and acquiring more effective ways of coping with problems. |
| *Family systems therapy* | The family is viewed from an interactive and systemic perspective. Clients are connected to a living system; a change in one part of the system will result in a change in other parts. The family provides the context for understanding how individuals function in relationship to others and how they behave. Treatment is best focused on the family unit. An individual's dysfunctional behavior grows out of the interactional unit of the family and out of larger systems as well. |

T A B L E    13-2
Key Concepts

| | |
|---|---|
| *Psychoanalytic therapy* | Normal personality development is based on successful resolution and integration of psychosexual stages of development. Faulty personality development is the result of inadequate resolution of some specific stage. Id, ego, and superego constitute the basis of personality structure. Anxiety is a result of repression of basic conflicts. Ego defenses are developed to control anxiety. Unconscious processes are centrally related to current behavior. |
| *Adlerian therapy* | Based on a growth model, this approach emphasizes the individual's positive capacities to live in society cooperatively. It also stresses the unity of personality, the need to view people from their subjective perspective, and the importance of life goals that give direction to behavior. People are motivated by social interest and by finding goals to strive for. Therapy is a matter of providing encouragement and assisting clients in changing their cognitive perspective. |

TABLE   13-2
Key Concepts *(continued)*

| | |
|---|---|
| *Existential therapy* | Essentially an approach to counseling and therapy rather than a firm theoretical model, it stresses core human conditions. Normally, personality development is based on the uniqueness of each individual. Sense of self develops from infancy. Self-determination and a tendency toward growth are central ideas. Focus is on the present and on what one is becoming; that is, the approach has a future orientation. It stresses self-awareness before action. It is an experiential therapy. |
| *Person-centered therapy* | The client has the potential to become aware of problems and the means to resolve them. Faith is placed in the client's capacity for self-direction. Mental health is a congruence of ideal self and real self. Maladjustment is the result of a discrepancy between what one wants to be and what one is. Focus is on the present moment and on experiencing and expressing feelings. |
| *Gestalt therapy* | Emphasis is on the "what" and "how" of experiencing in the here and now to help clients accept their polarities. Key concepts include personal responsibility, unfinished business, avoiding, experiencing, and awareness of the now. Gestalt is an experiential therapy that stresses feelings and the influence of unfinished business on personality development. |
| *Reality therapy* | The basic focus is on what clients are doing and how to get them to evaluate whether their present ways are working for them. People create their feelings by the choices they make and by what they do. The approach rejects many notions of conventional therapy (such as focusing on the client's past, feelings, or insight; transference; the unconscious; and dreams). |
| *Behavior therapy* | Focus is on overt behavior, precision in specifying goals of treatment, development of specific treatment plans, and objective evaluation of therapy outcomes. Therapy is based on the principles of learning theory. Normal behavior is learned through reinforcement and imitation. Abnormal behavior is the result of faulty learning. This approach stresses present behavior. |
| *Cognitive-behavior therapy* | Although psychological problems may be rooted in childhood, they are perpetuated through reindoctrination in the now. A person's belief system is the primary cause of disorders. Internal dialogue plays a central role in one's behavior. Clients focus on examining faulty assumptions and misconceptions. |

*(continued)*

T A B L E    13-2
Key Concepts *(continued)*

| | |
|---|---|
| *Family systems therapy* | Focus is on communication patterns within a family, both verbal and nonverbal. Problems in relationships are likely to be passed on from generation to generation. Symptoms are viewed as ways of communicating with the aim of controlling other family members. Key concepts vary depending on specific orientation but include differentiation, triangles, power coalitions, family-of-origin dynamics, functional versus dysfunctional interaction patterns, family rules governing communication, and dealing with here-and-now interactions. The present is more important than exploring past experiences. |

T A B L E    13-3
Goals of Therapy

| | |
|---|---|
| *Psychoanalytic therapy* | To make the unconscious conscious. To reconstruct the basic personality. To assist clients in reliving earlier experiences and working through repressed conflicts. To achieve intellectual awareness. |
| *Adlerian therapy* | To challenge clients' basic premises and goals. To offer encouragement so they can develop socially useful goals. To change faulty motivation and help them feel equal to others. |
| *Existential therapy* | To help people see that they are free and become aware of their possibilities. To challenge them to recognize that they are responsible for events that they formerly thought were happening to them. To identify factors that block freedom. |
| *Person-centered therapy* | To provide a safe climate conducive to clients' self-exploration, so that they can recognize blocks to growth and can experience aspects of self that were formerly denied or distorted. To enable them to move toward openness, greater trust in self, willingness to be a process, and increased spontaneity and aliveness. |
| *Gestalt therapy* | To assist clients in gaining awareness of moment-to-moment experiencing. To challenge them to accept responsibility for internal support as opposed to depending on external support. |
| *Reality therapy* | To help people become more effective in meeting their needs. To challenge them to evaluate what they are doing and to assess how well this behavior is working for them. |

T A B L E   13-3
Goals of Therapy *(continued)*

| | |
|---|---|
| *Behavior therapy* | Generally, to eliminate maladaptive behaviors and learn more effective behaviors. To focus on factors influencing behavior and find what can be done about problematic behavior. Clients have an active role in setting treatment goals and evaluating how well these goals are being met. |
| *Cognitive-behavior therapy* | To challenge clients to confront faulty beliefs with contradictory evidence that they gather and evaluate. Helping clients seek out their dogmatic beliefs and vigorously minimize them. To become aware of automatic thoughts and to change them. |
| *Family systems therapy* | Most approaches are aimed at helping family members gain awareness of patterns of relationships that are not working well and create new ways of interacting to relieve their distress. Some approaches focus on resolving the specific problem that brings the family to therapy. |

T A B L E   13-4
The Therapeutic Relationship

| | |
|---|---|
| *Psychoanalytic therapy* | The analyst remains anonymous, and clients develop projections toward him or her. Focus is on reducing the resistances that develop in working with transference and on establishing more rational control. Clients undergo long-term analysis, engage in free association to uncover conflicts, and gain insight by talking. The analyst makes interpretations to teach them the meaning of current behavior as related to the past. |
| *Adlerian therapy* | The emphasis is on joint responsibility, on mutually determining goals, on mutual trust and respect, and on equality. A cooperative relationship is manifested by a therapeutic contract. Focus is on examining lifestyle, which is expressed by the client's every action. |
| *Existential therapy* | The therapist's main tasks are to accurately grasp clients' being in the world and to establish a personal and authentic encounter with them. The relationship is seen as critically important. Clients discover their own uniqueness in the relationship with the therapist. The human-to-human client/therapist relationship and the authenticity of the here-and-now encounter are stressed. Both the client and the therapist can be changed by the encounter. |

*(continued)*

T A B L E    13-4
The Therapeutic Relationship *(continued)*

| | |
|---|---|
| *Person-centered therapy* | The relationship is of primary importance. The qualities of the therapist, including genuineness, warmth, accurate empathy, respect, and permissiveness, and the communication of these attitudes to clients are stressed. They use this real relationship with the therapist to help them transfer their learning to other relationships. |
| *Gestalt therapy* | The therapist does not interpret for clients but assists them in developing the means to make their own interpretations. Clients are expected to identify and work on unfinished business from the past that interferes with current functioning. They do so by reexperiencing past traumatic situations as though they were occurring in the present. |
| *Reality therapy* | Therapists show their concern for clients by a process of involvement throughout the course of therapy. They find out what clients want; ask what they are choosing to do; invite them to evaluate present behavior; help them make plans for change; and get them to make a commitment. |
| *Behavior therapy* | The therapist is active and directive and functions as a teacher or trainer in helping clients learn more effective behavior. Clients must be active in the process and experiment with new behaviors. Although a personal relationship between them and the therapist is not highlighted, a good working relationship is the groundwork for implementing behavioral procedures. |
| *Cognitive-behavior therapy* | In REBT the therapist functions as a teacher, and the client as a student. The therapist is highly directive and teaches clients an A-B-C model of changing their cognitions. In CT the focus is on a collaborative relationship. Using a Socratic dialogue, the therapist assists clients in identifying dysfunctional beliefs and discovering alternative rules for living. The therapist promotes corrective experiences that lead to learning new skills. Clients gain insight into their problems and then must actively practice in changing self-defeating thinking and acting. |
| *Family systems therapy* | The family therapist functions as a teacher, coach, model, and consultant. The family learns ways to detect and solve problems that are keeping members stuck, and it learns about patterns that have been transmitted from generation to generation. Some approaches focus on the role of therapist as expert; others concentrate on intensifying what is going on in the here and now of the family session. All family therapists are concerned with the process of family interaction and teaching patterns of communication. |

T A B L E   13-5
Techniques of Therapy

| | |
|---|---|
| *Psychoanalytic therapy* | The key techniques are interpretation, dream analysis, free association, analysis of resistance, and analysis of transference. All are designed to help clients gain access to their unconscious conflicts, which leads to insight and eventual assimilation of new material by the ego. Diagnosis and testing are often used. Questions are used to develop a case history. |
| *Adlerian therapy* | Adlerians draw from many techniques, a few of which are paraphrasing, providing encouragement, confrontation, interpretation, gathering life-history data (family constellation, early recollections), therapeutic contracts, homework assignments, paradoxical intention, and suggestions. |
| *Existential therapy* | Few techniques flow from this approach, because it stresses understanding first and technique second. The therapist can borrow techniques from other approaches and incorporate them into an existential framework. Diagnosis, testing, and external measurements are not deemed important. The approach can be very confrontive. |
| *Person-centered therapy* | This approach uses few techniques but stresses the attitudes of the therapist. Basic techniques include active listening and hearing, reflection of feelings, clarification, and "being there" for the client. This model does not include diagnostic testing, interpretation, taking a case history, and questioning or probing for information. |
| *Gestalt therapy* | A wide range of techniques is designed to intensify experiencing and to integrate conflicting feelings. Techniques include confrontation, dialogue with polarities, role playing, staying with feelings, reaching an impasse, and reliving and reexperiencing unfinished business in the forms of resentment and guilt. Gestalt dream work is very useful. Formal diagnosis and testing are not done. Interpretation is done by the client instead of by the therapist. Confrontation is often used to call attention to discrepancies. "How" and "what" questions are used. |
| *Reality therapy* | An active, directive, and didactic therapy. Various techniques may be used to get clients to evaluate what they are presently doing to see if they are willing to change. If they decide that their present behavior is not effective, they develop a specific plan for change and make a commitment to follow through. |

*(continued)*

T A B L E   13-5
Techniques of Therapy *(continued)*

| | |
|---|---|
| *Behavior therapy* | The main techniques are systematic desensitization, relaxation methods, reinforcement techniques, modeling, cognitive restructuring, assertion and social-skills training, self-management programs, behavioral rehearsal, coaching, and various multimodal-therapy techniques. Diagnosis or assessment is done at the outset to determine a treatment plan. Questions are used, such as "what," "how," and "when" (but not "why"). Contracts and homework assignments are also typically used. |
| *Cognitive-behavior therapy* | Therapists use a variety of cognitive, emotive, and behavioral techniques; diverse methods are tailored to suit individual clients. An active, directive, time-limited, present-centered, structured therapy. Some techniques include engaging in Socratic dialogue, debating irrational beliefs, carrying out homework assignments, gathering data on assumptions one has made, keeping a record of activities, forming alternative interpretations, learning new coping skills, changing one's language and thinking patterns, role playing, imagery, and confronting faulty beliefs. |
| *Family systems therapy* | There is a diversity of techniques, depending on the particular theoretical orientation. Interventions may target behavior change, perceptual change, or both. Techniques include using genograms, teaching, asking questions, family sculpting, joining the family, tracking sequences, issuing directives, anchoring, use of countertransference, family mapping, reframing, paradoxical interventions, restructuring, enactments, and setting boundaries. Techniques may be experiential, cognitive, or behavioral in nature. Most are designed to bring about change in a short time. |

T A B L E   13-6
Applications of the Approaches

| | |
|---|---|
| *Psychoanalytic therapy* | Candidates for analytic therapy include professionals who want to become therapists, people who have had intensive therapy and want to go further, and those who are in pain. Analytic therapy is not recommended for self-centered and impulsive clients or for severely impaired psychotics. Techniques can be applied to individual and group therapy. |
| *Adlerian therapy* | Can be applied to all spheres of life, such as parent/child counseling, marital and family therapy, individual counseling with children and adolescents, correctional and rehabilitation counseling, group counseling, substance-abuse programs, and dealing with problems of the aged. Being a growth model, it is ideally suited to preventive care and alleviating a broad range of conditions that interfere with growth. |

T A B L E   13-6
Applications of the Approaches *(continued)*

| | |
|---|---|
| *Existential therapy* | Can be especially suited to people facing a developmental crisis or a transition in life. Useful for clients with existential concerns (making choices, dealing with freedom and responsibility, coping with guilt and anxiety, making sense of life, and finding values). Appropriate for those seeking personal enhancement. Can be applied to both individual and group counseling, marital and family therapy, crisis intervention, and community mental-health work. |
| *Person-centered therapy* | Has wide applicability to individual and group counseling. It is especially well suited for the initial phases of crisis-intervention work. Its principles have been applied to marital and family therapy, community programs, administration and management, and human-relations training. It is a useful approach for teaching, parent/child relations, and working with groups composed of people from diverse cultural backgrounds. |
| *Gestalt therapy* | Addresses a wide range of problems and populations: crisis intervention, treatment of a range of psychosomatic disorders, marital and family therapy, awareness training of mental-health professionals, behavior problems in children, teaching and learning, and organizational development. It is well suited to both individual and group counseling. The methods are powerful catalysts for opening up feelings and getting clients into contact with their present-centered experience. |
| *Reality therapy* | Geared to teaching people ways to control their life effectively. It has been applied to individual counseling with a wide range of clients, group counseling, working with youthful law offenders, and marital and family therapy. In some instances it is well suited to brief therapy and crisis intervention. |
| *Behavior therapy* | A pragmatic approach based on empirical validation of results. Enjoys wide applicability to individual, group, marital, and family counseling. Some problems to which the approach is well suited are phobic disorders, depression, sexual disorders, children's behavioral disorders, stuttering, and prevention of cardiovascular disease. Beyond clinical practice, its principles are applied in fields such as pediatrics, stress management, behavioral medicine, education, and geriatrics. |

*(continued)*

T A B L E 13-6
Applications of the Approaches *(continued)*

| | |
|---|---|
| *Cognitive-behavior therapy* | Has been widely applied to treatment of depression, anxiety, marital problems, stress management, skill training, substance abuse, assertion training, eating disorders, panic attacks, performance anxiety, and social phobia. The approach is especially useful for assisting people in modifying their cognitions. Many self-help approaches utilize its principles. Can be applied to a wide range of client populations with a variety of specific problems. |
| *Family systems therapy* | Applications vary depending on the particular approach to family therapy. Useful for dealing with marital distress, problems of communicating among family members, power struggles, crisis situations in the family, helping individuals attain their potential, and enhancing the overall functioning of the family. |

T A B L E 13-7
Contributions of the Approaches

| | |
|---|---|
| *Psychoanalytic therapy* | More than any other system, this approach has generated controversy as well as exploration and has stimulated further thinking and development of therapy. It has provided a detailed and comprehensive description of personality structure and functioning. It has brought into prominence factors such as the unconscious as a determinant of behavior and the role of trauma during the first six years of life. It has developed several techniques for tapping the unconscious. It has shed light on the dynamics of transference and countertransference, resistance, anxiety, and the mechanisms of ego defense. |
| *Adlerian therapy* | One of the first approaches to therapy that was humanistic, unified, and goal-oriented and that put an emphasis on social and psychological factors. One of the major contributions is the influence that Adlerian ideas have had on other systems and their integration into various contemporary therapies. |
| *Existential therapy* | Its major contribution is a recognition of the need for a subjective approach based on a complete view of the human condition. It calls attention to the need for a philosophical statement on what it means to be a person. Stress on the I/thou relationship lessens the chances of dehumanizing therapy. It provides a perspective for understanding anxiety, guilt, freedom, death, isolation, and commitment. |

T A B L E   13-7
Contributions of the Approaches *(continued)*

| | |
|---|---|
| *Person-centered therapy* | Unique contribution is having the client take an active stance and assume responsibility for the direction of therapy. The approach has been subjected to empirical testing, and as a result both theory and methods have been modified. It is an open system. People without advanced training can benefit by translating the therapeutic conditions to both their personal and professional lives. Basic concepts are straightforward and easy to grasp and apply. It is a foundation for building a trusting relationship, applicable to all therapies. |
| *Gestalt therapy* | Main contribution is an emphasis on direct experiencing and doing, rather than on merely talking about feelings. It provides a perspective on growth and enhancement, not merely a treatment of disorders. It uses clients' behavior as the basis for making them aware of inner creative potential. The approach to dreams is a unique, creative tool to help clients discover basic conflicts. Therapy is viewed as an existential encounter; it is process-oriented, not technique-oriented. It recognizes nonverbal behavior as a key to understanding. |
| *Reality therapy* | Consists of simple and clear concepts that are easily grasped in many helping professions; thus, it can be used by teachers, nurses, ministers, educators, social workers, and counselors. It is a positive approach, with an action orientation. Due to the direct methods, it appeals to many clients who are often seen as resistant to therapy. It is a short-term approach that can be applied to a diverse population. Has been a significant force in challenging the medical model of therapy. |
| *Behavior therapy* | Emphasis is on assessment and evaluation techniques, thus providing a basis for accountable practice. Specific problems are identified, and clients are kept informed about progress toward their goals. The approach has demonstrated effectiveness in many areas of human functioning. The roles of the therapist as reinforcer, model, teacher, and consultant are explicit. The approach has undergone extensive expansion, and research literature abounds. No longer is it a mechanistic approach, for it now makes room for cognitive factors and encourages self-directed programs for behavioral change. |
| *Cognitive-behavior therapy* | Major contributions include emphasis on a comprehensive and eclectic therapeutic practice; numerous cognitive, emotive, and behavioral techniques; an openness to incorporating techniques from other approaches; and a methodology for challenging and changing faulty thinking. Most forms can be integrated into other mainstream therapies. REBT makes full use of action-oriented homework, listening to tapes, and keeping records of progress. CT is a structured therapy that has a good track record for treating depression and anxiety in a short time. |

*(continued)*

T A B L E    13-7
Contributions of the Approaches *(continued)*

| *Family systems therapy* | In all of the systemic approaches, neither the individual nor the family is blamed for a particular dysfunction. The family is empowered through the process of identifying and exploring interactional patterns. Working with an entire unit provides a new perspective on understanding and working through both individual problems and relationship concerns. By exploring one's family of origin, there are increased opportunities to resolve other relationship conflicts outside of the family. |
|---|---|

T A B L E    13-8
Limitations of the Approaches

| *Psychoanalytic therapy* | Requires lengthy training for therapists and much time and expense for clients. The model stresses biological and instinctual factors to the neglect of social, cultural, and interpersonal ones. Its methods are not applicable to clients in lower socioeconomic classes and are not appropriate for many ethnic and cultural groups. Many clients lack the degree of ego strength needed for regressive and reconstructive therapy. It is inappropriate for the typical counseling setting. |
|---|---|
| *Adlerian therapy* | Weak in terms of precision, testability, and empirical validity. Few attempts have been made to validate the basic concepts by scientific methods. Tends to oversimplify some complex human problems and is based heavily on common sense. |
| *Existential therapy* | Many basic concepts are fuzzy and ill-defined, making its general framework abstract at times. Lacks a systematic statement of principles and practices of therapy. Has limited applicability to lower-functioning and nonverbal clients and to clients in extreme crisis who need direction. |
| *Person-centered therapy* | Possible danger from the therapist who remains passive and inactive, limiting responses to reflection. Many clients feel a need for greater direction, more structure, and more techniques. Clients in crisis may need more directive measures. Applied to individual counseling, some cultural groups will expect more counselor activity. The theory needs to be reassessed in light of current knowledge and thought if rigidity is to be avoided. |
| *Gestalt therapy* | Techniques lead to intense emotional expression; if these feelings are not explored and if cognitive work is not done, clients are likely to be left unfinished and will not have a sense of integration of their learning. Clients who have difficulty imagining and fantasizing may not profit from techniques. |

T A B L E    13-8
Limitations of the Approaches *(continued)*

| | |
|---|---|
| *Reality therapy* | Discounts the therapeutic value of exploration of the client's past, dreams, the unconscious, early childhood experiences, and transference. The approach is limited to less complex problems. It is a problem-solving therapy that tends to discourage exploration of deeper emotional issues. It is vulnerable to practitioners who want to "fix" clients quickly. |
| *Behavior therapy* | Major criticisms are that it may change behavior but not feelings; that it ignores the relational factors in therapy; that it does not provide insight; that it ignores historical causes of present behavior; that it involves control and manipulation by the therapist; and that it is limited in its capacity to address certain aspects of the human condition. Many of these assertions are based on misconceptions, and behavior therapists have addressed these charges. A basic limitation is that behavior change cannot always be objectively assessed because of the difficulty in controlling environmental variables. |
| *Cognitive-behavior therapy* | Tends to play down emotions, does not focus on exploring the unconscious or underlying conflicts, and sometimes does not give enough weight to client's past. REBT, being a confrontational therapy, might lead to premature termination. CT might be too structured for some clients. |
| *Family systems therapy* | Limitations include problems in being able to involve all the members of a family in the therapy. Members may be resistant to changing the structure of the system. Therapists' self-knowledge and willingness to work on their own family-of-origin issues is crucial, for the potential for countertransference is high. It is essential that the therapist be well trained, receive quality supervision, and be competent in assessing and treating individuals in a family context. |

T A B L E    13-9
Contributions to Multicultural Counseling

| | |
|---|---|
| *Psychoanalytic therapy* | Its focus on family dynamics is appropriate for working with many minority groups. The therapist's formality appeals to clients who expect professional distance. Notion of ego defense is helpful in understanding inner dynamics and dealing with environmental stresses. |
| *Adlerian therapy* | Its focus on social interest, doing good for society, importance of family, goal orientation, and striving for belongingness is congruent with Eastern cultures. Focus on person-in-environment allows for cultural factors to be explored. |

*(continued)*

T A B L E    13-9
Contributions to Multicultural Counseling *(continued)*

| | |
|---|---|
| *Existential therapy* | Focus is on understanding client's phenomenological world, including cultural background. This approach leads to empowerment in an oppressive society. It can help clients examine their options for change, within the context of their cultural realities. |
| *Person-centered therapy* | Focus is on breaking cultural barriers and facilitating open dialogue among diverse cultural populations. Main strengths are respect for client's values, active listening, welcoming of differences, nonjudgmental attitude, understanding, willingness to allow clients to determine what will be explored in sessions, and prizing of cultural pluralism. |
| *Gestalt therapy* | Its focus on expressing oneself nonverbally is congruent with those cultures that look beyond words for messages. Provides many techniques in working with clients who have cultural injunctions against freely expressing feelings. Can overcome language barrier with bilingual clients. Focus on bodily expressions is a subtle way to help clients recognize their conflicts. |
| *Reality therapy* | Focus is on members' making own evaluation of behavior (including how they respond to their culture). Through personal assessment they can determine the degree to which their needs and wants are being satisfied. They can find a balance between retaining their own ethnic identity and integrating some of the values and practices of the dominant society. |
| *Behavior therapy* | Its focus on behavior, rather than on feelings, is compatible with many cultures. Strengths include a collaborative relationship between counselor and client in working toward mutually agreed-on goals, continual assessment to determine if the techniques are suited to the client's unique situation, assisting clients in learning practical skills, an educational focus, and stress on self-management strategies. |
| *Cognitive-behavior therapy* | The collaborative approach offers clients opportunities to express their areas of concern. The psychoeducational dimensions are often useful in exploring cultural conflicts and teaching new behavior. The emphasis on thinking (as opposed to identifying and expressing feelings) is likely to be acceptable to many clients. The focus on teaching and learning tends to avoid the stigma of mental illness. Clients may value active and directive stance of therapist. |

T A B L E   13-9
Contributions to Multicultural Counseling *(continued)*

| | |
|---|---|
| *Family systems therapy* | Many ethnic and cultural groups place value on the role of the extended family. Many family therapies deal with extended family members and with support systems. Networking is a part of the process, which is congruent with the values of many clients. There is a greater chance for individual change if other family members are supportive. This approach offers ways of working toward the health of the family unit and the welfare of each member. |

T A B L E   13-10
Limitations in Multicultural Counseling

| | |
|---|---|
| *Psychoanalytic therapy* | Its focus on insight, intrapsychic dynamics, and long-term treatment is often not valued by clients who prefer to learn coping skills for dealing with pressing daily concerns. Internal focus is often in conflict with cultural values that stress an interpersonal and environmental focus. |
| *Adlerian therapy* | This approach's detailed interview about one's family background can conflict with cultures that have injunctions against disclosing family matters. Counselor needs to make certain that the client's goals are respected. |
| *Existential therapy* | Values of individuality, freedom, autonomy, and self-realization often conflict with cultural values of collectivism, respect for tradition, deference to authority, and interdependence. Some may be deterred by the absence of specific techniques. Others will expect more focus on surviving in their world. |
| *Person-centered therapy* | Some of the core values of this approach may not be congruent with the client's culture. Lack of counselor direction and structure are unacceptable for clients who are seeking help and immediate answers from a knowledgeable professional. |
| *Gestalt therapy* | Clients who have been culturally conditioned to be emotionally reserved may not embrace Gestalt techniques. The quick push for expressing feelings could cause premature termination of therapy by the client. Some may not see how "being aware of present experiencing" will lead to solving their problems. |
| *Reality therapy* | This approach stresses taking charge of one's own life, yet some clients hope to change their external environment. Counselor needs to appreciate the role of discrimination and racism and help clients deal with social and political realities. |

*(continued)*

T A B L E   13-10
Limitations in Multicultural Counseling *(continued)*

| | |
|---|---|
| *Behavior therapy* | Counselors need to help clients assess the possible consequences of making behavioral changes. Family members may not value clients' newly acquired assertive style, so clients must be taught how to cope with resistance by others. |
| *Cognitive-behavior therapy* | Before too quickly attempting to change the beliefs and actions of clients, it is essential for the therapist to understand and respect their world. Some clients may have serious reservations about questioning their basic cultural values and beliefs. Clients could become dependent on the therapist for deciding what are appropriate ways to solve problems. There may be a fine line between being directive and promoting dependence. |
| *Family systems therapy* | Some approaches are based on value assumptions that are not congruent with the values of clients from certain cultures. Concepts such as individuation, self-actualization, self-determination, independence, and self-expression may be foreign to some clients. In some cultures, admitting problems within the family is shameful. The value of "keeping problems within the family" may make it difficult to explore conflicts openly. |

# CHAPTER FOURTEEN

# Case Illustration: An Integrative Approach in Working with Stan

# Introduction

The purpose of this chapter is to bring together the nine approaches that you have studied in an integrative fashion by using a thinking, feeling, and acting model in counseling Stan. At this point I recommend that you think concretely about how to blend the concepts and techniques of various theories in a way that makes the most sense to you. As a reference point, the chapter begins with an overview of some of the themes in Stan's life that have emerged from his intake interview, his autobiography, and his work with the therapists representing each of the models covered in this book.

## SOME THEMES IN STAN'S LIFE

A number of themes appear to represent core struggles in Stan's life. Below are some of the statements he has made at various points in his therapy:

- "Although I'd like to have people in my life, I just don't seem to know how to go about making friends or getting close to people."
- "When I'm with other people, I feel stupid much of the time."
- "I'd like to turn my life around, but I don't know where to start."
- "I'd like to find a career in working with people so that I can make a difference in their lives. I want to return a favor to a person who really helped me."
- "I worry about whether I'm smart enough to complete my studies and do what's needed to become a counselor."
- "Sometimes when I feel alone, scared, and overwhelmed, I drink heavily to feel better."
- "When I'm around a woman, I generally feel sweaty and terribly uptight. I'm sure she's judging me and will think that I'm not a real man."
- "I'm so afraid of getting close to a woman. If I were to get close, my fear is that she would swallow me up."
- "My divorce made me wonder what kind of man I was."
- "Sometimes at night I feel a terrible anxiety and feel as if I'm dying."
- "There have been times when I've fantasized committing suicide, and I wondered who would care."
- "I often feel guilty that I've wasted my life, that I've failed, and that I've let people down. At times like this, I get really depressed."
- "I like it that I have determination and that I really want to change."
- "I hate being a quitter."
- "I remember hearing from my parents that I couldn't do much of anything right."
- "My parents compared me unfavorably with my older sister and brother. I've never felt that I could measure up!"
- "I've never really felt loved or wanted by my parents."
- "I'd like to feel equal with others and not always have to feel apologetic for my existence."

- "I'd like to get rid of my self-destructive tendencies and learn to trust people more."
- "Although I put myself down a lot, I'd like to feel better about myself."

If I were Stan's therapist, we would explore many of these themes in our sessions. He will lead the way in therapy by the concerns he identifies. My job is to intervene in ways that will enable him to work through places where he is stuck. Many of these personal issues are connected, which will give some continuity to the work. My theoretical orientation will guide the focus of the therapy.

Table 14-1 provides a concise overview of the major emphasis of each theoretical orientation. The table illustrates how I am likely to work with Stan by selecting goals, key concepts, and techniques from the various approaches.

# Working with Stan: Integration of Therapies

In this section I work toward integrating therapeutic concepts and techniques from the nine theoretical perspectives. As I describe how I would counsel Stan on the levels of *thinking, feeling,* and *doing,* based on information presented in his autobiography, I will indicate from what orientations I am borrowing ideas at the various stages of his therapy. As you read, think about interventions you might make with Stan that would be either similar to or different from mine. At the end of the chapter are questions that can guide you as you reflect about being his counselor and working with him from an integrative perspective.

## A PLACE TO BEGIN

I start by giving Stan a chance to say how he feels about coming to the initial session. Questions that I might explore with him are:

- "What brings you here? What has been going on in your life recently that gave you the impetus to seek professional help?"
- "What expectations do you have of therapy? of me? What are your hopes, fears, and any reservations? What goals do you have for yourself through therapy?"
- "Could you give me a picture of some significant turning points in your life? Who have been the important people in your life? What significant decisions have you made? What are some of the struggles and conflicts you've dealt with, and what are some of these issues that are current for you?"
- "What was it like for you to be in your family? How did you view your parents? How did they react to you? What about your early development?" (It would be useful to administer the Adlerian lifestyle questionnaire.).

T A B L E    14-1
Major Areas of Focus in Stan's Therapy

| | |
|---|---|
| *Psychoanalytic therapy* | My focus is on the ways in which Stan is repeating his early childhood in his present relationships. I am particularly interested in how he brings his experiences with his father into the sessions with me. As it is relevant, I will focus on his feelings for me, because working with transference is one path toward insight. I am interested in his dreams, any resistance that he reveals in the sessions, and other clues to his unconscious processes. One of my main goals is to assist him in bringing to awareness buried memories and experiences, which I assume have a current influence on him. |
| *Adlerian therapy* | My focus is on determining what Stan's lifestyle is. As a part of conducting a lifestyle assessment, I will examine his early childhood experiences through his recollections and family constellation. My main interest is in identifying what his goals and priorities in life are. I assume that what he is striving toward is equally as valid as his past dynamics. Therapy will consist of doing a comprehensive assessment, helping him understand his dynamics, and then helping him define new goals and translate them into action. |
| *Existential therapy* | My aim is to be as fully present and available for Stan as possible, for I assume that the relationship that I am able to establish with him will be the source of our work together. An area that I am likely to concentrate on is how he finds meaning in life. He says he feels anxious a great deal, and this is an avenue to explore. Since he mentioned a fear of dying, and even entertained suicide as an option, I will certainly encourage him to explore his thoughts and feelings in these areas. I want to find out more about the nature of his fear of death and what keeps him alive, and I will of course assess the risk of suicide at the outset. We will also explore what quality of life he is striving for. I am interested in how he is dealing with freedom and the responsibility that accompanies it. Therapy is a venture that can help him expand his awareness of the way he is in his world, which will give him the potential to make changes. |

T A B L E   14-1
Major Areas of Focus in Stan's Therapy *(continued)*

| | |
|---|---|
| *Person-centered therapy* | Because I have a faith and trust in Stan to find his own direction for therapy, I will avoid planning and structuring the sessions. My main focus is on being real, on accepting his feelings and thoughts, on demonstrating my unconditional positive regard for him, and on respecting him as a person. If I am able to listen carefully and reflect what I am hearing, and if I am able to deeply empathize with his life situation, he will be able to clarify his struggles and work out his own solutions to his problems. Although he is only dimly aware of his feelings at the initial phase of therapy, he will move toward increased clarity as I accept him fully, without conditions and without judgments. My main aim is to create a climate of openness, trust, caring, understanding, and acceptance. Then he can use this relationship to move forward and grow. |
| *Gestalt therapy* | My focus is on noticing signs of Stan's unfinished business, as evidenced by the ways in which he reaches a stuck point in his therapy. If he has never worked through his feelings of not being accepted, for example, these issues will appear in his therapy. I will ask him to bring them into the present by reliving them, rather than merely talking about past events. I hope to help him experience his feelings fully, instead of simply gaining insight into his problems or speculating about why he feels the way he does. I'll direct him to pay attention to his moment-by-moment awareness, especially to what he is aware of in his body. We will concentrate on *how* he is behaving and *what* he is experiencing. |
| *Reality therapy* | Counseling will be guided by the principles of control therapy. First, I will do my best to demonstrate my personal involvement with Stan, by listening to his story. The emphasis is on his total behavior, including his doing, thinking, feeling, and physiology. I assume that if we concentrate on what he is actually doing and thinking and if change occurs on these levels, he will automatically change on the feeling and physiological levels. After he evaluates his present behavior, it is up to him to decide the degree to which it is working for him. We will explore those areas of his behavior that he identifies as not meeting his needs. Much of therapy will consist of creating specific, realistic, and attainable plans. Once he agrees to a plan of action, it is essential that he make a commitment to following through with it. |

*(continued)*

T A B L E    14-1
Major Areas of Focus in Stan's Therapy

| | |
|---|---|
| *Behavior therapy* | Initially, I'll conduct a thorough assessment of Stan's current behavior. I'll ask him to monitor what he is doing so that we can create baseline data to evaluate any changes. We will continue our work by collaboratively developing concrete goals to guide our work, and I will draw on a wide range of cognitive and behavioral techniques to help him achieve his goals. We may use techniques such as role playing, modeling, coaching, assertion training, carrying out homework assignments, and relaxation methods. I will stress learning new coping skills that he can use in everyday situations. He will practice what he learns in the office in his daily life. |
| *Cognitive-behavior therapy* | My focus is on the ways in which Stan's internal dialogue and his thinking processes are affecting his behavior. I will use an active and directive therapeutic style. Therapy will be time-limited, present-centered, and structured. My task is to create a form of collaborative empiricism in which Stan will learn to recognize and change self-defeating thoughts and maladaptive beliefs. We will concentrate on the content and process of his thinking by looking for ways to restructure some of his beliefs. Rather than merely telling him what faulty beliefs he has, I will emphasize his gathering data and weighing the evidence in support of certain beliefs. By the use of Socratic dialogue, I will try to get him to spot his faulty thinking, to learn ways of correcting his distortions, and to substitute more effective self-talk and beliefs. We will be using a wide range of cognitive, emotive, and behavioral techniques to accomplish our goals. |
| *Family systems therapy* | Stan has identified a number of strained relationships with his mother, father, and siblings. Ideally, we will have at least one session with all of the members of his family. The focus will be on his gaining greater clarity on how his interpersonal style is largely the result of his interactions with his family of origin. I am likely to focus on the degree to which he has developed his uniqueness, rather than seeing him as merely his parents' son. If I work individually with Stan, the emphasis can still be on the many ways in which his current struggles are related to the system of which he is a part. Through our therapy, he will learn to recognize the rules that governed his family of origin and the decisions he made about himself. Rather than trying to change the members of his family, we will largely work on discovering what he most wants to change about himself in relation to how he interacts with them. |

## CLARIFYING THE THERAPEUTIC RELATIONSHIP

I do not want to give the impression that I would bombard Stan with all of the preceding questions at once. Early in our sessions, however, those are some of the questions I have in the back of my mind. At the outset I work with him to develop a contract, which involves a discussion of our mutual responsibilities and a clear statement of what he wants from these sessions and what he is willing to do to obtain it. I believe that it is important to discuss any factors that might perpetuate a client's dependency on the therapist, so I invite his questions about this therapeutic relationship. One goal is to demystify the therapy process; another is to get some focus for the direction of our sessions.

In establishing the therapeutic relationship, I am influenced by the person-centered, existential, Gestalt, and Adlerian approaches. They do not view therapy as something that the therapist *does* to a passive client. Counseling is far more than administering techniques. It is a deeply personal relationship that Stan can use in his learning. Although I think it is essential for me to be familiar with the various theories of counseling and to possess specific skills in implementing techniques in a timely manner, I must apply this knowledge in the context of a working relationship characterized by mutual trust and respect. A few questions that I see as helpful to ask myself are: To what degree am I able to listen to and hear Stan in a nonjudgmental way? Am I able to respect and care for him? Do I have the capacity to enter his subjective world without losing my own identity? Am I able to share with him my own thoughts and feelings as they pertain to our relationship? This relationship is critical at the initial stages of therapy, but it must be maintained during all stages if therapy is to be effective.

My contract with Stan specifies his rights and responsibilities as a client and my role as his therapist. Expectations are explored, goals are defined, and there is a basis for therapy as a collaborative effort. This emphasis is consistent with several of the therapeutic approaches: Adlerian therapy, the behavior therapies, the cognitive therapies, and reality therapy. An excellent foundation for building a working partnership is openness by the counselor about the process of therapy. I think it is a mistake to hide behind "professionalism" as a way of keeping distance from the client. Therefore, I begin by being as honest as I can be with Stan as the basis for creating this relationship.

## CLARIFYING THE GOALS OF THERAPY

It is not enough simply to ask clients what they hope they will leave with at the conclusion of therapy. Typically, I find that clients are vague, global, and unfocused about what they want. Especially from behavior therapy, cognitive-behavior therapy, Adlerian therapy, and reality therapy I borrow the necessity of getting clients to be specific in defining their goals. Thus, Stan says: "I want to stop playing all these games with myself and others. I'd hope to stop putting myself down. I want to get rid of the terrible feelings I have. I want to feel OK with myself and begin living." My reply is: "Let's see if we can narrow down some of these broad goals into terms specific enough that both you and I will know what you're talking about. What exactly are these games you talk about? In what ways do you put yourself down? What are some of these terrible feelings that bother you? In what specific ways do you feel that you're not living now? What would it take for you to begin to feel alive?"

Again, I do not barrage Stan with all these questions at once. They are merely illustrations of ways in which I work with him toward greater precision and clarity. If we merely talked about lofty goals of self-actualization, I fear, we would have directionless sessions. Thus, I value focusing on concrete language and specific goals that both of us can observe and understand. Once this is ascertained, Stan can begin to observe his own behavior, both in the sessions and in his daily life. This self-monitoring itself is a vital step in any effort to bring about change.

GLIMPSES OF WORKING WITH STAN ON IDENTIFYING GOALS.   My main aim is to encourage Stan to assume responsibility from the onset of our relationship for what he wants to accomplish. A large part of our early work together consists of helping him get a clear sense of concrete changes he would most like to make and how he can make them happen. Following are a few interchanges focused on the process of defining goals that will give direction to his therapy:

*Jerry:*   What would you most hope for, through our work together?

*Stan:*   Well, I know I put myself down all the time. I'd really like to feel better about myself.

*Jerry:*   You put yourself down *all* of the time? Is what you've just said an example of how you are being hard on yourself right now?

*Stan:*   Well, once in a great while I don't put myself down.

*Jerry:*   If you had what you want in your life today, what would that be like? What would it take for you to feel good about yourself?

*Stan:*   For one thing, I'd have people in my life, and I wouldn't run from intimacy.

*Jerry:*   So this might be an area you'd be willing to explore in your sessions.

*Stan:*   Sure, but I wouldn't know where to begin.

*Jerry:*   I'll be glad to provide suggestions of ways to begin, if I know what you want.

*Stan:*   Well, for sure I'd like to get over my fears of being with people. All my dumb fears really get in my way.

*Jerry:*   I like it that you're willing to challenge your fears. Are you aware that you also just put yourself down again in labeling your fears as dumb?

*Stan:*   It just comes as second nature to me. But I really would like to be able to feel more comfortable when I'm with others.

*Jerry:*   How is it for you to be in here with me now?

*Stan:*   It's really not like me to do something like this, but it feels good. At least I'm talking, and I'm saying what's on my mind.

*Jerry:*   It's good to see you give yourself credit for being different in our interchange right now.

This process of formulating goals is not accomplished in a single session. Throughout our time together, I ask Stan to decide time and again what he wants from his therapy and to assess the degree to which our work together is resulting in his meeting his goals. As his therapist I expect to be active, yet it is important for me that he provides the direction in which he wants to travel on his journey. If he has clear, specific, and concrete goals for each therapy session, he will be the one who is providing this direction. Once I have a clear sense of the specific ways in which he wants to change how he is thinking, feeling, and acting, I am likely to become quite active and directive in suggesting experiments that can be done both in the therapy sessions and on his own outside of our sessions.

## IDENTIFYING FEELINGS

The person-centered approach stresses that one of the first stages in the therapy process involves identifying, clarifying, and learning how to express feelings. Because of my relationship with Stan, I expect him to feel increasingly free to mention feelings that he has kept to himself. In some cases these feelings are out of his awareness. Thus, I encourage him to talk about any feelings that are a source of difficulty. Again drawing on the person-centered model, I expect these feelings to be vague and difficult to identify at first.

Therefore, during the early stages of our sessions I rely on empathic listening. If I can really hear Stan's verbal and nonverbal messages, some of which may not be fully clear to him, I can respond to him in a way that lets him know that I have some appreciation for what it is like in his world. I need to do more than merely reflect what I hear him saying; I need to share with him my reactions as I listen to him. As I come to communicate to him that he is being deeply understood and accepted for the feelings he has, he has less need to deny or distort his feelings. His capacity for clearly identifying what he is feeling at any moment gradually increases.

There is a great deal of value in letting Stan tell his story in a way he chooses. The way he walks into the office, his gestures, his style of speech, the details he chooses to go into, and what he decides to relate and not to relate—to mention a few elements—provide me with clues to his world. If I do too much structuring too soon and if I am too directive, I will interfere with his typical style of presenting himself. So at this stage I agree with the Adlerians, who stress attending and listening on the counselor's part and who focus on the productive use of silence. Although I am not inclined to promote long silences early in counseling, there is value in not jumping in too soon when silences occur. Instead of coming to the rescue, it is better to explore the meanings of the silence.

## EXPRESSING AND EXPLORING FEELINGS

My belief is that it is my authenticity as a person that encourages Stan to begin to identify and share with me a range of feelings. But I do not believe that an open and trusting relationship between us is sufficient to change his personality and behavior. I am convinced that I must also use my knowledge, skills, and experiences.

As a way of helping Stan express and explore his feelings, I tend to draw heavily on Gestalt techniques. Eventually, I ask him to avoid merely talking about situations and about feelings. Rather, I encourage him to bring whatever reactions he is having into the present. For instance, if he reports feeling tense, I ask him *how* he experiences this tension and *where* it is located in his body. One of the best ways that I have found to encourage clients to make contact with their feelings is to ask them to "be that feeling." Thus, if Stan has a knot in his stomach, he can intensify his feeling of tension by "becoming the knot, giving it voice and personality." If I notice that he has moist eyes, I may direct him to "be his tears now." By putting words to his tears, he avoids merely abstractly intellectualizing about all the reasons *why* he is sad or tense. Before he can change his feelings, he must allow himself to *fully experience* these feelings. And the experiential therapies give me valuable tools for guiding him to the expression of feelings.

SAMPLE VIGNETTE IN WHICH I FOCUS ON STAN'S FEELINGS.   Following are some segments of our dialogue in a session where Stan becomes quite aware of what he is feeling as he talks about his relationship with his father:

*Jerry:*   You mentioned that your father often compared you with your brother Frank and your sister, Judy. What was that like for you?

*Stan:*   I hated it! He told me that I'd never amount to a hill of beans.

*Jerry:*   And when he said that, how did that affect you?

*Stan:*   It made me feel that I could never measure up to all the great things that Judy and Frank were accomplishing. I felt like a failure. [As he says this, he begins welling up with tears, and his voice changes.]

*Jerry:*   Stan, what are you experiencing now?

*Stan:*   All of a sudden a wave of sadness is coming over me. I'm getting all choked up. Wow—this is heavy!

*Jerry:*   Stay with what you're feeling in your body. What's going on?

*Stan:*   My chest is tight, and something wants to come out.

*Jerry:*   And what's there?

*Stan:*   I'm feeling very sad and hurt.

*Jerry:*   Would you be willing to try something? I'd like you to talk to me as though I were your father. Are you willing?

*Stan:*   Well, you're not mean the way he was to me, but I can try.

*Jerry:*   How old are you feeling now?

*Stan:*   Oh, about 12 years old—just like when I had to be around him and listen to all the stuff he told me about how rotten I was.

*Jerry:*   Good. Let yourself be 12 again, and tell me what it's like for you to be you—speaking to me as your father.

*Stan:*   There was nothing that I could ever do that was good enough for you. No matter how hard I tried, I just couldn't get you to notice me. [crying] Why didn't I count, and why did you ignore me?

*Jerry:*   Stan, I'll just let you talk for a while, and I'll listen. So keep on, telling me all the things you may be feeling as that 12-year-old now.

*Stan:*   All I ever wanted was to know that I mattered to you. But no matter how hard I tried, all you'd do was put me down. Nothing I ever did was worth anything. All you ever told me was that I could never do anything right. I just wanted you to love me. Why didn't you ever do anything with me? [Stan stops talking and just cries for a while.]

*Jerry:*   What's happening with you now?

*Stan:*   I'm just feeling so damn sad. As if it's hopeless. Nothing I can do will ever get his approval. And that hurts!

*Jerry:*   At 12 it was important for you to get his acceptance and his love. There is still that part in you that wants his love.

*Stan:*   Yeah, and I don't think there's much I can do now to get it.

*Jerry:*   So, tell him more of what that's like.

Stan continues talking to his "father" and recounts some of the ways in which he tried to live up to his expectations. He lets him know that no matter what he did, there was no way to get the acceptance that Frank and Judy got from him.

*Jerry:*   Having said all that, what are you aware of now?

*Stan:*   I'm feeling kind of embarrassed. I shouldn't have gotten so emotional and worked up over such a dumb thing.

*Jerry:*   You say you're embarrassed. Whom are you aware of?

*Stan:*   Well, right now of you. I'm such a wimp. You're probably thinking that I'm really weak and dumb for letting this get to me.

*Jerry:*   Tell me more about feeling weak and dumb.

Stan expresses that he should be stronger and that he is afraid I'll think he is hopeless. He goes into some detail about putting himself down for what he has just experienced and expressed. I do not too quickly reassure him that he "shouldn't feel that way." Instead, I let him talk, for this is what he so often feels. After expressing many of the ways in which he is feeling embarrassed, he wonders if I still want to work with him. At this point I let him know that I respect his struggle and hope that he can eventually learn to judge himself less harshly. Because this session is coming to an end, I talk with him about the value of releasing feelings that he has been carrying around for a long time, suggesting that this work is a good beginning. I am also interested in getting him to do some homework before the next session.

*Jerry:*   Stan, I'd like to suggest that you write a letter to your father . . .

*Stan* [interrupting]:   Oh no! I'm not going to give that guy the satisfaction of knowing that I need anything from him!

*Jerry:*   Wait. I was about to say that I hope you'll write him a letter that you don't mail.

*Stan:*   What's the point of a letter that won't be sent?

*Jerry:*   Writing him a letter is an opportunity for further release and to gain some new insights. I hope you'll let yourself write about all the ways you tried to live up to his expectations. Let him know what it felt like to be you when you were around him. Tell him more about you, especially how you felt in not getting those things that you so much wanted.

*Stan:*   OK, I'll do it if you think it might help.

In this session I might have made many different interventions. For the moment, I chose to let him "borrow my eyes" and talk to me as his father while he was 12 years old. I asked him to stay with whatever he was experiencing, paying particular attention to his body and to the emotions that were welling up in him. I see therapeutic value in letting him identify and express his feelings. It is premature to suggest problem-solving strategies or to attempt to figure everything out. My intent in offering him the homework assignment of writing a letter was to promote further work during the week. Writing the letter may trigger memories, and he may experience further emotional release. I hope this will help him begin thinking about the influence that his father had on him then and also now. At our next session I will ask him if he wrote the letter and, if he did, what it was like for him to do so. What was he feeling and thinking as he was writing to his father? How was he affected when he read the letter later? Is there anything that he wants to share with me? The direction of our following session could depend on his response. Again, he can provide clues to where we need to go next.

## WORKING WITH STAN'S PAST, PRESENT, AND FUTURE

DEALING WITH THE PAST.   Some therapies (for example, reality therapy and rational emotive behavior therapy) do not place much emphasis on the client's history. Their rationale is that early childhood experiences do not necessarily have much to do with the maintenance of present ineffective behavior. My inclination, in contrast, is to give weight to understanding, exploring, and working with Stan's early history and to connect up his past with what he is doing today. My view is that themes running through our life can become evident if we come to terms with significant turning points in our childhood. The use of an Adlerian lifestyle questionnaire would indicate some of these themes that originate from Stan's childhood. The psychoanalytic approach, of course, emphasizes uncovering and reexperiencing traumas in early childhood, working through the places where we have become "stuck," and resolving unconscious conflicts. Although I agree that Stan's childhood experiences were influential in contributing to his present personality (including his ways of thinking, feeling, and behaving), it does not make sense to me to assume that these factors have *determined* him. I favor the Gestalt approach of having him bring to the surface his "toxic introjects" by dealing in the here and now with people in his life with whom he feels unfinished. This can be accomplished by fantasy exercises and a variety of role-playing techniques. In these ways his past comes intensely to life in the present moment of our sessions.

DEALING WITH THE PRESENT.   Being interested in Stan's past does not mean that we get lost in history or that we dwell on reliving traumatic situations. In fact, by paying attention to what is going on in the here and now of the counseling session, we get excellent clues to what is unfinished for him in his past. There is no need to go on digging expeditions, because the present is rich with material. He and I can direct attention to his immediate feelings as well as his thoughts and actions. It seems essential to me that we work with all three dimensions—what he is thinking, what he is actually doing, and how his thoughts and behaviors affect his feeling states. Again, by directing his attention to what is going on with him during our sessions, I can show him how he interacts in his world apart from therapy.

DEALING WITH THE FUTURE.   Adlerians are especially interested in where the client is heading. Humans are pulled by goals, strivings, and aspirations. It would help to know what Stan's goals in life are. What are his intentions? What does he want for himself? If he decides that his present behavior is not getting him what he wants, he is in a good position to think ahead about the changes he would like and what he can do *now* to actualize his aspirations. The present-oriented behavioral focus of reality therapy is a good reference point for getting him to dream about what he would like to say about his life five years hence. Connecting present behavior with future plans is an excellent device for helping him formulate a concrete plan of action. He will have to actually *create* his future.

## THE THINKING DIMENSION IN THERAPY

Once Stan has gotten in touch with intense feelings and perhaps experienced catharsis (release of pent-up feelings), some cognitive work is essential. He needs to be able to experience his feelings fully, and he may need to express them in symbolic ways. This may include getting out his anger toward women by hitting a pillow and by saying angry things that he has never allowed himself to say. Yet eventually he needs to begin to make sense of the emotional range of material that is surfacing.

To bring in this cognitive dimension, I focus Stan's attention on messages that he incorporated as a child and on the decisions that he made. I get him to think about the reason that he made certain early decisions. Finally, I challenge him to look at these decisions about life, about himself, and about others and to make necessary revisions that can lead him to getting on with his living.

The Adlerian perspective is highly cognitive. After getting basic information about Stan's life history (by means of the lifestyle assessment form), I summarize and interpret it. For example, I find some connections between his present fears of developing intimate relationships and his history of rejection by his siblings and his parents. Thus, I am interested in his family constellation and his early recollections. Rather than working exclusively with his feelings, I want him to begin to understand (cognitively) how these early experiences affected him then and how they still influence him today. I concur with the Adlerians in their therapeutic interest in identifying and exploring basic mistakes. Here my emphasis is on having Stan begin to question the conclusions he came to about himself, others, and life. What is his private logic? What are some of his mistaken, self-defeating perceptions that grew out of his family experiences? An Adlerian perspective provides tools for doing some productive cognitive work both in and out of the therapy sessions.

From rational emotive behavior therapy I especially value the emphasis on learning to think rationally. I look for the ways in which Stan contributes to his negative feelings by the process of self-indoctrination with irrational beliefs. I get him to really test the validity of the dire consequences that he predicts. I value the stress put on doing hard work in demolishing beliefs that have no validity and replacing them with sound and rational beliefs. Surely, I do not think that he can merely think his way through life or that merely examining his faulty logic is enough by itself for personality change. But I do see this process as an essential component of therapy.

The cognitive-behavioral therapies have a range of cognitive techniques that can help Stan recognize connections between his cognitions and his behaviors. He should also learn about his inner dialogue and the impact it has on his day-to-day behavior. Eventually, our goal is some cognitive-restructuring work by which he can learn new ways to think, new things to tell himself, and new assumptions about life. This provides a basis for change in his behavior.

SAMPLE VIGNETTE IN WHICH I FOCUS ON STAN'S THINKING.   I have given Stan a number of homework assignments aimed at helping him identify a range of feelings and thoughts that may be problematic for him. In several of our sessions, he has talked about messages that he picked up about himself through his family. We have explored some specific beliefs he holds about himself, and he is beginning to recognize how his thinking processes are influencing the way he feels and what he is doing. Following are sample pieces of a session in which we focus on his cognitions:

*Jerry:*   Several times now you've brought up how you're sure you'd be judged critically if you allowed yourself to get close to a woman. Is this a topic you want to explore in more depth?

*Stan:*   For sure. I'm tired of avoiding women, but I'm still too scared of approaching a woman. Part of me wants to meet a woman, and the other part of me wants to run. I'm convinced that if any woman gets to know me, she'll see me as a royal wimp.

*Jerry:*   Really, *any* woman will see you as a wimp? Have you checked out this assumption? How many women have you approached, and how many of them have condemned you to eternal wimphood?

*Stan:* Well, it's not that bad! They never tell me these things. But in my head I keep telling myself that if they get to know the real me, they'll be turned off by my weakness.

*Jerry:* How about telling me some of the things that you tell yourself when you think of meeting a woman? Just let yourself go for a while, listing out loud some of the many statements that you make to yourself internally. Ready?

*Stan:* So often I say to myself that I'm not worth knowing. [pause]

*Jerry:* Just rattle off as many of these self-statements as you can. Don't worry about how it sounds. Rehearse out loud some of the familiar self-talk that keeps you from doing what you want.

*Stan:* What a nerd! Every time you open your mouth, you put your foot in it. Why don't you just shut up and hide in the corner? When you do talk to people, you always freeze up. They're judging you, and if you say much of anything, they'll find out what a jerk you are! You're a complete and utter failure. Anything you try, you fail in. There's not much in you that anybody would find interesting. You're stupid, boring, weak, and a scared kid. Why don't you keep to yourself so that others won't have a chance to reject you?

Stan continues with this list, and I listen. After he seems finished, I tell him how I'm affected by hearing his typical self-talk. I let him know that it saddens me to see how hard he is on himself. Although I have a liking for him, I don't have the sense that he will emotionally believe that I care about him. I let him know that I respect the way he doesn't run from his fears and that I like his willingness to talk openly about his troubles.

Stan has acquired a wide range of critical internal dialogues that he has practiced for many years. My hope is that he will begin to challenge those thoughts that are unfounded, that he will discover the nature of his faulty thinking, and that eventually he will restructure some of his beliefs. Along this line I work with him to pinpoint specific beliefs and then do my best to get him to come up with evidence to support or refute them. I am influenced by the constructivist trend in cognitive-behavior therapy. Applied to Stan, constructivism holds that his subjective framework and interpretations are far more important than the objective bases that may be at the origin of his faulty beliefs. Thus, rather than imposing my version of what may constitute faulty, irrational, and dysfunctional beliefs on his part, I pursue a line of Socratic questioning whereby I get him to evaluate his own thinking processes and his conclusions:

*Jerry:* Let's take one statement that you've made a number of times: "When I'm with other people, I feel stupid most of the time." What goes on within you when you say this?

*Stan:* It's like I hear critical voices, almost like people are in my head or are sitting on my shoulder.

*Jerry:* Name one person who often sits on your shoulder and tells you that you're stupid.

*Stan:*   My dad, for one. I hear his voice in my head a lot.

*Jerry:*   Let me be Stan for a moment, and you be your dad, saying to me some of those critical things that you hear him saying inside your head.

*Stan:*   What the hell are you going to college for? Why don't you quit and give your seat to someone who deserves it? You always were a bad student. You're just wasting your time and the taxpayers' money by pretending to be a college student. Do yourself a favor and wake up to the fact that you'll always be a dumb kid.

*Jerry:*   How much truth is there in what you just said as your dad?

*Stan:*   You know, it sounds stupid that I let that old guy convince me that I'm totally stupid.

*Jerry:*   Instead of saying that you're stupid for letting him tell you that you're stupid, can you give yourself credit for being smart enough to come to this realization?

*Stan:*   OK, but he's right that I've failed at most of the things I've tried.

*Jerry:*   Does failing at a task mean that you're right holding to the label of being a failure in life? I'd like to hear you produce the evidence that supports your interpretation of being stupid and of being a failure.

*Stan:*   How about the failure in my marriage? I couldn't make it work, and I was responsible for the divorce. That's a pretty big failure.

*Jerry:*   And were you totally responsible for the divorce? Did your wife have any part in it?

*Stan:*   She always told me that no woman could ever live with me. She convinced me that I couldn't have a satisfying relationship with her or any other woman.

*Jerry:*   Although she could speak for herself, I'm wondering what qualifies her to determine your future with all women. Tell me what study was conducted that proves that Stan is utterly destined to be allergic to all women forever.

*Stan:*   I suppose I just bought into what she told me. After all, if I couldn't live with her, what makes me think that I could have a satisfying life with any woman?

At this point, there are many directions in which I could go with Stan, designed to explore the origin of his beliefs and to assess the validity of his interpretations about life situations and his conclusions about his basic worth. In this and other sessions, we explore what cognitive therapists call "cognitive distortions," some of which are:

- *Arbitrary inferences.* Stan makes conclusions without supporting and relevant evidence. He often engages in "catastrophizing," or thinking about the worst possible scenario for a given situation.
- *Overgeneralization.* Stan holds extreme beliefs based on a single incident and applies them inappropriately to other dissimilar events or settings. For instance, because he and his wife divorced, he is convinced that he is destined to be a failure with any woman.

- *Personalization.* Stan has a tendency to relate external events to himself, even when there is no basis for making this connection. He relates an incident in which a female classmate did not show up for a lunch date. He agonized over this event and convinced himself that she would have been humiliated to be seen in his presence. He did not consider any other possible explanations for her absence.
- *Labeling and mislabeling.* Stan presents himself in light of his imperfections and mistakes. He allows his past failures to define his total being.
- *Polarized thinking.* Stan frequently engages in thinking and interpreting in all-or-nothing terms. Through this process of dichotomous thinking, he has created self-defeating labels and boxes that keep him restricted.

Over a number of sessions we work on specific beliefs. The aim is for Stan to critically evaluate the evidence for many of his conclusions. I see my role as promoting corrective experiences that will lead to changes in his thinking. I am striving to create a collaborative relationship, one in which he will discover for himself how to distinguish between functional and dysfunctional beliefs. He can learn this by testing his conclusions.

## DOING: ANOTHER ESSENTIAL COMPONENT OF THERAPY

Stan can spend countless hours in gathering interesting insights about why he is the way he is. He can learn to express feelings that he kept inside for so many years. And he can think about the things he tells himself that lead to defeat. Yet in my view feeling and thinking are not enough to a complete therapy process. *Doing* is a way of bringing these feelings and thoughts together by applying them to real-life situations in various action programs. I am indebted to Adlerian therapy, behavior therapy, reality therapy, and rational emotive behavior therapy, all of which give central emphasis to the role of action as a prerequisite for change.

Behavior therapy offers a multitude of techniques for behavioral change. In Stan's case I am especially inclined to work with him in developing self-management programs. For example, he complains of often feeling tense and anxious. Daily relaxation procedures are one way that he can gain more control of his physical and psychological tension. Perhaps by a combination of meditation and relaxation procedures he can get himself centered before he goes to his classes, meets women, or talks to friends. He can also begin to monitor his behavior in everyday situations to gain increased awareness of what he tells himself, what he does, and then how he feels. When he gets depressed, he tends to drink to alleviate his symptoms. He can carry a small notebook with him and actually record events that lead up to his feeling depressed (or anxious or hurt). He might also record what he actually did in these situations and what he might have done differently. By paying attention to what he is doing in daily life, he is already beginning to gain more control of his behavior.

This behavioral monitoring can ideally be coupled with both Adlerian and cognitive approaches. My guess is that Stan gets depressed, engages in self-destructive behavior (drinking, for one), and then feels even worse. I work very much on both his behaviors and cognitions and show him how many of his actions are influenced by what he is telling himself. For example, he wants to go out and apply for a job but is afraid that he might "mess up" in the interview and not get the job. This is an ideal time to use behavioral rehearsal. Together we work on how he is setting himself up for failure by his self-defeating expectations. True to the spirit of rational emotive behavior therapy, we explore his faulty assumptions that he *must* be perfect and that if he does not get the job, life will be unbearable. There are many opportunities to help him see connections between his cognitive processes and his daily behavior. I encourage him to begin to behave differently and then look for changes in his feeling states and his thinking.

With this in mind I ask Stan to think of as many ways as possible of actually bringing into his daily living the new learning that he is acquiring in our sessions. Practice is essential. Homework assignments ( preferably ones that he could give himself) are an excellent way for him to become an active agent in his therapy. He must do something himself for change to occur. I hope that he sees that the degree to which he will change is directly proportional to his willingness to get out in life and experiment. I want him to learn from his new behavior in life. Thus, each week we discuss his progress toward meeting his goals and review how well he is completing his assignments. If he fails in some of them, we can use this as an opportunity to learn how he can adjust his behavior. I insist on a commitment from him that he have an action plan for change and that he continually look at how well his plan is working.

SAMPLE VIGNETTE IN WHICH I CONCENTRATE ON STAN'S ACTIONS.    I am very interested in what Stan is doing and how his thoughts and emotions are affecting this behavior. In the following dialogue, our interchanges deal primarily with teaching him a more assertive style of behavior with one of his professors. Although this session focuses on his behavior, we are also dealing with what he is thinking and feeling. These three dimensions are interactive.

*Jerry:*   Last week we role-played different ways that you could approach a professor with whom you were having difficulty. You learned several assertive skills that you used quite effectively when I assumed the role of the critical professor. Before you left last week, you agreed to set up a time to meet with your professor and let her know how she affects you. When we did the role playing, you were very clear about what you wanted to say and strong in staying with your feelings. Did you carry out your plan?

*Stan:*   The next day I tried to talk to her before class. She said she didn't have time to talk but that we could talk after class.

*Jerry:*   And how did that go?

*Stan:*   After class all I wanted to do was make an appointment with her so that I could talk in private and without feeling hurried. When I tried to make the appointment, she very brusquely said that she had to go to a meeting and that I should see her during her office hours.

*Jerry:*   How did that affect you?

*Stan:*    I was mad. All I wanted to do was make an appointment.

*Jerry:*    Did you go to her office hours?

*Stan:*    I did, that very afternoon. She was 20 minutes late for her office hours, and then a bunch of students were waiting to ask her questions. All I got to do was make an appointment with her in a couple of days.

*Jerry:*    Did that appointment actually take place?

*Stan:*    Yes, but she was 10 minutes late and seemed preoccupied. I had a hard time at the beginning.

*Jerry:*    How so? Tell me more.

*Stan:*    I feel stupid in her class, and I wanted to talk to her about it. When I ask questions, she gets a funny look on her face—as if she's impatient and hopes I'll shut up.

*Jerry:*    Did you check out these assumptions with her?

*Stan:*    Yes I did, and I feel proud of myself. She told me that at times she does get a bit impatient because I seem to need a lot of her time and reassurance. Then I let her know how much I was studying for her class and how serious I was about doing well in my major. It was good for me to challenge my fears, instead of avoiding her because I felt she was judgmental.

*Jerry:*    It's good to hear you give yourself credit for the steps you took. Even though it was tough, you hung in there and said what you wanted to say. Is there anything about this exchange with her that you wish you could have changed?

*Stan:*    For the most part, I was pretty assertive. Generally, I blame people in authority like her for making me feel stupid. I give them a lot of power in judging me. But this time I remembered what we worked on in our session, and I stayed focused on myself, rather than telling her what she was doing or not doing.

*Jerry:*    How did that go?

*Stan:*    The more I talked about myself, the less defensive she became. I learned that I don't need to give all my power away and that I can still feel good about myself, even if the other person doesn't change.

*Jerry:*    Great! Did you notice any difference in how you felt in her class after you had this talk?

*Stan:*    For a change, I didn't feel so self-conscious, especially when I asked questions or took part in class discussions. I was not so concerned about what she might think about me.

*Jerry:*    What did your meeting with her teach you about yourself?

*Stan:*    For one thing, I'm learning to check out my assumptions. That frees me up to act much more spontaneously. Also, I learned that I could be clear, direct, and assertive without getting nasty. It was possible for me to take care of myself without being critical of her. Normally, I'd just swallow all my feelings and walk away feeling dumb. This time I could be assertive and was able to let her know that I needed some unhurried time from her.

Practicing assertive behavior is associated with working with the feeling and thinking domains. Had Stan not done as well as he did in engaging his professor, we could have examined what had gone wrong from his vantage point. We could have continued role-playing various approaches in our sessions, and then with new knowledge and skills and more practice, he could have tried again. The point is that if he hopes to make the changes he desires, it is essential that he be willing to experiment with new ways of acting, especially outside of the therapy sessions. In a sense, counseling is like a dress rehearsal for living. Stan exhibited courage and determination in carrying out a specific action plan, which is a catalyst for change.

## WORKING TOWARD REVISED DECISIONS

When Stan has identified and explored both his feelings and his faulty beliefs and thinking processes, it does not mean that therapy is over. Becoming aware of early decisions, including some of his basic mistakes and his self-defeating ideas, is the starting point for change. It is essential that he find ways to translate his emotional and cognitive insights into new ways of thinking, feeling, and behaving. Therefore, as much as possible I structure situations in the therapy sessions that will facilitate new decisions on his part on both the emotional and cognitive levels. In encouraging him to make these new decisions, I draw on cognitive, emotive, and behavioral techniques. A few techniques that I might employ are role playing, fantasy and imagery, assertion-training procedures, and behavioral rehearsals. Both reality therapy and Adlerian therapy have a lot to offer on getting clients to decide on a plan of action and then make a commitment to carry out their program for change.

EXAMPLES OF TECHNIQUES EMPLOYED IN THE REDECISION PROCESS.    In this section are examples of some of the experiments that I suggest for Stan during the therapy sessions and homework assignments geared to helping him apply what he is learning to situations in everyday life.

- I engage in a number of reverse role-playing situations in which I "become" Stan and have him assume the role of his mother, father, former wife, sister, older brother, and a professor. Through this process he gets a clearer picture of ways in which he allowed others to define him, and he acquires some skills in arguing back to self-defeating voices.
- To help Stan deal with his anxiety, I teach him relaxation methods and encourage him to practice them daily. He learns to employ these relaxation strategies in anxiety-arousing situations. I also teach him a range of coping skills, such as assertiveness and disputing irrational beliefs. He is able to apply these skills in several life situations.
- Stan agrees to keep a journal in which he records impressions and experiences. After encountering difficult situations, he writes about his reactions, both on a thinking and feeling level. He also records how he behaved in situations, how he felt about his actions, and how he might

have behaved differently. He also agrees to read a few self-help books in areas that are particularly problematic for him.

- As a homework assignment, I urge Stan to meet with people whom he would typically avoid. For instance, he is highly anxious over his performance in a couple of his classes. He accepts my nudging to make an appointment with each professor and discuss his progress. In one case, a professor takes an increased interest in him, and he does very well in her class. In the other case, the professor is rather abrupt and not too helpful. Stan is able to recognize that this is more the professor's problem than anything he is doing wrong.

- Stan wants to put himself in situations where he can make new friends. We work on a clear plan of action that involves joining a club, going to social events on campus, and asking a woman in his class for a date. Although he is anxious in each of these situations, he follows through with his plans. In our sessions we explore some of his self-talk and actions at these events.

## ENCOURAGING STAN TO WORK WITH HIS FAMILY OF ORIGIN

After working with Stan for a short time, I suggest that he take the initiative to invite his entire family for a session. My assumption is that many of his problems stem from his family-of-origin experiences and that he is still being affected by these experiences. I think it will be useful to have at least one session with the family so that I can get a better idea of the broader context. The following dialogue illustrates my attempt to introduce this idea to Stan:

*Jerry:* Our sessions are certainly revealing a good deal of unfinished business with several members of your family. I think it would be useful to bring in as many of them as you can for a session.

*Stan:* No way! I'm not going to jump in that snake pit.

*Jerry:* Are you willing to talk with me more about this idea?

*Stan:* I'll talk, but it won't do any good.

*Jerry:* What stops you from asking them?

*Stan:* They already think I'm nutty as a fruitcake, and if they find out I'm seeing a psychologist, that's just one more thing they can throw in my face.

*Jerry:* You think they'd use this against you?

*Stan:* Yep. Besides, I can't see how getting my family together is going to help much. My mother and father don't think they have any problems. I don't see *them* wanting to change much.

*Jerry:* I wasn't thinking of their changing but more of giving you a chance to say directly some of the things you've said about them in your sessions with me. It might help you gain clarity about how you are with them.

*Stan:* Maybe, but I'm not ready for that one yet!

*Jerry:*   OK, I can respect that you don't feel ready yet. I hope you'll remain open to this idea, and if you change your mind, let me know.

My rationale for including at least some of Stan's family members is to provide him with a context for understanding how his behavior is being influenced by what he learned as a child. He is a part of this system, and as he changes, it is bound to influence others in his family with whom he has contact. From what he has told me, I am assuming that he has unclear boundaries with his mother that have an impact on his relationships with other women. He is convinced that if he gets close to a woman, she will swallow him up. If he can gain a clearer understanding of his relationship with his mother, he may be able to apply some of these insights with other women. In many ways he has allowed himself to be intimidated by his father, and he still hears Dad's voice in his head. In much of his present behavior, he compares himself unfavorably with others, which is a pattern that he established in early childhood with his siblings. If he is able to begin dealing with the members of his family about some of his past and present pain, there is a good chance that he will be able to free himself of emotional barriers that are preventing him from forming those intimate relationships that he says he would like to have in his life. (For a more complete description of working with Stan from a family systems perspective, see Stan's case in Chapter 12.)

## WORKING WITH STAN'S DRINKING PROBLEM

Although each of the nine therapeutic approaches would address drug and alcohol abuse in different ways, all probably agree that it would be imperative at some point in Stan's therapy to confront him on the probability that he is a chemically dependent person. In this section I describe my approach to working with his dependence as well as giving some brief background information on the alcoholic personality and on treatment approaches.

SOME BASIC ASSUMPTIONS.   I would be sure to establish a good relationship with Stan before launching into the treatment phase of his possible alcoholism. He has given a number of significant clues suggesting that I should determine whether he is a chemically dependent person and, if so, what course of treatment would be indicated. From the information he has provided, it is clear that he has many of the personality traits typically found in alcoholics, including low self-concept, anxiety, sexual dysfunctions, underachievement, feelings of social isolation, inability to love himself or to receive love from others, hypersensitivity, impulsivity, dependence, fear of failure, feelings of guilt, self-pity, and suicidal impulses. In addition, he has used drugs and alcohol as a way of blunting anxiety and attempting to control what he perceives as a painful reality. He has switched from drugs to alcohol, which is a common attempt to control the disastrous effects of addiction.

Once our therapeutic relationship is firmly established, I confront Stan (in a caring and concerned manner) on his self-deception that he is doing something positive by not getting loaded with drugs but is merely getting drunk. He needs to see that alcohol *is* a drug, and I want him to make an honest evaluation of his behavior so that he can recognize the degree to which his drinking is interfering in his living. Although he resorts to excuses, rationalizations, denials, distortions, and minimizations about his drinking patterns, I provide some information that he can use to examine his confused system of beliefs. Johns Hopkins University Hospital in Baltimore has designed a questionnaire that is useful in assessing the preliminary signs of alcohol addiction. A few questions are "Have you lost time from work due to drinking? Do you drink to escape from worries? Do you drink to build up your self-confidence? Have you ever felt remorse after drinking? Do you drink because you're shy with other people? Does drinking cause you to have difficulty in sleeping?" From what we already know of Stan, it is likely that he would answer yes to several of these questions if he responded honestly. "Yes" answers to even one or two of these questions indicate enough of a problem to warrant further assessment for chemical dependency.

A SUPPLEMENTARY TREATMENT PROGRAM.   Stan eventually recognizes that he does indeed have a problem with alcoholism, and he says he is willing to do something about this problem. I tell him that alcoholism is considered by most substance-abuse experts to be a disease in itself, rather than a symptom of another underlying disorder, that it is a chronic condition that can be treated, and that it is a progressive disorder that eventually results in death if it is not arrested. It will be helpful for him to know that long-term recovery is based on the principle of total abstinence from all drugs and alcohol and that such abstinence is a prerequisite to effective counseling. In addition to his weekly individual therapy sessions with me, I provide him with a referral to deal with his chemical dependence.

I would encourage Stan to join Alcoholics Anonymous and attend their meetings. The 12-step program of AA has worked very well for many alcoholics. It is not a substitute for therapy, but it can be an ideal supplement. Once Stan understands the nature of his chemical dependence and no longer uses drugs, the chances are greatly increased that we can focus on the other aspects of his life that he sees as problematic and would like to change. In short, it is possible to treat his alcoholism and at the same time carry out a program of individual therapy geared to changing his ways of thinking, feeling, and behaving.

## MOVING TOWARD TERMINATION OF THERAPY

The process that I have been describing will probably take months, and it could even take a couple of years. My basic point has been to show that it is possible to draw simultaneously on a variety of therapeutic systems in working with Stan's thoughts, feelings, and behaviors. Although in this illustration I have described these three dimensions separately, do keep in mind that I tend to work in an integrated fashion in this way as well.

Eventually, this process leads to a time when Stan can continue what he has learned in therapy but without my assistance. Termination of therapy is as important as the initial phase, for now the challenge is to put into practice what he has learned in the sessions by applying new skills and attitudes to daily social situations. When he brings up a desire to "go it alone," we talk about his readiness to end therapy and his reasons for thinking about termination. I also share with him my perceptions of the directions I have seen him take. This is a good time to talk about where he can go from here. Together we spend a few sessions developing an action plan and talking about how he can best maintain his new learning. He may want to join a therapeutic group. He could find support in a variety of social networks. In essence, he can continue to challenge himself by doing things that are difficult for him yet at the same time broaden his range of choices. If he wants, he might take some dancing classes that he has previously avoided out of a fear of failing. Now he can take the risk and be his own therapist, dealing with feelings as they arise in new situations.

In a behavioral spirit, evaluating the process and outcomes of therapy seems essential. This evaluation can take the form of devoting a session or two to discussing Stan's specific changes in therapy. A few questions for focus are: "What stands out the most for you, Stan? What did you learn that you consider the most valuable? How did you learn these lessons? What can you do now to keep practicing new behaviors that work better for you than the old patterns? What will you do if you experience setbacks? How will you handle any regression to old ways or temporary defeats?" With this last question it is helpful for him to know that his termination of formal therapy does not mean that he cannot return for a visit or session when he considers it appropriate. Rather than coming for weekly sessions, he might well decide to come in at irregular intervals for a "checkup." Of course, he will be the person to decide what new areas to explore in these follow-up sessions.

## ENCOURAGING STAN TO JOIN A THERAPY GROUP

As Stan and I are talking about termination, he gives me clear indications that he has learned a great deal about himself through individual counseling. Although he has been applying his learning to difficult situations that he encounters, I am convinced that he would benefit from a group experience. I suggest that he consider joining a 16-week therapy group that will begin in two months:

*Jerry:* I've mentioned to you before that I think a group would be a good place for you to continue the work you've done in here. Have you given it more thought?

*Stan:* I did, and I have mixed feelings. I'd like the challenge of pushing myself to open up with others in a group, but the idea scares the hell out of me.

*Jerry:* Tell me more about your fears.

*Stan:* I understand that there will be both women and men in this group, and I'm still terribly anxious around women.

*Jerry:*   Then a group could give you a lot of opportunities to explore these fears and practice new behavior. In our individual sessions you and I did a good bit of role playing, and you did push yourself to try new behavior on the outside. In a group, you could work through some of the fears you've identified.

*Stan:*   But what if people in the group don't like me? You know how I'm still hung up on getting approval. I might be devastated if everyone in the group rejected me. What if I do my best to be open, and they tell me they don't like what they see?

*Jerry:*   Sounds to me as if you have plenty to work with in a group. You could explore how you seek approval from others, and at what expense. You could experiment with some new ways of behaving and see how others would respond. You could test your hypothesis that one person's rejection would devastate you.

*Stan:*   Well, the AA groups I've been going to have really helped. Maybe I should give it a try.

*Jerry:*   This will be a different kind of group. AA is more of a support group. In this therapy group you'll be exploring many of the intensely personal issues that you worked on with me. The value of a group is that you'll also learn from the other members.

*Stan:*   Do you think I'd fit into the group? I always worry when I'm in any group that somehow I don't belong and that I won't have anything in common with the others.

*Jerry:*   But you could always talk about your feelings of not fitting in. That would be a great place to begin.

*Stan:*   OK, but I wouldn't want to be looked at as being different. I hope I'd find others who had problems like mine.

*Jerry:*   I think you'd find that others are wrestling with similar problems. And even if your problems are different, you may share the same feelings.

*Stan:*   I want to say yes, but you've taught me to think about things before I commit myself. Let me do some thinking, and I'll let you know next week. How does that sound?

*Jerry:*   I like it that you're saying what's on your mind.

*Stan:*   Good. I'll give plenty of thought to it. I don't think I should back off just because I'm scared. After all, I was scared in my individual sessions with you, but I gained a lot of strength by dealing with my fears.

*Jerry:*   So let me know next week. If there's anything else you want to know about the group, feel free to call.

To me, progressing from individual therapy to a group seems useful for a client like Stan. Because many of his problems are interpersonal, I see a group as an ideal place for him to deal with them. The group will give him a context for practicing the very behaviors that he says he wants to acquire. He wants to feel freer in being himself, to feel easier in approaching people, and to be able to trust people more fully. He realizes that he has made gains in these areas, yet he has some distance to travel. In addition to a group experience, I will be working with Stan in the final phases of his therapy in finding some other steps that he can take to continue his growth. Together we will make plans for putting him into situations that will foster change. He might take skiing lessons, join a dance class, attend more parties, engage in volunteer work with children, and continue writing in his journal.

OUTCOMES OF STAN'S GROUP-THERAPY EXPERIENCE.    Stan decides to enter the 16-week group during the final stages of his individual therapy. I then see him individually for a couple of sessions six weeks after the group has ended to discuss his experience. Along with Stan, there were 11 other members. What follows are some reactions he shares with me about his significant learning. He focuses on his reactions to each group member in terms of what he learned from them or in his interactions with them:

- Emily, a single person at age 23, lives at home for convenience yet feels that this limits her greatly. Initially, Stan was intimidated by Emily, but he dealt with his feelings toward her at the second group session. He was able to role-play asking her for a date, and in the process he expressed his fear of being rejected by attractive women. He was able to identify with Emily's problems with her parents.

- Ed, age 60, has been divorced twice and now lives alone. He has a drinking problem and fears isolation and rejection. At the initial group meeting Stan felt close to Ed, which surprised him because of their age difference. As Ed worked in the group, Stan was able to do significant work with him, especially on the ways in which they had both resorted to alcohol to allay their depression and anxiety.

- Beth, age 55, devotes most of her life to taking care of her sons and others. Stan wanted to avoid her, until he figured out that her style of taking care of people reminded him of his mother's treatment of him. Beth did some emotional work with Stan as her son, and in turn, this triggered Stan's work with Beth as his mother. As a result of these exchanges, he acquired a new understanding of his mother, which allowed him to release some of the anger and resentment he had harbored toward her. Eventually, he took the initiative of talking to his mother, expressing to her many of the feelings he had had as a child.

- Robert, age 28, single, and a social worker, has trouble forming close interpersonal relationships with women. As he did with Ed, Stan felt connected to Robert in many ways. Robert's breakthroughs in the group were catalytic for Stan, who did some psychological working through of his fears of intimacy. The two men worked simultaneously with Emily, because they worried about her judgment and feared her rejection.

- Joanne, age 35, is struggling in her marriage and has just returned to college. She found herself becoming angry at Stan for what she regarded as his "passive style." This proved therapeutically useful for him, because it provided him with a safe context to explore his reactions to a woman who got mad at him.

• Sam, age 34, hates his job but doesn't have the confidence to seek new employment. Stan had trouble listening to Sam. He perceived him as a complainer and was put off by Sam's indecisiveness. In one session the two men worked on their reactions toward each other, and eventually Stan became aware that Sam's lack of confidence in himself served as a mirror for Stan.

• Sharon, age 25, feels guilty about letting her parents down. Stan identified with her guilt, but for different reasons. He has a chronic sense of guilt over not measuring up to his parents' expectations, especially in light of the accomplishments of his siblings. In one session, he worked with Sharon as his sister, telling her of his jealousy and resentment toward her. After role-playing with her at several sessions, he developed feelings of affection toward his "sister" and was able to tell her that he was sorry that he had cut her out of his life. A week later he arranged to meet Judy, and he was able to tell her some of what he had said in the therapy session. He also talked with her about the kind of relationship he would like to establish with her.

• Randy, age 47, a high school teacher, was abandoned by his wife. In a group session he dealt with Beth, who psychologically "became" his wife. He experienced an intense catharsis in which he was able to release pain and anger over his wife leaving and taking their children with her. Randy's work with Beth triggered Stan, and both men worked through much of the anger they felt about their divorces and how they felt stuck with their wives' treatment of them.

• Judy, age 38, is a university professor who is struggling to find a new meaning in her life. For much of the life of the group, Stan felt very awkward around her, feeling that he had to "prove" himself to her. In her presence he felt intimidated and inferior. He also perceived that she was judging him. It helped him feel more of himself with her when he finally checked out his assumptions about her. His work consisted of "becoming" Judy and saying to Stan all the judgments that he imagined she had made about him. When he finished being Judy in this experiment, she let him know that she felt uncomfortable around him because she felt he was avoiding her. She also told him that none of the judgments that he was attributing to her were ones that she held. From dealing with Judy, he learned about the power of projection.

• Boyd, age 22, came to the group because of his bouts with anxiety and depression. When he disclosed and worked on his fear over his suicidal thoughts and feelings, Stan shared his own concerns pertaining to suicide. Prior to Boyd's disclosure, Stan felt alone with this particular worry. He was afraid of mentioning it because he didn't want others in the group to see him as being sick.

In summary, although Stan had hesitations about joining the group, he was amazed at how much he identified with so many members. He had never imagined that he would talk so openly about his concerns, yet as others disclosed their struggles, he found himself touched time after time. The group afforded him multiple opportunities each week to work on his thoughts and feelings that emerged as others brought up their problems. He had the courage to tell others how he perceived them and how he felt affected by them. This gave him practice in dealing with his reluctance to form intimate relationships. By risking saying what was on his mind and in his heart, he took an active part in creating a trusting climate in the group that allowed him to tap deep emotions and work through some unfinished business to a greater extent than he had done in individual counseling. The purpose of the group was not to form friendships with group members but to teach members how to create friendships and how to become real with others outside of the group. Stan was able to carry to the outside world what he was learning in the group about overcoming his fear of approaching people. Besides feeling less isolated, he reported, he frequently took the initiative in meeting people in classes and in social situations. Stan felt enriched by the contact in his group.

## COMMENTARY ON THE THINKING, FEELING, AND DOING PERSPECTIVE

In applying my integrated perspective to Stan, I've dealt separately with the cognitive, affective, and behavioral dimensions of human experience. Although the steps I outlined may appear relatively structured and even simple, actually working with clients is more complex and less predictable. If you are practicing from an integrative perspective, it would be a mistake to assume that it is best to always begin working with what clients are thinking (or feeling or doing). Effective counseling begins where the client is, not where a theory indicates a client should be.

Applied to Stan, a client-centered focus takes into account factors such as his cultural background, his presenting problem, what he says he needs and wants at the initial session, and the clues he gives both verbally and nonverbally. I began by exploring his feelings, for as he was talking he teared up, and it was evident that he had a need to express feelings that had been bottled up for years. Some clients might leave counseling never to return if I attempted to call attention to their feelings at the initial session. Feelings might be too threatening for them, and in such situations it might be more appropriate to focus on underlying assumptions or thoughts. For others, a proper launching point might be what they are actually doing, with a discussion of how well it is working for them. By paying attention to the client's energy (or blocked energy), therapists have many clues to where to begin. If the client resists, dealing with the resistance in a respectful way could open other doors.

In summary, depending on what clients need at the moment, I may focus initially on what they are thinking and how this is affecting them, or I may focus on how they feel, or I may choose to direct them to pay attention to what they are doing. Because these facets of human experience are interrelated, one route generally leads to exploring the other dimensions. Thus, I frequently ask a client: "What are you aware of now?" or "What are you experiencing now?" If they say, "I'm thinking that . . . ," I may follow that path and ask them to say more about what they are thinking. If they say, "I'm feeling a tightness in my chest and . . . ," I am likely to ask them to stay with their bodily sensations for a bit longer and see where that leads them. If they say, "What I'm doing is . . . ," I generally encourage them to tell me more about how well their actions are serving them. If they say, "I'm feeling lonely and frightened . . . ," I may encourage them to stay with their feelings and talk more about what it is like to experience these feelings.

A client-centered focus respects the wisdom within the client and uses it as a lead for where to go next. My guess is that counselors often make the mistake of getting too far ahead of their clients, thinking, "What should I do next?" By staying with our clients and asking them what they want, we do not need to assume too much responsibility by deciding for them the direction in which they should be heading. Instead, we can learn to pay attention to our own reactions to our clients and to our own energy. By doing so we can engage in a therapeutic dance that is exciting for both parties in the relationship.

## FOLLOW-UP: YOU CONTINUE WORKING WITH STAN IN AN INTEGRATIVE STYLE

Think about these questions to help you decide how to counsel Stan:

- What themes in Stan's life do you find most significant, and how might you draw on these themes during the initial phase of counseling?
- What specific concepts from the various theoretical orientations would you be most inclined to utilize in your work with Stan?
- Identify some key techniques from the various therapies that you are most likely to employ in your therapy with Stan. What are a few cognitive techniques you'd probably use? emotive techniques? behavioral techniques?
- How might you invent experiments for Stan to carry out both inside and outside the therapy sessions? How are you likely to present these experiments to him?
- As you were reading about the integrative perspective, what ideas did you have about continuing as Stan's counselor?
- Knowing what you do about Stan, what do you imagine it would be like to be his therapist? What problems, if any, might you expect to encounter in your counseling relationship with him?
- What life experiences of your own might you draw from that would better enable you to empathize with Stan and work more effectively with him?
- What are your thoughts about ways in which you could pay attention to working with Stan from a thinking, feeling, and behaving perspective? What modalities might you emphasize?

# Where to Go from Here

At the beginning of the introductory course in counseling, my students typically express two reactions: "How will I ever be able to learn all these theories?" and "How can I make sense out of this mass of knowledge?" By the end of the course, these students are often surprised by how much work they have done *and* by how much they have learned. Although an introductory survey course will not make students into accomplished counselors, it generally gives them the basis for selecting from among the many models to which they are exposed.

At this point you may be able to begin putting the theories together in some meaningful way for yourself. This book will have served its central purpose if it has encouraged you to read further and to expand your knowledge of the theories that most caught your interest. I hope that you have made friends with some theories that were unknown to you before and that you have seen something of value that you can use from each of the approaches described. Further, I hope that this book has introduced you to some of the major professional and ethical issues that you will eventually encounter, that it has stimulated you to think about your position on them, and that you have been convinced that no single theory contains the total truth. You will not be in a position to conceptualize a completely developed integrative perspective after your first course in counseling theory. But the combination of this course and this book can provide you with the tools to begin the process of integration. With additional study and practical experience, you will be able to expand and refine your emerging personal philosophy of counseling.

Finally, the book will have been put to good use if it has stimulated and challenged you to think about the ways in which your philosophy of life, your values, your life experiences, and the person you are becoming are vitally related to the caliber of counselor you can become and to the impact you can have on those who establish a relationship with you personally and professionally. This book and your course may have raised questions for you regarding your decision to become a counselor. If this is the case, I encourage you to seek out at least one of your professors to explore these questions.

If you have read the chapters in the order presented in the book, I suggest that you make the time to reread Chapters 2 and 3, as they can help you put some of the personal and professional issues in perspective. As this point you may find it interesting to compare your thinking on the issues that were examined in these early chapters with your views when you began the course.

Now that you have finished this book, I would be very interested in hearing about your experience with it and with your course. The comments that readers have sent me over the years have been helpful in revising each edition, and I welcome your feedback. You can write to me in care of Brooks/Cole Publishing Company, Pacific Grove, CA 93950-5098, and you can complete the reaction sheet at the end of the book.

# Recommended Supplementary Readings for Part Three

These books can help you begin to integrate the various theories and apply them to your practice.

*Handbook of Psychotherapy Integration* (Norcross & Goldfried, 1992) is a superb resource for conceptual and historical perspectives on therapy integration. This edited volume gives a comprehensive overview of the major current approaches, such as theoretical integration and technical eclecticism, and it deals with issues pertaining to the development of integration. If you have time to read only one source on integrative therapies, this is my recommendation.

*Casebook of Eclectic Psychotherapy* (Norcross, 1987) is designed to define and illustrate major approaches to eclectic practice. This volume presents 13 cases and critical analyses on the practice of eclectic therapy in its varied manifestations.

*Therapy Wars: Contention and Convergence in Differing Clinical Approaches* (Saltzman & Norcross, 1990) presents leading psychotherapists of diverse persuasions discussing the same case from multiple theoretical orientations. The final two chapters summarize these exchanges with integrative implications.

*Systematic Treatment Selection: Toward Target Therapeutic Interventions* (Beutler & Clarkin, 1990) is an excellent source for readers interested in an integrated approach. The book describes a systematic eclectic psychotherapy that can be applied in a relatively consistent and reliable fashion. It attempts to define the ingredients of good therapy and to maximize their effective use by matching clients to both therapists and techniques.

*What Is Psychotherapy? Contemporary Perspectives* (Zeig & Munion, 1990) provides an overview of a wide range of therapy approaches, including psychodynamic therapy, humanistic and experiential approaches, behavior therapy, cognitive therapy, philosophically oriented psychotherapy, eclectic and integrative therapies, family and systemic therapies, group psychotherapy, and Ericksonian psychotherapy.

*Counseling Methods and Techniques: An Eclectic Approach* (Young, 1992) provides an eclectic perspective on the therapeutic relationship, assessment, goal setting, practicing new behaviors, and evaluating therapy.

*Videotape: The Art of Integrative Counseling and Psychotherapy.* Although there is no videotape demonstrating an integrative approach in working with Stan, I have made such a tape that illustrates my own integrative perspective in working with a hypothetical client, Ruth, entitled *The Art of Integrative Counseling and Psychotherapy.* In Part I ("Techniques in Action") there are short clips of therapy sessions from the initial to termination phases of Ruth's therapy. In Part II ("Challenges for the Counselor") the focus is on issues such as resistance, transference, and countertransference as they apply to working with Ruth. This video brings together several of the therapies that are discussed in this book. Information about this teaching supplement can be obtained from Brooks/Cole Publishing Company, Pacific Grove, CA, 93950.

# References and Suggested Readings for Part Three*

ARKOWITZ, H. (1992). Integrative theories of therapy. In D. K. Freedheim (Ed.), *History of psychotherapy: A century of change* (pp. 261–303). Washington, DC: American Psychological Association.

BEITMAN, B. D. (1992). Integration through fundamental similarities and useful differences among the schools. In J. C. Norcross & M. R. Goldfried (Eds.), *Handbook of psychotherapy integration* (pp. 202–230). New York: Basic Books.

BERGIN, A. E. (1988). Three contributions of a spiritual perspective to counseling, psychotherapy, and behavioral change. *Counseling and Values, 33,* 21–31.

BERGIN, A. E., & LAMBERT, M. J. (1978). The evaluation of therapeutic outcomes. In S. L. Garfield & A. E. Bergin (Eds.), *Handbook of psychotherapy and behavior change* (2nd ed.). New York: Wiley.

BEUTLER, L. E. (1983). *Eclectic psychotherapy: A systematic approach.* New York: Pergamon Press.

BEUTLER, L. E. (1990). Systematic eclectic psychotherapy. In J. K. Zeig & W. M. Munion (Eds.), *What is psychotherapy? Contemporary perspectives* (pp. 225–233). San Francisco: Jossey-Bass.

*BEUTLER, L. E., & CLARKIN, J. (1990). *Selective treatment selection: Toward targeted therapeutic interventions.* New York: Brunner/Mazel.

*BEUTLER, L. E., & CONSOLI, A. J. (1992). Systematic eclectic psychotherapy. In J. C. Norcross & M. R. Goldfried (Eds.), *Handbook of psychotherapy integration* (pp. 264–299). New York: Basic Books.

BRAMMER, L., SHOSTROM, E., & ABREGO, P. J. (1989). *Therapeutic psychology: Fundamentals of counseling and psychotherapy* (5th ed.). Englewood Cliffs, NJ: Prentice-Hall.

COHEN, L. H., SARGENT, M. M., & SECHREST, L. B. (1986). Use of psychotherapy research by practicing psychotherapists. *American Psychologist, 41*(2), 198–206.

CORSINI, R. J. (Ed.). (1981). *Handbook of innovative psychotherapies.* New York: Wiley.

ELKINS, D. N. (1994, August). *Toward a soulful psychology: Introduction and overview.* Paper presented at the meeting of the American Psychological Association, Los Angeles.

FAIVER, C. M., & O'BRIEN, E. M. (1993). Assessment of religious beliefs form. *Counseling and Values, 37*(3), 176–178.

FELDMAN, L. B., & POWELL, S. L. (1992). Integrating therapeutic modalities. In J. C. Norcross & M. R. Goldfried (Eds.), *Handbook of psychotherapy integration* (pp. 503–532). New York: Basic Books.

GARFIELD, S. L. (1980). *Psychotherapy: An eclectic approach.* New York: Wiley.

GARFIELD, S. L. (1986). An eclectic psychotherapy. In J. C. Norcross (Ed.), *Handbook of eclectic psychotherapy* (pp. 132–162). New York: Brunner/Mazel.

GARFIELD, S. L. (1987). Ethical issues in research on psychotherapy. *Counseling and Values, 31*(2), 115–125.

GARFIELD, S. L. (1990). Multivariant eclectic psychotherapy. In J. K. Zeig & W. M. Munion (Eds.), *What is psychotherapy? Contemporary perspectives* (pp. 239–243). San Francisco: Jossey-Bass.

*GARFIELD, S. L. (1992a). Eclectic psychotherapy: A common factors approach. In J. C. Norcross & M. R. Goldfried (Eds.), *Handbook of psychotherapy integration* (pp. 169–201). New York: Basic Books.

*GARFIELD, S. L. (1992b). Major issues in psychotherapy research. In D. K. Freedheim (Ed.), *History of psychotherapy: A century of change* (pp. 335–359). Washington, DC: American Psychological Association.

*Books and articles marked with an asterisk are suggested for further study.

GENDLIN, E. T. (1986). What comes after traditional psychotherapy research? *American Psychologist, 41*(2), 131–136.

GEORGIA, R. T. (1994). Preparing to counsel clients of different religious backgrounds: A phenomenological approach. *Counseling and Values, 38*(2), 143–151.

GINTER, E. J. (1988). Stagnation in eclecticism: The need to recommit to a journey. *Journal of Mental Health Counseling, 10*(1), 3–8.

GOLDFRIED, M. R., & CASTONGUAY, L. G. (1992). The future of psychotherapy integration. *Psychotherapy, 29*(1), 4–10.

* GOLDFRIED, M. R., CASTONGUAY, L. G., & SAFRAN, J. D. (1992). Core issues and future directions in psychotherapy. In J. C. Norcross & M. R. Goldfried (Eds.), *Handbook of psychotherapy integration* (pp. 593–616). New York: Basic Books.

* GOLDFRIED, M. R., & NEWMAN, C. (1992). A history of psychotherapy integration. In J. C. Norcross & M. R. Goldfried (Eds.), *Handbook of psychotherapy integration* (pp. 46–93). New York: Basic Books.

* GOLDFRIED, M. R., & SAFRAN, J. D. (1986). Future directions in psychotherapy integration. In J. C. Norcross (Ed.), *Handbook of eclectic psychotherapy* (pp. 463–483). New York: Brunner/Mazel.

GRIMM, D. W. (1994). Therapist spiritual and religious values in psychotherapy. *Counseling and Values, 38*(3), 154–164.

HERINK, R. (Ed.). (1980). *The psychotherapy handbook: The A to Z guide to more than 250 different therapies in use today.* New York: New American Library.

HINTERKOPF, E. (1994). Integrating spiritual experiences in counseling. *Counseling and Values, 38*(3), 165–175.

IMBER, S. D., GLANZ, L. M., ELKIN, I., SOTSKY, S. M., BOYER, J. L., & LEBER, W. R. (1986). Ethical issues in psychotherapy research. *American Psychologist, 41*(2), 137–146.

INGERSOLL, R. E. (1994). Spirituality, religion, and counseling: Dimensions and relationships. *Counseling and Values, 38*(2), 98–111.

KARASU, T. B. (1986). The specificity versus nonspecificity dilemma: Toward identifying therapeutic change agents. *American Journal of Psychiatry, 14*(3), 687–695.

KELLY, E. W. (1994). The role of religion and spirituality in counselor education: A national survey. *Counselor Education and Supervision, 33*(4), 227–237.

KELLY, K. R. (1988). Defending eclecticism: The utility of informed choice. *Journal of Mental Health Counseling, 10*(4), 210–213.

KELLY, K. R. (1991). Theoretical integration is the future for mental health counseling. *Journal of Mental Health Counseling, 13*(1), 106–111.

LAMBERT, M. J. (1992). Psychotherapy outcome research: Implications for integrative and eclectic therapists. In J. C. Norcross & M. R. Goldfried (Eds.), *Handbook of psychotherapy integration* (pp. 94–129). New York: Basic Books.

* LAMBERT, M. J., & BERGIN, A. E. (1992). Achievements and limitations of psychotherapy research. In D. K. Freedheim (Ed.), *History of psychotherapy: A century of change* (pp. 360–390). Washington, DC: American Psychological Association.

LAZARUS, A. A. (1986). Multimodal therapy. In J. C. Norcross (Ed.), *Handbook of eclectic psychotherapy* (pp. 65–93). New York: Brunner/Mazel.

* LAZARUS, A. A. (1989). *The practice of multimodal therapy.* Baltimore: Johns Hopkins University Press.

LAZARUS, A. A., & BEUTLER, L. E. (1993). On technical eclecticism. *Journal of Counseling and Development, 71*(4), 381–385.

* LAZARUS, A. A., BEUTLER, L. E., & NORCROSS, J. C. (1992). The future of technical eclecticism. *Psychotherapy, 29*(1), 11–20.

MacDONALD, D. (1991). Philosophies that underlie models of mental health counseling: More than meets the eye. *Journal of Mental Health Counseling, 13*(3), 379–392.

MATTSON, D. L. (1994). Religious counseling: To be used, not feared. *Counseling and Values, 38*(3), 187–192.

McBRIDE, M. C., & MARTIN, G. E. (1990). A framework for eclecticism: The importance of theory to mental health counseling. *Journal of Mental Health Counseling, 12*(4), 495–505.

MELTZOFF, J., & KORNREICH, M. (1970). *Research in psychotherapy.* New York: Atherton.

MESSER, S. B. (1986). Eclecticism in psychotherapy: Underlying assumptions, problems, and trade-offs. In J. C. Norcross (Ed.), *Handbook of eclectic psychotherapy* (pp. 379–397). New York: Brunner/Mazel.

MESSER, S. B. (1992). A critical examination of belief structures in integrative and eclectic psychotherapy. In J. C. Norcross & M. R. Goldfried (Eds.), *Handbook of psychotherapy integration* (pp. 130–165). New York: Basic Books.

MILLER, W. R. (1988). Including clients' spiritual perspectives in cognitive-behavior therapy. In W. R. Miller & J. E. Martin (Eds.), *Behavior therapy and religion: Integrating spiritual and behavioral approaches to change* (pp. 43–55). Newbury Park, CA: Sage.

MILLER, W. R., & MARTIN, J. E. (Eds.). (1988). *Behavior therapy and religion: Integrating spiritual and behavioral approaches to change.* Newbury Park, CA: Sage.

MORROW-BRADLEY, C., & ELLIOTT, R. (1986). Utilization of psychotherapy research by practicing psychotherapists. *American Psychologist, 41*(2), 188–197.

MURRAY, E. J. (1986). Possibilities and promises of eclecticism. In J. C. Norcross (Ed.), *Handbook of eclectic psychotherapy* (pp. 398–415). New York: Brunner/Mazel.

NANCE, D. W., & MYERS, P. (1991). Continuing the eclectic journey. *Journal of Mental Health Counseling, 13*(1), 119–130.

NORCROSS, J. C. (1986a). Eclectic psychotherapy: An introduction and overview. In J. C. Norcross (Ed.), *Handbook of eclectic psychotherapy* (pp. 3–24). New York: Brunner/Mazel.

NORCROSS, J. C. (Ed.). (1986b). *Handbook of eclectic psychotherapy.* New York: Brunner/Mazel.

* NORCROSS, J. C. (Ed.). (1987). *Casebook of eclectic psychotherapy.* New York: Brunner/Mazel.

NORCROSS, J. C. (1990). Eclectic-integrative psychotherapy. In J. K. Zeig & W. M. Munion (Eds.), *What is psychotherapy? Contemporary perspectives* (pp. 218–220). San Francisco: Jossey-Bass.

* NORCROSS, J. C., & FREEDHEIM, D. K. (1992). Into the future: Retrospect and prospect in psychotherapy. In D. K. Freedheim (Ed.), *History of psychotherapy: A century of change* (pp. 881–900). Washington, DC: American Psychological Association.

* NORCROSS, J. C., & GOLDFRIED, M. R. (Eds.). (1992). *Handbook of psychotherapy integration.* New York: Basic Books.

* NORCROSS, J. C., & NEWMAN, C. F. (1992). Psychotherapy integration: Setting the context. In J. C. Norcross & M. R. Goldfried (Eds.), *Handbook of psychotherapy integration* (pp. 3–45). New York: Basic Books.

NORCROSS, J. C., & PROCHASKA, J. O. (1988). A study of eclectic (and integrative) views revisited. *Professional Psychology: Research and Practice, 19*(2), 170–174.

PATE, R. H., & BONDI, A. M. (1992). Religious beliefs and practice: An integral aspect of multicultural awareness. *Counselor Education and Supervision, 32*(2), 108–115.

PATTERSON, C. H. (1986). *Theories of counseling and psychotherapy* (4th ed.). New York: Harper & Row.

PAUL, G. L. (1967). Outcome research in psychotherapy. *Journal of Consulting Psychology, 31,* 109–188.

PECK, M. S. (1978). *The road less traveled: A new psychology of love, traditional values and spiritual growth.* New York: Simon & Schuster (Touchstone).

* PROCHASKA, J. O., & DICLEMENTE, C. C. (1992). The transtheoretical approach. In J. C. Norcross & M. R. Goldfried (Eds,), *Handbook of psychotherapy integration* (pp. 300–334). New York: Basic Books.

* PROCHASKA, J. O., & NORCROSS, J. C. (1994). *Systems of psychotherapy: A transtheoretical analysis* (3rd ed.). Pacific Grove, CA: Brooks/Cole.

* SALTZMAN, N., & NORCROSS, J. C. (Eds.). (1990). *Therapy wars: Contention and convergence in differing clinical approaches.* San Francisco: Jossey-Bass.

SIMON, G. M. (1989). An alternative defense of eclecticism: Responding to Kelly and Ginter. *Journal of Mental Health Counseling, 11*(3), 280–288.

SIMON, G. M. (1991). Theoretical eclecticism: A goal we are obliged to pursue. *Journal of Mental Health Counseling, 13*(1), 112–118.

SMITH, D. (1982). Trends in counseling and psychotherapy. *American Psychologist, 37,* 802–809.

SMITH, M. L., GLASS, G. V., & MILLER, T. I. (1980). *The benefits of psychotherapy.* Baltimore: Johns Hopkins University Press.

STANLEY, B., SIEBER, J. E., & MELTON, G. B. (1987). Empirical studies of ethical issues in research. *American Psychologist, 42*(7), 735–741.

STILES, W. B., SHAPIRO, D. A., & ELLIOTT, R. (1986). Are all psychotherapies equivalent? *American Psychologist, 41*(2), 165–180.

STRUPP, H. H. (1986). Psychotherapy: Research, practice, and public policy (How to avoid dead ends). *American Psychologist, 41*(2), 120–130.

* STRUPP, H. H., & HOWARD, K. I. (1992). A brief history of psychotherapy research. In D. K. Freedheim (Ed.), *History of psychotherapy: A century of change* (pp. 309–334). Washington, DC: American Psychological Association.

* SUE, D. W., IVEY, A., & PEDERSEN, P. (1996). *A theory of multicultural counseling and therapy.* Pacific Grove, CA: Brooks/Cole.

SUE, D. W., & SUE, D. (1990). *Counseling the culturally different: Theory and practice.* New York: Wiley.

VANDENBOS, G. R. (1986). Psychotherapy research: A special issue. *American Psychologist, 41*(2), 111–112.

WEINRACH, S. G. (1991). Selecting a counseling theory while scratching your head: A rational-emotive therapist's personal journey. *Journal of Mental Health Counseling, 13*(3), 367–378.

* YOUNG, M. E. (1992). *Counseling methods and techniques: An eclectic approach.* New York: Macmillan.

* YOUNG, M. E., FEILER, F., & WITMER, J. M. (1989). *Eclecticism: New foundation for recasting the counseling profession.* Unpublished manuscript available from Mark Young, Graduate Programs in Counseling and Therapy, Stetson University, P. O. Box 8365, Deland, FL 32720.

* ZEIG, J. K., & MUNION, W. M. (1990). *What is psychotherapy? Contemporary perspectives.* San Francisco: Jossey-Bass.

ZOOK, A., II, & WALTON, J. M. (1989). Theoretical orientations and work settings of clinical and counseling psychologists: A current perspective. *Professional Psychology: Research and Practice, 20*(1), 23–31.

# SUBJECT INDEX